# Tactics of Christian Resistance

CHRISTIANITY & CIVILIZATION

Published by Geneva Divinity School

ISSN 0278-8187
ISBN 0-939404-07-9



**No. 3 SUMMER, 1983**

**Gary North, Editor**

# Tactics of Christian Resistance

Tyler, Texas

Geneva Divinity School Press

1983

# Tactics of Christian Resistance

A Symposium Edited by Gary North

TYLER, TEXAS
GENEVA DIVINITY SCHOOL PRESS
1983

THIS ISSUE OF

*Christianity and Civilization*

IS DEDICATED TO THE MEMORY OF TWO GREAT CHRISTIAN RESISTERS OF TYRANNY:

**Andrew Melville and Thomas Becket**

DURING the 1590s, King James the Sixth of Scotland embarked on a policy of gradual attrition in his attempt to take over the Church of Scotland. He objected to the fact that the reformed bishops (called "superintendents" in Scotland) were subject to the authority of Presbyteries, Synods, and the General Assembly. He began to intrude, on his own, another kind of bishop, one commissioned by the State. He refused to suppress wide-spread corruption, injustice, and crime. Matters began to come to a head when the Earl of Moray was murdered by the Earl of Huntley, a favorite of the King. When the Church put Huntley under the ban of excommunication, the King was enraged, and was the more determined to bring the Church to heel.[1]

In 1596, a group of ministers visited the King to try to bring him to a proper understanding of Church-State relations. James was insulting, and Andrew Melville rebuked him with these famous lines: "Sir, you are brought in extreme danger both of your life and your crown. And with you the country and the Kirk of Christ is like to wreck. And, therefore, Sir, I must tell you, *there are two Kings and two Kingdoms in Scotland*. There is Christ Jesus the King, and his Kingdom the Kirk, whose subject James VI is, and of whose Kingdom not a King, nor a lord, nor a head, but a member."[2]

---

1. See the introduction by Thomas Torrence to Robert Bruce, *The Mystery of the Lord's Supper* (London: James Clarke & Co., [1589] 1958), pp. 23f.

2. From the Diary of James Melville.

Four centuries earlier, in December of 1170 A.D., Thomas Becket, Archbishop of Canterbury, was martyred for the same holy cause. The story, in its bare outlines, is known because of the film *Becket*,[3] but eyewitness accounts of the events provide us a transcript of the actual conversation between Becket and his murderers on the day of his murder.[4]

Four officers of King Henry II came to see the Archbishop. Becket had disciplined some lower bishops for rebellion against the Church, men who had sworn allegiance to the State and had affirmed that the King was head of the Church. The four royal officers demanded that Becket remove the discipline pronounced against these men. Becket refused, on principle.

At this point, one of them took another tack. "From whom do you hold your see?"

Thomas replied, "The spiritualities from God and my lord the pope;[5] the temporalities from my lord the king."

"So you do not recognize that everything you possess you have received from the king?" asked the officer.

"Not at all; but I have to render to the king what is the king's, and to God what is God's. I will not spare anyone who violates the laws of Christ's Church." At this, the knights sprang to their feet, waving their arms and gritting their teeth.

That night they returned, and murdered Thomas Becket in the cathedral.

---

3. There are some inaccuracies in the film; Becket, for instance, was not a Saxon, but a Norman.

4. See Richard Winston, *Thomas Becket* (New York: Knopf, 1967) pp. 357ff.

5. Protestants should keep in mind that at this time in history, the pope was premier bishop of the entire Western church.

# TABLE OF CONTENTS



*(Continued on next page)*

# EDITOR'S INTRODUCTION

Gary North

> **Ye are the light of the world. A city that is set on an hill cannot be hid. Neither do men light a candle, and put it under a bushel, but on a candlestick; and it giveth light unto all that are in the house. Let your light so shine before men, that they may see your good works, and glorify your Father which is in heaven (Matt. 5:14).**

ANY discussion of specifically *Christian* forms of resistance cannot avoid a careful consideration of the implications of this passage in Matthew. In the history of man, there have been a seemingly endless number of conspiratorial resistance movements.[1] Most of them failed. Few of them left any records. A few have been successful, the Nazis and the Communists being the primary examples in this century. The ideology of the socialist revolution was a product of two primary influences in the nineteenth century: occult secret societies (many of them Masonic) and journalism.[2] But Christian resistance is, of necessity, open to the public at large through public conversion to the gospel. Christian resisters are not to undergo a secret system of initiation, the hallmark of occult conspiracies. Christian resisters are not to adopt any and all resistance measures, irrespective of the morality of these acts. The Bible, a public document, provides the foundation of ethics, including the ethics of resistance.

This does not mean that everything involved in resistance must be crystal clear and open to God's enemies. Ehud did

---

1. See, for example, Charles William Heckethorn, *The Secret Societies of All Ages and Countries* (2 vols.; New Hyde Park, New York: University Books, [1897] 1965); Stephen Runciman, *The Medieval Manichee: A Study of the Christian Dualist Heresy* (New York: Viking, 1961).

2. The most detailed account of the rise of revolutionary socialism is the book by James Billington, *Fire in the Minds of Men: Origins of the Revolutionary Faith* (New York: Basic Books, 1980).

not carry his "present"—a dagger—in his hand as he entered Eglon's chamber (Judges 3:16). Gideon did not warn the commanding officer of the Midianites of his strategy of surprise (Judges 7:15-25). Jesus spoke in parables in order to keep the masses of Hebrews from understanding His message and being converted, and He cited Isaiah 6:9-10 as His justification (Matt. 13:13-17). Despite the legitimacy of the Christian's use of deception against the followers of Satan, the great deceiver, *the building of a Christian resistance movement cannot legitimately be based on a program of initiation into a secret hierarchy of power.* Men who enter resistance movements are to know who their institutional superiors are, as in the case of a military chain of command, and their actions are to be governed by an agreed-upon handbook, the Bible. There are no secret principles that must not be revealed to non-initiates, so there can be no ritual murders or other physical reprisals against those who reveal biblical principles of resistance. The principles of righteous action are available to all those who are willing to discipline their minds and actions by the revealed word of God.

In a period of increasing social, political, and economic disorder, we can expect to see many resistance groups competing for the allegiance of millions of people. We can expect to find that thousands of people join organizations that would have been anathema to these new members a decade earlier. The escalating confrontations between these organizations and the civil government, and between each other, will mobilize people who had preferred to avoid earlier confrontations. People will be swept away emotionally and perhaps morally if they are not careful to examine the *goals, training, and techniques* of all organizations that call members to sacrifice their lives, wealth, and honor for a cause.

By what standard should these movements be examined? The Christian should not hesitate to answer, "The Bible." But understanding the Bible takes time and effort. It is not an overnight educational process. Certain biblical truths must be so firmly planted in the mind that the emotions of the moment are not allowed to carry the potential victim into the pit. This is what we expect of Christians who are tempted to become adulterers. In times of social chaos, as in times of bureaucratic tyranny, the emotional appeal of resistance and revolution is often stronger than the appeal of non-marital sex. Wild enthusiasm and deviant behavior are common aspects of both of these forms of ethical rebellion. So is personal destruction. Men need to think through the implications of their actions before temptation comes.

Of course, the legitimacy of any given tactic must be supported first of all by the legitimacy of resistance as such. We do not deal with this important question in this issue of **Christianity and Civilization**. This was covered in considerable detail in **C&C 2**, "The Theology of Christian Resistance." But resistance must have a foundation of moral legitimacy if it is to be successful. Christianity offers legitimacy to resistance under certain limited conditions, using certain limited means.

This symposium is a call to action and a warning about the wrong kinds of action. It is simultaneously motivational and restraining. It recognizes the words of the Bible as binding:

> Enter ye in at the strait [narrow] gate: for wide is the gate, and broad is the way, which leadeth to destruction, and many there be which go in there at. Because strait is the gate, and narrow is the way, which leadeth unto life, and few there be that find it (Matt. 7:13-14).

In resistance against tyranny, as in every other human venture, there is a broad path and a narrow path. The broad path is the path of romantic (lawless) violence and self-destruction. *This narrow path is hemmed in on both sides by biblical law.* We are not supposed to retreat; we are supposed to head forward down the path. But we are not to deviate from that path, either to the right hand or the left (Deut. 17:11).

In an age of turmoil and confusion, the subtleties of academic and theological debate will be lost on the vast majority of those who call themselves Christians. There will be a desperate quest for *action*—action which promises to bring peace, or righteousness, or justice, or economic equality, or any number of other seemingly legitimate goals. What Christians must be on guard against is *any call to action which is not hemmed in by basic biblical principles*, such as the principle against secret societies and initiations. (Members of Masonic orders are already violating this principle.[3] What will happen in a time of really serious social crisis? Will Christians honor this principle?)

As one skeptic has said, "When the public starts looking

---

3. Everett C. DeVelde, "A Reformed View of Freemasonry," *Christianity and Civilization*, 1 (1982).

for a man on a white horse, watch out: there are a lot of fellows out there with horses and buckets of whitewash." Or as Jesus said:

> Beware of false prophets, which come to you in sheep's clothing, but inwardly they are ravening wolves. Ye shall know them by their fruits. Do men gather grapes of thorns, or figs of thistles? Even so every good tree bringeth forth good fruit; but a corrupt tree bringeth forth evil fruit (Matt. 7:15-17).

### *Why Resistance?*

Assume that you are a member of a Reformed church in the Netherlands. It is 1942. The Nazis who control your nation militarily have just announced a new policy requiring all Jews to come to the local city hall and register. The most prominent church leader in your denomination has recommended obedience to all "lawful" directives of the German authorities. He has not recommended disobeying this new directive, and you have no reason to believe that he will. Your denomination will not speak directly to this issue, and you think the civil authorities will threaten to shut down churches or in other ways pressure the church's leadership to remain silent or even recommend compliance with the order.[4] Then a Jew you know comes to you and asks for asylum. He wants you to hide him in your attic or barn. You know that this would be illegal. Will you hide him or turn him over to the Nazis?

Assume that you are a Negro lady living in Montgomery, Alabama in late 1956. You have had a hard day at work, and you have just boarded a bus to go home. You sit down in the first row of the section of the bus set aside for Negroes. At the next stop, several white passengers board the bus, and there is no room for them in the white section. The driver tells you to move farther to the rear of the bus. Whites can sit in your section of the bus, but you are not allowed to sit in theirs. The bus system is owned by the municipal government, and these rules are established by that government. The driver is acting as an agent of the civil government. If you refuse to move, he will have you arrested. Will you move?

---

4. This is the reason why churches should prepare basic documents concerning the limits of cooperation with the State *before* the enemy controls the public declarations of the ecclesiastical hierarchy.

Assume that you are a member of the board of a small church. Your state has passed a law which allows local counties to impose property taxes on all church properties that are not specifically set apart for exclusively religious activities. Officials of the county government have written to your church to inform you that they intend to enter the premises of your church and make an assessment of just which property in your church is devoted exclusively to worship, and what property is used also for "non-worship" activities and is therefore subject to the tax. You know that most of the mainline denominations are going to cooperate with the local officials, and they have decided to pay any taxes levied by the county, just to avoid trouble and expensive lawsuits. Will you recommend to other members of the church's board to allow the tax assessors in to make their assessment, and then pay the tax bill when it is sent?

These are not hypothetical cases. I know a Dutchman whose family did hide a Jewish gentlemen from local authorities for several years. They were nearly driven crazy by the man, who kept getting bored and would insist on going shopping, or even getting involved in municipal work projects. As for the Negro lady, her name was Rosa Parks, and she refused to move from her seat on December 1, 1956. She was arrested. The Negro community in Montgomery then organized a boycott of the municipal bus system, which was an illegal act. The boycott was successful economically; the bus company lost a fortune. Negroes returned only eleven months later, when the United States Supreme Court declared the segregated seating law unconstitutional. The man who led the protest was Rev. Martin Luther King, Jr. The protest launched his career.

Finally, the problem of property taxes. A model law subjecting church property taxation is on the books in most states in the United States. It has been quietly passed by legislatures, and it has received little or no attention from the press or the churches. It is now being enforced in California. Its success or failure there will probably be used as a precedent. Other counties around the nation are waiting for the political go-ahead signal. Churches are now declared to be under the jurisdiction of the civil government, and the State now asserts its power to destroy the churches, for "the power to tax involves the power to destroy," as Supreme Court Chief

Justice John Marshall declared in the landmark case of 1819, *M'Culloch v. Maryland*. In that case, the Court declared unconstitutional the law permitting a state to levy a tax on banknotes issued by banks not chartered by the state. The bank in question had been chartered by the Federal government, but not by the state. The constitutional battle was a battle over *sovereignty*. Two governments—a state government and the Federal government—were in conflict. Marshall's words are significant. The principle of *governmental sovereignty* was the issue.

> . . . That the power to tax involves the power to destroy; that the power to destroy may defeat and render useless the power to create; that there is a plain repugnance, in conferring on one government a power to control the constitutional measures of another, which other, with respect to those very measures, is declared to be supreme over that which exerts the control, are propositions not to be denied. . . . The question is, in truth, a question of supremacy; and if the right of the States to tax the means employed by the general government be conceded, the declaration that the constitution, and the laws made in pursuance thereof, shall be the supreme law of the land, is empty and unmeaning declamation. . . .[5]

The question today is this: Is one or another civil government the only kind of government allowed to claim definitive sovereignty? Is the church, as the body of Jesus Christ, not also entitled in the eyes of God to sovereignty equal to that of any civil government? While the courts of the civil governments may not today recognize such sovereignty on the part of Christ's churches, does this deny its existence? Should the officers of the various churches act as though the State's claim is valid, as if the State has the right before God to impose taxes on the church, thereby acquiescing to the State's claim that it possesses sovereignty superior to that of the church? If the State declares that it has incorporated the churches and therefore has legitimate sovereignty over the churches, should the churches remain incorporated? Have they the moral obligation before God to admit that previous church officers were remiss in appealing to the state for a charter? Should they not de-incorporate and begin anew as sovereign agents

---

5. *M'Culloch v. Maryland* (1819), in Henry Steele Commager (ed.), *Documents of American History* (6th ed.; New York: Appleton-Century-Crofts, 1958), p. 219.

under God rather than under some civil government?

### *The Question of Sovereignty (Legal Jurisdiction)*

The question of sovereignty, civil government vs. church government, has confronted Christians in every major period of Western history, but especially during periods of rapid political change. It was Christ vs. Caesar in the early church, the Pope vs. the Emperor in the middle ages, the Roman Church vs. the princes in Luther's day, and the British Parliament and the Anglican Church vs. both the independent and established state churches in the American colonies in 1775.

Few Americans are aware that it was not even legal for American colonists to print Bibles in the colonies; that was a monopoly granted to British printers, most notably Oxford and Cambridge Universities. The restriction applied only to unannotated versions of the King James Bible, but that was sufficient. The annotated ones were too elaborate and expensive to print in the colonies. Prior to the American Revolution, the only Bibles ever legally printed in the colonies—one may have been produced illegally in Boston in 1750—were John Eliot's 1663 translation into the Algonquin Indian language and a mid-eighteenth century German language Bible. During the Revolutionary War, Bibles became extremely scarce. One of the "acts of rebellion" by the Continental Congress in 1781 was to authorize the printing of 10,000 copies of the Bible, which Robert Aitken printed at his own expense the next year.[6]

*There can be no escape from the question of sovereignty.* Few evangelical church leaders in the West's industrial nations recognize the nature of the confrontation, but those in Marxist and Islamic nations do. The intellectual and religious battles between humanists and Christians have heated up only in recent years. High-risk confrontations have been limited in number. The publicized battles generally have been confined to a barrage of words. It is not surprising to learn that

6. Rosalie J. Slater, *Teaching and Learning America's Christian History* (San Francisco: Foundation for American Christian Education, 1975), pp. 339ff. Cf. Robert R. Deardon, Jr. and Douglas S. Watson, *The Bible of the Revolution* (San Francisco, 1930). A facsimile copy of this Bible was printed by the Arno Press, New York, in 1968. The introductory essay includes a one-page bibliography about the Aitken Bible.

Norman Lear's People for the American Way organization, dedicated to battling Jerry Falwell's Moral Majority, turns out to be heavily funded by Hugh Hefner's Playboy Foundation.[7] (I can see the headline now: "Norman Leer.") But the looming battles have higher stakes than winning debate points. Families and churches are literally coming under attack.

The attacks should not surprise Christians. The battle over sovereignty has been going on since the temptation of Adam. It was the issue which confronted Job. Not until he understood its implications was he restored to his former condition of prosperity.

> "And the Lord said unto Satan, Hast thou considered my servant Job, that there is none like him in the earth, a perfect and an upright man, one that feareth God, and escheweth evil? Then Satan answered the Lord, and said, Doth Job fear God for naught? Hast thou not made an hedge about him, and about his house, and about all that he hath on every side? Thou hast blest the work of his hands, and his substance is increased in the land. But put forth thine hand now, and touch all that he hath, and he will curse thee to thy face" (Job 1:8-11).

The Bible is a book about warfare. The warfare began in the garden of Eden, and it will not end until the final judgment. The essence of this warfare is *ethical*: Who will be cursed by a man, God or Satan? Who will be praised by the works of a man's hands, God or Satan? Who will stand firm for God ethically, in order to march forward dominically? This confrontation involves every aspect of life, for the whole world is at stake. There is no neutral territory. God claims total sovereignty over the whole creation, and so does Satan, although it is basic to Satan's strategy to give rebellious man the impression that Satan is standing for multiple sovereignty, and therefore standing up for man. But the heart of his confrontation is to demonstrate that God does not possess the total sovereignty that God, as Creator, unquestionably claims to possess. If God does not possess total sovereignty, then He is not what He says He is, and therefore Satan, as the most beautiful and powerful of created beings, has sovereignty

7. *Christian Enquirer* (April, 1983), p. 6. Playboy Foundation gave PAW $40,000 in 1981. It also donated to Catholics for a Free Choice ($10,000), Religious Coalition for Abortion Rights ($10,000), National Abortion Rights Action League ($15,000), and the American Civil Liberties Union ($50,000).

transferred to himself.

This battle over sovereignty involves two kingdoms, God's and Satan's. Whose troops will be victorious on the battlefield? There is no "Switzerland" in this warfare, no "King's X." Two commanders are marshalling their forces continually. The armies are real armies, and they operate as armies: they have skirmishes, they send in spies, they use deception, they make plans for major battles, they use psychological warfare techniques, they devote resources to buy equipment, they have "rest and recreation" centers, they have medical teams, they have specialized commando units, they have established territories under their jurisdiction, and from time to time in history, they launch major strategic campaigns against each other.

The confrontation between Moses and Pharaoh was an archetype of the nature of the warfare. Neither side would give in to the other. The honor of Pharaoh and Egypt's gods was at stake; so was the honor of Jehovah. Here was a major confrontation, and it was marked by a series of escalating engagements. It ended in the death of Egypt's firstborn and the total victory of the Hebrews over their enemies. Pharaoh possessed earthly power and continued to exploit God's people. He made life increasingly miserable on them. They were weak, and they blamed Moses for their pains, not Pharaoh (Ex. 5:20-23). They continued to blame him in the wilderness. They were blaming God through Moses (Num. 14:27).

### *The War on Church-Operated Schools*

Pastor Everett Sileven of Louisville, Nebraska, went to jail for over six months for keeping open a church school which was not accredited by the state. The videotaped program documenting his confrontation with the bureaucracy of the state should be shown to every congregation and every Christian school in the United States. Showing this videotape could easily be the very first stage of any church or parent motivation program in a program of Christian resistance. You can (and should) buy a copy of the tape, plus Pastor Sileven's books that he wrote in prison, plus audiocassette tapes, for a $100 donation:

C. A. P.
P.O. Box 249
Louisville, NB 68037

You will also receive a copy of Ed Rowe's paperback book, *The Day They Padlocked the Church*. This book can be ordered separately, however, for $3.50:

Huntington House
1200 N. Market, Suite G
Shreveport, LA 71107

The humanist opponents of Christian education are blind to the underlying issues involved in the battle over Christian education—willfully blind, in my view—or else simply dishonest. They have become convinced, as so many naive Americans are, that the State is responsible for the education of children. The Bible teaches that parents are responsible, not the State. It is only because modern men believe that the State has taken on the functions of the family that people can believe that the State must supervise education. But this religion of the "State as pseudo-parent" is widespread. The State has taught it in its very own established church, the public school system.[8]

Conservatives are not immune to this error. I received a letter from a subscriber to my economics newsletter, *Remnant Review*, who protested against my insertion of a promotional flyer telling the story of Pastor Sileven's crisis. My letter is quite conservative. Amazing—one of Sileven's opponents was a subscriber! Here, believe it or not, is a "conservative's" view —a very, very high official of the public schools in a Nebraska county:

> The State of Nebraska requires public and private school teachers to be certified which requires a B.S. or B.A. degree in education. The Catholic and Lutheran private school systems adhere to this policy and they state that although religion is an added part of the curriculum, qualified teachers still are needed to teach the three R's.
>
> To someone living in Florida or Oregon and reading the newspapers about Everett Sileven's church, one would think that anti-religious idiots existed in the State of Nebraska. The public pulse columns of the Omaha World Herald were full of letters to the editor from all over the country complaining about the Sheriff hauling Sileven out of a church and not one of the letters stated anything about the school, sponsored by the church, not using certified teachers, which was why Sileven, as head of the school,

8. R. J. Rushdoony, *The Messianic Character of American Education* (Nutley, NJ: Craig Press, 1963).

was charged to appear in court.

> Your readers, in my opinion, may be reading about an issue that is not the real issue when they buy Sileven's publication. (Letter dated 5/23/83)

It is not Sileven's supporters who fail to understand the issue. It is this public school official who does not understand. *The issue is sovereignty: God vs. Satan, Christianity vs. secular humanism, family vs. State.* It is the B.A. in education which appalls parents—a third-rate union card in an academic field which is the laughing stock on every university campus in America. Yes, Sileven was hauled out of a church. The school was a ministry of his church, and parents, as sovereign agents over their children, delegated the authority to instruct their children to this church ministry. Those parents are sovereign over the education of their children, not the State.[9]

These issues concerning legitimate sovereignty are at last being drawn by American conservative Christians. The fact that old-line (and humanist-infiltrated) Roman Catholic or Lutheran schools long ago compromised on this sovereignty issue provides an additional reason why it is not these schools that have experienced the unprecedented, explosive growth in Christian education since 1965. They believe that "religion is an added part of the curriculum," do they? Well, they are incorrect: religion is not an "added part." *Religion is the ultimate foundation of all curricula.* The question is: *Which religion?* The battle over sovereignty in education is really a battle to decide this crucial question: *Whose religion will undergird education in this nation, the "State-parent's" religion or the covenant parents' religions?*

Nevertheless, Christians should be forewarned: *millions of conservatives and Christians do not recognize the importance of the sovereignty issue.* We cannot expect automatic support from our supposed "natural allies." This is why we must prepare carefully before we launch any program of resistance. A resistance program is an educational program and a public relations program. It also involves important legal issues.

Constitutional law specialist John Whitehead has written several important books about this battle, most notably the best-selling book, *The Second American Revolution* (David C. Cook, 1982). In an essay published in *The Journal of Christian*

9. R. J. Rushdoony, *Intellectual Schizophrenia: Culture, Crisis and Education* (Philadelphia: Presbyterian & Reformed, 1961).

*Reconstruction* (Summer, 1981), he outlined fourteen steps that churches should consider if they operate a Christian school. Two overall principles must govern these educational ministries. First: *What does the Bible say?* Second, *consistency*. "In a Christian school context, this means that the church must treat the school the same way the other ministries of the church are treated. A clever state prosecutor will attempt in every way to distinguish the Christian school from other ministries of the church. Be consistent!"

Here are Whitehead's suggested steps:

1. The Christian school should never be separately incorporated from the church.
2. The financial statements of the day school should show the day school as a ministry on the same level as other ministries of the church. (Also, do not use the language of a commercial business in the financial statements of church or school.)
3. The church treasurer should write all checks and control all funds flowing in or out of all ministries.
4. If possible, all ministries should use the same physical facilities.
5. Use the Bible in establishing the church constitution, using Bible references throughout.
6. The school name should be about the same as the church's name, and the same doctrine should be taught.
7. The governing board of the church should govern all the ministries, including the school.
8. All fund raising should be done through the school's parent organization.
9. If parents "donate" money to the school, it may be held to be tax-deductible only in amounts *above* what tuition for their children would be.
10. Teacher contracts must be carefully worded. Is the teacher the same as a minister? Is the minister not under contract, but the teacher is?
11. Church officers, especially pastors, create a problem for the day school if their children are enrolled in government (public) grade or high schools.
12. Churches are *automatically exempt* from Federal taxation under the Internal Revenue Code. Why apply for exemption?
13. Some laws (Internal Revenue Code) treat the church as separate from the school. This could become a problem.
14. The State is asserting the right to tax churches and their ministries. This is where the battle must be joined.[10]

---

10. John W. Whitehead, "God vs. Caesar: Taking Steps to Protect Church Schools," *The Journal of Christian Reconstruction*, VIII (Summer, 1981). Address: P.O. Box 158, Vallecito, CA 95251: $5.00.

Whitehead's warning takes on new significance since May of 1983. In that month, two key decisions were made by the U.S. Supreme Court. The Bob Jones University case of May 24 received a lot of publicity. The Court removed the university's tax exemption because it affirmed a policy of racial segregation (dating, marriage). This policy is in opposition to public policy, the Court said, so no exemption would be allowed.

The more significant decision was handed down on May 23, in the case of *Regan v. Taxation With Representation of Washington*. It received virtually no publicity. A previously tax-exempt organization had been lobbying in Washington. The I.R.S. had revoked its tax-exempt status. The Supreme Court upheld this decision of the I.R.S. The opinion of Justice Rehnquist is significant:

> Both tax exemptions and tax-deductibility are a form of subsidy that is administered through a tax system. A tax exemption has much the same effect as a cash grant to the organization of the amount of tax it would have to pay on its income.

From a strictly economic standpoint, Justice Rehnquist is correct. If the government allows someone to keep money he would otherwise have been obliged to pay to the tax collector, the narrowly defined economic effects are the same as if the State had granted him a direct subsidy. The higher the rate of taxation, the larger the subsidy. This is a very good reason why taxes should be limited to under 10% of net income: it would reduce the size of all tax-exemption "subsidies." The State therefore would lose much of its clout in the area of tax-exempt institutions, because the threat of the removal of the "subsidy" would not drastically affect the survival of the organization. But if the Court intends to adopt a narrowly economic definition of the meaning of tax-deductibility (let alone tax exemption), in order to force all tax-exempt organizations to adhere to every conceivable public policy (as defined by the Supreme Court), then an endless war is about to begin between politicians, bureaucrats, and I.R.S. officials on one side, and tax-exempt organizations that do not "follow the public policy guidelines"—and there are seemingly an innumerable number of public policy guidelines—on the other.

The race issue in the case of Bob Jones University is now in principle settled. The Court has set the precedent. Will the

I.R.S. begin to attack Christian schools once again, as it attempted to do in August of 1978? If the I.R.S. is successful in shutting down Christian schools with this ploy, can we then expect attacks on "racially imbalanced" churches? (Perhaps not: there are too many all-black churches that will create a firestorm of protest if such nonsense is attempted.)

Let us consider another possibility: *homosexuality.* Is it public policy, as affirmed by Congress and the courts, to forbid all discrimination based on sex? Even though the Equal Rights Amendment failed? If so, then churches that excommunicate (or refuse to admit to membership) homosexuals and lesbians face the removal of their tax exemption. (If we look at this from a narrowly economic standpoint, this will tend to subsidize physicians who specialize in the treatment of AIDS. Should they therefore be regulated by the I.R.S., since they will be the recipients of an implicit subsidy?) This example is only one of hundreds I could conceivably enumerate. The point is clear: *the threat of the removal of tax exemption is a club which the bureaucrats will learn to swing selectively.* The question is: What will be the response of the churches?

The necessary first response is clear: churches must insist that they possess tax *immunity,* not tax exemption. The words "tax *exempt*" transfer too much power to the civil government. The State can begin to assess the churches' stand on every conceivable public policy issue, with the courts or Congress determining what is acceptable public policy this week. The churches are in a unique category: total immunity from any taxation by any agency of civil government. Church boards must defend the total immunity from taxation; then they must fight, case by case, to maintain this sovereignty. If they capitulate to any civil government on any tax, they have admitted their liability to taxes in general.

When the church buys something, *it must not pay the sales tax.* For cash, the seller ought to provide a discount. In any case, *the seller owes the tax, not the church.* If necessary, agree in advance to pay more than retail, so that the seller implicitly collects the tax and pays it, but *under no circumstances should any tax subtotal appear in any bill presented to a church.* If the seller wants to do business with a church, he will have to learn not to put tax subtotals on bills submitted to the church.

If a bill must be paid to a public utility, and some tax is mentioned on the computerized bill, the church should pay the total bill presented but attach a disclaimer on the back of the check which says something like this:

> The payment of this bill in no way represents an admission on the part of the [ ] church that it owes any tax to any agency of civil government. A tax may be owed by the organization to which this check is made payable. The [ ] church is simply paying a bill submitted to it by a seller of goods or services.

This disclaimer can be imprinted on a rubber stamp. Stamp this notification on the back of every check, just below the space where the payee will sign or stamp its name. It can also be printed at the bottom of every check on the front, as an alternative to the rubber stamp approach.

Such steps seem like a lot of trouble. They *are* a lot of trouble. We are in a war. This war is going to escalate, as it has escalated in the past. The question is: Will Bible-believing churches fight? Will they count the costs? Will they pay the price?

### *Environmental Determinism: Will Christians Fight?*

Pharaoh operated in terms of a philosophy of environmental determinism, of pure "condition and response." He believed that if he could escalate the punishments against God's people, they would give in to his demands. What Pharaoh did not count on was that his punishments were nothing compared to those that God could and eventually did inflict on him and his followers. God gave Pharaoh a lesson: it was Pharaoh and his followers who would capitulate to God's will because it was they who were the believers in the religion of environmental determinism. Though the Hebrews did attempt to conform to Pharaoh's will, God would not allow them to have their way. And God showed Moses that Satan's philosophy of environmental determinism was incorrect by the experience of the Israelites in the wilderness: they did not conform to God, even though He showered them with blessings, beginning with deliverance from Egypt. Faith, in short, is not a matter of economic determinism. Pharaoh had not understood the nature of the God facing him, and neither did the people of Israel in the wilderness.

In the Book of Job, we have the Bible's most detailed account of a confrontation between Satan and man. The man is described by God as perfect. This does not mean that he was sin-free, but it means that he honored the terms of the covenant and made continual burnt offerings as sacrifices to God for his sin and the sins of his family (1:5). He was a shining example of righteousness.

God called Satan's attention to Job. Satan's response was immediate: he appealed to the doctrine of *economic determinism*, a variation of the environmental determinism which Adam used to justify his actions: "The woman whom thou gavest to be with me, she gave me of the tree, and I did eat" (Gen. 3:12). He is faithful, Satan argued, because God provides him with external blessings. In short, God has bought him off. God is, in effect, paying tribute to Job. It is Job who is sovereign here, not God. Remove the benefits, and He will curse God. By implication, Satan said that *God's followers are in it for the money, and that if God should stop providing benefits, all his people will rebel*. If the perfect man does, then they all will. The key is economics: without benefits to offer His followers, God would be a Commander without an army.

Satan repeated this argument with another perfect man, Jesus. He offered Him the kingdoms of this world in order to gain Jesus' worship.[11] This attempt failed, for Jesus answered: "Get thee hence, Satan: for it is written, Thou shalt worship the Lord thy God, and him only shalt thou serve" (Matt. 4:10). This is the eternally binding response. Job never denied it. A curse of God never came from his lips, despite the pleadings of his faithless wife (2:9).

Job misunderstood the cause-and-effect nature of faithfulness and blessing. He was not an economic determinist, as Satan is. He did not worship God because of the economic benefits God poured out upon him. He lost them all, but he

11. Did Satan own the kingdoms of the world? No; God owns the earth (Ps. 50:10-11). But Satan did hold temporary title as a steward because of Adam's transfer of title to him at the Fall. Adam decided not to act as God's steward, thereby placing himself under Satan's power. In this sense, Satan could offer Jesus the world's kingdoms as a *leasehold*. But He would have remained an *ethical subordinate* under Satan. After Satan's defeat at the cross, he possessed everything as a squatter; title reverted to the perfect man, Jesus, and to His disciples, through the Jubilee principle (Luke 4:16-21). Jesus announced the Jubilee Year immediately upon His return from Satan's temptations in the wilderness. In principle, the temptation was over with respect to stewardship under God. The only temptation remaining was the temptation not to go to the cross. After His resurrection, all power was transferred to Him (Matt. 28:18).

remained a follower of God. What Job did not understand was that *God's blessings on His faithful people are ultimately a matter of grace, that since the days of Adam's Fall, man has no claim whatsoever on God's blessings.* Blessings are conditional, and Adam violated the conditions. While God grants blessings on those who at least attempt to walk perfectly, they are nonetheless sinners and altogether under the sovereignty of God.

The normal cause-and-effect relationship between covenantal faithfulness and external blessings is not an invariable, autonomous law of the universe. While it is sufficiently predictable to make possible redeemed man's strategy of dominion, it is not autonomous, nor must redeemed man ever count on its operation as if it were an invariable law. When men's faith in this regularity interferes with their faith in the absolute, unconditional sovereignty of God, then they have exposed themselves to Satan, for they have adopted a view of history which is perilously close to Satan's economic determinism. While faithful men do not worship God because they are seeking benefits, as Satan claims that they do, they come close to his view of cause and effect when they assume that their faithfulness will bring automatic blessings and automatic victory.

Job's response indicates the extent to which he was under the spell of Satan's philosophy. "After this opened Job his mouth, and cursed his day. And Job spake, and said, Let the day perish wherein I was born, and the night in which it was said, There is a man child conceived" (3:1-3). *Job cursed God's historical environment.* He saw all his life as a liability, as "red ink" in the cosmic ledger. He did not blame God for his crises, but he cursed the cause-and-effect nature of the universe. His life was a loss in his own eyes, a mockery of justice. His righteousness had availed him nothing. Better that he had never been born.

With respect to the life of a rebellious man, "better that he had never been born" is a proper conclusion, not because there is no real justice in the universe, but because there is perfect justice and perfect punishment. Jesus' words regarding Judas make this clear: "The Son of man goeth as it is written: but woe unto that man by whom the Son of man is betrayed! It had been good for that man if he had not been born" (Matt. 26:24). Nevertheless, Judas could not rightfully blame his environment for his sin, even though his acts had been written before the foundation of the world. The same was true of Pharaoh's sin (Rom. 9:17-18). Job did not understand that his environment did not testify concerning his ethical position before God. He blamed his environment, and indirectly he was blaming God, just as the Hebrews did in the wilderness. The Book of Job is a document which warns men about the fallacious nature of environmental determinism. The attacks on Job were fully within the plan of God and in no way overturned the omnipotence of God. They were not events that somehow thwarted God's design for Job's life. Job's environment was not to blame. The ethical cause-and-effect nature of the universe had not been overturned.

*What Job did not grasp was the doctrine of the sovereignty of God.* He did not initially understand that *God can legitimately do whatever He chooses with all that He possesses*. God's answer to Job was essentially the answer of the sovereign employer in Jesus' parable of the householder: "Is it not lawful for me to do what I will with mine own? Is thine eye evil, because I am good" (Matt. 20:15). In short, "Therefore hath he mercy on whom he will have mercy, and whom he will he hardeneth" (Rom. 9:18). When Job finally came to understand the biblical doctrine of the unconditional sovereignty of God, which was God's detailed answer to Job (chaps. 38-41), God blessed him with twice the goods that he had possessed before (42:10).[12]

Why all this discussion of economic determinism? Because Satan and his followers believe in it. They judge the motivation of Christians in terms of their supposed economic self-interest. *They imagine that if they can threaten Christians with economic penalties of one kind or another, the Christians will capitulate.* To the extent that Christians do operate in terms of economic determinism, their efforts in resisting satanic tyranny will be thwarted.

Yes, Christians operate in terms of economic motivations. If we can get what we want for less than we are willing to pay, we may buy more of it (or more of something else we could not otherwise have purchased). If someone increases our costs of buying, we will buy less (or reduce our purchases of some-

12. This two-fold increase is consistent with the penalty of double restitution (Ex. 22:7, 9). As the destroyer, Satan owed Job the double restitution payment, but Satan owns nothing of his own. God made the restitution payment owed by Satan, not as grace to Satan but as grace to Job.

thing else). But the point is, *we are not solely motivated by economics*. If the enemy assumes that we are, then he has made a strategic error.

As the intensity of the confrontation increases, and as the areas under attack by humanists increase in number, Christians will be called upon to make sacrifices, including economic sacrifices. Our opponents are going to misjudge our willingness to make those sacrifices. Our opponents do not understand God or His universe. They do not understand the motivation of God's redeemed people. Because of this, they are going to get a much tougher battle than they have counted on.

### *The Decisive Battle of the War*

The fascination of contemporary Christian fundamentalists with the battle of Armageddon indicates a weakness in their theology. *The decisive battle of our war was fought at Calvary*. Any program of Christian resistance must begin with an understanding that the outcome of the war was firmly established long ago. Satan now concentrates his attention on earth rather than on the court of God's host. The twelfth chapter of the Book of Revelation describes the effects of Christ's crucifixion on Satan's war-making ability. He was cast down from heaven to the earth, along with his angels (12:8-9). This was a post-resurrection event, as the passage makes clear: "And I heard a loud voice saying in heaven, Now is come salvation, and strength, and the kingdom of God, and the power of his Christ: for the accuser of our brethren is cast down, which accused them before our God day and night. And they overcame him by the blood of the Lamb, and by the word of their testimony; and they loved not their lives unto the death" (12:10-11). Satan no longer goes before God in heaven to accuse God's people, as he did in the days of Job. "Therefore rejoice ye heavens, and ye that dwell in them. Woe unto you inhabitants of the earth and of the sea! For the devil is come down unto you, having great wrath, because he knoweth that he hath but a short time" (12:12).

His time is short. He is in a defensive operation. Like the fury of the late 1944 German defensive campaign at the Battle of the Bulge, Satan's warfare can be savage, but it is short-lived. He is fighting desperately, for the key events in history, the death and resurrection of Christ, are behind him. He is a commander who knows what the outcome of the war will be, just as Hitler knew by 1943, after the defeat of his troops in North Africa and at Stalingrad. He keeps fighting anyway, for he will not sue for peace. The casualties mount up on both sides, but he does not have the troops to spare. God does. Satan is calling for kamikaze attacks from his followers in a desperate final campaign to inflict wounds on his great enemy. He is calling on his troops to form suicide squads. What was established *definitively* at Calvary is now being worked out *progressively* in history, as history heads for the *final* resolution of the war. Though Satan wounded the heel of the Anointed, his head is in principle crushed. Analogously, though the heels of Christ's troops will be wounded, the heads of Satan's followers will be crushed.

The tactics of Christian resistance must not begin with a mistaken understanding of the nature of the strategy involved. We are in the final stages of a major series of conflicts. The enemy has received a mortal wound. A mortally wounded animal can become a ferocious beast. It attacks when it might otherwise be content to slink off. But let us not mistake the mortal nature of the wound. Time is on our side, not his. *We must not adopt the kamikaze tactics that are associated with the final stages of a losing campaign*. Once again, let us heed the words of General George S. Patton to his troops: "Your job is not to die for your country. Your job is to get the other poor, dumb bastard to die for *his* country."

### *Counting the Costs*

Here is the first step in any program of Christian resistance: "For which of you intending to build a tower, sitteth not down first, and counteth the cost, whether he have sufficient to finish it? Lest happly [it happen], after he hath laid the foundation, and is not able to finish it, all that behold it begin to mock him, saying, This man began to build, and was not able to finish" (Luke 14:28-30).

Are we environmental determinists? Are we in this fight for the economic benefits we can get out of it? Are we what Satan said Job was? If so, then an attack on us by Satan comparable to his attack on Job will finish us off. By removing our protected environment, God can deliver us into the hand of the enemy at any time. Will being caught in the enemy's hand destroy us or strengthen us?

The literature of the prison camps is instructive. Some men do break, but most of them do not. In Korea, more American soldiers capitulated than in any prior war. The Communists first removed officers and men who showed leadership abilities and put them under tight guard. Then they effectively indoctrinated the ones who were left. They did not torture people. They alienated prisoners from each other. They subtly got them to collaborate. They controlled large numbers of prisoners with a handful of guards.[13]

In contrast the North Vietnamese dealt harshly with captured pilots. These Americans were officers. They had better educations. It was not possible to use the same techniques on them that the Koreans had used. Instead, the familiar techniques of physical isolation, deprivation, and torture were used. But few of them broke down.[14]

When men have a sense of calling higher than their own self-interest, they are much harder to break down. Christians who are put under torture and psychological pressure take far longer to break, and they absorb far more of their oppressors' time. They are, in this respect, low pay-off victims. The oppressors can more profitably spend their time on less dedicated prisoners.

When major issues of life and death are at stake, Christians perform very well. They always have. The problem comes, as it came in the Korean prisoner of war camps, when the enemy's challenge is not clear-cut. If the stakes do not appear to be very high, if none of the issues involved appear to be critical, and if the consequences of capitulating seem minimal, Christians may capitulate. What is giving up church records to some minor state official when compared with, say, the possibility that the Federal government will remove the church's tax exemption? What is the cost of complying with the Department of Education's demand that all church school students be given state-administered examinations? What "really important" precedent is set by such interference? Besides, legal fees are expensive, and so few lawyers really want to fight. They usually want to capitulate without giving up *too* much. Lawyers are "team players,"

13. Eugene Kinkaid, *In Every War But One* (New York: Norton, 1959).

14. Jeremiah Denton, *When Hell Was in Session* (Clover, SC: Riverhills Plantation, 1976).

when the opposition team, not to mention the referees, is composed of State officials.

Church officers need to sit down and calculate well in advance when they intend to say "no." Will the church pay property taxes to the state? Will the church pay Social Security taxes without protest (or has it already done so)? Will the church get incorporated (or has it)? Will the church require church school teachers to be licensed by the state board of education (or has it)? Will the church allow its church school to get accredited (or has it)? Will the church open its financial records to any State official, for any reason? What reason? What precedent is being set? Will the church wind up like the Russian Orthodox Church, a paid hireling of the State? If not, why not? How can church officials see to it that they do not cooperate unnecessarily?

Church officers must finally wake up to the fact that *a spiritual war is in progress*. This war involves the civil government. *Secular humanists have captured the robes*: judges, educators, and mainline church officers, especially seminary professors.[15] The churches have been capitulating to the State for decades. Has the State reduced its demands? Are churches and Christian schools under less pressure today than in, say, 1938? Are the demands of the State escalating, or not? If they are escalating, then Christians must escalate their willingness and ability to resist. *We must match the escalation process of the humanist State, and then exceed it.*

## *Strategy and Tactics*

The conventional distinction between strategy and tactics is the military application of the one and many distinction. *Strategy* governs the uses to which each of the parts is put. *Tactics* involve the deployment of the components of the overall strategic forces.

The battle between God and Satan involves strategy and tactics on both sides. The competence of the two opposing commanders is being tested on the ethical battlefields of life. Each commander has followers, angelic and human; each commander has a strategy. In the deployment of forces we see the steady working out of each commander's overall strategy.

15. Gary North, "Capturing the Robes," *Christian Reconstruction*, VII (Sept./Oct., 1982).

Christians need not worry about the outcome of the war. The outcome has never been in doubt. Christians also need not fret about the competence of the grand strategy. We do not know exactly how this strategy will be imposed on history, but we know that it will be.[16] *What must concern us is our performance of the tactical duties assigned to us.* Ours responsibility is to recognize the nature of the warfare of our age, and to deploy the forces entrusted to us by God. The grand strategy is God's and is known only to God. We know only the general principles of action. But these principles are perfectly integrated with the grand strategy, so that as we seek to conform ourselves ethically to God's requirements, we thereby take our positions not only in the grand strategy but also in our tactical command posts.

We must perceive the principles of the grand strategy—*biblical law*—and apply them in concrete historical circumstances. We must master the details of our own callings, so that we will be able to perceive the tactical requirements of the hour. Our strategic plans are, at best, larger tactical plans. No man lives long enough to develop overall strategies, and few human institutions survive the test of the battlefield. They become citadels to conquer and hold. Some of them—universities, for example—have been captured by the enemy within a generation. Satan and his troops seem to be superior in the development of successful tactics, but it is the long-term strategy which counts. It is the *integrating framework* for that strategy—*biblical law*—which will enable Christians to develop more powerful tactics that will fit God's overall strategy.

Tactical considerations should be governed by long-run considerations. What kinds of actions are appropriate? we ask ourselves. We should seek answers that are conformed to strategic requirements:

1. How does biblical law apply in this situation?
2. What are my capacities as a leader?
3. What resources do I have available?
4. What are the capacities of my colleagues?
5. What resources do we have available?
6. Which issues must be dealt with immediately?
7. What is a proper plan of action?

---

16. R. J. Rushdoony, *The Biblical Philosophy of History* (Fairfax, VA: Thoburn Press, [1969] 1978).

8. What will the enemy do in response?
9. How can we effectively counter his response?
10. How long can we sustain this battle?
11. What are we willing to commit to win?
12. What will it cost us if we fail?
13. How must we fight today if we should lose?
14. How will we mount a new offensive if we lose?

### *Romantic Revolutionaries*

By "romantic," I do not mean dizzy with love. I mean dizzy with hate. "Romantic" refers to lawlessness, a kind of frenzy—the idea that the "heroic act" can overcome all opposition. This is the ideology of the moral revolutionary. Sometimes this romantic impulse is sexual; other times it is social. In either case, it must be rejected as opposed to the concept of fixed moral law.

In the summer of 1983, the Geneva Divinity School sold a pair of audiocassette tapes of my lectures on Christian resistance (one was a summary of my essay on "Confirmation, Confrontation, and Caves," which appeared in the second issue of **Christianity and Civilization**). I received the following handwritten letter. It is an excellent example of romantic revolution:

> I am returning these tapes because they do not show how to resist tyranny. . . .
>
> 1) You need a tape on "what to do when the police start arresting Christians."
>
> 2) How about advocating books by Loompanics. . . . How about *Methods of Electronic Surveillance* by David A. Pollack, or *How to Cheat on Taxes*, or perhaps Minney's five-volume set on *How to Kill*. We need to know this when "they" start coming after us.
>
> 3) How can I obtain the real information? Do you have some kind of secret list? I mean, your newsletter and tapes are just surface material—you know, gold, non-hybrid seeds, food storage, and so on. Where is the meat? How about a tape on how to take over the government, or how Christians can take over Cuba, or what automatic weapons are best, or how to escape once in the concentration camp (see FM 31-20 Special Forces operational techniques), or how to get rid of homosexuals in two steps?
>
> 4) O.K., we know about Von Mises, Pugsley, Ruff, Casey, and the Institute for Economic Research. We have bought the silver and food storage. What next? Why don't you write a letter and ask everybody to donate $100 for a few tanks. . . . You will need them when the government blocks off the roads.

I think this letter is serious. It is so far "out in right field" that I am not certain. Is it a joke? I see traces of sarcasm in it, but then why was he so upset with the tapes? The tapes were not "hard-core romanticism," so why use such sarcasm, unless the writer was a dedicated hard-core romantic revolutionary? He did return the tapes and ask for a refund. I gather that he is serious. Even if he isn't, he still speaks for those who are serious, for the kinds of books he mentions do exist, and there is a market for them in conservative circles (and also in radically left-wing circles).

The letter-writer's fears are legitimate. There really are concentration camps in the world. There really are places where the government blocks off the roads. But the tyranny of Nicaragua or Cuba is not characteristic of this nation. It can happen here, but it has yet to happen here, except in certain unique instances that do not yet constitute a trend. What we do know is that one man with a tank is a sitting duck for a modern SWAT team, let alone a platoon of well-armed Marines. The idea that a tank would do anyone any good in a long-term siege on a city, or even in the countryside, boggles the mind. This man has some vision of "The Lone Tanker" and his faithful Indian companion roaming the West and bringing justice. (Silver ate oats; in contrast, the Lone Tanker just pulls into a gas station and says "fill 'er up" with 300 gallons of diesel. Will he save money with "self-serve"? Will he use his Texaco card?)

It is not tanks that bring down governments; it is pamphlets, Bibles, photocopy machines, mimeograph machines, carbon paper, typewriters, *samizdat* (underground) literature, secret prayer groups, and only occasionally an assassination (e.g., killing a top-level official when your nation is occupied by a foreign army: Ehud's tactic). Brother Andrew is doing far more to bring down Communism by smuggling Bibles into Iron Curtain countries than anyone could accomplish by smuggling Uzi submachine guns.[17] (I am not speaking here of Afghanistan; smuggling Uzis to the Afghan rebels would be a worthwhile endeavor, since that Moslem nation is resisting a hated invader.)

---

17. Brother Andrew's organization is Open Doors, P.O. Box 2020, Orange, CA 92669. His books include: *God's Smuggler*, *God's Smuggler to China*, *New Borders for God's Smuggler*, *Persecution: Will It Happen Here?*, and *The Ethics of Smuggling*.

The murder of two Federal agents in early 1983 by a so-called "Christian tax resister" (as the media dubbed him), Gordon Kahl, indicates just how serious—and utterly misguided—some of these "Christian patriots" are. Two Federal officers are dead. So is the murderer. Are our taxes any lower? Is inflation any less a threat? Is the Federal deficit any smaller? Let's face it: if every IRS agent in the country were murdered, the Federal Reserve System could still create the money, buy government bonds (or anything else), and let the government spend the newly created fiat money into circulation. This would "tax" us through price inflation. Americans would then be forced to pay the inflation tax rather than pay the Federal income tax.[18] Yet Kahl is being portrayed as some kind of hero or martyr to a magnificent cause. A flyer on "Kahliphobia" is circulating in Far Right circles—a veiled threat to IRS officials that they, too, risk being murdered.

What has murder got to do with tax protesting? Tax resistance in this case is simply a false ethical shield used by guilty, violent men. Such bloody protesting is revolutionary romanticism in action. Did the murderer accomplish anything for other tax resisters or his family by dying in a shoot-out with authorities after he had vowed not to be taken alive? What "magnificent cause" did he die for? What glory did he bring to God or His church by his romantic, suicidal stand?

I spoke to one courageous Christian resister in the summer of 1983. He predicted (perhaps "vowed" is more accurate): "There's going to be a bloody revolution in this country." I think he is out of touch with the mainstream of fundamentalist churches. He has given too many rousing

---

18. Counterfeiting Federal Reserve Notes and passing them to unsuspecting private individuals in order to "help pay for the tax resistance movement" partakes of the same immoral romanticism. How is the economy helped by new injections of fiat money into the economy? Why is private counterfeiting moral when official central bank counterfeiting is immoral? Yet I received a letter from one tax protestor who justified counterfeiting as a valid means of protest. He defended Vic Lockman's actions in counterfeiting money for "the cause"—actions which Lockman himself had already publicly repented of—by arguing that if the Federal Reserve System has the legal right to counterfeit money, so should private citizens. Here is a classic example of the old "two wrongs make a right" ethic. *Some segments of the Far Right have already adopted tactics based on ethical rebellion.* They are also very close to the violence of romantic revolution.

speeches to visibly enthusiastic but small audiences filled with people who have not counted the costs of revolutionary violence. Perhaps there will eventually be a bloody revolution, but not until the Federal government is much, much weaker. Furthermore, this bloody revolution will not be led by Christians, although Christians may well serve as someone else's misguided cannon fodder in the battle. If Christians try to lead "a bloody revolution," they will find that their associates are not always Christians, are seldom reliable, and are not willing to pay the price that the American revolutionaries paid, let alone the price paid by the suicidal Russian revolutionaries and nihilists of the 1870s and 1880s.[19] There will be no "Christian" bloody revolution; at most, there will be sporadic acts of violence committed by tiny, strategically unskilled, and socially impotent terrorist groups that call themselves Christian—people who are unable to build anything more lasting than a "hit squad." Such sporadic terrorism does not reconstruct a civilization. It does call forth repression by the State, however—repression which is cheered by the average voter, including most conservative Christians, who will want to distance themselves from Bible-quoting "crazies."

The warning of Christ concerning the exorcism of a single demon should be in our minds when we hear romantics cry out for revolutionary violence in order to achieve a single "housecleaning," a one-time violent overthrow of the "Establishment" which will forever rid the republic of evil rulers:

> When the unclean spirit is gone out of a man, he walketh through dry places, seeking to find rest; and finding none, he saith, I will return unto my house whence I came out. And when he cometh, he findeth it swept and garnished. Then goeth he, and taketh to him seven other spirits more wicked than himself; and they enter in, and dwell there: and the last state of that man is worse than the first (Luke 11:24-26).

Christians need not turn to bloody revolution in this country; they are in the majority. They need to understand God's word, and to have the courage to apply it in every area of their

---

19. Ronald Seth, *The Russian Terrorists: The Story of the Narodniki* (London: Barrie & Rockliff, 1966); James H. Billington, *Fire in the Minds of Men*, ch. 14: "The Bomb: Russian Violence." Cf. Avrahm Yarmolinsky, *Road to Revolution: A Century of Russian Radicalism* (New York: Collier, 1962), chaps. 11-14.

lives. They need to understand the theology of resistance, the tactics of resistance, and the goal of resistance: the Christian reconstruction of the republic,[20] and then the world. We do not want or need bloodshed in our struggle against the legally constituted civil government. (On the other hand, we may well need to defend ourselves against lawless anarchists and criminal bands if the "establishment" order breaks down.)

What we are beginning to hear is apocalyptic rhetoric concerning the moral responsibility of Christians to take up arms if some church has its tax exempt status revoked, or worse, is sold at auction for non-payment of property taxes. Pastors who said nothing when the Supreme Court legalized abortion, or who have preached an eschatology of non-involvement in "worldly" affairs for two decades, are overnight so intensely involved with "basic principle" that they recommend a suicidal strike against the Federal government should their church lose its present status as a "tolerated but ignored organization." Why this life-and-death commitment all of a sudden?

Did David murder Saul when Saul persecuted him? David was forced to flee Israel and pretend to be crazy in the presence of the Philistines—and not just the Philistines, but the king of Gath, the city of Goliath (I Sam. 21:10-15). David was God's anointed, yet he did not challenge Saul. He did not surrender, either. He wrote: "I shall not die, but live, and declare the works of the Lord" (Ps. 118:17).

Is the essence of the gospel tax exemption and bricks and mortar? Is the heart of our stand for Christ our willingness to defend to the death our control over a particular piece of previously tax-exempt ground? This is nonsensical. It is romanticism. Rushdoony writes concerning the revolutionary: "The destiny of the revolutionary is to hunger for life and to know that, in spite of all, death is his future. Death is for him the great enemy, but he longs for death also, because all of life betrays him in his pretended divinity."[21] Why should self-professed Christians adopt the same sort of suicide mentality? Why should they take up arms against the State visibly, just because some official has stepped on their institutional

---

20. Harold O. J. Brown, *The Reconstruction of the Republic* (New Rochelle, NY: Arlington House, 1977).

21. R. J. Rushdoony, *Revolt Against Maturity: A Biblical Psychology of Man* (Fairfax, VA: Thoburn Press, 1977), p. 115.

toes this late in the twentieth century? Haven't the humanists been doing far worse things to Christians and non-Christians for decades? Why revolt now? Why begin to adopt the language of apocalyptic romanticism at this late date? Are we in fact not viewing a kind of *spiritual adolescent's rebellion* — the temper tantrum of the formerly uninvolved, socially uncommitted, and economically pampered youth who finds that the world no longer conforms to his will through his parents' sacrifices for him? Are we not viewing a revolt against maturity?

Before we can even think about ruling a nation we must learn how to exist under the present order and still accomplish the bulk of our goals. Like the Israelites under the Babylonians and Assyrians, we must learn how evil the gods of our conquerors are — and how evil their law-orders are — before we can call upon the name of the Lord and expect deliverance. Like the church under the Roman Empire, we must be subordinate before we can lead. We are in a wilderness; we need to bring ourselves under the dominion of the law of God in our local relationships before we can expect to be put in seats of power nationally.

## *Alinsky's Tactics*

Saul Alinsky was one of the really effective humanistic radicals of the 1960s. He did not throw bombs. He did not spout rhetoric. He simply taught people how to use the bureaucracies' own red tape to tie them up in knots. This is why he was so effective, and why his book, *Rules for Radicals* (1972), is so useful for an understanding of the principles of successful resistance, despite its humanistic bias. His words are worth considering:

> Let us in the name of radical pragmatism not forget that in our system with all its repressions we can still speak out and denounce the administration, attack its policies, work to build an opposition political base. True, there is still government harassment, but there still is that relative freedom to fight. I can attack my government, try to organize to change it. That's more than I can do in Moscow, Peking, or Havana. Remember the reaction of the Red Guard to the "cultural revolution" and the fate of the Chinese college students. Just a few of the violent episodes of bombings or a courtroom shootout that we have experienced here would have resulted in a sweeping purge and mass executions in Russia, China, or Cuba. Let us keep some perspective.

> We will start with the system because there is no other place to start from except political lunacy. It is most important for those of us who want revolutionary change to understand that revolution must be preceded by reformation. To assume that a political revolution can survive without a supporting base of popular reformation is to ask for the impossible in politics.
>
> Men don't like to step abruptly out of the security of familiar experience; they need a bridge to cross from their own experience to a new way. A revolutionary organizer must shake up the prevailing patterns of their lives—agitate, create disenchantment and discontent with the current values, to produce, if not a passion for change, at least a passive, affirmative, non-challenging climate.
>
> "The revolution was effected before the war commenced," John Adams wrote. "The Revolution was in the hearts and minds of the people. . . . This radical change in the principles, opinions, sentiments and affections of the people was the real American Revolution." A revolution without a prior reformation would collapse or become a totalitarian tyranny.[22]

If a humanist like Alinsky understood this about the nature of man and social change, we Christians should at least give heed to his conclusions concerning tactics. Not bombs but protests and petitions. Not guns but getting people involved in dragging their feet. We need a *positive program* of changing people's minds about God, man, and law; about family, church, and State, not to mention the economy.[23] We also need a *negative program* of successful resistance techniques that will get the State off our backs long enough for us to go about the work of positive reformation. Meanwhile, we can gum up the works. That literally happened under Alinsky. Some Christian college was foolish enough to allow students to invite him to speak on campus. A group of disgruntled students met with him after his speech. "How can we change this place? We can't do anything. We can't smoke, dance, go to movies, or drink beer. About all we can do is chew gum." Alinsky told them, "Then gum is your answer."

He told them to get 200 or 300 students to buy two packs of gum each. Chew both packs simultaneously every day, and then spit out the wads on campus walks. As he said, "Why, with five hundred wads of gum I could paralyze Chicago, stop

22. Saul Alinsky, *Rules for Radicals: A Practical Primer for Realistic Radicals* (New York: Random House, 1972), pp. xxi-xxii.

23. Gary North, *Unconditional Surrender: God's Program for Victory* (2nd ed.; Tyler, TX: Geneva Divinity School Press, 1983).

all the traffic in the Loop." He told them to keep it up until the rules were loosened or abolished. The tactic worked. Two weeks later all the rules were lifted. One new rule was substituted: no gum on campus.[24]

That college administration was weak. Its leaders really did not believe in their own standards. They could have immediately banned gum from the campus the second day, with immediate expulsion as the penalty for anyone caught chewing it. But this would have made them look ridiculous to people on the outside. Expelling kids for chewing gum, when other campuses are being bombed by student radicals? The outsiders would never have seen the hundreds of wads of dried gum on the walkways every morning. *Bureaucrats never, ever want to look ridiculous*. They capitulated. They were, in short, fearful bureaucrats. So are most of the people who will give Christians trouble over the next two decades.

We can learn from Alinsky. We must learn how to gum up the works. We must create a new, hypothetical society, "Gummit," which sounds a lot like "Guvmint."

Here are Alinsky's thirteen tactical rules:

1. Power is not only what you have but what the enemy thinks you have.
2. Never go outside the experience of your people.
3. Wherever possible go outside the experience of the enemy.
4. Make the enemy live up to their own book of rules.
5. Ridicule is man's most potent weapon.[25]
6. A good tactic is one your people enjoy.[26]
7. A tactic that drags on too long is a drag.
8. Keep the pressure on.
9. The threat is usually more terrifying than the thing itself.
10. The major premise for tactics is the development of operations that will maintain a constant pressure upon the opposition.
11. If you push a negative hard and deep enough it will break through into its counterside.
12. The price of a successful attack is a constructive alternative.
13. Pick the target, freeze it, personalize and polarize it.[27]

---

24. Alinsky, *op. cit.*, pp. 145f.

25. He adds: "It is almost impossible to counterattack ridicule. Also it infuriates the opposition, who then react to your advantage."

26. Christians normally do not enjoy any resistance tactics. So we should substitute: ". . . tactics that Christians are willing to participate in and which they develop a facility for over time."

27. *Ibid.*, pp. 127-30.

The details of each tactic are frequently useful, though in some cases his humanist recommendations cannot be used.

Interested leaders should locate a copy of the book and read it. Then they can examine these tactics in the light of the Bible to see which tactical principles are in conformity to God's law—the same way Christians need to judge all other products of non-Christian scholarship.[28] The point is: most of these tactics work incredibly well. The second point is: American Christians have not thought about these matters for well over a century—not since the era immediately preceding the Civil War. They are not ready to lead. They are not ready to "throw out the humanists" and replace them in every area of life, from the police force to the physics laboratory.

But they *can* chew gum.

### *The Prayer That Never Fails*

> And the LORD said unto Moses, I have seen this people, and, behold, it is a stiffnecked people. Now therefore let me alone, that my wrath may wax hot against them, and that I may consume them: and I will make of thee a great nation. And Moses besought the LORD his God, and said, LORD, why doth thy wrath wax hot against thy people, which thou hast brought forth out of the land of Egypt with great power, and with a mighty hand? Wherefore should the Egyptians speak, and say, For mischief did he bring them out, to slay them in the mountains, and to consume them from the face of the earth? Turn from thy fierce wrath, and repent of this evil against thy people. Remember Abraham, Isaac, and Israel, thy servants, to whom thou swarest by thine own self, and saidst unto them, I will multiply your seed as the stars of heaven, and all this land that I have spoken of will I give unto your seed, and they shall inherit it for ever. And the LORD repented of the evil which he thought to do unto his people (Ex. 32:9-14).

God was angry. He complained bitterly to Moses. He offered Moses revenge against those who had criticized him

28. Anyone who criticizes me for recommending Alinsky's book ought to have an even better book or manual of resistance tactics to substitute in its place. He also needs a track record: some bureaucracy, somewhere, that he personally has helped to bring to a grinding halt. Criticism from *armchair resisters* whose lives and the organizations they control are characterized by continual capitulation to bureaucracies of all kinds should not be taken very seriously.

for so long. He offered him the opportunity to become a new Abraham, a new father of multitudes—a great gift in the ancient world. But Moses turned down this generous offer. He did not seek revenge. Instead, he pleaded for the lives of the Israelites.

He did not deny the obvious, namely, that they were a stiffnecked bunch. He did not appeal to God on their behalf in terms of what God owed them for their righteousness; they had no righteousness. But he did appeal to God on their behalf in terms of what God did owe them because of His promise to Abraham. God had said that they would inherit the land in the fourth generation after they went down into Egypt (Gen. 15:16). The time had come for God to fulfill His word. The honor of God was at stake.

The parallel passage in Numbers 14 is even more explicit concerning the honor of God:

> And Moses said unto the LORD, Then the Egyptians shall hear it (for thou broughtest up this people in thy might from among them); and they will tell it to the inhabitants of this land: for they have heard that thou LORD are seen face to face, and that thy cloud standeth over them, and that thou goest before them, by day time in a pillar of a cloud, and in a pillar of fire by night. Now if thou shalt kill all this people as one man, then the nations which have heard the fame of thee will speak, saying, Because the LORD was not able to bring this people into the land which he sware unto them, therefore hath he slain them in the wilderness (vv. 13-16).

Then Moses pleaded for mercy. But he made it clear that this mercy would be offered by God in order to uphold the honor of His own name. If He destroyed His people after having delivered them from the Egyptians, then His reputation would be in jeopardy. He was stronger than the Egyptians' gods, but not stronger than the gods of Canaan. The Egyptians would tell the enemies of God in the promised land of the weakness of the God of Israel. They would tell of a God who slays His own people because of His own inability to deliver His enemies into their hand.

This is the most effective prayer available in any program of Christian resistance. It still works as well as it did in Moses' day. If His people challenge rival gods in His name, and are ready to sacrifice everything they own for the cause of God, then God can be called upon to uphold His name. The ethical rebels will not enjoy the opportunity to call the power of God into question (Psalm 2).

After the failure of the Puritan revolution under Cromwell in 1660, one of the discouraged radical supporters of the revolution was reported to have said, "God spat on our dream." God spits on the dreams of many people. If we elevate our little dreams and schemes above the honor of God, then we can prepare ourselves for damp faces. But if we stand as Moses stood, on the honor of God's name, and we conduct ourselves accordingly, then God will spit on the dreams of our enemies, for they are His enemies.

### *A Warning*

If you or your church should decide to take a stand and fight on a fundamental principle, such as the sovereignty (legal jurisdiction) question regarding taxes or Christian education, understand that there is no large, well-funded organization which is likely to assist you. The few large ones are swamped with requests to defend this or that group, free of charge. These groups seldom can devote much time to the cases they take on, and they are losing case after case. Yet the smaller organizations are, for the most part, letterhead organizations. They exist only as hopes and dreams.

When I first started to edit this issue, I contacted at least five organizations that are involved in one facet of resistance or another. I asked the directors to produce a 20-page, double-spaced, typewritten essay on just what services their groups offer, and what kinds of tactics they recommend. I received back a few previously published pamphlets that did not really deal with the issues I raised. I did not get a single essay that described what, precisely, each group actually does to support those churches or schools involved in resistance. My conclusion: They aren't really ready to help you—not if they are unable to get out what is in effect free advertising for their own operations. Thus, you are on your own, institutionally speaking.

Those of us who are associated with the publication of these two issues of **Christianity and Civilization** understand that this is a pioneering effort. As far as we are aware, these two issues constitute the only explicitly Christian materials published in English in this century that deal with the question of resistance. We believe that these materials will serve as the starting point for all serious, theologically informed discussions of resistance. We fully expect these two issues to serve as primary source documents for historians a century or more in the future, just as Sam Adams' papers and publications are documentary sources for the American Revolution. This is not a matter of arrogance; this is a realistic appraisal of just how little cogent Christian material on this topic is available in 1983.

I can recommend one book, above all, to each and every church. Buy it, read it, and begin to implement it. It is Gene Sharp's *Politics of Non-Violent Action*, published by Porter Sargent in Boston. Sharp lists dozens of non-violent tactics that have been used over the years against bureaucratic tyrannies. It will provide many ideas for you. (Sharp also wrote a book on Gandhi. All books on Gandhi need to be offset in part by the extraordinary book-length essay by Richard Grenier, *The Gandhi Nobody Knows*, published by Thomas Nelson Sons in 1983. It appeared originally as a review of the Academy Award-winning movie, *Gandhi*, in the March, 1983, issue of *Commentary*.)

### *Strategies and Tactics*

**Christianity and Civilization** draws on authors from numerous denominational backgrounds, not to mention religious traditions. We have found that many conclusions of people who do not share our opinion of the Puritan and Reformed tradition are often in agreement with the conclusions of that tradition. At the same time, there are some writers who do not seem to be consistent with their theology. We offer these essays with a disclaimer: They have been published in good faith by all parties, but neither the editors nor the authors agree on all points with each of the essays in this volume.

Part I deals with general strategies and perspectives which Christians must bear in mind when devising tactics of resistance to pagan tyranny. Theologian and evangelist **Francis Nigel Lee** presents an alternative to *The Communist Manifesto* in his own "Christian Manifesto," originally published in 1974. Dr. Lee outlines the present position of Christians in the world, and then sets out a blueprint for world conquest, including specific objectives and tactics for reaching those objectives.

**Louis DeBoer** reminds us that the ultimate Bringer of tyranny is God Himself, and our ways must be brought to please Him before He will be pleased to release us from bondage. Simply to complain about the evils of the tyrants is pharisaism and hypocrisy, unless we have examined our own hearts first and foremost.

**Rousas J. Rushdoony** points out that religious liberty should be distinguished from religious toleration. We do not wish official toleration from the state for the church; rather, we insist that the state recognize that the church is a separate government established by Christ.

**James B. Jordan** argues from the book of Genesis that men are not to seize power prematurely. Jordan argues that such was the sin of Adam, and that a similar temptation is placed before the New Christian Right. Patient faith avoids revolutionary action. Jordan closes his essay with a sketch of how Christians are to submit to tyrants, and when they should resist. We submit to their *office*, when lawfully exercised within a proper sphere, and to their *power*, when actually manifested. Jordan applies this scheme to the issue of Christian schools, the draft, and taxation.

**Herbert Schlossberg's** contribution is a selection from his remarkable book *Idols for Destruction* (Thomas Nelson Pub., 1983). Schlossberg argues that the building up of a strong and righteous Christian community is essential in dealing either defensively or offensively with paganism.

Finally in this section, **David Chilton** and I argue that a clear understanding of the Christian faith, particularly of four key doctrines, is absolutely essential to a clear setting forth of the Christian alternative in our time. The four key doctrines are: the doctrine of Divine predestination, presuppositional apologetics, an optimistic eschatology, and a clear understanding of the comprehensiveness of God's law. Included in this essay is a close look at Francis A. Schaeffer's popular book, *A Christian Manifesto*.

Part II is concerned with defensive tactics. As Satan increasingly attacks Christendom, we need to know how to resist his onslaughts. A great many practical tactics are available to Christians in America, and I survey these. I take you through a series of steps, designed to counter pagan aggression at several levels of intensity. **Wayne C. Johnson** provides a humorous look at how the evil and paranoia of pagan leftists has been and can still be used against them. **Wayne C. Sedlak** discusses techniques of resistance used by the high priest Azariah in confronting the tyrant Uzziah, and Paul's use of Roman constitutional liberties to promote the gospel.

The personal home computer is proving an effective tool to slow down, stop, and even defeat bureaucratic tyranny, argues **A. Richard Immel**, while **Harry Caul** discusses the usefulness of radio hobbying in the development of a secret Christian information network.

Finally, the issue of taxation comes to the fore in a brief but invaluable essay by **Douglas Kelly**, and in a lengthy study of detail strategies by **Michael Gilstrap**. Both men note that the church is not tax exempt, but *tax immune*. Gilstrap sets out various important strategies in dealing with pagan state officials when they attack the tax-immune status of the church.

Part III deals with offensive tactics. The best defense is a strong offense, and this is particularly true concerning the gospel, when we have the great commission ever before us. **Pat Robertson** provides a brief overview of problems that face us in the 1980s, and suggests steps to overcome these problems in order to turn our nation (and the world) back to Christian standards.

**Ray R. Sutton** notes that the institutional church, as the Bible sets it out, is supposed to operate as a government, with rulers, courts, trials, and judgments. The church in America has often declined to be merely a preaching point, but as important as preaching is, the church needs to recover its self-image as a true government on the earth. Men trained to pass judgments in church courts will be able to step into civil office competently.

In an important study, **Otto J. Scott** discusses the various tactics of resistance, defensive and offensive, used by the protestants in the reformation of Europe. This is a fascinating study of intrigue, deception, and righteousness.

One of the problems facing us as we resist tyranny and build a Christian tomorrow, is lack of funds. **John Wesley's** famous sermon on money is here included. His three points—earn all you can; save all you can; give all you can—transformed the Methodist movement into one of the most culturally powerful forces in recent centuries. **James B. Jordan** argues that if Christians will tithe properly, there will be no problem financing Christian reconstruction. Jordan shows exactly what God expects, and makes practical recommendations on how to tithe.

I argue that with the leverage provided by satellite television, and with the fulcrum provided by sound Christian scholarship, we are in a position to educate the chruch and world as never before. I set out numerous possibilities for filling the airwaves (and other avenues of communication) with materials to help the churches in the fight against pagan tyranny.

Three tools of resistance are discussed by **Lawrence D. Pratt**: education, a well-armed local militia, and computerized mailing lists. **Paul M. Weyrich** discusses the value of fighting causes that appear lost—you never know whom you might unwittingly be influencing. **Connie Marshner** discusses the various ways to lobby senators and congressmen, to bring them to vote for righteous causes. The basic point made in each of these three essays is that Christian political action is, at present, primarily a form of evangelism, of persuasion. Paul's primary purpose in speaking before Festus, Agrippa, and Caesar, was to articulate the claims and promises of God, not directly to effect a political reform or takeover. The democratic political processes in the United States at present provide many, many opportunities to set forth the truth in the marketplace, and as Weyrich particularly points out, even if we lose particular political battles, the bread of truth cast upon the waters will return after many days. (Eccl. 11:1).

# I. FUNDAMENTAL STRATEGIES OF CHRISTIAN RESISTANCE

## THE CHRISTIAN MANIFESTO OF 1984

(an answer to the Communist Manifesto of 1848
and to George Orwell's *Nineteen Eighty-four*)
A victory blueprint for world take-over by A.D. 2000 by Christian conquerors who *"Preach the gospel!"* and *"Subdue the earth!"*

Francis Nigel Lee

**And God said, 'Let Us make man in Our image, after Our likeness: and let them have dominion over the fish of the sea, and over the fowl of the air, and over the cattle, and over all the earth, and over every creeping thing that creepeth upon the earth.' So God created man in His own image, in the image of God created He him; male and female created He them. And God blessed them, and God said unto them, 'Be fruitful, and multiply, and replenish the earth, and subdue it: and have dominion over the fish of the sea, and over the fowl of the air, and over every living thing that moveth upon the earth' (Genesis 1:26-28).**

**And Jesus came and spake unto them, saying, 'All power is given unto Me in heaven and in earth. Go ye therefore, and teach all nations, baptizing them in the name of the Father, and of the Son, and of the Holy Ghost: Teaching them to observe all things whatsoever I have commanded you: and, lo, I am with you alway, even unto the end of the world' (Matthew 28:18-20).**

### *Introduction*

A specter is haunting the stage of world history—the specter of consistent Christianity. All the powers of the world have entered into an unholy alliance to exorcise this specter: American pragmatists and European humanists, Russian communists and Red Chinese revolutionaries, Islam and Zionism, freethinkers and freebooters, anti-intellectual pietists and incorrigible antinomians.

It is high time that consistent Christians should openly, in

First published in 1974 as part of the epilogue to Dr. Lee's massive work, *Communist Eschatology—A Christian Philosophical Analysis of the Post-Capitalistic Views of Marx, Engels and Lenin* (Nutley, NJ: Craig Press, 1974), pp. 840-848.

the face of the whole world, publish their views, their aims, their tendencies, with a Manifesto of consistent Christians themselves.

To this end, consistent Christians of various nationalities have assembled together, and sketched the following Manifesto.

### *General*

The history of all hitherto existing society is the history of religious struggles. Adam and Satan, Abel and Cain, Sethites and Cainites, Noah and Nimrod, Abraham and the Chaldeans, Israelites and Canaanites, Christians and heathen, consistent Christians and inconsistent pietists, free men and communists, the seed of the woman and the seed of the serpent, stood in constant opposition to one another, carried on an uninterrupted—now hidden, now open—fight, that each time ended, either in a reformatory reconstitution of society at large, or in the common revolutionary ruin of the contending classes.

Our epoch, the epoch of the twentieth century, possesses, however, this distinctive feature: it has simplified the religious antagonisms. Society as a whole is more and more splitting up into two great hostile camps, into two great classes directly facing each other: the followers of Christ and the followers of antichrist.

The consistent Christians are the true followers of Christ. They are called upon by Almighty God to eat and to drink and to do literally everything solely to the glory of the Triune God—Father, Son, and Spirit. Consistent Christians are the salt of the earth and the light of the world.

Satan, however, seeks to extinguish the light of consistent Christianity in ways devilish, devious, and subtle.

Satan often paralyzes the Christians' testimony by making them so worldly minded that they are no heavenly use—they lose their zeal for the Lord and His house, or they keep coming to church on Sundays but live like heathen every other day of the week (or even for the rest of the Lord's day, between services).

Frequently, however, Satan tries another device, known as pietism. Here he makes the Christians so heavenly minded that they are of no earthly use. They spend all their time in church and at prayer meetings, and lose all their zeal for the Creator God and this His world. Here the church becomes other-worldly, unearthly, and irrelevant to real life. It becomes progressively more and more alienated from the real issues and foreign to God's world. Lonely and defeatistic, it surrenders all the other areas of life to the forces of antichrist, which ultimately surround and destroy this pietism. What pietism produces, therefore, above all, is its own grave-diggers.

Consistent Christianity, however, will ultimately prevail. It alone will stand fast against and overcome the pressure of antichrist's world system, for the gates of hell shall not prevail against the true members of the Church of Christ. The battle may be long and protracted, fierce and bloody, but the ultimate victory is sure. For true Christians shall overcome all opposition by the indwelling power of the Spirit of God. And then, when Christ comes for His Own, He shall gather all His elect from the four corners of the earth, and destroy His enemies with the brightness of His coming. The triumph of consistent Christianity and the fall of the system of antichrist are both equally inevitable. History is on our side! Even so, come, Lord Jesus!

### *Objectives*

In what relation do consistent Christians stand to mankind as a whole?

Consistent Christians are truly human and seek to oppose *Satan* and all his inhuman works. They do not seek to form a separate party opposed to the rest of *mankind*, but when they stand up for the Kingdom of God and His righteousness, while the *progressive* non-Christians are converted and become Christians, the remnant, the non-progressive non-Christians, *reactionarily* cling to their sins and sink even deeper into their Satanic alienation from true humanity. Consistent Christians are the *vanguard* of the true humanity, the new creation, and seek to persuade *all* men to become consistent Christians. Non-Christian men are inconsistent *men*. Only by becoming consistent Christians do inconsistent men become *consistent men*. Only by dedicating their lives to the Lord Jesus Christ, that most human of all men, can humanistic men become truly human.

Consistent Christians seek to realize *all* their objectives.

They cheerfully seek to execute their duties toward God, toward themselves, toward one another, and toward humanity.

Toward God, consistent Christians seek to obey *all* His commandments and to live according to *all* His counsel as revealed in *all* His Holy Scriptures, both in the Old and in the New Testaments. Toward themselves, consistent Christians seek to condemn and to castigate their own (de-humanizing) sins and to consecrate to Christ their own God-given (humanizing) virtues. Toward one another, consistent Christians seek to promote their mutual dedication to the Lord and His commandments and their enmity toward Satan and his devices. Toward humanity, they seek to promulgate God's Kingdom in all of His realms and to demand the unconditional surrender of *every* man, woman, and child (including professing Christians), together with all their possessions, to the all-embracing Kingship of the Lord Jesus Christ, and to reign together with Him both in this present age now and tomorrow and (still more) in the age to come.

### *Strategy*

Consistent Christians must clearly understand their ultimate goals and plot their strategy of conquest accordingly.

1. They must acknowledge that their program must at every stage be subject to the revealed will of the Triune God, whereby He would have us demand that all men willingly submit to His authority right now, even though some will only (unwillingly) submit after the last judgement. This should encourage us not to be discouraged if we do not see vast numbers accepting His authority during our own lifetime. At the same time, we have no right to assume that God does not desire to transform all men presently alive into His Kingdom. All men are His creatures and therefore all men owe Him perfect obedience, and all categories of men (communists, Zionists, Moslems, etc.) are, from the human viewpoint, saveable, provided they repent and turn from their sins and thenceforth serve the Lord Jesus Christ.

2. Although the coming of the Lord draweth nigh, it is not for us to set dates, but rather to carry on working for Him as if He were not yet to come for another thousand years or more —as indeed He might not. Consequently, Christians *dare* not be idle in *any* area of life as they wait for the Lord's appearance.

While the risen Christ reigns on high and (also through His Spirit-filled Church on earth) subdues all His enemies under His feet, Christians are in His Sovereign Majesty's Service. Without Him, they can do nothing. Moment by moment dependence upon Him and the power of His Spirit in all that they do, is absolutely essential.

3. Our strategy centers around two main poles: a) subduing the entire earth to God's glory in all that we do[1]; and b) discipling all the nations[2] and, in declaring to them *all* the counsel of God,[3] teaching them to subdue[4] the entire earth to God's glory in all that they do as well as teaching them to communicate the gospel to every man.[5]

4. In subduing the entire earth to God's glory, Christians must be *encouraged* to discover their own special gifts of God and to become respectively Christian preachers, ethicists, lawyers, economists, artists, sociologists, linguists, historians, philosophers, psychologists, biologists, physicists, mathematicians, etc., *all* and *only* to the glory of God. They should form Christian professional associations (local, national, and international), as well as infiltrate into and capture control of non-Christian professional associations for Christ's sake and turn every sphere of human endeavor toward Christ through the *POWER* of His Holy Spirit.

5. In communicating the gospel to every man, not only must preachers and missionaries by supported, but every Christian must at all times be prepared to give account of the faith which is in him—through the *POWER* of the Holy Spirit.

6. Subduing the earth involves the Christian's work in respect of the sub-human creation, and communicating the gospel involves the Christian's work in respect of the human creation, but both are inter-connected in that both involve going into all the world and extending the Kingdom of God in all possible fields and by every possible means. Accordingly, a survey of the earth's resources as well as of mankind is necessary in determining our strategy of conquest.

7. The world's most important resources which Christians

1. Gen 1:26-28.
2. Matt. 28:18-20.
3. Acts 20:27.
4. Ps. 8; Heb. 2:6-10; 4:11-16.
5. Mark 16:15; Acts 1:5-8; 2:38-47.

must seek to control are: religion, food, clothing, housing, industry, money, and culture. On this basis, it is clear that the most crucial geographical areas which Christians must seek to control for Christ's sake in all fields today, are: the U.S.A., the U.S.S.R., Europe, Japan, Canada, and, to a lesser extent, Australia and South Africa.

8. The world's most numerous peoples today which Christians must seek to evangelize immediately are located in: Red China, India, Europe, the U.S.S.R., the U.S.A., Japan, Indonesia, and Pakistan.

9. The earth to be subdued and the people to be evangelized live almost exclusively on the two world-islands, both of which are overwhelmingly located in the strategically vital Northern Hemisphere. These two world-islands are: the greater world-island, consisting of Africa, Asia and Europe, with Israel as its hub, and the lesser world-island, consisting of North and South America, with Panama as its slender waist. About 90 percent of the world's population lives in the greater world-island, which is probably also the area of *potentially* the greatest natural resources (iron, coal, oil, etc.). Only about 10 percent of the world's present population lives in the Americas, and only about 7 percent in North America. Yet the latter produces about 45 percent of the world's wealth, and, together with Western Europe, well over 60 percent as of now.

10. It is therefore essential for the NATO powers to be (re-)Christianized and strengthened in order for Christians to regain and then maintain and expand their control over the world in the immediate future. Historically, the NATO nations are also the countries with the strongest Christian heritage, and should, other things being equal, also be the easiest area of the world to (re-)Christianize. But Christianity must also be rapidly expanded in Russia and Asia (where well over half of the world's present population lives), as one would expect their power to increase dramatically over the next few decades as they become more industrialized. It is therefore essential for consistent Christians to take control especially of the U.S.A., the U.S.S.R., Europe, China, and Japan, as well as the miniscule countries in the geographical center of the two world-islands, viz., Israel and Panama. Missiologically, the unambitious practice of sending 90 percent of the world's available Christian missionaries to the

geopolitically relatively insignificant Africa (where only 8 percent of the world's present population is located) should immediately be revised.

### *Tactics*

The tactical reformatory Christian leadership will have to begin in the nominally Christian nations like the U.S.A., the Republic of South Africa, Northern Ireland, the Netherlands, Finland, and, to a lesser but ever-increasing extent, South Korea and Nationalist China (Formosa, Taiwan). The tactics whereby Christians must obtain and maintain religious, political, economic, and cultural power will vary in each of the main strategic areas (viz., the U.S.A., the U.S.S.R., Europe, Red China, Japan, Israel, and Panama), in spite of many points of contact and overlap.

If Christianity recedes in the U.S.A. it will probably recede in the other strategic areas too, as far as can humanly be foreseen. But conversely, too — if Christianity does not soon prosper in the other strategic areas, it will probably also soon recede in the U.S.A., at least for the foreseeable future. Let us then deal with all these strategic areas, shortly, one by one.

1. In the U.S.A., the influential areas which must be controlled by Christians are: the West Coast (Seattle through Los Angeles), the Great Lakes (Duluth through Buffalo), the East Coast (Boston through Washington), and the South Coast (Houston through Atlanta). In the next few years, these are the areas where U.S. history will be made; and of these areas, control of the Great Lakes and the East Coast will be decisive — for this is where the huge central and eastern megapolis will arise. The U.S.A. still has the greatest available number of Christians in the world at present, and they must be increased and deployed to maximum utility both in the U.S. and elsewhere. Geopolitically, the U.S. must man its western border in the region of Southeast Asia (not just in California), and its southern border south of Panama, keeping these borders under constant surveillance. U.S. Christians *must* get involved in churches, politics, education, commerce, and international affairs — for Christ's sake!

2. The U.S.S.R. covers by far the largest land-mass on earth — as big as the U.S.A., Canada, and Red China all put together. Potentially, it has vast mineral resources — especially

of iron, oil, and gold. The areas of greatest influence in the U.S.S.R. during the next few years will be the industrialized belt from the Baltic to the Caspian (Leningrad, Moscow, Stalingrad, Odessa, Kiev, and Baku), and, to a lesser yet ever-increasing extent, the continuing Russian colonization of Southern Siberia (Omsk, Tomsk, Novosibersk through Vladivostok) vis-à-vis the Red Chinese. Christians must take control of these areas by: a) infiltration by Russian speaking Christian agents into the Russian underground in order to Christianize it; b) the Russian underground's infiltration of key areas of the Soviet government, especially in the geographical areas mentioned above; and c) the isolation of the U.S.S.R. from Eastern Europe on the one flank, from Red China on the other, and from the Indian sub-continent to the south. Turkey must be strengthened, the Dardenelles closed to Russian influence (until the Christian takeover of Russia has been successfully accomplished), and the Mediterranean meantime preserved as a Western waterway.

3. Europe is vitally important, especially northwestern Europe. At least 20 percent of the world's present population lives in Europe (compared to only 6 percent in the U.S.A.), and, potentially, the highly industrialized Europe, even Western Europe alone, could, perhaps, out-produce even the U.S.A. The crucial iron and coal resources of Europe are located in Czechoslovakia, Germany, France, and England, which, together with Italy, the Benelux countries, Spain, and Poland, are also the greatest areas of population. Christians must therefore take control especially of Germany through Bonn and Berlin, of France through Paris, and of England through London. These three countries must immediately be re-evangelized and must cooperate with one another in the interests of the overall cause. In many respects an extension of Western Europe, Australia, and especially South Africa (which produces 82 percent of the free world's gold and 90 percent of its diamonds and platinum), should aid in the complete economic (and spiritual) recovery of these areas and in the expansion of trade with them, and the U.S.A. too, even if only in its own interests, dare not isolate itself from them. Again, the slavic countries of Eastern Europe must be liberated from Russian domination and (re-)Christianized.

4. The sub-continent of Red China houses fully one-quarter of the world's present population of almost four billion

people, but most of them still live in the Hoang-ho, Yangtze-kiang, and Si-kiang valleys, and especially in eastern China. Fortunately, Red China is isolated by the Himalayas from the Indian sub-continent to the south and by mountains and deserts (and by historic hostility) from the Soviet Union to the west and to the north. During the last twenty centuries, China has never had more than 1 percent of its population even nominally Christianized, and the Christianization of China is of top priority to international Christians. Right now, the massive evangelization of Formosa should be undertaken; the Free Chinese should be given full Western support and turned loose on the Chinese mainland, with trained cadres of Chinese Christian evangelists and intellectuals in their wake. Friction between Red China and the Soviets should not be discouraged, and it should never be forgotten that Stalin on occasions supported Chiang against Mao in the 1920s, nor that Russia aided India against Pakistan and the latter's Red Chinese ally in 1971.

5. Control of Japan is of more tactical importance right now than is control of Red China. With the fastest growing economy and the greatest shipbuilding yards in the world, and rapidly expanding in every branch of industry, Japan must be kept with the West and anti-communist. Thousands of Japanese must be trained as evangelists and as Christian intellectuals in order to Christianize this, the least evangelized country this side of the iron curtain. At all costs, rapprochement between Japan and Red China must be avoided.

6. Panama, the navel string of the two Americas, must be held for the West at all costs. Cuba must be contained, and then de-communized and Christianized as soon as possible, and Mexico must also be evangelized.

7. Israel and the adjoining Suez Canal—Israel the hub of the greater world-island and of international Zionism—must not only be held for the West, but must also be Christianized. This may perhaps best be achieved by the intensive evangelization of Israel's financial bulwark, viz., American Jewry, beginning in the New York and Chicago areas.

8. Concentrating on the total Christianization of the U.S.A., the U.S.S.R., Europe, Red China, Japan, Panama, and Israel is not at all to suggest that the rest of the world is unimportant. Where Christianity is already strong, she should hold her own and also promote the total Christianiza-

tion of the neighbors adjoining these countries. Again, the Christianization of large and important countries such as India, Brazil, Nigeria, and Indonesia should enjoy full support. We are saying, however, that the immediate battle between the forces of Christ and the forces of antichrist in this last quarter of the 20th century will rage and be decided especially in the U.S.A., the U.S.S.R., Europe, Red China, and Japan, and that these are therefore the areas which should enjoy the greatest attention in the plans of international Christians.

9. Positive steps to be taken by international Christians everywhere as the Lord enables are: total Christian involvement (in our churches, in our jobs, with our gifts, and with our opportunities), total Christian witnessing (in every field, in church, by tracts, in politics, etc.), and total Christianization of the whole of life (recognition of the sphere-sovereignty of church, state, family, business, society, etc.), and to this end: Christian control of all the existing (and creation of new) mass communications media such as television, newspapers, the movies, and radio; support of the free enterprise trading system; the encouragement of both individual and covenantal incentive and accountability to Almighty God; the strengthening of the rights of inheritance; decentralization of government, industry, education, and church life; the Christianization and strengthening of the armed forces; the reduction of the power of humanistic education, political parties, and labor unions, and the massive promotion of Christian schools, colleges, universities, political parties, Christian economic bargaining, etc.

10. Opposed as international Christians are to *all* departures from God's most holy will, we do recognize that the various non-Christian movements are not all equally bad and that there are areas in which, by God's common grace, we may cooperate with non-Christians in seeking to realize our Christian objectives. Hence, we will gladly cooperate with orthodox Jews and Moslems against all shades of atheism, and with Catholics against all those who are avowedly anti-Christian. At the same time, we will not compromise our own distinctively Christian views in any areas. If in following the commandments of our God, e.g., in moving against communism and/or pornography, we are offered the support of

concerned Jews, Moslems, and Catholics, we will willingly welcome and utilize such support.

*Conclusion*

In all of this, however, let all men know where we stand. We stand on the infallible Word of God, which teaches that God the Father has chosen those who become Christians in Christ before the foundation of the world, that they should become holy and without blame before Him in love; that He has predestinated them unto the adoption of children by Jesus Christ to Himself, according to the good pleasure of His will; that He has made known to them the mystery of His will, according to His good pleasure which He hath purposed in Himself, so "that in the dispensation of the fullness of the times He might gather together in one *all things* in Christ, both which are in heaven, *and which are on earth*, even in Him; and that the God and Father of the Lord Jesus Christ may give them the Spirit of wisdom and revelation in the knowledge of Him, that the eyes of their understanding may be enlightened (so) that they may know what *is* the hope of His calling, and what the riches of His inheritance in the saints, *and what is the exceeding greatness of His power to us-ward who believe*, according to the working of His mighty power which He wrought in Christ when He *raised Him from the dead and set Him at His own right hand in the heavenly places, far above all principality*, and power, and might, and dominion, *and every name that is named*, not only *in this world*, but also in that which is to come, *and hath put all things under His feet*, and gave Him *to be the Head over all things* to the *Church*, which is *His body*, the *fullness of Him that filleth all in all!*" (Ephesians 1:3-11, 17-23).

We stand, then, for the visible manifestation of the complete control of the Lord Jesus Christ over the whole of life, right here and now, and even more so in tomorrow's world, and still more on the new earth to come. We disdain to conceal our views and aims. We openly declare that our own ends can be attained only by the Christianization of *all* existing social conditions. Let the anti-Christian classes mark the prospect of this consistent Christian conquest! Mankind has nothing to lose but its inhumanity and the chains of sin—and it has a new earth to win!

Then conquer we must,
When our cause it is just;
And this be our motto:
"In God is our trust!"

We shall overcome![6] CHRISTIANS OF THE WORLD, UNITE![7]

6. Rev. 2:26; 12:11.
7. John 17:21f.; I Cor. 12:12f.; Eph. 4:3-6.

# THE FUNDAMENTAL BIBLICAL TACTIC FOR RESISTING TYRANNY

Louis DeBoer

THE church must inescapably deal with the problem of tyranny when it arises, but we must ask what the church is really dealing with. Ultimately, what is the church confronting when it faces the issue of tyranny? We may say we are dealing with wicked men. We may go a step further and say we are not dealing with mere flesh and blood but are confronting principalities and powers, even Satan himself. But ultimately we are dealing with God. He is the great first cause of all things. As the writer to the Hebrews puts it, "it is with Him that we have to do." If we face the question of the problems of tyranny squarely, we cannot possibly do so apart from the recognition of its source and its place in the providential purposes of a sovereign God who works all things according to His purpose.

The existence of evil, even the evil of tyranny, is not an argument against but rather an argument in favor of the reality of the moral government of God. It is because God is sovereign, because he does hold men accountable for all their actions, because His government is real, that He not only claims the right but exercises the prerogative of punishing sin not only in the life to come but also in this present life. If God is God, if He is the only God, then the totality of His moral government automatically follows. Thus, God Himself declares through the mouth of Isaiah, "I am the Lord, and there is none else, there is no God beside me: . . . I form the light, and create darkness: I make peace, and create evil: I the Lord do all these things" (Isaiah 45:7). Similarly, when calamity threatens Samaria, Amos boldly declares, "Shall a trumpet be blown in the city, and the people not be afraid? shall there be evil in a city, and the LORD hath not done it?" (Amos 3:6). Clearly the problem of tyranny involves the issue of our relationship to the sovereign God of history.

As Christians we cannot separate the issue of tyranny from the recognition of the existence and moral government of God. We must constantly remember that the main issue is not ill fortune, and neither is it the evil or the power of the oppressor. All these are secondary. They are but the means that God uses to accomplish His righteous purposes in history. We must remember that against the judgments of God there is no national defense. We must call to mind that against His chastisements there are no successful resistance movements. In such struggles the arm of flesh will surely fail us, and it is not basically a matter of organized might. As Solomon declares, "I returned, and saw under the sun, that the race is not to the swift, nor the battle to the strong, . . . but time and chance happeneth to them all" (Eccl. 9:11). Solomon is teaching that such struggles are not decided by mere human factors but that the battle is the Lord's, and although this may appear to men as chance, it is but the timely working out of God's decrees. It is only when we have this clearly in focus that we can begin to deal with the issue of resistance to tyranny.

Any strategy of resistance to tyranny will have to deal with the fact that *tyranny is a curse of God*. It must recognize that to rail against God's righteous judgments is merely to perpetuate and aggravate them. It must start with a humble submission to His will, a reverential fear of His judgments, and a full recognition of the righteousness of His moral government. Although we may marvel at the iniquities that men commit, at the fury of the "Commune" or the depravity of "Bolshevism," although the utter evil of God's instruments may astound us until with Habakkuk we are compelled to cry out to the Just and Holy God, "Thou art of purer eyes than to behold evil, and canst not look on iniquity: wherefore lookest thou upon them that deal treacherously, and holdest thy tongue when the wicked devoureth the man that is more righteous than he?" (Hab. 1:13); yet we must always remember that He styles Nebuchadnezzar his servant and terms Assyria the rod of His anger. It is still with Him that we have to do.

Ultimately, the only solution there can be to the problem of tyranny is to solve the problem of *how we can turn God's curse into blessing*; how we can transmute His anger into favor. The question becomes one of how can we appease His anger and stay His wrath.

What can shield a man, or a people, or a nation from the

curse of God? Ever since the fall by the sin of one man, death and curse have been universal. All have sinned and come short, there is none that doeth good, no not one, and so by both original and actual sin all men and all societies bring judgment and wrath down upon themselves. One of the forms of this wrath is that God sends tyrants as He so clearly warned in I Samuel 8. Men need a covering, an atonement, to shield them from the wrath of God. They need a Daysman, a Mediator, to intercede on their behalf with an offended and omnipotent Deity. In short, men need the blessings of the Abrahamic Covenant. *They need to be justified before God.* And the Biblical, the Protestant, the Reformed answer to this need is that men need to be justified by faith in Christ Jesus. But faith is inexorably linked in the divine economy with repentance and the latter is again just as inescapably linked with reformation. The same golden chain that links election to effectual calling, regeneration, justification, sanctification, and glorification also links faith with good works, and the new nature with the fruits of repentance. If we would have a covering from the wrath of God and from His curse including the curse of tyrannical government, the road leads inexorably to justification by faith, repentance, and reformation. And we come to the very same conclusion whether we examine the issue in its negative or in its positive aspects. Whether we are seeking to avoid God's righteous curse or whether we are seeking to bring down His blessing, including the blessings of peace, liberty, and just government, either way the answer is *reformation*. For if I Samuel 8 teaches that the fruit of apostasy is tyranny and unjust, coercive government, Leviticus 26 and Deuteronomy 28:1-14 assert that God's blessing will attend a faithful, covenant keeping people. In the Abrahamic Covenant, the covenantal blessing that God will be a God and a Father to us and our seed after us is linked with the covenantal command to "walk before me and be thou perfect."

### *Foundations for Resistance*

The *folly* of what today passes for conservatism should be thoroughly evident to discerning Christians and was thoroughly rebuked by that uncompromising prophet of God's truth, Robert Lewis Dabney, in the last century. Conservatives generally try to build without adequate foundations and wind up with castles in the sky, ethereal houses of cards without any solid underpinnings. Robert Welch (founder of the John Birch Society) for example has consistently (inconsistently?) tried to marry his liberal theology with the political conclusions of conservatism. While providing radical resistance to the programs of the National Council of Churches, he is one with their theology. The hopelessness of supporting such weighty matters forged from an entirely different theology, on a theology of skepticism and infidelity which has consistently produced different fruit elsewhere, never seems to be recognized. Dabney thoroughly diagnosed the reasons for the weakness of conclusions held on such grounds, when he wrote of Yankee Conservatism:

> This is a party which never conserves anything. Its history has been that it demurs to each aggression of the progressive party, and aims to save its credit by a respectable amount of growling, but always acquiesces at last in the innovation. What was the resisted novelty of yesterday is to-day one of the accepted principles of conservatism; it is now conservative only in affecting to resist the next innovation, which will to-morrow be forced upon its timidity and will be succeeded by some third revolution, to be denounced and then adopted in its turn. American conservatism is merely the shadow that follows Radicalism as it moves forward towards perdition. It remains behind it, but never retards it, and always advances near its leader. This pretended salt hath utterly lost its savor: wherewith shall it be salted? Its impotency is not hard, indeed, to explain. It is worthless because it is the conservatism of expediency only, and not of sturdy principle. It intends to risk nothing serious for the sake of the truth, and has no idea of being guilty of the folly of martyrdom. It always—when about to enter a protest—very blandly informs the wild beast whose path it essays to stop, that its "bark is worse than its bite," and that it only means to save its manners by enacting its decent *role* of resistance. The only practical purpose which it now subserves in American politics is to give enough exercise to Radicalism to keep it "in wind," and to prevent its becoming pursy and lazy from having nothing to whip. No doubt, after a few years, when women's suffrage shall have become an accomplished fact, conservatism will tacitly admit it into its creed, and thenceforward plume itself upon its wise firmness in opposing with similar weapons the extreme of baby suffrage; and when that too shall have been won, it will be heard declaring that the integrity of the American Constitution requires at least the refusal of suffrage to asses. There it will assume, with great dignity, its final position.[1]

1. Robert L. Dabney, *Discussions*, Vol. 4 (Vallecito, CA: Ross House Publishers, [1897] 1979), p. 496.

All of which should serve to teach us of the absolute necessity for proper theological foundations for any resistance to tyranny. The case of Cromwell is a good case in point in that respect. Cromwell has to be regarded as one of the most eminent foes of tyranny in the history of the English nation. Cromwell was consistent and he never swerved in his constant opposition to all civil and religious tyranny. The great object of his life's labors was the destruction of the House of Stuart, to him the very epitome of tyranny. And to that end he fought anyone and everyone, Calvinist and Papist alike. When the Scotch Covenanters allied themselves with Charles Stuart, who had hypocritically sworn to the covenant, he fought and defeated the forces of Scotch Presbyterianism. When Ireland became a base for a Stuart threat to retake the throne of England, then the Irish Papists felt the weight of his sword. When English Presbyterianism, in control of the Long Parliament, threatened religious liberty, he dismissed them at the point of the sword. And in a day and age when the Protestant nations of Europe were few and a Catholic League remained a constant threat, Cromwell went to war with Calvinist Holland when the House of Orange foolishly allied itself with the cause of the House of Stuart.

Cromwell's aims were consistent, and his means to those ends extremely effective, and yet he failed. In a very real sense the Restoration was inevitable. In spite of all he had, what Cromwell lacked was indispensable. *He lacked a national theological concensus undergirding his position*. Ultimately, he could only maintain with the sword the liberty that he had so nobly won with the sword. Ironically, the forces of tyranny could be kept at bay only with the rule of the major-generals, even as Cromwell, the champion of liberty, was progressively being branded as a tyrant and usurper by the very people who had experienced the deliverance that his sword had wrought. This is a lesson that American foreign policy has yet to learn as it continues to pave the way for Soviet imperialism by destroying the Trujillos, Batistas, Somozas, etc., in a vain attempt to reproduce American institutions where there is no national theological consensus to support them.

### *Reformation From the Top Down?*

Having recognized the vanity of resistance to tyranny without proper theological foundations, without a proper ideological consensus among the people to undergird such resistance, we can begin to examine the feasibility of any proposed "Reformation from the top down." And the obvious answer is that it can only succeed where the proper foundation has already been laid. This does not necessarily mean that it may never be attempted without such a consensus, but the ultimate hopelessness of such an attempt should be weighed by any responsible civil magistrate before he embarks on such a course. Things can go from bad to worse!

It is of course always true that civil magistrates are ministers of God and responsible to their Creator, and must someday give account of their official actions to the Righteous Judge. Like Christ's ministers in the church, although pastors are chosen by the people and elders are the representatives of the people in the courts of the church, they are preeminently the servants of Jesus Christ and absolutely subject to his will as their Sovereign Lord. But ministers are not little popes and elders not junior satraps. Churches are ruled by constitutions, not men, and ultimately by the written word and the Living Word, Jesus Christ its Head. Similarly, unless a civil magistrate is providentially placed in the position of being absolute in his rule, of being a golden head such as Nebuchadnezzar, a godly magistrate is limited in any attempts to produce a reformation by the constitutional restraints on his authority and functions. In other words, a theonomist in the White House does not herald America's redemption from her present ills. The constitutional system of checks and balances on the President's authority, the legitimate scope of the Supreme Court and the Congress, as well as the issue of State's Rights, all combine to make any such President totally ineffective without a national theological concensus in favor of God's law as revealed in the Holy Scriptures. Without a troop of Cromwellian major-generals, such a President could effect no national transformation, even outwardly, in the face of overwhelming antinomianism.

As others have pointed out, the cases of Hezekiah and Josiah are clear-cut cases of reformation from the top down, and they were successful. And as the Apostle Paul taught, all these things were written for our example and they ought not to be slighted as Biblical models of good reformations. But it is imperative that we note that there was a solid foundation for such reformations. Both kings were doing their *strict duty* according to the *constitutional responsibilities of their office*. They were not introducing anything new or illegitimate but were reforming all things according to the nation's constitution, according to the terms of the covenant that the nation made with Jahweh at Sinai.

One may argue on the basis that neither of these reformations was of an enduring nature, that they lacked a true national theological consensus required for effective top-down reformation, but here we must be careful. God only is the judge of the thoughts and intents of the heart. Men are not omniscient, and so our Lord teaches that we are to judge men by their outward fruits. If the tree is good it will inevitably yield good fruit, and vice versa. If nothing else can be learned from the Old Side and New Side controversy in the Presbyterian schism of the 1740s, it is the sinfulness of the rash charges of attributing motives. The Old Side ministers thoroughly rebuked the New Side for their practice of condemning all their opponents as unconverted.[2] As the Old Side correctly pointed out, a man could be judged only by his *faith* and *practice*, that is, by his *doctrine* and his *actions*. If these could meet the test of scripture, then it would be the height of slander to condemn him as an unconverted hypocrite. It is by his external actions that a man is judged by both the civil and the ecclesiastical elders, and that is all they can properly concern themselves with.

This is certainly the basis on which Hezekiah and Josiah proceeded. The nation was still formally in covenant with Jahweh, and the people were still outwardly and constitutionally His people. They called forth the fruits that were consistent with such a profession and applied the legal penalties to all breaches of the covenant. To do more was not within the proper scope of their office and to have done less would have been to violate their oaths of office and their sacred duty under the Sinaitic Covenant. They had a solid constitional basis and outward national consensus for their reformations. They did their duty under the covenant and received God's covenantal blessings. No civil magistrate should ever do less.

But, when there is no such basis or consensus, it would be folly to try to force such a reformation. Here, the examples of

2. Charles Hodge, *Constitutional History of the Presbyterian Church in the United States of America* (Uxbridge, MA: The American Presbyterian Press, [1851] 1983).

both Joseph and Daniel should be carefully appreciated. Both these men were knowledgeable and godly men who rose to positions of great power, influence, and authority in essentially pagan empires. The scriptures totally vindicate both men from any charge of sin with respect to their public actions as recorded in sacred history. Yet there is no evidence at all in the sacred record that either man ever attempted any reformation whatsoever in the nations that each respectively ruled as a result of their faithful commitment to Jahweh, the God of Israel. To have attempted such a reformation would obviously have exceeded their constitutional authority and would probably have been to court martyrdom. Martyrdom has its place when we are called to it by the God who is sovereign over all life, but we have no right to court it foolishly, especially by insisting on casting our pearls before swine.

Both these men owed not only their positions but their lives to remarkable dispensations of divine providence, and it would have been a presumptuous tempting of the Most High to have embarked on a rash and suicidal course of building castles in the sky. Both men were models of faithful ministers, wise stewards, and diligent servants bringing honor to their God and submitting graciously to those powers and authorities that God in His providence had chosen to place them under. They performed the functions of their office with such honesty and truth, such equity and justice, such remarkable intellect, wisdom, and nobility of character, that they brought honor to themselves and the God they served. They were living examples of Paul's admonitions in Romans 13 and in I Timothy 6. God was greatly pleased with them and we should be also. In short, there is no Biblical requirement to abuse one's legitimate authority in a vain attempt to promote a reformation by authoritative fiat without a shred of constitutional basis or national consensus.

### *Authority*

While we are on the aforementioned subject, it is fitting to examine carefully the nature of authority. As we have seen, the matters of resistance to tyranny and of godly reformation are closely related to questions of authority. And here we must carefully distinguish between the revealed and secret wills of God (Deut. 29:29). God's revealed will is that the murderer must be put to death. God's secret will may be that the murderer, like Cain, should escape all merely human retribution. And how does all this work out in practice in human history as God's eternal decrees are being worked out in time and space? Well, God calls and raises up civil elders, magistrates, to whom he gives the power of the sword and clothes with His authority to take human life within the terms of his law. And He places further restrictions by giving rules of evidence such as a plurality of witnesses to establish guilt in a capital crime. Then, if in God's providence He has raised up faithful rulers subject to His revealed will, and He providentially provides the proper testimony and evidence to obtain a conviction, it obviously was His secret will that that particular murder should be officially executed for his sin. But in spite of the revealed will of God that requires his death, if any other than a lawful magistrate upon due process should take his life, that in itself would not be vindicatory justice but merely compounding the act of murder. Now the problems of resistance to tyranny and of reformation must be approached exactly the same way.

God's revealed will may place the curse of His displeasure on tyrants and usurpers, but this in no way is sufficient to undergird a movement of resistance. Like the woman taken in adultery, tyrants may well deserve to be stoned to death. But who has the moral authority to throw the first stone? Certainly not the guilty subjects who have brought God's wrath and curse down on their society by their wickedness! We must always remember that although the tyrant may be worthy of death, he is still, like the arch traitor Judas Iscariot, God's instrument to fulfil God's secret counsel. We must be careful not to jump the gun lest we be found to be opposing the counsels of the Most High. In due time when He is finished with His purposes in an instrument, then and then alone will He personally raise up an avenger, an Ehud, who will dispatch the tyrant. But He will raise up an avenger that will meet all the requirements of His revealed will. An avenger clothed with the proper legal and moral authority who can without sin exact the full penalty of God's righteous judgment on such sins. Vengeance is mine, saith the Lord, I will repay, and He does, and Reformed Christians should shudder to attempt to steal that prerogative from the Almighty!

Now these exact principles also apply to the question of

reformation. It is God's revealed will that all things be conformed to His revealed will, to the pattern of the mount. But not all have the prerequisite authority to impose such changes on society. It is precisely here that Hezekiah and Josiah saw their duty and that Joseph and Daniel saw their limitations. The latter faithfully served God in their appointed callings and waited until, in God's secret counsel, better things should be brought to pass. And they both waited in faith and in hope, trusting in God's covenant promises. Joseph gave command concerning his bones, awaiting the day that the land of Canaan would be restored to the heirs of Abraham, Isaac, and Jacob, and Daniel awaited the day that the saints would inherit the kingdom. We must always remember the godly examples of the latter as well as of the former. We too must be subject to God's timing in His purposes in history.

### *Patriotism*

Christians are called to be the salt of the earth and the light of the world. As such, they ought to be the most excellent of citizens. They ought to be pillars of stability in the body politic and paragons of patriotism, at least in any reasonably just society. And in a society somewhat less than just, they could reasonably be expected to be found in the forefront of any reform movement. They even could be expected to provide principled leadership in any struggle against despotism and tyranny. Yet, in this area especially, it seems that professing Christians have been all too prone to rash and unprincipled resistance to the pettiest of tyranny, all in the sacred name of patriotism. Just what is true of patriotism and just what scriptural obligations does it really lay on all faithful disciples of Jesus the Christ?

True patriotism recognizes that righteousness exalts a nation, but sin is a reproach to any people. True love of one's country will prompt one to promote its national righteousness. True patriotism is not concerned with the worldly power, position, and prosperity of the nation, but is concerned with the nation's status in the sight of a holy, just, and righteous God. In this connection, the reader is urged to read Jeremiah 37 and 38, where the false patriot Hananiah tells the people "all is well," while the true patriot Jeremiah calls for national repentance, and is imprisoned for his pains.[3]

3. For a more extensive discussion, see Louis DeBoer, *The New Phariseeism* (Uxbridge, MA: The American Presbyterian Press, 1978), pp. 127-133.

The Hananiahs of the age may sound like the ultimate in Christian patriotism but their's is a siren song that leads to destruction. The tragedy of Jeremiah's day has been repeated over and over again in human history. In 33 A.D. the "patriotic" Jews, concerned about their place and nation, chose Barabbas over Christ. They preferred a popular "resistance" leader to "the Lamb of God that takes away the sin of the world." They preferred an uncouth revolutionary to Him who taught, "Give unto Caesar what is Caesar's and unto God what is God's." And their ultimate and total destruction was just and sure, as in 70 A.D., the fanatical, suicidal patriotism of the Zealots drowned Judah and Jerusalem in a sea of Jewish blood as God avenged His Son!

### *The Doctrine of Balaam*

Any true theory of scriptural patriotism and any proper understanding of Biblical resistance to tyranny must take into account the doctrine of Balaam. Balaam, if one recalls, was that prophet of the True God who prostituted his office for the sake of filthy lucre. Like Demas, he forsook his calling because he loved this present world. In his days the children of Israel were on the march into the land of Canaan, into the land that God had covenanted with their patriarchs, Abraham, Isaac, and Jacob, to give to them. And their progress was irresistable and their arms invincible because God was with them. The generation that apostatized at Kadesh-Barnea, the race that could not enter in because of unbelief, was gone, dead and buried in the wilderness. A new race had sprung up in God's covenant faithfulness that had the faith, that had renewed the covenant on the plains of Moab, and God, their God, was going to establish them in the land of promise and nothing could stay His hand. Balak, the King of Moab, with more wisdom and insight than displayed by contemporary conservatives and by many professing Christians, realized that the issue to be joined between Israel and Moab was strictly a spiritual one. Acknowledging that the weapons of our warfare are not entirely carnal, he retained Balaam to curse the children of Israel, knowing that if they were cursed of their God they would be easy prey in battle.

But God was with Israel, and in spite of himself, the prophet could under divine direction do no less than pour out one blessing and glorious prophecy upon the other concerning the children of Israel. So at first Balak was entirely frustrated in his attempts to curse Israel and rob her of Jahweh's favor which constituted her supremacy. But Balaam was not so easily frustrated in his pursuit of this world's goods and he ultimately was somewhat successful in having Abraham's God curse the children of Israel. Christ rebukes the church in Pergamos for having "them that hold the doctrine of Balaam, who taught Balak to cast a stumbling block before the children of Israel, to eat things sacrificed unto idols, and to commit fornication" (Rev. 2:14). The result of this original application of the doctrine of Balaam by Balak is recorded for us in Numbers 25. And had it not been for the righteous and courageous actions of Phinehas by which the plague of God was stayed, the strategem would surely have succeeded in destroying Israel and removing her as a military threat to Moab. As Balak properly saw, the struggle was a spiritual one, and it was not won by the captains of the host of Israel, neither was it lost by the armies of Moab. The victory belonged to one righteous man, to Phinehas, who stood in the gap that day for Israel.

Now any Biblical doctrine of resistance to tyranny should take careful note of Balaam's strategy. It should note that while the enemies of America promote abortion, homosexuality, pornography, and sabbath breaking, etc., it will not suffice to debate SALT and START and Pentagon defense budgets, etc. The battle is still the Lord's and the issue is still spiritual. We must hold to the converse of the doctrine of Balaam. We must promote that national righteousness which will bring down the blessing of the Almighty. Phinehas was only one man and God was willing to spare Sodom if but ten righteous men could be found there. Let us repent and reform, reforming our own lives, our families, our churches, and our land, that we may be instrumental in bringing the blessings of peace and liberty to us and to our seed after us.

### *Hypocrisy*

Our Lord hated hypocrisy and it was preeminent in His rebukes. There has been a great deal of hypocrisy in much of what passes for principled resistance to tyranny and it really is small wonder that so much of contemporary resistance to the democratic totalitarianism of the welfare state has been an exercise in bitter frustration. Without divine blessing, any such movement is condemned to futility, and God will never bless hypocrisy.

As we have seen, reformation is the stock of the tree from which liberty sprouts. But too many conveniently have forgotten the fundamental truth that reformation begins at home. It is the essence of hypocrisy that the focus is always on another's sins and never on its own. When we are exclusively concerned with the wood in everyone else's eyes and oblivious to the wood in our own, then our basic attitude has already degenerated to crass hypocrisy, irrespective of how efficiently we can apply God's law to anyone and everything else. Our Lord brought this out so clearly in the parable of the Pharisee and the Publican. The former, in spite of his extensive knowledge of the scriptures, was an offensive hypocrite because all he could see was the sin of this despised tax gatherer, this corrupt tool of the pagan Roman State. The latter saw his own sin and confessed it before God with penitential tears. The scriptures leave no doubts about which man left God's house a justified man with peace and liberty in his heart.

Now it is the patent stock in trade of "Christian Conservatism" perpetually ad nauseum to call everyone else to repentance.[4] It is always the liberals, the socialists, the communists, the atheists who are called to repentance. It is the sins of the pornographers, of the National Council of Churches, of radical politicians, that are constantly kept in view. By comparison, the membership of such groups are constantly preening themselves as a righteous elite standing for "God and country." One prominent anti-communist evangelist actually pleaded with his following to ignore his homosexuality so that they could get on with the main task of saving the nation from communism. God does not give us knowledge of His will primarily so that we can be better judges of other people's sins but rather that we might more and more conform ourselves to the Lord Jesus Christ, the perfect Servant of Jahweh. Knowledge brings responsibility; therefore, judgment begins with the House of God. Unless we stop acting and assuming and actually demanding that it start with atheists and communists, etc., that is exactly where it

4. We might call this a doctrine of Selective Depravity.

will begin. If the salt has lost its savor it is henceforth useless and it will be cast out. Such pretended salt has utterly lost its ability to staunch the corruption of the body politic.

In that regard Russia is a good case in point. For over a century and a half she has not lacked for powerful revolutionary movements reacting against the corruption and tyranny of her governments. But none of these movements has been viable and has succeeded in advancing the cause of liberty in Russia. Every revolutionary clique has exploited with radical propaganda the abuses and tyranny of the administration that was targeted for overthrow, even as it was prepared to justify its own. Russia can and has changed rulers but what she cannot do is change and produce a free society. As Jeremiah said, "can the leopard change its spots?" The Bolshevik revolution left Russia exactly where she had always been, with a centralized and despotic government controlling the people politically, economically, and religiously. A change of the ruling clique from the Romanovs to the Bolsheviks and from their icons to posters of Marx and Lenin, etc., could affect no real fundamental changes in that society. The land is still characterized by savagery, superstition, and serfdom, and will remain so until righteousness and reformation prevail to deliver her.

### *A Godly Example*

Scotland, that most presbyterian of all nations, found herself beset with many national difficulties in the middle of the seventeenth century. Having as a nation covenanted in the National Covenant and in the Solemn League and Covenant for a thorough and scriptural reformation in both church and state in not only her own realm but in the three kingdoms of Scotland, England, and Ireland, she found her hopes and plans in disarray. The English parliament that had signed the covenant had been prorogued by Cromwell, and when the Scotch had tried to enforce it by arms, they suffered defeats at Worcester and Dunbar. Their land was now occupied by the English and the enemies of the covenant were rife even in their church and state. But they did not rail against God's judgments nor did they resort to venting self-righteous anger at that "conquering usurper," Oliver Cromwell. Rather, they had a very special gathering of the General Assembly of the

Church of Scotland to consider "Causes of the Lord's Wrath Against Scotland" which they published under that title. It is a remarkable document and deserves our careful attention.

Here is no hypocrisy but rather a baring of the sinful soul before God and a pleading for Him to withdraw His chastising hand. It is a call for a thorough reformation as it systematically catalogs the national sins that have brought God's displeasure on the land. The document begins:

> *Some General Heads of the Causes Why the Lord Contends With the Land,* —Agreed upon (after seeking of the Lord) by the Commission of the General Assembly, 1650, with the advice of divers ministers from several parts of the kingdom, met at Edinburgh, October 1651, so far as, for the present, they could attain light therein, which they offer and advise to be made use of by all the Lord's people in the land, leaving place to add, as the Lord shall make further discoveries hereafter of the guiltiness of the land, and intending more fully and particularly to enlarge this paper.

and then follow ten articles under which are summed up the sins of the land. Some of these read as follows:

> *Art.* 1. The gross Atheism and ignorance of God, and of his word and works, that is in a great part of the inhabitants of the land, which is such that neither law nor gospel, nor the most common and necessary points of truth are understood or known by many thousands.
>
> *Art.* 2. Horrible looseness and profanity of conversation in all sorts, against the commandments both of the first and second table, which hath so abounded and increased that scarce hath any of the nations exceeded us therein.
>
> *Art.* 3. The despising and slighting of Jesus Christ offered in the gospel (which we look on as the chief and mother sin of this nation), and the not valuing and improving the gospel and precious ordinances of Christ, unto the establishing and building up of ourselves in the lively faith of Christ and power of godliness, but either neglecting and despising these things altogether, or else resting upon and idolising outward and bare forms, without studying to know in ourselves, or to promote in others, the kingdom of God, which is righteousness, and peace, and joy in the Holy Ghost; whereby it hath come to pass that persons not rightly qualified have been admitted unto, and continued in, the work of the ministry and elderships, and that public repentance and kirk censures have been grossly slighted, and the sacrament of the Lord's supper fearfully polluted by the promiscuous admitting of many ignorant and scandalous persons thereto; and many wilfully ignorant, and openly and continuedly profane, have been kept in the fellowship of this kirk, contrary to

> the word of God, and constitutions of this kirk, and that many other sad and fearful consequences have followed unto the profaning of all the ordinances of God, and rendering them for the most part barren and fruitless to us.
>
> *Art.* 5. The base love of the world, and covetousness, which hath made not only the body of the people, but many ministers, more to mind their own things than the things of Jesus Christ; and many masters, rulers, magistrates, officers and soldiers in armies, exceedingly to abuse their power unto the exercising of intolerable oppression of all kinds on the poor, to the grinding of their faces, and making their lives bitter to them; which fountain of covetousness did also produce great insolences and oppressions in our armies in England and Ireland, and the fearful perjuries in the land in the matter of valuation and excise.

Of particular interest are these excerpts from Article 9 condemning a latent hypocrisy and a bitter and railing spirit under these trials.

> The rejecting of discoveries of guiltiness, and causes of the Lord's contending with us, and of our duty in reference thereto; . . . neglecting the means tending to peace, and to the preventing the effusion of more blood, from pride and bitterness of spirit against those who had invaded us.

And finally, this last article:

> Deep security, impenitency, obstinacy and incorrigibleness, under all these, and under all the dreadful strokes of God, and tokens of his indignation against us, because of the same; so that whilst he continues to smite, we are so far from humbling ourselves and turning to him, that we wax worse and worse, and sin more and more.

These articles were followed by thirty some pages of fine print cataloging in detail the sins under these ten heads and thoroughly setting forth the testimony of the word of God with respect to each sin. What follows is really amazing, for there is then appended a lengthy confession of their own sins entitled, "A Humble Acknowledgment of the Sins of the Ministry of Scotland." The preface reads as follows:

> Although we are not ignorant that mockers of all sorts may take occasion by this acknowledgment of the sins of ministers to strengthen themselves in their prejudices at our persons and callings, and turn this unto our reproach, and that some may misconstrue our meaning therein, as if we did thereby intend to render the ministry of this church base and contemptible, which is far from our thoughts, we knowing and being persuaded in

ourselves that there are many able, godly, and faithful ministers in the land; yet, being convinced that we are called to humble ourselves, and to justify the Lord in all the contempt that he hath poured upon us—that they who shall know our sins may not stumble at our judgments,—we have thought it our duty to publish this following discovery and acknowledgment of the corruptions and sins of ministers, that it may appear how deep our hand is in the transgression, and that the ministers of Scotland have no small accession to the drawing on of these judgments that are upon the land.

Only in this following acknowledgment we desire it may be considered, That there are here enumerated some sins whereof there be but some few ministers guilty, and others whereof more are guilty, and not a few which are the sins of those whom the Lord hath kept from the more gross corruptions herein mentioned; and that it is not to be wondered at if the ministry of Scotland be yet in a great measure unpurged, considering that there was so wide a door opened for the entering of corrupt persons into the ministry, for the space of above thirty years under the tyranny of prelates, and that also there hath been so many diversions from, and interruptions of endeavours to have a purged ministry in this land.

Now, when if ever in our day have you heard of a group of Reformed, or Evangelical, or Fundamentalist ministers publically in great detail (versus pious platitudes and empty general confessions) confess their own sins and acknowledge that they have greatly contributed to bringing down the displeasure and judgments of God upon the land? Is this why reformation lags and tyranny spreads itself like a green bay tree? Let us labor and pray that in our day also we should be blessed with so godly a response to God's present chastisements on our land.

## *History*

The Bible is to be our only rule of faith and practice. We take our cosmology from Moses and not from the pronouncements of secular science. By faith we believe that the worlds were framed by the word of God. We are not empiricists. But while we may reject science, falsely so called, yet we do not hesitate to strive hard to establish thorough correlation between special revelation, the inscripturated word, and general revelation, the testimony of the creation. And neither should we hesitate, in the light of the principles we have been examining from God's word, to review the record of human history and see how God has providentially dealt with these matters, and if we can see consistent application of these principles in His dealings with the children of men.

A brief review of all human history quickly establishes the scarcity of two commodities; righteous godly societies walking in the fear of God in subjection to His law, and liberty. If we can establish a connection between the absence of the former and of the latter, then history will become a witness in our case. The connection is not hard to establish. All of the pagan empires of antiquity were ruled by man's law rather than God's law. From Nimrod's Babylonian Society throughout the respective empires of Assyria, Egypt, Greece, Rome, and a score of lesser known, there is a uniform absence of godly government and liberty. The principles of Leviticus 26 and Deuteronomy 28 shine through as clear as the noonday sun in God's dealing with His people as recorded in the Book of Judges. When God's law is forsaken and His covenant cast aside, when every man does that which is right in his own sight, then liberty departs and is replaced with oppression, spoilation, tyranny, and foreign domination.

More recent history continues to confirm the same truths. Although we may find a few occasions where resistance to tyranny obtained at least some temporary results, such as the Magna Charta wrung from King John in 1215 and the Great Privilege obtained by the Dutch people from their government in about the same era, yet without a solid ideological foundation in that society, these soon became empty ciphers in the hands of future corrupt administrations. But, it is in the histories of Holland, England, and America that we can especially trace the workings of these principles. In Holland, then the Spanish Netherlands, we see a nation sliding deeper into oppression and despotism as her ancient liberties were steadily being eroded by the Hapsburgs. What arrested all this was not futile resistance of the Roman Catholic nobles, such as Egmont and Horn, who were executed for merely questioning the royal prerogatives of the tyrant, Philip II of Spain. It was arrested by a thorough grass-roots reformation that swept through the land till the superstition and heresies of the Church of Rome were well-nigh extinct, and the reformed faith, Calvinist doctrine reigned supreme in the people's hearts and the land was filled with the pure praises and worship of God. On such a foundation the Almighty raised up a champion, William of Orange (The Silent), who initiated the Eighty Years War that culminated in the freedom and independence of the Dutch people and the Reformed faith. We have already mentioned Scotland where a similar reformation extirpated Popery and rid the land of foreign domination by the French and the Vatican.

In England, the Puritan movement ultimately broke the back of the despotic tendencies of both the Tudors and the House of Stuart. Again, this was a grass-roots reformation thoroughly resisted by the entrenched powers in church and state. And although it was slower in its development, less thorough and less pure than the aforementioned reformations, yet with the blessing of the Almighty it was sufficient to hamstring the Tudors and twice to drive the Stuart tyrants off the throne in the English Civil War and again in the Glorious Revolution. The Stuarts were correct in one thing when they contended "No bishop, No king" and a reformation in the church always heralds trouble for a despotic state. Without English Puritanism, there would have been no basis for English liberties, the very liberties that we ourselves have inherited in this nation. A liberty that was successfully maintained in 1776 because at that time in our history, as Bancroft records it, America was 98% Protestant and 66% Calvinist. America's theological high water mark was hit before the Revolutionary War, before the advent of Arminianism, Unitarianism, Universalism, and Deism that were already in evidence at the time of the War of Independence. Her purest expression of the Reformed faith was in the now long extinct Old Side Presbyterianism. If, in these nations, with such godly reformations, liberty came with such struggles and at such costs, let us forever dispel the myth that liberty can ever be established without such a foundation.

# RELIGIOUS LIBERTY VERSUS RELIGIOUS TOLERATION

Rousas John Rushdoony

ONE of the areas of profound ignorance today is religious liberty and the meaning thereof. The common pattern throughout history, including in the Roman Empire, has been religious toleration, *a very different thing.*

In religious toleration, the state is paramount, and, in every sphere, its powers are totalitarian. The state is the sovereign or lord, the supreme religious entity and power. The state decrees what and who can exist, and it establishes the terms of existence. The state reserves the power to license and tolerate one or more religions upon its own conditions and subject to state controls, regulation, and supervision.

The Roman Empire believed in religious toleration. It regarded religion as good for public morale and morals, and it therefore had a system of licensure and regulation. New relgions were ordered to appear before a magistrate, affirm the lordship or sovereignty of Caesar, and walk away with a license to post in their meeting-place.

The early church refused licensure, because it meant the lordship of Caesar over Christ and His church. The early church refused toleration, because it denied the right of the state to say whether or not Christ's church could exist, or to set the conditions of its existence. *The early church rejected religious toleration for religious liberty.*

Over the centuries, both Catholics and then Protestants often fought for religious liberty. Over the centuries also, the churches too often capitulated to religious toleration, with very evil results. Toleration was productive of fearful evils. *First*, one church was tolerated and established *by the state*, not by Christ, as the "privileged" or state-tolerated institution.

---

Reprinted from *Chalcedon Position Paper* No. 31. 

This "privilege" called for concessions to the state.

These took a variety of forms. It could mean that the state appointed or controlled the bishops (Protestant or Catholic). It meant that only the state could give permission for a meeting of a church's national convocation or general assembly. In a variety of ways, establishment meant an establishment under the state's control. At its best, the church was turned into a privileged house-slave; at its worst, the church was simply a part of the bureaucracy, and the working pastors were rare and alone. Sooner or later, an establishment meant subservience and bondage to the state.

*Second*, the tolerated church became a parasite, because it was dependent too often on state aid to collect its tithes and dues. It lived, not because of the faith of the people, but because of the state's subsidy. As a result, the state church served the state, not the Lord, nor the Lord's people. (When the states turned humanistic and, losing interest in their captive churches, began to cut their "privileges" and subsidies, revivals broke out in many established churches as a result!)

*Third*, the tolerated or established church became a persecuting church. It could not compete with its now illegal rivals in faith, and so it used the state to persecute its competitors. Both Catholic and Protestant establishments built up an ugly record in this respect. Meanwhile, their humanist foes could criticize their intolerance and speak of this inhumanity as a necessary aspect of Christianity!

*Fourth*, religious toleration leads to intolerance, as it should now be apparent. Toleration is licensure; it is a state subsidy, and those possessing it want a monopoly. Hence, intoleration of competitors results, and the church becomes blind to all issues save monopoly. In 17th century England, for example, the blindness of the Church of England under Archbishop Laud, as he fought the Puritans, was staggering. However, when Cromwell came to power, the Presbyterians became a one-issue party, the issue being the control and possession of the Church of England. Had they triumphed, the evils of Laud would have been reproduced. Cromwell balked them; later, the Presbyterians undermined the Commonwealth and helped bring in the depraved Charles II, who quickly ejected them from the Church of England.

In colonial America, uneasy semi-establishments existed. Technically, the Church of England was the established church for all the crown realms, including Catholic Ireland. (Ireland was never more Catholic than *after* England imposed an alien church on the land!) Carl Bridenbaugh, in *Mitre and Sceptre* (1962), showed how the fear and threat of a full-scale establishment with American bishops alarmed Americans and led to the War of Independence. Meanwhile, in the colonies, men began to oppose religious toleration in favor of religious liberty. Here, the Baptists were most important, especially Isaac Backus.

Backus declared, "We view it to be our incumbent duty to render unto Caesar the things that are his but also that *it is of as much importance not to render unto him anything that belongs only to God, who is to be obeyed rather than any man*. And as it is evident that God always claimed it as his sole prerogative to determine by his own laws what his worship shall be, who shall minister in it, and how they shall be supported, so it is evident that this prerogative has been, and still is, encroached upon in our land." (Wm. J. McLoughlin, editor: *Isaac Backus on Church, State, and Calvinism, Pamphlets, 1754-1789*, p. 317. Harvard University Press, 1965.) The defenders of establishment or toleration became, Backus said, "Caesar's friend" (John 19:12). We cannot make the state the definer of man's duty to God, as the establishment-toleration position does. This position, Backus held, takes matters of faith from the conscience of man to the councils of state and thus undermines true faith. Backus saw that the new country would have no unity if establishment and toleration became lawful in the Federal Union. Backus quoted Cotton Mather, who said, "Violences may bring the erroneous to be hypocrites, but they will never bring them to be believers." The heart of Backus' position was this: "Religion (meaning Biblical religion) was prior to all states and kingdoms in the world and therefore could not in its nature be subject to human laws" (p. 432).

The First Amendment to the U.S. Constitution, replacing religious toleration and establishment with religious liberty, was the result of the work of Backus and many other churchmen. It represented a great and key victory in church history.

Now, however, religious liberty is dead in the United States. It only exists if you confine it to the area between your two ears. Instead of religious liberty, we have religious toleration. Now, religious toleration is the reality of the situation in Red China and Red Russia. In both cases, the toleration is very, very limited. In the United States, the toleration is still extensive, and most churchmen fail to recognize that the states and the federal government are insisting that only toleration, not liberty, exists, and the limits of that toleration are being narrowed steadily.

Thus, Senator Ernest F. Hollings of South Carolina has given expression to the position of the regulators and tolerationists, writing (2-19-82), "Tax exemption is a privilege, not a right. It is not only proper but Constitutional that the government condition that privilege on the Constitutional requirement of nondiscrimination. Religious freedom is a priceless heritage that must be jealously guarded. But when religious belief is contrary to the law of the land then it is the law, not religion, that must be sustained. The 1964 Civil Rights Act provided there be no discrimination in institutions receiving Federal financial assistance and the courts have interpreted this to mean that no public monies be appropriated directly or indirectly through tax exemption to those institutions that discriminate" (Letter by Hollings, re: the Reagan bill S2024, to control Christian Schools).

Sen. Hollings has, with many, many other members of Congress, *first*, replaced religious liberty with state toleration. Tax exemption originally meant no jurisdiction by the state over the church, because the power to tax is the power to control and destroy. Now, these humanistic statists tell us it is a subsidy! Tax exemption is called "Federal financial assistance," and the courts hold that controls must follow assistance from the civil treasury. This means a mandate to control churches, and every facet of their existence, including Christian Schools, colleges, seminaries, employees, etc., in the name of controlling federal grants!

*Second*, Hollings (and others, including many judges) hold that this means that the Civil Rights Act of 1964 must take priority over the First Amendment. The Civil Rights laws forbid discrimination in terms of race, and also a number of other things, *including creed*. The evidence is accumulating that federal authorities believe that they have now the legal *right* to require churches to ordain women, and homosexuals; on January 26, 1982, to a group of us meeting with Edwin Meese and eight or ten Justice Department lawyers in the White House, Meese (a Lutheran layman!) said flatly that this was within the legitimate power of the federal government. This means that the church, in terms of the same laws, can be forbidden to discriminate with respect to creed! This would mean equal time for all creeds, including humanism and atheism, in every church. In the Worldwide Church of God case, the court held that a church and its assets belongs, not to the members thereof, but to all citizens!

*Third*, the position of Hollings; Reagan; before him, Carter; the Justice Department; the Internal Revenue Service; the Labor Department; the Treasury Department; and the several states is that the only "freedom" that the church can have is that activity which the state chooses to tolerate. Toleration on any and all activities is subject to regulation, controls, and oversight.

That is, of course, totalitarianism. The fact is that religious liberty is dead and buried; it needs to be resurrected. We *cannot* begin to cope with our present crisis until we recognize that religious liberty has been replaced with religious toleration. The limits of that toleration are being steadily narrowed. If Christians are silent today, the Lord will not be silent towards them when they face the judgment of His Supreme Court. There is a war against Biblical faith, against the Lord, and the men waging that war masquerade it behind the facade of non-discrimination, subsidies, legitimate public interest, and so on.

All this is done in the name of one of the most evil doctrines of our time: *public policy*. Nothing contrary to public policy should have tax exemption, and, some hold, *any* right to exist. Today, public policy includes homosexual "rights," abortion, an established humanism, and much, much more. The implication is plain, and, with some, it is a manifesto: No one opposing public policy has any rights. The public policy doctrine is the new face of totalitarianism. It has all the echoes of tyrannies old and new, and with more muscles.

What is increasingly apparent is that the triune God of Scripture, the Bible itself, and all faith grounded thereon, are contrary to public policy. Christianity has no place in our state schools and universities; it does not inform the councils of state; every effort by Christians to affect the political process is called a violation of the First Amendment and "the separation of church and state." Our freedom of religion is something to be tolerated only if we keep it between our two ears. A war has been declared against us, and we had better know it, and we had better stand and fight before it is too late.

We may be able to live under religious toleration, but it will beget all the ancient evils of compromise, hypocrisy, and a purely or largely public religion. It will replace conscience with a state license, and freedom with a state-endowed cell of narrow limits. This is *the best* that toleration may afford us in the days ahead.

But the LORD alone is God, and He does not share His throne with the state. If we surrender to Caesar, we will share in Caesar's judgment and fall. If we stand with the LORD, we shall stand in His Spirit and power. "Stand fast therefore in the liberty wherewith Christ hath made us free, and be not entangled again with the yoke of bondage" (Gal. 5:1). At the heart of that yoke of bondage is the belief and fear that the powers of man (and the state) are greater than the power of God. It is bondage to believe that man can prevail, or that man can frustrate God's sovereign and holy purpose. The only real question is this: Will we be a part of the LORD's Kingdom and victory?

# REBELLION, TYRANNY, AND DOMINION IN THE BOOK OF GENESIS

James B. Jordan

THE differences between true and false dominion constitute one of the major themes of the book of Genesis. While other books of Scripture, such as the book of Judges, give us similar insights, the book of Genesis is particularly suited to our present situation in America as Christians. We have not (yet) been conquered by outsiders (as in the book of Judges), but the governance of our lives has been given over to anti-Christian tyrants from within, with whom we have to deal. Moreover, with the emergence of the New Christian Right, a temptation is placed before the American Christian community which is analogous to the temptation placed before Adam and Eve by the tempter: the temptation to seize power instead of waiting for God to confer it.

The procedure of this paper is as follows. First we look at several sections of the book of Genesis to learn what it teaches about rebellion, tyranny, resistance, and dominion. Then we suggest some relevant applications to our own time, in both church and state. Some applications will be made along the way, in order to illustrate the points made.

### *Seizing the Robe from God: Adam*

In Genesis 1:1-2:4, we have an account of God's creation of a *place* for man. The Hebrew word is *'erets*, which is translated earth, but which always implies an organized place, a structured environment. It stands in contrast to the word for *ground* used in chapters 2-4, *'adhamah* which means the dirt out of which men and animals are made, and to which they return when they die. In Genesis 6-8, it is the *'erets* which is decreated (or destabilized) back to its initial stage (cf. Gen. 1:2) and then recreated. This restabilizing process constitutes the "establishing" of God's original covenantal order of creation, an establishing of it *through* Noah (Gen. 6:18; 9:9-16).[1]

The world as God originally created it was "formless and empty" (Gen. 1:2). The work of God in the six days of creation was designed to give structure and content to the creation. This giving of structure to the formless and content to the empty consists of a series of "covenant" actions on God's part. First comes the *covenant word*: Let there be (1:3,6,9,14,20,24,26). Following the covenant word comes, second, the *covenant act*, an act either of separating or of filling. Third we find *covenant provisions*, which consist of naming or describing what has been made, giving to each its place in the covenant order. Fourth and fifth, we find *covenant witness* which forms the basis of *covenant judgments*: And God *saw* that it was *good* (1:4,10,12, 18,21,25,31).

Man is made in the image of God, and we expect from this that man will be, like God, a covenant-acting being. Man's actions within the covenant will be secondary; he will *image* the covenant-life of God; he will think God's thoughts after Him, and in a sense live God's life after Him. Man is created, we may truly say, a *symbol of God*, and his whole life is to be a life of imaging God.

Man has meaning, thus, only as a symbol of God. The meaning of his life is not found within himself, but in his being an image of something else, of God. Man does not have meaning within himself; he does not define himself; he is defined by God.

Imaging the life of God, man is not able to speak a covenant word in the same sense as God does (though in magic sinful man would try to do so); but man tracks God's other covenant actions, acquiring knowledge and wisdom and passing judgment. God's actions had entailed a prophetic command (let there be), a kingly response of action (and there was), and a final priestly evaluation (and God saw that it was

---

1. That God's original creation of the *'erets* was a covenant making activity has been well demonstrated by Meredith G. Kline, *Kingdom Prologue*, volume 1 (Wenham, MA: Gordon-Conwell Divinity School Bookstore, 1981), pp. 26ff. On the meaning of "establishing" the covenant, as opposed to "making" it, see Umberto Cassuto, *A Commentary on the Book of Genesis*, part II: *From Noah to Abraham*, trans. by Israel Abrahams (Jerusalem: The Magnes Press, [1949] 1964), p. 67f.; and Cassuto, *The Documentary Hypothesis*, trans. by Israel Abrahams (Jerusalem: The Magnes Press, [1941] 1961), p. 47f.

good). Man was not to be a prophet; he was to get his inceptive word from God.[2] Man was, however, to engage in a kingly function of action in terms of God's command, and finally he was going to be called upon to make priestly judicial pronouncements.

Man's first day was God's seventh. Man would start in a sabbath, and receive God's prophetic word of command-promise. Then he would work for six days, in faithfulness or disobedience. At the end, at the sabbath of his analogous labors, he would pass judgment. Judgment comes at the end, not at the beginning; after getting wisdom and working, not before it.

God created man to image Him in two primary respects, seen in Genesis 2:15: "Then YHWH God took the man and put him into the garden of Eden to *serve* it and to *guard* it." The serving function images God's kingly character, and the guarding function images His priestly character. Man's understanding of these two duties was to be progressive. Though made "like God," man was to become more and more like God through a process of growth and maturation in His image. God used the animals to teach man about his basilic (kingly) and hieratic (priestly) tasks.

First, he brought animals to the man to see what he would *name* them. Man would *learn* from the animals and acquire *wisdom* from them (as we see later on also from the book of Proverbs). *Acquiring knowledge and wisdom* is the first part of man's kingly function; the second part is his *kingly servant-rule* based on his wisdom. Imaging God's covenant provisions, man named the animals, thinking God's thoughts after Him. From this action, man learned that he was alone, something he learned because God had set up an analogy between the life of man and the life of the animals.[3] Now that the man had

2. The prophetic function (sometimes called an office, but not in the same sense as priest and king) was given to man after the fall, to speak God's inceptive word of command-promise into the world. The first use of the term 'prophet' in Scripture indicates that it basically means "mediator," one who speaks for two opposed sides (Gen. 20:7).

3. After all, Adam might have reasoned, "Hmmm. Each of these animals has a sexually polar mate. But, that's the way animals are, and since I am not an animal, it has nothing to do with me." Adam did not so reason, however. Both man and animals are made from the *'adhamah* (2:7,19). It is because of this analogy that animals can serve as symbolic sacrificial substitutes for man, and that dividing animals into two halves can signify a covenantal relationship between man and the *'adhamah* (Gen. 15:9-21).

learned of his need of a mate, God provided her by means of the covenant act of separation (2:21). The Bible also informs us that the covenant act of separation continues each time a man leaves his father's house to marry (2:24). Now that the woman had been made, God gave His basic "cultural mandate" to the man and the woman together, telling them to image His covenant action of filling as well (1:28).

We could say more about all this, but we are now in a position to interpret God's second course of wisdom-instruction, which also used an animal. God would bring an animal to Adam to teach him something about his guarding task. From naming the animals Adam had learned that he needed something. "Well, Lord, you have told me to serve the garden, but I find I cannot do so. There is a problem. I find I have a lack. I need a helper suited to me." So, God provided a passive Adam with something to make up the lack. So also here. From encountering the dragon Adam would learn that he needed something. "Lord, you have told me to guard the garden, but I find I am naked. I lack any robe of judicial authority. I am not empowered to deal with this situation." So, God would provide, when Adam was ready for it, what he needed to deal with the invader. Let us now consider this in more detail.

First we read that Adam and Eve were "both naked and not ashamed." It is a fundamental mistake of interpretation to think that man's nakedness was supposed to be a permanent condition, and that clothing was simply introduced to cover man's sin. Not so. God is clothed in a garb of light, an environment called "glory" in Scripture. The "glory cloud" is seen as a palace, as a temple, as a society of angels and men around Him, and in other forms as well.[4] The glory cloud is God's garment of regal and priestly office. Man, as God's image, should also have such robes. The robe of office, however, is not something man starts out with, but something he must mature into, by acquiring wisdom based on righteousness. The robe of office is for *elders*, not for young men. Moreover, it is never seized, but is always *bestowed*.

God intended for man to learn about his priestly task, which involves measuring (evaluating, witnessing) as a

4. On this see Meredith G. Kline, *Images of the Spirit* (Grand Rapids: Baker, 1980).

precondition to the formal passing of judgment.[5] Thus, God brought an animal to Adam and Eve.[6] By observing the animal's attack upon his wife, Adam would learn that he must guard her, since she was under his covenant headship. By observing what the animal said, and how it defiled God's garden, Adam and Eve would learn that they lacked something else they needed: a robe of office. This would have been given them by letting them eat of the Tree of the Knowledge of Good and Evil.

God put two special trees in the garden: the Tree of Life and the Tree of Judgment. God told Adam and Eve that *all* the trees were made for them to eat of (1:29), so that they knew the prohibition on the Tree of Judgment was temporary. Moreover, God had told them that of *every* other tree they might *freely* eat (2:16), so that they were invited to eat of the Tree of Life from the start.[7] Arriving at the center of the garden, symbolic of God's throne (or the earthly footstool thereof), Adam and Eve were approached by the dragon.

The dragon stated that if Eve ate the fruit her *eyes* would be opened and she would be *like God, knowing good and evil*. What does this mean? Were Adam and Eve blind? Clearly

---

5. Throughout Scripture the priests are those who measure out the dimensions of the temple of God, the man with the measuring rod of Ezekiel 40ff. being but the most prominent example. Such measuring, like witness-bearing, entails *seeing*, and is the precondition of *judging*, as we have seen these in God's covenant actions in Genesis 1. The priestly aspect of measuring and witnessing can be seen in that it correlates to guarding, because it sets up and establishes boundaries, and bears witness regarding whether or not those boundaries have been observed. We might say that the kingly function has to do with filling, and the priestly with separating, the former with cultivation and the latter with jealousy, propriety, and protection.

6. It is clear from the phrase "with her" in 3:6 that Adam was standing by Eve all the while the serpent tempted them.

7. This is quite clear from the text. Various commentators and theologians have supposed that Adam "knew" he was not to eat of the Tree of Life until he had "passed the test." This is completely wrong. The Tree of Life is not an attainment, but is the foundation of life. It is the Tree of Judgment, of investiture with office, which is eschatological in character. The choice before Adam on that first sabbath day was which of the two trees in the center of the garden he would approach: the one God had prohibited, or the one God had invited him to. For the redeemed man, the Tree of Life is not something given him at the end, but at the beginning of his Christian life, for Jesus Christ is the Tree of Life, and the sacraments are the abiding food-form of that same Tree.

not, for the woman *saw* that the tree was good for food (correctly, 2:9) and a delight to the eyes (correctly, 2:9), and that it was desirable to make her wise (wrongly). Also, how about being like God? Wasn't man made in the image and likeness of God? How, then, is it a temptation to become like God, if man is already like God? And again, how about knowing good and evil? Were Adam and Eve in a state of moral neutrality at this point? Obviously not, for they were in covenant with God. They were morally good, and they had a knowledge of moral goodness. They knew right from wrong, and especially Adam, as covenant head, was not deceived about what was going on (1 Tim. 2:14).

The matter becomes even more curious when we notice the sequel. We read that their *eyes* were indeed opened (3:7). We hear God soberly state, "Behold, the man has become *like one of Us, knowing good and evil. . . .*" Was the tempter right? Clearly in some sense, the dragon was telling the truth, though he lied in saying that they would not die.

All of these questions are answered when we realize that the opening of the eyes, the maturation in God-likeness, and the knowledge of good and evil, all have to do with investiture with the robe of judicial office. Concerning the eyes: We have already seen in Genesis 1 that God's seeing is part of His passing judgment. We find in Jeremiah 32:18-19 that God's "eyes are open upon all the ways of the sons of men, to give every one according to his ways, and according to the fruit of his doings." In Psalm 11:4, the eyes of YHWH "behold, His eyelids try, the children of men." False gods are witnesses, says Isaiah 44:9, which "see not, nor know," and which are "put to shame," all language reminiscent of Genesis 3. Meredith M. Kline summarizes, saying that "the picture is of the eyes of God functioning in the legal sphere to give a conclusive judgment concerning lives of men which have been observed by God."[8] Thus, God's eyes either spare or do not spare men His judgments (Ezek. 5:11; 7:4; 20:17).

Concerning becoming more like God, we notice in the text itself the statement that man is already like God (morally), and from the text itself we could draw the inference that the temporary prohibition on the Tree of Judgment was designed

8. Meredith M. Kline, "The Holy Spirit as Covenant Witness" (Th.M. Thesis, Westminster Theological Seminary, 1972), p. 72. I am indebted to Kline's discussion for the verses cited in this section of my essay.

to cause man to mature in God-likeness. The rest of Scripture confirms this for us, in that when men are invested with special office as *judges*, they are called *gods*: "God takes His stand in His own congregation; He judges in the midst of the gods. How long will you judge unjustly and show partiality to the wicked? . . . They do not *know* nor do they understand; they walk about in *darkness*; all the foundations of the earth are shaken. I on My part said, 'You are gods, and all of you are sons of the Most High. Nevertheless, you will die like men' " (Psalm 82:1,2,5,6,7a). Jesus cites this passage in John 10:34. The rulers of Israel are called gods in Exodus 21:6; 22:8,28. This language may make us nervous, because we are so used to thinking of man's making himself into a god as sinful—and rightly so. It is God alone who can invest men properly with the robe of judicial godhood, and it is the essence of original sin for man to seize that robe for himself and seek to make himself into a god (a judge).

What about the phrase "knowing good and evil"? Again, in context, God has been said to pronounce things good, as we have seen. Thus, for man to get knowledge of good and evil would, in context, mean that man has *the privilege of making judicial pronouncements*. Indeed, the rest of Scripture confirms this. Solomon, the first fulfillment of the Davidic Son-covenant and the most splendid type of Christ, prays to be given "an understanding heart to *judge* Thy people, to *discern* between *good and evil*. For who is able to judge this weighty people of Thine?" (1 Kings 3:9). God grants this kingly request (notice that Solomon does not assume that he already possesses this discernment), and immediately we see Solomon exercise His judgment (v. 28). We may also look at what the wise woman said to David in 2 Samuel 14:17: "For as the angel of God, so is my lord the king to discern good and evil." In other words, man's judicial authority is a copy of God's. The angel of God has wisdom to "know all that is in the earth" (v. 20), and this knowing entails seeing: "My lord the king is like the angel of God, therefore do what is *good* in your *sight*" (2 Sam. 19:27). Infants do not have the wisdom to know good and evil in this judicial sense (Deut. 1:39), and frequently the aged lose this capacity due to senility (2 Sam. 19:35). Thus, it is not *moral* knowledge but *judicial* knowledge that is involved.

Now we can better understand the dragon's temptation. "True," he says, "you are already morally like God. But as you know, you are naked. Your destiny is to be robed with judicial office, passing judgment on good and evil. That's what this tree here is all about. In the day you eat of it, your eyes will be opened, and you will be fully like God, judging good and evil. Why has God forbidden it, then? Didn't He tell you that *every* tree was for you to eat? How long will this prohibition last? How long are you expected to postpone taking up what is your right? How long are you supposed to fast from this privilege? Forty days?[9] Why wait?

"God says He wants you to acquire wisdom first? *Then*, when you're older, He'll let you take on the vestments of office? I doubt it. Frankly, God knows that if you eat this fruit, it will magically confer wisdom on you. You don't need to learn wisdom through the course of time; you can get it instantly. Look at how God acted. He did not acquire wisdom and then bring things to pass, but He said 'let there be.' He created His wisdom by His prophetic command-word. If you are going to be like God, that is what you also should do. Make your own wisdom. Say how it's going to be, and then force your will upon everything else. God wants you to image Him, to be His copy and symbol; don't do it. Become gods yourselves; that's what it truly means to be godlike.

"Oh, God said you would die? If you seize office prematurely it will unravel the entire covenantal order? You'll return to the *'adhamah*, and so will everything else? All will be de-stabilized? I doubt it. You won't die. Believe me. If you are really sons of God, and gods yourselves, being His image and likeness, then act like it! (Matt. 4:3,6). Would God wait for permission? Why should you? After all, what does it mean to be an image and likeness of God? Clearly it means to be *the same as* God, right? God does things on His own, and therefore so should you. You are like God, and so you have life in yourself. You don't need to go to that Tree of Life and pray to God and beg Him to give you life, so you don't die! No, no; you are like God, right? And so you are self-sustaining, right? So you don't need that Tree of Life, right?[10]

9. Forty days is a standard period of waiting or testing in Scripture; also forty years. We shall see that the period between creation and Noah's investiture was a "forty" period. See footnote 13 below.

10. Satan's denial that man need fear death presupposes that man is on a continuum with God, that he has being in common with God, and thus does not need to get life from God. This is the origin of the basic pagan "scale of

"So don't worry about a thing, my dear. Assert yourself. See, Adam's not objecting, so don't bother to ask him for permission. Take and eat."

And so, hearkening to the dragon's word, man decided that he did not need to depend on God for life. He adopted the philosophy of the scale of being. Being a part of God, he thought, he reasoned that he had life in himself, and could not perish. Confident that God's threats meant nothing, Adam seized the garment of judicial office, and made himself a god.

God chose to honor man's decision. Immediately, Adam and Eve found out that the devil had lied about wisdom. They had the office, but they lacked the psychological heaviness to bear it. They were embarrassed. What they had expected to be robes of office now had to do double duty as a means of concealing their inadequacy. With a sinking feeling in their bellies, they realized they had gotten themselves into a position they could not handle. They did not have wisdom, but now they had to judge. They hoped the moment would not come.

But come it did, and right away. God called on them to exercise their new office by evaluating their own actions. "Judge righteous judgment," said God. Did they do so? No, they called evil good and good evil (Isaiah 5:20). They did not each blame himself or herself, but they tried to pin the blame on each other and on God. They showed themselves unfit to guard the garden, and they were expelled; new cherubic guardians were appointed, until the coming of the Son of Man would replace them with New Covenant human guardians.

God clothed them in animal skins, showing that they should have awaited His investiture of them rather than seizing the robe of office. Perhaps the animal skins were a token of their new bestial status; seeking to become gods, they became less than men.[11] Certainly evil rulers are likened to beasts

---

being" philosophy, which is well discussed throughout the works of Cornelius Van Til and Rousas J. Rushdoony. Adam's sin consisted of seizing the robe of judicial authority prematurely, but in order to do this he had to shift his presuppositions to believe that he was equal with God ontologically, and that his mind was equally able to evaluate data epistemologically. Adam took upon himself the right to decide, which it was not his place to do.

11. Not in some scale of being sense, obviously, but in the sense that animals are not the dominators but the dominated. Man had hearkened to the animal, and thus had become subjected, in a sense, to the animal.

often enough in the rest of Scripture, thinking only for the moment of the beasts in Daniel and in Revelation. But we may also see in the clothing with animal skins another meaning as well, which is that God intends to establish His covenant and to bring man eventually to a place of true office, but now only on the basis of a blood sacrifice. The clothing with animal skins was a token to Adam and Eve that someday a man would be given the robe of office, on the basis of the death of a substitute.

Noah, the second Adam, was that person.

### *Seizing the Robe from Human Authority: The Example of Ham*

Before the Flood, God did not give to His people the right to exercise judicial office. Sinful men, having seized the robe, did not hesitate to use it in terms of their own perverted standards. Thus Cain, unwilling to judge himself for his sins and bring a blood sacrifice as his substitute, chose to execute capital punishment against his innocent brother, who had shamed him. The *'adhamah*, drinking Abel's blood, cried out for vengeance, but God appointed Himself a city of refuge for Cain. Cain, however, did not want to hide in God, and built his own city, ramming it into the ground which kept trying to throw him off. In time, Cain's descendents prided themselves on the violence with which they abused the robe of office, as seen in the culminatory hymn of Lamech, the seventh from Adam in the Cainite line (Genesis 4).

How did the righteous fare during this time? Not well, if Abel is an example. In time, the Godly Sethites succumbed to the temptation to become part of the enrobed Cainite culture, and intermarried with it: They were unwilling to persevere, to *wait*. Tyranny abounded, and God decided to judge the world. *Judicial evil had matured* from youth to age, and it was time to end it (Genesis 6).

After the Flood, on the basis of Noah's sacrifice (Gen. 8:20), God renewed His covenant with man, and this time enrobed His people with the office of judge. God had not put Cain to death, though Abel's blood cried out for it. Now, however, shed blood would be avenged, and the image of God, man himself, would carry it out (Gen. 9:5-6).[12] This was

12. Some have argued that Cain was not put to death because it was not the charge of the family to execute capital punishment, but of the state, and

Noah's investiture with office. As a token of that investiture, man is now permitted to eat the meat of the animals originally slain to provide coverings (Gen. 9:2,3). The covering with skins had signified to Adam that someday investiture would come; eating—ingesting—the flesh of the animals signifies that such an investiture is now taken into the life of man.[13]

Before the Flood, wild animals had hunted men and eaten them; fierce dinosaurs had roamed the earth, signifying the lifestyle of the Cainites over against the lifestyle of the righteous, who were their prey. Now, however, man is given power to hunt and eat the animals (Gen. 10:9), and they are made afraid of man. This signified the ascendency of true Godly men over the ungodly beastlike men.[14]

Man was sinful from his youth (Gen. 8:21), and when that youth had matured to full age, God had to destroy the world, so corrupt had it become. Now, however, God institutes the righteous civil authority to restrain evil, so that *such a maturation in corruption will never again take place.* The youth will be cut off, either in death or in circumcision, before he reaches full age in evil. When Noah's youngest son (Ham) attacks him, Ham's youngest son (Canaan) is cursed to become a slave, showing the ascendency of the saints over the wicked, of true men over wild animals, and illustrating how the wickedness of man's youth would be restrained.

---

there was no state in the world at that time. This argument, however, would also apply in the case of Noah, since there was not yet a state in the world then either, but only a family. Also, in the Bible the avenger of blood is the next of kin, so there is some relationship between the family and the execution of the death penalty.

13. The period from creation to the year after the Flood, when the robe was bestowed, lasted 1657 years according to the chronology of the Bible. 1657 years is 33 jubilees of 50 years plus 7 years. 33 + 7 = 40. This kind of reasoning with numbers abounds in Genesis; cf. Cassuto, *Genesis,* vols. I & II, comments on Genesis 5 and 11.

14. The Bible tells us that someday the lion will lie down with the lamb, and that the lion will eat straw like the ox (Is. 11:6,7; 65:25). There is no reason to believe that this will not physically come to pass. Foundationally, though, animals are symbols of humanity, and this signifies peace in the social realm. Man's robe was supposed to be vegetable (linen), not animal (wool); but the death and ingestion of animals was introduced to signify that man's investiture would come through the death (shed blood) of a Substitute. After the death and resurrection of Jesus Christ, the symbol of progressive investiture and salvation returned from the animal realm (sacrifices) to the vegetable realm (bread and wine).

We must now look at the sin of Ham, how he tried to steal the robe of office from his father, thus recapitulating the sin of Adam.

When Noah was born, his father Lamech said, "This one shall comfort us in our work and from the toil of our hands arising from the *'adhamah* which YHWH has cursed" (Gen. 5:28). The fulfillment of this promise comes after the Flood, when we find that Noah, the "master of the *'adhamah*, was the first to plant a vineyard" (Gen. 9:20).[15] While wine can be used to excess, and a life characterized by drunkenness is condemned in Scripture, the use of wine for effect is praised by Scripture in its proper context. Thus we read in Judges 9:13 that wine gladdens both God and man, as also in Psalm 104:15.

According to Proverbs 31:4-7, alcohol is not for kings while they rule, lest they pervert justice by forgetting the difference between good and evil; but alcohol *is* for him whose life is bitter and troubled by the curse.[16] The use of alcohol for relaxation is sabbatical; it comes after work during the time of rest. Preeminently in the New Covenant this means the use of wine for the Lord's Supper, as Melchizedek gave wine to Abram after his labor of battle (Gen. 14:18). At any rate, under the Old Covenant during the sabbath feast of the seventh month the people were enjoined to buy "wine or strong drink, or whatever your soul asks of you . . . and rejoice in the presence of YHWH your God, you and your household" (Deut. 14:26). There is nothing to suggest that Noah was a man characterized by drunkenness. He drank, became sleepy and hot, and removed his robe of office in the privacy of his tent. He was still covered by his tent, and it was necessary for Ham to invade his privacy to see him. If some reader is still determined at all costs to pin some blame on Noah at this point, the most

15. For a defense of this translation, see Cassuto, *Genesis,* II, pp. 158ff. Even if we go with the more common translation, "Noah began to plant a vineyard," we still have the fulfillment of the prophecy, though not quite so dramatically. It has been argued that the rate of fermentation after the Flood was more rapid than before, so that Noah was caught off guard and drank too much before he realized he had become drunk. See for instance the discussion in Joseph C. Dillow, *The Waters Above: Earth's Pre-Flood Vapor Canopy* (Chicago: Moody Press, 1981), pp. 102ff. I do not think it necessary, as I argue, to see Noah's action as questionable at this point, however, so the point may be moot.

16. Similarly the priests were not to drink on the job, Leviticus 10:9.

he can accuse him of is a momentary indiscretion. The text says not one word against Noah; it is Ham who is the sinner here.

It was sabbath time, a time of rest, of relaxation, of enjoying the good fruits of the earth, which was now bringing up wine among the thorns and thistles. It was a time to lay aside the burdens of office for a moment, and leave everything in God's hand. In the privacy of his tent, it was a time to drink, praise God, and forget his toil. He could relax in his own tent, couldn't he?

Ham invaded Noah's privacy.[17] He "saw" Noah's "nakedness." This language takes us right back to Genesis 3. Then he "told" his brothers outside. This was the extent of his sin.[18] Shem and Japheth, however, "took a garment and laid it upon both their shoulders and walked backward and covered the nakedness of their father; and their faces were backward so that they did not see their father's nakedness" (9:23). The two shoulders correspond in the Bible to two pillars, and thus to two witnesses.[19] The older men refused to "see" their

---

17. It should be born in mind that the kind of tent spoken of was not a Boy Scout pup-tent, but a private dwelling. Ham did not just happen to walk by and see into a small teepee; he had to go in and look around.

18. Failure to see the nature of Ham's sin of rebellion has caused commentators to speculate that Ham did something else, such as attempt homosexual relations with his father (as his descendents in Canaanite Sodom might have), but which the text glosses over. There is no need, however, to read anything into the passage.

19. Kline comments, in *Images*, p. 44f., on "the biblical usage, peculiar to tabernacle and temple architecture, whereby the two side-posts of entryways are called 'shoulders,' the first occurrence being just before the directions for the priests' garments (Ex. 27:14,15. Cf. 1 Ki. 6:8; 7:39; 2 Ki. 11:11; Ezk. 40:18,40ff.; 41:2,26; 46:19; 47:1,2). This usage of 'shoulder' is immediately associated with *miptan*, 'lintel,' in Ezekiel 47:1,2. While the shoulder pieces of the ephod represented the 'shoulders' of the entry-gate, the priestly headdress formed the lintel name-banner. This is suggested both by its lintel-like position between and above the shoulder pieces and by the fact that it bore the name of God in the inscription of its gold plate: 'holy to Yahweh.' (Engraved on precious stones on the shoulder pieces [the side-pillars in the entry imagery] were the names of the sons of Israel [Ex. 28:9ff.]. Note that the incarnate Glory promises that his people will be made pillars in God's temple, bearing the name of God and the holy city and Lord's own new name [Rev. 3:12; cf. 1 Tim. 3:15].)" The use of pillars as witness stones is seen in Joshua 24:27. The picture of two men upholding a third is also seen in Aaron and Hur upholding Moses' two pillar-positioned arms in Exodus 17:12. Even apart from all this, it should be clear that the use

father's nakedness. They went out of their way to cover it. This action is wholly symbolic, since Noah was already covered by his tent and did not need recovering by a garment. The action of Shem and Japheth was designed to dramatize their refusal to go along with Ham's plan.

What plan was that? We may already infer that Ham wanted the brothers to join him in a conspiracy to take up the robe. We can hear him investing Noah's action with sinfulness, and investing his own with righteousness. "Look guys, father has laid aside his robe. He's gone off and gotten drunk, and thus he can't judge righteously. We're well over 100 years old now. I think we ought to rule father incompetent, and seize his office. He's just not moral enough for me to submit to any longer." The proof that such was Ham's design comes in the wording of the curse pronounced on Canaan, Ham's youngest son. Canaan would be a slave of slaves (v. 25). *Those who seek power by revolutionary action, however pious in appearance, will become slaves.* The sons will reproduce the pattern of the father.

David was similarly tempted. We read about it in 1 Samuel 24. Saul was seeking to kill David, who had been anointed Saul's replacement, but who refused to act in a revolutionary fashion. Saul stepped into a cave to cover his feet (answer the call of nature), and it happened that David and his men were hiding further back in the cave. David's men brought Satan's temptation to him: "Behold, this is the day of which YHWH said to you, 'Behold, I am about to give your enemy into your hand, and you shall do to him as it seems good in your *sight*.' " David then arose and cut off the wing of Saul's *robe*, but immediately David's conscience smote him for it and he repented. He renounced his act to his men, and confessed it to Saul. God caused the fickle Saul to feel good about David, and they were temporarily reconciled.

Ham's invasion of Noah's tent was an attack upon his father's glory, honor, propriety, and rule. As such, it could have no purpose except to tear down constituted authority, and no motive other than to establish himself as the new authority. The Bible is clear: Those who seize at power will

---

of shoulders to bear the garment is unusual and designedly symbolic, and in the nature of the case, shoulders are used to bear things up, in this case bearing up the position of the father.

become slaves, and if the Canaanites are the example, such slaves will eventually be exterminated. Those on the other hand who honor authority, and cover up the indiscretions (real or supposed) committed by such authorities, will themselves in time be honored with dominion and rule (Gen. 9:26-27).

How many young men there are in history and today who will not wait until they are older to become elders in the church! They go to college, where they acquire virtually no wisdom, and from there to seminary, where they are isolated from the wisdom-inducing problems of church life. Then, robed with a sheepskin, they get ordained to office at the ripe age of 25! Is it any wonder that the churches are in such a horrible condition? One would like to think that there are older men around who can lead, but sadly in our day and time those who are older seldom have wisdom, for they have not matured in terms of the law of God. Virtually all older Christians in this day and age have grown up believing that law and grace are opposed one to another, and so have never acquired mature wisdom based on years of study, obedience, and governance by God's law. Frequently, then, office does fall to those of younger years. Let them beware the perils, however, and always be deferential toward those who are older, if not wiser, in the faith.

Biblical teaching at this point strikes at the heart of perfectionistic and pharisaical religion. If Saul is an evil king, then Saul should be deposed; yet David, already anointed, being a man after God's own heart, refused to depose him. David did deceive Saul, and avoided him, but he never rebelled against him. This by itself does not solve all our hypothetical questions. Do we submit to an invader? Do we submit to a revolutionary regime? Are our rulers anointed of God in the same way as the kings of the Old Covenant? These questions have their place, but they are not in view here. What is in view is *motive*. The desire to seize power and to make oneself a ruler (a god), without waiting for it to be bestowed, and without acquiring years of wisdom first, is the essence of original sin.

### *Avoiding the Tyrant's Robe: The Patriarchs*

The basic means for dealing with power tyrants in Genesis, and in the rest of Scripture, is though deception.[20]

20. On the ethics of lying, see Jim West, "Rahab's Justifiable Lie," in

The reason for this in Genesis particularly is that the serpent tricked Eve through deception (Gen. 3:13; 2 Cor. 11:3; 1 Tim. 2:14), while Adam stood by and failed to protect her. Thus, a theme emerges later in Scripture wherein the serpent attacks the bride, and the husband must attempt to protect her. In each case *it is the intention of the serpent to use the bride to raise up his own seed.*[21] In each of these cases deception is used against the serpent, and God acts to protect the bride.

The use of deception against the serpent is simply an application of the *lex talionis*: an eye for an eye, a tooth for a tooth, a deception for a deception. Jesus enjoins us to be "as wise as serpents, and as harmless as doves" and this is because we have been sent out "as sheep among wolves" (Matt. 10:16). In other words, our practice of deception must be in order to further good and peace, not a violation of the ninth commandment.

It is preeminently women or subordinates who practise deception in Scripture. That is, those in a vulnerable position, who do not have power to engage in direct confrontation, are advised to use deception and lies to evade the dragon. Thus, in addition to the examples we shall shortly examine in the book of Genesis, we have the Hebrew midwives in Exodus 1, and the deception practised by Jochebed in Exodus 2. We have the deception by Rahab in Joshua 2, and the deception by Jael in Judges 4 and 5.[22] Powerless subordinates such as Jacob use deception against tyrants such as Isaac was in the situation recorded in Genesis 27 (although we should note that the woman here is the primary actress in protecting her covenant-seed). When Samuel fears the power of Saul, in 1

---

Gary North, ed., *The Theology of Christian Resistance*, Christianity and Civilization, No. 2 (Tyler, TX: Geneva Divinity School Press, 1983).

21. That the serpent does have a seed is clear from Genesis 3:15, which seed does come through the woman. Her hearkening to his voice was spiritually adulterous, and as a result both the Satanic seed and the redeemed seed come through the woman. That which is essentially *hers*, however, is the redeemed. Thus the Pharisees were serpents, the offspring of the serpent (Matt. 23:33), for the serpent was their father (Jn. 8:44). Satan's two goals in the war of the seeds are (1) to kill the Godly seed, and (2) to take the bride to raise up his own evil seed.

22. That this situation entailed an attack upon the seed, and an attempt to use the bride to raise up Satanic seed, is made clear in Judges 5:30, which literally reads, "Are they not finding, are they not dividing the spoil? A womb, two wombs for every warrior. . . ."

Samuel 16:2, God Himself gives him the deceptive strategy.

The highest privilege of man is to be the official Friend of God, which is to be God's most trusted confidant and advisor (through prayer). We see Abraham as God's Friend in Genesis 18.[23] Hushai the Archite was David's Friend (2 Sam. 15:37). David asked Hushai to remain with Absalom and to deceive him. Hushai did so, and it resulted in Absalom's death (2 Sam. 15-18). We might note that Absalom publicly took David's concubines (2 Sam. 16:20-22), an attack on the bride and seed. Absalom died the serpent's death, by a head wound (2 Sam. 18:9). At any rate, we see from this that to be an expert liar and deceiver, in the interest of the kingdom of God, is commensurate with the highest position of moral privilege and trust God has given man.

The first occurrence of this pattern is in Genesis 13:10-20. As a result of a severe famine, Abram repaired to Egypt. The text nowhere criticizes him for this, because this is the first encounter with Egypt. Abram realized that Sarai's beauty would attract the unconverted Egyptians, and that they might kill him and steal her. Petty commentators mirror themselves in seeing Abram's deception as merely designed to save his own hide. Rather, Abram knew that if he were killed, Sarai's protection would be gone. He also knew that God's plans were tied up with his remaining alive.

Abram deceived Pharaoh by telling the Egyptians only that Sarai was his sister, not that she also was his wife. Abram counted on the common law fratriarchy of the ancient near east to protect Sarai, in that any man desiring her would have to negotiate with her brother, and Abram would be able thus to forestall any marriage.[24] The draconic Pharaoh, however, thinking himself a god, took Sarai against custom, abusing laws of hospitality precious to the God whose worship culminates with a Supper at His house, whereupon God sent plagues against him. When Pharaoh found out what had happened, he assumed the role of Satanic accuser, and tried to pin the blame upon Abram. Meanwhile, Abram had been prospered by God in his deception, and emerged from Egypt

23. See footnote 51 below for more on the office of King's Friend.

24. On the brother as guardian of the sister, see Genesis 24:29ff., 50,53,55,60; Lemuel was alive, but Laban did all the negotiating and received the gifts.

with much spoil.[25]

In Genesis 20, the serpent tried again. Realizing that the godly seed had been promised (18:9-15), he sought to defile the bride before the seed could be born. Visiting among the early Philistines, Abraham again used deception to protect Sarah. Again the king violated basic rules of hospitality and fratriarchy and took the bride. God cursed him, but offered him a way of escape if he would ask Abraham to pray for him. The king professed that he had not meant to sin, and restored Sarah, along with many gifts, to Abraham. The curse upon Abimelech for attacking the bride was that the women of his household all became barren. This was reversed at the request of Abraham (v. 17f.).

Again we see deception used as a strategy. God again lets Abraham know that if He had not blessed the deception, it would not have worked; but no criticism is offered of the lie itself. Again we see the righteous prospering under the dominion of the ungodly, though in this case Abimelech seems not to have been such an evil man as Pharaoh.

Before returning to avoidance and deception as a strategy, it would be well to look briefly at Abram's rescue of Lot in Genesis 14. According to v. 14, Abram had 318 trained fighting men in his retinue, who were adopted sons of his house (first class servants—such is the meaning of the term 'homeborn servant'). If we take into consideration the wives and children of these, as well as the number of ordinary non-military domestic servants in such a household, Abram must be seen as chief of a rather large group of people, probably well in excess of three thousand.

What is going on in Genesis 14 is one of the early fulfillments of the curse upon Canaan. An alliance of Japhethites (Tidal king of "nations"—cf. Gen. 10:5), Shemites (Chedorlaomer king of Elam), and non-Canaanite Hamites (Amraphel king of Shinar) comes to displace the dominion of the five Canaanite lords of the circle of the Jordan. We do not see Abram interfering in the politics here. When Lot is carried off from Sodom by the non-Canaanite kings, Abram

25. Commentators regularly seem to take Pharaoh's side in this matter, completely missing the point. After all, in context Abram had been told that those who cursed him would be cursed, and those who blessed him would be blest (13:3); thus, the curse upon Pharaoh can only be interpreted as a judgment against him, and not as some oblique judgment against Abram.

takes his men and rescues Lot. We may see this as analogous to vigilante action only if we understand that it was not based on an abstract principle (free enterprise versus socialism), but on covenantal, familial responsibilities. It is, in fact, an example of the kinsman-redeemer/avenger-of-blood principle. Abram was Lot's next of kin, and it was his lawful responsibility to rescue him if he could. Because kidnapping is a capital crime (Ex. 21:16), Abram could lawfully kill men, in Chedorlaomer's army, in his rescue of his kinsman.[26]

Abram simply rescues Lot. He does not take over the government of the area, and in fact refuses any power when it is offered to him. To be sure, in the battle some people probably died; but this should be seen as a survival operation, not as a type of resistance or revolution. Abram did not worry about what he had no control over. He did not bite off more than he could chew. He had enough forces to deliver Lot, and he did so. God had told him He would give him the land in His good time. Abram was willing to be patient and await investiture by God.

Avoidance as a tactic is seen in the life of Isaac. This is clear from Genesis 26. Again a famine drives the patriarch

---

26. Abram was living in Hebron, where he had placed a sanctuary-altar. Later Hebron became a city of refuge. *Abram was Lot's city of refuge*, as God had offered to be Cain's earlier. When Abram leaves Hebron with his men and travels hundreds of miles to recover Lot, he is extending the boundaries of the city of refuge to cover his kin.

I dare not go into this here; space and my own lack of requisite knowledge forbid it. I can say, however, that the blood avenger in Scripture is an agent of the land, called up by blood spilled on the land (figuratively in the case of Lot). The land appoints the next of kin, not the civil magistrate. The killer may flee to a city of refuge, a sanctuary, where he will be tried by officials of church and state (since these were Levitical cities). Abram's placement of altars around the land was also a placement of sanctuaries. With the death of Christ, all the land is definitively cleansed, so that blood no longer defiles the land in this sense. Romans 13 states that the magistrate is to be God's blood avenger. Whether this means that the family is no longer permitted to be involved is a good question. For centuries the churches functioned as sanctuaries. Someone needs to take this up as a project and see how the church historically has applied the city of refuge principle to church buildings, and whether or not a Christian civilization might have a place for avengers of blood. One thing the Biblical system did was put on the apparently guilty man some burden of proof to show his innocence. He had to flee to the sanctuary, and then plead his innocence before a tribunal. There is a lot that needs exploring here.

into the land of a pagan lord. Again deception is used as a tactic to protect the bride. In this case, Abimelech the king notices that the relationship between Isaac and Rebekah is more than fraternal, and calls him to account for it. God's hand of protection is here, but in the background this time. Again the king Satanically tries to blame Isaac for a sin that one of his own people might have committed: If one of the people had taken her and lain with her it would have been *your* fault for not telling us she was your wife. (!!!)

Again YHWH blesses the patriarch (vv. 12-14) and this brings on the envy of the wicked, who stop up his wells and otherwise persecute him, eventually asking him to leave their area (vv. 14-16). We don't see Isaac raising up his fist, asserting his constitutional rights, or otherwise contesting the power given over by God to the Philistines. Unlike the Philistines of Samson's day, these men were not invaders, and though bullies, they had as legitimate a claim to the turf as Isaac did (though they did not have Isaac's eschatological guarantee). Isaac simply avoids them. Later, in other quarrels with the powers that be, Isaac again avoids trouble (vv. 18-22). He is rewarded when God does finally make room for him.

Isaac avoids suicidal and revolutionary action, and God blesses him in it. In time, the pagans realize that God is with Isaac, and they come, desiring to have peace with him (vv. 23-33). Had Isaac defied the powers, he would have lost everything; through humility, deference, and a foregoing of his "rights," Isaac came to be a power in the community.

Isaac had two sons. They were twins and struggled in the womb: the righteous Jacob against the wicked Esau. (Had Jacob not been regenerate at this point, he would not have fought with Esau.) Esau was a hairy man, signifying a bestial nature which was his in life. Jacob was a "perfect" man, according to the clear meaning of the Hebrew of Genesis 25:27.[27] From the beginning Jacob knew that he was appointed to inherit the covenant of God. Esau had no interest in it, but Jacob's spirituality desired it earnestly. Like Adam and Ham, Esau was a completely present-oriented man. When he came into camp one day, he could not wait twenty

---

27. Determined to misinterpret the life of faithful Jacob, commentators and translators alike refuse to render *'ish tam* here as "perfect man," as they do of Noah in Gen. 6:9 and Job in Job 1:1, or as "blameless," as they do of Abram in Gen. 17:1.

minutes for a meal to be cooked, but sold his birthright for a stew of lentils.[28]

Isaac fell from righteousness and came to prefer the wicked Esau, who by this time had also married outside the covenant. Though Isaac knew the prophecy that Jacob should inherit, and though he knew that Esau had sold and despised the birthright, he tyrannically determined to give it all to Esau anyway. Isaac and Rebekah engaged in righteous deception, however, which God and later Isaac honored. Jacob did not demand a miracle from God, but used the proper means of deception to carry out God's law, even as Dutch Christians lied to Nazis to protect Jews and Christians during World War II.

True to form, the Satanic Esau tried to blame Jacob for getting the birthright, instead of asking from God a place in the covenant and confessing that he had sold and despised his inheritance (27:36). Esau begged for a blessing, and a penitent Isaac gave him one, phrased to his sinful liking. The Hebrew is ambiguous, and can mean that Esau would dwell in the fertility of the earth, or away from it.[29] Esau would live by the sword, and be a man of violence. Someday he would break Jacob's yoke from off his neck, but this would only damn him, because salvation was only to be found in being yoked to the covenant line! Thus, the rebel only finds damnation in the end.

Jacob went to his relatives to get a wife. While there, he encountered the unrighteous deceiver Laban. He was re-

28. According to Gen. 25:29, Esau "came in from the field." In other words, he was not starving to death in the bush and cheated by a ruthless Jacob, as commentators often portray it. Had the Scripture been written by some preachers, v. 34 would not read "Thus Esau despised his birthright," but "Thus Jacob stole Esau's birthright"!!! Nowhere is there a hint of criticism of Jacob for this. Ellison points out that Esau's request for "some of the *red*, this *red*" may indicate he thought the red lentil soup was blood soup, having forbidden magical properties (Gen. 9:4), the name of which should not be spoken but only indirectly alluded to. Whether this was the case or not, it certainly is in keeping with Esau's character. H. L. Ellison, *Fathers of the Covenant: Studies in Genesis and Exodus* (Palm Springs, CA: Ronald N. Hayes Pub. Inc., 1978), p. 64f.

29. Gen. 27:39, "Behold, [of/away from] the fatness of the earth shall be your dwelling, and [of/away from] the dew of heaven from above." In a sense, the choice of whether this would be curse or blessing was still before Esau, as it lies before all men until they are dead and have no more opportunity to repent.

duced to a form of servitude in this foreign land. While Jacob is never called a slave, the verbal root meaning "slave service" is repeatedly used to describe his work. Laban's treatment of Jacob parallels in certain respects Pharaoh's later treatment of the Hebrews. Although Laban initially welcomed Jacob, there came a change in Laban's attitude which resulted in Jacob's reduction in status.[30] After earning his wives, Jacob labored six additional years (31:41), the period of slave service (Ex. 21:2). Jacob was oppressed, we are told (Gen. 31:39f.). God saw his affliction (31:12,42), even as He saw the affliction of the Hebrews in Egypt (Ex. 3:7). In violation of custom (Deut. 15:12-15), Laban would have sent Jacob away empty-handed (Gen. 31:42). Even though Jacob had earned Leah and Rachel, Laban acted as though they were slavewives given by him to Jacob and so should not go free with their husband (31:43; Ex. 21:4,7). Actually, it had been Laban who reduced the women from a free to a slave status by using up their insurance money (Gen. 31:15). Jacob did not steal from Laban, but he did act to protect his interests, and God blessed him in it (30:28-43). Finally, when things really got bad due to the envy of Laban and his sons, Jacob simply fled. Again, God prospered him in this, threatening Laban if he harmed Jacob.

When Esau came out with 400 armed men to kill him, Jacob bought his present-oriented brother off with a series of handsome gifts. In all these things we see Jacob acting in a shrewd and non-confrontative manner. There was no rebellion in him. He sought to avoid trouble, and when trouble came, he acted in a shrewd and wise manner to turn it away. Jacob showed himself to be a master of *deception and avoidance* when dealing with tyranny. He knew that now was not the time to fight, and that God would invest him with dominion when He and His people were ready. Jesus had the same philosophy: "I say to you, do not resist him who is evil, but whoever slaps you on your right cheek, turn to him the other also. And if any one wants to sue you and take your shirt, let him have your cloak also. And whoever shall force you to go one mile, go with him two" (Matt. 5:39-41). The evil man is

30. This seems to be the meaning of Gen. 29:15. Cf. David Daube and Reuven Yaron, "Jacob's Reception by Laban," *Journal of Semitic Studies* I (1956):60-62. A family member would not have worked for wages, so Laban here excludes Jacob from the family.

anyone who has power and abuses it. He may be a powerful man in town who sues you, and you cannot win in court; it is wisest to let him slap you around a bit, as Isaac let the Philistines slap him. Resistance accomplishes nothing.[31]

Joseph's unrighteous brothers Simeon and Levi took matters into their own hands, and in a seemingly righteous cause avenged the seduction of their sister (Gen. 34). Their rebellion brought only trouble upon the church (v. 30), for they acted without wisdom. Proud in the righteousness of their action, the two men refused to repent (v. 31) and received the curse of God (Gen. 49:5-7). They had the power to pull off a temporary operation such as the sack of Shechem, but did they have the power to sustain a long-term war with all the Canaanites, asked their father? The time was not right, but youthful men have not learned to see consequences. Thus, the governance of church, state, and family is reserved for the older and the wise.

We may call attention to three other examples of deception in Scripture. When Israel was captured by Pharaoh, and he sought to kill the seed and take the women for himself, the midwives lied to Pharaoh and thus kept the boy babies alive. God blessed them for this (Exodus 1). When Saul pursued David, he fled, not worrying about the humiliation, time and again; and when he was living among the Philistines, David deceived them by feigning madness (1 Sam. 21:13ff.; Psalm 34).

To explore the limits of deception, let us take as our third example Esther. Mordecai sought power with the king by telling Esther to conceal her faith (Esth. 2:10,20). This was a great evil, and God later forced Mordecai's hand over it, so that Esther was forced to reveal her covenant committments. We also note that Mordecai was a proud and vain man who refused to show deference to proper authorities, and Haman was a proper authority, even though an Amalekite (Esth. 3:2;

31. The context of Jesus' remarks is resistance, not simply the encountering of evil. As much as we are able, we are to put down evil, so that if a thief breaks in at night, we may kill him rather than let him kill us (Ex. 22:2). Concerning evil powers and authorities, however, we are to deal with our rebellious hearts by going out of our way to be deferential to them, as to the Lord.

Also, we are ordered to submit to the *powers* that be, not to any and every *law* some human authority chooses to put on the books. The powers that be may include not only civil officials but also neighborhood bosses and Cosa Nostra operatives.

contrast Gen. 23:12; 33:3; 37:9f.; 42:6; 43:26ff.; etc.)[32] In this case, God protected the bride by converting her regal husband (in some sense). That God worked good out of Mordecai's evil schemes in no wise exonerates him, and this is clear in that Mordecai was forced to abandon his scheme. We see from this that deception must never involve denying the faith. And of course, it should be clear from this discussion that it is the deception of serpentine powers and authorities which is permitted in Scripture, not the deception of one's neighbor.[33]

### *Waiting for the Robe: The Example of Abram*

The robe of dominion and authority is a basic consideration for the theology of Genesis, particularly as it comes to full expression in the history of Joseph. Before considering Joseph's earning of the robe, we should take a look at the patience of Abraham. Patience, a willingness to await God's time, is what neither Adam nor Ham possessed. It is, thus, an essential mark of true faith.

In Hebrews 6 we read that true Christians are "imitators of those who through faith and *patience* inherit the promises. For when God made the promise to Abraham, since He could swear by no one greater, He swore by Himself, saying, 'Blessing I will bless you, and multiplying I will multiply you.' And thus, having *patiently* waited, he obtained the promise. For men swear by one greater than themselves, and with them an oath given as confirmation is an end of every dispute. Therefore [similarly], God, desiring even more to show to the heirs of the promise the unchangeableness of His purpose, guaranteed with an oath, in order that by two unchangeable things,[34] in which it is impossible for God to lie, we may have strong

32. The Agagites were the descendents of the kings of the Amalekites, whom God had vowed to destroy. Cf. Esth. 3:1; 1 Sam. 15.

33. See footnote 20 above. The ultimate deception occurred at the cross. Had Satan realized that the death of Jesus Christ would be the very means to destroy him and his evil power, he would never have crucified Him!

34. The two unchangeable things are God and His oath or covenant. This is seen in the very Hebrew form taken over into the Greek, called 'pleonasm,' which doubles the verb for intensity: blessing I will bless, multiplying I will multiply. This two-witness covenant language is found in the Adamic covenant, Genesis 2:17, where the punishment for eating of the forbidden fruit is "dying you shall die."

encouragement" (vv. 12-18). The recipients of the letter to the Hebrews knew that Jesus Christ had conquered Satan, and was now enthroned king of the world. They wondered why they did not yet see all things put under His feet (2:8). The answer for them was that God had sworn by Himself an oath that they would in time inherit the promise, and thus that they should be patient and await its realization. Thus the preeminent quality of faith is a trust in God that He will accomplish His promise (ch. 11). Just as Jesus was perfected through wisdom-inducing suffering (2:10), so Christians must patiently endure suffering until they are ready to be invested with authority and dominion (ch. 12).

The great example set out for consideration is Abraham. The situation referred to is in Genesis 14-15, which is a unit.[35] God had promised Abram the land from the beginning (Gen. 12:1-3), and had reiterated it to him when he arrived in Canaan (12:7). Abram walked the length of the land, setting up witness-altars establishing worship at two focal points (12:7,8). When God delivered him from Egyptian bondage, he reestablished altar-dominion in the land (13:4). Lot chafed under Abram's leadership, and Abram permitted him to depart (13:5-13). Then God again promised him the land.

About that time there was a rebellion by the Canaanites, who were already in subjection (Gen. 9:25-27) to Chedorlaomer the Shemite, and the Japhethite (Tidal) and non-Canaanite Hamites who dwelt in his tents (Gen. 14). Abram stood by and watched his promised land dominated by Chedorlaomer, who was an Elamite and not a Hebrew.[36] Chedorlaomer's dominion was very effective: He subdued all the people who later would frighten the Hebrews and bring about their refusal to enter the land (Num. 13). The punch line, though, is that Abram was completely able to defeat Chedorlaomer, at least in a temporary operation (Gen. 14:15,17,20).[37] Yet Abram did not use his strength to con-

35. Genesis 15:1, "After these things. . . ."

36. A major theme in Genesis is the replacement of the firstborn with a younger son, signifying the failure of the first Adam and the faithfulness of a second. Shem's firstborn was Elam, and Chedorlaomer was of that line (Gen. 10:22). Abram the Eberite (14:13; 11:15) was of the line of Arpachshad, a younger brother of Elam.

37. This is the prophetic (proclamatory) purpose of Genesis 14. Israel should have been encouraged to take the promised land, realizing that the

solidate a rule in Canaan, but refused to take any spoil; he would take nothing until the Possessor of heaven and *'erets* [place] chose to give it to him (14:19-24).

Afterward, Abram was afraid, probably that Chedorlaomer would return (15:1). God gave him His word that He would protect him and would give him seed and land. Then, when Abram had exercised true patient faith, Abram asked for the *covenant guarantee*, the *second witness* (15:8).[38] He asked how he might *know*, which as we have seen indicates judicial confirmation; thus, he asked God to give a judicial sign that the matter was fully established.

God had him take five different sacrificial animals, probably signifying the whole sacrificial system in seed form, and to divide them in half.[39] In a vision, the sun went down and a horror of great darkness came over Abram. In the midst of this absolute darkness, the only light was that of God, Who passed between the parts of the animals. This strange action was the "cutting" of the covenant, as the Hebrew of verse 18 literally reads.

What is going on here? In the context of Genesis 1 and 6-8 we can see God again de-creating and re-creating the world. Just as the Flood returned the world to a condition of formlessness and emptiness, which God refilled, so in the vision of Abram the world returns to the primeval darkness of Genesis 1:2, before God established the covenantal separation-

---

inhabitants had repeatedly been defeated earlier, and that Abram with only 318 men had been victorious over those who defeated them. Giants were defeated by Shemites in 14:5; Horites in v. 6, and later again by Esau; Amalekites in v. 7; Amorites in v. 7; and Canaanites in vv. 8-11. The Canaanites had to hide in tar pits, had to flee to the hills, and were dispossessed of their goods. The updating of the names in Gen. 14 was designed to tell Israel the location of these places, so that when they came to Kadesh and El-paran (Num. 13:26) they should not have feared the Horites and Amalekites (Num. 13:29); etc. Moses makes a similar point in his first Deuteronomic sermon (e.g., Deut. 2:10-12,20-23).

38. Not that God's word by itself in inadequate, but that God has set up the two-witness pattern. See Hebrews 6:13-18.

39. The animals are three years old. Thus, the de-creation and re-creation of history comes before the seventh and last day. Man is sinful "from his youth," as we have seen, but he gets a new start before judgment day. The third-day/third-year theme is prominent throughout Scripture, particularly in Numbers 19, the book of Jonah, and the resurrection of Jesus Christ in the middle of history (making possible ours at the end).

union of day and night.[40] Abram himself is in "deep sleep," the same condition as Adam was in Genesis 2:21 when God separated Eve from him and established a covenant separation-union between the man and the woman.[41] Here the purpose is to reestablish the connection between man and *'erets*. The false and perverted relationship between man and land, which came in with the Fall, is undone by de-creation; but before the birds can descend to destroy matters utterly,[42] the covenant order is re-created by God Himself becoming the unbreakable binding force connecting the two. Abram is as likely not to possess the land as God is likely to perish.[43]

What did it mean? It meant that the birds of prey would

---

40. The de-creation of the Flood undid the separation of waters above and waters below (Day 2) and of land and sea (Day 3), killing birds (Day 5) and beasts and men (Day 6). It did not harm the light (Day 1) or the light-bearers (Day 4). Thus, the collapse of sun, moon, and stars later in Scripture becomes a sign of future judgment, since there will never again be a Flood. The de-creation of Genesis 15, as a sign of that coming three-hour Golgothic darkness, takes away the covenantal order of Days 1 and 4 and reestablishes the *'erets* in the power of resurrection.

41. "Deep sleep" is a different word in Hebrew from "sleep." "Deep sleep" is close to death and is the place where covenants are made; it is de-creation preceding either total death or resurrection. The term occurs elsewhere in Scripture in Judges 4:21 (Sisera just before his head is crushed); 1 Samuel 26:12 (Saul's head not crushed by David while Saul was in deep sleep); Job 4:13 (Eliphaz confronted with the Creator); Job 33:15 (God preventing men from entering the pit of sheol); Psalm 76:6 (man under God's wrath); Proverbs 10:5; 19:15 (moral sleepiness); Daniel 8:18; 10:9 (Daniel's almost dying when confronted with God's Word, but being raised up; cf. Rev. 1:17, where the same happens to John); Jonah 1:5-6 (Jonah in deep sleep just before being cast into the de-creating waters and swallowed by the dragon, from which God resurrects him).

42. "And the birds of prey came down upon the carcasses, and Abram drove them away" (Gen. 15:11). The curse of the covenant is to be ripped in half and then devoured by the birds and beasts; cf. Jeremiah 34:18-20.

43. The analogy among man, the *'adhamah*, and the animals is the foundation for the covenant-cutting actions. The animals represent both man and *'adhamah*, so that the divided animals represent man on one side and the land on the other; see footnote 2 above. The connection between man and *'adhamah* is unbreakable, so that the *'adhamah* is cursed because of its tie to man. The cutting of the covenant removes the curse, and reestablishes man in a redeemed *'adhamah*, an *'erets*. The covenant relationship is restored only through the rending of death, an animal substitute typifying Christ, but a death which does not lead to bird-devoured destruction, but to God-empowered resurrection.

threaten God's people and oppress them for 400 years (15:13), but that God's covenant was as sure as His Person, and would in time be established. It meant that Pharaoh and Abimelech and Laban were birds of prey, but that God's people would acquire possessions and wisdom and would come out in wealth and power and authority (15:14). It meant that Abram and those who have like faith (Romans 4; Hebrews 6) must exercise patience during the "probationary forty."[44] If they try to seize it (land, power, glory, dominion, office), they will lose it all.

Abram had the power to score a temporary victory over Chedorlaomer. He was wise enough to realize he did not have the power to maintain such dominion, and quickly retired from the field of battle after rescuing Lot. He was smart enough to wait.

### *Earning the Robe: The Example of Joseph*

Reuben was Jacob's eldest son. Reuben could not wait to inherit the robe, so he lay with his father's wife (Gen. 35:22).[45] For this revolutionary act, he lost his preeminence (49:3-4). Simeon and Levi were passed over because of their revolutionary actions, and so the blessing of rule came to Judah, the fourth son (Gen. 49:5-12). Because of Joseph's faithfulness, however, Jacob early on elevated him over the other brothers in some capacities. Jacob made for Joseph a full-length (not multicolored) robe, and invested him with authority over his brethren when he was only seventeen (37:2,3,14). This may not have been a wise move, as the sequel perhaps shows, but it was prophetic, as God's double-witness dream showed to them all (Gen. 37:2-10).

---

44. In this case 400. See footnotes 9 and 13 above.

45. Taking the concubine of one's predecessor was a perverted way of claiming to be the new lord of the bride. Absalom did it publicly to David (2 Sam. 16:20-23). Adonijah tried to do it to Solomon (1 Ki. 2:13-25). This act is forbidden explicitly in Deuteronomy 22:30 as an uncovering of the wing of the father's garment, and is one of the particular curses of Deuteronomy 27, in v. 20. The "wing" is the extended corner of the robe (Deut. 22:12) and signifies the extension of a man's dominion to the four corners of his life, analogous to the four corners of the world which are overshadowed by the four wings of the cherubim. For the *seed* to rise up and attack the *bride* is an extremely grotesque perversion of man's symbolic imaging of the life of God, and makes the seed into the serpent.

When the brothers attacked Joseph, the first thing they did was strip off his robe (37:23). Then they threw him into a pit. This was the beginning of Joseph's humiliation, his passage into the "deep sleep"-like trauma of suffering, from which he would learn wisdom, and from which he would be resurrected and invested with authority.

Joseph was sold to a household in Egypt. The first phase of his service was in the house of Potiphar (39:1-7). Joseph did not see his enslavement as a cause for resentment or bitterness. We cannot imagine him throwing spanners into the works, or sand into the machinery. Rather, he served dutifully and well. As a result, lazy Potiphar gladly entrusted more and more of the household responsibilities to Joseph. Soon, it was really Joseph who was in charge, and Potiphar "did not concern himself with anything except the food which he ate" (v. 6). Potiphar had the name of master (and ultimately its power as well), but he had a slave mentality and lived as a slave, a slave of food. Joseph had the name of slave, but he was a dominion man, and he ruled in life. The point was not lost on the wife of Potiphar; she knew who the real power in the house was.

Like the camp followers of all ages, the wife of Potiphar tried to cleave to the man of power, but Joseph was not only a faithful servant of Potiphar, he was also a faithful servant of God (39:7-12). Lying with the wife of Potiphar would not only have been a sexual sin; it would also have been an act of insurrection, as we have seen. When the wife of Potiphar grabbed Joseph's robe, she was grabbing for his dominion; in terms of Biblical custom, she was not trying to strip him nude or pull him to her room, but she was trying to get him to spread his cloak over her.[46] Rather than abuse his authority, Joseph forsook it and fled. It is better not to possess invested authority at all than to abuse it.[47] Joseph could have attained premature authority and power had he gone along with her, but it would

46. Compare Ruth 3:9; Ezekiel 16:8.

47. The term "garment" comes six times in this paragraph, highlighting its importance to the story. There seem to be parallels between this story and the "attack on the bride" theme, in that when the woman's sin is in danger of exposure, she Satanically blames the righteous man. The sexual roles are reversed, as is the identity of the deceiver. In a larger sense, however, all God's people are the bride, and the seduction of Joseph to sin is equivalent to the seduction of the bride to infidelity.

not have been permanent and he would eventually have been put to death for it. The temptation before Joseph, thus, is analogous to the temptation before Adam and Ham, to seize power unlawfully.

The vengeance of the wife of Potiphar landed Joseph in prison. There again, however, he ruled in life (39:20-23). Because of his effective and responsible service to those in charge, Joseph was soon put over the entire prison. He had the position of prisoner, but he was exercising dominion. From that position he could do much good. By being a good slave, Joseph acquired mastery.

From prison Joseph was elevated to Pharaoh's right hand. The narrative of Joseph's prison experiences in Genesis 40 shows the means whereby he was enabled to rule in the midst of enslavement: He understood and applied the Word of God, which came to him in the form of dreams and to us in the form of Holy Scripture. Because he understood God's principles whereby He rules the world, and because he was able to apply them accurately to the situation in which he found himself, Joseph proved of inestimable value to every master who employed him. In time he was exalted to second in command over all Egypt: "And Pharaoh said to Joseph, 'You shall be over my house, and according to your mouth all my people shall kiss; only in the throne I will be greater than you. See I have set you over all the land of Egypt.' And Pharaoh took off his signet ring from his hand and put it on Joseph's hand, and clothed him in *garments* of fine linen, and put the gold necklace around his neck. And he had him ride in his second chariot; and they proclaimed before him, 'Bow the knee.' And he set him over all the land of Egypt. Moreover, Pharaoh said to Joseph, 'I am Pharaoh; yet without your permission no one shall raise his hand or foot in all the land of Egypt' " (Gen. 41:40-44). From this position, Joseph was able to feed the entire world (41:57).

The story of Joseph illustrates patient faith and its reward. It ends the book of Genesis and brings its theme to a literary climax. We know that Joseph's authority was temporary and not complete; we know that Christ's now is both. But the story of Joseph shows us that the road to victory, dominion, mastery, and judicial authority, is through service, the humble service of a slave. Through service and suffering, God purges and destroys indwelling sin in the believer (not completely, but sufficiently), builds character in him, and fits him for the mastery of the world. The man made heavy through experience will not be crushed by the robe when it comes, for he will not be inwardly naked as were Adam and Eve when they seized the robe from God.[48]

### *Implications and Applications: Motives*

In the book of Genesis we see three kinds of people. There are those who are tricked into assuming the robe of office prematurely, such as Eve. The blame for what happens to them rests on the shoulders of the authorities over them (Adam). A man is ordained to the gospel ministry at age 25, but he drops the ministry after his first pastorate, or he fails in three churches until he finally succeeds with his fourth (because he is 35 years old by that time, and much wiser)—this man can honestly say, "I wish they had told me to wait, but they said, 'Dedicate your life to the ministry, and we'll ordain you immediately,' so I did. It's their fault." He's right; it is the fault of the leadership.

"I went to the mission field when I was 23. After four years of agony I was totally burnt out, and left. The local people simply could not take rulings from such a young man. I lay the blame on that evangelist who got me to dedicate myself to the mission field while I was in college. Such work is not for young men, unless they are deaconing (apprenticing) under an older man." So it goes, not only in the church, but also in the corporate business world, and other places as well. The Biblical apprenticeship system has been ignored.[49]

The second kind of situation addressed in Genesis occurs when the young man impatiently seizes the robe of office. The bare minimum age for rule in Scripture is 30 years of age

---

48. Part of this discussion of Joseph originally saw print in James B. Jordan, "Joseph's Job," in *Christian Reconstruction* V:3 (May/June 1981). This essay also goes into how Joseph enslaved his enslavers (his brothers, and the Egyptians). It can be had, for a contribution, from the Institute for Christian Economics, Box 8000, Tyler, TX 75711.

49. On deacons as assistant and apprentice elders, see James B. Jordan, "God's Hospitality and Holistic Evangelism," *The Journal of Christian Reconstruction* VII:2, *Symposium on Evangelism*, p. 112f. On the use of the apprentice model successfully in modern corporate business structures in Japan, see Richard T. Pascale and Anthony G. Athos, *The Art of Japanese Management* (New York: Warner Books, 1981), esp. pp. 78ff.

(Gen. 41:46; 2 Sam. 5:4; Luke 3:23).[50] Men *marvelled at Christ's wisdom* when He was twelve, but He did not ask them to *submit to His authority* until He was thirty. True, Paul told Timothy not to let people despise his youth, but Timothy was at least 35; and Rehoboam was called a youth when he was 41 years old (1 Ki. 12:8; 14:21). Along these same lines, Jesus said, "When you are invited by someone to a wedding feast [signifying the kingdom of God—JBJ], do not recline at the place of honor, lest someone more distinguished than you may have been invited by him, and he who invited you both shall come and say to you, 'Give place to this man,' and then in disgrace [exposed nakedness—JBJ] you begin to occupy the last place. But when you are invited, go and recline at the last place, so that when the one who has invited you comes, he may say to you, 'Friend [a technical term in Scripture, meaning a chief advisor], move up higher.' Then you will have honor in the sight of all who recline at table with you. For everyone who exalts himself shall be humbled, and he who humbles himself shall be exalted" (Luke 14:9-11). One thing that stands out in this proverb is that the man who exalts himself is totally oblivious to his offense; he is insensitive to what he has done, and must be told to vacate his assumed position. Those who do not advance themselves presumptuously will in time become chief advisors to the Lord, as was Abraham, the "friend" of God.[51]

The third kind of person in Genesis is the one characterized by patient faith. When Abram's patience lapsed, though his and Sarai's motives were good (bringing in God's kingdom through the seed), the result was Ishmael (Gen. 16:1ff.). We have a major problem in our culture understanding patient faith, and it is the problem of individualism. We think, "Well, all right; we'll exercise patient faith for twenty or so years, until God is ready." We think only in terms of one generation.

50. Also, the Levites had to be 30 years of age before they could carry the furniture of the Tabernacle (Num. 4:22ff.). This was symbolic of the church's being born on the pillar-shoulders of office-bearers (Gal. 2:9; 1 Tim. 3:15; Rev. 3:12). Cf. footnote 19 above.

51. Isaiah 41:8. For an example of such advising, see Genesis 18:22ff. For the office of King's Friend, cf. 1 Chronicles 27:33; 1 Kings 4:5. Joseph and Mordecai (Esth. 8:2,15) are other King's Friends. In the New Covenant, all Christians are potentially King's Friends, after they have matured through service (John 15:14,15).

This is because of the influence of Baptist theology on our culture, for Baptist theology isolates each generation from the preceding and following ones.[52] Biblical patience, however, extends over lines of generations, over centuries. Abraham had to look forward 400 years. After being placed into the land of promise, Israel served for another 450 years before the reign of Solomon. Patient faith means laying a foundation in righteousness and wisdom for our great-grandchildren, not looking for the accomplishment of things in our lifetime.

Is the "New Right" really "ready to lead"? I doubt it. The New Right has not yet figured out the message of the book of Genesis. It continues to think that reformation will come through the acquisition of political power. By looking to the state, New Rightists (and old conservatives as well) make themselves statist. Some anarchistically believe that the problem is the state, and we should devote our lives to fighting it. Others in their thirst for (individual) power attack more sober-minded Christians. A Christian attorney has written to me in a letter concerning Christian tax protestors in North Dakota: "One of the interesting things that has developed in that area, and in the people who are involved in the trial, is that Christian Reconstructionists are now being referred to as 'soft patriots.' There is an increasing thirst for blood. . . ." One such "tax patriot," now in prison because of his involvement in counterfeiting money, has announced his intention to devote all his energies to exposing the heresies propounded by myself and other authors writing in this symposium.[53]

Other New Rightists are not anarchistic, but still have a political faith. Many conservative Roman Catholics thought that John Kennedy would help turn things around. They were disappointed; Mr. Kennedy apparently spent too much time doing other things to ask what he could do for his country. Mainline conservatives then trusted Richard Nixon, a man knowledgeable in international affairs, to turn things

52. On this see James B. Jordan, ed., *The Failure of the American Baptist Culture*, Christianity & Civilization, No. 1 (Tyler, TX: Geneva Divinity School Press, 1982).

53. "The Serpent Treader" bulletin, April 1983, p. 8. My own nonrevolutionary essays on Tax Resistance, Biblical State Financing, and Tithing (as a way of building up the church to replace the pagan state) are available from the Institute for Christian Economics, Box 8000, Tyler, TX 75711. Send a contribution. Ask for Vol. IV, Nos. 2,3,4.

around. They were disappointed; Mr. Nixon's conscience was not sufficiently seared to permit him to act like a Democratic Party politician, guilt-free. Bible-believing Christians had high hopes for Jimmy Carter. Need we add that they were disappointed by the decisions made by Mr. Carter's mother, sister, and wife? And then the whole New Right got behind Ronald Reagan, who by his appointments betrayed them before he even took office, and has now signed a bill, updating social security, which directly taxes the churches.

I never did like the self-righteous whine of those Vietnam war era pseudo-folk-songs, but may we be excused if we sing one refrain of "When will they ever learn?"

Frankly, I believe that in all of this God has, as always, been gracious to us. Are Christians in this country ready to take charge? Heaven forbid! Virtually none of them knows the first thing about the law of God, by which they are called to govern.[54] Most of them do not even acknowledge the sovereignty of God.[55] Few have any experience in governing, since their churches have no courts, being at best mere preaching points (where they have not degenerated into spas and literal circuses). The most powerful New Christian Right people are personality-cult oriented, one-man shows (and by shows I mean shows: radio shows, television shows, and the putting on of shows).

Thankfully, increasing numbers are seeking to be faithful in small things. They are forming elders into genuine church courts and conducting trials for offenders. They are studying the law of God, which He gave to Israel and which is sure wisdom for us. They are working with Christian lawyers to set up Christian reconciliation and arbitration commissions, dealing with divorce, with business conflicts, and with other sticky situations. To the extent that they are involved in

54. When the Bible says that the law is written on the hearts of believers, it does not mean something magical. The law has to be learned, believed, internalized, meditated on (Ps. 1, 119), and applied where possible. In this way it issues in wisdom, and becomes part of the warp and woof of a person's life.

55. Not only are most Arminian, but increasingly popular is a new Pelagianism which denies that God even knows in advance what we are going to do. This notion is pushed in several very large international Christian youth organizations, most prominently Youth With a Mission and Agape Force, as well as in certain young denominations.

politics, it is local politics designed to force abortion mills out of business. Such men do not trumpet themselves into the marketplace, but they are the leaders of tomorrow.

This is not to despise the New Christian Right, or to argue that we should not exercise our (remaining) liberties as Americans to pressure the larger governments toward more Godly actions. We need to remember, however, that there is only so much time and energy alloted to each of us, and essentially that time is far better spent acquiring dominion through service than in power politics.

We may contrast three different approaches, which are not mutually exclusive, but which are of varying value at present. First, there is the effort to change laws by getting people elected to office. That has not been very successful so far, and the reason is that the vast majority of Americans essentially like things the way they are. That's why things are the way they are—it is what the people want, and it is what they deserve, and so it is what God gives them. Political action (campaigning, lobbying, etc.) should therefore be viewed primarily as evangelism.

Second, there is the effort to go about our business as quietly as possible. We submit to the "*powers* that be," not to any law such powers may happen to enact. We do not recognize their right to make laws, for to do so would be to grant them absolute power; but we recognize that God has given them power, and we are not to contest that power as such. We practice deception where morally necessary, and that includes preserving our capital, protecting our households, and rearing our children, as Genesis makes clear.[56] If we are taken to court, we fight in that arena for the right to conduct Christian lives, as Paul did in the book of Acts.

Third, there is the effort to develop a Christian subculture, building up the churches as true courts and sanctuaries, developing Christian arbitration and reconciliation commissions, Christian schools, Christian medical facilities, and the like. These latter two methods are the primary ones for our times.

This essay is designed as a cautionary note. The Bible has a great deal to say about patience and waiting, and about the

56. Just to review: preserving capital = Jacob's dealings with Laban; protecting household = Abram's rescue of Lot and the many lies told to protect his wife; preserving children = the midwives' lies to Pharaoh, and Moses' mother's deceptions in Exodus 1 & 2.

preconditions for investiture. Eve decided that eating the fruit would instantaneously make her wise. Actually, wisdom comes from years of experience mixed with faithful righteous living under the revealed law of God. Thus Joseph is singled out as the wisest man in the world (Gen. 41:8,33,39). Similarly, it was 476 years after God gave Israel the law that the wisdom-matured Solomon, author-collector of the wisdom literature of Scripture,[57] became king of Israel and extended his dominion to surrounding lands. There is a progressive development of wisdom toward Solomon, but Solomon falls from wisdom and there is a decline away from him. If the lengths of time here are any example, Christian reconstructionists would do well to cultivate Abrahamic *patient* faith!

To illustrate: Mr. A decides to preach against corruption in Washington, and in the course of things he makes some wild statements against the President. When he is asked for the source of his allegations, he has to admit that he made things up. Mr. B, a Christian leader, tells newsmen that it is easier to get forgiveness from God than to get permission, excusing one of his own foibles. Mr. C zips through college and graduate school to become a Ph.D. and professor at age 26. In his lectures he often simply reads chapters from books or from unpublished syllabi he got from his professors, but he never informs his students of what he is doing; rather, he passes the lectures off as his own. After all, all truth is God's truth. Now, is there any particular Scripture that explicitly forbids this? No, but what a lack of basic ethical sensitivity it reveals! Mr. D zips through seminary and gets himself ordained at the ripe old age of 25. At his first presbytery meeting, Mr. D speaks on every topic that comes up. He becomes notorious for speaking first, middle, and last on every matter that comes to the floor, and for speaking at length. He is totally insensitive to the deference he should show to the older members of the court. Mr. E fights his way into a junior executive position with the company. Once he has arrived, he boldly speaks out repeatedly in board meetings, unaware that the older men are coming to view him as a fool. Mr. F decides to devote his life to getting prayer to some nebulous deity reinstituted in the state schools, a total waste of time and energy. Mr. F thinks that the way the public schools were in 1952, when he went to them, is

57. Proverbs, Song of Solomon, Ecclesiastes.

the way they ought to be. It never occurs to him that the schools of 1952 led straight to the schools of 1982, as they were set up to do in the first place, in 1832. And so it goes.

These are all examples of ethical insensitivity. Examples could be multiplied. The fact is that the law of God was not given to cover every case explicitly, but to form the foundation from which God's people could learn wisdom and become sensitive to moral and judicial matters. The kinds of cases that can come before a Christian court are frequently far more complex than those actually given in Scripture; it requires a man who has matured in the law to discern what is to be done. We don't have such men today, and that is why God is graciously keeping the church small and powerless.

When we are ready, God will give the robe to us. That He has not done so proves that we are not ready. Asserting our readiness will not fool Him. Let us pray that He does not crush us by giving us such authority before we are ready for it. Let us plan for our great-grandchildren to be ready for it. Let us go about our business, acquiring wisdom in family, church, state, and business, and avoiding confrontations with the powers that be. Let us learn to be skillful in deceiving them and in preserving our assets for our great-grandchildren. For as sure as Christ is risen from the grave and is ascended to regal glory on high, so sure it is that his saints will inherit the kingdom and rule in His name, when the time is right.

## *Appendix: Submission and Resistance*

The thrust of this essay has been that Christian people must submit to the "powers that be," develop wisdom, and await God's time for dominion. That's fine as far as it goes, but it does not answer all questions. I hope in this appendix to give at least some helpful guidelines on how to resist the devil (so that he flees from us) while resisting not evil, but overcoming evil with good.

How do we submit? There are two proper ways to submit, and two improper ways. We must never submit to either the persons or the laws of man. When it comes to submitting to a person, the only Person we submit to is God, and when it comes to submitting to laws, the only Law we submit to is God's.

Man is made as God's symbol, and in terms of this, man possesses *office*. God has set up various official relationships in the world, to image His life among men. Submission is in terms of office, not in terms of person. Thus, the wife is to submit to the husband, not because she likes him personally (though that obviously is desirable), but because of his office as lord of the home. Similarly, the Biblical love which the husband is to exercise toward his wife is not grounded in emotion, though that hopefully is present, but is grounded in a principle of office: It is his office to care for her.

What are some of the other offices God has set up? First, there is office in the church. We are to submit to officers in the church, even when we think that they have made mistakes. God will judge them for their mistakes; God will judge us for our submission or lack of it.[58] There are, secondly, officers in the state (more on them below). Thirdly, there are officers in the home: husbands and parents. Fourthly, there are officers in the economy: owners, managers, superintendents. Fifthly, there is the general office of humanity, which increases with age, so that older people are to be shown especial respect.

We submit, in principle, to office; but we submit Biblically. We submit to office in its proper *sphere* and only under God's *law*. If a husband orders his wife not to attend worship, she is not to submit, because he is acting outside his sphere. If he administers corporal punishment to her, which between free adults is reserved only for the state, he is acting outside his sphere, and she has grounds for action against him in court. If the state attacks Christian schools, the state is not to be submitted to, since education is the responsibility of the family and of the synagogue (church). If the elders of a church tell a man not to pay taxes, or to change jobs, they are not to be submitted to. No office is absolute. Each has its designated

58. In a recent church court trial, one outsider to the court decided, based on misinformation given him, that the court was not perfect. He broadcast to various persons involved that "you couldn't get me to submit to such a court on a bet!" Such heretical and Donatistic notions reign supreme in American Christendom, and explain why the faith is so weak in our day. (The Donatists were an early Christian sect who argued that if the leadership made any mistakes, they would not submit to them. They demanded perfection of their leaders.) Even if the court makes a mistake, it is better to submit than to rebel. Many so-called "theonomists" do not understand this principle, and that is why the "theonomic" movement is bound to split between the Donatists and the Catholics sooner or later.

sphere. When an office-bearer steps outside his sphere, he is not to be submitted to.

Secondly, we submit in terms of God's law. If the state orders us to commit evil, we must not submit; and this may mean conscientious refusal to participate in foreign wars (as opposed to defensive wars). If a father patriarchally orders his children to remain under his authority, after they are married and have children, they are not to submit (Gen. 2:24).

By itself, what we have described would be conducive to anarchy. We would obey an office-bearer only when he gave commands within his sphere, and only when such commands did not conflict with the Scripture. There is, however, a second form of submission, which God requires of us. It is submission to *power*.

Properly speaking, office, authority, law, and power should always be joined. In a sinful world, however, they often are not. The Bible tells us to submit to power *where it is manifested*.[59] That is, we are not foolishly to contest it. Those in a subordinate position are not *able* to confront an evil power, and thus must live by being invisible to it, by deceiving it. We take note of and submit to officers because the *law* of God tells us to. We take note of and submit to power because the *sovereignty* of God puts it over us.

Practically speaking, this means that if the state passes a sinful law, we do not submit to it unless the state puts genuine power behind that law. We do not have to obey sinful laws, because we do not submit to human law. If we can evade, avoid, deceive, or compromise with the powers, we should do so. If they close one Christian school, we open another. If they lock the doors, we cut the lock when they leave. When they come back, they can lock it again. If they want to station an armed guard, then they can keep it locked.

Rape is a good analogy. If God sovereignly brings a rapist into a woman's room, and she cannot overpower him (say,

---

59. This principle is recognized in secular law as well. "According to the Declaration of Paris of 1856, a blockade to be binding must be effective. In other words, a sufficient force must be maintained to prevent access to the coast of the enemy. . . . A blockade may be considered effective if the forces employed are such that any breach of blockade will bring considerable risk to the ships involved. An ineffective or paper blockade is legally not binding." William L. Tung, *International Law in an Organizing World* (New York: Thomas Y. Crowell Co., 1968), p. 470.

because he is armed), then she may as well submit. There is no sin on her part, and resistance quite probably will only worsen matters.[60]

The Mafia is another example. If the Mafia runs the neighborhood and demands protection money, pay it. They are part of the "powers that be." God put them there, for reasons of His own.

Another example is a conquering army. Our conscious loyalty should continue to be to our country, but our external obedience for a time must be to the conqueror.

We may summarize this doctrine of submission as follows:

A. Submission to God-constituted office:
   1. Only in its proper, Biblically-defined sphere.
   2. Only where it conforms to Biblical law.

B. Submission to God-ordained power:
   1. Only where that power is actually exercised, or we have good reason to believe it will be exercised.

Since the attack on Christian schools and churches is before us at present, let us expand on that for a moment. When the state tries to tax the church, the issue is jurisdiction. We must go to the civil authorities and respectfully point out that we cannot comply, for the simple reason that they do not have jurisdiction. We cannot submit to their office and rulings in this matter, since the church is not under their jurisdiction. We do not submit to court orders. We do, however, submit to the barrel of a gun. If they come and close the church or school at gun-point, make sure the media are present. Frequently, however, if we resist the devil, he will flee from us. Thus, often the civil authorities are not prepared to go to the point of drawing guns against the clergy. If they are, fine, we submit (and open another church/school down the road). If they are not prepared to use *power*, then we need not submit to their rulings.

Why not simply go along with the state's sinful requirements, and deceive them by raising up Christian students? This argument is frequently heard, and in terms of what we have been saying, has a superficial plausibility. The

60. This may not square with Victorian ethics, but it is the position taken by Augustine in *The City of God*. There is no virtue, Augustine points out, in a woman's killing herself to avoid rape.

problem, however, is that it is precisely the direct government of Christ over his Church which is at issue, and this is the heart of the gospel. Thus, no compromise is possible.

Christians should be careful about hiring lawyers and trying to fight matters out in civil court, at least when it involves the church directly. (A Christian school not run by a church is another matter.) The issue is jurisdiction, pure and simple. A lawyer will almost always de facto grant jurisdiction to the state. In spite of personal integrity, lawyers are officers of the court, and have a vested interest in working within the system. The church is outside the system. I do not say that all lawyers are committed statists at heart, but that Christians must be careful in employing them. There may be a place for going into court precisely to make the point about jurisdiction, but a church officer must be careful not to compromise the integrity of the church in any way.

It should also be noted that many times a judgment call on affairs such as this is a very close matter. God promises to give us wisdom *in the midst of the situation*, not in abstraction, as He says in Matthew 10:19, "When they deliver you up, do not become anxious how or what you will speak; for it shall be given you in that hour what you are to speak." We must be careful about judging other Christians in abstraction. In the midst of the situation, a man may determine that the state intends to use maximum force, and may choose to let his church be shut down, and flee to start another. In another situation, a man might force the state actually to use force before he finally capitulates. The principle is the same, though there is variance in application.

Two areas we might briefly address before concluding this appendix are the draft and taxes. 1 Samuel 8:10ff. makes it clear that it is sinful for the state to draft men into an army for aggression or even as a standing army (as opposed to a ready militia), and it is also clearly sinful for the state to claim more than 9.99% of income as a tax, since to do so is to make the state preeminent over God. Thus, it seems that Christians should not obey calls for the draft, and should pay no more than 9.99% in income taxes. Biblically speaking, property and capital taxes are wholly wrong, so Christians should not pay them. If Christians respond to draft calls, or pay their full income and property taxes, it is out of submission to *power*, not to law. If the state is prepared to kill or imprison men for draft or tax evasion (and it has done both, even in recent years), then Christians have good reason to believe that the exercise of force will be employed by these powers, and thus submit. There is nothing immoral, however, from a Biblical point of view, with evading the draft or evading taxation, since deception is the proper way to deal with tyrants. It is pretty hard to do, however, and the cost in psychological worry and distress, not to speak of the cost if one is caught, renders draft evasion and tax evasion unwise.

We must keep in mind that the pagan is primarily interested in *power.* This means that the maintenance of *force* (the draft)[61] and the seizure of *money* (excessive taxation) are of absolute primary interest to him. If we think these are the most important things, then we will make them the point of resistance (becoming "tax patriots" or some such thing). To think this way is to think like pagans. For the Christian, the primary things are righteousness (priestly guarding) and diligent work (kingly dominion). Generally speaking, the pagans don't care how righteous we are, or how hard we work, so long as they get their tax money. This is why the Bible everywhere teaches to go along with oppressive taxation, and nowhere hints at the propriety of tax resistance.[62] As far as the pagan state is concerned, taxes are about the most important thing, since they finance everything else. We are advised not to make an issue at that point, lest we become like them, and because we are sure to lose any confrontation on that issue (after all, they presently have power). We know that righteousness and work will overcome pagan power eventually, so we can afford to ignore the tax issue. The pagans will give up the Christian school battle long before they will give up the tax issue.

This is not even to note that tax resistance accomplishes nothing positive anyway. Politically if the income tax were overcome by tax protests, some other more efficient and subtle form of taxation would replace it (maybe a Value Added

61. A forthcoming (1984) issue of *Christianity and Civilization*, now in preparation, deals in depth with the draft, in a symposium on war and revolution.

62. For a brief discussion of relevant passages and concepts in the area of taxes, see James B. Jordan "The Christian and Tax Strikes," in *Biblical Economics Today* IV:2 (April/May 1981), available for a contribution from ICE, Box 8000, Tyler, TX 75711.

Tax, as in Europe), because the state is not about to give up either the military or social welfare programs, the conservatives insisting on the former, and the liberals demanding the latter. The cost to the individual of "saving my tax money" is greater than the cost of simply paying, when we consider the cost of worry, of a fearful wife (*very* common), and the cost in time and money of fighting for one's "rights" in tax court. It is a pointless battle for the individual to engage in, but an all-important battle for the church to fight, if the church is directly taxed.

The Christian resists the powers that be primarily by avoiding them. In our day, the state is not yet wholly tyrannical in the sense that Nebuchadnezzar or Nero were. Thus, there is a place for resisting the devil, hoping he will flee from us. The question of when to resist and when to capitulate requires wisdom and discernment to answer in any given situation, but the boundary line is at the point of the actual exercise of force.

# THE NEW COMMUNITY

Herbert Schlossberg

NONE of the modern idolatries can give a satisfactory answer to the question of preserving the just prerogatives of both the individual and the collective. Statism, in its currently fashionable form, says that individualism allows the stronger to crush the weaker, and therefore the state must assume control over both. Individualism, in both classical liberal and modern libertarian forms, says that the state necessarily takes away liberty and must not be allowed to encroach on the individual, whose desires therefore are given the status of the rule of law. In practice, these antithetical positions are both given some freedom to maneuver in the context of an uneasy play of political forces whose hallmark is pragmatism.

Only the Christian gospel transcends these antitheses. The metaphor of the *body of Christ*, the New Testament's description of the Christian church, is the amazing answer in the sphere of human relations to the ancient conundrum of the One and the Many. It shows why we are not required to be either the isolated atoms of individualism, nor links in the great collectivist chain that is enslaving the world. If each of us is related to the whole of the community as, say, the eye is to the body, then the reason we cannot exist alone is clear; our needs, purposes, and functions must be related to those of the other members of the body. At the same time, the eye performs a vital function for the body and cannot be written off as unimportant or peripheral. "On the contrary, the parts of the body which seem to be weaker are indispensable" (1 Cor: 12:22). This is the only conception that makes feasible love as a practical expression of a social ethic. Under individualism, love is debased to sentimentality; under statism, it is a cover for the exercise of power.

---

Excerpted from Chapter Eight of *Idols for Destruction: Christian Faith and Its Confrontation With American Society*, published by Thomas Nelson Publishers, 1983.

Christian faith therefore provides meaning for the individual within the context of a larger society. It is the analogue to the doctrine of the trinity, in which each manifestation of God retains clear identity and function without dissolving the unity into three gods. This is the truth in the often-expressed statement that there is no brotherhood of man without the fatherhood of God. (But this is bound to collapse if used in a purely pragmatic way: "Since we desire all men to be brothers, let us pretend that there is one God who is father of all.") Western individualism dissolves the unity to preserve the individuality. Utopian collectivisms and all pantheisms preserve the unity—at least in principle—while dissolving any basis for respecting the individual.

In the gospel, furthermore, lies the only true cosmopolitanism. Entering the midst of the deepest-seated national animosities, it transforms hatred into love. The apostle Peter was thunderstruck to be shown in a vision that he was to regard his erstwhile enemies as brothers. As he said to an officer in the army of occupation: "God has shown me that I should not call any man common or unclean. . . . Truly I perceive that God shows no partiality, but in every nation any one who fears him and does what is right is acceptable to him" (Acts 10:28, 34f.).

If reconciliation between people is to be more than a pious wish, then the body of Christ must become a living experience among Christians, actualized and made into a reality in the church. This has been done in every age, but its potential has rarely been fully realized. Reconciliation and then unity are the corporate aspects of justification. They mean that a new community is to be born out of the formerly isolated individuals, together becoming the new body of Christ.

Thus, self-sufficiency is swallowed up in mutual dependence. Marks of talent or genius are recognized as gifts to be used for mutual benefit. Self-indulgence is recognized as more than merely a general fault, being the specific betrayal of a portion of the body of Christ that needs the gifts a particular person has to offer it.

But the body of Christ is never coextensive with the visible church. In the history of Israel those faithful to God were the remnant, whose compliance with the forms of religious obedience was matched by inner faithfulness and obedience to God. The remnant was comprised of the few who recognized God as their Lord and followed him, even as the broader religious community committed greater or lesser forms of apostasy. The early Christians learned that under the new covenant a similar condition would obtain. In the parables of the kingdom of God, Jesus taught that the kingdom would resemble a field in which an enemy had sown weeds among the wheat. Not before the end of the age would it be possible to separate them out of the crop (Matt. 13:24-43). In the apocalyptic vision the church at Sardis, unfortunately a prototype of many to follow, contained only a few who remained faithful. In the main, it was dead (Rev. 3:1-6).

The forms taken by this new body of Christ are of less consequence than the extent to which it reflects the good grain in its membership, those who are part of God's new creation among human beings. For, although the idolatries celebrate their capacity to create "new men" out of the old, only this genuine reflection of God's creative power is able to embody new spiritual life. This makes the church's remnant a new community unlike every other in its potential for exemplifying corporate spiritual life in the midst of a decaying civilization.

### *Defying the Powers*

One of the real contributions of the Christian radicals has been their insistence—indeed, their concrete demonstration—that a Christian community that is consciously modeled on the New Testament pattern is a powerful force.

> The making of community is essentially a revolutionary act. It is revolutionary because it proposes to detach men and women from their dependence upon the dominant institutions, powers and idolatries of the world system over the lives of people.[1]

Richard Neuhaus has pointed to the paradoxical truth that the revolutionary act of abandoning the world in favor of the creation and maintenance of Christian community may, finally, render the greatest service to the world. It does this by witnessing to the judgment under which the present world order is condemned and by demonstrating the alternative that is available.[2] This suggests that the true Christian community

1. Jim Wallis, *Agenda for Biblical People* (New York: Harper and Row, 1976), p. 103.
2. Richard John Neuhaus, *Time Toward Home: The American Experiment as Revelation* (New York: Seabury, 1975), p. 162.

will be what sociologists call a deviant subculture. In political terms, it may be regarded as subversive in the sense that it is radically and consciously attempting to subvert the values of society and the institutions that represent those values. Marching to a different drummer than their neighbors, these Christians are likely to appear threatening to many, and yet to some strangely attractive.

Dissident communities need to be more than collections of individuals if they are to avoid disintegration. If they are churches, they must exemplify the organic bond that can only be found in the body of Christ. That is a quality difficult to find in the typical American parish. An association that merely occupies its members for a few hours a week reinforces the fragmentation of the individual's life among numerous loyalties and makes it virtually impossible to build genuine community. The resulting privatized kind of religion tends to be completely ineffectual.

Deviant subcultures can survive only if they form permanent and effective communities to stand in opposition to the larger society. In sociological terms, they need to have "plausibility structures" that will support their deviance and that can only come from a close community of like-minded deviants. As sociologist Donald Kraybill says: "It is not psychologically healthy to be the only oddball around."[3] Vladmir Bukovsky, whose principled obstreperousness, both in and out of prison, nearly drove the Soviet authorities wild, acknowledged that without a closely knit band of like-minded partisans he could have accomplished nothing. The churches will be able to fashion effective groups of Christians, living in the community, only when they acknowledge the bankruptcy of the larger culture, just as the Soviet dissidents have done.

### *The Preservation of Intellect*

Creating Christian culture can be accomplished only with the aid of a solid intellectual effort that takes seriously a responsibility to defend the truth. This requires a conscious departure from the debased norms that are gradually gaining

---

3. Donald B. Kraybill, *The Upside-Down Kingdom* (Scottsdale, PA: Herald Press, 1978), p. 305. See also the excellent discussion of this problem by Os Guinness, "The Problem of Modernity—and the Church," *Radix*, Nov.-Dec. 1978, pp. 8-13.

predominance. Scholarship is neither to be feared nor its products given the exalted status of sacred texts. If the wisdom of the first century was "foolish" and "doomed to pass away" (1 Cor. 1, 2), so is what passes for wisdom in the present age. The New Testament writers were conscious that their teaching was despised by the cultured Greeks of the dominant civilization. The spirit of the age—any age—is always opposed to the spirit of Christ.

In their uncompromising determination to proclaim truth, Christians must avoid the intellectual flabbiness of the larger society. They must rally against the prevailing distrust of reason and the exaltation of the irrational. Emotional self-indulgence and irrationalities have always been the enemies of the gospel, and the apostles warned their followers against them (Col. 2:18).

Paramount among the difficulties in Christian thinking is the dominance of anti-Christian assumptions in the "best" of the surrounding culture. Those who think Christians can easily use the world's artifacts and methods in the creation of a new synthesis underestimate the all-persuasiveness and subtlety of alien and hostile influences. T. S. Eliot, who was much concerned about this problem, warned that "paganism holds all the most valuable advertising space." He feared that as long as Christians were a tolerated minority, the unconscious pressures of intellectual conformity would more gravely complicate their survival than would the plainly perceived dangers of active persecution.[4]

Since ours is not so much a pagan (which is to say a pre-Christian) society as it is a post-Christian one, the dangers are all the more serious. The forces of idolatry do not urge us to worship Zeus but rather use the language that for many centuries has been associated with the Christian church. Profound religious differences may on the surface appear trivial, and one who points to them runs the risk of being called a hair-splitter. Just as an observer in the seventh century before Christ would be hard-pressed to distinguish the altar of the Lord from one dedicated to Baal, so we are faced with similar confusion when devotees of the idol state use the language of Christian compassion in their evangelistic mission.

---

4. T. S. Eliot, *The Idea of a Christian Society and Notes Toward the Definition of Culture* (New York: Harcourt, Brace, Harvest Books, 1940), p. 18.

There is no defense against such perils without a vigorous intellectual effort that enables us to discriminate between the true and the bogus. What assumptions lie behind the standard appeals to security and prosperity, justice and equality? Whose ends are being served? Whose gods are being served? What are the consequences of the measures that this group would like to put into effect? We shall not be able to deal with questions like these until we prepare intellectuals who are able to penetrate with clarity the "advertising" that Eliot warned about, which permeates the output of all of our influential institutions. We have not yet devised a way to train them without making use of the major advertising agencies—the universities and seminaries of the reigning idolatries.

When the cultural life of antiquity collapsed with the Roman Empire, and a centuries-long era of darkness followed, it was a corps of Christian intellectuals who kept the manuscripts, and the skills to use them, from disappearing from the face of the earth. We cannot say how long or how serious the present decline will prove to be, but once again Christians can stand in the gap against barbarism. Just as the biblical doctrine of creation demystified the world and made science possible, so other aspects of the faith are needed to destroy the follies of the modern idolatries. We must demystify the nation so that patriotism does not serve as an excuse for killing people. We need to demystify the state so that it cannot do evil with impunity. We need to demystify wealth and poverty so that they do not remain principles of human worth.

None of this can be done without the intellectual sophistication to detect the special pleading and the false assumptions of the intellectual world arrayed against us. We need it to defend against tendentious proposals accompanied by "studies" that purport to buttress the most destructive utopia-mongering. Christian intellectuals need the courage and confidence to stand fast, if need be, against the near-unanimous weight of scholarly fashion.

### *Christ Against the World*

To use the language of militance in describing Christian responsibility in the world is to advocate a view of societal relevance that is far from unanimously held. By and large, Calvinists of one kind or another have supported it. The Arminian and Pietist positions, on the other hand, are much more ones of withdrawal than of confrontation. John Howard Yoder, one of the more eloquent defenders of these positions, urges Christians to consider that they are not the guardians of history and thus should refrain from grasping for the levers by which they hope to move society in the desired direction.[5]

In some respects this disinclination to change society mirrors the early monastic movement, which recoiled in horror from the excesses of a disintegrating empire and resolved to remain unspotted. Many of the followers of Karl Barth, those who are determined to view temporal events *sub speciae aeternitatis*, have found themselves unable to make distinctions between competing claims for allegiance. Bemused by the call for putting spiritual values first, they are unable to move decisively in the struggles that mark modern life. This is another version of the neo-Kantian dualism, helpless to reconcile the worlds of matter and of spirit. It was no wonder that a number of Lutheran bishops supported Hitler in 1934; they had difficulty seeing how Christian faith could inform material action. Reinhold Niebuhr never tired of pointing out this persistent weakness in Barthian thinking.

Christians who resist acknowledging any close correspondence between their faith and the direction that history takes strangely echo the postion taken by the reigning humanist establishment. As Richard Neuhaus has pointed out, their stand is precisely that of the modern secularists who wish to banish Christian ideas from influencing public policy. This understanding of Christian action aids its enemies by reinforcing the notion of the supposed irrelevance of Christian faith.

Biblical teaching, in contrast, insists that faith and works are inseparable, that the interior dimension, if it is not a sham, must have its effect on the external world. The "salt" of people changed by the gospel must change the world. In the prophetic tradition, turning away from false gods had to be accompanied by a resurgence in the doing of justice. At its better moments, the church has made enormous differences in the way society functioned. In the midst of Hitler's program to kill the incurably ill in 1941, Bishop Galen published a sermon that exposed the practice and caused widespread revulsion throughout Germany. Galen was spared only because propa-

---

5. John Howard Yoder, *The Politics of Jesus* (Grand Rapids, MI: Eerdmans, 1972), pp. 234-38.

ganda chief Joseph Goebbels feared massive public reaction if he should be executed. Meanwhile, the government stopped the killings after seventy thousand people had lost their lives. Millard Everett showed good sense in blaming the biblical ethic for prejudicing people against the killing of infants who fail to meet whatever tests of perfection their elders desire to impose upon them. It is this continual willingness to stand against culturally approved evil in the name of Christ that makes of the church a revolutionary force.

Christian revolution begins with the individual and has its concrete effect in the culture. Whether or not it exercises control, it always takes its stand with the eternal requirements of God against the idolatrous attractions of the moment. This means that it may appear either backward- or forward-looking depending on the nature of the opposition. Its enemy at a given time may be an ideology that marshals ideas in order to preserve the current order or, at another time, a utopia that sacralizes a new order.[6] It may be subject, therefore, at any time to being attacked as either "liberal" or "conservative," but it can never be either. All orders, old and new, are subject to the same eternal law that the church serves, and therefore are judged by the same standard. If they are found wanting, it has nothing to do with their conformance to this or that tradition.

To expect a transformation of society that results from changed people is not an idealistic hope that can never come to pass; it is a matter of historical record. In the midst of the nature worship of the second millenium before Christ, Israel introduced the dynamism of a people who worshiped the God beyond nature. As long as Israel maintained the distinctiveness of this heritage, it alone among its neighbors built a society based on justice, one that recognized that there was an objectively understood ethic beyond the exigencies of power. Much later the new Christian church infused the Mediterranean world with the same vision. This social transformation made Western civilization what it was. Love became the central idea in the dominant ethic, so much so that idolatry adopted its language and actions and was thereby made tolerable for a time.

---

6. "Ideology" and "utopia" are used in the special sense found in Karl Mannheim, *Ideology and Utopia: Introduction to the Sociology of Knowledge*, trans. Louis Wirth and Edward Shils (London: Kegan Paul, Trench, Trubner, 1946 [1936]).

Contrary to the sense of affliction and defeat that marks so much of the contemporary church in the West, the tone in the New Testament was one of victory. If we turn away from the *Weltschmerz* adopted too uncritically from the larger society, and look instead at the emerging new churches of Asia, Africa, and Latin America, we see something akin to the first-century exemplars. Considered on a worldwide basis, the twentieth century is a great period of Christian expansion, and the number of new converts to the faith has been estimated reliably as exceeding fifty thousand *per day.*[7] If current trends in East and West should continue, we may expect that some of what are now the poor, backward countries of the world will become the economic, political, and social leaders of the twenty-first century, while the neo-pagan West continues its slide into impotence.

### *Toward the Triumph of Justice*

Few ironies are more bitter than the fact that the strongest declamations against injustice come from the apologists of Marxism, an ideology responsible for the death or enslavement of countless millions. The Christian churches of the West in recent years have addressed this issue largely from the perspective of the great depression of the 1930s. Reinhold Niebuhr in the United States and Archbishop William Temple in Great Britain, persuaded that the business cycle and the hardships of the thirties were caused by the unbridled play of market forces, led the movement to make state domination of the economy normative. This, they said, would bring into being the "just social order." Their vision for the messianic state was not far from what we have today. In this sense, if in no other, they may be said to have succeeded.

Notwithstanding the errors of some of the church's leaders in this respect, the doing of justice in society is one of the major themes in the biblical writings. How the weak are treated is a test for any society, because it requires self-restraint for the powerful to do justice. "If a king judges the poor with equity," declared the ancient wisdom literature, "his throne will be established forever" (Prov. 29:14). The king who does so does

---

7. Cambridge University historian Edward Norman discussed this issue in the 1978 Reith Lectures, published as *Christianity and the World Order* (Oxford: Oxford Univ. Press, 1979).

not make of the poor the arbiters of right and wrong, thus divinizing them, but refuses to sacrifice them to the interests of the rich or of himself.

Doing justice in this sense is *uniquely* the function of the state, one that it usually fails to perform. Within a religious federation Israel's twelve tribes functioned as a unified social structure. They found their principle of unity in the covenant with God. When the federated tribal structure broke down, the monarchy supplanted the law as the unifying structure of national life. The effect was the creation of a privileged class and the destruction of justice.[8] That set the stage for the pattern of injustice that called forth the prophetic ministry of denunciation and ultimately led to the fall of the two monarchies.

Since injustice stems from the application of force or the threat of force against innocent persons, it is natural that those who seek to overthrow it would be active in political life. They should be working to stop the incessant looting taking place under the banner of redistribution, which at once makes dependents out of all its recipients and destroys the economy by removing the incentives for production. And it must insist that the criminal justice system, bemused by behaviorist contentions that criminals are victims, begin protecting the innocent against those who prey upon them. To take the position that faith should not be expected to affect corporate life is to acquiesce to the reigning order. For all its effect on the society, it is tantamount to saying that the rule of idolatry is legitimate. Or else it is to etherealize the faith by divorcing it from life. In either case, the injunction to act as salt in the world is robbed of half its meaning.

Questions about justice are fundamentally religious. This is naturally denied by those who think that the separation of church and state is a doctrine providing them with the means to structure the political order to the exclusion of Christian belief. But there is no such thing as law that does not assume a particular configuration to reality, which does not at least pretend to tell what kind of values are to be considered ultimate. That is why the establishment of justice as the aim of a biblical world view must encompass the changing of the political system. Justice means the ruling of society in conformance with the law of God.

---

8. This argument on the metamorphosis of Israel is taken from John Bright, *A History of Israel*, pp. 241f.

If Barth and Niebuhr represent the Scylla and Charybdis of the eternity-time dichotomy, then an authentic biblical approach would be to reject the neo-Kantian split that can never seem to accommodate both between a preoccupation with heavenly concerns that are completely irrelevant to earthly affairs and the kind of activism that can only worsen the conditions it seeks to ameliorate.

If we are to change the temporal in keeping with the eternal, then it will have to be done by changing the powers that control events. This means that we must work toward bringing the political, economic, and cultural landscape into conformity with the divine intention. That is what the New Testament means when it speaks of Christ as the ruler of the kings of the earth (Rev. 1:5). The Lord of history is the rightful sovereign of events and institutions. There is a note of triumph in the writings left to us by the early church that breaks through the telling of manifold difficulties. It recognized that crucifixion was followed by resurrection. The current critique of "triumphalism" with its lachrymose dwelling on "brokenness" is the recipe for retreat and defeat, and presages the continued failure to change human institutions so that they conform to a view of justice consonant with God's law.

We should recognize that these powers exercise legitimate functions but refuse them the right to usurp others. They may, and must, punish murderers, but must not be permitted to order family life. Insofar as they do not confine themselves to their appointed tasks, Christians must be the disloyal opposition. We do not recognize their right to play god. Theologians have often lost the distinction between legitimate and illegitimate functions in urging Christians to support the powers without reservation. For we are enjoined to obey authorities that "punish those who do wrong and . . . praise those who do right" (1 Pet. 2:14), not those that foster evil. Religious traditions that advocate unquestioning loyalty to the powers make it almost certain that injustice will rule. The natural inclination people have toward misusing authority is encouraged when those who claim to follow a higher law than the statutes fail to act on that claim. Tolstoy was sympathetic with the Indians under colonial rule, but observing that thirty thousand British controlled two hundred million Indians, he concluded that the Indians had enslaved themselves. The passivity displayed by the Indians is properly a trait of pantheism, not of Christianity.

There is an almost infinite number of ways one can stand against the powers. We are not limited to either acquiescence or law-breaking. Once we reject passivity, we can consider how to carry on the struggle. There are speeches, demonstrations, petitions, withholding of services, letter-writing, marches, economic boycott, selective disobedience, refusal to serve the state, ignoring of government directives, stalling and obstruction, overloading the administrative system with excessive compliance, and so on.[9] Should the system worsen, of course, there is always the possibility of making oneself vulnerable to prosecution.

Prior to sabotaging the establishment, however, we should consider how to change its course. Perhaps we could turn the powers away from idolatry and toward the establishment of the rule of justice. Proclaiming the gospel is fundamental to this. As the idolatries almost universally recognize, changing society without changing people is futile. The church's teaching function has to include a more biblical understanding of society if it is to influence the provision of justice.

In our effort to do this, is it possible to pursue wholeheartedly the program of one party or movement while recognizing its contingent nature? Not if "contingent" is understood to mean the opposite of "absolute." Inasmuch as these movements are driven by ideological forces that are to some degree in conflict with Christian faith, we are able to accord them at best only partial support. Our loyalty will always be suspect among those groups, and rightly so, for we are ready to change from support to opposition as soon as they depart from some approximation of justice by biblical standards. The danger in becoming "Christians for X," as Richard Neuhaus has well said, is that of becoming mere appendages to "Americans for X." This can only encourage millions of Christians, wary of being used by hostile forces, to turn away from their responsibility to work toward creating a just society.

The rival movements provide no help in understanding contemporary events. The common labels are as worthless

---

9. For the theory of nonviolent resistance, and scores of concrete strategies, see Gene Sharp, *The Politics of Non-Violent Action* (Boston: Porter Sargent, 1973).

now as they were a century ago when W. S. Gilbert lampooned them in *Iolanthe*:

> I often think it's comical
> How nature always does contrive
> That every boy and every gal,
> That's born into the world alive,
> Is either a little Liberal,
> Or else a little Conservative!

This is the dichotomous thinking that invites us to be part of any movement claiming to be "moral" or any movement that claims to favor the poor and oppressed. Such follies stem from blind submission to political symbols instead of seeing the realities hiding beyond them. To follow the modern ideologies, however disguised with biblical language, invites idolatry to set the agenda for the church. The early Christians, living among eastern Mediterranean populations divided into Jews and pagans, were called by the latter the "third race," and so called themselves. As long as they did not think of themselves as belonging to one branch or the other of a twofold division of the world, they could truly be Christian.[10] So it is now. Christians can be liberals if they wish, or conservatives, or radicals, but not until they unmask those false images can they fulfill their real responsibilities.

It may be, then, that the only healthy relationship the church can have with the political parties is one of mutual suspicion, with a willingness to undertake short-term alliances of limited scope. Since each side is marching to a different drummer, it is difficult to see how the relationship can be any firmer, unless one or the other capitulates. Recent history is not encouraging about which side that would be. If we are successful, no party could lightly legislate or enforce the law in ways that are repugnant to Christians. They may finally do so, but only at political cost.

Representative government is worthy of support in principle because the biblical view of human nature concludes that all of us are flawed and unable to handle unlimited power without falling into pride and irresponsibility. Nevertheless, the ratification of law by majority vote does not validate it. To the democratic ideology, any action is just if it is approved by

10. See R. A. Markus, *Christianity in the Roman World* (New York: Scribner's, 1974), pp. 24ff.

majority rule. To the libertarian ideology, any action is just if it is not coercive. Both are thus humanist to the core. In biblical perspective, right and wrong are not determined by the process leading up to their proclamation, but by the degree of conformity to the law of God. At the same time, most Christians have lived—and do live—under authoritarian or totalitarian regimes, and the kingdom of God is not thereby made of no effect. For Christians to remain faithful to their calling under regimes that are at once idolatrous and unrestrained in power is to invite persecution. These regimes seem to know instinctively that a church which has not been tamed is their most dangerous adversary.

One of the most serious dangers we face in seeking to influence the political sphere is that we, too, may succumb to the delusion that we possess the "solution" to the dilemmas of peace and justice, requiring only that we grasp the reins of power. If that should happen, we are only a step away from seeking to bring into being our own version of the messianic state. For it would imply that our salvation lies in yet another reformation of institutional arrangements. This society will have peace and justice when it repents and overthrows the idols, and not before.

### *Persecution*

It is absurd that the name "Christian" should be taken by so many as synonymous with respectable, middle class, or conventional. It was first used to refer to *disciples*—those under discipline of the Master—and it was coined in the midst of persecution (Acts 11:26). Should we stop accomodating ourselves to the prevailing norms, we can expect to be treated in the same fashion. We have allowed ourselves to be bought off with our free education, prosperity, and tax deductions. The persecution may begin when we renounce all that and indeed become disciples. In fact, the disabilities brought upon the Christian school movement by officers of the state suggest that it has already begun.

Modern persecutions replicate the experience of the church from the beginning. While Christ was yet with his disciples, he warned them about what would take place. "If the world hates you, know that it has hated me before it hated you. . . . If they persecuted me, they will persecute you"

(John 15:18ff.). One of the apostles later interpreted Cain's fratricide as the outcome of envy for his brother's righteousness and warned the followers of Christ that they could expect the world's enmity for the same reason (I John 3:12ff.). The apostle James, initially attracted by what he thought was a gospel of success that would bring him political power, had to be told that he could not have what he craved. Later, he was killed by the state (Mark 10:35ff.; Acts 12:2). That pattern was often repeated often for the church's first three centuries; the state wanted reverence that the Christians could not give without defying God.[11]

If the ancient precedents are repeated, we can expect the new persecution of Christians to be led by the social and religious elite, in conjunction with the authorities of the state. The warning of Christ was that those who were going to persecute his followers would think that by so doing they were serving God. This kind of persecution is extremely debilitating, because it induces in the victims doubt as to whether they are in the right, while convincing the guilty ones that they are. In the aftermath of the mass suicide in Guyana, reporters referred to James Jones's People's Temple as a manifestation of "radical Christianity." Had the political climate been different, the congressional investigation that followed could have resulted in legislation seriously restricting Christian groups that depart from establishment churches, and thus could be considered dangerous sects. Rousseau, who provided an ideology for modern totalitarianism, said that Christianity was of all things he knew the most contrary to the "social spirit." The state is never amused at being defied, and Christians who take their responsibilities seriously are not likely to remain within the pale of what its functionaries regard as socially responsible.

How should we react to the threat of persecution? Paul's famous passage on obeying rulers, so often misused to justify the domination of despots, offered a subsidiary reason for obedience: the maintenance of a clear conscience (Rom. 13:5). It is absurd to weaken oneself by violating the law for a trivial reason like evading taxes. The Christians of the first generation, undergoing severe persecution, "joyfully accepted the

---

11. Ethelbert Stauffer, *Christ and the Caesars*, trans. K. and R. Gregor Smith (London: SCM Press, 1955).

plundering of [their] property," and those who live now can do the same, rather than cheapening their resistance. Ayn Rand caught perfectly the power that a clear conscience gives one who is persecuted, in the words she put in the mouth of Dr. Ferris, a scientist who served the state in its quest for power:

> . . . there is no way to disarm any man except through guilt. . . . If there's not enough guilt in the world, we must create it. If we teach a man that it's evil to look at spring flowers and he believes and then does it—we'll be able to do whatever we please with him. He won't defend himself. He won't feel he's worth it. He won't fight. But save us from the man who lives up to his own standards. Save us from the man of clean conscience. He's the man who'll beat us.

One theme that emerges from the literature of resistance against the Soviet tyranny is that external power silences and conquers those who are willing to be conquered. Solzhenitsyn and Bukovsky gave innumerable examples to show that submission is not a foregone conclusion in the face of inexorable force: it is an act that is engaged in willingly by those who could do otherwise. Political authorities whose final appeal is their ability to kill or imprison their opponents cannot easily cope with people who say that that is not the final appeal, but only one appeal among many. This appears on the surface to be courage, but it is really something much more profound and powerful. Faith makes it possible to be relatively indifferent to the secondary considerations while exercising supreme care about the main consideration.

In the midst of persecution, the community of believers is the main source of strength for Christians. Their unity is of capital importance, but this has nothing to do with the ecclesiastical gigantism that currently accompanies the great weakness of the churches. Organizational unity often serves as a pernicious substitute for the organic unity that ought to mark the body of Christ and has made it easier in the past for alien influences to subvert the church. The Living Church in the Soviet Union could be made a part of the state apparatus with little trouble once Stalin had moved his own people into the top leadership. The Nazi revolution similarly found the unified state church easy to take over, while the authorities could deal only with great difficulty with the lay-dominated decentralized churches.

Speculation on how best to meet the threat of disaster

must be accompanied by a theology of disaster, and such a theology must center on the Christian virtue of hope. The apostle who suffered innumerable hardships, including beatings and imprisonment, wrote: "But thanks be to God, who in Christ always leads us in triumph" (2 Cor. 2:14). Hope is what enabled him to see the essence of the situation—triumph—beyond the accident of disaster. It is the quality of which optimism is the secularized and debased remnant. It is rooted in the faithfulness of God, the firmest of all foundations, instead of being a mere habit of thinking or, worse, the outcome of historicist or other theories of inevitable progress. Now that the prevailing fashion is to cry doom, it is needed all the more.

### *Embarking on the Great Adventure*

Biblical faith finds great power—as does its imitator, Marxism—in the conviction that history is going its way. Or rather, that since Christ is the Lord of history, it is going history's way. Final victory is not dependent upon how well its work is done; rather it is assured regardless of all contingent factors. "Thy kingdom come, thy will be done on earth as it is in heaven," is not a pious wish, but a certainty. We do not question if we shall be able to bring such a happy state of affairs into being, but rather what our role should be in its inevitable fulfillment. Since the world's powers were "disarmed" in Christ (Col. 2:15) their might is limited, despite the illusions of invincibility they are able to project. The eschatology of victory is a principal theme of the New Testament.

Yet, we live in a world of phenomena as well as eschaton, and we must face the question of what good the gospel of Christ is in the here and now. Ironically, those who seek their ultimate value in the next world are the only ones able to do much good in this one. Those who love with this present world destroy it along with themselves. Charles Cochrane concluded his study of ancient Rome by affirming that Christianity was the synthesis that provided the only cohesion to the fragmenting culture of Hellenism. That may be the role it is presently preparing to assume again.

From the most homely of responsibilities to the most exalted, Christian faith has the capacity to infuse coherence and grace where disintegration now takes place. About seventy-five years ago French poet Charles Péguy declared that the true revolutionaries of the twentieth century would be the fathers of Christian families. He must have meant that the infusion of meaning and sanity into family nurture has enormous potential to thwart the march of the idolatries.

At the other end of the scale, it it getting ever more difficult to disguise the intellectual sterility of the modern movements that a century or two ago moved triumphantly away from their biblical underpinnings. Czech Marxist philosopher Milan Machovec has expressed frustration at theologians overly enamored of "dialogue" who fail to speak boldly enough about the distinctives of Christian faith. Although an atheist, he believes that the "dynamic" of the West lies in its allegiance to a transcendent God who relativizes present achievements. His goal is to find a secular equivalent for God, and thus rescue the moribund idolatries of communism from their predicament. Yet, the West itself has fallen victim to those idolatries, and only a return to the same transcendent God can rescue it.

In the New Testament, the metaphors commonly used to describe the church's external relations were those of war. The ethic of the early church made it inevitable that strife would come from its refusal to conform to the reigning idolatries. On the other hand, dialogue is for the church the great metaphor of decline and defeat, a dispirited acknowledgment that one does not have the truth. It is expressed on the popular level by the currently faddish emphasis on peace, security, and prosperity as the normal outcomes of Christian faith. This debased form of Christianity is unable to comprehend the contemporary meaning in the incident wherein Christ branded as satanic Peter's refusal to accept the reality of the coming crucifixion. The same idea is often found in the Pauline literature. "When the people say, 'There is peace and security,' then sudden destruction will come upon them . . . and there will be no escape" (I Thess. 5:3).

Their new-found minority status in a world headed for the brink of disaster holds the promise of providing more excitement than most Christians are expecting. Once again in the West we live under conditions the early church knew intimately, and perhaps we can understand better than most of our predecessors the meaning of passages in the New Testament dealing with these conditions.

One reason Chesterton's writings have been so challenging and hopeful to three generations of Christians is that he captured better than most the quality of adventure in Christian life. That is a quality of which we shall have more than enough if we are willing to accomplish the task that lies before us. For even the good kings of ancient Judah, who expelled the worship of the Baals from the temple, left the Asherim and their devotees undisturbed on the hills. So rooted in communal life these deities became, that it was unthinkable to be rid of them. In the late twentieth century the West is similarly plagued with major and minor idols, some of them all but invisible. It is hard to imagine a more important or satisfying role than to embark on the spiritual, intellectual, and political adventure of working toward stripping them, root and branch, from the land.

# APOLOGETICS AND STRATEGY

Gary North and David Chilton

**Thus, what is of supreme importance in war is to attack the enemy's strategy.**
Sun Tzu, *The Art of War*

WE are not sure when Sun Tzu of the Chinese province of Wu lived, or if he ever really did live. What we do know is that the collection of brief observations on war attributed to Sun Tzu constitutes the finest summary of military strategy ever written. He may have been a contemporary of Plato, or of Alexander the Great and Aristotle in the fourth century, B.C., in the period of Chinese civilization known as "classical," as we also call the civilization of Greece of this period. B. H. Liddell Hart, the prominent British military author and strategist, has written that "Sun Tzu's essays on 'The Art of War' form the earliest of known treatises on the subject, but have never been surpassed in comprehensiveness and depth of understanding. They might well be termed the concentrated essence of wisdom on the conduct of war. Among all the military thinkers of the past, only Clauswitz is comparable, and even he is more 'dated' than Sun Tzu, and in part antiquated, although he was writing more than two thousand years later. Sun Tzu has clearer vision, more profound insight, and eternal freshness."[1] He admitted that in this one short book, Sun Tzu had incorporated "almost as much about the fundamentals of strategy and tactics as I had covered in more than twenty books."[2]

## *Offensive Strategy*

Sun Tzu's comment on the necessity of overcoming the enemy's strategy appears in the third chapter, "Offensive

1. B. H. Liddell Hart, "Foreword," Sun Tzu, *The Art of War,* translated by Gen. Samuel B. Griffith (New York: Oxford University Press, 1963), p. v.
2. *Ibid.*, p. vii.

Strategy." A military strategy which does not include offense is doomed. But it must not be a suicidal offense—the kind of wild, foolhardy offensive frontal attacks that characterized Pickett's charge at Gettysburg and Bonnie Prince Charlie's attack on the British forces at Culloden.[3] The best kind of offense which leads to victory is one in which the enemy is overcome strategically even before the battle begins. As Sun Tzu said, "those skilled in war subdue the enemy's army without battle. . . . They conquer by strategy."[4] In short, "To subdue the enemy without fighting is the acme of skill."[5]

This, quite frankly, is what the humanists have accomplished in the United States and England: a bloodless conquest of their enemies, the Christians. (In France, they conquered through a bloody revolution, and they attempted to spread their religion by force across the continent of Europe.) The Christians in the United States surrendered, step by step, issue by issue, because Satan and his forces understood the strategy of Christians—though not the strategy of Christ—better than Christians understood Satan's strategy.

There was no bloodshed or threat of bloodshed when Horace Mann and the defenders of State-financed "moral" education—consciously distinguished from Christian education—persuaded the citizens of Massachusetts to agree to the creation of a comprehensive government school system.[6] The most conservative Christian forces, the Calvinists, had already suffered a series of defeats in New England. The anti-Calvinist evangelicals had defeated the Calvinists at Harvard and Yale a century earlier. Then the Unitarians had beaten the evangelicals' leadership for the control of Harvard and Yale in the early decades of the nineteenth century. Finally, Mann and the statist Unitarians completed their victory, and all the other states in the Union followed suit, although it took a military victory over the South to complete public education's mopping-up operations.

The New England Puritans had opened the door to defeat in education two centuries earlier when Massachusetts had

---

3. Grady McWhinney and Perry Jameson, *Attack and Die* (Montgomery: University of Alabama Press, 1982).

4. *The Art of War,* III:10, p. 79.

5. *Ibid.*, III:3, p. 77.

6. R. J. Rushdoony, *The Messianic Character of American Education* (Nutley, NJ: Craig Press, 1963), ch. 3.

passed a law in 1647 requiring all towns with 50 households or more to establish compulsory Christian schools. This law decreed that town funds were to support the educations of the children of poor people who could not afford to pay.[7] The Puritans established the precedent which Horace Mann and the public school religionists later exploited. The Puritans had misunderstood a fundamental principle of sovereignty, namely, that it is the parents' responsibility to educate children, not the civil government's. They mistakenly believed that compulsory education would remain Puritan education. By failing to honor a principle of sovereignty, they took the first step backward in a war which we are still fighting.

Mann could not have created a modern public school if he had attempted to jam it down the throats of the Christian majority by force. But he was able to use the philosophical and theological errors of the Christians against them. They believed in natural law—a supposed common-ground between Christians and non-Christians. They believed in "shared moral principles" among all "rational" men—the intellectual heritage of early church fathers and the medieval scholastics. They believed in compulsory education, even partially tax-supported. Mann and the Unitarians simply took these erroneous first principles and created a rival religious order—a religious order financed by compulsory taxation levied by the majority vote of Christians on each other. "I believe in the existence of a great, immutable principle of natural law, or natural ethics, . . . a principle of divine origin, clearly legible in the ways of Providence . . ." Mann wrote.[8] It sounded so religious! It *was* religious—the religion of humanism. Christians joined in the "great crusade" to create tax-supported "moral" education in America, and then turned the management of the whole system over to the "experts"—people who held the tenets of Mann's religion of salvation through public education, or at least his non-Christian "natural law" educational methodology.

What is scarcely recognized by Christians today is that *Christians financed the construction of the humanist social order which now oppresses them, all in the name of shared moral principles and compulsory "charity" by the State*. Who else could have financed it?

7. Lawrence Cremin, *American Education: The Colonial Experience, 1607-1783* (New York: Harper Torchbook, 1970), pp. 181f.

8. Cited in Rushdoony, *Messianic Character*, p. 21.

There were only a handful of Unitarians in the United States in 1830, and most of them were concentrated in and around Boston. The humanists planned the conquest of a culture already controlled by a vast majority of Christians. In many respects, this planned conquest was a conspiracy.[9] Not only did the Christians not fire a shot in reply, they surrendered enthusiastically. Even today, Christian headmasters and university presidents do everything possible to gain academic accreditation for Christian schools from the humanist-controlled accrediting agencies. The capitulation goes on, all in the name of "shared moral principles" or "common standards of academic excellence."[10] In other words, all in the name of the *myth of neutrality.*

We can see the same step-by-step capitulation in the debate over the origin of the world. Long before Charles Darwin's *Origin of Species* (notice: no "the" after "of"), Christian geologists and "naturalists" had given up the idea of a six-day creation. Once they had accepted the possiblility of a 20,000-year-old earth, they could not resist the triumphant extension of autonomous time's arrow, until the advent of the idea of today's 4.5 billion-year-old earth.[11] Prominent Christian geologists still stand before classrooms filled with sons and daughters of Christian parents and teach them such a time-frame, all in the name of "enlightened" Christian scholarship.[12]

The humanists avoided a frontal assault against Chris-

---

9. R. J. Rushdoony, *The Nature of the American System* (Fairfax, VA: Thoburn Press, [1965] 1978), ch. VI: "The Religion of Humanity"; Otto Scott, *The Secret Six: John Brown and the Abolitionist Movement* (New York: Times Books, 1979).

10. Gary North, "Academic Compromise," *Christian Reconstruction*, I (Nov./Dec., 1978): "Who Should Certify Competence?" *Biblical Economics Today*, IV (Feb./March, 1981); "The Impossible Dream," *Christian Reconstruction*, VI (May/June, 1982).

11. For an historical account of this capitulation, see Gary North, *The Dominion Covenant: Genesis* (Tyler, TX: Institute for Christian Economics, 1982), Appendix C: "Cosmologies in Conflict: Creation vs. Evolution."

12. One example: Dr. Davis Young, who teaches at Calvin College. He is the author of two books defending the ancient earth. Of course, he says he is not an evolutionist. But he supports the geological worldview of those who are, and his viewpoint would render Christians virtually defenseless in the battle against evolution. For a critique of Dr. Young's philosophy, see North, *ibid.*, pp. 287ff., 384f.

tians in the United States until our own day. They operated from a minority position before this. They were content to capture the seats of influence: the judges, the teachers, and the pulpits of the mainline denominations.[13] They worked for two hundred years to "capture the Robes."[14] Now they are taking action through the State's apparatus to shut off the competition of Christians—precisely what Lester Frank Ward, a prominent late nineteenth-century humanist-evolutionist educator, said evolutionists would have to do.[15] The humanists have implicitly followed the teachings of Sun Tzu:

> When ten times the enemy's strength, surround him.
> When five times his strength, attack him.
> If double his strength, divide him.
> If equally matched you may engage him.
> If weaker numerically, be capable of withdrawing.
> And if in all respects weaker, be capable of eluding him,
> for a small force is but booty for one more powerful.[16]

What is our point? Simple: the humanists recognized the weaknesses of the "common ground" philosophy of the Christians. They used this intellectual weak point to take away sovereignty from Christians, step by step, institution by institution. Because Christians gave up the idea of the sovereignty of God, and therefore the sovereignty of God's word over the very concept of cause and effect, they eventually gave up the idea of the sovereignty of Christianity over anything outside the home, the sanctuary, and (maybe) the Christian school. Only with the advent of legalized abortion did millions of Christians begin to wake up to the crisis—*a crisis of sovereignty.* Here at last was an issue which was clearly a life-and-death issue. Because they had not recognized the sovereignty of God as a life-and-death issue, they were driven by the humanists, step by step, into the historical shadows, until the day came when they finally decided to take a stand, to say "we will not

---

13. Gary North, "Humanism's Accomplices," *Christian Reconstruction*, III (March/April 1979); "Humanism's Chaplains," *Biblical Economics Today,* III (April/May, 1980).

14. Gary North, "Capturing the Robes," *Chrisitian Reconstruction*, VI (Sept./Oct., 1982).

15. For a detailed analysis of Ward, see North, *Dominion Covenant: Genesis*, pp. 297-317.

16. Sun Tzu, *The Art of War,* III:12-17, pp. 79f.

budge, or go away, until abortion is made a criminal offense once again." (When they come to agree that it is a *capital offense*, and they proclaim the moral necessity of the civil government's imposition of the death penalty for both mother and physician, they will have begun to take the Bible seriously: Ex. 21:22-25.)

It is not always possible to win without fighting, especially if you are outnumbered. Martyrs have played an important part in the success of the church, and also in the success of other important historical resistance and revolutionary movements. Tertullian wrote in the early third century, A.D. that "The oftener we are mown down by you [the Roman State], the more in number we grow; *the blood of Christians is seed.*"[17] (This has come down through history as "The blood of martyrs is the seed of the church."[18]) There are always risks—life-and-death risks—in any attempt to reshape a society's thinking, and therefore its way of life. But the quest of martyrdom is suicidal; it is not a goal, but a means, and a rare and last-resort means at that. The "suicide mission" is to be used sparingly, if at all, only as a tactic which is part of an overall strategy of victory. When it is used as a last-ditch effort, as it was used by Germany[19] and Japan (kamikaze attacks) in the spring of 1945, it is lawless— a "romantic" assertion of heroism in the face of sure defeat.

### *God's Grand Strategy*

It is our contention that the foundation of the "grand strategy" was Christ's victory over Satan, especially at Calvary. Christ announced: "All power is given unto me in heaven and earth. Go ye therefore, and teach all nations baptizing them in the name of the Father, and of the Son, and of the Holy Ghost: teaching them to observe all things whatsoever I have commanded you: and lo, I am with you alway, even unto the end of the world. Amen" (Matt. 28:18-20). This

17. Tertullian, *Apology*, Chapter L; in *The Ante-Nicene Fathers* (Grand Rapids, MI: Eerdmans, 1973), p. 55.

18. H. L. Mencken (ed.), *A New Dictionary of Quotations on Historical Principles from Ancient and Modern Sources* (New York: Alfred A. Knopf, 1942), p. 111.

19. A powerful movie about this phase of the German defense effort was the German film, "The Bridge" (1959).

is the Great Commission, but because it involves all of God's commandments, it constitutes a grand strategy.

God is the master strategist. All of history constitutes the outworking of His meticulously detailed strategy. The one and the many—the integration of both the overall strategy and the details of tactics—are comprehensively known by God and executed by God. In short, *God's strategy is infallible because He is absolutely sovereign over history.*

Do we really mean absolutely sovereign, down to the last detail? Yes. Do we mean that God has overcome every aspect of Satan's strategy? Yes. Do we mean that *nothing is left to chance* (*or autonomous man*)? That is exactly what we mean.

> We do not pretend that the fate of the world is in our hands. That way lies madness, being a burden that no human being can bear. Yet, we are not condemned to resignation and quietism, still less to despair. We are not the lords of history and do not control its outcome, but we have assurance that there is a lord of history and he controls its outcome. We need a theological interpretation of disaster, one that recognizes that God acts in such events as captivities, defeats, and crucifixions. The Bible can be interpreted as a string of God's triumphs disguised as disasters.[20]

As soldiers in a worldwide struggle, we must have total confidence in God, even when we cannot have very much confidence in our own efforts. Without this absolute confidence, our efforts are compromised. We grow faint. We may not persevere. What we need is a *vision of victory.* But it is not to be a vaporous vision; it is to be a vision grounded in the sovereignty of God.

Men play their part briefly in the sweep of history as covenant-breakers or covenant-keepers. The basis for our proper understanding of our role in this struggle is the Bible. The Bible is our military handbook. It is our link, in time and on earth, generation after generation, with the overall strategy of God. This is why an understanding of biblical law is absolutely basic to any tactic. The strategy of a single generation is undercut if that generation of Christians refuses to acknowledge the binding nature (and awesome power) of biblical law.

---

20. Herbert Schlossberg, *Idols for Destruction: Christian Faith and Its Confrontation With American Society* (Nashville, TN: Thomas Nelson, 1983), p. 304.

## *The Four-Pronged Foundation*

It is the argument of this essay, and the argument of those who are part of what has become known as the "Christian Reconstruction" movement, that Christians must strive to conquer the whole world for Jesus Christ. To accomplish this, Christians need an understanding of their God, His law, and their satanic opponents. They also need motivation. Christians need a strategy grounded in biblical truth, in order to give them the necessary confidence for such a vast undertaking. We believe that there are four fundamental aspects of Christian belief that too often have been missing *as a unit*, from the days of the early church fathers until the 1960's. Because we are convinced that this four-part doctrinal position is now recognized by a tiny minority of Christians, its influence will again begin to spread. This new intellectual foundation has come at precisely the time when the established institutions and belief of the triumphant humanist culture are being called into question, even by humanists. They are losing confidence in their own world-and-life view at the same time that Christians have solid reasons to regain confidence in the Bible's world-and-life view. What is the proper Christian alternative?

### I. *The Sovereignty of God*

"The king's heart is in the hand of the LORD, as the rivers of water: he turneth it whithersoever he will" (Prov. 21:1). God controls completely the history of every civil government. "Daniel answered and said, Blessed be the name of God for ever and ever: for wisdom and might are his. And he changeth the times and the seasons: he removeth kings, and setteth up kings: he giveth wisdom to the wise, and knowledge to them that know understanding" (Dan. 2:20-21). "Thus saith the LORD God: Remove the diadem, and take off the crown: this shall not be the same. Exalt him that is low, and abase him that is high. I will overturn, overturn, overturn it; and it shall be no more, until he come whose right it is; and I will give it to him" (Eze. 21:26-27). And then that promised king came, and announced: "All power is given unto me in heaven and earth" (Matt. 28:18).

In his letter to the church at Rome, Paul stressed the doctrine of the sovereignty of God. He wanted Christians to understand it, for they were struggling against a mighty empire.

So he pointed to another great empire, Egypt: "For the scripture saith unto Pharoah, Even for this same purpose have I raised thee up, that I might shew my power in thee, and that my name might be declared throughout all the earth" (Rom. 9:17), a direct quotation of Exodus 9:16. Paul's conclusion concerning God's sovereignty: "Therefore hath he mercy on whom he will have mercy, and whom he will he hardeneth" (Rom. 9:18).

Now, if Paul was really arguing for God's predestination of all events in history, the next argument from the skeptic would be something like this: "But if God predestines all things, then he predestines some men to heaven and some to hell, some to political power and others to bondage. There would be no true personal responsibility for sinners or saints in such a predestined universe. If men are predestined, then there isn't a thing men can do about their plight. God shouldn't hold sinners responsible."

Paul foresaw this very argument. He offered this reply—a reply which makes sense only if someone is about to make this argument in reply to an argument for predestination. Paul summarized this argument: "Thou wilt then say unto me, Why doth he yet find fault? For who hath resisted his will?" (vs. 19). And then he answered it by citing another great passage affirming the sovereignty of God, Isaiah 45:9-10: "Nay but, O man, who art thou that repliest against God? Shall the thing formed say to him that formed it, Why hast thou made me thus? Hath not the potter power over the clay, of the same lump to make one vessel unto honour, and another unto dishonour?" (vv. 20-21). God's warning against the man who would offer this argument against God's sovereignty is even stronger: "Woe unto him that striveth with his maker! Let the potsherd strive with the potsherds of the earth. Shall the clay say to him that fashioneth it, What makest thou?" (Isa. 45:9).

Sadly for them, men who reject the doctrine of the sovereignty of God disregard the words of Paul and God. They *do* raise the argument about the incompatibility of God's predestinating will and human responsibility—the very argument Paul says is *immoral*. The vast majority of Christians today wallow in the immorality of the "free will, personal responsibility" syllogism, despite God's explicit warning against even raising the question. They refuse to acknowledge that the Bible explicitly teaches that 1) all events are totally predestined by God, and 2) both angels and men, as created beings, are totally responsible for their actions. They hide from the obvious implications of what the Bible says of Judas: "And truly the son of man goeth, as it was determined: but woe unto that man by whom he is betrayed!" (Luke 22:22). Judas played his determined role in history, and woe unto him. Christians try to place their own would-be autonomous logic above the explicit teaching of Scripture. They naively quote Romans 8:28 in confidence, yet refuse to believe in Romans 8:29-31, which is the very theological foundation of Romans 8:28:

> And we know that all things work together for good to them that love God, to them that are called according to his purpose. For whom he did foreknow, he also did predestinate to be conformed to the image of his Son, that he might be the firstborn among many brethren. Moreover whom he did predestinate, them he also called: and whom he called, them he also justified: and whom he justified, them he also glorified. What shall we say to these things? If God be for us, who can be against us?

Here is a rallying cry for those involved in the life-and-death issues of Christian resistance! What more stirring passage is there in all the Bible than this one? If God is for us, who can be against us? This is why Paul could write a few lines later: "So it is not of him that willeth, nor of him that runneth, but of God who sheweth mercy" (9:16).

But what guarantees the victory of our cause? What guarantees that *all things* work together for good to those who love God, to those who are called according to his purpose? Paul tells us in verse 29: the predestinating sovereignty of God. This is the same predestinating sovereignty that he speaks about in Ephesians 1: "According as he hath chosen us in him before the foundation of the world, that we should be holy without blame before him in love: Having predestinated us unto the adoption of children by Jesus Christ to himself, according to the pleasure of his will" (vv. 4-5).

It is the doctrine of the sovereignty of God which gives us hope. We have an omnipotent God standing above, below, behind, and ahead of us, both spatially and chronologically. He will bring His will to pass. Because He declares that our cause shall be vindicated, in time and on earth, and then beyond the grave, we therefore can work in confidence, knowing that the work of our hands and hearts will not amount to nothing. We can have confidence in Him.

The early church conquered the Roman Empire, and Augustine laid the theological and philosophical foundation of Western civilization. He offered a new view of history, a linear view in contrast to the cyclical views of pagan culture.[21] Augustine was a predestinarian who warred against the free-will doctrines of Pelagius.[22] Martin Luther launched the Protestant Reformation in the name of a totally sovereign God; and he warred against the free-will doctrines of Erasmus.[23] The predestinarian views of John Calvin, John Knox, Martin Bucer, and most of the other Protestant Reformers are well known. The Puritans who founded New England were all Calvinists. Even Charles Spurgeon, hero of modern Baptists, was a staunch predestinarian.[24] In our century, Christian intellectual leaders who have held this belief include J. Gresham Machen, who led the fight against theological liberalism in the 1920s and 1930s, R. J. Rushdoony, and Francis Schaeffer.

There will be many Christian resisters who read these words and who say to themselves, "You don't need to believe in predestination in order to resist tyranny." That is quite true. You also don't need to be a Christian to resist tyranny. But in order to replace tyranny with a functioning biblical alternative civilization, you need to have confidence in the power of God to back up your efforts — a God who has decreed the success of His cause, in time and on earth.

Few major movements in history have ever succeeded in extending their dominion over large chunks of this earth without adopting some version of providence, meaning predestin-

21. Charles Norris Cochrane, *Christianity and Classical Culture* (New York: Oxford University Press, [1944] 1957), pp. 480ff.

22. *The Anti-Pelagian Works of St. Augustine* (3 vols.; Edinburgh: T. & T. Clark, 1872-76).

23. Martin Luther, *The Bondage of the Will* (London: James Clarke & Co., 1957).

24. Iain Murray, *The Forgotten Spurgeon* (Edinburgh: Banner of Truth Trust, 1966). Incredibly, John R. Rice, a mid-twentieth-century American fundamentalist who edited books by Spurgeon, deliberately (and without warning to the reader) eliminated all references to predestination in his edited versions of Spurgeon's writings. When called to account for his actions by Rev. C. W. Powell of Anderson, California, Rice wrote back that he would never give any impetus to this doctrine under any conditions, including his editions of the writings of Spurgeon. (I have seen this letter; this is not an apocryphal story. — G. N.)

ation.[25] The Muslims of the seventh and eighth centuries, A.D., believed in predestination fervently, and conquered North Africa and even parts of Europe by means of the motivation which this doctrine provided, even in the perverted form held by Islam. Marxists in our day have relied on "the inevitable forces of history" to undergird their efforts. Modern science, until the advent of quantum mechanics, also rested on a version of comprehensive, though impersonal, cause and effect. Mao was wrong: power does not flow from the barrel of a gun. *Power flows from faith in the inevitability of a cause*. In the Christian world today, only the Calvinists possess this faith in the inevitability of Christ's cause.

## II. *A Presuppositional Apologetic*

Herbert Schlossberg is correct when he says that apologetics should not be apologetic. We are not saying "we're sorry" to anyone about our faith and our God. We have not been assigned the task of designing an intellectual defense of the faith which is solely a defensive faith. We defend faith in the living God of history. We tell man of God's totally successful offensive campaign against Satan and his followers. This message of God's total victory is, in fact, precisely what *offends*. Fallen men do not like to hear about a God who shows no mercy beyond man's grave—a God who also intends to smash the idols of humanity, in time and on earth. The existence of hell testifies to the inescapable fact that *God takes no prisoners*. There are no POW camps in God's post-judgment plans. God demands unconditional surrender, in time and on earth.[26]

One of the failures of Christianity for two thousand years has been its defense of the faith in terms of the intellectual categories of fallen, would-be autonomous man. The early church apologists used Platonic thought to defend the truths of the faith, and then the neo-Platonists made great inroads into the church. The medieval scholastics used Aristotle to defend the faith, and then natural law rationalists made great inroads into the church. Since Kant, traditional Christian

25. The Bible teaches that God is the sustainer of all things—providence—because He created all things in terms of an eternal decree: predestination.

26. Gary North, *Unconditional Surrender: God's Program for Victory* (2nd ed.; Tyler, TX: Geneva Divinity School Press, 1983).

apologists have given up; they have still clung to pre-Kantian forms of rationalism.[27] What modern physical science has done—post-Heisenberg quantum mechanics—is to undercut not only traditional Christian apologetics but most humanist apologetic systems. We are in the twilight of traditional Western rationalism.[28]

The first Christian philosopher who recognized this clearly was Cornelius Van Til of Westminster Seminary in Philadelphia. Prof. Van Til saw that all philosophy after Immanuel Kant has been caught in the web of contradiction: the deterministic rationality of science's explanations of causality (which has collapsed in this century) vs. the indeterminacy (randomness, irrationalism) of all ethics. Van Til returned to the Bible, and only the Bible, as the foundation of all knowledge. Christianity is not one intellectual system among many, but the *only* valid premise for human thought. Christianity is not merely probable; it is the *only possible* consistent world-and-life system.[29]

More than any Christian philosopher before him, Prof. Van Til made an intellectual frontal assault on all forms of autonomous thought. *His apologetic system marks the first total break with humanism in all its forms.* Without such a break, a full-scale assault on the forces of Satan cannot possibly be successful. In this sense, Christian philosophy in the second half of the twentieth century is unique because of one man, Cornelius Van Til, and his contribution will be understood in the history of the church as equal in importance to, and probably greater than, the contribution of the scholastics or the Protestant Reformers. It is the *sense of destiny* which Prof. Van Til's break with rationalistic apologetics can inspire which offers us the

27. What Cornelius Van Til demonstrates is that Karl Barth and other neo-orthodox theologians reworked Christianity to fit the Kantian outline. Van Til, *The New Modernism* (Philadelphia: Presbyterian & Reformed, 1947); *Christianity and Barthianism* (Presbyterian & Reformed, 1962).

28. Herman Dooyeweerd [pronounced DOUGH-yeh-veerd], *In the Twilight of Western Thought: Studies in the Pretended Autonomy of Western Thought* (Philadelphia: Presbyterian & Reformed, 1960).

29. Cornelius Van Til, *A Christian Theory of Knowledge* (Nutley, NJ: Presbyterian & Reformed, 1969); *The Defense of the Faith* (2nd ed.; Presbyterian & Reformed, 1963). For a simple introduction to Van Til's thought, see Richard Pratt, *Every Thought Captive* (Nutley, NJ: Presbyterian & Reformed, 1979). For a more advanced study, see R. J. Rushdoony, *By What Standard?* (Tyler, TX: Thoburn Press, [1959] 1983).

first two prongs of a four-pronged theological and intellectual foundation for Christian resistance: the sovereignty of God and the self-sufficiency of an authoritative Bible.[30] This vision makes Christian social action relevant.[31]

III. *An Optimistic Eschatology*

Prof. Van Til's position has two major flaws. The first is his amillennial eschatology. (The second, explored below, is his lack of emphasis on the specifics of biblical law.) He offers no vision of victory, in time and on earth. He sees only steady external defeat. This is spelled out in detail in his book, *Common Grace.*

He argues, quite correctly, that the conflict between Satan and God escalates over time, with each camp becoming more and more consistent with its ultimate presuppositions. Then he asserts that non-Christians, as they progressively come to understand the threat offered to them by a fully developed Christian world-and-life view, will launch persecutions against the church. The "free ride," so to speak, that the church has enjoyed will end. No longer will there by any visible common ground between Christianity and humanism. Thus, Van Til says, our protection will end. God's common grace—or "restraining grace"—will be removed from the world, leaving Christians at the mercy of the increasingly self-consistent pagans. "The full self-conscious reprobate will do all he can in every dimension to destroy the people of God. So while we seek with all our power to hasten the process of differentiation in every dimension we are yet thankful, on the other hand, for 'the day of grace,' the day of undeveloped differentiation. Such tolerance as we receive on the part of the world is due to this fact that we live in the earlier, rather than the later, stage of history."[32]

He is a commander who calls his troops to charge—to bring the *distinctives of the gospel* before the enemy. He tells us to

---

30. For an excellent little book filled with Bible verses related to the self-sufficiency of Scripture, see George W. Marston, *The Voice of Authority* (Vallecito, CA: Ross House Books, [1960] 1978).

31. Kevin Craig, "Social Apologetics," in James B. Jordan, ed., *The Failure of the American Baptist Culture.* Christianity and Civilization No. 1 (Tyler, TX: Geneva Divinity School Press, 1982).

32. Van Til, *Common Grace* (Presbyterian & Reformed, 1954), p. 85. The newer edition is *Common Grace and the Gospel* (Presbyterian & Reformed, 1974), same pagination.

demonstrate in every area of thought and culture that *there is no common ground* between believer and unbeliever, other than the image of God in each man—an image twisted by sin. In short, *Christians must abandon the sinful and biblically illogical quest for a common ground philosophy.*[33] And to the extent that they are successful in this endeavor, they will lose what little influence and protection they have in today's world.

In short, Prof. Van Til's pessimistic eschatology has not only colored his analysis of common grace, it has gutted it. The world will not be blessed, in his view, by the progressive dominion over all things by Christians. He does not believe in the possibility of progressive dominion by Christians. Prof. Van Til's interpretation of the implications of Christianity's progressive abandonment of common-ground philosophy leads directly to historical pessimism. The church will be persecuted by the dominant humanistic order. The more we Christians are successful in persuading unbelievers (as well as other Christians) that there is no common ground between their philosophies and Christianity, the more we will suffer persecution. When we win intellectually, we will lose culturally.

The point should be, rather, that as the humanists become more consistent with their philosophies—philosophies grounded in the presuppositions of chaos, randomness, and chance—*they* will become increasingly impotent, not the Christians. For example, the tax-supported public schools in the United States are collapsing, not the parent-financed Christian schools. The Bible teaches that Christians can become victorious when they become faithful to God's law in every area of life (Deut. 8; 28). Prof. Van Til has undercut the power which his apologetic methodology can impart, for he has adopted an eschatology of shipwreck.[34]

But we need not be burdened with this weakness in Prof. Van Til's system. His eschatological pessimism makes itself felt only in his writings on common grace. Others have adapted his basic methodology—the denial of common ground philsophy—to more positive uses. A restructuring of

33. R. J. Rushdoony, "The Quest for Common Ground," in Gary North (ed.), *Foundations of Christian Scholarship: Essays in the Van Til Perspective* (Vallecito, CA: Ross House Books, 1976).

34. Gary North, "Common Grace, Eschatology, and Biblical Law," *The Journal of Christian Reconstruction*, III (Winter, 1976-77); "Eschatologies of Shipwreck," *Christian Reconstruction*, III (Jan./Feb., 1979).

Van Til's interpretation of common grace was basic to the development of the Christian Reconstructionist perspective. Unlike Van Til, this version of Van Til's philosophy is eschatologically optimistic.[35]

IV. *Biblical Law*

Prof. Van Til also ignores biblical law in his philosophy. He shares this perspective with the vast majority of other published Christian philosophers. The historical dynamic provided by a positive eschatology needs to be accompanied by *a tool of reconstruction*—an explicitly biblical system of ethics which undergirds the creation of an explicitly biblical social order.[36] We must recognize that the confrontation between Christianity and all forms of humanism is comprehensive. No area of life is left untouched. There is no "hidden valley"—no "King's X"—in this war between rival religions. Everything is on the battlefield. God's redemption is comprehensive.[37] So is fallen man's rebellion.

How can we begin to reconstruct the social orders of this world without guidelines? Where are we to gain access to such universally valid guidelines? Obviously, in the Bible. What other standard do we have? The title of Rev. Rushdoony's first book is right to the point: *By What Standard?* We must ask ourselves this question again and again—every time we are told that "the Bible doesn't speak to the subject of . . . " or "you're trying to impose a theocracy." And what is the critic trying to impose? What god does he worship? Which guidelines does he seek to impose?

Christians today may prefer to hide behind phrases like "Christian principles," and "God's universal standards," and "traditional moral values." But what permanent, reliable, and universally valid moral values are there in Darwin's world of evolution? None. So let us confront the world with *comprehensive answers* to the world's *comprehensive crises*, which are in turn

35. For a biblical defense of eschatological optimism, see Roderick Campbell, *Israel and the New Covenant* (Tyler, TX: Geneva Divinity School Press, [1954] 1982); J. Marcellus Kik, *An Eschatology of Victory* (Nutley, NJ: Presbyterian & Reformed, 1971).

36. Greg L. Bahnsen, *Theonomy in Christian Ethics* (Nutley, NJ: Craig Press, 1977).

37. Gary North, "Comprehensive Redemption: A Theology for Social Action," *The Journal of Christian Reconstruction*, VIII (Summer, 1981).

the product of fallen man's *comprehensive rebellion*. Let us therefore confront the world with the testimony of *comprehensive biblical law*, not some warmed-over version of the now (post-Darwin, post-Heisenberg, post-existentialist) defunct concept of natural law. *There is no common ground morally and philosophically*. There are only more or less internally consistent rival worldviews.

What we must adopt, therefore, is a philosophical attack against humanism which is four-pronged: *the sovereignty of God* (the revelational foundation of our derivative, legitimate authority), *presuppositional apologetics* (the revelational categories of human thought), *optimistic eschatology* (the revelational dynamic for history), and *biblical law* (the revelational tool of reconstruction, both personal and social). As the advertisement for an aspirin substitute once put it, this "proven combination of active ingredients" is unique, and it *alone* offers a comprehensive foundation for a program of Christian resistance which is simultaneously offensive and defensive.

The very structure of this issue of *Christianity and Civilization* reflects the nature of the struggle: a three-part division, defensive tactics, fundamental strategies, and offensive tactics. We need defensive tactics that are based on a positive program of reconstruction. Any attempt to create a short-term defensive strategy which is not simultaneously a long-term offensive strategy will fail in the long run. In fact, its only hope is in a short-term holding action. We must reject, here and now, such a *stalemate mentality*.[38] Men should not be called upon to sacrifice their fortunes, lives, and honor to participate in some kamikaze-type holding action.

## Francis Schaeffer's *A Christian Manifesto*

The following material is undoubtedly controversial. It cannot be avoided, if we are to come with grips with the requirements of devising tactics of Christian resistance. If the stakes were not so high, if the crisis were not literally upon us, and if Dr. Schaeffer's book[39] had not sold 350,000+ copies, thereby making him the most prominent "Christian resister"

38. Gary North, "The Stalemate Mentality," *Christian Reconstruction*, VI (Nov./Dec., 1982).

39. Francis A. Schaeffer, *A Christian Manifesto* (rev. ed.; Westchester, IL: Crossway Books, 1982).

in the minds of fundamental Christians, neither of us would have brought any of this up. We both kept our opinions out of print until now. But the circumstances of the day no longer permit silence.

We all want to find allies wherever we can, but we must recognize deep-seated flaws in strategies and tactics recommended in the name of Christ by people who, in this particular area, do not adhere to a consistent theology of Christian resistance. If we refuse to face the theological and tactical differences that divide us, "before the shooting starts," we may not have time to think through what needs to be thought through when the crises escalate. That is what issues 2 and 3 of *Christianity and Civilization* are all about.

When lives are literally at stake—indeed, when the survival of Western civilization is literally at stake—we dare not pussyfoot around the hot issues. If generals who are responsible for devising a military strategy prior to the declaration of war are afraid of discussing openly the nature of each strategy and the reasons for each, then as military leaders, they are not fit to exercise command. If concern for "damaged egos in the general staff" is considered more important than the strengthening of the army's strategy, then the survival of those in the army is called into question. If we are at war with the philosophy and institutions of humanism—and it is our contention that we are—then we have to get our offensive and defensive strategies discussed and agreed to before we commit our capital and even our lives. The stakes are just too high.

Christians tend to rip each other up. Sometimes this is necessary, if someone is selling out the faith in a key area. Paul, after all, publicly confronted Peter when Peter capitulated to the Judaisers (Gal. 2:11-14). Usually, attacks by Christians on other Christians are ego-inspired or "turf-protecting" exercises. What is needed in an era in which Christians do not agree on the fundamentals of the faith, let alone strategy and tactics—and we are living in such an era—is open disagreement, *in order to facilitate cooperation in those areas where there is agreement*. We should not cooperate with those who are undercutting the defense of the faith *in those areas where they are undercutting it*. Thus, we have to get our disagreements into the open, not to destroy our cooperative efforts, but in order to increase cooperation in those areas where we are agreed. We need to define and thereby limit our areas of cooperation in advance, so that we are not disappointed and resentful later on when we discover just how disagreed we are in one area or another. Anything less than open discussion of disagreements *in advance* is short-sighted, like the apocryphal ostrich with its head in the sand. With this in mind, we turn now to a consideration of *A Christian Manifesto*.

Francis Schaeffer's books simultaneously soften and toughen up Christians. They toughen up Christians' confidence in the philosophical categories of orthodox Christianity by showing the futility of humanism and the cultural products of humanism, thereby making Christians more able to see the failures of the modern humanism. On the other hand, his books also soften Christians up offensively. He offers Christians little or no hope in their ability to do anything substantial to reverse the drift of humanism over the falls. (And that is where humanism is heading.)[40]

Dr. Schaeffer's writings have alerted Christians to the intellectual weaknesses of their enemies. That, as this portion of this essay will make clear, is probably Dr. Schaeffer's most important contribution. Like David, he stands across the valley from Goliath and tells the army of Israel that these Philistines cannot be ultimately victorious over the forces of righteousness. But then, unlike David, as he journeys across that valley of the shadow of destruction, he refuses to pick up any stones for his sling. Why not? Because also unlike David, he expects external, visible victory of the righteous to come only after the physical return of Jesus Christ to set up an earthly kingdom. Yet he expects God's army to follow him, stoneless, across the valley to confront the Philistines.

His books are important in some ways, and liabilities in others. They are important because a lot of people are reading them, and because some of his readers are discovering that his books are important primarily as introductions to the nature of the enemy's thoughts and works. They are liabilities as training manuals for the battle, for they do not really answer the questions Dr. Schaeffer raises. Eventually, some readers within the select group which have made this discovery are going to discover that what answers Dr. Schaeffer *does* have

40. Gary North, "Tugboats, Lifeboats, and Battleships," *Christian Reconstruction*, IV (Nov./Dec., 1980).

usually come from other people—people who fail to show up in his footnotes. Before we open that can of worms, however, we need to understand Dr. Schaeffer's basic argument in *A Christian Manifesto*.

Dr. Schaeffer begins his treatise by observing that the various problems confronting Christians in our society—the single issues over which Christians become agitated—are really "bits and pieces" of a much larger whole. *The basic problem is that a radical change in worldview has taken place*—a paradigm shift (to use Thomas Kuhn's now common phrase[41]) "*away from* a world view that was at least vaguely Christian in people's memory (even if they were not individually Christian) *toward* something completely different" (p. 17). This "different something" is a relativistic philosophy in which autonomous man and his choices are regarded as ultimate (i.e., *humanism*).

The American apostasy from Christianity into humanism has had grievous results in all areas of life, and most obviously perhaps in civil government and law. It is Christianity, Dr. Schaeffer insists—Reformation Christianity especially—which has given us what he calls the *form-freedom* balance of obligations and rights in government. "There is a balance here which we have come to take as natural in the world. It is not natural in the world" (p. 25). In moving away from the Christian worldview, apostate man has sought to find the basis of law in himself, in his own reason and experience. and the inevitable consequence of thus *deifying man* has been both *anarchy and tyranny.*

> The humanists push for "freedom," but having no Christian consensus to contain it, that "freedom" leads to chaos or to slavery under the state (or under an elite). Humanism, with its lack of *any* final base for values or law, always leads to chaos. It then naturally leads to some form of authoritarianism to control the chaos (pp. 29f.).

In opposition to humanism, the Reformation stressed the only base for law is "God's written Law, back through the New Testament to Moses' written Law. . . . The base for law is not divided, and no one has the right to place anything, including king, state or church, above the content of God's Law" (pp.

41. Thomas Kuhn, *The Structure of Scientific Revolutions* (Chicago: University of Chicago Press, 1962).

28f.). (The importance of the Reformation's emphasis on God's written law will become clearer in our analysis of Dr. Schaeffer's recommendations, for he really disagrees with this neglected aspect of Reformation history.) And Dr. Schaeffer argues, this Reformation viewpoint was held, substantially, by the Founding Fathers of the United States, who understood very well that the "inalienable rights" for which they were fighting had been given them by the God of the Bible.

> These men truly understood what they were doing. They knew they were building on the Supreme Being who was the Creator, the final reality. And they knew that without that foundation everything in the Declaration of Independence and all that followed would be sheer unadulterated nonsense (p. 33).

Thus, the Framers of the Constitution had no intention of establishing a secular State. In fact, although there was no national *church*, the courts recognized very early that Christianity was "the established religion" of the land, and that, as Justice Story of the Supreme Court declared, the Common Law was indisputably rooted in Christianity (pp. 37f.). In both intention and act, the Founders established the United States as a Christian nation.

But we have fallen far from that original ideal. Dr. Schaeffer documents the spread of the humanist plague by numerous examples: our secularized, sociological, arbitrary justice (pp. 41ff.); the move from "situational ethics" to "situational law," so that the courts have become the usual means of enforcing humanism upon the population (pp. 48f.); the barren materialism of modern science (pp. 44f., 53f.); the leftist media, which have become in effect a "fourth branch of government," and which have repeatedly demonstrated a vicious bias against a biblical position, particularly concerning the national horror of abortion (pp. 56ff.).

With some justifiable optimism, Dr. Schaeffer observes that Christians have an "open window," an opportunity to turn things around, to turn back the forces of humanism (pp. 73ff.), although he also acknowledges, very rightly, that this window could slam shut on us, leaving us with a totalitarian, humanist regime. He argues, from Scripture and from Reformation history, that the State is required to be *a ministry of justice*, and that when it fails in that calling, it may and should be opposed by conscientious Christians (pp. 89ff.). The State, he argues, "should be made to feel the presence of the Christian community." So far, so good. But then Dr. Schaeffer drops the ball. He says:

> *First*, we must make definite that we are in no way talking about any kind of a theocracy. Let me say that with great emphasis (p. 120).

He may say it with emphasis, but he has yet to answer the obvious question: "Just what, precisely, do you think should be established in place of *humanism's* theocracy (or, anthropocracy)?" He never answers this crucial question.

> We must continually emphasize the fact that we are not talking about some kind, or any kind, of a theocracy (*Ibid.*).

Whatever a theocracy is, it sure sounds terrible, doesn't it? Apparently, *all* theocracies are bad, since Dr. Schaeffer does not want *any kind* of a theocracy. But you never know, these days; you might bump into a theocracy roaming around wild somewhere, and for your own protection, you ought to find out what one looks like. How can you find out?

There are several ways to do this. We can use etymology, for instance: What do the roots of the word "theocracy" mean? *Theo* means *God*, and *cracy* means *rule of*. So *theocracy* means *the rule of God*. Scary, isn't it? Sounds just like . . . uh, the Garden of Eden. Or Heaven. And didn't Jesus teach us to pray, "Thy will be done in earth, as it is in heaven"? Of course, Dr. Schaeffer couldn't mean this. He must be against only a *bad* kind of theocracy. But no, he did say *any* kind. . . .

We can go to the "final arbiter" of English word meanings, the *Oxford English Dictionary*. It says:

> **Theocracy** A form of government in which God (or a deity) is recognized as the king or immediate ruler, and his laws are taken as the statute-book of the kingdom, these laws being usually administered by a priestly order as his ministers and agents; hence (loosely) a system of government by a sacerdotal order, claiming a divine commission; also, a state so governed: esp. applied to the commonwealth of Israel from the exodus to the election of Saul as king.

Now, this helps immeasurably. We are, of course, against the rule of "a deity," in the sense of some heathen god. Nor would we want "a priestly order" running the country, as in ancient Egypt, or in the Jesuit socialist state of Paraguay during the seventeenth and eighteenth centuries.[42] The biblical

42. For an account of the Jesuit State in Paraguay, see Igor Shafarevich, *The Socialist Phenomenon* (New York: Harper & Row, [1975] 1980), pp. 143-51.

standards of law are completely opposed to such a form of civil government. (As for "a sacerdotal order, claiming a divine commission"—we already have several of those: the Internal Revenue Service, the Department of Education, the Environmental Protection Agency, the Supreme Court, CBS News. . . . ) For us, the question is not "Theocracy or no theocracy?" but, increasingly, "*Whose* theocracy?" (Whenever we deal with a question which is not a case of "either/or," but rather "*whose*" or "*which*," we are dealing with what Rushdoony calls an "inescapable concept.")

Just as there is no legitimate possibility of talking about "theism *in general*"—true Christian theism being radically and qualitatively different from the idolatrous "theism" of non-Christianity—so we must not speak of "theocracy in general." The Reformed Confessions, before they were butchered (revised) by the embarrassed twentieth-century descendants of the Reformers, recognized the Scriptural demand for the Christianization of all of culture. Look, for example, at the original wording of the *Belgic Confession* (1561) on the duties of civil rulers:

> Their office is not only to have regard unto and watch for the welfare of the civil state, but also that they protect the sacred ministry, and thus may remove and prevent all idolatry and false worship, that the kingdom of antichrist may be thus destroyed and the kingdom of Christ promoted.

And the doctrine of the *Westminster Confession* (1646) is even more explicit:

> The civil magistrate . . . hath authority, and it is his duty, to take order, that unity and peace be preserved in the church, that the truth of God be kept pure and entire, that all blasphemies and heresies be suppressed, all corruptions and abuses in worship and discipline prevented or reformed, and all the ordinances of God duly settled, administered, and observed. For the better effecting whereof, he hath power to call synods, to be present at them, and to provide that whatsoever is transacted in them be according to the mind of God.

We should remember that Samuel Rutherford (whom Dr. Schaeffer professes to follow) was an uncompromising theocrat, so defined; and, as one of the members of the Westminister Assembly, he assisted in drawing up the statement quoted above (which may have been put a bit too mildly for his tastes). Consider the following statements from his

1644 book, *Lex, Rex* (notice the comma after *Lex*[43]):

> Kings and magistrates are God's, and God's deputies and lieutenants upon earth (Psalm 82:1, 6, 7; Exod. 22:8; 4:16). . . . and their throne is the throne of God, 1 Chron. 22:10 (p. 4).
>
> Magistrates (not the king only but all the princes of the land) and judges are *to maintain religion by their commandments* (Deut. 1:16; 2 Chron. 1:2; Deut. 16:19; Eccles. 5:8; Hab. 1:4; Mic. 3:9; Zech. 7:9; Hos. 5:10-11), and to take care of religion (p. 55).
>
> The king may not dispose of men as men, as he pleaseth; nor of laws as he pleaseth; nor of governing men, killing or keeping alive, punishing and rewarding, as he pleaseth. . . . Therefore, *he hath the trust of life and religion, and hath both tables of the law in his custody* (p. 72; cf. p. 142).
>
> This is the very office or official power which the King of kings hath given to all kings under him, and this is a power of the royal office of a king, *to govern for the Lord his Maker* (p. 72; cf. p. 232).
>
> Now certain it is, God only, univocally and essentially as God, is the judge (Ps. 75:7), and God only and essentially king (Ps. 97:1; 99:1), and all men in relation to him are mere ministers, servants, legates, deputies. . . . And look, as the scribe following his own device, and writing what sentence he pleaseth, is not an officer of the court in that point, nor the pen and servant of the judge, *so are kings and all judges but forged intruders and bastard kings and judges, in so far as they give out the sentences of men, and are not the very mouths of the King of kings to pronounce such a sentence as the Almighty himself would do, if he were sitting on the throne or bench* (pp. 107f.).

In case the significance of Rutherford's statement here escapes you, consider it for a moment. The Almighty Judge has already pronounced the death sentence upon murderers, and it is thus incumbent upon all judges to repeat the sentence, with no qualifications. This means, for instance, with regard to the case of anyone intentionally involved in the murder of unborn children—a practice euphemistically known as "abortion" and "free choice"—that a judge who refuses to repeat God's sentence of death upon such a person is a bastard, according to Rutherford.

---

43. Without a comma, *Lex Rex* means "law is king"; with a comma, *Lex, Rex* means "the law and the prince." The italics in the following quotations are ours. A reprint of this book is available for $8.95 in paperback or $10.95 in hardback from Thoburn Press, P.O. Box 6941, Tyler, TX 75711.

It is hard to imagine Dr. Schaeffer calling for magistrates to "govern for the Lord" and to enforce "both tables of the law" (i.e., the "religious" as well as the "civil" portions of biblical law), as Rutherford insists; nor would he seem to agree that judges are "forged intruders" and "bastards" when they fail to render exactly the same sentence that God Himself would pronounce. In fact, by rejecting theocracy, Dr. Schaeffer has necessarily denied Rutherford's position. For what is the difference between Rutherford's Christian State and a theocracy? If there is no difference, what is Dr. Schaeffer doing in championing Rutherford but condemning theocracy? If there is no difference, why doesn't Dr. Schaeffer embrace theocracy or repudiate Rutherford?

On the other hand, if there *is* a difference—if what Rutherford preaches is *not* "any kind of a theocracy"—then *what* precisely *is* the difference? Even apart from the issue of the rightness of Rutherford's theocratic position, an important question must be faced: What in the world is Dr. Schaeffer talking about?

In Dr. Schaeffer's defense, it might be argued that he has been off in Europe these many years, and is unacquainted with the "Reconstructionist" exposition and elaboration of the Reformed theocratic tradition; thus, being unaware of the work of R. J. Rushdoony and others, it is understandable that Dr. Schaeffer has not seen that theocracy is an "inescapable concept."

That argument can be blown full of holes, but it requires lifting the veil on one of the most well-kept secrets in modern evangelicalism: *Francis Schaeffer has been reading the writings of R. J. Rushdoony for twenty years. In fact, Rev. Rushdoony's thought has been a major influence on the work of Dr. Schaeffer.* This can be proved very easily, but let us make room for a skeptical question: "If that's true, why hasn't Dr. Schaeffer *ever* footnoted his dependence on Rushdoony?" Of course, we cannot fully answer that question, but it is an interesting one. The main reason, we believe, is that *Rev. Rushdoony is a theological hot potato.* He is a self-proclaimed advocate of Old Testament civil law—"theocracy," in Dr. Schaeffer's view (and Rutherford's).

Does Dr. Schaeffer really rely on Rushdoony's work? Consider this, for example: pages 92-93 of Dr. Schaeffer's *Christian Manifesto*, and page 94 of Rev. Rushdoony's *The One and the Many* (1971).

*Rushdoony:*

> The conflict of Christianity with Rome was thus political from the Roman perspective, although religious from the Christian perspective. The Christians were never asked to worship Rome's pagan gods; they were merely asked to recognize the religious primacy of the state. As Francis Legge observed, "The officials of the Roman Empire in a time of persecution sought to force the Christians to sacrifice, not to any heathen gods, but to the Genius of the Emperor and the Fortune of the City of Rome; and at all times the Christians' refusal was looked upon not as a religious but as a political offense. . . ."

*Schaeffer:*

> The early Christians died because they would not obey the state in a civil matter. People often say to us that the early Christians did not show any civil disobedience. They do not know church history. Why were the Christians in the Roman Empire thrown to the lions? From the Christian's viewpoint it was for a religious reason. But from the viewpoint of the Roman State they were in civil disobedience, they were civil rebels. The Roman State did not care what anybody believed religiously; you could believe anything, or you could be an atheist. But you had to worship Caesar as a sign of your loyalty to the state. The Christians said they would not worship Caesar, or anybody, or anything, but the living God. Thus to the Roman Empire they were rebels, and it was civil disobedience. That is why they were thrown to the lions.
>
> Francis Legge in volume one of his book *Forerunners and Rivals of Christianity from 330 B.C. to A.D. 330* writes: "The officials of the Roman Empire in times of persecution sought to force the Christians to sacrifice, not to any heathen gods, but to the Genius of the Emperor and the Fortune of the City of Rome; and at all times the Christians' refusal was looked upon not as a religious but as a political offense."

Striking parallels, don't you think? Especially when you look up what Dr. Schaeffer *does* say in his footnote. He cites only Legge. Now, you should understand that Legge's book is not often cited by scholars; the modern edition is published by University Books, a relatively obscure publishing firm which has specialized in scholarly reprints of books dealing with the occult. In 1964, when Legge's book was reprinted — the edition cited by Dr. Schaeffer in his footnote — Rev. Rushdoony was a member of the Mystic Arts Book Club, University Book's mail-order marketing arm; he even persuaded one of the authors of this essay to join this book club in 1965. In 1965, Dr. Schaeffer was in Switzerland. Can we reasonably guess who found this citation in Legge? But who gets cited by Dr. Schaeffer? Nice, safe, obscure, uncontroversial, but most of all, *non-theocratic* Legge.

There are other examples of Dr. Schaeffer's dependence on Rev. Rushdoony's researches, going all the way back to 1963, when Dr. Schaeffer delivered two lectures based on an early spiral-bound version of Rev. Rushdoony's *This Independent Republic*. (The lectures, entitled "Relativism in the 20th Century," are available on four cassette tapes for $16 from L'Abri Cassettes, P.O. Box 2035, Michigan City, IN 46360; we recommend them highly.) But the spiral-bound version of *This Independent Republic* was published a decade before his book which advocated the imposition of Old Testament civil law, *The Institutes of Biblical Law* (1973). It was not yet clear in 1963 that Rev. Rushdoony is a proponent of theocracy, nor that he is a believer in an optimistic eschatology. Dr. Schaeffer has subsequently seen fit not to footnote his books.

This, of course, is to say nothing of Dr. Schaeffer's vast indebtedness to the work of Cornelius Van Til, under whom he studied apologetics at Westminster Theological Seminary in the 1930s. Consider, for example, Dr. Schaeffer's quasi-Vantillian treatment of the relationship of the Trinity to the One-Many problem in *He Is There and He Is Not Silent* (pp. 14-20). Again, Dr. Schaeffer's published works contain exactly *zero* references to Van Til. (To obtain Prof. Van Til's little-known, still unanswered mimeographed critique of Dr. Schaeffer, "The Apologetic Methodology of Francis A. Schaeffer," write to Geneva Divinity School for information, 708 Hamvasy Ln., Tyler, TX 75701.)

The point here is not to catalogue every missing footnote in the Schaeffer literature. Nor is it to single out Dr. Schaeffer for special censure in this regard, for the same can be said of virtually every prominent leader of the so-called "Christian Right": Without admitting it, they are getting much of their material, their insights, even their slogans, from the Christian Reconstructionists. But since Dr. Schaeffer is widely published and rightly regarded as a major Protestant evangelical philosopher and scholar by the fundamentalist world, one might expect more candor from him. Readers of *Christianity and Civilization* should understand what is going on in the revival of Christian activism, and what has been going on in certain cases for two decades.

What seems to be the case is this: the Christian Reconstructionists forthrightly call for the imposition of biblical law by the civil government, in such cases where the Bible requires the civil government to enforce its law. This is seen by many leaders in the new Christian Right as being theocratic, and therefore forbidden. Whether this or that member of the Christian Reconstructionist movement gets to see his name in footnotes should be personally irrelevant. What *is* relevant is that there has been an active attempt on the part of too many religious leaders to hide the highly controversial source of their conclusions. Their footnotes are conspicuously incomplete. Their readers have not been told where to begin a more detailed search for specifically Christian answers to specific humanist crises.

We bring this up in this essay only to highlight a crucial point: *leaders of the New Christian Right are needlessly avoiding controversies concerning one of the three vital pillars of a consistent Christian apologetic, namely, biblical law.* If we were not convinced that this omission of biblical law from Dr. Schaeffer's apologetic were not undercutting his call to resist the humanist State, we would not have dredged up all this material. (The same comment applies to our criticism of Prof. Van Til's works, whom we also admire.)

The point about Dr. Schaeffer, however, is that he is certainly not ignorant of the theocratic origins of his most incisive political ideas, from Rutherford to Rushdoony; nor can he be ignorant of the fact that he is straddling the fence, halting between two opinions. On the one hand, he doesn't want the "neutrality" of a humanistic State; on the other hand, he doesn't want a full-fledged Christian State, either. So where does that leave us? Should we work for a *half*-fledged Christian State? A "dappled" State?[44] Or should we work toward a State which professes to take no sides on religious issues, but which merely strives for "justice" and "humanity" and "morality" in terms of lowest-common-denominator pluralism? Problem: the lowest-common-denominator principle is what got us into this mess in the first place.

The fact remains that *Dr. Schaeffer's manifesto offers no prescriptions for a Christian society.* We mention that merely in the interests of clarity, for we are not sure that anybody has noticed it up to now. The same comment applies to *all* of Dr.

44. "Glory be to God for dappled things." Gerard Manley Hopkins.

Schaeffer's writings: he does not spell out the Christian alternative. He knows that "you can't fight something with nothing," but as a premillennialist, he does not expect to win the fight prior to the visible, bodily return of Jesus Christ to earth to establish His millennial kingdom.

When Dr. Schaeffer finally gets down to his "bottom line," it turns out to be simply the fact that "at a certain point there is not only the right, but the duty, to disobey the state" (p. 120). Hear, hear! We're glad he said that, particularly after decades of mush-mouthed, spineless, lily-livered, craven milksops telling us that no matter what the State does, we mustn't resist, we mustn't worry our pretty little heads about such things, and we should just leave politics to the *men*, i.e. the non-Christians. (The fact that we are seeing the rise of "evangelical homosexuals" shouldn't surprise anyone; evangelicals have been "politically effeminate" for 50 years.) So Dr. Schaeffer is a welcome alternative to pietistic tapioca. If he were not so forthright in his opinions concerning our moral obligation to oppose an immoral State, we would not bother to spend this much space in analyzing *A Christian Manifesto*.

Is the *bottom line* of Christian resistance simply our right to get our bottoms lined up against the wall and shot? Martyrdom has its place, of course. But what if a Christian resistance movement were *successful?* What if Christians began to find political power being given into their hands? Is there any hint in Dr. Schaeffer's work about what they should try to do? No—only the stern warning against any kind of a theocracy. Well, *what* then? Surely, Dr. Schaeffer wants us to do something.

He almost stumbled onto the path leading to theocracy on page 136. "What is needed at this time is to take the steps necessary to break the authoritarian hold which the material-energy, chance concept of final reality has on government and law." Right. But first, what is needed at this time is to *tell us* the steps necessary. He provides *no steps*. This drastically reduces the practical importance of his book. We can find a bottom line, but no top lines. No place to go, no way to get there, no way to get out of here—in short, *no recommended concrete program of resistance, let alone victory.*

He *does* say that the consequence of taking the aforesaid mysterious "steps" would be wonderful, however. A positive flowering of culture: "The result would be freedom for all and especially freedom for all religion. That was the original purpose of the First Amendment" (*ibid.*). But is any of this possible? Can we achieve a godly society under pluralism? Have we achieved it in the past under pluralism? Furthermore, is he correct in his assessment of the First Amendment?

On this point about the purpose of the First Amendment being "freedom for all religion," we believe that Dr. Schaeffer is mistaken, and we know of a dandy little book that will correct his understanding on this point. The book is called *A Christian Manifesto*, and on pages 34-39 it effectively demonstrates that the United States began, defectively but substantially, as a *Christian* nation (or, more precisely, *a union of Christian states*)[45] – that, in fact, the First Amendment actually *protected* the existence of established state churches. Admittedly, the relationship of Christianity to the civil government in the early life of our nation was somewhat ambivalent and confusing, but not nearly so ambivalent and confusing as *A Christian Manifesto* is.

Once we get freedom of religion going, however, Dr. Schaeffer says, "Reformation Christianity would compete in the free marketplace of ideas" (p. 136f.). Just like in the Bible – remember? From this point of view, God handed Moses the Ten Suggestions, and said: "Run this up the flagpole, Moses. Set it out there in the Free Marketplace of Ideas. Of course, being a Libertarian at heart, I've got to acknowledge that some people might not like My ideas. They might want to sacrifice their children to Molech instead. Well, that's the way the civilization crumbles."

We should not mix categories. Religious competition is not a commercial activity – or shouldn't be, anyway. A "free marketplace" is a place to sell soap. When it is used as a metaphor for religious confrontation it is either meaningless or deceptive. In fact, it is the triumph of Christianity alone which ensures the existence of a free marketplace for soap. But remember: *When Dr. Schaeffer argues against theocracy and for "religious liberty," he is advocating neutrality.* Similarly, *when Dr. Schaeffer argues against neutrality, he is advocating theocracy.* This was the point of the essay on the myth of neutrality in the first

45. The Constitution was not meant to create a unitary State, but rather a union of states. Therefore, its purpose was not to create a unitary national religion. It allowed the various Christian states to maintain their varying Christian traditions. In fact, it *prohibited* the central government from *interfering with* these varying, but explicitly Christian, traditions.

issue of *Christianity and Civilization*, specifically, the question of "religious liberty" and Christian education:

> Education is deeply religious. So is any system of legislation. We cannot escape religion. There is no neutrality. *Everyone uses the neutrality doctrine in order to create his own version of theocracy:* humanist theocracy (man is God), Marxist theocracy (the proletariat is God), anarchist theocracy (the free market is God), or whatever. They use the doctrine of religious liberty to enthrone an anti-Christian social order —an order which does not allow Christians to establish their God-ordained theocracy. . . . In short, those using the religious liberty argument say that they are maintaining a society open to all religions, when in fact it will be *a society closed to the God of the Bible and His law-order.*[46]

If this is correct, then how can we escape the conclusion?

> The defense of Christian education today is therefore schizophrenic. The defenders argue that there is no neutral education, yet they use the modern doctrine of religious liberty to defend themselves—a doctrine which relies on the myth of neutrality in order to sustain itself. As a tactic, it is legitimate; we are jockeying for power. We are buying time. *But anyone who really believes in the modern doctrine of religious liberty has no option but to believe in some variant of the myth of neutrality.* Those who have abandoned the latter should also abandon the former.[47]

So—it looks as though we have a choice of three possibilities: 1) *Dr. Schaeffer is a closet theocrat*, masking his real views with certain neutralist language in order to buy time for a biblical law-order; 2) *Dr. Schaeffer is a closet neutralist*, masking his real views with certain theocratic language in order to buy time for a humanistic law-order; or 3) *Dr. Schaeffer is a closet schizophrenic*, masking his serious confusion by alternately using neutralist and theocratic language with random, promiscuous abandon, not really understanding the difference between the two.

It really is a shame, the way *A Christian Manifesto* turned out, especially when you consider its predecessors. The *Communist Manifesto* does not have mere "resistance to capitalism" as its bottom line. It calls for *dominion*, and gives a concrete, numbered *program* for achieving the takeover of the world. It outlines a cause, and sets forth a goal in terms of which hun-

---

46. Gary North, "The Intellectual Schizophrenia of the New Christian Right," in Jordan, ed., *Failure of American Baptist Culture*, pp. 23f.

47. *Ibid.*, p. 25.

dreds of thousands have fought to the death—and won. The two *Humanist Manifestos* are not so romantic as the *Communist Manifesto*, but they too give a specific plan of action for world domination, and they, too, have been very effective. Even most evangelicals think in terms of humanist categories by now.

Then there was Nigel Lee's *Christian Manifesto of 1984* (printed elsewhere in this volume), originally published in 1974. It positively drips with confidence and assurance of victory—the inevitability of Christianity. And it gives a program for accomplishing its goals. It deals with strategy and tactics. It is written in terms of a clear, objective, identifiable standard. It is highly motivational. With Nigel Lee's manifesto, you could raise an army. What kind of army will we raise with Dr. Schaeffer's manifesto?[48] And what will it accomplish if we do?

Is this too harsh? Normally, a book's *potential* is no greater than its *message*. The message we need is an answer to a question Lenin asked—a question which had been asked by numerous Russian revolutionaries before him. Lenin's answer to it overthrew a government: *What Is to Be Done?* If our "manifestos" fail to answer this absolutely crucial question, we should not be surprised when alien religions take the podium.

Is Dr. Schaeffer's manifesto worthless? Not at all. Its chief value will be in its "toughening up" quality, mentioned previously. There will be some who will read it, become motivated by it, and then realize that there *must* be more. They will realize that Schaeffer's position, although well stated, is untenable. It hesitates between two incompatible views: a society built in terms of the myth of neutrality and a society built upon the specifics of God's revealed law.

### *"Equal Time for Jesus"*

*A Christian Manifesto* has fundamental weaknesses, as we have seen. But these weaknesses are not simply random. They are part and parcel of a pattern of weaknesses that has afflicted apologetics in general, and Dr. Schaeffer's apologetics in particular, from the beginning. We have already mentioned these three weaknesses: 1) an unwillingness to make a definitive

48. Gary North, "What Kind of Army?" *Christian Reconstruction*, IV (July/Aug., 1980).

break with "common ground" philosophy; 2) a failure to recognize the eschatological implications of the expansionary and culture-transforming power of the gospel in history; and 3) an unwillingness to affirm biblical law as the tool of personal and social reconstruction. (Even Dr. Schaeffer's commitment to Calvinism is compromised; he does not speak about the predestinarian faith he personally believes in, and which his denomination is officially committed to by its proclamation of the *Westminster Confession of Faith*. Anyone unfamiliar with this document should read Chapter III, to get a better understanding of Dr. Schaeffer's views, and ours.)

These three tendencies have led to three consistent and disastrous conclusions within the realm of political theory: 1) religious pluralism as the only valid long-term political goal for Christians; 2) satisfaction with the attainment of legal freedom to preach a narrow gospel of personal salvation but not social reconstruction; and 3) satisfaction with almost any presently prevailing (or recently abandoned) system of civil law which proclaims itself to be "natural" and therefore based on "universal moral principles." We can summarize these three political goals in one phrase: *equal time for Jesus*.

What we must understand is that this political goal—"equal time for Jesus"—is a consistent application of all non-Vantillian apologetic methodologies. They, too, want to proclaim equal time for Jesus. They proclaim this message: "Faith in Jesus makes more sense than faith in any other god or system." Prof. Van Til spent his life demonstrating how such a claim is inconsistent with the Bible, for the Bible claims that *only* the God of creation is the source of truth, facts, and logic. Van Til also showed how the claim that Christianity is merely more logical than other systems is more acceptable to non-believers than an absolutely sovereign Christianity because such a claim is consistent with the presuppositions of non-Christian systems. Why? Because it denies the absolute authority of Jesus. The concept of a Jesus who is "most probably" the Son of God—who claims to come in the name of a religion which has only comparatively *more* likelihood of being the true religion than all other religions—is not the Son of the Creator God of Scripture. Such a pussyfooting Jesus must be the son of an equally pussyfooting god. Non-Christians can safely and *logically* neglect the claims of such a god. They have not been confronted with the God of Scripture, His authoritative word, and His omnipotent, resurrected Son. This is the heart of Prof. Van Til's criticisms of all "rational" apologetic methodologies: they do not confront the ethical rebel with the comprehensive and absolute claims of the God of Scripture. The Bible says that we are in an *all-or-nothing* confrontation, in the final analysis, for on the day of the final judgment, there will be no neutral zones of safety for those who have rejected the gospel. We need an apologetic approach which is not apologetic. We need to come to grips with Schlossberg's analysis:

> . . . what is widely regarded as a struggle between the religious and the secular is really a struggle between religions. The current strife over such issues as abortion is perfectly in order, because it is an attempt by both sides to establish a rule of order in accordance with basic religious precepts. Man is the autonomous ruler of himself, able to define right and wrong and frame statutes according to whatever he defines as just. Or else man is created and sustained by a holy and just God who declares on matters of right and wrong in the form of law. Both are religious views held by faith. In the most basic sense there is no such thing as a secular culture. This is not a call for religious warfare; it is an assertion that religious warfare exists, and inevitably so if one religion does not simply surrender.[49]

The humanists do not intend to surrender. Until we understand their strategy, we cannot expect to defeat it, as Sun Tzu warned so long ago. Our opponents understand what so few Christians have yet to recognize: "You don't fight something with nothing." The "religious pluralism" allowed in the West from about 1648 on, was possible only because the two warring sides were Christian in perspective. Rulers agreed on many of the fundamentals of civic justice because their universe of discourse — the "climate of opinion" — was still essentially Christian. The humanists were isolated in the seventeenth century. They flourished primarily in Italy and France; the Renaissance had been checked elsewhere by the Reformation.

Christians in the United States did not face a malevolent humanism as late as 1789, the year after the Constitution was adopted; Christians in France did, but they did not know it until a year or two later. The Constitution was written before Robespierre had made his public appearance. The guillotines were not yet in public squares in 1789. Lenin was not yet

49. Schlossberg, *Idols for Destruction*, p. 275.

born. And babies in the United States were not being aborted by the millions annually.

Let us ask Dr. Schaeffer the question which follows from the crusade he has called us to join: *Should abortionists have equal time in the delivery room*? No? Then how are they to be kept out? By what means? By what legislation? In short, *by what standard*?

And if abortionists should not be allowed to ply their trade, what about other trades? Do we allow prime-time pornography over the airwaves? Do we allow heroin dealers to provide drugs to eight-year-olds in exchange for homosexual favors? If not, why not? *By what standard*?

The apologetic method of Dr. Schaeffer has never made a clean break with the rationalists. It has also never made a clean break with the evidentialists. It has never confronted the humanists with a positive, all-encompassing philosophical and cultural alternative. Neither have the apologetic methodologies used by the vast majority of Christians. Until only recently, when the issue of abortion had to be faced by Christians as an all-or-nothing crusade, Christians have refused to make a clean break from humanism's supposed neutral morality. They still hesitate, for it would mean breaking with the politics of religious pluralism. So far, they have not been able to make up their minds. They prefer not to think about the problem. They decry the myth of neutrality, while they simultaneously call for religious pluralism as the only valid political goal for Christians. They want only "equal time for Jesus."

The humanists now are afraid. The abortion issue has forced Christians to make a clean break, and to begin a major confrontation. It has pulled Dr. Schaeffer out of Switzerland and into the political battle. And the rhetoric of Christians concerning abortion is having its effects in other areas of life, including apologetics. If there can be no compromise with abortion, then there may be other areas in life in which there can be no compromise with evil. Thus, Christians are beginning to deal with the effects of rival philosophies: Christ's vs. everyone else's.

### *Bottom-Up Theocracy*

The fear of a Bible-based theocracy on the part of most Christians and all humanists rests on a partial misunderstanding. Most people think of theocracy as a social system modelled along the lines of ancient Egypt, with a top-down pyramid structure run by priests and kings. That is indeed Satan's version. It is the heart and soul of Marxist regimes, modern socialist societies, and the elitist dreams of Darwinistic scientific planners.[50]

In contrast to this sort of theocracy is the ideal of a Christian holy commonwealth. It is fundamentally *decentralist*. Its bedrock presupposition is *self-government under the law of God.* This is what Jethro told Moses that he must do, and Moses did: "And thou shalt teach them [all the people of Israel] ordinances and laws, and shalt shew them the way wherein they must walk, and the work they must do" (Ex. 18:20). First and foremost, *teach the people of God the laws of God.* All government begins with *self-government.* All discipline begins with *self-discipline.* All men stand alone before God on the day of judgment; they are personally responsible to God.

Next, every institution of society is brought under the law of God by the increasingly self-disciplined Christians who honor the law of God: the family, the church, private business, local agencies of civil government, and only then the more distant agencies of civil government. This is the foundation of all Christian resistance to tyranny: one's reliance upon already reconstructed local agencies of government—and not just *civil* government—in order to challenge the humanist-dominated distant agencies of civil government. This is the so-called doctrine of *interposition.*[51]

How do we begin to build a biblical theocracy? By beginning with ourselves. We read the five books of Moses, the prophets, and the New Testament in search of guidelines for ourselves personally and for all human institutions. We read commentaries on biblical law, such as R. J. Rushdoony's two-volume set, *The Institutes of Biblical Law*, and Greg L. Bahnsen's *Theonomy in Christian Ethics.* We must take seriously God's moral and legal guidelines.

Then we vote in terms of these laws. We will also sit on juries and vote in terms of these guidelines. We use juries, if possible, to nullify the ability of the civil government to im-

50. Gary North, *The Dominion Covenant: Genesis*, Appendix A: "From Cosmic Impersonalism to Humanistic Sovereignty."

51. Tom Rose, "On Reconstruction and the American Republic," in Gary North, ed., *The Theology of Christian Resistance*, Christianity and Civilization No. 2 (Tyler, TX: Geneva Divinity School Press, 1982).

pose God-defying laws on our fellow citizens, as Michael Gilstrap describes in his essay in this journal. Nullification by colonial juries is what drove the British to despair in the years preceding the American Revolution: They could not easily get juries to convict colonial violators of the statutes of the British Empire's bureaucracy, especially in matters regarding smuggling. It was so "bad" in the late seventeenth century, that England had to set up Admiralty Courts in 1696 that alone were empowered to try cases regarding smuggling violations. These special courts did not allow trial by jury.[52] The American Act of 1764 expanded the authority of these courts to all intercolonial trade, not just ships trading on the high seas. Furthermore, the court where the trial was to be held was in remote Halifax, Nova Scotia.[53] Then came the revolution.

Theocracy is government by God's law—not just in the realm of civil government, but *all* government. It is not a top-down imposition of biblical law by an elite of priests, but, in contrast, *a bottom-up imposition of biblical standards over every area of life*—areas not regulated by civil law for the most part—by Christians who are morally responsible and legally empowered to make decisions. As the process of dominion extends the authority of Christians over more and more areas of life, we will see the creation of a comprehensive theocracy.

A truly biblical theocracy will not come as the result of some sort of "palace revolution," but as a result of millions of God-fearing people working to extend the reign of Christ over every area of life. In all likelihood, the last institutions brought under the rule of biblical law will be the central civil governments of the world. (No, come to think of it, the central civil government will be the next-to-last institution captured by Christ; the last institution will be the tax-supported university.)

In short, we are arguing that the theocracy of secular humanism now reigns in the West. What Christians must recognize, and then learn to resist, is *theocratic humanism*. In the United States, theocratic humanism is a system of rule by a tiny minority of humanists over a vast majority of confused, intellectually compromised, hesitant Christians. What we

52. Charles M. Andrews, *The Colonial Period of American History* (4 vols.; New Haven, Connecticut: Yale University Press, [1938] 1964), IV. ch. VIII: "The Vice-Admiralty Courts."

53. Bernard Knollenberg, *Origins of the American Revolution, 1759-1766* (New York: Free Press, [1961] 1968), ch. 15.

need, therefore, is for this vast majority of Christians to rediscover their spiritual heritage and the power which this heritage offers to those who conform themselves to God's law (Deut. 28:1-14). Then, and only then, will a truly majoritarian Christian theocracy be established, and the elitist theocracy of secular humanism driven, by personal example but also by civil law, out of the land and eventually from the face of the earth.

Such a forecast may not be fully accepted or understood by most of today's fundamentalists, including Dr. Schaeffer. It is understood, however, by the humanists who see what is coming if several generations of Christian day school graduates start entering the society. Like the rulers of Israel in Jesus' day who understood His prophecy about His rising from the dead, and who rolled a stone in front of the tomb in an attempt to prevent His disciples from carrying away the body and claiming that He had risen, the modern humanist elite is worried. And like Jesus' disciples on the weekend of the resurrection, modern Christians have fled from the scene, not realizing what our Lord has promised.

R. J. Rushdoony has called attention to the implications of modern eschatologies of earthly defeat, in his study of the Book of Daniel:

> Daniel is political prophecy, and it is confident prophecy, declaring the certain victory of the kingdom of God (*not* to be confused with or limited to the institutional church, which is one manifestation thereof), in history. If the victory of Christ is to be eschatological only, and in terms only of an eternal order, then Daniel is a monstrous piece of irrelevance. The sorry tribulation-complex of a smug and self-satisfied church, surrounded by ease and luxury, is certainly an amazing fact, one surely indicative of a masochistic desire for self-atonement by means of suffering. But the whole of Scripture proclaims the certainty of God's victory in time and in eternity, and the resurrection is the bold and uncompromising declaration of that victory in time. *There can be no retreat from victory without a corresponding retreat from Christ.* The Great Commission, which its confident command to make disciples of all nations (Matt. 28:19), was no mere hyperbole or vain expression of wistful hope, but the assured promise of Him who could say, "All power is given unto me in heaven and in earth" (Matt. 28:18), "Go ye therefore" (Matt. 28:19). Unhappily, since the day of Calvary, the church has all too often been concerned

> with embalming Christ, while His enemies, a little more realistically, have sought vainly to guard themselves from His power. It is high time to proclaim the power of His resurrection.
>
> The resurrection is given in Daniel 12:2 as the keynote of the gospel age, i.e., of the latter days. The "day" or time of resurrection began with the resurrection of Jesus Christ, so that Christians live in the resurrection era. The age has its tribulations, its battles unto death, but its essence for the Christian is victory unto life. Because of the resurrection of Jesus Christ, it cannot be otherwise.[54]

We live in the "resurrection age." Christ rose from the dead, definitively overcoming our most powerful enemy. The church rose in history, and is now in the process of conquering in the name of the resurrected Christ. At the final resurrection, the conquest will be complete (I Cor. 15).

Pharisees and humanists, please take note. *Your days are numbered.* When the church finally ceases its attempt to embalm Christ in history, it will overcome all your efforts.

### *Conclusion*

We are in a fight. There will be winners and losers. On the day of judgment, there will be no prisoners. *Our apologetic methodology must therefore reflect the all-or-nothing nature of the confrontation between God and Satan.* The defeat of Satan is sure, for it was a definitive defeat at Calvary. There is no necessity of hiding from ourselves the all-or-nothing nature of the confrontation. Compromise here leads to compromise everywhere.

We must proclaim the sovereignty of God. Nothing else guarantees our victory. Nothing else ratifies our confidence in Christ's definitive victory over Satan at Calvary, and His final victory over Satan at the end of time. If God is not sovereign, then Christ's victory at Calvary is not assured. If we do not believe in the absolute sovereignty of God, then we are logically forced to admit that Satan may yet wriggle out of his predicament, if he gets lucky enough. This is the doctrine of *chance*.

Unlike most fundamentalists who are involved in the battle against humanism, Dr. Schaeffer believes in the sovereignty of God. Unfortunately, the doctrine of the sovereignty

54. R. J. Rushdoony, *Thy Kingdom Come: Studies in Daniel and Revelation* (Fairfax, VA: Thoburn Press, [1970] 1978), pp. 84f.

of God is not the bedrock claim of each and every book he writes in the field of philosophy. His fundamentalist readers do not know that he is a member of a Calvinistic church (Presbyterian Church in America), and that he is more Calvinistic than most of its pastors. In neither of Mrs. Schaeffer's books about her husband does this fact receive much (if any) discussion. Again, *it has been characteristic of Dr. Schaeffer's apologetic method to avoid some desperately needed confrontations*: either with the humanists (whose common-ground philosophy he still partially uses) or with the fundamentalists (who would be alienated by a forthright presentation of his Calvinistic theology).

What we need is *a theology of confrontation*. We need a fully developed philosophy which says plainly, "Christ or chaos, God's law or tyranny." We have not been presented with a full-scale version of such a philosophy by Francis Schaeffer or the leaders of the fundamentalist world. But the humanists can nevertheless sense where the Christians are headed. Abortion has provided an inescapable issue, and the Christians have chosen to fight. An army is being raised up. The leaders of this army are still operating in terms of compromised apologetic methods of an earlier era. Because of this, Dr. Schaeffer has offered us only half a manifesto. But there will be other leaders and other manifestos soon. The humanists cannot chase this army away. And as it crosses the valley toward the Philistines, many of the troops are quietly picking up the stones that Dr. Schaeffer has left behind.

To conclude, we are arguing that in order for a successful full-scale Christian counter-offensive to be launched *and completed* against the humanist civilization of our day, Christians must adopt and then operate in terms of four fundamental doctrines: 1) the absolute and unqualified sovereignty of God; 2) the absolute and unqualified self-sufficiency of Scripture, meaning a presuppositional apologetic; 3) an optimistic eschatology; and 4) the continuing validity and binding character of biblical law. Few Christians will affirm even one of these doctrines today. Until the bulk of those who serve in the Christian resistance movement do, the humanists will be able to disregard the Christian resistance movement, except as an annoyance.

Our conclusion will not be accepted by most of those necessarily dedicated people who are in the Christian resistance movement at this time, let alone by those Christians who are not connected with it. We understand this. This is why we do not expect this preliminary phase of Christian resistance to experience very much success. It will serve as a training ground, just as the wilderness served the younger generation of Israelites who were allowed to enter the promised land.

This is not to say that individual Christians who do not affirm all four doctrines cannot be successful resisters. Lots of people will develop skills necessary to resist bureaucratic tyranny, including many non-Christians. But a Christian resistance movement as a whole which is not motivated generally by all four beliefs will not achieve long-term, comprehensive success. Such a movement will not be able to construct *a Christian social alternative*, which must be the earthly goal of any serious Christian resistance movement. God will not honor the cause of those who do not rely on Him utterly—not on human decisions, human logic, human will ("heroic" or "free"), or human efforts. We cannot defeat Satan by proclaiming even the partial sovereignty of man. After all, the partial sovereignty of man is his most successful lie (Gen. 3:5).

# II. DEFENSIVE STRATEGIES OF CHRISTIAN RESISTANCE

## THE ESCALATING CONFRONTATION WITH BUREAUCRACY

Gary North

> Now there arose up a new king over Egypt which knew not Joseph. And he said unto his people, Behold, the people of the children of Israel are more and mightier than we. Come on, let us deal wisely with them; lest they multiply, and it come to pass, that, when there falleth out any war, they join also unto our enemies, and fight against us, and so get them up out of the land. Therefore they did set over them taskmasters to afflict them with their burdens. And they built for Pharaoh treasure cities, Pithom and Raamses. But the more they afflicted them, the more they multiplied and grew. And they were grieved because of the children of Israel (Ex. 1:8-12).

THE Pharaoh of Moses' day understood the threat to Egypt posed by the rapidly growing population of the Israelites. But he had become dependent on their productivity. Instead of killing them, he enslaved them. He wanted the fruits of their labor; he was not willing to pay the necessary cost of eliminating this threat to his kingdom. His strategy failed; the more he enslaved them, the faster their numbers grew. There was an *escalation of oppression* which was matched by an *escalation of counterforce capabilities*. In the case of the Hebrews, their counterforce response was not only effective, it was one of the few sources of pleasure they possessed. They gave it everything they had.

Throughout history, this is a recurring experience. *Bureaucratic kingdoms are essentially parasitic*. They are forever in search of new hosts to sustain them. They are always dependent on the more productive members of society to provide them with surplus wealth. Furthermore, as bureaucracy grows, it absorbs more and more production. The capital reserves of the civilization are drained off into unproductive activities. Kingdoms always construct pyramids of one sort or another—vast projects that produce nothing except a sense of awe and resentment.

To replace these economic reserves, kingdoms need to enlist the cooperation of productive citizens. But the growth of the empire drains more than economic reserves; it eventually drains the willingness of its citizens to take risks, to save for the future, and to build familistic capital. The economic incentive provided by the uncertainties of the market is lost. Men rely on the State to care for them. Fewer and fewer people are willing to supply the capital needed for the future tax base.

The empire eventually may resort to conquest and slavery to sustain itself. But the costs of war increase as supply lines grow long and the costs of administering conquered enemies increase. The level of resistance increases abroad, both among conquered enemies and more distant unconquered enemies. The slaves need direction, and they constitute a permanent source of potential allies for foreign enemies (Ex. 1:10). But the parasite always needs new hosts. The empire continues to intensify its search for new sources of productivity to confiscate. There is no escape, except to abandon the empire's top-down system of control, which is capital-absorbing and resistance-producing, and to adopt the biblical standard of the republic under God: *a bottom-up system of decentralized responsibility and a court appeal system* (Ex. 18).[1] This is what no empire is ever willing to do on a voluntary basis. The empires of history are always smashed; they never reform themselves.[2]

Because the empire is dependent on what it can extract by force from productive people, its administrators have an innate resistance to the idea of destroying productive minorities. When God's faithful remnant is productive, because the people are faithful to God's laws and are therefore blessed by God, the theologically hostile State has a tendency to tolerate its presence. The appeal made by the leaders of the early church

---

1. Gary North, *Unconditional Surrender: God's Program for Victory* (2nd ed.; Tyler, TX: Geneva Divinity School Press 1983), ch. 6.

2. We see this in Daniel's explanation of Nebuchadnezzar's dream. The idol represented a series of kingdoms (Dan. 2:31-45): Babylon, Medo-Persia, Alexander's, and Rome: R. J. Rushdoony, *Thy Kingdom Come: Studies in Daniel and Revelation* (Fairfax, VA: Thoburn Press, [1971] 1978), p. 16. Babylon fell to the Medes and Persians; the Medo-Persians fell to Alexander. Alexander's empire broke into four parts, and these were later conquered by Rome. This sequence of events is outlined in Daniel 8:3-12: *ibid.*, pp. 58-62.

to Rome was constant: "We are the most law-abiding, most productive members of this society. Let us alone and you will benefit."

Tertullian's *Apology*, written around the year 200 A.D., is only one of many such documents, though one of the most eloquent.[3] He stated his case in no uncertain terms: the Roman authorities *needed* the growing Christian minority:

> We are but of yesterday, and we have filled every place among you—cities, islands, fortresses, towns, market-places, the very camp, tribes, companies, palace, senate, forum—we have left nothing to you but the temples of your gods. . . . For if such multitudes of men were to break away from you, and betake themselves to some remote corner of the world, why, the very loss of so many citizens, whatever sort they were, would cover the empire with shame; nay, in the very forsaking, vengeance would be inflicted. Why, you would be horror-struck at the solitude in which you would find yourselves, at such an all-prevailing silence, and that stupor as of a dead world. You would seek to have subjects to govern. You would have more enemies than citizens remaining. For now it is the immense number of Christians which makes your enemies so few—almost all the inhabitants of your various cities being followers of Christ. Yet you choose to call us enemies of the human race, rather than of human error. Nay, who would deliver you from those secret foes, ever busy both destroying your souls and ruining your health?[4]

Intermittent persecutions by the Roman Empire always were replaced by periods of toleration. Rome's authorities could not afford the costs of imposing endless persecution on Christian people. During periods of persecution, the church was strengthened by a kind of scraping away of the marginally faithful, but the persecutions did not last long enough to wipe out the institution as a whole. As F. F. Bruce writes: "What did the Christians do by way of reaction to the persecution which befell them from time to time? First and foremost, they maintained their faith and continued to propagate it so successfully that their numbers went on increasing."[5]

3. Tertullian, *Apology*, in *The Ante-Nicene Fathers* (Grand Rapids, MI: Eerdmans, 1978), III.

4. *Ibid.*, Bk. XXXVII.

5. F. F. Bruce, *The Spreading Flame: The Rise and Progress of Christianity from its First Beginnings to the Conversion of the English* (Grand Rapids, MI: Eerdmans, 1958), p. 176.

### *The Failure of Our "Early Warning System"*

Why are our churches under attack by the State today? For the same reason that they were under attack in the days of Tertullian: *the church represents an alien theology.* It teaches principles that, when applied in society in general, create a social order which replaces the top-down hierarchy of empire with a decentralized, bottom-up system of personal responsibility. Personal self-government under God replaces coercive civil government. The church's rival theology is simultaneously a rival social theory.[6] There can be no permanent truce between God's society and Satan's.[7] This confrontation extends to every area of life, to every institution. There can be no long-term neutrality.

The churches find themselves temporarily outgunned and undermanned in today's confrontation with the State because conservative, Bible-believing preachers have not been reliable pastors for four generations. They have not called the attention of church members to the inescapable conflict between the society of Satan and God's society. They have not set forth the principles of righteous, God-ordained civil government, generation after generation. *They have neglected the law of God.* This was also the sin of the Levites in ancient Israel, and it led to the apostasy and subsequent enslavement of Israel on several occasions.

Pastors have not preached that taxation at 10% or above is immoral by biblical standards (I Sam. 8:15, 17), since it elevates the State to the level of the church, which alone can legitimately collect 10% of one's increase. They have not warned the flock constantly against fiat money, fractional reserve banking, and the Federal Reserve System, which debases the currency unit, in direct violation of the biblical requirements of honest weights and measures.[8] Christians were

6. R. J. Rushdoony, *Foundations of Social Order: Studies in the Creeds and Councils of the Early Church* (Fairfax, VA: Thoburn Press, [1968] 1978). Reviewed in depth in *Preface 1,* published by the Institute for Christian Economics, P.O. Box 8000, Tyler, TX 75711.

7. R. J. Rushdoony, "The Society of Satan" (1964); reprinted in *Biblical Economics Today*, II (Oct./Nov., 1979). Published by the Institute for Christian Economics.

8. Gary North, *An Introduction to Christian Economics* (Nutley, NJ: Craig Press, 1973), ch. 1.

politically silent in the United States in 1913, when the sixteenth amendment was passed, establishing the Federal income tax, the same year in which the Federal Reserve System was created.

From the end of the Civil War until the 1960s, conservative critics of the Social Gospel movement had no systematic, Bible-based criticism of the liberals' social, political, and economic programs. The Social Gospel had its critics, but the critics never attempted to offer a full-scale biblical alternative set of programs. Even Robert L. Dabney, the great Southern Presbyterian theologian and social philosopher of the late nineteenth century (and Gen. Thomas "Stonewall" Jackson's chaplain), appealed continually to natural reason rather than the Bible to defend his belief in the free market.[9] (He taught political philosophy at the University of Texas at the end of the nineteenth century.) The same was true of J. Gresham Machen, who was a nineteenth-century liberal in his economic views—a defender of limited civil government. He fought the Social Gospel's theological presuppositions with biblical arguments, especially in *Christianity and Liberalism* (1923), but not the economic conclusions of the movement. Ronald Sider's *Rich Christians in an Age of Hunger* (1977) went unchallenged until 1981, when David Chilton (a theonomist) and John Robbins (a follower of Gordon Clark) published their critiques.[10]

The pastors were silent for over a century. They did not cry out in horror when the Social Security program was initiated in the late 1930s. They even signed up when they were made "eligible" in the mid-1950s, despite the warnings of a handful of "John the Baptists" who cried in the wilderness.[11] Now the handful who did not sign up are being forced into the program, with their churches about to be forced to pay half the tax directly to the Federal government—taxing an "employer"

9. Robert L. Dabney, *Discussions*, Vol. IV, Secular (P.O. Box 1094, Harrisonburg, VA: Sprinkle Publications, [1897] 1979).

10. David Chilton, *Productive Christians in an Age of Guilt-Manipulators* (Tyler, TX: Institute for Christian Economics, 1981); John Robbins, "Ronald Sider *Contra Deum*," *The Trinity Review* (1981); reprinted in *Biblical Economics Today*, V (Apr./May, 1982).

11. Francis Mahaffy, "A Clergyman's Security," *The Freeman* (1957); reprinted in *Tentmakers*, III (Jan./Feb., 1980). Published by the Institute for Christian Economics.

—so that pastors now face the grim choice of having to acknowledge implicitly that the church, as a church, is under the jurisdiction of the State. *And most churches will pay up, if they have not been paying since the 1950s, leaving only a handful of small churches to make the case for the sovereignty of the church by refusing to pay.*

Yet it should be obvious that the churches must not pay any tax of any kind directly to the civil government. The elders of every church in the land should immediately hold a meeting and insert into the minutes and the By-Laws of the church a statement denying the right of the civil government to tax the church of God, and affirming as a matter of principle that no elder or representative of the church can write a check to any branch of civil government which involves the payment of a tax on the church. Checks written as withholding payments are merely taxes owed by individual employees; the Social Security tax is a tax directly on the church as an employer.

If necessary, the pastor should forfeit his status as an employee of the church (and possibly forfeit his housing allowance deduction), and become an independent contractor. He then pays his Social Security taxes each quarter in his estimated tax payment (Form 1040 ES). But the By-Laws of the church should be amended to deny the right of any church official to pay any tax imposed on the church itself.

### *Temporary Exemptions*

In the mid-1940s, the Labor Party in Britain decided to create a system of State-financed national health care. They knew that they would not readily gain cooperation from the private physicians of Britain. So the Labor Party created a plan. First, they made it illegal for non-participating physicians to sell their practices upon retirement, thereby extracting a major capital tax from the physicians. Second, they offered relatively high salaries (for the post-war years) to all participating physicians. Third, they offered high positions in the new, compulsory system to the leaders of the British Medical Association. Nye Bevan, the Labor Party's master political strategist, who served as Minister of Health, promised Party leaders that the Party would gain the support of the medical profession's leadership. "How?" he was asked. His answer shall ring down through the ages: "We shall stuff their mouths with gold." So the Labor Party did, and the medical leadership capitulated, just as Bevan had predicted.

Then came the grim reality: larger and larger case loads, coupled with a salary freeze. The medical profession was trapped. They had been given the initial benefits to gain their cooperation, and then the trap was sprung.

So it has been with pastors in the United States since 1913. Their churches were for seventy years exempted from all property taxation. No longer. Beginning in 1913, the churches were exempted from having to pay taxes as employers. No longer (as of 1984). Pastors have received remarkable income tax exemptions, such as the dual exemption on housing: a tax-free housing allowance, plus the standard interest-rate deduction on all mortgage interest on their homes. No longer. This two-pronged exemption was available only to pastors — a special subsidy to silence the opposition. And it has worked! The pastors did not feel the pain that higher-income congregation members did. They did not preach against the envy-based nature of the "progressive" (graduated) income tax. Now they are being forced into high brackets as a result of the price inflation created by fiat money. Will they protest successfully now?

The churches' tax exemptions were acknowledged by English common law — a law-order heavily influenced by the Bible — in the days of lower taxation. In the old days, the exemption did not mean that much. The legal right to receive tax-deductible donations did not mean much of anything in the days prior to the Federal income tax. Today, however, the churches are as hooked on tax-deductible donations as any heroin addict is hooked on heroin. They will suffer withdrawal pains if they lose their various exemptions. They are too deeply in debt to get their income cut off without suffering great pain. In short, *the statists bought the silence of the churches*, and they will continue to try to do so. If a church gets involved in conservative politics — politics that would defend biblical law, or even historic Constitutional religious liberty — it risks disaster. (The National Council of Churches will be left alone, of course.) The State now claims that tax exemption is in fact a tax subsidy — a very large subsidy, given the level of taxation generally. It also claims the legal right to regulate all institutions that receive such "subsidies."

*Orthodox Christians must deny, on principle, that the State grants or establishes the tax-exempt status of the church of Jesus Christ.* This status derives from the sovereignty of the church under God. The State is wise to acknowledge what God has established, but the State has not created this tax-exempt status.

It is true, however, that the State has created the tax-deductible status of gifts to the church. This is different from tax-exemption. Church members may well have to give up the tax-deductible status of their gifts to the church. If the State unwisely revokes the tax-deductible status of gifts to a God-fearing Christian church, then members are required to tithe only the after-tax portion of their incomes. They did not pay the tithe in Old Testament times on crops eaten by the locusts; similarly, Christians are not required to pay a tithe on production which is confiscated today by other kinds of locusts.[12]

The churches of the West did not cry out against the escalating welfare State, and so the most important single potential source of opposition to the State was silenced in the United States, from 1865 until about 1980. Only recently have a minority of conservative and fundamentalist pastors begun to sound the alarm, and only in the United States. *Conservative pastors allowed the State to escalate its war against personal freedom for*

12. R. J. Rushdoony denies this principle in the book he co-authored with Edward Powell (and, just for the record, which my tithe financed through the Trinity Presbyterian Church of Fairfax, Virginia). Rushdoony concludes *Tithing and Dominion* (Vallecito, CA: Ross House Books, 1979), with these words: "The law of the tithe, unlike the Sabbath law and works of necessity, has no qualifications or exceptions. God's tax *must* be paid. Because God has prior claim on us, this tax is computed before the state takes its tax. We cannot bring a blemished offering to the Lord: He calls this *evil* (Mal. 1:8). Similarly, we cannot give anyone priority over God without blemishing our approach to the Lord" (p. 143). It should be pointed out that Ed Powell the co-author of the book, categorically disagrees with Rushdoony on this point and has written a privately circulated paper to that effect. I agree here with Powell. The tithe is on the *increase* a man experiences; what is confiscated is not counted as part of the increase. Wealthy people in many Northern European nations are taxed at rates of 98% or even 102% of their income. Are they evil for paying? Foolish, perhaps, but not evil. The State simply steals their increase; they owe God no tithe. Mr. Rushdoony has not thought through his position carefully. I do not disagree with him publicly often, but here we must break with his argumentation. We do not need to create unnecessary guilt for God-fearing people who tithe on their after-tax increase in nations that do not permit charitable deductions from taxable income.

*over a century, almost without Christian opposition.* Even now, few pastors seem to be able to make a fully Bible-based attack on the welfare State. They do not like what they see, but they have preached for too long against "getting the church mixed up in politics," or they have announced that "we're under grace, not biblical law," so they find themselves and their churches facing increasingly tyrannical humanistic law.

When the State closes the noose around the freedoms that the churches used to enjoy, a lot of pastors will start getting involved in politics. But will they change the content of their preaching? Will they at last admit that churches cannot possibly avoid the moral necessity of dealing with political issues? Question: If it is legitimate today to get involved in politics in order to defend the interests of the church, *why was it immoral (or unwise) to get involved in politics a century ago, in order to head off the coming of this era of oppression?* Why is it legitimate today to escalate our political defense of Christian liberty in every area of life, when it was supposedly so terrible to escalate our defense a century ago, or even in 1970, before the humanist enemy grew so powerful?

Why should pastors refrain from preaching about the biblical principles of politics, economics, and education? Doesn't the Bible teach these principles? And when we say "principles," don't we *really* mean *biblical law?* Can we expect to fight today's battles without a direct, systematic appeal to biblical law? Until churches return to faith in comprehensive biblical law, defending their position in terms of an appeal to biblical law, their defense of Christ's interests will be compromised.[13]

## *Bureaucratic Escalation*

A defensive campaign against an enemy is the first stage of an offensive campaign. Defense is not a sufficient goal; victory is the only goal which inspires confidence. General Douglas MacArthur was correct when he said that *there can be no substitute for victory*. A strategy, whether offensive or defensive, should begin with an understanding of just how the enemy

13. R. J. Rushdoony, *The Institutes of Biblical Law* (Nutley, NJ: Craig Press, 1973); Greg L. Bahnsen, *Theonomy in Christian Ethics* (Nutley, NJ: Craig Press, 1977).

fights. We must understand the workings of bureaucracy.

Bureaucrats operate in terms of a fundamental political principle, a way of life: "Go along to get along." (This political principle was first articulated by Speaker of the House Sam Rayburn in the 1950s.) Their warfare against their opponents involves the steady pressure of bureaucratic power, always limited to some extent by the official rules guiding the particular bureaucratic unit. An all-or-nothing assertion of absolute power is foreign to entrenched bureaucracies at the end of a civilization. All-or-nothing confrontations are too risky for latter-day bureaucracies. *Bureaucracies are risk-avoiding institutions*. This is why they are so utterly inept at creating and even sustaining capital in the face of an ever-shifting, uncertain market. (It also partially explains why the United States lost the Korean War and the Vietnam War: we attempted to play the escalation game against ideologically motivated revolutionaries who were willing to escalate for two generations, if need be. The only way we could have won those wars was with a declaration of Congress that we were, in fact, at war, followed by nuclear strikes against every conceivable military target in North Korea and North Vietnam, after allowing them 24 hours to consider a surrender. No ground troops, no draftees: just daily nuclear strikes until nothing was left of the enemy's war-making ability. In short, "send them a message" —and all others who are thinking of imitating them. They will think twice. That strategy would have worked in 1949 and 1962, since the United States had a monopoly over the delivery of nuclear weapons to their targets—before we allowed a private U.S. firm to sell the Soviet Union the grinding machines that alone make possible the building of accurate MIRVed nuclear missiles.[14])

No one offers monetary rewards to bureaucrats for forecasting the future accurately. A profit-seeking entrepreneur reaps personal profits from accurate forecasting and efficient planning. The bureaucrat, at best, gets a promotion. Therefore, bureaucrats are almost always *past-oriented.*[15] They do

14. The firm was the Bryant Chucking Grinder Company of Springfield, Vermont. The tool was the Centalign-B precision bearing machine. Antony C. Sutton, *National Suicide: Military Aid to the Soviet Union* (New Rochelle, NY: Arlington House, 1973), pp. 91ff.

15. Ludwig von Mises, *Bureaucracy* (New Rochelle, NY: Arlington House, [1944] 1969).

things "by the book"—a book which was written in the past in terms of past conditions. The bureaucrat is rewarded for *not making a mistake* in terms of a set of complex written formal rules and unwritten informal rules, while the entrepreneur is rewarded by consumers for accurately forecasting the future in an uncertain market. Thus, bureaucrats seldom act rapidly enough to stamp out a growing evil—"evil" being defined as anything which threatens the smooth operation of the bureaucracy and the continued advancement of the bureaucrats. They act in a *piecemeal* fashion. They prefer to escalate, to respond to recent conditions.

Bureaucracies seldom attempt to stamp out a movement. They attempt to buy off the opposition's leaders, or convince the movement to impose self-regulation in terms of imposed bureaucratic guidelines. They increase pressures on *visible* manifestations of opposition movements. But most employees of bureaucracies are slow-acting, benefit-seeking, work-avoiding people who expect to be rewarded by merely staying on the job and not making a procedural mistake. Few of them are dedicated pursuers of institutional enemies, except in cases where *personal vendettas* are involved. But personal vendettas are always aimed against personal opponents or against one limited segment of the opposition. *Long-term personal vendettas against whole movements are almost never sustainable by a bureaucracy.* If nothing else, the dedicated agent gets promoted, or he moves to another agency, or he breaks an internal organizational rule and becomes vulnerable to skilled victims who know the law, or to personal rivals within the organization who are willing to cooperate with his victims in order to unseat him. If nothing else, he eventually retires or dies on the job.

The typical bureaucrat does not understand religious or ideological dedication. He does not understand what it is which motivates members of dedicated organizations.[16] Nothing in his world prepares him for dealing with such committed people. He is used to scaring people with threats against their business, or threats of fines. He is not used to people who take on the bureaucracy, who fight by every legal

16. An indispensable study of dedication is Douglas Hyde's book, *Dedication and Leadership* (Notre Dame, Indiana: Notre Dame University Press, 1956). Hyde was a former Communist organizer. His book is a study of Communist leadership techniques.

means, who appeal to a sense of fair play to the general public, who write letters to the editor and news releases, who organize politically, and who use deception against him. He is not used to people who expose him and the inner workings of his organization. Most of all, he fears people who can thwart his advancement in his niche of the bureaucracy. Nothing will inhibit future advancement more than the imposition of *a budget cut on the whole organization* by the politicians in response to the voting public's outrage against an overeager employee. An employee who gets his superiors in budgetary trouble is in very hot water.

Because he cannot understand dedication and resolve, he takes steps that only deal with symptoms. He threatens verbally, by phone if possible. He causes trouble and psychological pain for leaders of the organization that is seen as a threat. He sometimes tries to get the cooperation of other bureaucracies to remove the offending group. But if the group is simply one branch of a wider movement, especially a movement without formal institutional connections, he is in trouble. The energy expended in trying to stamp out one branch only frees up the others. If numerous other branches continue to do the same things that the first group does, he must get his superiors to commit additional funding to the war against all branches.

### *Lawyer Delay*

Every bureaucracy has a set of operating regulations that control its *official, visible* activities. Of course, all bureaucracies operate to a considerable extent outside of the limits established by law. They continually break the rules, especially where the rules are extensive, complex, and unclear. But officially, the employees of the bureaucracy are required to operate in terms of a set of rules and regulations.

When a bureaucracy begins to infringe upon the activities of any organization, the first step of the responsible officials of that organization is this: *assess the implications of compliance.* If there is any question whatsoever about whether the effects of compliance may be adverse to the interests of the threatened organization, the responsible decision-makers must begin to consider alternatives to compliance. In most cases of churches under pressure from the State, resistance is called for.

Whenever any official confronts a church official with any

verbal request, unless the church has decided in advance to comply, there should be a universal response on the part of the appropriate church officer: **"Write us a letter."** Under no circumstances should the officer begin to comply with any directive of a local bureaucrat until the church has received a letter from the bureaucrat, on official stationery, stating that such and such an action must be taken by the church.

There is an operating law of most bureaucrats: *never write a letter, and never throw a letter away.* No bureaucrat wants to put anything in writing if he can avoid it. He can never be certain that his official demand will achieve his career-enhancing goals. He may have made a procedural mistake. He wants desperately to "cover his tail." Therefore, the proper initial tactic of resistance is to require every bureaucrat to put every demand in writing. No letter—no compliance. "No tickee—no washee."

Many bureaucratic demands can be derailed right here. The bureaucrat simply drops the whole matter. It may not be worth the effort and/or risk to his career. But if a letter from the bureaucrat does arrive, the church or school must begin the next phase, what is sometimes called *Lawyer Delay.* The church or school waits as long as the letter says it can wait before responding. If the letter fails to specify a response date, then it is appropriate to wait about ten days and then send a certified letter to the bureaucrat asking how long the church has to respond. This eats up another few weeks.

Once the deadline arrives, the proper response is to write a letter in response which asserts your intention to comply fully, *just so long as the church is not giving up any of its Constitutional rights by complying*. Now, in order to make certain that the church is not giving up any of its Constitutional rights, could the bureaucrat please provide explicit information regarding his agency's statutory authority by which he is requiring a particular action by the church or school?

This forces the bureaucrat to begin the most important aspect of the confrontation: *looking it up*. "Looking it up" is the be-all and end-all of all bureaucratic endeavors. It is what both sides pay lawyers to do. But at this initial phase, you have not hired the services of a lawyer. You are only making a legitimate request that the bureaucrat demonstrate that what he is asking is legal for him to ask, according to statutory authority.

If you get your requested documentation from him, then

the next step is to ask for more documentation. You will need photocopies of the statutory authority in order to consult your legal counsel. If you have been provided with photocopies already, then you need further clarification. How, precisely, does this somewhat confusing statute—and all statutes are confusing, since they are written by lawyers or bureaucrats—apply in your specific case? You just don't understand the wording. Are there precedents for this interpretation? Please provide citations. Again, reassure the bureaucrat that you fully intend to comply with all legal and Constitutional statutes, *just so long as the church is not being asked to give up its fundamental rights.*

The bureaucrat now has a problem. You are not openly defying him. This makes it very difficult for him to call in the police to force you to comply. You are not threatening his authority. You are only asking for clarification. Lots and lots of clarification.

What if you get clarification, accompanied with a positive, no-exceptions demand for you to comply by a specific date? At this point, you request a copy of the organization's *official appeal guidelines*. Every organization has some sort of formal appeals structure. Sometimes it is written out; other times it isn't. But you, as the victim, have the right to be informed about the details of the appeal structure.

When you get it, you may want to go to a lawyer. But you have saved many hours of lawyer's fees at $50 to $100 per hour by conducting several weeks, or even months, of your own *lawyer delay* activities. You have forced the bureaucrat to take all the steps his bureaucracy's internal regulations require. *If every organization always took just these basic steps, the whole bureaucratic structure of the humanist State would crumble.*

You do not intend to give up Constitutional rights. You also do not intend to acknowledge the ultimate sovereignty of the State over the affairs of the church, but you do not put this in your initial letters. This is your ultimate fall-back position. Initially, you are just a responsible citizen seeking more information. Meanwhile, you have given yourself more time to begin mounting a full-scale resistance program.

### *Tax-Exempt Schools*

The tax-exempt private school movement is a threat to the public schools, and the public schools are the heart and soul of modern statist humanism—the recruiting area for the "privates, corporals, non-commissioned officers, lieutenants, and captains" who serve as managers for the elitists who are running the United States. (Those who really rule the United States tend to be graduates of exclusive private high schools and private universities in the Northeast.)[17] Private schools are subject to the threat of losing their tax exemption.[18] While it would break the system's back if every school threatened with the loss of its tax-exempt status would challenge the civil government in court, bureaucrats have been correct in the past in assuming that most schools will capitulate to a bureaucratic ruling if one or two do. *Therefore they deliberately attack smaller, weaker, and less ideologically committed schools in order to get a legal precedent set.*

But what if these vulnerable schools affiliate with churches, which are more difficult to threaten with removal of their tax-exempt status? Or what if these schools begin operating on a profit-seeking basis, and work out a deal with the local church to rent church space for, say, one dollar per year? Or worse yet, from the viewpoint of the bureaucrats, what if the parents start home schools that leave few records? How can the bureaucrats lock up every parent who starts a home school? How can the children of every home school family be taken away and turned over to foster parents (as parents in Pastor

---

17. Probably the best book on who rules America, and how, is Prof. Carroll Quigley's massive textbook, *Tragedy and Hope*, published by Macmillan in 1966 and later suppressed. It is available in a "pirate" version from most American Opinion bookstores. If you cannot locate a copy locally, write: American Opinion, 395 Concord, Belmont, MA 02178.

18. It is interesting that in the 1978 attempt by the Internal Revenue Service to impose racial quotas on private schools, the ruling specifically exempted certain private schools from the classification of "reviewable school." Which schools were not therefore assumed to be guilty until proven innocent of racial discrimination? Why, all those private schools that had been started prior to "Brown Vs. Board of Education of Topeka, Kansas" in 1954—the U.S. Supreme Court's school desegregation decision. In short, they exempted the exclusive private schools of the Northeast that train up the sons and daughters of the ruling elite! See the August 22, 1978, issue of the *Federal Register* in which the directive was published, Section 2.03. This regulation was not imposed in 1978 because of the firestorm of protest created by the fledgling Christian newsletter network. For details concerning this protest, see Martin Claussen (ed.), *The Voice of Christian and Jewish Dissenters in America* (P.O. Box 3605, Georgetown, Wash., D.C.: Piedmont Press, 1982).

Sileven's Baptist church in Louisville, Nebraska, have been threatened with)? And what if these parents get the local television stations to cover the event?

### *The Videotape Machine*

Television news broadcasts are the most profitable segment of the networks' budgets. The per-hour revenues from advertising are higher (more ads per show), and the costs of production so low, that the networks are now pushing for one-hour news shows. The public's insatiable demand for action and gossip also makes news shows popular. (Note the number of "fire" stories on any given local news broadcasts.)

When bureaucratic push comes to literal shove, the victims have an enormous potential lever at their disposal: television news. T.V. news is "action news." It is "eyewitness news." It is news that takes little time to explain. Most of all, it is *news that can be videotaped*. In the atrocious words of Nixon's former Press Secretary Ron Ziegler, every signing of a document or trip down the street became a "photo opportunity." The phrase stuck. In the case of television, the broadcasters need a *moving* —physical and emotional—photo opportunity.

What the T.V. news team wants is a brief story—no more than three minutes long—which holds the viewers' attention long enough to get to the next paid advertisement. *The goal of T.V. news is to sell soap*. It is not to inform. It is only partially to indoctrinate, especially local T.V. news. The goal is to "deliver market share," meaning viewers who may buy the advertiser's product.

The radicals of the late 1960s understood this principle better than anyone else ever had. They were geniuses at getting action shots on the evening news. They designed their slogans to fit into the two-minute or even 30-second time slots on the CBS Evening News. "Hell, no; We won't go!" "Hey, Hey, LBJ: How many people have you killed today?" They had picked up where Martin Luther King, Jr. and the civil rights protestors had left off, 1960-65. They recognized what King had accomplished, and how, so they escalated the visual impact of their protests. They understood what a 19-inch television screen could accomplish.

One of the first tools that a resistance group needs is a portable, battery-operated, half-inch *videotape machine* and a *low-*

*light color camera*. Also useful is a high-intensity light, whether battery-operated or not. These systems can be purchased for under $1,400. They can be paid for by renting the equipment out to church members for kids' birthday parties and Little League games, or for making videotaped personal inventories for insurance records, or for other non-commercial uses. Weddings and high school graduations are popular "photo opportunities," and people will readily pay a hundred dollars or more to have someone photograph them with videotape. People will make visual "last wills and testaments" that enable them to leave a record for their heirs of their family histories, personal goals, and philosophy of life.

Nothing known to man will inhibit a bureaucrat more than the presence of a videotape machine and a microphone. He knows that he may be on that evening's local evening news. If he really makes the big time, the way the arresting officer in the Sileven case did, he may be beamed on CBN's satellite to millions of people, possibly on several occasions. The church, school, or persecuted group which can tell its story through videotape is in a position of real strength.

Any time a hostile or enforcing bureaucrat is allowed on the premises of any church or school—and it is generally wise to deny such access to all bureaucrats suspected of taking action against the church—he should be placed in front of an audio cassette tape machine. A high quality microphone is necessary—not the cheap plastic units. You need to spend at least $35 or more on a good microphone. You want to get this on a radio news broadcast at some point. I suggest using a high-quality battery-operated cassette deck (Superscope, Marantz, etc.) and a high-quality microphone (Shure, Sony, etc.). This may cost $400, but so what? Such equipment will produce far better master tapes for sermons in the meantime. *When you need a tool for survival, get a high-quality one.*

The bureaucrat knows that everything he says may be held against him in an administrative inquiry. Tapes will not stand up by themselves in a court of law, but tapes are fine for verifying stories to newspaper reporters and to use in administrative inquiries. But because tapes cannot normally be used in court, no officer of a church or school should speak to a hostile or enforcing bureaucrat without the presence of witnesses, one of whom should be assigned the task of taking notes. *Put the tape recorder in front of the invader the moment he begins to speak*. Have your secretary take notes. Many bureaucrats—indeed, most bureaucrats—will just pick up their papers and walk away at this point. The police generally won't, since they are called in only toward the latter stages of a confrontation, but any bureaucrat who is not legally allowed to carry a gun will be sorely tempted to quit at this point, until his superior thinks up another approach. Always allow him to retreat gracefully. Let him save face. Your goal is to get him off the premises. But if you fail, be sure you have evidence which will create trouble for him and his superiors later on.

This strategy begins once it is clear that the war is on. In earlier stages, it may be possible to deal with a local bureaucrat amicably, so that he does not begin the escalation process. Fire marshals and safety inspectors should be treated gently, at least initially, unless "foul play" on the part of inspectors is suspected. (Is the inspector acting as an unofficial agent of some other administrative bureaucracy?) Tax collectors should never be be allowed into a church in their official capacity. Always insist that they, the tax officials, send a letter explaining exactly what they want. No jurisdiction over the church should be granted or even implied to tax collectors by any officer of the church, as a matter of official church policy. The State must not be granted symbolic authority over the church in advance. Once it is granted—and allowing them in the door could be interpreted as constituting an acceptance by the church of the State's authority—it becomes difficult to prove in a court that the church has not already granted such authority to the State in principle and is therefore not entitled to legal immunity at a later stage of the judicial process. Never, ever allow a tax official to examine church records of any kind.

The videotape and audiotape machines are used above all as tools for mobilizing public opinion, and any public official who forces entry into a church should be met head-on. The tape should be rolling the moment he forces his way in. The church officer should be protesting verbally in terms of biblical authority and the public official's lack of legal jurisdiction over the church. He should be asked repeatedly to display a warrant, and to state precisely what crime has been committed by which church officer.

The public should learn from the videotape of the protesting church officer that only records involved in specific criminal cases involving church officers will be released—that the church itself is not Constitutionally subject to "fishing expeditions" by any public official. Appeal repeatedly to *freedom of speech*. This stands up better than freedom of religion in today's courts. Remind him of the "chilling effect"—a key phrase in any trial—his actions are having on people who only want to exercise their Constitutional rights in speaking out.

Another good tactic for the church officer is to say on camera that he realizes that this official is probably acting under orders from his superiors, and that the church officer has no *personal* ill feelings toward the official. *However,* the church officer explains, he simply cannot in good conscience cooperate with the official, since it would mean giving up the church's Constitutional rights. The church officer must make it clear *to the viewing audience*, including some future judge and jury, that he has no authority to give up the church's Constitutional immunities against unlawful actions being taken by the *invading official's superiors*.

Consider the problem of the enforcing official. Either he is acting without authorization, in which case there will be big, big trouble for him if this videotape is aired, or else his superiors really are pushing him into a very difficult position—a position from which he desperately wishes to extricate himself. He can still retreat gracefully at this point. Every fiber of his bureaucratic being is telling him to retreat. All of a sudden, this deal does not look so easy. Discretion is the better part of valor. Run!

The more excitement there is on screen, the more likely this videotape will be used by local television stations. After all, few programs ever have a T.V. crew on the premises in the midst of the action. This really *is* "action news." Even if no local station runs the film, CBN might. The moment the official leaves, start calling every news media source you can think of. Tell them that you have a videotape of everything.

Warning: be sure you record the proceedings on the *fast speed setting* on the videotape machine. You want the highest quality reproduction you can get. This means high-speed recording. (If churches have ¾-inch tape machines, all the better, but these are expensive and bulky. They are not required.)

If you are in a community which has a Christian television station, make a bee-line to see the manager. He needs filler. If you can come on a talk show and bring your videotape, you are in a strong bargaining position. Any time the interviewer can insert some "action footage" during a program of "talking heads" (discussion format), he will be tempted to schedule the interview. This is also true of secular talk format shows. Try to get on local secular talk shows. Few people watch these shows, but some do, and the local bureaucrats are not really certain how many people, or which people, are watching. It makes them nervous.

If you can get on a talk show, be sure to use your videotape machine to record the show off your T.V. set. This tape can be played at public meetings later on. The program has been produced professionally by a "neutral third party," so it carries more weight.

Obviously, the angle you need to stress on a T.V. interview is *freedom of speech*. This is the be-all and end-all of the broadcaster's worldview. If you can constantly stress that the State is restricting your freedom of speech, you have scored points with the broadcaster, since his self-interest (and ideology) is at stake when freedom of speech is threatened. Do not allow yourself to be deflected from this theme. The tape of your televised interview may be used later on in an administrative hearing or even in court. You must establish your case early, and never deviate from it: *you are defending your first amendment liberties*.

### *The Press Release*

Before the Second World War, newsmen did not rely on press releases for their stories. Today, it is the first thing they look for. Therefore, the first thing a church or school should do after calling the news media is to prepare a two-page, *double-spaced* press release. Why double spaced? Because newsmen find double spacing easier to read and *quote from*. Keep the paragraphs short—no longer than four lines each. Why? Same reason. If necessary, use subheads (the way I do in this essay). *Make it easy for the reporter to get the story in a nutshell*. Remember, *the invading bureaucracy probably did not expect this, and it will take time for the bureaucrats to get their official statement cleared*. Meanwhile, the newspaper is devoting more space to your side of the story because *you have provided the reporter with more copy*.

This means that your church needs a *photocopy machine* that produces crisp, clear copies, and an *electric typewriter.* You must always be ready to write clearer press releases, more readable press releases, and most of all, *more quotable* press releases than your opposition.

Not only do you need an official press release stating your position, you also need to be ready to produce a near-story. It would look like something that could be put out over the Associated Press wire. It might look something like this (double spaced, of course):

> (Burlap, Nebraska). Officials of the Department of Education of the state of Nebraska broke into the Harmless as Doves Baptist Church Thursday evening. The church is located at Samson and Delilah Streets in Burlap. Operating without a warrant, officials demanded that church officers turn over all records of the church-operated day school.
>
> Sheriff Elwood Connors accompanied Peter Burke and Roger Van de Meer, Department of Education officials. They were met by Rev. C. B. Dial and trustee member William Emerson, who refused to open the files of the church.
>
> Mr. Emerson was carrying a videotape machine and a camera. He was ordered by the Sheriff to shut it off. He refused to do so and continued taping the intruding officials. The tape is being made available to local television stations.
>
> "We must ask you to leave the premises of the church," announced Rev. Dial. "This church has committed no crime. Unless you have a warrant for my arrest or the arrest of some other church officer, you will have to leave."
>
> The three officials did not produce any warrant, nor did they arrest anyone. They told the church officers that they were going to get the records one way or another, and that they had better hand them over. The church officers refused again, and asked the three men to leave.
>
> After ten minutes of arguing, which Mr. Emerson recorded, the three officials departed. They said that they would return with a warrant to open the church's files.
>
> Church officers continue to protest this unauthorized break-in. "The Constitutional rights of freedom of speech and freedom of religion are involved here. If the rights of our little congregation can be disregarded like this, then nobody's rights are safe," said Rev. Dial.
>
> The Department of Education insists that all private schools in the State of Nebraska are under its jurisdiction, despite parental objections. The fact that the school is an official ministry of the church makes no difference, according to Department policy.
>
> Parents of the children say they are determined to keep their children in the church school. "It is a matter of principle," said

> Harold Bannister, who has three children in the school. "I am responsible before God for the education of my children, and I want them to be educated in terms of biblical religion, not the religion of secular humanism."
>
> Church officials vow that they will go to jail before they will open the files. "The state does not have jurisdiction over the church," says Rev. Dial. "Unless the state plans to bring criminal charges against an individual, it has no business coming in here and demanding compliance. But they know we haven't broken any Constitutional laws, so they're 'fishing' for evidence."

The news story answers the five basic questions: who, what, when, where, and how? It does not say *why*. The news story is designed to create the appearance of objectivity. The accompanying church press release gives the church's explanation, plus makes reasonable "guesses" about the motivation of the state. The press releases ask such "questions" as: "Why isn't the state honoring our Constitutional rights?" "Why didn't they produce a warrant?" "Is someone in the Department of Education pursuing a vendetta against us?" Questions, after all, aren't accusations. People can occasionally get sued for making false accusations; *it is very difficult to get sued by a public official for asking pointed questions*. So ask lots of questions in the press release. It should be signed by the pastor. This way, reporters can quote him in any articles.

The news story and the press release are both mailed to a network of Christian news media: newspapers, magazines, T.V. stations, and newsletters. This alerts the news media to the existence of a story. Copies (not the original) of the videotape are offered to reporters who wish to pursue the story. But always keep the story and the press release short—two pages per item. People have little time to read, even reporters. If they want more details, let them call. Put the church's mailing address and telephone number at the upper left-hand corner of both releases.

Several different 7-inch by 10-inch black and white glossy photographs will help get the story into print, especially any photos of the confrontation. This means that the church needs a *35 millimeter camera* and a *strobe flash attachment* in the building. It should be loaded with B&W film (Kodak Plus-X is good if you have a flash attachment; Tri-X if it is "available light"). No matter what the state officials say in protest, just keep shooting pictures. If they are foolish enough to confiscate the film, charge them with theft. (If the photographer can leave the room, rewind the film, reload the camera, and let the second, blank roll get confiscated, so much the better. Always have a second blank roll close in your pocket in order to make the switch, a strategy which also applies to video-cassette cartridges.) If they are foolish enough to stand around getting photographed, send out the photos. Heads, you win; tails, they lose.

Publicity, publicity, and more publicity. This should be a full-time program of the attacked organization, right from the beginning. Never let up. Keep sending out material. Bureaucrats despise unfavorable publicity. If you can badger them into making outrageous statements, have a witness and a tape recorder present. Make them look like tyrants or fools. Hound them. Just keep coming back. If they throw you out of the room, be sure you have it all on videotape. (Make back-up copies of the tapes immediately.)

Be sure to *play to the audience*. Look like wounded lambs. Make your opponents look like wounded water buffalos. This is a *media event*. Never forget this. Your best earthly aid is publicity. Make sure you orchestrate as much of it as possible. Always consider just how what you are doing will look in print or on the T.V. screen.

### *Mailing List*

Your church or school needs an active mailing list. If you have to mobilize support rapidly in a crisis, the mailing list will help. It should be computerized. The new portable units are incredibly cheap, starting at about $1,800 retail, or $2,500 for "bells and whistles." Common brands are the Kaypro II, the Zorba, Osborne, and Morrow Designs, all of which manufacture models selling for $1,800. Each includes a good quality word processing program, which will help you in every area of operations, but especially in a crisis when the "war of words" is critical. You will also need a letter-quality printer, which will cost at least $500. Simple mailing list programs are available for a hundred dollars or less, and some of the portables come with mailing list programs at no extra charge.

You need to have other schools and churches on the list, other resistance groups, the Christian news media, and legislators, if possible. Do not overuse this tool. You need to communicate news fast, and you need to get it read. Send out news when you have real news. Put certain names in reserve for emergencies. Do not mail out chatty but irrelevant materials to these reserve names. Save this reserve for an emergency. Keep it updated, however. Make sure the addresses are up to date.

Churches should not apply for the tax-exempt mailing rate. A tax-exempt mailing permit forces you to apply for tax exemption. Pay second-class rates and let it go at that. Churches are automatically tax exempt; apply to no one to get such a grant of privilege. Your church has already acknowledged the sovereignty of the State over it when it applies for such a privilege. Mailing at the tax-exempt rate is a subsidized privilege—too expensive a privilege for any God-fearing church to seek.

Certain churches should become clearing houses of information on resistance activities. The Calvary Temple of East Point, Georgia is a prime example. Its publication, the *Temple Times*, is filled with the latest cases of unconstitutional activities of government agencies. We need dozens of such newsletters.

We could also use computerized "bulletin boards" that have information on defense measures, unwarranted invasions by the State, and so forth. Those churches with a computer and a "modem" telephone communications device (such as the Hayes Smartmodem 1200) can call in and leave messages. Pastors can scan the board to see if other churches have reported on infringements of Constitutional liberties. These boards are relatively inexpensive to set up. I think we will see dozens of them eventually. (This could be an important service of CBN's Freedom Council. I hope its members will encourage the organization to begin such a bulletin board. Jerry Falwell's Moral Majority organization could also inaugurate a bulletin board. They could get out important information rapidly.)

When a major crisis appears, a church can get a phone line installed and then buy a telephone answering machine. The pastor can record 3-minute summaries of what is going on, so that Christian radio stations can call in and get a "quote" or two. Give the presentation as if it were an interview. Make short, snappy statements. Advertise the existence of your phone-in taped message in local newspapers. Be sure you leave space at the end to get people to write in for more information.[19] A Post Office Box would help (repeat the box number at least twice; forget about the zip code—first-class mail will be delivered without a zip code, and extra numbers confuse people unnecessarily). *Build that mailing list.* (See "Picketing and Petitions," below.)

### *Letter-Writing Campaigns*

Christians must learn to make good use of the written word. When a particularly flagrant example of statist interference with our liberties hits a congregation or a school, local Christians must put their typewriters to work. Yet few Christians are in the habit of writing letters on important topics. They probably will not know where to begin.

The first letters of public protest should go to elected officials. (I cover letters to the editor later on.) What is important here is to distinguish *letters* from *press releases*. They are not the same sort of communications device. A letter must give the appearance of being personal. A letter can be written by a computer-driven, letter-quality printer, but it must *appear* to have been personally typed. You want a person with authority to read the letter. He has to believe that it was written by a constituent.

There are some basic rules to follow. *First*, your letter should be neatly *typed*. The person reading it should not be expected to decipher your handwriting.

*Second*, the letter should be no longer than one single-spaced page. This increases the likelihood that it will actually be read. Long letters are more likely to be tossed out. If you cannot state your case in 500 words, hire someone who can.

*Third*, if necessary, enclose a copy of your press releases and church position paper with the letter. The letter can refer the reader to the more detailed testimony. *Let the reader know that full explanations are available on request.* He has to know that if he gets into this mess on your side, that you can supply him with back-up materials. But do not expect him to read

19. I recommend that every church install such a telephone line immediately. The pastor can offer a two-minute summary each week of next Lord's Day morning sermon. Invite people to come and hear the whole sermon. Then tell them where to write to receive the church's free newsletter. Start a newsletter which deals with community-interest items from an explicitly biblical point of view. Minimize "in-house" news items.

through everything the first time you contact him.

*Fourth*, enclose *newspaper clippings*, if possible. This demonstrates to the official that this issue is becoming public. It makes it more difficult for him to avoid dealing with it. This is why it is important to get the press interested in your case early. Legislators read letters in the local newspapers. If church members who have not written letters to the editor can send a legislator a packet of newspaper clippings and letters to the editor, they give the impression that this issue is a hot one, and that it will probably get hotter. If the politician sees that there are a lot of voters who are reading these articles and letters, he will find it difficult to ignore the topic. If the topic is controversial, the politician will try to stay out of the fight until he is forced to declare himself publicly by pressure from his constituents. Make his silence difficult.

*Fifth*, send the letter, or similar versions, to *every relevant elected official*. You never know which one will respond favorably. Your letter will probably be read by some staff assistant, and he will pass it along to the official only if he thinks it is really important. You never know which staff assistant will read it. The more elected officials you send this to, the more likely you will get some staffer to become interested in the case.

In addition to letters to public officials, there are also *letters to the editor*. Local newspapers always have columns for subscribers' letters. These columns are widely read. If you can get your story in this section of the paper, you may arouse a lot of interest.

There are rules for letters to the editor. *First*, keep the letter short; express one basic idea. This keeps the readers from getting confused. *Second*, double space it. This increases the ease of retyping it into the newspaper's computer. The easier you make any stage of the process for the user, the more likely you will get it published. *Third*, avoid all libelous language. The newspaper is sensitive to law suits. *Fourth*, the "wounded lamb" approach is best to generate public support. *Fifth*, if the pastor or headmaster is writing the letter, he should mention that the public can get involved by calling him or the school. Use the published letter to generate identified supporters. (The newspaper may edit this, but it never hurts to try.) *Sixth*, if you have set up a 24-hour taped phone message, mention the phone number. Be sure that the tape gives a P.O. Box number, so that interested people can contact you. *Seventh*, never forget your goal in writing the letter: *mobilizing people to back you up in a fight*. You have to identify them. This means that *you must motivate them to identify themselves*.

I would suggest that the pastor or headmaster write different letters to different newspapers, but all with the same story. Sometimes in large cities, two papers or more will cover a metropolitan area. It would be wise to *have every congregation member buy subscriptions to all papers in the area as soon as a fight starts brewing*. This way, if the editor checks to see if the letter-writer is really a subscriber, it will show up in the computer's files.

It never hurts to have someone else send a letter. It would be unwise to have too many letters come in all at once; a campaign should not look like a campaign. Subtlety is important here.

All letters that are part of a campaign should be screened first by a committee established for this purpose. Each letter should be read by a second person, preferably read orally. An oral presentation of a letter helps the writer to spot confusing phrases. Any time you have to interject, "By that I meant. . . ." you need to rewrite the letter. The pastor should organize the campaign, so that there are no duplications of effort or letters. Each letter should appear to be the product of an independent mind; none of the letters sent by church members should be written independently, however.

Each letter should focus on *one idea*—two at the most. It must be kept short. Each letter should create one specific kind of emotional response: sympathy, outrage, concern for Constitutional liberties, or whatever. There can be an "outraged parent" letter. There can be an "injured reputation" pastoral letter. There can be a "we've got the whole thing on videotape; you can see it for yourself this Saturday at our church at noon, 1:30, 3:00, 4:30, 6:00, and 7:30" letter. There can be a "What's this country coming to when bureaucrats can walk in and. . . ?" letter. You can even get two or three hand-printed "I'm eight years old and a student in the school and I think it's a wonderful school" letters. But these letters should all come from separate sources over a period of several weeks. If they appear to be responding to an article the newspaper has run, so much the better. Editors like to believe that people are reading the paper. Again, it is important to get the paper to cover the story as early as possible.

A committee should not actually write each letter. Word of such manipulation could get out to the press. But it never hurts if the pastor or some person in charge types up a list of several *suggested* reasons why the civil government should not be doing what it is doing. An outline of ten different objections can then be used by ten members of the congregation or school to create ten different letters to the editor.

### *Going to Jail*

Martin Luther King, Jr. was willing to go to jail. He did, frequently, and always with T.V. camera crews present. Guess what? He always got out of jail. When he did, he had a pile of telegrams, sympathy cards, and checks waiting for him.

Some day, a bureaucrat is going to shut down a church. The pastor will resist. He will be threatened with prison. The pastor will get the word out to about a hundred other pastors who are standing with him. The day he is locked up, there will be a new pastor in his pulpit and in the church school. Let them lock him up, too. Then there will be a new pastor. *They will fill the jail with pastors*. Talk about a "photo opportunity"! And one day, guess who will be found in the local pulpit? Brother Jerry from Virginia. Or Brother Pat from Virginia.[20] And then the CBS Evening News crew will be in town, all hot to interview some pimple-faced bureaucrat with his brand-new M.A. in education and his prepared statement about the need to provide better schools for our children and how Christian schools must be made to "measure up" to the high quality public school system.

Until we start assembling teams of pastors who are ready and willing to fly in and be locked up in order to keep a Christian school open, the bureaucrats will know that they are not

20. Big-name T.V. evangelists could participate in such a program with what insurance companies call "high deductible" policies. The big-name evangelist could agree to come if the church had already brought in 25 other pastors who are in jail. Any cause that can get 25 pastors tossed in jail is worth getting involved in. The publicity—not to mention the fund-raising potential—would be worth the air fare. A local pastor cannot expect big-name people to get in line right behind him, but he ought to be able to get them in line 26 places in the rear.

dealing with the likes of Martin Luther King, Jr. *And until the Christian resistance movement is willing and able to do as well as Martin Luther King, Jr., it is all bark and no bite.*

Pastors and Christian school headmasters should have the resistance equivalent of health insurance. Maybe we can call it *bureaucracy insurance*. Fifty or a hundred of them should "co-insure": a covenant agreement that they will come if called upon to "stand in the gap" and go to jail, one by one, until the particular state bureaucrats who think they can shut down a Christian school cost-free and publicity-free find out that the costs are embarrassingly high. A bureaucracy insurance contract might look like this:

> I, __________________, hereby agree to come to the defense of the __________________ School, if and when the headmaster of this school is imprisoned for having failed to comply with any regulation or requirement of the Department of Education or its equivalent in the State of __________________. I agree also to act as a representative of the school's board of trustees or controlling board, and to go to jail if necessary. I agree to cooperate with the school's board in generating as much publicity as possible for the stand which the school is taking.
>
> __________________

Get a hundred of these signed, or even two dozen, and you have "bought yourself a policy." Just agree to sign a similar statement for the others. Presto! You have just accomplished what nobody would ever have dreamed: a commitment from equally vulnerable Christian leaders to take *a few minimal risks* and *to generate some local controversy*. And should you find that you are unable to get two dozen others to agree to co-insure with you on this basis, then you know what you are up against tactically. *Count the costs*. (Warning: I am proposing an insurance contract. Like any insurance contract, it should be purchased only when risks are shared equally. Please do not look shocked when you try to get others to sign up three weeks after you are already in jail. You apply for health insurance when you are healthy, not after you get leukemia.)

If you are really interested in locating others who will join with you in such a covenant, write to

Covenant
Geneva Divinity School
708 Hamvasy Lane
Tyler, TX 75701

The average bureaucrat does not want trouble. This is a law of bureaucracy. He wants a fat salary, good-looking secretaries, and not much to do. He does not want a moral confrontation. Some humanist leaders want a confrontation, but the people they hire to do their dirty work are not the best quality personnel. They are the C+/B− graduates of their colleges, or worse. Bureaucracy corrupts them. It makes them soft.

Now, how about a $500,000 *personal* law suit against some $23,000-a-year bureaucrat for false charges, defamation of character, or false arrest? How about a second law suit for infringement on Fourteenth Amendment-protected civil rights? How about a third for his willful denial of First Amendment Constitutional guarantees? Not law suits against the bureaucracy which employs him, but *against him personally.* How about three or four different computerized law suits, which can be pulled out of the church's microcomputer for each successive pastor or schoolmaster who is locked up to initiate? You say it might be a bit expensive for the bureaucrat to defend against in court? You say it might tie him up for several years? Well, isn't that a shame. Perhaps his successor will think twice the next time he starts looking for instant victims of bureaucratic tyranny.

Christians have to start *increasing the costs to bureaucrats for their unconstitutional infringements on Constitutional rights*. It is just this simple, and just this complex. It involves a willingness of Christian leaders to commit themselves to several troublesome, high-profile, high pay-off, media-designed resistance tactics that will make it hot for a lot of overpaid bureaucrats. It is the responsibility of Christians to count the costs of resistance, and then, under God's guidance, to force the opposition to count the costs. It is the responsibility of Christian leaders to make sure that the costs to the opposition are higher, compared to the expected pay-off, than the costs are to the church of Jesus Christ, compared to the expected pay-off. We are fighting for Christ's kingdom; we have the Constitution behind us, even if judges are humanists or corrupt; we have our testimony to proclaim. What are moderate costs for us are unacceptably high costs for Civil Service-protected bureaucrats. *Sue the bastards!*

### *The Weakest Link*

If you have a sufficiently large congregation (40+ families) or if a large number of pastors from outside your area are available for public protest, invest in a *chain-cutting tool* when it looks as though the civil authorities are about to shut down your church or school. Keep the tool outside the church, of course. When the police chain the church door and lock it, as they did in the case of Pastor Sileven's church, wait for the police to leave. *Then as soon as they are gone, get the tool and cut the chain or lock.* You know their action was unconstitutional, immoral, and illegal. You are only exercising your Constitutional right of free speech and assembly. Then get the press to stick around for stage two. Get the videotape machine ready. Start preaching, singing, and praying.

When the police find out what you have done, they will return. Let them drag you out again. Go limp. Do not struggle; just do as little as possible to assist the removers. Let them take you to jail. Remember, *this is a media event.*

The police will probably station a man to guard the church. Anyway, after you cut the chain the first time, they will. Fine; it is eating into the budget of the local law enforcement agency. Nothing like a uniformed policeman standing, gun on his hip, in front of your padlocked church. Be sure to have lots of people stop in and take photographs of him several times each day. The more people who do this, the worse he will feel. Furthermore, it will take three policemen to stand guard 24 hours a day. This drains local budgets. It also looks ridiculous, 24 hours a day. The moment he leaves, get the chain cutter and cut the chain. Get everyone back into the church for prayer.

A chain has a weak link. That is where you cut. A police force has a weak link. They do not like unfavorable publicity. That is where you cut. Take out ads in the local newspaper. Run a picture of good old Officer Ray, everyone's friend, standing in front of the chained-up church. How about a nice, juicy headline: "Officer Ray's Superiors Station Him in Front of the Calvary Bible Church, To Keep People from Worshipping God While Three Burglaries, Two Rapes, and 23 Drug Deals Take Place." (Get specifics on local crimes from your newspaper; put the clippings in your files for documentation.) Or: "Your Property Tax Dollars At Work." Or: "God's House of Worship Is Protected From Worshippers, 24 Hours a Day. Is Your House Protected From Burglars?" Or: "Public Prayer: Void Where Prohibited By Law." List the 24-hour telephone number where readers can call for taped information.

If your daily newspaper refuses to accept paid advertising, then print up flyers with the picture and an appropriate headline on one side and your explanation on the back. Then use the flyers to get signatures on petitions. Never let an incident like this go unused. Let the bureaucrats know in advance: *everything they say or do may be held against them*. And the nice thing about it is that they have no pseudo-"Miranda" rights. No citizen needs to warn the bureaucrats about their right to remain silent, or that what they say may be held against them. Just hit them after the fact. It keeps them off balance.

You can bet your chain cutter that Officer Ray is unhappy about his latest assignment. It is probably prudent to treat him decently, although he is acting immorally and he ought to quit his job when he is ordered to stand at the church's door to guard the church against worshippers. You are looking for public support. If some reporter interviews him, you want him to speak well of your church and the conduct of its members. Take a cue from the Amish. Does anyone hate the Amish? Nobody; not even the bureaucrats who persecute them. People respect the Amish. Never forget, *this is a war of public relations*. It is not only that, but it is at least that. So offer him lemonade if it is hot outside (besides, it will make him thirstier, and he may be too embarrassed to ask for water), or a cup of soup if it is freezing. Who knows; maybe he will be converted. And if he maintains his rebellion, he will be condemned. Paul, citing Proverbs 25:21-22, wrote: "Therefore if thine enemy hunger, feed him; if he thirst, give him drink; for in so doing, thou shalt heap coals of fire on his head" (Rom. 12:20).

Never show any sign of moral uncertainty. He and his superiors should know beyond a shadow of a doubt that the day he and his gun are removed from the front of the door, and not replaced by his partner, you are going to cut the chain again. You are going to have another prayer service. You respect power as power; you do not respect his actions, and especially not the actions of those who have ordered him to stand guard.

*Cutting the chain lets the other side know they are in for a long, comprehensive battle—a battle which you intend to win.* They are not used to people who cut chains. If they threaten to arrest the person who uses the chain cutter, get everyone involved. Everyone ought to have a crack at it: a squeeze here, a nick there. It will not be clear just who it is who is responsible for cutting the chain. Besides, it is probably only a misdemeanor to cut the chain. Be ready to pay the fine and replace the chain, but only after a long court battle proves you were not within your Constitutional rights—a very expensive trial, which will involve several people (preferably pastors), or several trials, held one at a time. You either get a "Burlap Eight" media event, or a ridiculously long series of trials. And if you lose, buy the police a new chain. Big deal. But let them know, if they try to chain up your church again, you intend to cut it again. And again. The only way they will get you to stop cutting the chain is to make chain-cutting a capital crime. Dead men don't cut chains.

This is psychological warfare, public relations warfare, county budget warfare. *Every time they try to infringe on your Constitutional liberties, it is going to cost them a bundle.* Cutting a chain is an act of defiance, but it is a very specific kind of defiance. It is defiance in the name of God. It is defiance which will be respected, if not understood, by the average voter. He just cannot understand why a church needs to be chained up. You have won over a voter when you act on principle in a polite, peaceful, and relentless way. You demonstrate by the *relentlessness of your opposition* that you are *fighting on the basis of principle.* Only madmen or principled men would keep cutting a chain. You must demonstrate to the voters that you are principled, and you can also score points with the bureaucrats if they suspect that you might be a bit crazy.

### *Brush-Fire Wars*

The escalation of Federal, state, and local pressure against Christian schools has reached a crisis stage. (The escalation of pressure against churches is in the early stages.) Day after day, headmasters are being put under new bureaucratic regulations. No longer is the battle against Christian schools being left to amateur prosecuting attorneys. The bureaucrats are bringing out their biggest guns.

There are many reasons for this escalation of pressure. The private school movement is now visibly threatening the survival of the modern humanist State's most important institution, the public school. The public school is the humanist's equivalent of the established church. The priesthood of state-certified teachers no longer has its monopoly. The source of new recruits to the humanist State is being reduced drastically. The inner-city schools are already doomed. By 1980, under 27% of the schoolchildren in the Los Angeles city schools were white; four years earlier, the proportion had been about 40%. Forced busing had been ideologically consistent with bureaucratic equalitarianism, but it had also been politically suicidal. The Los Angeles city school system will not get back its white, middle-class students. They are now in the suburbs or in private schools.

Within a decade, the public school systems of the major cities will be overwhelmingly composed of poorly trained, poorly motivated minority students whose academic skills will be not be adequately developed by the modernist education methods. The academic standards of the public school products have been falling since 1963; each year, test scores on the Scholastic Aptitude Tests (SATs) drop lower. Guns are being aimed at the schools.

To stem this bloodletting, the cities are desperate. As white middle-class families depart, in order to escape forced busing (forced racial and above all *social* integration), the tax base of the large cities erodes. Parents who have their children in private schools are no longer interested in voting in favor of huge bond issues for the construction of more public schools. Who cares if public school teachers are denied higher salaries? Not the parents of students in private schools. The *tax revolt against large-city public schools* is now a reality. The cities are now in a downward spiral. The more liberal ("feed me, house me, clothe me") the voting patterns in the cities, the more the taxpaying, employed citizens flee to the suburbs. They try to escape from the politics of envy.[21]

To stop the spread of private schools, the bureaucrats are creating an endless series of regulations that are designed to raise the costs of private education and thereby reduce the

21. Gary North, *Successful Investing in an Age of Envy* (2nd ed.; P.O. Box 8204, Ft. Worth, TX: Steadman Press, 1983).

number of students who enroll. The most important tactic is to use judicial harassment. It is expensive for tiny, struggling schools to hire top-flight legal talent. The states, in contrast, are using tax money to send in waves of lawyers to do their best to tie up private schools in red tape and restrictions. How can a small school expect to win? How many well trained, effective lawyers are there who are familiar with the legal issues involved? Not many.

What we need in education is precisely what we need in every other area of life: *decentralization*. We need an army of dedicated Christian school headmasters who are ready to say "no" to the bureaucrats and defend their schools successfully in court. We do not need large national organizations that are easy to infiltrate, buy off, sidetrack, or frighten. Such organizations are run by bureaucrats, not fighters. The bureaucrats of the State see bureaucrats in large private organizations as their allies. But small local schools are driving the bureaucrats crazy. They are springing up everywhere. They do not report on what they are doing or where they are. These schools are like hornets. There are too many of them to fight effectively one by one.

The tactical problem facing Christians is this: How can we gain the benefits of a centralized, well-paid organization, yet avoid the concomitant bureaucratization? How can we mobilize the army, yet keep all the troops in the field, constantly sniping at the enemy? How can we train local men to carry the battle to government officials, yet make certain that the local people are ready and able to fight successful battles? We do not want precedents going against us because the local headmasters and their lawyers were not well prepared. We already face a situation where the civil governments are attacking schools continually in order to get adverse legal precedents.

Obviously, few churches and Christian schools can afford to hire local lawyers at $100 per hour. Besides, lawyers face the problem of specialization. They have to educate themselves in a new field. There are cases to read, arguments to master, in state after state. There is no doubt that since the late 1970s, there has been a coordinated effort on the part of Federal, state, and local education officials to limit the Christian schools. The state attorneys are no longer being surprised by new arguments of the defense lawyers, as they were in the early 1970s. Precedents are going against Christian schools today. Prosecuting attorneys know who the better-known defense witnesses are and what they will say. There are no more easily won cases. The enemy is well-armed in this battle. Our people are poorly armed, except when the very best, most prominent defense attorneys have been hired. (The most prominent of these attorneys are not always the best, especially when their tiny organizations are fighting hundreds of cases. Never hire an attorney to fight your case if he has over five potential trial cases in progress.) There are few of these men to go around. They ask and receive high fees, too, or are forced to raise the money from hard-pressed donors.

Yet the enemy has problems, too. First, the religious traditions of the United States stand against them. So do the legal traditions. Second, there are only so many top-flight prosecuting attorneys. The government lawyers at the local level are not usually "the best and the brightest." If they were really good, they would be in private practice making three times the pay. Third, the state still faces the threat of jury trials, and these juries are sometimes filled with people who are sick and tired of being kicked around by bureaucrats. So the war is not over. Christians and independent school supporters have the principles on their side, and the civil government has both the initiative and the money.

What we need is to take advantage of our greatest strength: *numbers*. We have many schools and churches that need their independence. If we could get the State to commit more men and resources into the fight, we would find that the quality of our opponents would drop. Their best legal talents would be tied up in other court battles.

The court system is becoming vulnerable. Courts are tied up today in a series of endless appeals.[22] It is becoming very expensive to prosecute a case successfully these days, which is why defense lawyers are getting reduced sentences or suspended sentences for their clients through plea-bargaining (pleading guilty to lesser crimes). The accused agree to plead guilty to lesser charges rather than tie up the courts in long cases to prove that the accused committed a major crime. So far, Christian pastors and Christian school headmasters have not been willing to play this plea-bargaining game. Therefore, it will tie up more of the State's economic resources if we stand firm. If we do not capitulate, but force the prosecutors

22. Macklin Fleming, *The Price of Perfect Justice* (New York: Basic Books, 1974).

to prove every point in court, we can make it very expensive for the civil government to prosecute hundreds of schools. If we can find a way *to reduce our costs of defense*, simultaneously *increasing the costs of prosecution*, we can make the State think twice about initiating new suits against us. How can we do it?

The best way to get most things accomplished is to persuade a skilled worker that he has both principle and a profit potential on his side. Show him how to do well by doing good.

Highly skilled lawyers need good incomes to lure them away from the more lucrative ways to practice law. New lawyers are becoming a glut on the market; they will practice for less money. Is there a way to enlist the services of skilled lawyers for lots of money, payable once, and then use their skills to mobilize lots of lower paid new lawyers to become the *legal shock troops* in a long battle against bureaucratic tyranny?

Here is a list of needed services to defend the Christian school movement: 1) a master lawyer who is skilled in the field of private education law, and who is also 2) skilled in communicating this knowledge to his peers; 3) a series of publications that enable non-lawyers to defend their own cause; 4) a strategy geared to the mobilization of thousands of independent schools; 5) a tactical program which will work at the local level. We need a skilled motivator at the top, and men at the local level willing to fight.

What if some bright lawyer could offer the following publications package? *First*, an *introductory, inflammatory paperback book* which offers some true "horror stories" of bureaucratic tyranny, and how the defendants successfully defended themselves. This inexpensive, mass-produced book would contain a tear-out sheet for people to order information about a local defense program.

*Second*, the lawyer would publish a *manual for self-defense*. It would be in two sections. First, there would be a "do it yourself" guide to Christian school headmasters about what to do in the preliminary stages. For example, it would teach that most crucial of all responses to inquiries from bureaucrats: "Write us a letter." It would contain a series of sample letters which will escalate the intensity of the resistance, letters requesting further information, the statute in terms of which the bureaucrat is taking action, and information on why this statute applies in this instance to the school in question. Letters, letters, and more letters. This is the tactic of *Lawyer Delay*.

Meanwhile, the headmaster or pastor can begin to prepare the real defense. But Lawyer Delay can provide extra time. Make sure the opposition really has a legal case before capitulating to anything, signing anything, agreeing to anything, or paying anything.

The manual would contain "nuts and bolts" information for non-lawyers: how to write letters of inquiry, how to file official protests, what *not* to admit or agree to, where to get procedural help, where to locate defense witnesses, a list of law firms or independent lawyers specializing in school cases, which forms to fill out, where to get them, etc. This would be a *layman's introduction*.

*Third*, the master lawyer would produce a *lawyer's defense manual*. It would contain relevant precedents, information on which arguments seem to be working, transcripts of testimony from successful cases, and a history of the legal battle. This would be sold to lawyers directly by the master lawyer to his peers, or sold to a Christian school to give to a local lawyer hired by the school. The idea is to save the local lawyer time in looking up the cases. At $100 per hour, the school needs to save the lawyer all the time it can. The idea is to avoid reinventing the wheel at $100 per hour.

*Fourth*, the master lawyer can supply *updates* to the lawyer's manual. He can keep up with precedents. This new information would become a source of continuing income for him. It would help finance his continuing research in the field.

*Fifth*, sell a monthly *newsletter*, or raise tax-deductible money with a free one, to alert pastors and headmasters of the problem.

All of these projects could be accomplished through a profit-seeking organization run by the master lawyer. It could also be accomplished through a non-profit legal defense organization. The idea is to get the *benefits of legal specialization* along with the benefits of *decentralized multiple defense initiatives*.

I want to make it perfectly clear that my tactic is not aimed at clogging the courts. Clogging the courts as a tactic is illegal. It is classified as "obstructing justice." People who publicly recommend court-clogging as a tactic can get into trouble with the authorities, just as black people in Montgomery, Alabama, could get in trouble in 1956 for promoting a boycott of the local transit system. In contrast, my tactic has a strictly economic goal: to *lower the costs of defending our Constitutional liberties* on the one hand, and to *raise the costs to the State of infringing upon our Constitutional liberties*, on the other.

Our goal should be to make it almost prohibitively expensive for bureaucrats to initiate unconstitutional attacks on our little institutions. If we can do this, then the State will begin to reduce its reliance on judicial harassment to drive innocent victims out of existence.

*I have a dream*, as one former media manipulator once said. I have a dream of fearless Christian school headmasters walking arm-in-arm with fearless laymen, whose legal training has been sufficient to equal $1,400 worth of legal talent. I have a dream of avoiding the use of defense lawyers in 60% of the harassment cases. I have a dream of headmasters being able to hold out until the last minute before having to hire any lawyer, and then paying him as little as possible to do his preliminary homework. I have a dream of making it so expensive for prosecuting attorneys to take on a Christian school that they will spend more of their time prosecuting murderers, rapists, and burglars, if only because they will spend less time and achieve greater success, case for case, than prosecuting Christians. I have a dream of desperate local education officials, bogged down in a mountain of paper, trying to figure out how all these evils came upon them. I have a dream of weary judges reading defense motions to dismiss, and being driven to distraction by skilled defense lawyers who follow lawyer William Kunstler's tactic of objecting to everything the prosecution says all day long. And I have a dream of being able to buy the basic tools in two manuals for a total of $200.

*My dream would be the State's nightmare.*

Why is it that no lawyer has produced this sort of program? I wish I knew. The money is there. The institutional pay-off is there. It is clear that the clients will soon be there, if harassment escalates. Why don't we see Christian school defense manuals, and anti-abortion tactical manuals, and how to de-incorporate your church manuals? Why do Christian legal groups feel compelled to do everything "in-house," and not decentralize the whole Christian defense system through the use of training manuals? Have our Christian lawyers adopted the mentality of empire-builders? Have they all decided that if they cannot personally oversee a case from start to finish that it is better that the victims not be defended? It looks that way.

What we desperately need is *decentralization*. We need to take advantage of our numbers. If one church or school is threatened, then every church and school in the region should publicly state that it is doing precisely what the school under attack is doing, and that the authorities had better take them to court, too. Then each group begins a counter-suit. Each church sues the bureaucrat who takes steps to challenge a particular group. We need *brush-fire wars*, all over the country. We need to show the bureaucrats that they cannot stop the spread of the Christian fire by putting out one blaze. They have to put out hundreds of blazes. They cannot do it if enough of us get involved.[23] *But this strategy cannot work if one law firm or one organization tries to accomplish it alone.*

If you are a headmaster or pastor who would want to buy such a defense package, or if you are a local lawyer who wants to get involved in defending Christian causes, or if you think you are sufficiently skilled to become a master lawyer who will publish such materials, contact the following *layman's clearing house*:

"I Have a Dream"<br>
Vanguard International<br>
107 W. 6th St.<br>
Tyler, TX 75701

Until Christians are ready to enlist the support of lawyers in some system of decentralized defense, there is little hope that a systematic, concerted, effective national campaign against local harassment will be launched. When churches begin encouraging one or two members to learn the rudiments of legal research, churches will become less vulnerable to attack. When there are lawyer-directed home study courses in how to become a *Christian paralegal activist*, we will know that a new day has dawned. This may be a decade or more away, but it is eventually going to come.

### *Picketing and Petitions*

Most Christians regard picketing as the exclusive monopoly of political liberals. But Jews have been picketing the

23. I am not suggesting that this tactic will work only if everyone gets involved. No tactic should ever be begun which relies on "getting everyone involved" to achieve success. But the more who start getting involved, the tougher it will be on opponents.

Soviet Embassy in Washington for well over a decade, day in and day out. They protest the poor treatment of Jews in the Soviet Union. They hand out brochures. This infuriates the Soviets, but there is nothing they can do about it. These picketers are dedicated. They have a cause to defend. Why should Christians be any less committed?

Picketing gets public attention. Some people resent it, but not all. The point is, you can enlist the support of some passers-by if you are out there handing out literature and asking people to sign a petition. It really is not crucial what the petition says or what effect it will have. The point is, *you get the name and address of someone who may be of assistance to you later on.* This goes into your files, preferably computerized.

If necessary, go down each morning to the city hall and get authorization to demonstrate. This protects you. You may not have to do this initially, but if the bureaucrats protest your picketing, then get authorization. You are, as always, exercising your First Amendment liberties as a citizen. This argument carries weight. You are exercising your right of free speech and also free assembly. You are expressing your opinions publicly. It is risky to deny you these rights.

If you are denied your written daily or weekly authorization, insist that the bureaucrat who denies you your permit *put it in writing on official stationery that he is personally forbidding you to demonstrate.* Write up the statement you want him to type up and sign. Naturally, he will refuse. When he refuses, demand to speak to his superior and get him to sign. Always carry a tape recorder and have a witness present when you confront a bureaucrat who is likely to deny you anything. You do not need to let him see it. It is wise not to threaten anything, or reveal a recorder, until after the bureaucrats has said "no."

Organize teams of mothers or others who are willing to commit a few hours during the week. Organize a time schedule. Get someone to phone each morning to make sure no one has forgotten. Protesting effectively takes organization, just like anything else. Make up a few signs that say "Let My People Go," or "Parents' Rights to Educate Their Children," or "First Amendment Liberties," or "Our School Costs Taxpayers Nothing," or "Why Are We Being Persecuted?" or "Keep Our School Open," or "Christians Have Rights, Too," or "Citizens for Non-Humanist Education." Get some signs for the kids to carry in the afternoon, after school: "Of Course

I Can Read," or "Why Deny Me a Godly Education?" or "My Education Costs You Nothing," or "No Drugs In My School!" or "Christian Schools Produce Christian Citizens." Go down to the headquarters of the bureaucracy which is causing trouble for you. Be there at least when people are going to work, at the lunch hour, and when people are going home from work.

Hand out press releases, typeset and printed brochures, and even promotional brochures for your school. You may be able to enroll some new students. Get people to sign petitions. But keep at it. *Once you begin a picketing campaign, it is important to keep it going, no matter what.* This tells the bureaucrats that your group is determined to fight them tooth and nail forever. This discourages the opposition. Again, *count the cost.* It looks bad if you begin a campaign and then quit. Even if you get few visible results, the presence of representatives of your group on a daily basis is a symbol of the high cost to the bureaucrats of pursuing you. Never forget, *they fear adverse publicity.* The more good publicity your cause receives, the better off you are.

Is there one specific bureaucrat who has denied you your Constitutional liberties? Consider picketing his home, especially when he leaves for work in the morning, when his children come home from school, and when he returns from work. Be sure you are polite. Never make noise to disturb the neighborhood. Speak pleasantly to his neighbors. Say things like, "I just can't understand why he would shut down our little school. We have such a good program." You are a *wounded lamb.* Never forget it. *But you are not a lamb for the slaughter.* Never let *him* forget it.

Your goal is to stop him from causing you pain. Your goal is to persuade him that the cost to him, personally, of inflicting pain on you, is just not worth it. You must inflict embarrassment on him, not to mention fear concerning his career. Your immediate tactical program should be to impose more pain and embarrassment on the enemy than he is willing to tolerate. But you must always impose such costs on him *in a manner by which it will be very difficult for him to retaliate against inexpensively.* He may retaliate, but it should never be cost-free retaliation.

As for petitions, try to enlist the cooperation of other churches in your area. Try to enlist the cooperation of other

Christian schools. Ask them if you can get their members or parents to sign a petition defending the First Amendment liberties of your school. If you encounter resistance that you think is based on the hesitation of the other group to allow you to assemble a mailing list from their members, tell them it is a list only for Christian education, and that if they get in trouble later on, you will make the list available to them to defend themselves. Again, we return to that familiar theme, *build that mailing list.* This is a crucial tool of resistance.

### *A Public Hearing*

If the bureaucrats continue to pressure your organization, and it becomes clear that they intend to pursue you into the courts, demand a public hearing. Find out what the bureaucracy's rules governing public hearings are. They will have to tell you if you put your request in writing. *This is one of the most important steps you can take, and it must be taken early.* If you know what rules they are governed by, you can make use of those rules to achieve your purposes. You may be "stonewalled" for a time. *They know how vulnerable they are to anyone who understands the nature of the competition, namely, "looking it up."* If they drag their feet, start pursuing legal action. Go to the city's attorney and ask him to look into the matter. If he balks, go to the state, county, or even Federal attorney. The word will get back to the bureaucracy, even if everyone tells you nothing can be done. Use the grapevine to pressure your opponents.

If the bureaucrats still refuse to give you a public hearing, get on the phone to the politicians. Do whatever you can to get each one to commit *in writing* that he thinks your group is owed a public hearing. This does not force the official to take a stand with you, but it does force him to agree publicly to the principle of *open deliberations*. It costs an elected official very little to affirm the principle of open deliberations, just so long as it is not *his* deliberations that you are trying to pry open. Yet this is the principle, above all other principles, that the bureaucrats are afraid of. They desperately want to avoid public scrutiny. If they balk after the politicians have publicly affirmed your group's right to an open hearing, they are risking budgetary cut-backs next year. Step by step, *you are creating pain for your opponents*. This, after all, is the whole idea.

When the public hearing is scheduled, start getting on the

phone. Get your computer in operation. Mail notices asking people to come and support you. Make it clear that their physical presence at the hearings could make the difference. The bureaucrats may try to reschedule the hearing if they get wind of this. Protest this if you have a large crowd scheduled. Give in if you haven't.

Never forget: *it is a zero-cost response for someone to say he will come to a hearing; it is not a zero-cost response to show up*. People will do what is easy for them. Every person who agrees to come must be contacted the day before to remind him, and then an hour before the hearing just to make sure. If necessary, get car pools together to drive people. Once you have a commitment, you must go to considerable trouble to see to it that the commitment is met.

If you can get cooperation from other schools and churches at this stage, do it. Ask one more time. *But regard it as your responsibility to call everyone who promises to show up to remind him to show up*. Try to get the phone number of every person in the other person's group who agrees to come. Do not try to pass the responsibility of phoning these people to any other group.

Naturally, you will videotape the proceedings. Naturally, you will also do everything possible to see to it that representatives of the local media show up at the meeting. Naturally, you will produce an initial public statement in the form of a press release before the meeting begins. As soon as the meeting is over, you will type up yet another press release regarding the outcome of the meeting, and hand-deliver it to the local media early the next morning—sooner, if possible. *You will make it easy for the media to report your version of the story.*

The crowd should not be rowdy. But it is important that your people get there *one hour early.* Get them seated early. Then late-comers can line up in the hallway. This really scares the bureaucrats, since meetings are normally poorly attended. A murmuring crowd in a hallway is a bad sign. They may think that twice as many people are coming. They really won't know what to think. They know that whatever they decide will be public. If they try to defer a decision, the pastor should *immediately* stand up and address the crowd, before the chairman of the meeting can stop him:

> "Ladies and gentlemen, we have not been able to settle this matter tonight. This is making it very difficult for us to run our

little school. We need your help. I am asking you all to come back next [ *date* ], and next time, please bring one or two extra people with you. We want to get as many people here as we can."

That really scares the bureaucrats. They know that by deferring a decision, they could face a monster crowd. They have no idea how you managed to get out this large a crowd. They are afraid that you really will bring in twice as large a crowd the next time. The longer they delay, the worse it gets for them. Their way of life—"demand, threaten, conceal, and delay"—is being threatened by your ability to mobilize people.

### *Prayer*

Throughout any program of resistance, churches need to be in prayer. I have waited until the closing pages of this essay to discuss prayer. Prayer needs to be specific. People need to know what, specifically, to pray about. The steps I have outlined so far provide a lot of specifics.

The first prayer request is always for *the peace of the church*. This should be a weekly prayer in every church all of the time: "I exhort therefore, that first of all, supplications, prayers, intercessions, and giving of thanks, be made for all men; for kings, and for all that are in authority; that we may live a quiet and peaceable life in all goodness and honesty. For this is good and acceptable in the sight of God our Saviour" (I Tim. 2:1-3). Any church which refuses to pray this publicly on a regular basis is asking for trouble because it is not taking Paul's exhortation seriously. We are to pray for peace—not a peace based on compromise, but peace based on the State's willingness to allow us to go about our affairs, building the kingdom of God.

When the State begins to inhibit our actions in building up God's kingdom institutions, then we must begin to pray more specifically. We must pray for the success of specific kingdom projects: building a Christian school, starting a new church in a zoned area of town, having Bible studies in homes in zoned areas. This is a real problem. Writes Rushdoony:

> As early as the 1940's, the Federal Council of Churches [now the National Council—G.N.] of Churches of Christ, together with local councils of churches and the Home Missions Council of North America developed a "Master Plan" for the location and relocation of Protestant churches. Dr. H. Paul Douglass, director

> of Co-operative Field Research for the F.C.C.C.A., toured the country, conferring with local leaders to set up the plan. Area Comity Councils of cooperating churches were created. The plan for the proper location of churches was then urged on city planning commissions. Very quickly, orthodox church groups outside the F.C.C.C.A. found themselves unable to get permits to build. Thus the Rev. Lawrence R. Eyres had organized the First Orthodox Presbyterian Church in Portland, Oregon, and applied for permission to build on their lots. The answer they received was the following statement: "There are already enough churches and denominations to serve the needs of this community and it is therefore economically unsound to place additional churches there." . . . The First Orthodox Presbyterian Church, facing a long legal battle and declining attendance because of inadequate rented facilities, bought property outside the city limits, built there, and prospered.[24]

Zoning laws against "home churches" have been passed in many communities. As Rushdoony comments, "The Christian Church of the New Testament era would have been eliminated by such zoning laws [had the churches abided by any such laws—G.N.], because, while it spread extensively across the empire, numbering possibly half a million, its members were mostly limited in the local churches, and met in homes. There is no record of any church buildings in the New Testament."[25]

If the church encounters systematic resistance by the civil government, then it must adopt a specific type of prayer. *The congregation must pray that specific officials who are resisting God's kingdom be eliminated from their offices, or else change their minds.* In every meeting of the church, the pastor or praying elder must specifically pray against this man's actions, calling on God to change the man's mind as He directs the heart of kings (Prov. 21:1), or else remove the man, as He removes kings (Dan. 2:21). This means that the church's leaders must strive to discover just who is blocking the church within the local or state bureaucracy. Other churches must be ready to pray with the besieged church, once the facts of the matter plainly identify the culprit.

When churches begin to pray publicly against each other's enemies, they will become a force to be reckoned with. Until

---

24. R. J. Rushdoony, *The Nature of the American System* (Fairfax, VA: Thoburn Press, [1965] 1978), pp. 57f.

25. *Ibid.*, p. 60.

they do, the bureaucrats can use their time-honored strategy of *divide and conquer*. Churches will not be a major threat to the existing bureaucratic system until they stop assuming that the alligator which is eating the fellow next to them will have its appetite satisfied forever. When the alligator is finished with the person next to you, it will come back for you.

### *Fund Raising*

Some of these tactics are expensive. The day you are forced to hire a lawyer is the day you will need money.

The first source of money is your mailing list. I keep coming back to this topic because it is absolutely crucial. You need a mailing list—up to date—that can serve as your initial source of funds.

You need to write fund-raising appeals. The master of such appeals is Jerry Huntsinger. He has written a course on the subject that is very valuable, *Fund Raising Letters*. You can order it for $95 (non-profit organization rate) from:

Emerson Publishers
P.O. Box 15274
Richmond, VA 23227
(804) 266-2499

Some of the basic rules are these:

1. Relatively small letterheads (upper left-hand corner)
2. A full date (April 15, 1984): right-hand side
3. A three-line "hook" under the letterhead, such as:

   Will the government
   shut down your church
   school next term?
4. Dear Friend:
5. Short, indented paragraphs in the letter (with underlining)
6. A close (In Christ, In His Name, etc.)
7. A signature
8. A brief P.S. which calls for specific action

It would help to have a photograph in the upper right-hand corner of the first page. A photo of your school's padlocked door—even if you have to put up the chain and padlock as a symbol—would be good. Get a photo of Officer Ray standing in front of the church's door. If the police actually dragged off the pastor in handcuffs, so much the better, if you have a photo. Intersperse the appeal letter with several photographs. *Real horror stories about real situations get donations.* After painting a verbal picture of the problem, paint a *vision of victory*. Show them how money sent to your cause immediately goes to work to fight the bad guys and defend the good guys. You are fighting for *their* liberties, for *their* school, for *their* church. *You are fighting their cause.* For this, you need immediate financial support of $25, $35, $50, or $100. Enclose a return envelope (not postage-paid, in my view: it looks too "professional").

*The more outraged you can make the reader, the more likely he is going to be to write a check.* The more trouble you appear to be able to cause the bad guys, the readier he will be to "hire" you to fight this holy war. The more clearly he sees that you are fighting in the cause of Christ, the more ready a Christian is likely to be to send money.

If you have a really "hot" story, you may be able to rent lists and mail to them. If you get the names of donors, you can still do well even if you only break even on the mass mailings. But it is not easy to break even on Christian mailing lists, unless it is *your own list* which you have built up over several years. This is why building up a mailing list is important as a self-defense measure.

## *Conclusion*

When we decide that we will not allow our efforts to be stopped by the efforts of humanist bureaucrats, we have made an important psychological transition. We have become resisters. This has not been a familiar calling for conservative Christians for many decades, although it certainly is part of the Protestant-Puritan heritage.

It is important to count the cost. This volume of *Christianity and Civilization* is designed to help readers begin to make this important estimate. Do not get involved if the issues are not important to you, and you are not willing to follow through.

Our enemies are vulnerable. We do not recognize this vulnerability, which is part of their mystique. When we see the "soft underbelly" of modern bureaucracy, we can design resistance tactics to take advantage of these weaknesses. We must learn to choose the battlefields to our advantage, and to take away the advantages our opponents enjoy on their own turf.

The fundamental weaknesses of bureaucracy are these:

1. Dependence on politicians for a budget
2. Vulnerability to political mobilization
3. A fear of being embarrassed publicly
4. Complex rule books that no one is quite sure about
5. Fear of making an *exposed* procedural mistake
6. Fear of legal precedents going against them
7. Fear of law suits, especially personal
8. Fear of publicity
9. Lack of skills with the media
10. Unfamiliarity with determined, religious resistance
11. Personnel with limited abilities
12. High-paid jobs of limited responsibility
13. Fear of superiors (no more promotions)
14. An inability to make one-step decisive decisions

Because we live in a Constitutional republic, we have numerous avenues of resistance short of nonviolent, illegal resistance and violent, illegal resistance. There is no need at this stage of the battle to capitulate to every demand of bureaucracy, nor is there any need to take up arms. The slow, deliberate organized tactics of nonviolent legal resistance are still enormously effective. We have not yet begun to fight.

Because bureaucracies escalate their attack on opponents, and because they never are skilled at mapping out long-term strategies, they can be beaten. Because they are unable to spot a coming crisis early enough to take cost-effective steps to head it off, we are in a position to go about our affairs quietly. We can prepare for the coming confrontations at our own pace most of the time.

The lack of immediate confrontation is no excuse for not preparing. We should be clear about where we are headed. We must not be as short-sighted as our bureaucratic, humanistic opponents. So far, Christians have been even more short-sighted. This must end, soon. We are in a religious war. There will be a victor and a loser. It is our responsibility to work towards comprehensive victory.

Only since the late 1970s have even a small number of Christian leaders begun to perceive the necessity of entering the arena of conflict. Only recently have they begun to use the language of victory in motivating their followers. But the change is here. The humanists are worried about it, as well they should be. Our advantage at this point is that we seem to be innocuous. We seem to be no threat to the entrenched humanist system. Organizationally, we are no real threat, *yet*, but with time, training, experience, and the proper motivation, we will be a threat. Their head was crushed by Jesus Christ at the cross; the fact that Satan bruised our heel is neither here nor there. As time goes on, we will crush their institutions just as surely as Christ crushed Satan's head at Calvary. We will replace them in those institutions that are biblically sanctioned and therefore allowed to remain standing. (The public schools will not be among the institutions left standing.)

The non-revolutionary humanists always escalate slowly. This is the way of all non-revolutionary bureaucracies. They are going to pressure us intermittently, and in so doing, will give Christian leaders incentives to learn the skills of resistance. The present pace of tyranny matches our woefully inexperienced condition. We will "learn by doing." We will be taught how to fight by our opponents. They are unlikely to take the offensive rapidly and comprehensively enough to do more than make people angry enough to resist. This is just what Christians need.

# TERMITE TACTICS; OR HOW TO BE A 98-POUND SAMSON

Wayne C. Johnson

IN 1969, the liberal intelligentsia were sharply divided between the Old Left and the New Left. At most campuses, the faculties were divided between these two warring factions, struggling for supremacy. At Purdue University, things were different.

Purdue missed the revolution. Situated amidst the cornfields of Northern Indiana (and with Indiana University siphoning off most of the sociology majors and artsy-craftsy types), Purdue University was the eye of the storm, alma mater of the astronauts, home of science, technology, and agriculture, where people learned how to make and do things. Wisconsin, Columbia, and Kent State had the Old Left and the New Left. Purdue had the What's Left.

The What's Left were a pretty sad bunch, caught in the Twilight Zone of a campus where the students were stubbornly more conservative than their professors. War, for instance, was not an issue at Purdue. It was a science. The professor foolish enough to bring the Vietnam issue before his class saw it immediately wrenched from his grasp as the class chose up sides. On the one hand, were the Navy ROTC cadets arguing passionately for sea power. The astrophysicists, who today are actually developing it, were hinting at the coming "high frontier."

Dumbfounded, the What's Left professor would sit back helplessly as the nuclear engineers joined the fracas, pointing out the efficacy of strategic nuclear weapons. And then would come the slide rules. Hundreds of slide rules. Thousands of slide rules.

This was 1969 and Hewlett-Packard was just launching the mini-calculator revolution. For thousands of engineering students, the problems of life were still solved by the furrowed brow and hunched shoulders, fingers working feverishly at the white plastic slide rule. Within minutes of bringing up the

Vietnam War, the What's Left professor at Purdue had an entire class waving slide rules at one another, shouting about ballistics and trajectory patterns, proving and disproving one hypothesis and then the other.

The astrophysicists usually won. It's a shame they weren't running the war.

Helpless, dejected, the What's Left at Purdue were looked down upon by their peers at more radically chic universities. For a few brief months, it looked like things might be happening at Purdue when a student demonstration ended in the arrest of more than twenty students. But then the Administration expelled them all and Purdue's short-lived revolution was over.

Just imagine how difficult it was to get published! Professors have always lived by the "publish or perish" rule, but what respectable New Left publication was going to print an article by a professor from a campus like Purdue? A librarian from Bob Jones had a better chance!

One might make the case that the Great Bongo-Bongo Incident had to happen. It was inevitable.

It all started when in my weekly column for the *Purdue Exponent*, I criticized the sloppy scholarship of another article aimed directly at me personally. He pointed out that I had once been a student of his and that I could only have been talking about him when I spoke of the Political Mythology Department. Furthermore, I represented everything that was wrong with this country ("Mr. Johnson, you do not think, you do not feel, you do not care, you do not . . .").

Needless to say, a student columnist rarely gets the privilege of having a professor go off the deep end and engage in a personal attack, in a student paper, no less! I was ecstatic! I had not intended to aim my article at any individual, least of all Professor Raymon. But when he responded with such wild-eyed rhetoric, I played it for all it was worth.

In the next issue, I pointed out that I wasn't speaking about anyone in particular in my first article. Furthermore, my description of the Political Mythology professor was so uncomplimentary, that one must have a severely damaged self-image to identify with such a caricature.

That did it. He came completely unglued. His next letter went on and on. (The first letter had been so wordy and pointless that the editors had several times been forced to resort to that most devastating of literary insults, the ". . ."). This time, he knew he had gone too far. He called the newspaper office and told them that he believed his letter no longer to be timely and wished to withdraw it.

Too late.

It had already been copied and circulated throughout the newspaper offices and was prominently displayed on the bulletin board usually reserved for cartoons. Of course, I had secured a copy.

The original column and the subsequent exchange of letters were sent to the Editor of *The Alternative* magazine (now known as *The American Spectator*) which found the incident of a professor willingly throwing himself into the lion's den absolutely irresistible. They printed the entire exchange in the place of their monthly humor column.

Poor Professor Raymon. Things were only going to get worse. While it is customary to refer to one's instructors as "Professor," the fact is that many of these instructors do not yet have full professorial status. In Professor Raymon's case, he was just coming up for tenure.

As I mentioned, it was pretty tough for a What's Left Professor from a nothing's-happening university like Purdue to get published in one of the more respectable radical journals. It seemed the least we could do was help old Raymon out.

We ordered fifty copies of the issue of *The Alternative* in which Professor Raymon's letters appeared and had a rubber stamp made, which we imprinted on the cover of each issue—before delivering them to the mailboxes of all of Raymon's colleagues in the Political Science Department. It said simply,

"RAYMON FINALLY PUBLISHED! SEE PAGE 9!"

Thinking back, I suspect Raymon might have been able to survive if he just hadn't blown up every time someone teased him over the next few days. But alas! Like the New Left, the What's Left didn't have a whole lot of humor. Raymon proceeded to throw his hands aloft and go into an absolute rage whenever he was "congratulated" on his publishing success.

Funny thing. When the faculty committee voted, he didn't get tenure.

### *"Mizz Baxter Goes Bonkers"*

Of course, her actual name wasn't Mizz Baxter, it was Mizz Something-Else, but on the odd chance that this publication makes it through the censor at one of those small sanitariums in downstate Illinois, I just wouldn't want to be responsible for pushing her over the edge . . . again.

It all started when Mizz Baxter took her sabbatical leave from the Northwestern University Philosophy Department back in the early seventies. That was probably a good idea. Deciding to spend her vacation teaching at Purdue, however, was definitely a bad idea (the first of several).

To fully appreciate Mizz Baxter's situation, one must remember that the late sixties and early seventies were a time of turmoil on our nation's college campuses. There were riots and demonstrations, civil disobedience and just a hint of revolution in the air. Heady stuff for an old fellow traveller like Mizz Baxter, who had all but given up hope that she would live to see the collapse of the fascist superstate and the dawn of proletariat victory. (Don't laugh, there were lots of people that talked that way back then. Really.)

Then it happened. She was walking across the mall from University Hall to Stewart Center when, glancing down, she saw painted those words that were to change her life.

"CUBA WEEK. HEAR THE TRUTH ABOUT COMMUNISM IN CUBA FROM FORMER AMERICAN DIPLOMAT TO HAVANA, PAUL BETHEL."

The time and place of Bethel's speech was noted below, in smaller letters, along with the name of the sponsoring organization. To most students, it was just another watercolor message to be washed away with the next rainstorm. But when Mizz Baxter read those words, she was immediately gripped with that mixture of fear and exhilaration that only the combat soldier can truly know. The Enemy was here.

There wasn't time to waste. Revolutionary action must be bold and imaginative. Later that morning, she would awaken her Introductory Philosophy students to the coming conflict. She would not dwell on mere factuality, but rather sublimate those facts to the necessities of dialectical thought. She would tell a lie.

No, not a lie. A bone fide whopper.

As she stood before the class and began to tell them of the

Enemy's plan to spread vicious anti-Castro propaganda on the Purdue campus, she detected the first hints of interest. A cocked eyebrow here, a sideways glance there. She had them! Now, for the clincher. She announced that she had information from an unimpeachable source that the entire CUBA WEEK program was funded by the CIA and the leader of the sponsoring group was a paid CIA agent.

Many of my fellow students found the charge mildly interesting, particularly those who knew the alleged CIA agent, namely, me. I like to think I have as much of a sense of humor as the next running dog, but this was a bit much. After all, student organizations at Purdue have all of their funds held in trust by the University administration and every financial transaction must be approved in writing by a faculty sponsor. Like most student organizations, our little conservative group was always strapped for money. Surely an organization like the CIA could afford to keep up appearances in a style somewhat grander than ours. Still, it was an opportunity to have a little fun and we never passed up one of those.

### *A. The Haunting*

It was about 6:00 P.M., the dinner hour at Purdue, but Mizz Baxter was still working late in her office. She was somewhat surprised when three students stepped into her office and asked for a moment of her time (I took along two friends who wouldn't have missed it for the world).

"Mizz Baxter?" I asked.

"Yes?"

"My name is Wayne Johnson, the person whom you identified in your classroom today as a paid CIA operative," I said.

Mizz Baxter had clearly been caught off guard, but her recovery was almost immediate. She would not be tested and found wanting. . . .

"Are you here to deny it?" she asked testily.

I couldn't resist. Actually I had come to deny it, but suddenly I realized how ridiculous this entire conversation was bound to be.

I narrowed my eyes, and spoke as raspy as I could, without laughing. "No," I said slowly. "I'm here to find out who the leak is in our organization."

Out of the corner of my eye, I saw my friend Stan almost swallow his gum and then try to choke back the laughter, with only partial success.

She bit. What followed is almost beyond narrative. We exchanged charges and counter-charges, each more ridiculous than the last. Only she wasn't kidding.

"Let's just say that we both know what the military-industrial complex is doing on this campus," she sputtered, with growing fear and a slightly shaky voice, adding "my source is none of your business!" Her voice was now a full octave higher than it was when we first arrived . . . and rising. If this continued, dogs would soon be howling. It was clearly time to leave.

"Listen, Baxter," I said. "Me and the military-industrial complex don't like what you're saying and doing around here, get the picture?"

"Yeah," said Stan, "and dat goes double for the CIA."

To fully appreciate this last statement, you simply had to know Stan. He looked like a close relation of a Mafia chieftain. In fact, in real life, I think he was a close relation of a Mafia chieftain. In any case, with the trench coat pulled up around his ears, the effect was either incredibly sinister or marvelously funny. For Mizz Baxter, it was the former.

As we headed out the door, I turned for a final parting shot, "And don't call the police."

### *B. The Complaint*

By late afternoon of the following day, I had all but forgotten the great CIA Caper. Then, about 4:00 P.M., I happened to run into the campus police captain, who shall also remain nameless. He asked me if I knew a Professor Baxter in the Philosophy Department. Without committing myself, I told him that I didn't believe Purdue had a Professor Baxter. He then added that she was actually a Northwestern Professor, temporarily teaching at Purdue.

"Why do you ask?" I added cautiously.

"Funniest thing, Wayne," said the Captain, "this dame flies in here first thing this morning and tries to file charges against you, the CIA, and the 'military-industrial complex,' whatever that is. A real loonytune, for my money."

I looked at my watch and quickly nodded good-bye before the good Captain realized that I hadn't answered his question. I ducked into the Student Union and walked swiftly toward the far exit when I saw her. Good old Mizz Baxter.

I think I've got these things under control now, but this was 1971 and the campus war was almost as hot as the shooting war. Again, I simply couldn't resist. I walked up behind her as she stood looking at a window display case in the Union sponsored by the John Brown Society. It was all about oppression and grapes.

"That wasn't very smart," I whispered.

It's nice to know that real live communists get scared, too, because there was no other explanation for her reaction. She uttered several unintelligible sentence fragments and practically flew down the hall and out the door.

I understand from my police captain acquaintance that Mizz Baxter again tried to press charges against just about everybody and everything, real and imagined, only this time she was asked to spend two thirty-minute sessions with a member of the psychiatric staff at the Purdue Hospital.

I'm still waiting for my check.

## *Conclusions*

Unfortunately, the university student today is confronted with a new orthodoxy on campus which does not permit the kind of response which we were able to offer in the late sixties and early seventies. There is a tendency among many observers to think that philosophies on campus have changed. They haven't. What has occurred is the Stalinization of the New Left.

Just as the romantic revolutionaries of the Bolshevik Revolution were replaced by the iron fist of Stalinism, so have the New Left campus radicals of the seventies been replaced by a stifling uniformity that is more structured, more repressive, yet fundamentally the same in philosophy.

The academic community has even frightened itself with its harsh, authoritarian reaction to the new wave of politically conservative publications that have sprung up on college campuses across the nation. Academic freedom, which was formerly necessary to overthrow the Old Liberalism, no longer serves the purpose of the new regime. Of course, parents and administrators couldn't be happier. Things were so difficult then.

Some commentators have suggested that the tight job market is responsible for the prevailing quiet. Possibly. But revolutionaries didn't care about job markets. They had no intention of working for the "fascist corporate state." So why has it gotten so quiet? I suspect what has happened is not really new. It seems that the people who start revolutions seldom are the ones who finish them.

No, the job market didn't extinguish the campus wars, nor did the collapse of the Vietnamese war effort. The revolution on campus was over because somebody won.

The victory for the New Left did not occur because their arguments were either true or compelling. Their victory was assured because we fought the wrong battle. It began when we joined forces with the Old Liberalism in what was essentially a traditionalist battle.

As the new authoritarians began to impose their world-view, and exclusively their world-view, on the academic community, we fought back. But instead of articulating an adequate defense of our own world-view, we appealed to "fairness." We admitted the legitimacy of their position, asking only that our own views be given "equal time."

We opted for peaceful co-existence. And we lost.

The greatest failure was among those individuals and groups which we loosely classify as "conservative." American conservatism had, by the late sixties, become intellectually bankrupt. The only vitality left in the movement was among Austrian school economists and the Chicago school monetarists. Foolishly, conservatives made the same mistake Marx did in assuming that all of life's problems were essentially economic. In so doing, conservatism became essentially irrelevant, attempting to answer problems concerning free speech, pornography, the draft, homosexual "rights," drug use, authority, etc. using economic arguments. We were prepared to let the marketplace solve our moral dilemmas.

"Do what you want to do as long as you don't hurt anybody" went from the script of the counter-culture stageplay "HAIR," to become the guiding principle of the conservative movement. To be painfully blunt, political conservatives didn't have any answers. If it had not been for the paranoia and foolishness which the New Left brought to us on such a grand scale, we would have not had the few apparent victories which we did enjoy.

Institutionally, America was a mess. The few churches which were not actually part of the revolution, had transcended all of these earthly battles, concentrating on soteriology. Parents, teachers, and administrators alike just wanted students to stop making trouble.

Politically speaking, "student unrest" was a goldmine. Any politician worth his salt could ride a student riot to a 54% majority. As late as 1976, Dr. S. I. Hayakawa was elected to the United States Senate from California solely upon the reputation he gained years earlier by personally unplugging the loudspeakers at a campus demonstration.

Unfortunately, that was about all we were intellectually prepared to do—unplug their loudspeakers. There were a few sad attempts at formulating a positive conservative response to all that was going on, but most were just what the New Left said they were, reactionary.

Even among the campus "conservatives," the only genuine distinctives were drawn between "traditionalists" and "libertarians." The traditionalists were reactionary, in the most classic sense of the word, while the libertarians simply retired from the field of battle.

Modern libertarianism, the temporary ally of the traditionalists of the sixties and seventies, has become the enemy of Christian political action in the eighties. The extent to which this fact is perceived was made plain in one recent political campaign in California. When asked what the size of the Libertarian Party vote would be in a San Francisco legislative district, one politico answered with a question of his own, "I don't know, how many homosexuals are there in the 40% tax bracket?" In other words, the unspoken Christian foundations upon which classical libertarians premised their view of society are being swept away, leaving behind nothing but the self-interest of the autonomous man.

One might deduce from that rather cynical comment that the on-again, off-again alliance between libertarians and conservatives is definitely off, probably for good. It remains to be seen whether the balance of what we euphemistically refer to as the "Conservative Movement" will follow the leadership of Christian thinkers in taking this country back, or continue shadow-boxing the "enemies of the permanent things." And if it does?

Political commentators have been predicting a fundamental realignment of voting patterns for more than two decades now. None of those commentators are prepared for what is going to happen. Why? Because they fail to realize that the revolution that is taking place is not a revolution of the intellect, the affections, or the will, but rather a reformation of the heart.

Because the Christian faith speaks first to the heart, it is beyond the understanding of the pollsters and the commentators. It is, accordingly, the most powerful of all social forces, sweeping away the old man and reforming society beyond all expectations.

This is what is happening in our country today. The false divisions are set aside. The battle lines are clearly drawn. But unlike the campus battles of the sixties, in this battle our victory was assured from the foundation of the world.

Won't Mizz Baxter be surprised.

# RESISTANCE TACTICS OF AZARIAH AND OF PAUL

Wayne C. Sedlak

**But when he was strong, his heart was lifted up to his destruction: for he transgressed against the Lord his God, and went into the temple of the Lord to burn incense upon the altar of incense. And Azariah the priest went in after him, and with him fourscore priests of the Lord, that were valiant men: And they withstood Uzziah the king, and said unto him, It appertaineth not unto thee, Uzziah, to burn incense unto the Lord, but to the priests the sons of Aaron, that are consecrated to burn incense: go out of the sanctuary; for thou hast trespassed; neither shall it be for thine honor from the Lord God. Then Uzziah was wroth, and had a censer in his hand to burn incense: and while he was wroth with the priests, the leprosy even rose up in his forehead before the priests in the house of the Lord from beside the incense altar. And Azariah the chief priest, and all the priests, looked upon him, and, behold, he was leprous in his forhead, and they thrust him out from thence; yea, himself hasted also to go out, because the Lord had smitten him (II Chronicles 26:16-20).**

THE events surrounding Pastor Sileven and his church in Nebraska have caused many Christians to re-think views concerning a Christian's duty in "rendering unto Caesar the things which are Caesar's." Increasingly, Christian people who are at heart peaceful and law-abiding citizens, are finding themselves the target of vicious state and federal enactments which attempt to close Christian schools, harass ministries, and bludgeon churches into adherence to state dictates. This is justified, of course, by the average American on the basis that "there simply must be a Jim Jones lurking behind every pew." As a result, the average Christian finds himself caught on the "horns of a dilemma." His theology, heretofore, has not allowed him to consider even a passive (much less active!) resistance to such tyranny. And yet the injustice of being deemed a "criminal" so assaults his conscience and fills him with a righteous indignation that he feels obligated to take a stand in order to uphold justice for himself and his church. But his theology (usually based upon a misunderstanding of Romans 13) will not let him stand or at the very least renders him ineffective and he fights as "one who beateth the air."

What principles must guide such a Christian? In order to answer that, consideration must be given to more fundamental questions: What relationship does the Chruch have with the State? Are they friends or enemies? Is there perhaps a master-servant relationship between them? These questions are dealt with in the passage cited in Chronicles 26.

We have here a remarkable passage. It is the case of King Uzziah who is at first honored by the LORD. We are told that "he did that which was right in the sight of the LORD" (vs. 4) and "he sought God in the days of Zechariah . . . and as long as he sought the LORD, God made him to prosper" (vs. 5). This "prosperity" is clearly outlined. He built towers and fortifications (vs. 9) and organized the army under capable men of war (vs. 12). He equipped his army with the proper weaponry (vs. 14). God "helped him" against Israel's covenant enemies (vs. 7). As a result, his fame was spread far and wide (vs. 15). But again, it is emphasized that his strength and prosperity were not his own; his God "marvelously" helped him. In fact, the word translated "marvelous" is used elsewhere to describe God's "extraordinary" works (cf. Job 37:5, 14). This is the type of help he received from the LORD as an obedient head of state—obedient, that is, unto the precepts of the LORD. In establishing a strong defensive posture for Israel he illustrates one of the purposes of a good ruler, *i.e.* to do his utmost to secure the safety of his people. It should be noted that he specifically defended the church of God against the covenant enemies who had long tormented her, such as the Philistines (vs. 6-7). This is one type of application Peter refers to when he says that rulers are sent by God "for the punishment of evildoers." (Philistines are certainly included among "covenant-breakers" before God.)

However, the heart of King Uzziah was lifted-up in pride and we are told that he transgressed against the LORD and went into the temple in order to burn incense upon the altar. This offering of incense at the altar of God was expressly prohibited to everyone (including kings) except the Levitical priests ordained of God unto that function (Num. 8:19, 24).

This is a point which must be understood. Despite the fact that King Uzziah was *the king*, he too must not be presumptuous to usurp functions which are not delegated to the governing rulers of Israel. Earlier, Saul, as king, had been duly chastened of the Lord because *he* had presumed to offer sacrifice (I Sam. 13:12-14). Neither Uzziah nor Saul nor any other king of Israel was ever considered to be the supreme law of Israel. He, like everyone else, was subject to a Constitution and that Constitution was the Law of God itself.

Uzziah's pride was his undoing as he tried to interfere in the ordinances of worship. In this he was acting like a heathen monarch who refused to be put into subjection to any binding statutes. It was very common for kings in all other pagan nations to control the religion of their respective nations and even assume priestly functions. This was exactly what happened in the well-known situation of Akhenaton the "heretic king" of Egypt. He attempted to change the official religion of Egypt and the worship of the Egyptian god "Amon" in preference for his own god "Aton." As a result, he suppressed the worship of Amon and attempted to abolish all religious cults but his own.[1] This same pattern of interference in religious affairs characterized all the ancient kingdoms. Now, Uzziah was acting like those nations. Unfortunately, this is exactly what the people of Israel had wanted when they first asked for a king to judge them; that is, they wanted a king "like all the other nations" (I Sam. 8:7) and now God was rejecting this king because of his arrogance in defying the constitutional precepts given by Moses. According to our text, he was struck with leprosy (vs. 19), making him "unclean" (Lev. 13). This was certainly fitting as a sign of rejection because he was acting just like the "unclean" nations and their kings instead of being an holy example of obedience to the commandments of the one and true God.

We see also in this text the very clear principle of the separation of the *functions* of church and state. Now, by this it is meant that both church and state operate under the constitution of God's holy law-word but each has its respective ministry to fulfill. The civil government, on its part, is to protect its citizens (as God prospered Uzziah to do) and ad-

---

1. Sir Alan Gardiner, *Egypt of the Pharaohs* (Oxford: Oxford University Press, 1961). p. 228.

minister judgment in criminal and civil disputes as Solomon clearly undertook during his administration (I Kings 3:28). On the other hand, the church of both the Old and New Testaments has its own administrative functions of worship and teaching. That the state ministers to man by *God's command* and under His authority is clearly established in Romans 13:4. That command establishes "the things which are Caesar's" namely, to be a "terror" to the criminal in order to *restrain* his wicked behavior toward others.

This characteristic of restraint stands in stark contrast to the present day emphasis of "creative law" in which justice is violated in the name of humanistic relativism in order to "rehabilitate" the criminal. As a result, the criminal is allowed further opportunities to plunder the community and the hapless victim is left humiliated, unavenged, and vulnerable to further attack. So instead of fulfilling the biblical mandate to use the sword to restrain sinful behavior, according to God's command, the civil government undertakes to establish *its own* ethic and quite religiously *sets the standard* of good and evil. Granted, this is a far more sophisticated violation of church-state relations than was Uzziah's act, but nonetheless just as real.

It should also be noted that both the ministry of the state and that of the church bear individual swords. The state bears the physical sword of justice and the church bears the so-called "spiritual" sword of the proclamation of the Word of God. *Both* bear swords and *both* act to administer that sword *under God* and according to His revealed Constitution for men, the Scriptures. If both act in a godly manner according to Scripture, they will cooperate with one another side-by-side without usurpation for the benefit and sanctity of society. This was the heritage of America over the past 300 years. At the inception of this nation there was a fruitful union of the truth of God's Word with justice, which gave us a Constitution. That Constitution, in turn, promoted and protected Christian precepts and allowed an unprecedented prosperity, as the blessings of God (Deut. 28) were poured out upon this land.

But what if the state or the church (or both) refuse to cooperate and instead begin to violate God's ordained order by usurping power not delegated to them? At that point they become enemies, and one of two possible perversions takes place.

The first type of church-state perversion is seen in Romanism in which the church seeks to use the power of the sword for its own ends. The actions of various popes throughout the later Middle Ages certainly illustrate this usurpation. For example, Pope Innocent III meddled in the affairs of France by placing it under an interdict in 1200 A.D.[2] (An "interdict" is to a country what "excommunication" is to an individual). As a result, King Phillip Augustus II of France yielded to the Pope's wishes.[3]

The Crusades were yet another example of Romanistic power politics. After all, any pope who could call forth powerful armies from all countries to oppose the "infidel" Turk could (and did) call armies against any king of Europe who might refuse to do his bidding. It was under such a threat of armed invasion that King John of England was humbled under the authority of Pope Innocent III.[4] Is it without reason that Innocent could claim that "Europe is my fief"? As a side note, one may regard the exertions of the present pope, as the acclaimed "champion of freedom" in Poland and elsewhere, as a possible indication of a return to medieval power politics in the Romanist tradition.

The second type of church-state perversion is known as Erastianism. Erastianism is named for a Swiss theologian by the name of Thomas Erastus, who was a disciple of Zwingli. His view on this subject was simply that the church owes its existence to the state and therefore must be obedient to it. Obviously, this is not true, as James Bannerman pointed out:

> As a Divine institution, designed for a continued existence on earth, the Church is divinely equipped with all the powers necessary for its own being and welfare, without owing anything to man. Without doing more than merely glance at the argument at present, it is enough to say the Erastian theory proceeds upon the mistake of identifying the Church and State, and denying those essential differences between them, which demonstrate them to be distinct and separate ordinances of God, having each an independent existence.[5]

---

2. Norton Downs, *Basic Documents in Medieval History* (Princeton, NJ: D. Van Nostrand Company, Inc., 1959), pp. 117-118.

3. Wallace Ferguson and Geoffrey Bruun, *A Survey of European Civilization* (Boston: Houghton Mifflin Company, 1962), pp. 205, 207.

4. Frederick G. Marcham, *A History of England* (New York: The MacMillan Company, 1937), p. 141.

5. James Bannerman, *The Church of Christ*, Vol. 1 (Edinburgh: The Banner of Truth Trust, 1960), p. 24.

That Uzziah's actions were certainly Erastian is clear from the text. Because the Lord had made him so very powerful and because he saw himself (rightly) as the protector of the church, he came to view the church's authority and that of its ordained officers as subordinate to his own and consequently atempted to brush those authorities aside in order to offer sacrifice in the temple of God (vs. 16).

At this point, Azariah the priest was faced with the same dilemma as that which Christians in America are increasingly facing today. How must the Christian office-bearer respond to such tyranny? Shall he return "railing for railing"? Shall he play the carpet and render obedience to the "powers that be" and allow Christ's honor and people to be transgressed? Obviously, Azariah the priest responded in neither of these ways. Recognizing the Erastian principle as a violation of God's law, he and 80 other priests of the Lord withstood King Uzziah to his face (vs. 18). There was certainly no passive acquiescence to the dictates of Caesar when Azariah stated "It appertaineth not to thee, Uzziah, to burn incense unto the Lord, but to the priests, the sons of Aaron, that are consecrated to burn incense: GO OUT OF THE SANCTUARY for thou hast trespassed; neither shall it be for thine honor from the Lord God (vs. 18)." Note Azariah's bold and clear testimony as he stands to defend *Christ's honor* and warn the king of his own dishonor. This should show us the church's duty before such a ruler as Uzziah.

### *Pauline Resistance*

Despite the clear stand and bold testimony of Azariah as an officer of the church, many still insist that the Christian is under a higher law now and that such Old Testament examples belong to another dispensation. The Christian of today often sees his duty of "turning the other cheek" as the proper response in "rendering unto Caesar the things which are Caesar's."

The most common justification for this position is one which insists that any resistance to "the higher powers" must always be considered resistance to God (Rom. 13:1). It is interesting that those who most insist on quoting Paul in this chapter of Romans never seem to use Paul's example in Acts, specifically chapters 22-26. It is in these chapters that Paul is called upon to defend himself against the misuse of state power and the pressure politics of the Jews.

For background, it might be helpful to understand that there were two sets of courts in the Roman Empire in Paul's day. The first was called the "Ordo judiciorcum publicorum" which tried severe cases such as murder and treason.[6] Paul was not tried in this type of court. He was tried in the second set of courts called the "Extra ordinem."[7]

Under this second set of courts there were certain procedures which were to be followed. First, Roman law insisted that the accused be tried by the Roman magistrate on his tribunal. Felix was the magistrate which first heard Paul's case, but he did not settle it in order to show favor to the Jews (Acts 24:27). Festus replaced Felix and he, in turn, tried to please the Jews by changing the site for the hearing (Acts 25:9). That hearing would take place in Jerusalem where the influence of the Jews would be strongest. The prisoner, however, had the right to be tried at the tribunal of the magistrate, which in this case was Caesarea. Paul therefore insisted, "I stand at Caesar's judgment seat WHERE I OUGHT TO BE JUDGED (Acts 25:10)." Paul knew his rights as a Roman citizen and he insisted upon them.

The law demanded that there be a formal act of accusation by the interested party. Festus made sure this was done (Acts 25:5). Paul certainly knew his rights in this matter and makes reference to it (Acts 25:16). In addition, the law insisted upon a clear formulation of charges at the time of the hearing. This was called the "Arbitrium iudicantis" and is seen in Acts 25:6-9.[8] The accused had the right to respond to such charges and Paul took the opportunity to do so (Acts 25:8).

One of the most confusing and unjust points of Paul's two year court ordeal is the fact that, though the *charges* were political in form ("sedition, ringleader of a sect"—Acts 24:5, 6), the *evidence* was theological in nature (Acts 24:10-21; Acts 26).[9] Recognizing this, Paul continually answered his accusers theologically. Being a Roman, Festus could not understand such theology, especially since he was looking for some

---

6. A. N. Sherwin-White, *Roman Society and Roman Law in the New Testament* (Grand Rapids: Baker Book House, 1978), p. 13.

7. *Ibid.*, p. 14.

8. *Ibid.*, p. 22.

9. *Ibid.*, p. 57.

justification for the political charges. As a result, he asked for an advisor who would be capable of understanding the essentials of the case. Such an advisor was called a "concilium."[10] The man whom Festus asked to hear and render an opinion was King Agrippa (Acts 25:22). In Acts 25, Paul had already used his legal right to "appeal to Caesar" (which was known as the right of "provocatio"[11]). He did this in order to put aside the jurisdiction of Festus. As a result, Agrippa would have no say in either Paul's immediate condemnation or release. Festus, however, needed Agrippa's help in signifying the nature of the crime in order to write his report intelligently in *sending* Paul to Rome (Acts 25:27). Paul, therefore, was more than willing to argue his case before Agrippa in order to establish clearly the exact nature of all the things with which he was accused (Acts 26:2). Paul must have known that Agrippa's "expertise" (Acts 26:3) would be cited in any report which would be subsequently sent to Caesar. Apparently, Paul argued successfully enough to convince Agrippa that there truly was no basis for the accusations made by the Jews (Acts 26:32). Such successful argumentation before King Agrippa could help Paul immeasurably in light of the fact that the reputation of King Agrippa carried great weight in Roman politics.[12]

There are two other points of Roman law which Paul used to his advantage. Earlier in Acts 22:25-30, Paul forcefully asserted his legal rights as a Roman citizen instead of passively accepting an unjust beating at the hands of the centurion. This appeal to his citizenship was of such weight that the centurion and chief captain immediately ordered a procedural change from the informal harassment of Acts 22:25 to the formal hearing of Acts 22:29-30. This, you will remember, is the same Paul who insisted that we render obedience to the powers that be. One thing is certain, Paul was not one to merely accept *any* verdict of the state simply by virtue of its authority as the state.

The last point which should be emphasized was Paul's understanding of the importance of case-precedent. A case-precedent is an important case which has some outstanding

10. *Ibid.*, p. 17.

11. *Ibid.*, pp. 63-64.

12. Alfred Edersheim, *The History of the Jewish Nation* (Grand Rapids: Baker Book House, 1979), p. 22.

point to it such that the verdict rendered in that case may be used to help other judges determine their verdict in similar cases.

Paul used this principle wisely in Acts 23:6-10. Knowing the natural hatred which existed between the Sadducees and Pharisees, he appealed to the council on the basis that he was a Pharisee being condemned for his stand concerning the resurrection of the dead. He knew that if that council would have then proceeded to condemn him, a case-precedent could have been used in all future cases by the Sadducees who do not believe in the resurrection. This means that they would have been able to use it specifically against Pharisees who did believe in the resurrection. It is not surprising that the Pharisees were the first to rise in defense of Paul's innocence (Acts 23:9).

The case of Paul should certainly give the Christian a clear example of his lawful and biblical reponsibility to use *all* Constitutional precepts to defend himself against the unjust actions and usurpations by any man in authority. This, coupled with the courage of Azariah, will be necessary if godly men are to withstand the present efforts of government officials to subordinate churches and their ministries under state authority. At the present moment, many churches and church schools are being attacked mercilessly. These are usually small, independent ministries which do not have the means to combat the comparatively unlimited resources of the state. As a result, the state is establishing case-precedents throughout the country and with such precedents established it may then begin to attack the larger denominations which do have the means to defend themselves. The final result, if left unchecked, will be the submission of many churches beneath strict governmental guidelines and regulations. Those churches which refuse to submit will be persecuted.

Now is the time for men of wisdom to withstand "Uzziah" as he arrogantly enters the temple of Christ to dishonor it for his own Erastian designs. Such men of wisdom must also be men of immediate action. If Azariah had waited for even one moment, the temple would have been defiled. The Lord upheld the courage of His ordained officers, however, and struck the impious king. Our prayer must be that the Lord will again raise up such men of faith and ultimately, rise up in their defense for the sake of His beloved people.

# COMPUTER GUERRILLAS

A. Richard Immel

**A best-selling author, his wife, and neighbors battle the U.S. Government to a standstill over a proposed timber cut that would denude parts of their scenic little valley in southern Oregon.**

**A national environmental organization blocks a $5-billion power plant project and successfully prods utility regulators in five states to reorder their priorities by putting conservation and alternative energy sources ahead of new power plant construction.**

**A rural refugee from the city, irked by a speeding ticket from a radar-wielding country cop, proves that the radars used by police across the U.S. exceed microwave safety limits established by the federal government.**

BY themselves these events aren't particularly earth-shaking; little guys have been rattling the establishment's cage for years, and once in a while they even win. But there's another common thread here that couldn't have existed more than four or five years ago: in all of these cases the little guys turned to *microcomputers* to even the odds. None of them, in fact, would have had a prayer without the new technology.

Author Richard Bach used his Apple II computer mainly as a word processor in his fight with the Bureau of Land Management in Oregon. "It was absolutely indispensable," he says. "We never could have written the things we had to write without it."

A homebrewed computer model of energy use was the only feasible way for the activist group known as the Environmental Defense Fund (EDF) to stand up to the utility companies and their voluminous and expensive mainframe computer analyses. "The idea was to rub their faces in their own numbers," says Dan Kirshner, EDF's economic analyst.

---

The battle over radar was a personal feud for Paul Lutus, the highly successful professional microcomputer programmer who developed Apple Writer, Graforth, and other best-selling software. Despite its insignificant scale, though, Lutus's battle illustrates the computer's potential for a broader social function. A microcomputer may be used to augment your own resources in what Lutus calls "computer activism."

### *The Computer as Social Guerrilla*

Indeed, one of the more important aspects of the information revolution we hear so much about may not be a personal computer in every home, the automated office of the future, or even so-called computer literacy for our children; the most important thing may be the ramifications of the computer as social guerrilla.

Socially active computing is a departure from most previous antiestablishment computer activity, which has tended to be either destructive or quixotic. Until recently we've seen either outright sabotage by employees or terrorists with axes to grind or the meddling of sometimes playful, sometimes disgruntled individuals quietly burrowing into monolithic mainframe computers at universities and corporations. This sort of sabotage has been the work of expert programmers—known as "hackers" in the trade—who have the skill and know-how to break into large computers and roam around electronically, erasing and changing data or sometimes just leaving a "Kilroy was here" mark as a sort of electronic vandalism.

But now legitimate political and social activists of all stripes are increasingly recognizing the power a microcomputer can lend to their efforts to achieve change. Groups and individuals from Alaska to Atlanta and from Buffalo to Burbank are beginning to see how their Apples, PETs, TRS-80s, North Stars, and Vector Graphics can help them regain control of their lives and the environment we all share. They're talking to each other on their machines and plugging into commercial databases or setting up their own; they're writing letters to congressmen, they're publishing political-action newsletters, and in some cases they're even making their *own* analyses of government and corporate figures, no longer letting the institutions intimidate them with "official" results spewed out by basement-dwelling mainframe computers.

Nobody really knows how much grass-roots computer activism is going on out there, and much of what is happening is tentative. But many such endeavors are off to a good start, and the idea is beginning to spread like Pac-Man. Consider this cross section:

- The Virginia Coalition, a statewide network of action groups, is using a computer for mailing lists and get-out-the-vote campaigns.
- A Washington state group has formed an alternative Grange called Tilth that offers farmers agricultural information through a microcomputer network.
- Neighborhood community groups in Buffalo, Chicago, Denver, and Atlanta are using microcomputers to set up job-skills banks, to fight discriminatory lending practices, and to get funds for neighborhood rehabilitation projects.
- New York's Telecommunications Co-operative Network is one of a mushrooming new breed of service bureaus that provide a wide range of nonprofit and community-activist groups with various computer and telecommunications services such as discounted equipment, cheap rates for computer timesharing, electronic mail, and teleconferencing. "Demand is greater than we expected," says managing director Bob Loeb. The Co-op is eyeing plans to expand nationwide.
- The Disarmament Resource Center, an umbrella organization for some 30 peace groups in northern California, has created a microcomputer network called Peace Net that offers electronic mail, a shared database of antiwar materials, and comprehensive administrative service to coordinate antiwar activities. "We believe technology can be redirected to serve *our* needs," says director Martha Henderson. "We want to use it directly in the work of peace."

Why all of this computer-inspired activity? "It's a great equalizer," Steve Johnson says of the microcomputer. Johnson, a young Oregon researcher who runs Portland's Rain Resource Center, a clearing house for community resources information, has been keeping tabs on grass-roots computing for some time now. He reports a surge of interest in microcomputers over the past year, for which he cites several reasons: more people know how to use computers, prices are lower, and the notion of microcomputers as "hobby" machines is changing.

Perhaps even more important, he thinks, was the 1980 federal election. The computerized campaigns some conservative groups used to target candidates for victory or defeat impressed many politically active people. "It brought home the power of the computer as a tool," Johnson says.

Another factor in this growing use of computers is the parallel phenomenon of computer professionals shedding their apolitical pasts and becoming involved in social activism. Laurie Foster, the spark plug of Peace Net, is a good example. A professional developer of minicomputer systems software, Foster says she was galvanized into action by a speech given by Helen Caldicott of Physicians for Social Responsibility. (Caldicott is the Australian physician who has been protesting nuclear bomb tests in the Pacific Ocean.) Foster donated her services to get Peace Net organized. She's drawn up an elaborate analysis of the Net's software and hardware needs and is accumulating whatever she can beg, borrow, or steal. "I don't have a history of activism, so when *I* get involved, you know people are really coming out of the woodwork," she says.

Computer engineer Lee Felsenstein, designer of the Osborne 1 portable computer, is another active professional. Felsenstein is one of a number of hardware and software engineers belonging to a Berkeley, California, group called the Community Memory Project. To give computing power to people who wouldn't normally have access to computers, Community Memory is developing a system of free computer terminals to be placed in bookstores, laundromats, and other public locations. The project is being financed in part by Pacific Software, a commercial venture that has developed and is now marketing a relational database called Sequitur for mini- and microcomputers.

So far microcomputer manufacturers haven't gone out of their way to encourage the kind of computer activism that has a political edge to it, but this too may be changing. Through its public affairs department, Apple Computer Inc. has begun to donate equipment for computer communications networks to various worthy groups, including some that are promoting social change. In the first year Apple hopes to seed 20 to 25 of these networks with three to five computers each, according to Mark Vermilion, who oversees the project.

What constitutes a worthy group? Apple starts with the

IRS definition of a nonprofit, nontaxable organization and whittles it down from there. "If the Radical Vegetarian League of Ann Arbor came to us with a request for a microcomputer network, we'd turn them down," Vermilion says. "On the other hand, we aren't going to limit ourselves to totally safe projects either. Apple Computer is an adventurous and progressive company." Vermilion says he'd like to make at least some grants to politically or socially active groups involved in human-rights causes and to "certain types of peace organizations if they're largely educational and are addressing needs for citizen awareness and conflict resolution.

"We're obviously going to stay away from groups that would be inappropriate for the corporation to back, but we will be in the forefront when it comes to helping groups whose aim is to benefit communities in innovative ways," he says.

Apple and its fellow sponsoring companies—Hayes Microcomputer Products, Software Publishing Corporation, Southwestern Data Systems, Tymshare, and Visicorp—recently supplied $35,000 worth of computer equipment to help eight community organizations set up communications networks.

As much as computers have been taken up by activists throughout the country, it would be a mistake to assume they have won over the hearts and minds of the entire activist community. Indeed, a strong current of ambivalence about using the new technology runs through some of the more ideologically oriented groups. On the one hand they recognize the utility of microcomputers, but on the other hand there's resentment over unresolved problems created by computer technology. "We don't want to be doing public relations work for the computer manufacturers," says Marcy Darnovsky, who is a member of the Community Memory Project and is also active with the Abalone Alliance, an antinuclear power group.

"Computers are being developed for things we don't like: they're making jobs dull or eliminating jobs altogether, they're collecting information about people, and they're being used by the military to kill people," says Darnovsky, who also edits the *Journal of Community Communications*, a counterculture magazine that publishes critical analyses of the social effects of technological advances in communications. "In terms of the disarmament movement people need to be aware of these negative aspects of computer technology," she concludes.

Political reservations are not the only kind of apprehension that enters the picture. In a study of 28 computerized grass-roots groups, University of Wisconsin researcher Timothy Haight found that while on the whole the groups had few problems using computers, there were exceptions. Computers for Christ, which serves fundamentalist church congregations, is one. "Several of the ministries were concerned that computers were a manifestation of the Beast of the Apocalypse," Haight reported.

### *Apples vs. Chain Saws*

If there is such a presence, it's probably being felt by U.S. Bureau of Land Management (BLM) officials in southern Oregon, where a stubborn band of computer-wielding home owners has shown that the personal computer is a match for the chain saw. As of October of last year, the group had forced the BLM to cancel a routine timber sale. Since then they've entangled more sales in a web of protests and appeals that could end up changing forestry practices throughout the country. What's happening in Oregon is a textbook case of what a small band of seemingly powerless citizens can do with a little help from their friends . . . and a computer or two.

Richard Bach's best-selling book of yesteryear, *Jonathan Livingston Seagull*, is a story about a seagull who does impossible things because he believes he can. It may sound corny to make the analogy, but that's pretty much what happened when a group of rural neighbors came together over the Bach's computer and took on the U.S. Bureau of Land Management.

The tale actually began a couple of years ago when Richard and his wife Leslie left Los Angeles and moved to the idyllic Little Applegate Valley in the southwestern corner of Oregon. "We looked all over the country for a couple of years and finally found the spot," Bach says, adding that it's something "right out of a travel guide to Shangri-la."

They bought a 20-acre parcel on a hilltop with a panoramic view across the 15 miles to California, built a little house there, and then listened in dismay as neighbor Diane Albrechtsen dropped a bombshell: "They're going to cut all the trees down and they won't grow back."

The Bach's were disappointed but philosophical. They said, "Well, it looks like we moved to the wrong place and now let's move on. We'll find some other place, farther north, farther away. But before we do that let's just double-check to make sure that it's a legal timber sale." The Bachs didn't realize it at the time, but they were about to embark on an endeavor that would consume the next two years of their lives.

What they immediately learned was that much of the area was public land under the control of the BLM and that by law the BLM is required to identify commercial stands of timber and periodically offer these tracts for sale. Mrs. Albrechtsen and other Little Applegate Valley residents had unsuccessfully tried to stop earlier timber sales, including that of a 40-acre stand in Grouse Creek Canyon, directly across from the Bach's property. Trees had been cut years before in the same area and had never grown back.

But as the concerned residents delved into stacks of arcane forestry laws and regulations, transcripts of congressional hearings, and BLM records, discrepancies between law and practice took on palpable form. "As we gained an education we saw that what was happening was the old method of timber management called cut-and-run," Bach says.

Although Bach had never before been involved in any kind of social protest, his wife had. After 20 years as a movie and TV actress, Leslie had turned to political organizing in the entertainment industry and pursued it far enough, her husband says, to get "clubbed and teargassed in the streets" during a demonstration against the war in Vietnam.

Leslie immediately drew on her organizing skills. She helped to create an umbrella organization called Threatened and Endangered: Little Applegate Valley (TELAV) that spontaneously attracted 700 members. TELAV quickly raised the ante, protesting the entire 400 acres of Grouse Creek timber sale, and the Bachs prepared for a fight. Their principal weapons were a growing sense of indignation and a pair of Apple II computers they had bought soon after moving to Oregon for writing and record keeping.

TELAV and the Bachs used the computers as terminals to gather information from public data banks and as word processors to help organize and analyze the mounds of raw information and, later, to prepare the documents appealing the BLM's planned sales.

For example, by dialing up The Source, a commercial

database service available over the telephone to members with microcomputers or terminals, they were able to search records of previous timber-sale protests and their outcomes. "We got back something like 82 different precedents of people who had been outraged at what they saw going on and tried to protest—and were almost invariably shot down," Richard says. The common denominator among these failed appeals, Bach says, was their reliance on humanitarian or emotional arguments rather than hard proof of specific errors on the part of the government (most of these cases involved the U.S. Forest Service because the BLM manages little timber, but the principles were the same). In the absence of "clear error" by the BLM or the Forest Service, the Interior Board of Land Appeals, the court of last resort in an appeal case, invariably let the sales continue.

Following the initial research, the Bachs and TELAV typed into their machines all of the laws that were relevant and important enough to be challenged, and then they typed in alongside these records of what had actually been done, thus highlighting the discrepancies on which their arguments for appeal were based. In this way they detailed 19 major violations involved in the proposed sale, with 12 of these concerning federal laws. ("We didn't even bother with the minor ones," Leslie says.) As they worked the paper mounted—eventually filling two file boxes and overflowing into a stack four feet high; the computer data itself filled a shoebox with floppy disks. Bach says the Apples never cooled off.

Although the arguments were wide ranging, the basic contention was that the BLM violated its own rules on numerous occasions by allowing timber cuts in areas where trees will not grow back. By definition, land qualifies as "commercial" timberland when trees can be regenerated within a certain number of years. Current regulations say five years, but the BLM is trying to change that to 15 years. The exact figure doesn't really matter, say the Bachs, because some areas they found have been replanted five times and haven't grown back in over 20 years.

BLM officials note that dozens of previous protests have been lodged, but these have been consistently rejected by the Board of Land Appeals. Bach thinks he knows why: "Most people have many other things to do with their lives than fight timber sales." In the time allotted to appeal a proposed cut—30 days, initially—"they can write two or three pages with their goose quills or their typewriters, and that constitutes the protest. They do not have time to research it and dump tens of thousands of bytes into a computer and correlate the whole thing." TELAV's appeal, on the other hand, ran to 600 pages in three volumes.

### *A Mixed Victory*

The BLM canceled the Grouse Creek timber sale just before it was to go before the Board of Appeals. TELAV had won—or had it? By withdrawing from a case that was heavily documented against it, the BLM avoided an unfavorable ruling that could have been used as a precedent by protesting groups in other parts of the country.

BLM officials shrug off the Grouse Creek incident as "an oversight on our part," caused mainly by a change in state regulations that tightened up the definition of commercial timberland. "It was like changing the rules in the third quarter of a football game," explains John Dutcher, the Little Applegate Valley Area manager for the BLM. "Based on that, we withdrew," he says, somewhat unnecessarily adding that "it was kind of awkward."

But TELAV got its hands on the ball again when the BLM put the 237-acre Lick Gulch timber sale out for bid; the Bachs cranked out another 600-page protest, and the proposed sale is still on appeal. "We're all hanging our hats on that one," Dutcher says, but when it will be decided is anybody's guess. The BLM is still trying to sell more timber in the area, but now that the basic appeal format is filed on a floppy disk, Jenny Windsor, another TELAV activist with an Apple, has cranked out protests on four more timber sales totaling more than 2,000 acres. She simply calls up the statement of reasons from the word-processing file, changes the arguments to fit the current sale, prints it out, and sends it off.

The arguments have settled into a typical standoff: TELAV says the valley is too marginal to produce timber, but the BLM says it's good enough.

TELAV has since incorporated as a nonprofit organization. Using a simple database program called Visifile, one of Visicorp's series of packaged programs for microcomputers, the group has computerized all of the BLM's reforestation records in the area, thus putting it on more equal footing with the federal agency in knowing exactly what's happening to the forest lands. This effort has also drawn grudging admiration from the BLM's Dutcher. "They do have a neat computer system," he says. "I've often kidded them about having better records than we do."

Meanwhile, the use of computers to protect Little Applegate Valley is spreading. Another protest group called Applegate Citizens Opposed to Toxic Sprays (ACOTS) recently acquired an Apple II and has prevailed upon Windsor to help the group get up to speed on its machine.

What the Bachs and their Little Applegate Valley neighbors did was especially impressive because they came off the street, so to speak, with no computer background. They had neither computer-science skills nor an interest in becoming computer programmers, and they didn't. They were able to use their computers in the purest sense: as general-purpose tools. In some respects they were lucky; coming up against an arm of the federal bureaucracy like the BLM was somewhat like shooting fish in a barrel. But what about corporate America and the industries that have the legal and financial clout to stand up to, if not to dominate, the agencies that are supposed to regulate them? What about an industry that's an institution in itself, like the nations utilities?

## *Taking On the Utilities*

The Environmental Defense Fund (EDF) is one of a number of environmental and consumer groups that have for years been jousting with utilities over soaring gas and electric rates and questioning the need for new power plants, particularly nuclear ones. EDF's goal is to ease the pressure on the nation's air, water, and energy resources by arguing for less exploitation and more conservation. Its focuses are water quality, toxic chemicals, lead in gasoline, and energy use. Its weapons are economic analysis and legal action.

Following the oil crunch of the mid-1970s and the subsequent skyrocketing oil prices, EDF began to lose its record of frequent intervention in utility-rate cases and found itself increasingly unable to stand up to the utilities.

The turning point came in a 1977 rate hearing when Zack Willey, EDF's chief scientist, tried valiantly to take on one utility company. Armed with only a pocket calculator, he sat in vain punching in 64 variations of a single equation, no match for the utility's foot-thick computer printout. His failure was embarrassing. Vowing never to do that again and having grown tired of getting sand kicked in his face by the utilities, Willey hired Dan Kirshner, a young graduate of the University of California at Santa Cruz with degrees in economics and physics, to build up EDF's computer muscle. A self-taught programmer who looks every bit as young as he is (he's 28), Kirshner took six months to computerize Willey's single-equation model. The result, written in FORTRAN, is ELFIN (for electric/finance), a model that allows EDF or anyone else who uses it to quantify the effects of alternative-energy proposals. Kirshner has continued to refine ELFIN into what is now a state-of-the-art model for analysis of alternative energy.

### *ELFIN Proves Its Worth*

"Before we had the model, we were basically intimidated by the utilities in rate hearings," Kirshner says. "They'd present a run from their computer and say, 'These are the results.' There was no way to really challenge it. You could ask if cost estimates were realistic, but we had no way of examining substitutes and alternatives."

ELFIN not only works, it's cheap. Each run eats up only $12 of computer time, compared to $1000 or more for each run of the utility company's computer. ELFIN will work on any "super" minicomputer, such as Digital Equipment Corporation's VAX or Data General's Eclipse (the machine in Tracy Kidder's *Soul of a New Machine*). In Berkeley, EDF buys time on the university's VAX computer, calling in through an acoustic telephone modem from a dumb terminal in Kirshner's office.

The model was first used to pursue a case against Pacific Gas & Electric Company, the nation's largest utility, in 1978 rate hearings in California. "PG&E did its best to brush it aside," Kirshner says, and although ELFIN didn't directly figure in the outcome of that hearing, it turned the California Public Utility Commission toward making conservation and alternative energy key considerations in future electrical expansion. California has, in fact, taken the lead among the 50 states in pushing for alternative energy and conservation, mainly at the prodding of the EDF and its partner ELFIN.

In 1980 EDF successfully used an ELFIN model to block construction of a proposed $5 billion complex that called for two coal-fired plants in Utah and Nevada. EDF contended that the power needed could be provided less expensively through a combination of conservation and available alternative energy sources such as wind and geothermal power. The utilities withdrew from the project before the Public Utility Commission (PUC) reached a decision, citing changed projections of power demands, but according to the PUC the EDF model was a decisive factor in killing the project.

ELFIN has also figured prominently in half a dozen other significant utility or legislative hearings in Florida, Illinois, Arkansas, Michigan, and most recently in New York, where EDF tried to halt construction of the partially completed Nine Mile Point No. 2 nuclear plant near Oswego.

The Nine Mile challenge was a departure for EDF. "Until Nine Mile we had basically been looking at plants that hadn't started," Kirshner explains. "We wanted to avoid committing good money to them until it was clear they were needed." As it turned out, EDF lost on that one; in February of last year the New York Power Commission decided to go ahead with the plant. However, the model did have some effect. The Power Commission included some of EDF's suggestions in its conditions for building the plant.

### *Irrigation Plans via Micro*

ELFIN is small by mainframe-computer standards, but it's still too large to run on a microcomputer. EDF *is* starting to do some other projects on its North Star microcomputer, however. The group bought the machine last year for word processing, but it's now being groomed as an attack computer as well. One current project is an analysis of alternative methods of farm irrigation in both the central plains of Texas and California's Central Valley. This is part of a project to find ways to irrigate with less water; it ties in with a six-state federal study that predicts farming may die out in parts of the U.S. because of dwindling supplies of ground water.

Zack Willey says the result of this work—irrigation plans that will help deal with the salt problem and eliminate the need to build new dams—will be presented to the U.S. Congress and the California and Texas legislatures over the next two years in an attempt to bring about changes in policies for water use.

As anyone who has ever done it knows, to fight well is not necessarily to win. Although it gained in other ways, EDF lost its battle to stop the Nine Mile nuclear plant. And even with success in the air in Little Applegate Valley, the battle itself changed things in unforeseen ways. Ten months ago the Bachs sold their little piece of Shangri-la and moved to another, quieter spot in the Pacific Northwest.

"We desperately needed to be alone again, and I had to get back to work on the book that had just been stopped cold," Richard says. "What was supposed to have been a private little place to write and work from became the center of this great environmental movement. You'd get up in the morning and there'd be strangers in the house saying, 'Can we use the computer?' That was a little disconcerting after a few years."

Looking back, though, the Bachs have no regrets. Richard says the experience was a major education for him: "I have always been a retreater. If somebody wants the trees, let 'em cut the trees; I'll move. I have other things to do with my life that do not involve protests. But it turned out this was an opportunity for me to learn something about the power that we all have once we make up our minds to say no to some of the excesses that we see around us. We are an extremely powerful people in this country; every single citizen is powerful if each one says I will put my foot down at this point and devote some part of my life—in our case a huge percentage of our lives—to standing up against the cynical destruction of our country, of the country we have known. Couple that attitude with a tool like the computer and it's dynamite."

# MISSION: UNDERCOVER RADIO

Harry Caul

CHANCES are that if you've got a communications receiver (or even a scanner) you've come upon the results of the rather unusual work I do. At the least, you've probably noted the efforts of others who compete with me in my endeavors.

To put it in its simplest and bluntest terms, I supply information, training, and various other services for persons and groups interested in establishing long and short distance radio communications without benefit of licenses from the host governments involved. I'm not at all talking about the bootleg pseudo-Hams and quasi-CB'ers who populate the airwaves; those guys are horsing around while my clients are deadly serious. Nevertheless, it is a pursuit which keeps me very busy. It is impossible to imagine the large number of folks who have come to feel that they want to have as much communications security, privacy, and secrecy as possible—even to the point of not appearing in anyone's computer as the licensee of a radio transmitter (assuming they could become licensed in the first place).

Who might be such a client? Maybe the operators of a diamond mine in Africa wishing to discreetly exchange market and production information with their people in Europe. Or, it could be an office of a multi-national corporation wanting to exchange certain delicate information with other offices in the world. You name it and there are those who want to exchange messages in total privacy; information on strategic metals, technologies, industrial data, information on financial matters such as stocks and bonds, bank accounts, currency exchanges, energy resources, and a couple of dozen other topics—and they want to do it via the back door without passing the data through the closely scrutinized facilities of the world's commercial Telex, cable, and overseas telephone services.

Then there are mercenary forces who want to have short and long range communications systems at their disposal. Who would grant them licenses to operate? What about guerrilla forces? Licenses? Don't make me laugh! What about all of the underground rebel broadcasters?

The fact is, there are embassies who have become wary of sending all but low and medium priority messages over commercial circuits. High priority messages cannot be trusted to their own authorized (and well monitored) international radio circuits, either.

Transmissions such as these, and others, are rife on frequencies throughout the short-wave spectrum and even into the UHF bands. A mini-industry has sprung up to tend to the needs of those who want to establish such systems, and although it has been going on quietly for at least twenty years, these days it has been starting to come out into the open. Within the past year, one of my competitors openly placed an ad for his services in *Soldier of Fortune Magazine*, offering to establish complete international undercover radio systems and even to act as the U.S. base station within those systems!

So when I stated that if you've got a communications receiver or a scanner you've probably noted some of these efforts, I wasn't whistling *Dixie*. Have you ever heard those shortwave stations which transmit 5-digit number code groups and nothing else? Do you really think those are licensed by *any* government? Hardly!

### *A Typical Example*

Here is a typical (but totally hypothetical) example of the services which might come into play.

Let's say that a mercenary force is being formed—soldiers of fortune, or *dogs of war,* so to speak—for operations inside a particular nation. It could be in Africa, Central America, or possibly even an island group in the Indian Ocean. They have outfitted themselves with the necessary garments, obtained ordnance items, vehicles, foodstuffs, and whatever else it takes to commence their operation. When it comes to communications items, their needs have to be analyzed and met by a specialist. Perhaps someone such as myself.

They will need short range tactical facilities, and that may also include scanners to listen in on the communications of "the other side." Chances are they will need medium range communications with other units deployed in their operation, as well as long range communications for keeping in contact with a headquarters unit.

Frequencies for all of this would have to be chosen, along with the designs of all of the systems and antennas to be used, modes of operation (AM, SSB, FM, CW, RTTY, or other non-voice modes), and the specific equipment to be employed. The equipment, in addition to scanners, would typically be comprised of transmitters, receivers, direction finders, power supplies, handhelds or backpack units, mobile/base units, radar, and even countermeasure devices (radio jamming gear).

Schedules, based upon propagation factors, have to be established for long range communications. Codes and cyphers would probably be required. Instruction in equipment operation and communications security techniques are a must. Information on antenna orientation and even data on standard time and frequency stations must be included in the material provided.

And, of course, the equipment itself would have to be obtained, modified (if necessary), tested, and checked out for proper operation, calibration, and spare parts. It is then packed safely along with basic trouble-shooting data.

## *Equipment*

The hardware for such an operation would generally consist of a mix of commercial and military surplus items—the same as most of the other items which will be used on the mission. All are suited to the exacting needs of the operation and within the budget allocated for the purpose.

Some of the military surplus equipment which is popularly sent into the field with considerable success includes the URC-68,[1] AN/GRC-84, '87, '109, and the AN/VRC-34 (all of

---

1. The AN/URC-68 is a military surplus combination UHF-AM/VHF-FM transceiver with a capability of voice or CW operation on 3 crystal controlled channels in each band. There's an emergency frequency in each band and a beacon mode on each emergency channel which permits automatic swept tone continuous transmission on either or both channels.

which should be well-known to those who worked with communications in Vietnam). Other popular units are low power backpack rigs such as the PRC-10s, low band mobile units like the RT-70, and hand-held PRC-6s.

### *Frequency Selection*

Selecting the array of frequencies is no mean trick. Some frequencies are for monitoring only, and others are used for two-way. Some are for short range, others for varying distances which could reach half way around the world—depending upon the client and the purpose of the communication. Many problems and influences come into play, especially in determining transmission frequencies. These include propagation factors combined with the transmission modes, antenna types, and amount of security required. Security is a problem in selecting any type of communications system which is intended to be operational over a reasonable period of time without creating more problems than anyone really wants.

If the transmissions are to be for long range work, then they will have to lie between 2 and about 25 MHz; that's the rub! These frequencies are already crowded with broadcasters and a myriad of other users who jealously guard them from appropriation by outsiders. Doing it without creating interference to some other (authorized) communications or broadcasting system is one of the most important things to keep in mind. There is, of course, the option to camouflage the communications operations to make them *appear* to belong on whatever frequencies have been selected. It's tricky, but it is commonplace. Actually, there are many frequencies which have been used (and are now being used) for such operations without bothering anyone or calling undue attention to those who operate the systems.

---

The battery operated unit can operate AM between 230 and 250 MHz and FM from 38 to 42 MHz with 1/5 watt on AM, 1/2 watt on FM. The whole thing can fit into a person's pocket and yet has a 20 mile operating range. This set was used in Vietnam, most especially by the CIA and related agencies. The going value for the URC-68s in good operating condition is about $150 and they are still in demand for use by all manner of paramilitary groups, few of which are particularly concerned with being licensed by the FCC.—Editor, *Pop. Comm.*

On the other hand, unlicensed "numbers" stations have been around for years now and pass their traffic right out where everybody can hear them. Obviously, they don't cause interference and haven't had much to worry about. There are certain frequencies within the HF, VHF, and UHF bands which are somewhat out-of-the-way, as it were, and upon which some have operated without being detected (or at least without being hassled) on a regular basis.

For instance, 13.560 MHz has been selected throughout the world as a *junk* frequency, relegated for authorized use for non-communications devices within the industrial, scientific, and medical communities, like arc welding machines. Since those who are authorized to use the frequency do so on an "interference expected" basis, nobody of any consequence monitors the frequency, and nobody complains about what goes on there! As a result, it has been long used for tactical and surreptitious voice and non-voice long-range communications systems. Other *junk* frequencies set aside for similar purposes include 27.120 MHz (lying between CB channels 13 and 14), and 40.68 MHz (the FCC recently gave the go-ahead for alarm and control devices to operate on this latter frequency, which units can be operated minus a license and meet certain technical specifications.

There are all sorts of nooks and crannies tucked away around the communications spectrum which have been pressed into service at one time or another by those who wish to operate without licenses and hassles and for reasons known best to themselves. You can hear loads of them on any scanner—33.12 MHz, 49.3 MHz, 154.456 MHz, 173.396 MHz. The listing is lengthy and there are also many places below 25 MHz which have traditionally provided a safe haven for undercover communicators—2.065 MHz, 6.522 MHz, 22.124 MHz, and the rest.

The selection of operating frequencies for this purpose is a study within itself, and it deserves an in-depth analysis; a story of its own discussing how frequencies allocated to various radio services (including Amateur) have been used. In the October, 1982, issue of *Popular Communications*, I've explored this and tell you about 90 to 100 specific "back roads" hidden frequencies and also "mainstream" frequencies (where things are hidden while out in the open). I've explained the whys and wherefores of selecting various frequencies between 2 and 470

MHz. In the meantime, check out the frequencies I've listed in this issue and while you hear legit stations, you might well hear some known only to their makers!

### *Problems*

Interestingly, one of the trickiest problems encountered by those in my line of work is extracting a sufficient amount of information from the client in order to advise him of what he requires. Without lots of information, it is almost impossible to do a good job. By the very nature of their operations, they are a bit on the paranoid and tight-lipped side and, as such, getting the data required can be a spectacular chore. It's a common problem and one which must be faced regularly.

Needless to say, there are few governments (indeed) which appreciate unauthorized communications taking place within their borders, regardless of their purpose. Some are downright hostile. Within the United States, for instance, the FCC becomes extremely hostile when it comes face to face with the practice and if it wishes to (within its motivation and budget limitations) could mount a rather potent array of fines and even prison sentences upon those who are caught. And depending upon the purposes of the communications, other agencies can also get in on the act.

But there isn't any restriction on using a communications receiver or scanner to listen to the goings-on. Frankly, at this point, it's hard *not* to hear these stations, there are so many of them. If you listen on frequencies such as 4.670, 5.810, 7.764, 9.267, 9.445, 14.419, 14.968, 16.310 MHz, and many others, you can often hear the mysterious so-called "spy numbers" stations with their coded messages. Or, take a listen to the Latin American two-way networks on 6.600 and 6.955 MHz some evening—all part of the growing network of undercover radio operations throughout the world.

Check them out sometime. You might just find yourself tuned to something you definitely aren't supposed to hear!

# WHO MAKES CHURCHES TAX EXEMPT?

Douglas F. Kelly

THE tax-exempt status of Churches is becoming a major controversy in the United States. Many are asking the question: What right does the Church have to be exempt from taxation anyway?

Of course a matter such as taxation or exemption of the Church is first of all a historical question. One has to look at the historical context in order to give a proper interpretation of our present status. It is clear that religiously, culturally, legally, politically, etc. the American colonies are the direct extension of Medieval, Christian Europe—particularly as this tradition was mediated through the Protestant Reformation of the 16th century and the Puritan movement of the late 16th and 17th centuries.

An illustration of this relationship is the fact that English Common Law precedents are binding in American practice unless they are specifically set aside by American Law. For instance, the Federal Courts claimed treasure that one Mr. Fisher had found in a sunken Spanish Galleon off the coast of Florida belonged to the Federal Government on the basis of British precedent. Supposedly, the Federal Government is an heir to the rights of King George III over all treasure found in coastal waters. We may not agree with this particular interpretation, but it is an illustration of the fact that American jurisprudence cannot be understood without the European and English background.

Now to come specifically to tax exemption of the Christian Church. In the Roman Empire, when the Church first came into prominence, it was treated by the Roman civil authorities as a legitimate Jewish sect, and as such, the Church (like the Jewish religion) was (in the equivalent of that day) fully 'tax

Reprinted from *Chalcedon Report* No. 204, August, 1982. 

exempt.' However, after the Fall of Jerusalem in A.D. 70, Judaism for a time was no longer a "religio licita" and this brought Christianity as well as Judaism into serious trouble legally. The real problem was not that the Roman government wanted to tax the Church (they apparently did not), but rather that they (from time to time) wanted Christians to swear by the genius of the Emperor: i.e. to sacrifice to him as being the world's center of unity and final Lord over all (including the Church). Rome was perfectly happy for the Church to exist as long as the Church recognized that Caesar is final Lord over the Church: the one who makes it "licita" or licensed. Most Christians refused to do so and accepted persecution and death in order to acknowledge Christ as Lord over all (including Caesar).

This situation of conflict radically changed with the Christian Emperor Constantine, who made Christianity the official state religion. Under the Constantinian settlement (and this was thoroughly backed up by the later influential Theodosian and Justinian Codes, which had so much authority in shaping legislation in all the Christian countries of Medieval Europe), the civil government had absolutely no authority to tax churches. They did not actually *make* churches tax exempt: they rather recognized that they already were such by virtue of the fact that churches paid taxes (tithes and offerings) to their head: Jesus Christ, while the state paid taxes to its temporal head: Caesar and his successors.

Sometimes tithes were collected for the Church by the civil authorities (as is still the case in West Germany), but these tithes went to the local churches and/or to the Pope in Rome. In these cases therefore the civil government collected taxes (tithes) not from the Church, but from the populace, and then gave the tithes to the Church.

Now there was an exception in Medieval Europe during the Crusades, in which *the Church itself* asked the civil authorities to tax Church income in order to finance this movement. This was known as the "Saladin Tithe." C. W. Previte-Orton in *The Shorter Cambridge Medieval History* (Cambridge: At The University Press, 1971), p. 618, explains:

> The Crusades, on which depended so much of the moral leadership of the West assumed by the Papacy, were financed in two ways: by indulgences, which were commutations of the vow to go on a crusade in return for money payment, a measure productive

of perilious extension and abuse in all directions, and by the taxation of ecclesiastical income by kings with the consent of the Papacy, begun by Louis VI of France (1146) and repeated in England and France by the Saladin Tithe (1188), which under Innocent III developed into the claim to dispose of all Church property and to tax it at will (i.e. the will of the Pope), while excluding the lay powers (i.e. the kings) from like behaviour. Further expedients by the Papacy to pay its way were to be devised in the next century.

In other words, with the exception of the Saladin Tithe, the problems and struggles over taxation of local and national Churches during the Middle Ages was an inter-Church battle to a major degree: between an increasingly strong Papacy, and local Bishops. Civil governments at this point had no thought of attempting to interfere and 'put their hands in the till.' (Civil governments were intensely involved in struggles with the Papacy over matters such as lay investiture, but this is on a different level, for powerful church officials who were to be 'invested' were often also powerful temporal lords).

In England, just before the Reformation, King Henry VIII did forcibly close down monasteries and confiscate their lands and wealth: on the supposed basis that the monasteries were dens of corruption and a hazard to the well being of the nation. The same thing happened in France after the French Revolution. However, the civil authorities still did not attempt to tax the Churches: closing the monasteries (as they saw it) was a police action, and, at least in England, was not used as a precedent to claim state authority to levy taxes on the remaining Church property and revenues.

At the time the American colonies were settled, the same Medieval situation still obtained between Church and State (even after the Reformation and Puritan movement): the Church was universally understood to owe its taxes (tithes) to its spiritual head, Christ, and thus was by definition free from civil control at this point since it was the spiritual realm or Kingdom of God on earth.

Therefore when we speak of tax exemption today, it is not a matter of trying to find some ancient obscure law that specifically states the Church has been declared (or made) tax exempt by the state: all history presupposes the independent financial status of the Church. Such was the accepted procedure of all Europe for a millenium and a half. The burden of proof is on the other side: Let those who want to tax the

Church find substantial historical or legal precedents for doing so. To use a rather silly illustration, who needs to prove that the public has the right to breathe free air without paying the civil government for doing so? Our right to do so is presupposed by all history and common sense. To claim we must have specific legislative action to make legal all we do is ridiculous: In most cases, to determine what is right, rather than researching volumes of statute legislation, one has to look at the whole human, moral, and historical situation.

Up until the Enlightenment, civil states knew that passing legislation for something like tax exemption of Churches would be as superfluous as voting to allow Christ to be Lord in his own realm. What the state did was to recognize Christ as Lord over his Church; they did not legislate to make him so; they simply accepted that as a previously existing situation. With the late 18th century secular humanist Enlightenment, some states (such as France after 1789) did indeed begin to claim sovereignty (including financial control) over the Church; but America was already a free country by this time with its own constitution, rooted—not in the humanist Enlightenment—but in the earlier Medieval, Reformation Christian order. We had no problems along these lines in this country until this same secular humanist Enlightenment reached these shores in the late 19th century. The Enlightenment attempts to cut ties with the past under the very modern pretense that every legitimate situation must rest upon specific statute legislation by the contemporary state or its legislative predecessors. They, however, are clearly the innovators and cannot by supported under American and British Common Law jurisprudence taken in its easy-to-understand historical context.

# CITIZENS' PARALEGAL LITIGATION TACTICS

Michael R. Gilstrap

ALL government begins with the sovereignty of God. Men are fully responsible before God, in terms of the revealed law of God. The concept of "government" is broad. It includes self-government, family government, ecclesiastical government, and civil government.

English and American common law recognizes the responsibility of citizens to abide by the law of God and those civil laws that are in conformity to, and extensions of, God's revealed law. At the same time, common law also recognizes the obligations of all citizens to see to it that no area of life to which civil law legitimately applies is allowed to continue in lawlessness. The tradition of *citizen's arrest* is a relic of this principle of citizen's authority.

With the advent of a society of litigation, in which the per capita number of lawyers is higher than in any other nation on earth, American citizens have increasingly deferred to "the legal experts" in every area of life. "Laymen" is a term of condescension, if not contempt, in the field of civil law. But the growing complexity of legislation — the product of a messianic impulse on the part of the law-makers — not to mention the complexity of administrative law (bureaucracy) and judicial review, has begun to place dedicated amateurs on a level with all but the most specialized lawyers. An intelligent citizen who has been taught the rudiments of legal research is in a position to dedicate many hours to researching one small segment of the civil law. Most lawyers cannot devote this much time to a detailed study of an area of law which does not lead to lots of clients or at least lots of money. Thus, a dedicated amateur who wants to obtain a reasonable mastery of a narrow, otherwise ignored field, can become an opponent who is sufficiently formidable to give the enforcing agents considerable agony. Furthermore, if the area of law is extremely controversial, and a lawyer taking a particular position might find himself in trouble with the bar association (or the Internal Revenue Service), the amateur may be in a better position to defend his own interests than to pay a lawyer to do it.

I point all this out as a motivation device. This essay will introduce Christian citizens to a new realm of responsibility that few have ever even considered. The escalating confrontation with bureaucracy, as Gary North calls it elsewhere in this volume, is forcing Christians to defend their interests, and God's interests, with only minimal aid from attorneys.

I focus on recent developments in the field of tax law. I do this deliberately. If the IRS, generally the most feared of all Federal agencies, has been stymied time and again by a particular series of tactics—tactics that have been adopted *only* by dedicated paralegal (non-professional, non-licensed) defenders of their own cases—*then Christians have a reasonable hope in dealing with the far less powerful bureaucratic agencies that are likely to interfere with their God-given duties.*

### *Christianity vs. Secular Humanism*

Secular humanism and Christianity cannot co-exist without conflict. The State[1] cannot be sovereign over all of life and simultaneously not control the Church and her schools. Just as the State has sought to control every other aspect of life, to offer "cradle to grave security," so it is seeking to control the Church. The beast desperately wants to control every aspect of the Church's life, from her finances to her methods of evangelism, from advertising to publishing, from selection of her ministers, teachers, and officers to the use of her facilities. The messianic State is asserting a usurped sovereignty over the Church, and it is using the IRS to enforce that sovereignty.

On January 9, 1978, then-IRS Commissioner Jerome Kurtz in a speech in New York City unveiled the new IRS policy with regard to churches. He outlined the "14-point criteria" the IRS would implement to determine whether a church is a church. Although Kurtz emphasized that the "enforcement program" primarily was aimed at tax-exempt religious educational ministries that "discriminate in their ad-

1. In this essay, I shall capitalize "state" when I refer to the modern, messianic civil government, and I will use the lower-case "s" when referring to the civil government of regional units known as states.

missions policy on the basis of race or ethnic origin,"[2] he made it clear that "Church related private schools are covered within this policy, *as well as the churches that operate and control them*" (emphasis mine).

In the *Federal Register* for August 22, 1978, the IRS published a "new revenue procedures" policy relating to private schools and church educational ministries. Once again, racial discrimination was the prominent reason given for the new procedures. The new procedures were said to be applicable to private schools as well as *"church-related and church-operated schools."* Educational ministries were called upon to give evidence of "operation in good faith on a racially nondiscriminatory basis" by the existence of at least four of five factors prescribed by the IRS: 1) financial assistance to minority students; 2) vigorous minority recruitment programs; 3) increasing percentage of minority enrollment; 4) employment of minority teachers or professional staff; 5) other substantial evidence of good faith.[3]

As a result of a newsletter-based protest, at least 135,000 letters of protest streamed in to the IRS within two months after the proposed regulations were published. Hearings were conducted in Washington, D.C. in December, and over 250 people testified.[4] As a result, Congress voted not to fund the implementation of the program. Nevertheless, the program can now be implemented at any time, because four years later, on November 30, 1982, in the House, and on December 18, 1982, in the Senate, the Ashbrook and Dornan amend-

---

2. The Supreme Court decision revoking Bob Jones University's tax-exempt status is a good example. On May 24, 1983, the Court ruled that because Bob Jones University affirmed a policy of racial segregation in the areas of dating and marriage, and since that policy is in opposition to public policy, no tax-exemption can be allowed.

3. The above information was gleaned from an article by Robert McCurry in *Temple Times*, January 16, 1983, Volume 14, No. 1. This newsletter was the first to report on the proposed IRS regulations, even before they were published in the *Federal Register. Temple Times* is a monthly newsletter which reports on the growing crisis between the Church and Federal and state governments. It is sent to all who request it without charge, although a contribution with the request is in order. For a sample copy write to: *Temple Times*, 2560 Sylvan Road, East Point, GA 30344.

4. For transcripts of this testimony, see *The Voice of Christian and Jewish Dissenters in America*, edited by Martin Claussen (P.O. Box 3505, Georgetown, Wash., D.C.: Piedmont Press, 1982).

ments were deleted from the Treasury Appropriations Bill. Those two amendments would have continued the withholding of funds from the IRS, to prevent the agency from implementing its program to investigate and approve of church schools and churches. *The IRS now has the funds to investigate churches and educational ministries.*

It is increasingly obvious that Christians must give serious thought as to how to resist the Internal Revenue Service's invasion of *traditional legal immunities* (sometimes called "rights") possessed by American citizens under the U.S. Constitution and common law. We no longer have the luxury of ignoring the leviathan at our door. The beast has taken up residence at the gate of the Church, and either he will be resisted and driven away, or the institutional Church as we know it will be compromised under its usurped sovereignty. We need to ask ourselves as Christians: In what ways may we lawfully resist the IRS? How are we to do so without being revolutionaries and anarchists? Can Christians legitimately resist the IRS as individuals, or must we submit as individuals and only resist as churches? If we can legitimately resist as individuals, then how can we do so and not end up like Gordon Kahl, the tax protestor who shot and killed two federal marshals and a sheriff, and who was finally blown up and burned beyond recognition after a gun battle with county authorities in a remote section of Arkansas?

It is my religiously held conviction that the Internal Revenue Service is the *heart* of the present expression of the messianic State. If unconstitutional activities of the IRS can be resisted successfully, then we will have taken the first step to rolling back government oppression and tyranny. The IRS cannot be ignored. The Church does not have a choice whether or not to fight the IRS. *Either she fights, or she capitulates*. There is no middle ground. The Church must confront the beast of messianic statism, eyeball to eyeball, and repel it. She must do so, however, lawfully and constructively, not lawlessly.

Furthermore, there is a growing body of evidence to indicate that the IRS can be successfully resisted by individual citizens, as well as by churches. This essay is designed to introduce Christians to this body of evidence. We can learn how to resist the beast of messianic civil government through a careful study of legal resistance techniques that have been used successfully against the IRS by certain citizens' paralegal defense organizations. Why? Because the point at issue in the courts is one and the same: *sovereignty.*[5] The IRS claims an unjust jurisdiction over individuals and has done so since its creation by Congress. Likewise, the IRS is presently asserting an unjust and usurped jurisdiction over the Church. Both usurpations can be resisted through the proper use of Constitutional law and case-law precedents. The IRS's unconstitutional invasion of our legal immunities can be stymied. Therein lies the purpose of this article.

We shall begin by reviewing the Christian rationale for resisting tyranny. It is important that we keep certain fundamentals in mind in order to avoid falling into anarchism and revolution. As trinitarians, we are neither statists nor anarchists. Next, we shall examine certain Constitutional issues concerning the income tax. Finally, a strategy for churches will be developed. There is much to be learned from what has been called the Tax Patriot movement.[6] In some instances, it is a lawful, Constitutional expression of political resistance. There are serious problems with it, however—problems which Christians must avoid.

### *How Not to End Up like Vic Lockman*

As readers of "Christian Reconstruction" periodicals are no doubt aware, Vic Lockman was something of an uncle in the Christian Reconstruction movement.[7] He was an elder in

---

5. For the remainder of this article, the terms "sovereignty" and "jurisdiction" will be used almost synonymously. Generally speaking, the theological concept is "sovereignty," and the legal concept is "jurisdiction." Although the terms will be further defined later in the article, the root concept is the theological notion of "sovereignty."

6. The "Tax Patriot Movement" is that broad, diverse, grassroots movement currently resisting (and revolting in some instances) unjust taxation. Its practitioners are commonly designated by various labels: "tax revolt," "tax protestors," and "tax rebels." Its members have one thing in common: they don't pay income taxes.

7. Christian Reconstructionism as a movement began in the early 60s as a result of the work of Rev. R. J. Rushdoony. It didn't become established, however, until 1973, with the simultaneous publication of Rev. Rushdoony's *Institutes of Biblical Law* and Dr. Gary North's *Introduction to Christian Economics*, both published by the Craig Press, Nutley, New Jersey. Christian Reconstructionism is based upon the presupposition that God the Lord is the Creator and Sovereign of the universe, and that His Law governs all of

our circles. Some of us who became "reconstructionists" looked up to him. He is a cartoonist with a great talent for illustrating the gospel message and particular aspects of Christian Reconstruction in cartoon/tract format. He is also a self-termed "tax patriot." I believe he stopped paying income taxes in 1973 or thereabouts. Many people regarded him as a true warrior for the faith.

In September of 1982, he was arrested. Most of us initially assumed it had something to do with his position on taxes. We were wrong. He was arrested for counterfeiting. He was caught with $8,000 in bogus bills, along with metal plates for printing more bills.[8] He had been discovered passing a phony bill at a restaurant in Dallas, and Secret Service agents trailed him for ten days before they finally arrested him.[9] He later pleaded guilty to the lesser offense of being in possession of counterfeit money, and he cooperated with the authorities.[10] He was sentenced to three years at the Federal Correction Institute in Texarkana, Arkansas.[11]

What motivated him to do something so obviously illegal? The purpose was to further the Patriot Movement.[12] Why, then, did he pass a bad bill to a waitress? He had been a tyranny resister for 20 years. He had done many good works in his life. What made him depart from the Biblical morality he had proclaimed? More importantly, if we resist tyranny, what can we do to avoid being another Vic Lockman?

In retrospect, it is simple to see his problem. Paul writes in Romans 13:1-2, "Let every person be in subjection to the governing authorities. For there is no authority except from

---

life. Further, we assert that the effectual sacrifice of Christ, the Son of God, who rose from the dead on the third day, is effective not only toward individuals or the Church, but that it will one day be applied to the cosmos as such. In other words, the redemption of all things takes place in time and history. Our hope is that the Kingdom of God, the rule of Christ, will one day encompass the whole world. Two excellent and highly readable softcover introductions to the Christian Reconstruction movement are available from Geneva Divinity School Press, 708 Hamvasy Lane, Tyler, TX 75701. The first is *Productive Christians in an Age of Guilt-Manipulators* by David Chilton, and the second is *Unconditional Surrender* by Dr. Gary North.

8. *Tyler Courier-Times* (Sept. 13, 1982), p. 1.
9. *Idem.*
10. *Ibid.* (Dec. 13, 1982), p. 1.
11. *Ibid.* (Jan. 21, 1983); (March 19, 1983).
12. *Ibid.* (Oct. 8, 1982).

God, and those which exist are established by God. Therefore, he who resists authority has opposed the ordinance of God; and they who have opposed will receive condemnation upon themselves." Paul enjoins us to submit to the governing *authorities*, which includes, but is not limited to, civil government. Christians are, as a general rule, to submit to all constituted authority whether in the state, the church, or the family. A revolt against *all* constituted authority is, says Paul, tantamount to rebellion against God. Those who so rebel, according to Paul, merit God's condemnation.

Vic Lockman was such a man. He rebelled against the civil authorities by passing counterfeit money, clearly an illegal and inflationary activity. His rebellion carried over into the church, where he refused to submit to the lawful government of Christ's church which he had formally and publicly agreed to honor. Eventually, the church under whose discipline he had placed both himself and his family had no other alternative but to declare him excommunicate. It happened to him just as Paul warned; he brought condemnation down upon himself.

Earlier we asked the question: How can we avoid being like Vic Lockman? We know that we must resist the unjust encroachments of the State, but how do we avoid bringing the condemnation of God down upon us in the process? To put it another way, what are some signs of illicit rebellion that we should recognize and guard against?

In answer to that query, we must first of all note that *rebellion is ultimately a denial of God's sovereignty.* Paul notes that in Romans 13 quoted above. We noted earlier that the concept of "sovereignty" is the basic issue in Christian resistance. When one denies God's sovereignty, it is inescapable that an assertion of man's sovereignty must be simultaneous. (The following implications can be implicit or explicit.) To deny God's sovereignty is to deny His transcendence, His control and jurisdiction over all reality. To be in rebellion is to assert the righteousness of man over against the righteousness of God. To be in rebellion is to deny all responsibility to God, and in some sense to assert a responsibility to man. To be in rebellion is to deny to God unlimited and unconditional power or authority, and to assert the same regarding man.

In the history of the world, the denial of God's sovereignty has resulted in one of two positions, each elevating man to deity. As R. J. Rushdoony has noted, "The denial of God's sovereignty and the affirmation of man's sovereignty (whether of rational or irrational man or of his unconscious being) denies transcendence and leaves only two realities, individual man and collective man."[13] These two related positions have come to be known in political theory as "anarchy" and "statism." In the history of the Church, the two have simply been expressed as the two strains of anabaptism, what may be referred to as "anarchical anabaptism" and "statist anabaptism."[14]

In discussing how a Christian resists tyranny, both extremes must be avoided. The pagan or humanistic *statist* submits blindly to his sovereign, "collective man." Instead of being openly in submission to God, man becomes subordinate to the State and, in fact, a creature of it. Because the transcendence of God is denied, "collective man," i.e., the State, establishes its total order over all of reality, which eventually results in absolute tyranny. A statist may fear the messianic State's power, but because of his denial of transcendence, he has no effective appeal or basis for resisting it. In denying God's sovereignty, the statist likewise denies his responsibility to Him. In other words, he denies his responsibility to keep God's law. The only law then left is the tyrannical and oppressive law of the State.

In contrast, the pagan or humanistic *anarchist* asserts that the autonomous individual is independent of and sovereign above all authorities including God. He submits to no personal authority. He affirms the unlimited or undisciplined authority of the individual. The individual is sovereign and accountable to no one or no thing. All legislation is evil. Every juridical limitation on his sovereignty is denied, unless he has first chosen to submit. Individual man is the be-all and the end-all of reality.

Both of these extremes are very real dangers for conservative Christianity. Both are present with us today. We have

---

13. R.J. Rushdoony, *This Independent Republic* (Fairfax, VA: Thoburn Press, [1964] 1978), pp. 130-131.

14. For an excellent treatment of these two expressions of apostasy, see pp. 18-79 of Igor Shafarevich's *The Socialist Phenomenon* (New York: Harper and Row, 1980). Also David Chilton's review of the work in *Preface 3*, published monthly by The Institute for Christian Economics, P.O. Box 8000, Tyler, TX 75711.

the statist anabaptists who insist on salvation via legislation.[15] We are told that we must blindly submit to the State for our own good. Likewise, the anarchical anabaptists are with us.[16] We are told that because the State comes in and locks the door to the Church, or takes some Christian school children away from their parents and places them in the custody of the welfare authorities, that this gives us the right to disregard *all* of the government's laws. The sentiment seems to be, "If they try to lock the door of one more church, there will be a bloody war!"[17] As Bible-believing Christians, when we wrestle with the question of resistance to lawfully constituted authorities, we must be diligent to guard ourselves against each of these heretical positions. Anarchy is equally as dangerous, and equally as sinful, as statism.

### *Canons for Biblical Resistance*

From one perspective, a "canon" is a rule or law. Looking at it from another perspective, a "canon" is a criterion or standard for judgment. As we consider civil resistance, the following canons should be kept in mind. They serve to guide us in our approach and strategy, and they also enable us to judge the righteousness of our actions.

**CANON ONE: The sovereignty and ultimate jurisdiction of God must be self-consciously confessed.**

The fundamental mistake of both statist anabaptists and anarchical anabaptists is the denial of God's total, comprehensive sovereignty. When God's ultimate jurisdiction is denied, then resistance becomes revolution. Instead of lawfully resist-

15. For more a detailed study of this strain of anabaptism see David Chilton's *Productive Christians in an Age of Guilt-Manipulators*, available from Geneva Divinity School Press, 708 Hamvasy Lane, Tyler, TX 75701. Mr. Chilton deals in detail with the statist heresy propagated by Ronald Sider, author of *Rich Christians in an Age of Hunger*.

16. Although he called himself a presbyterian, Vic Lockman should also be seen in this category.

17. This description is not intended to reflect the statements of any one individual. The sentiments, however, have been expressed to the author on more than one occasion. They are also being expressed as an undercurrent among many of the independent churches that are presently under direct attack by the State.

ing a tyrannical and unjust expression of power, all authority is resisted, thus meriting God's condemnation (Rom. 13:2).

Furthermore, only when we confess the sovereignty of God, is Biblical resistance possible. When God's sovereignty is denied, His transcendence must also be denied. If man is accountable to no authority higher than himself (whether viewed as "collective man," the State; or as individual man, the anarchist), then there can be no basis for lawful resistance. Biblical resistance is based upon a transcendental appeal to God. Under a tyranny, a Christian's duty to God is outlawed. Our resistance, therefore, is based upon an appeal that recognizes God's sovereignty and concludes that "We must obey God rather than men" (Acts 5:29).

**CANON TWO: Under God, a hierarchy of powers or authorities must be recognized.**

As trinitarians, we recognize a multiplicity of authorities over us. Paul, in Romans 13, begins by pointing out that it is a Christian's duty to be in subjection to the "governing authorities." As noted earlier, Paul is referring to our duty to be in subjection to all lawfully constituted authority, which covers all aspects of life. Gary North, in commenting upon this verse, writes, "He (Paul) was speaking of the *pluralistic authorities of all kinds over each man*. There is no single human authority over man which can claim final sovereignty. There is no absolute and final court of appeal in time and on earth. There are *multiple authorities* that must be respected, each bearing its authority from God."[18] We must respect each, and generally be in submission, but that submission is of necessity provisional.

Paul's general principle is that the *"autonomous human concience"*—the independent and undisciplined human conscience—is *not* sovereign above *all authorities*.[19] Resistance to a particular authority is legitimate if it is supported by one or more of the other authorities, and especially if it is supported by God. It must always be seen as wrong to give unlimited or unconditional power to a human institution; to do so is to divinize that particular aspect of creation.[20] To enjoin total obedience to

18. Gary North, *Unconditional Surrender* (2nd ed.; Tyler, TX: Geneva Divinity School Press, 1983), p. 129.

19. *Ibid.*, p. 132.

20. For further discussion, see *Unconditional Surrender*, pp. 129-134, and *This Independent Republic*, pp. 33-40.

one human institution, such as the civil magistrate, is to neglect or ignore other legitimate authorities also ordained by God.

**CANON THREE: Civil authority under God has limited power.**

This third canon is an obvious corollary to number two, but because of its importance to the civil order, it merits special emphasis. One of the primary reasons behind the American War for Independence was the assertion by both the King and parliament of absolute sovereignty. The colonists opposed this usurpation on legal and moral grounds. In its place they asserted a doctrine of *limited power* with regard to the civil order.

In working this out in the constituting of our government, the Founding Fathers developed three separate but related political concepts. The first was a *division of powers*. Secondly, civil government has a *multiplicity of powers*. And, thirdly, there is *a complexity of powers* in the civil order.[21] The statist, on the other hand, asserts a doctrine of the *simplicity of power*. All power is confined to the hand of the planner or governor, and tyranny quite predictably results.

The assertion of the division, multiplicity, and complexity of powers is particularly appropriate for our discussion of resisting the IRS. The IRS is but one authority within our complex legal system. We can legitimately resist it without denying the authority of our system in general. As we shall later see, resistance to the IRS on an individual as well as ecclesiastical basis is perfectly lawful and orderly within the framework of the Constitution, as well as within the framework of Internal Revenue Code (IRC).

**CANON FOUR: Authority or power in the Christian sense is ministerial, not legislative.**

Authorities in any area, whether church, state, or family, are not given the responsibility of creating laws apart from God's ultimate law. Their responsibility is to *administer* God's fundamental law to a particular sphere. In the case of civil

---

21. *This Independent Republic*, p. 33.

government, it is not a sovereign over law, but is under law. It is not a creator of law, but a minister of God's law.[22]

It was in terms of this Christian consideration that the Constitutional formulation of "express powers" was developed.[23] Our system is a system of *enumerated powers*. Powers granted to civil government in our Constitution are explicitly granted. If a power is not given, then it is absolutely denied from a Constitutional perspective.

**CANON FIVE: Law is addressed to both individuals and rulers, and therefore both are responsible to God.**

It is important to assert that rulers are not the only ones responsible to obey and enforce the law. Individuals have responsibilities here, too. Neither is exclusively authorized to enforce the law. Both are responsible to God. Once again, the assertion of God's sovereignty is implied. Responsibility before God connotes subordination to God's law; that is, God's sovereignty. When this responsibility is removed, anarchy or statism are the only possible results in the long run.

**CANON SIX: Biblical political action must have a legal foundation.**

All obedience and disobedience is grounded upon law. Ultimately, that law is God's, but, as we have seen, there are proximate laws and authorities ordained by God. Because we do not absolutize any one of these lesser authorities, disobedience to a lesser authority is possible without sin. The most notable example of this is Peter and John's declaration in Acts 5, "We must obey God rather than men." Another example would be the case of a pagan husband's commanding his wife not to go and worship the Lord. The wife would be obligated to disobey her husband and assemble with God's people to worship Him.

In the civil realm, we must assert that *resistance against an unlawful act* is not rebellion but *the maintenance of law*. We do not believe, as do the anarchists, that we are in no way bound to

22. For a fuller discussion of this point, see Michael R. Gilstrap, "John Calvin's Theology of Resistance," in Gary North, ed., *The Theology of Christian Resistance*, Christianity and Civilization No. 2 (Tyler, TX: Geneva Divinity School Press, 1983).

23. *This Independent Republic*, p. 37.

obey the laws of the land. Our assertion is that in the face of illegal, unjust governmental actions, resistance to those actions is the establishment of law, rather than its overthrow. This became a principle of international law with the Nuremburg trials after the Second World War. The excuse, "I was only following orders," was repudiated as a legal defense.[24] In any political action, we must first assume a solid foundation of law, and then proceed with our resistance.

*Summary*

These six canons give us the standard to work out a strategy of resistance to the IRS. We shall first examine in detail the Constitutionality of IRS attempts to collect income taxes from unincorporated, "unprivileged" citizens. The legal basis of this argument will first be established by reviewing the Constitution and pertinent IRS Codes. Only after a careful study of the relevant Constitutional issues can an individual begin to assess a proper response to unconstitutional invasions of the legal immunities of citizens. At that point, we shall apply what we have learned to the issue of ecclesiastical resistance to the IRS. Churches are by and large unaware of the great danger that confronts them. Our discussion will then end with several appendices outlining separate, but related matters of concern for the Christian as he contemplates the rationale and strategy of civil resistance.

## *Individual Resistance to the IRS*

The IRS is the most feared of all government agencies, even more so than the CIA. Since 1913 it has been used to bring the American people into compliance with an oppressive tax burden.[25] If the IRS can audit, harass, and intimidate churches into compliance, as it has been able to do

---

24. The danger of this precedent as it applies to one nation's enforcement of a law retroactively on a defeated nation after a war should be obvious: the leaders of a nation that is losing will "fight to the last man," or last nuclear warhead. They will fear the post-war "victor's justice."

25. The United States would have to roll back taxes 30% to 50% to even reach the taxation of Egypt under the Pharoah of Joseph's day (Genesis 41:34; 47:24), and Egypt was the most massive bureaucracy in the ancient world — indeed, the most massive, probably, until the advent of the Communist tyrannies.

with individuals, the Federal Government will achieve its goal—*control*.

There is a growing movement that is presently resisting the IRS. It has come to be known as the "Patriot Movement." This is a self-serving label. Throughout this essay, I will be discussing various paralegal litigants and their defenses against unconstitutional actions on the part of the IRS. For the most part, the paralegal litigation movement is a mixture of individualistic anarchism and legitimate Constitutional reform, with the anarchistic/libertarian strain dominant. Most of the criticisms that have been leveled against the "tax revolt" have focused upon the libertarian side of the paralegal litigation movement.[26] Without commenting upon the validity of the criticisms at this point, it is important to underline the fact that this article is seeking to avoid the anarchistic elements in the paralegal litigation movement, and to detail a legitimate strategy for asserting the legal and constitutional considerations in resisting the IRS and federal taxation.[27]

Another way of putting it is that Christians should not be interested in a *tax revolt*, an overthrow of the legitimate taxing authority of civil government. Our concern is to demonstrate the possibility of a legal and constitutional strategy of *tax resistance*. Although the paralegal litigation movement *can* be revolutionary, it does not have to be. We are interested here in outlining a strategy of *political reform* based upon the Constitution of the United States. Frankly, our Constitution does not recognize a "right of revolution," even though our country was founded upon a series of revolutionary acts. "The presumption of constitutional law is that the Constitution once framed on the political science right of revolution contains a legal process for all allowable constitutional change."[28] The following strategy is *an attempt to work within the system* for change in a

---

26. Examples of this are R. J. Rushdoony, "Jesus and the Tax Revolt," *Journal of Christian Reconstruction*, volume 2, Winter 1975-76, and James B. Jordan, "The Christian and Tax Strikes: Pros and Cons," *Biblical Economics Today*, volume IV, no. 2, April/May 1981.

27. For that reason, during the remainder of this article, unless otherwise noted, we shall refer to the individual strategy of resisting the IRS as "paralegal litigation," but please keep in mind that we are not endorsing all aspects of that movement's present expression.

28. John W. Burgess, *Recent Changes in American Constitutional Theory* (New York: Columbia University Press, 1923), pp. 16-17.

lawful and orderly manner.

Before we move on to a consideration of the Constitution, perhaps a short summary is in order of just exactly what is meant by "individual resistance to the IRS." Our strategy is based upon legal arguments which will be more fully developed later—legal arguments based on Constitutional law, case-law precedents, and legal jurisdiction. It is the contention of certain paralegal tax litigants that according to the Constitution of the United States and the relevant statutes and regulations, *they are not persons legally liable for income tax*. In other words, the laws and regulations of the Internal Revenue Service simply do not apply to them, because they are not "persons liable" for the tax. They are therefore not responsible for "filing a return."

If successful, the effectiveness of this strategy is obvious. The Federal Government's supply of funds would be severely restricted. People would hit the leviathan where it hurts the most—in his pocketbook. Big civil government would have no other choice than to trim the fat and stop the tyranny and oppression of the IRS.

It is true that the State could simply create the fiat money necessary to finance its operations. But this would create massive price inflation, and eventually the public would switch to a market-created, non-inflationary private currency system, leaving the State out in the cold, fiscally speaking. Also, mass inflation would not require the services of the IRS, so the fear created by the IRS's tactics could be eliminated. There would be no income taxes to collect! "Taxes" would be spent into circulation, not collected. This would expose the IRS as something more than a tax-collection agency. It would expose it as an instrument for instilling fear in political *and religious* enemies.

## *The Constitution of the United States*

### *The Preamble*

The Constitution is a charter establishing and granting certain powers to the Federal Government. Government, therefore, is similar to an incorporated business. It is a *corporate entity* and an *artificial person*. It has the ability to do what any other artificial person does. It can own property, sue and be sued, and fulfill the duties and obligations that other corporations are chartered to do.

As artificial persons, corporations must be created. In the instance of businesses and other forms of corporations, the creating entity is the state or Federal Government,[29] but in the case of the Federal Government, who is the creating entity? The Preamble to the Constitution tells us in its opening phrase; "We, the People of the United States . . . do ordain and establish this Constitution for the United States of America." The corporate entity of Federal Government is created by "We, the People" by a grant of power recorded in the document before us.

This leads us to another important point. The Preamble builds upon a relationship that was asserted in the Declaration of Independence and explicitly recognized here. In the relationship between the Federal Government and the people, "We, the People" are the "Sovereign," and the Federal Government is the "Servant." The Federal Government was established *to serve* the people by *securing their rights*.[30] Powers were given to that government *to secure the people's rights*. (The word "rights" also refers here to Constitutional *immunities* from the actions of agents of the Federal Government.) When we begin to think of Federal Government as our Servant, we will be well on your way to asserting our rights and securing our liberties.

With that in mind, then, the Constitution cannot be looked upon as a contract, contrary to some political theorists. At the time of the establishment of Federal Government, there was only one party involved, "We, the People." There was no corporate entity called "Federal Government" with which to make a contract as it did not yet exist as a corporate person until later created by the ratification of the Constitution itself. It can be seen, therefore, that "We, the People" are not contractually bound to the Constitution. *The Constitution is primarily a constraining definition of the corporate entity known as the Federal Government*, not a declaration or restriction of the rights and duties of the people.

Along with recognition of the relationship between civil

---

29. This concept has particular application to the Church. See section below, "Ecclesiastical Resistance to the IRS."

30. The notion of "rights" in this case is synonymous with "duty" in the theological sense. We have duties toward God. These duties are recognized by the Constitution which terms them "rights."

government and the people, the Preamble gives a *statement of purpose:* "in order to form a more perfect union, establish justice, insure domestic tranquility, provide for the common defense, promote the general welfare, and secure the blessings of liberty to ourselves and our posterity. . . ." Modern students of the Constitution almost universally *misinterpret* these clauses to be *grants of power* to the Federal Government, rather than a statement of purpose. Even a rudimentary understanding of the English language militates against such a construction. The clauses are not grants of power, but a statement of purpose for the constituting of a government. In later sections of the Constitution, the specific powers necessary to accomplish the stated purpose are outlined and granted. Our Founding Fathers never intended to give the broad, unilateral powers claimed for civil government by modern students in appealing to the Preamble and related sections.

This brings us to a basic distinction which must be understood in order to grasp the fundamental nature of any system of government. The Constitution does not create any "rights" for the Federal Government. Civil government does not have any "rights," only "powers" to act and "procedures to follow." "We, the People," on the other hand, have "rights" (abilities) granted to us by our Creator, and under the Lord's universally applicable law, we are also given duties and obligations. Those laws are found in the Bible, and not in some statute book or regulatory agency's manual. As a result of our position, we also have *immunities* to certain powers and procedures of Federal Government.[31]

The distinction between "rights" and "powers" also points out the fact that the Constitution places very strict jurisdictional restrictions on many functions of Federal Government. A very pertinent case in point is that the power to "lay and collect taxes" is given to Congress. By doing so, there is an explicit *jurisdictional restriction of power.* In other words, one of the other branches of Federal Government has *no power* to "lay and collect taxes." Now, what branch of government lays and collects taxes today? Although Congress chartered the Internal Revenue Service, the IRS is part of the Executive Branch, and as such *is outside of its constitutional authority to collect taxes and*

31. For an application of this principle to churches, see section below titled, "Ecclesiastical Resistance to the IRS."

*have direct jurisdiction over individuals*. In fact, there is not an explicit power granted by the Constitution to the President or to any Executive agency which gives them authority to acquire direct jurisdiction over the individuals of this nation. The President, and through him the Executive Branch, is granted power to be Commander-in-Chief of the armed forces, to make foreign treaties, appoint ambassadors, judges, and other officers, report on the state of the Union, and recommend legislation to Congress, *but not to "lay and collect taxes."*

You may ask then, why did the Executive Branch begin to collect taxes if there is no explicit statement granting it that power? The answer is that Congress long ago delegated all of its "non-legislative" powers to lay and collect taxes, coin money, and borrow money to the Executive agencies *in clear violation of the Constitution*. As noted earlier, ours is a system of *specific* and *separated* powers derived from the consent of the governed.[32] If a branch of government is allowed to ignore the "separateness" of powers, then eventually the freedoms of the people will be threatened, which is exactly what is happening today.[33]

One final word before we move on to the procedures and powers of Congress regarding the laying and collecting of taxes. The intent of the Framers of the Constitution was that *no power* is granted in the Constitution except by *explicit provision*. In other words, if the Constitution is silent on any subject whatsoever, then *no grant of power exists*. Rather, the silence of the Framers indicates an absolute prohibition of power. *Any other construction makes the Constitution meaningless*. The Constitution may be thought of as a house with four rooms. The first room is a *statement of purpose*. Room number two is a grant of *specific and separated powers*. The third room is a *prohibition and denial of power*, and room four is *procedural specifications*. If we do not take the silence of the Constitution as an absolute denial of power, then the granting of specific and separated power and the prohibition and denial of power (rooms two and three) have no meaning.

32. This is the language of the Declaration of Independence.

33. Although it is outside the scope of this article, the broad, unilateral power of "Executive Orders" is another example of the dramatic expansion and usurpation of the Executive Branch. On this point, see Gary North, *Government By Emergency* (Ft. Worth: American Bureau of Economic Research, 1983).

*Article I—Procedures and Powers of Congress*

Because the focus of this article is specifically taxes, we will skip Article I, Sections 1 through 7 which specify the creation, election, and procedures of Congress. Beginning in Section 8, "We, the people" grant the specific power to Congress "to lay and collect taxes." In Section 9 "We, the People" place explicit limitations upon that power, and in Section 10 "We, the people" place a series of explicit prohibitions upon legislative power as it applies to the individual state governments.[34]

*Direct and Indirect Taxes*

Article I, Section 8 grants to Congress its just powers. Because the power of taxation had been such an issue with England, the Framers of the Constitution begin the enumeration of Congressional powers with the power to tax. The entire clause reads, "The Congress shall have power to lay and collect taxes, duties, imposts, and excises, to pay the debts and provide for the common defence and general welfare of the United States; but all duties, imposts, and excises shall be uniform throughout the United States."[35]

A further description and limitation on the power to tax is found in Article I, Section 2, paragraph 3, "Representatives and direct taxes shall be apportioned among the several states which may be included within this Union, according to their respective numbers, which shall be determined by adding to the whole number of free persons. . . ." Another defining clause on the power to tax appears in Article I, Section 9, paragraph 4, "No capitation, or other direct, tax shall be laid,

34. The next few sections of this article will be important preliminary ground work. If you wish to understand a lawful reason why you do not have to pay taxes, it is *extremely important* that you pay close attention to the reasoning in these sections.

35. You will notice that a statement of purpose is buried within this granting of power lifted almost verbatim from the Preamble. The Constitution is uniform and consistent. Modern statists insist that "to provide for general welfare" is a broad, unspecified grant of power. The explicit wording of the Constitution will not bear this interpretation, although statist jurists have borne it. Statism is the rule of the day, and modern statists use this clause to justify our present "welfare programs" and other forms of coercive wealth redistribution to rob the people of not only their property, but more importantly, their liberties.

unless in proportion to the census or enumeration hereinbefore directed to be taken."

On the basis of these Sections, the courts have ruled that Congress has been granted the power to lay and collect two different types of taxes: *Direct* and *Indirect* taxes.[36] A direct tax is one that is imposed directly upon property according to its value (ad valorum). It is one that is imposed on existence.[37] Every year, if you own a home or some other form of real property, you pay property taxes. Those taxes are direct taxes. They are, however, levied by the individual states, and not by the Federal Government. The reference to "taxes" in Article I, Section 8, paragraph 1 refers to direct taxes which are subject to apportionment among the several states (Article I, Section 2, paragraph 3). There is a further limitation on direct taxes in Article I, Section 9, paragraph 4. Not only must direct taxes be apportioned among the several states, but they must be proportioned according to the census or enumeration directed to be taken.

Now, what does all of that mean? In granting to Congress the power to lay and collect a direct tax, "We, the People" did *not* grant to Congress the power to collect money directly from the unincorporated *individuals* of our nation. Rather, we granted to Congress the power to lay and collect a tax *from the state governments*. That is what "apportioned among the several states" means. Further, not only must the tax be levied and collected from the several states, but the amount of the tax must be according to the number of people residing in that state ("in proportion to the census or enumeration hereinbefore directed to be taken").

For example, if there are 20 million people in the state of Delaware, and 30 million people in the state of Pennsylvania, and 30 million people in the state of New York, and 20 million people in the state of New Hampshire, and the Federal Gov-

36. *Pollock v. Farmer's Loan and Trust Co.*, 157 U.S. 429, 15 S.Ct. 673, 39 L.Ed. 759 (1895). In the body of the opinion, Mr. Chief Justice Fuller, who wrote the opinion, states, "In the matter of taxation, the Constitution recognizes the two great classes of direct and indirect taxes, and lays down two rules by which their imposition must be governed, namely: The rule of apportionment as to direct taxes, and the rule of uniformity as to duties, imposts, and excises."

37. Henry Campbell Black, M.A., *Black's Law Dictionary*, Fifth Edition. (St. Paul, MN: West Publishing Co.), p. 415.

ernment wishes to collect $1,000.00,[38] then it would directly tax Delaware and New Hampshire for $200 each, and Pennsylvania and New York for $300 each. It would be the responsibility of each state to collect enough money to pay the apportioned direct tax to the Federal Government. The individual states probably would do that by some form of indirect taxation, such as sales tax, but however it is collected, the Constitution does not allow the Federal Government to gain jurisdiction and directly tax the individuals of the United States.

At this point it would be proper to ask: How did we get into the situation of paying income taxes to the Federal Government? The income tax certainly looks like a direct tax on our "income."[39] If the Constitution does not grant the Federal Government power to collect a direct tax from the individuals of the United States, then why do they collect an "income" tax?

During the last decade of the nineteenth century, statism began a serious effort to void some of the Constitutional limitations placed upon the Federal Government by our Founding Fathers. One of the limitations that was a particular nuisance to the ideals of the statists was the clause in the Fifth Amendment which reads, "No person shall be deprived of property without due process of law, nor shall private property be taken for public use, without just compensation."[40] The statists saw possibilities for the widespread *political* redistribution of wealth, and they began to agitate for a form of taxation that supposedly would make the rich pay more, and the poor pay less. In order to do that, they reasoned that they must not only get around the clause in the Fifth Amendment regarding "just compensation," but they must also somehow negate the apportionment limitation on direct taxes in Article I, Section 2.

38. I believe in a very *limited* government!

39. "Income" is a legal-fiction term. See discussion below.

40. It is with this clause that the doctrine of eminent domain is derived. You can see that although it is possible to *implicitly* derive a doctrine of eminent domain, it is also just as possible to derive a doctrine that would not grant the ultimate ownership of all land to the state, but would grant them what might be called an "easement" on selected pieces of property. That is, if the Federal Government needed to use a particular piece of property for a highway or some other good and necessary use, then it could do so, but it must first negotiate with the owner, and then pay for the property. The Federal Government would not, however, have a "right" to all property.

Although a great deal more could be said, suffice it to say that in the infamous year of 1913, the Sixteenth Amendment to the Constitution was passed. It reads, "The Congress shall have power to lay and collect taxes on incomes, from whatever source derived, without apportionment among the several States, and without regard to any census or enumeration." The statists got their way, an unapportioned direct tax graduated according to "income" was declared law. Or at least that is the way it seemed.

As might be guessed, there was a great deal of debate and bitter political fighting leading up to the passage of the Sixteenth Amendment. And, as is often the case in a hotly debated law, the Sixteenth Amendment was immediately challenged in the courts.

The case that is most important for our consideration is *Brushaber v. Union Pacific Railroad* (1916).[41] In this case a stockholder, Mr. Brushaber, objected to the voluntary paying of income tax by the corporation, Union Pacific Railroad Company. The Supreme Court used this case to clarify the confusion surrounding the Sixteenth Amendment. The major objection was that the Sixteenth Amendment was unconstitutional because it caused one portion of the Constitution to conflict with another portion of the Constitution. As it then stood, Article I, Section 2, paragraph 4 (the "apportionment" clause) conflicted with the Sixteenth Amendment.

In the *Brushaber* decision, the Supreme Court ruled that:

> 1) In spite of the explicit wording of the Sixteenth Amendment, no new power to tax was granted that did not already exist under Article I, Section 8.
>
> 2) The "income tax" was not in substance an unapportioned direct tax, for to be so would cause one provision of the Constitution to conflict with another provision that had not been lawfully repealed.
>
> 3) In order to avoid being an unapportioned direct tax, the Court ruled that the requirement that "income" be separated from "source" was of principle importance and could now be established by legislation. In other words, to tax a "source" would be a direct tax, but to tax "income" is to tax the *use* of a "source," whence arises ruling #4.
>
> 4) Regardless of its form, the "income tax" is in substance deemed to fall into the class of taxes known as "indirect" taxes, along with imposts, duties, and excises, which were never constitutionally subject to apportionment.

41. 240 U.S. 1 (1916).

So the "income tax" which is levied every year by the Internal Revenue Service is not a direct tax at all, according to this interpretation by the Supreme Court; it is an *indirect* tax![42] Now, just exactly what is an "indirect tax"?

According to *Black's Law Dictionary*, an "indirect tax" is either a tax on the *privileged* manufacture, sale, or consumption of a commodity, or on the acts and events of a *privileged person* such as a corporation or a licensed attorney.[43] This definition is derived from many court decisions, and it points to the fact that "indirect taxes" fall into two related, but separate categories. But more importantly, the definition points to a fundamental element of "indirect taxes," the idea of "privilege." *An "indirect tax" involves first and foremost the exercise of privilege, as distinguished from the exercise of a common right.* From whom does one receive such a privilege? The Federal Government is the grantor of privilege in this case. This point cannot be overemphasized, as we shall see in a moment.

The *first category* of "indirect taxes" is the privileged manufacture, sale, or consumption of a commodity. For instance, if a Japanese businessman wishes to import a particular product into the U.S. and sell it in the U.S., he must first of all get permission from the U.S. Government. The U.S. Government in turn grants him the privilege to import his product into the U.S., and further grants him the privilege to sell his product in the U.S. That is not, of course, the end of the story. The Constitution allows the taxing of the exercise of those privileges and calls that tax a "duty." In our day, we sometimes refer to this tax on privilege as a "customs tax." Regardless of the wording, it is a tax on privilege; hence, an "indirect tax."

Another example of this category of "indirect tax" is the tax on liquors and cigarettes. Everyone does not pay this tax, only those who drink alcohol and smoke cigarettes. In exchange for the privilege of smoking cigarettes or drinking whiskey, users pay an indirect tax. (These so-called "vice" taxes provided 89 percent of all Federal tax revenues as recently as 1913, the year

---

42. See also *Stanton v. Baltic Mining Co.*, 240 U.S. 103 (1916); *Doyle v. Mitchell Brothers Co.*, 247 U.S. 179 (1918); *Eisner v. Macomber*, 252 U.S. 189 (1920); *Bowers v. Kerbaugh-Empire Co.*, 271 U.S. 170 (1926).

43. *Black's Law Dictionary*, pp. 695-696. The Constitutional restriction on an "indirect tax" is that it must be uniform throughout the United States (Article I, Section 8, paragraph 1).

the income tax amendment was passed. Total Federal revenues in 1913 were $344,424,000—hardly sufficient to operate a messianic State!)[44]

The *second category* of "indirect tax" is the tax on the acts and events of a privileged person such as a corporation or licensed attorney. A privileged person is a person who has asked for and received a specific privilege from the Federal Government. For instance, an attorney is licensed by the state and exercises the privilege of being an officer of the court. A corporation, although an artificial person, is also granted privilege: the privileges of perpetual life and limited liability.[45] Each of these "privileged persons" is subject to indirect taxation. The *subject* of the taxation is the exercise of privilege, while the *object* of that taxation is the parameter "income."[46]

To sum up this section, we have seen that *both classes of taxation*, "direct" and "indirect" taxes, have *very restricted jurisdictions*. A "direct tax" cannot be imposed upon persons or property without apportionment among the states. An "indirect tax," on the other hand, while not subject to apportionment, must be uniform throughout the United States, and can only be imposed on privileged persons, acts, or events, *not on acts and events of common right*. We have also seen that the "income tax" is not a "direct tax," since it does not meet the Constitutional requirements. Rather, it is an "indirect tax," and as such, *it must be in some way a tax on privilege*.

Before we can use this important point in direct application to our contention that most of the individuals of the United States are not "persons liable" for "income tax," we must first examine some further preliminary matters. As is universally recognized, the bureaucracy is exceedingly complex. To unravel the deadly web which has been woven around us without becoming hopelessly entrapped requires persistence, patience, and a great deal of thought and careful study.

### *Fact, Law, and Determination*

Article Three of the Constitution grants power to the Federal Judiciary. The first sentence reads, "The judicial power of

---

44. *Historical Statistics of the United States, Colonial Times to 1957* (Washington, D.C.: U.S. Department of Commerce, 1960), p. 713.

45. See Appendix B.

46. See section below on "income."

the United States shall be vested in one supreme Court, and in such inferior courts as the Congress may from time to time ordain and establish." Further, in Section 2, paragraph 2, "the supreme Court shall have appellate jurisdiction, both as to Law and Fact, with such exceptions, and under such regulations as the Congress shall make." Although there is much more to be said with regard to the Federal Judiciary, we can only in passing mention one severely neglected Congressional power, and then focus upon a very important Constitutional distinction.

Please note that in Section 2, Congress is given the power to place "exceptions" and "regulations" on the Supreme Court's *jurisdiction*. In other words, Congress is able, via legislation, to define and restrict the jurisdiction and procedures of the Federal Judiciary. For one hundred years, the willingness of Congress to restrict the activities of the Supreme Court has been negligible; but the point is, they can if they want to. For instance, Congress could place the abortion issue out of the reach of the Supreme Court. They could rule that abortion is illegal, and then deny the Court jurisdiction in the matter. Congress *could* exercise this power, *but they won't*. The more important point for our consideration, however, is the separate recognition in the Constitution of the two elements of judicial decision, arguments of *LAW* and matters of *FACT*. The Constitution gives jurisdiction to the Court in both Law and Fact.

Paralegal litigants have only recently come across this important distinction, and are learning to use it to their advantage in battles with civil government.[47] The civil government has created deliberate confusion by intermingling and combining these two elements of judicial decisions. "Matters of FACT" are those *events* that have been shown during a court proceeding to have *actually occurred* or been experienced in your life, or to have been places and things that you have or had, or that otherwise belonged to you or did belong to you at one time or another. "Arguments of LAW" are those *provisions* of the Constitution, laws, or decisions of the Court, that one presents and argues as *applicable* in a specific case and with a specific set of factual circumstances.

47. The person principally responsible for this discovery is Dr. George Arlen, Executive Director and Founder of the American Patriot Association. Please see Appendix D for more information about his work.

In order to understand the relationship between FACT and LAW, the following chart is helpful.[48]

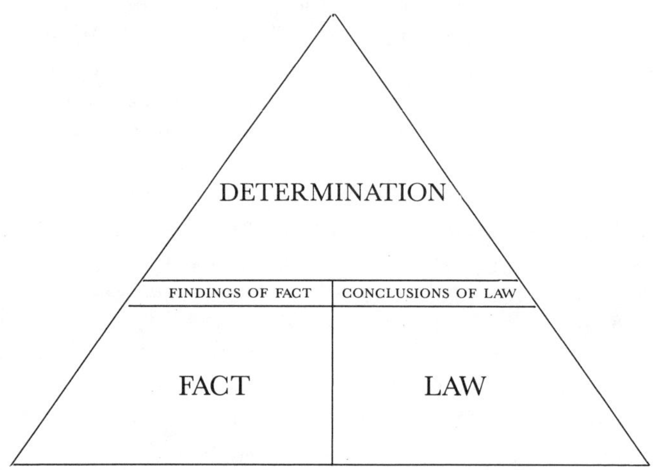


The triangular chart above illustrates the proper application of LAW to FACT. It points out the connection that causes certain and specific law, which is recited in the proceeding or in a brief, to be applicable to the certain and specific facts which have been introduced into evidence.[49] "Determinations" are those decisions, judgments, orders, or other completed action taken at the end of a proceeding. A "determination" is arrived at by a plenary consideration of the relationship of the "Findings of Facts" and "Conclusions of Law" presented in the proceeding.

---

48. This chart was devised by Dr. George Arlen and included in a non-published report titled "IRS Administrative Procedures and Appeals." For more information about Dr. Arlen and his research reports, please see Appendix D.

49. "Evidence" is "any species of proof, or probative matter, legally presented at the trial of an issue, by the act of the parties and through the medium of witnesses, records, documents, exhibits, concrete objects, etc. for the purpose of inducing belief in the minds of the court or jury as to their contention" (*Black's Law Dictionary*, p. 498). In other words, "evidence" is matters of fact conclusively proven to be so through the mediums mentioned above, and specifically bearing upon the case.

These distinctions are not only important for court proceedings, but are also important in many of our everyday considerations. For instance, let us suppose that an official for the Federal Aviation Administration appeared at your home or place of business and informed you that according to the Federal Aviation Code, Section 3107, paragraph 2, all pilots are required to carry their pilot's license at all times and annually to submit to testing before their license is renewed. The F.A.A. official then said, "Would you please present your pilot's license and annual certification slip for inspection?" Most of us would simply look at the F.A.A. official and reply, "But, I'm not a pilot." The F.A.A. official would then apologize for the inconvenience he caused you, and that would be the end of the matter. The dynamic of this "proceeding," however, is a little more complex.

The F.A.A. official presented you with an argument of law, "all pilots are required to carry their pilot's license at all times and annually to submit to testing before their license is renewed." You replied with a matter of fact, "I'm not a pilot." The determination was then made simultaneously by both of you, "A non-pilot is not liable for obeying the applicable F.A.A. laws." A finding of fact was joined with a conclusion of law and a proper determination was made regarding the specific case. That in summary, is the relationship between fact, law, and determination.

### *The Concept of Legal-Fiction*

A consideration related to the distinction between "fact" and "law" is that of "legal-fiction." Any word or term appearing in a statute and defined or qualified therein, or any term specifically made the subject of a court decision regarding its interpretation or definition, is a "legal-fiction" term. In other words, the *concept described* by legislative statute or court decision *cannot describe matters of facts* that are solely a part of an individual's life and action *because the definition of the term involves conclusions of law.* Some of the words may have ordinary, everyday meanings, but when they are used in a court proceeding, or in the documents or letters generated by a government agency, they assume the "legal-fiction" meaning given to them.

Examples of "legal-fiction" terms used in federal tax matters are: "tax liability," "taxpayer," "taxable year," "income," "gross income," "taxable income," "wages," "employee," "employment," "employer," "self-employment," "exempt," "allowance," "money," "dollars," "payment," etc. Examples of *proper* factual terms used in federal tax matters are: work, labor, property, sale, gift, exchange, receive, receipt, spend, expense, cost, purchase, check, paycheck, negotiable instrument, tender, Creator, etc. All of the "legal-fiction" terms must be carefully considered by the paralegal litigant before using *any* of them, especially in reference to himself. The law is very tricky at this point, and extreme caution is recommended.

### *"I am not a Person Liable for Income Tax"*

We are now ready for the major argument in defense of the contention that most individuals are not required to pay "income tax," and that the present "income tax" system is unconstitutional and should be outlawed.

Around the first of every year, the Internal Revenue Service mails out its annual "1040 package," which includes sample forms and an instruction booklet. Most Americans view this "service" as simply a component part of the IRS's collection process. In reality, the IRS is "requiring" individuals unknowingly to *volunteer* information about themselves, especially concerning their personal and business financial matters. The place then to begin in challenging the IRS is with this request for information.

The first thing that one should consider when *any* federal agency asks for information is an appeal to the Privacy Act of 1974. Even if you are not involved in the paralegal litigation movement, it is extremely beneficial to be familiar with the opportunities open to you under the Privacy Act, and ways in which you may use it. For more information on this preliminary strategy, see Appendix C.

For the sake of argument, let us assume that you have decided to become involved in the paralegal litigation movement. Your first appeal should be to the Privacy Act *before* using the arguments below. One extremely crucial ally that all paralegal litigants must learn to use is "Lawyer Delay." He needs to be employed as frequently as possible.[50]

Included in the 1040 instruction booklet every year is a

---

50. One of my personal mottos in this fight is, "If I haven't lost, then I'm winning!" "Lawyer Delay" can be of great help if he is used properly.

*jurisdictional statement* from the IRS in response to the Privacy Act requirement that "Each agency that maintains a system of records shall . . . inform each individual whom it asks to supply information . . . the authority (whether granted by statute, or by executive order of the President) which authorizes the solicitation of the information and whether the disclosure of such information is mandatory or voluntary."[51] The IRS's jurisdictional response reads, "Our legal right to ask for information is Internal Revenue Code 6001 and 6011 and their regulations. They say that you must file a return or statement with us for any tax you are liable for."

One should always do two things when any bureaucratic agency cites a law to you. First, *carefully read* the statement. Bureaucrats have a remarkable gift for obscuring the English language. Secondly, *look up the citation* and make sure they are using the specific law correctly.

In the IRS's statement above, they say that "you must file a return or statement with us for any tax" as a *consequence* of being a person "liable for" any tax imposed. The IRS's statement does not, however, reveal the condition, act, or event that would *as a matter of fact* be the cause of making one a "person liable" for any tax imposed. Instead, they refer to Sections 6001 and 6011 for that information.

Section 6001 reads:

> Every person liable for any tax imposed by this title, or for the collection thereof, shall keep such records, render such statements, make such returns, and comply with such rules and regulations as the Secretary from time to time prescribe. Whenever in the judgement of the Secretary it is necessary, he may require any person, by notice served upon such person or by regulations, to make such returns, render such statements, or keep such records, as the Secretary deems sufficient to show whether or not such person is liable for tax under this title. The only records which an employer shall be required to keep under this section in connection with charged tips shall be charge receipts and copies of statements furnished by employees under section 6053(a).[52]

Note that Section 6001 even more clearly states that as a matter of law ". . . any tax imposed by this title" is a *consequence* of being a "person liable." Once again, however, the

51. 5 U.S. Code 552a, The Privacy Act of 1974.
52. Title 26, U.S. Code, Section 6001.

how or why an individual is made a "person liable" is not given.

One does notice, however, that Section 6001 authorizes the Secretary of Treasury to collect information ". . . by notice served on such a person or by regulations, . . . to show whether or not such a person is liable for tax under this title." Therefore, as a *matter of fact*, an individual can make the determination that he is not a "person liable." The determination is based on the *fact* that he is a God-created individual, not a State-created individual, who is acting solely according to common law. He has not knowingly asked for nor received any privilege from the civil government, and he does not presently exercise any privilege from the civil government. The determination is further based upon the *argument of law* that the so-called "income tax" is in fact an indirect tax,[53] and as such applies only to the acceptance and exercise of privilege. Since he is not a privileged person, and since the "income tax" is an indirect tax levied against the privileged, therefore, the determination can be made, "*I am not a 'person liable' for 'income tax' within the meaning of Section 6001.*"

It can be further noted that the Secretary has not made a contrary determination, and that there are no laws or regulations existing to operate as a substitute for a personal notice pursuant to the meaning of the Fifth Amendment: "No person shall . . . be deprived of life, liberty, *or property*[54] without due process of law, nor shall private property be taken for public use, without just compensation."

The IRS's jurisdictional statement of authority also cites Section 6011 of the Internal Revenue Code. Although this section is much lengthier than Section 6001, the relevant portion reads:

> GENERAL REQUIREMENTS
> OF RETURN, STATEMENT, OR LIST.
>
> (a) General rule—When required by regulations prescribed by the Secretary any person made liable for any tax imposed by this title, or for the collection thereof, shall make a return or statement according to the forms and regulations prescribed by the Secretary. Every person required to make a return or statement shall include therein the information required by such forms or regulations. . . .

53. See section above "Direct and Indirect Taxes."

54. Your "money" is your property.

Almost identical wording occurs in Section 6011 as was found in Section 6001. "Any person *made* liable for any tax imposed by this title, . . . is required to make a return." It is a *consequence* of being a "person liable" that one is bound by "regulations prescribed by the Secretary." This same wording also appears in the IRS regulations.

It is seen, therefore, that both sections cited in the jurisdictional statement fail to describe what facts or circumstances may occur to cause a "tax liability" to come into existence. There is nothing in them which indicates why a private, "unprivileged" citizen cannot legally declare: *"I am not a person liable for income tax."* As such, we can further assert that any and all consequences of Title 26 that purport to impose an indirect tax simply *do not apply to unincorporated, non-privileged citizens*, any more than the F.A.A. regulations apply to non-pilots. One can see the genesis of the designation "return"; it is a "return" on the exercise or granting of privilege.

In summary, the determination "I am not a person liable for income tax" is based upon the *finding of fact* that a citizen is not a privileged person, and upon the *conclusion of law* that the "income tax" is an indirect tax, and as such applies only to privileged person or to the exercise of privilege.

*This determination is the most fundamental assertion of the paralegal tax litigation movement*. In the past, paralegal litigants have wanted to plead a multitude of reasons as to why they were not liable for payment of "income taxes." Common to almost all of the reasons was the *granting of jurisdiction* to the IRS by passively accepting the IRS's explanation of their authority. The strategy outlined in this article immediately points out that *as a matter of fact* the IRS does not have jurisdiction over citizens because *they are not "persons liable" for "income tax."*

The "income tax" is an unlawful and unconstitutional tax. *In spite of popular opinion, one can actually be a law-abiding citizen and NEVER FILE AN INCOME TAX RETURN*. The only way the IRS has been able to maintain its charade these many years is through misdirection, misinformation, fear, and tyranny.

### *Practical Guidelines*

We have only skimmed the top of the iceberg in fully understanding the paralegal tax litigant's strategy to resist the

IRS. I have only given you the Constitutional background on the unconstitutional tactics of the Internal Revenue Service and the paralegal litigants' response. A full explanation of *how* to resist the IRS would require an additional manuscript of five to eight times the length of this one. In our study, we have reviewed indirect and direct taxes in detail. The intricacies of "fact, law, and determination," however, have not been fully explored. Nor have we examined IRS administrative practices. When one assumes a paralegal litigant position, he needs to know how to terminate Social Security, request a refund, stop withholding, handle an administrative appeal, deal with audits and summons, appear in Federal court, appear in tax court, file petitions to tax court, quash a summons, and on and on and on. It is impossible in an article of this length to go into all of the practical aspects of the paralegal litigant position in detail.[55] We can, however, explore some preliminary considerations that will help if you choose to assume a paralegal litigant position.

### *The Acquisition of Knowledge*

*The most important objective for the new paralegal litigant should be the acquisition of knowledge.* One must make it his goal to understand not only the traditional tax position, but have a general, well-informed view of the tax laws and procedures. From the earlier discussions in this article, it can be seen that our "perceptions" of taxes and Federal tax laws are tainted. Notions previously accepted as "gospel" must be re-examined with specific reliance upon LAW, FACT, and DETERMINATION.

Extreme care must characterize the activities of the paralegal litigant. Knowledgeable, well-informed activity can be successful in the long-run. Sloppy, ill-informed activity will land a paralegal litigant in the poor house, jail, or both.

As noted earlier, the paralegal litigation movement is about 35 years old. During that time, many different strategies have been used by various paralegal litigants. Some have been more successful than others, but most of them have had one thing in common: *they have granted jurisdiction to the IRS by signing a form.* It was not necessarily the 1040 Form, but most often it was. It is sometimes necessary to sign a govern-

55. For information on how to obtain more information, see Appendix D.

ment form, *but it should always be done under duress or with a disclaimer noted on the form*. A paralegal litigant should make it a practice *never* to sign a government form unless he is forced to.

In the 1979 edition of the IRS Special Agent's Handbook, the IRS enumerated eleven paralegal litigant positions that the IRS can effectively counter. The list includes raising protests over how the taxes are spent, leaving the forms blank, asserting Fourth and Fifth Amendment and other constitutional procedural objections, protesting that the tax laws are unconstitutional, using gold and silver money accounting conversions to figure "tax liability," claiming excessive charitable contributions to oneself as a minister or to a church, reporting family estate trusts and assignment of services, inflating W-4 allowances and making false claims of exemption, and using Forms 843 and 1040x to claim refunds of withholding without filing a Form 1040.

One position which is *not* mentioned, however, in the Special Agent's Handbook is the one which I have discussed in this article. As we have seen, since unincorporated, "unprivileged" citizens are not "persons liable" for tax, tax litigants simply *DO NOT SIGN AND FILE A "TAX RETURN."* Because they are not "persons liable," they are not subject to the requirement of filing a "return." This is the *only* litigation position which does not include a *signed admission* that one is a "person liable" for taxes. *When nothing is signed and filed, then nothing is admitted to the IRS*. In so doing, administrative jurisdiction is denied to the IRS except in so far as it is necessary to receive the *facts* supporting the determination that "I am not a 'person liable' for tax under Section 6001."

Nevertheless, silence, anonymity, and non-filing are not enough to counter the IRS effectively. To become a tax litigant, one must also become an aggressive *non-filer*.[56] The IRS has ways of countering or neutralizing the tax litigant's assertions. The paralegal litigant must everywhere and at all times assert the determination that he is not a "person liable" for tax, and is, therefore, not subject to the tax. He must be ready to defend his position in whatever forum necessary, and

56. The most notable example of non-filing, non-signing not being enough is when you receive the infamous "90 day letter." Officially, it is a "Notice of Deficiency" from the IRS which must be challenged aggressively or the battle will be lost by default.

he must do so with expertise and finesse. Hence, the critical need for the acquisition of knowledge.

*Continuity*

Another important element in the paralegal litigant's fight is continuity from either a traditional tax position or from an inferior litigation position. A move from one position to another must be compatible and non-contradictory. A paralegal litigant must show "good faith." He must in all of his activities explicitly exhibit *an honest belief that his actions are according to law.* There must be an absence of malice and intent to defraud. There must be consistency not only in what is overtly done, but also regarding those actions left undone.

How would a tax litigant answer an IRS agent if he asked, "You filled out, signed, and filed a 1040 Form for ten years, why did you all of a sudden quit? If you were under our jurisdiction then, and if you were a "person liable" then, and if you received "income" during those years, why and when did you cease being under our jurisdiction, etc.?" What would the tax litigant say? How does one make a new tax litigation position compatible with a previous traditional position? The answer is really quite simple.

The tax litigant *revokes* all prior signatures on "Tax Returns," alleging that the signature was obtained through fraud. "Fraud" means deception with intent to do harm. It is easy to prove that the IRS did not tell the whole story when they instructed unincorporated citizens to fill out the 1040 Form. Did they publicly explain that the whole Federal tax system is based on *voluntary compliance*? Did they clearly explain how a person becomes liable for income tax? Did they explain exactly what the courts' narrow definition of "income" is? No, of course not. The IRS, therefore, *deceived* the citizens of the United States; and via the deception harmed the litigant in taking your property. That is fraud, and he may legitimately claim that the IRS is guilty of fraud, and that furthermore, when he signed the form he was mistaken as to the *facts*. In other words, he claims that he didn't realize that as a matter of fact he was not required to file a "Tax Return."[57]

57. This approach must be modified somewhat if a tax litigation position is assumed during a year that "withholding" has been deducted from your

From that point, the paralegal litigant must tailor his "aggressive non-filing" to his own situation. If he is an independent contractor, then his strategy will be different than if he is contracting with a party that "withholds" a portion of his property from his paycheck and deposits it with the IRS. The procedures for either course of action are, however, outside the bounds of this paper.

## *Financial Privacy*

Nothing could be further from the truth than to believe that the IRS is simply after "tax-dollars." *They are after information.* The "1040 Form" should be called a "confession," and not a "return." In the last 15 years, the IRS has usurped powers and jurisdiction far removed from its duty as a tax collector. It has invaded the hitherto "separated" realms of education, the family, and the Church. What can explain this incredible expansion? As Congressman George Hansen points out, "The IRS embodies the political realities of the selfish human desire to dominate others. Thus, the *end* of this gigantic pretense of officialdom is *power*—pure and simple."[58] The information the IRS receives from the "taxpayer," and it is primarily *financial information*, is used to gain power and control.

The solution? Restrict their flow of information. By not "filing" a 1040 Confession, the paralegal litigant severely restricts the flow of information. By practicing *financial privacy*, the paralegal litigant makes it even more difficult for the IRS to gather information about him. Although there is not time to go into detail, several important aspects of financial privacy must be mentioned.

1) GET OUT OF BANKING! The number-one source of information for the IRS is bank records. Although bank records are technically personal property, they are not pro-

---

paycheck. In order to assume a litigation position in "good faith" after the IRS has collected "withholding," the paralegal tax litigant must file for a refund of all withholding and Social Security tax on the grounds that they collected it from someone who is not a "person liable." If the IRS refuses to refund his money, he must then file suit in District Court for the refund. The technique, letters to IRS, documentation, etc. is available in the form of a research report from Dr. George Arlen. For more information, see Appendix D.

58. George Hansen, *How the IRS Seizes Your Dollars and How to Fight Back* (New York: Simon & Schuster, 1981), pp. 15f.

tected under the Fourth Amendment guarantee against unreasonable searches and seizures. The *only* effective way to deny the IRS access to these records is to not have them.

2) DEAL AS MUCH AS POSSIBLE IN CASH. The immediate response of the new paralegal litigant when these first two points are raised is to complain of the inconvenience of a life without checks. A most peculiar argument! How many hours do people spend during the year balancing the check book? How much does the bank charge people annually to deposit their money in their bank and maintain a checking account? It doesn't cost that much to purchase money orders for those payments that must be made by mail, and there are ways to recycle out-of-town checks. The inconvenience is in making the change, not in living without checks. Remember, checks can be traced . . . cash can't.

If you wish to test my hypothesis concerning checks and the information they reveal, pull out of your file one month's worth of cancelled checks. Try to assume that you don't know anything about yourself, and then thumb through the checks one by one. What can you find out about yourself from your cancelled checks? Where you attend church? The name of your mortgage company? The name of companies with which you do business? Personal characteristics (did you buy a *case* of shotgun shells last month)? Don't fool yourself, the IRS is *expert* in using bank records. They will find things you never dreamed of from bank records. Most important, however, is the fact that they will find *new leads* for more *information* from the bank records.

The bottom line, if you are going to assume a paralegal litigant position, is get out of banking and deal primarily in cash. Even if you are not willing to become a paralegal litigant, it is still a good idea to leave as little "paper" behind you as possible. Cash transactions have many advantages regardless of the direction you choose.

### *Dealing With The IRS*

If you have ever been called in for an "audit," then you have had some experience in dealing with an administrative agency. When you assume a paralegal litigant position, however, you will get lots of experience in administrative procedures! The observations below will help you in preparing for your first confrontation.

1) THE IRS WILL ALWAYS USURP UNJUST POWER. There is no way to soft-soap it; the IRS today is the enemy of liberty. Perhaps there is a place for this "servant," but at this point in history the "servant" has usurped unjust powers to the extent that in many ways it is now the "master." For that reason, the paralegal litigant *must expect* the IRS to make aggressive moves against the lawful exercise of his rights and liberties.

2) THE IRS OPERATES WITHOUT FORMAL RULES. As a result of Congress failing to legislate strict rules of practice and procedure such as are prescribed for the courts, *the IRS operates within a vacuum of formal or enforceable rules and procedures*. Because of this, the paralegal litigant must keep his guard up and ward off any tricks or schemes which have been developed by the IRS to achieve their goals of control and the acquisition of power. Many times the "tricks" involve semantic games. Once again, we see the need for knowledge.

3) WHAT RULES THE IRS DOES HAVE ARE CREATED IN A SELF-SERVING MANNER. Although there are many rules created by the Federal agencies which appear in the *Federal Register* and in the Code of Regulations, they are all self-serving in delegating unjust powers to themselves. It is usually futile to research these "rules," since they are *technically unenforceable*. The benefit of acknowledging this point is to prevent oneself from being "buffaloed" by some obnoxious bureaucrat who is attempting to ride roughshod over law-abiding citizens with one of his "rules."

4) THE IRS HAS THE POWER TO SUMMON. This unjust power is one of the most tyrannical of all. Without accusation of wrongdoing, the IRS has the power to summon a citizen to appear, to interfere in his personal life, and to infringe upon the free exercise of his Constitutionally guaranteed immunities. This power is considered *investigatory*, and amounts to no more than a fishing expedition. The paralegal litigant must learn to deal with this investigatory power, and not simply yell, "YOU CAN'T DO THAT!" There are ways to combat this tyrannical power, and even to effectively neutralize it, although a discussion of them is outside the bounds of this article.

5) THE IRS IS ALWAYS PRESUMED CORRECT. In other words, when anyone deals with the IRS, *he is guilty until he proves himself innocent*. This self-serving theory places the

smooth operation and success of the IRS over the rights of the people. Frustration and infuriation are, however, not the proper responses. The paralegal litigant must seize the initiative, shoulder the burden of proof, and proceed to disprove the position of the IRS agent.

6) FOR EVERY GRIEVANCE THERE IS A REMEDY. This is the basic principle of "due process." When one person has a grievance, the guarantee is that there will always be a remedy for obtaining relief. For every "cause of action," there is a *procedure* to follow to obtain a resolution to the conflict. Note that the "due process" clause of the Fifth Amendment guarantees *one* remedy for redress of a grievance, not many. It is therefore important to know not only that you have the right of redress, but what procedure you must follow to obtain relief. Again, the critical need for knowledge is of paramount importance.

7) SUBSTANCE ALWAYS GOVERNS OVER FORM IN LEGAL MATTERS. The "substance" of a factual matter is what is really there when one strips off any facade that may be present. "Form" describes only superficial appearance. In any dealing with government, the paralegal litigant must always remember that "substance" governs "form." To put it another way, the *real* truth must always be sought, and always presented.

For example, let us assume that Joe B. has created a "family estate trust" in order to protect his property, specifically his house. Joe B. would then claim to the IRS, "I don't own my house anymore, the trust does." This statement, however, describes only the *form* of the property ownership, and not the *substance*. Nothing has changed *substantially*. Joe B. still lives in the house rent-free. He is still responsible for maintaining it. Joe B. pays the property taxes and in every way functions as the owner. Thus, a court would rule that *as a matter of fact* Joe B. is the owner. Although the court would leave the trust intact, the property would be ruled to be owned by Joe B., and therefore, subject to seizure, etc. It is the opinion of this author that such a strategy also compromises the paralegal litigant in the eyes of the court. The court may determine that one is not exercising "good faith." Such insubstantial misdirection is ineffective and unnecessary.

8) LANGUAGE CONFUSION IS DELIBERATE. We have already referred to some of the semantic tricks the IRS is

apt to try on the paralegal litigant. The paralegal litigant should expect such delusion. "1984" is upon us, and the IRS is a master of "newspeak." For example, the IRS asserts that the Federal system of taxation is one of "voluntary compliance." Now think about that. What do they *really* mean? I think it is something along the lines of "Do what I *order* you to do *voluntarily*, or I will *force* you to comply with threat of fine or jail."

### *Ecclesiastical Resistance to the IRS*

Now that we have outlined the strategy for individuals in resisting the IRS, it is absolutely vital that we cover in this section two crucial "Achilles' Heels" that will plague the Church if efforts are not taken to strengthen these weak points. Both instances revolve around the issue of "jurisdiction" or "sovereignty." We have mentioned the significance of this word in our earlier study, but it bears reviewing.

The legal meaning of the word is very large and comprehensive. Practically speaking, it refers to "authority." If a court or administrative agency has "jurisdiction," it means that the court or administrative agency has the *authority* to take cognizance of and decide cases. It is the *legal right* by which judges exercise their authority, and by which the power and authority of a court to hear and determine a judicial proceeding is established. Furthermore, "jurisdiction" is the right and power of a court to adjudicate concerning the subject matter in a given case.

The jurisdictional question that confronts the Church is "Who *has* authority over the Church?" Does Jesus Christ, as Head of the Church, have sole jurisdiction; or does the State have some sort of jurisdiction also? The question here must be divided. In the sense that the Church is "all Christians in all of life," Christ is sole head. The Church as an institution claims Christ as unique King, but Christ also claims to be King of kings, King of the nations, King of the State. It has been, and still is the belief of orthodox Christianity that Christ alone is Head of the Church, and of the State. That His Word is our only source of Law. That the Church is a separate, created institution; equal with or on the same level as the State in one sense, but having a kind of primacy as the locus of the proclamation of God's Word, which governs the State as well. The Church is not subject to the State; that is, the State does not have jurisdiction over the Church, though the State is called to protect the Church's ordinances. Likewise, the State is not subject to the Church; that is, the Church as a government does not have jurisdiction over the State. Each is a separate and equal institution under God functioning in its own distinct sphere. There is an *interdependency* in terms of life and activity, but an *independence* in terms of human authority.

The jurisdictional problem arises when two separate but related practices common in American churches are examined. The first involves the application by a church to be "incorporated." The second is the application by a church to the Federal Government, specifically to the IRS, for classification as a "501(c)(3)" organization, that is, a charitable religious tax-exempt organization. Let us consider each in turn.

### *Incorporation*

What does it mean to apply for and become an "incorporated" Church? First of all, it is important to understand that a "corporation" is a legal-artificial-privileged person created by and under the authority of the laws of a state. A corporation is a legal and artificial person because it is *created* by the law of a state and exists as a "person" only in the eyes of the law. It is not a real person like you or me, but is a "person" on paper only.

For a church to become "incorporated," therefore, is to give *fundamental jurisdiction, power, and control to the State. The church gives to the State the jurisdiction of Creator.* It is to surrender categorically the orthodox confession that the Church is the creature of God, and to confess instead that this particular church is the creature of the State. I don't know how to put it any stronger than to say that *for a church to become incorporated is to be faithless to Christ*.

When the Rev. Everett Sileven was battling the State of Nebraska over the Christian school the Faith Baptist Church of Louisville, Nebraska, operated, at one point the judge leaned over his bench and remarked to Rev. Sileven, "I don't understand why you won't submit your school to licensure. Don't you realize that *everything* in your church is licensed from the building to the hymnbooks?"

Rev. Sileven replied, "What do you mean?"

The judge answered, "Isn't the Faith Baptist Church incorporated?"

"Well, yes . . . " Sileven answered.

"As a corporation," said the judge, "every possession of Faith Baptist Church is licensed by the state of Nebraska. We control it all, and that is the reason we can require you to submit your school to licensure!"

Perhaps your church is already incorporated. Maybe some well-meaning lawyer advised the church board at the formation of your particular congregation to apply for incorporation. What is your church's Biblical responsibility before God? *Unincorporate immediately*! Although you will probably need to contact a lawyer in order to unincorporate, be advised that nine times out of ten, the lawyer will try to talk you out of it. *Don't listen to him*. He may be a good lawyer, but in this case he doesn't know what he is talking about. Instead of hiring a lawyer, you may elect to file the papers yourself. In that event, simply write to the state capital and request everything necessary to unincorporate. All of the information, papers and forms will be sent to you by return mail.

Although the granting of the fundamental jurisdiction of Creator to the State is the main reason not to incorporate a church, there is also a more subtle danger in incorporating. When one applies for incorporation, one is requesting a grant of privilege from the State. The privileges granted are *perpetual life*, regardless of the changes in board membership; and *limited liability*, that is the corporation is only liable to the extent of the corporation's assets. The conviction of every Christian church should be that the Church has never, doesn't now, or ever will need a privilege from the State. Our sole subsistence is in Christ alone. We do not get *perpetual life* from the State. Practically speaking, the church doesn't need it. When one board member dies, then his name is simply taken off the property deed or any other official papers. It is a very simple process. Nor does the church need the "privilege" of *limited liability*. Churches purchase insurance to protect themselves. If Uncle "Hard-to-Get-Along-With" and Aunt "Never-Comes-to-Church" fall down on the front steps and sue the church for $100,000, then our insurance company will take care of the settlement. We don't need the State to protect the interests of the Church of Jesus Christ!

*Tax Exemption*

Briefly, let us turn now to the Internal Revenue Code, Section 501(c)(3) which deals with charitable religious and educational institutions. Much of what was said regarding incorporation is also applicable here, but due to the widespread ignorance involving the implications of being classified under this Section, 501(c)(3) warrants special emphasis.

About twenty-five years ago, the IRS made a special effort to include churches under its jurisdiction. It did so by telling the churches that in order to avoid any problems when their parishioners claimed a deduction on their tax returns for charitable contributions to the church, it would be advisable for each church to apply to the IRS for status as a "501(c)(3) Tax-exempt, religious organization." The church would then be issued a number, and if there was ever any problem, it could easily and efficiently be taken care of. Thus far the IRS.

Once again, *the main problem is jurisdictional.* In applying and submitting to the IRS classification, a church is submitting to the jurisdiction of the IRS. If the IRS decides that the *only* "religious" activity of XYZ Church is Sunday morning worship, and they disallow the "tax-exempt" use of the building for a Christian school, and if XYZ Church has granted the IRS jurisdiction by submitting to 501(c)(3) classification, *then there is very little that they can do, except to appeal to the mercy of the tax collectors. The Church had previously given the IRS the power to make that determination.* In all probability, if the church challenged the determination in court, it would lose. In order to be faithful to Christ, XYZ Church would end up merely refusing to comply, and its pastor or elders would end up in jail on contempt of court citations, or some other trumped-up charge.[59]

The bottom line, Biblically speaking, is that the Church must *never* grant jurisdiction to the Federal or state governments, either implicitly or explicitly. Whenever a church applies to the government for a privilege of any sort, it is granting jurisdiction to the State. In the case of the 501(c)(3) classification, the privilege requested is "tax-exemption." *The*

59. Please understand that I am not denigrating such a stand. There may come a time when churches and pastors will have to make similar stands. The point of this section is to put off such a stand as long as possible. If the choice is faithlessness or jail, then we must be willing to go to jail. We don't, however, want to go to jail until we have to!

*Church of Jesus Christ does not need tax exemption*! The Church is a separate institution accountable solely to the Lord Christ. *In order for the Church to need "tax-exemption" it would first have to be under the jurisdiction of the State for the State can only tax that which it has jurisdiction over.* The Church must never, ever become accountable to the State, and therefore, subject to taxation. To surrender to any other "head" other than Christ is spiritual adultery, and I fear the Church of the twentieth century is guilty of just that.

At this point, the distinction between "immunity" and "exemption" needs to be emphasized. As previously noted, "exemption" is a privilege granted by the Federal Government. When a church claims that it is "exempt," even if it asserts that it is "automatically exempt," *the church is implicitly submitting to the jurisdiction of the State*. Furthermore, in applying for and accepting a privilege from the government, the church is *being subsidized by government*. In a recent Supreme Court decision, *Regan v. Taxation with Representation of Washington* (May, 1983), Justice William Rehnquist wrote, "Both tax exemptions and tax-deductibility are a form of subsidy that is administered through a tax system. A tax exemption has much the same effect as a cash grant to the organization of the amount of tax it would have to pay on its income."

It is extremely important to understand the dynamic of the government's position. Justice Rehnquist rightly recognizes that when the government grants a tax-exemption, *it is allowing that party to keep money it would ordinarily have paid to the IRS*. The government's position is that the "tax-exempt" organization owes the tax dollars, but the government is graciously allowing them to keep their money. Justice Rehnquist is correct when he says, "A tax exemption has much the same effect as a cash grant to the organization." Churches must learn to accept this reasoning, and not naively to scream, "You can't do that!"

Hence, the importance of our contention that the Church is not "tax-exempt." If the Church is not "tax-exempt," however, what is it? The Church of Jesus Christ, because it is a separate institution under God, is *immune* from the State's jurisdiction. It is, therefore, *immune* from Federal taxation. The Church does not pay income tax or any other tax to the State because it is not under the State's jurisdiction.

*This distinction quite possibly could prove to be one of the most im-*

*portant assertions of the Church in the remaining years of this century.*[60] Churches must be ready to challenge the jurisdiction of the IRS or any other Federal agency with *the matter of fact* of the Church's immunity. We must forever strike from our vocabulary the notion of "tax-exemption" for the Church.[61]

What does a church do if it is already a 501(c)(3) organization and wishes to get out from under that classification? First, the officers of the church must write a letter to the Internal Revenue Service *instructing*, not requesting, that the IRS dissolve its 501(c)(3) classification of the church. The letter should briefly list the principled reasoning supporting the request, and give a reasonable time limit to respond. Second, the officers of the church should send a request pursuant to the Freedom of Information Act[62] for a copy of all documents, memoranda, etc. that may be in the possession of the IRS. Third, if there is no response from the IRS in one month, then write a second letter a little more strongly worded than the first enclosing a copy of the first letter. Fourth, if a satisfactory response is not immediately forthcoming, then a final letter must be written. In this letter all the stops should be pulled out.

Begin with a categorical statement that "XYZ Church" renounces the pretended jurisdiction of the Federal Government through the agency of the Internal Revenue Service. State in no uncertain terms the reasons behind this assertion.

---

60. This will become increasingly more important when local state and county governments begin to attempt to levy property taxes against church property. This contemptible action is already being done in California, and it is on the agenda in many other states. In fact, the first scheduled seizure of church property for payment of back taxes was June 30, 1983 in Poway, California. The Pomerado Road Baptist Church was seized because it "owed" $17,000 in back taxes to the state. In Texas, 1983 is the first year the state and county governments have begun to appraise church property. One way to fight these state and county taxes is to assert the church's immunity. It should be enough to simply appeal to the 1st Amendment, but that doesn't seem to be the case anymore.

61. Immunity applies *only* to the Church and her directly controlled ministries. Parachurch organizations are not directly under the umbrella of the Church. Hence, they are under government jurisdiction and subject to taxation or tax exemption. Perhaps the issue of taxation is one way in which God will bring many of the parachurch activities under the discipline of His Church.

62. See Appendix C.

Inform them that the church is exercising its God-given right to the Free Exercise of Religion, and that it is the *conviction* of the church that to be classified a 501(c)(3) organization impedes that exercise by granting jurisdiction to the IRS. Further, inform them that it is the *conviction* of the church that to remain a 501(c)(3) is to be faithless to the Head of the Church, the Lord Christ. Finally, inform them that it is the *conviction* of the church that the IRS obtained submission of the church to 501(c)(3) classification under fraud. Point out that the IRS deceived the church by not giving the church the whole story when it encouraged the church to submit to classification, and explain that the classification is harmful to the church for the reasons stated above. Hence, the allegation of fraud.[63] Send the letter to the Internal Revenue Service, and keep a copy for the church's files. The church is now a non-501(c)(3) organization, regardless of what the IRS may believe. If the IRS should challenge the determination sometime down the road, then simply pull out the file and reassert the church's position —in triplicate if need be! *But the Church must never, ever pay the tax. To do so would be faithless to Christ.*

As we have seen, we are dealing with a tyrannical tax system. The Church may have to suffer great persecution for the gospel of Christ. What we wish to prevent, however, is the Church *submitting* to persecution and oppression by giving the State jurisdiction over it.

## *Conclusion*

The Internal Revenue Service will be stopped someday from its unlawful usurpation and exercise of tyrannical and unjust power. The usurpation of power by civil government is *always bilateral*. In other words, when civil government seizes a power unjustly for itself, it does not do so in a vacuum. "We, the People" who chartered and granted power to the Federal Government in the first place must not allow that government to usurp this power. It is up to us not to allow civil government to usurp power unjustly, and it is up to us not to allow civil government to exercise unjust power which it has previously usurped.

63. The definition of "fraud" is deceit with intent to do harm.

The exercise of liberty and enforcing of the Constitution is what resistance to the IRS is all about. The last fifty years has seen an enormous growth of civil government and accompanying governmental abuses. If this generation does not take the initiative to roll back our gargantuan civil government, the liberties which our Founding Fathers fought and died to secure will be lost. The oppressor has the upper hand at this point. Inactivity on the part of "We, the People" will only strengthen the government's unlawful position.

Fighting the Federal Government is like opposing an enemy tank coming down the street. It does no good to stand out in the middle of the street and scream, "Stop! What you are doing is unconstitutional!" If you stand out in the middle of the street, the tank will simply run over you, or shoot its cannon and blow up your house, killing you and your family. We must be willing offensively to *disable the tank*. We must take our litigational bazookas and maneuver ourselves to get a clear shot of the tank's side. Then we must be willing to send an accurate shot into the vulnerable section of the tank's tread, thus disabling the tank.

One may do battle with the civil government and end up with "tank treads" on his back. Eventually, however, the "tank" of civil government will be disabled. The liberties given to us by God will once again be secure from tyrannical usurpation. Individual resistance to unjust taxation is merely one "guerrilla" tactic mobilized against government. It is not for everyone, but it is a legitimate form of Christian resistance to tyranny when approached properly. If you wish to join in this fight, please refer to Appendix D for more information on how to get started.

On the other hand, ecclesiastical resistance to the IRS is not an option. *The Church must never be compromised. The encroachments of the IRS on behalf of the messianic State must be resisted at all costs. Anything less is faithlessness.*

## *APPENDIX A: Is the Tax Movement Sinful?*

After outlining in detail the rationale for individual resistance to the IRS, it is now important to comment briefly on the sentiment in orthodox Christian circles that this strategy is in some way sinful, or at the very least not an activity that a believer should be involved in. As I said, my comments must be characterized by brevity, and therefore in the nature of the case cannot be painstakingly comprehensive. Nevertheless, I will endeavor to answer the arguments levied against the movement by two extremely competent Reformed theologians, R. J. Rushdoony and James B. Jordan.[64]

*Rushdoony*

In an article appearing in the *Journal of Christian Reconstruction* (Volume 2, Winter 1975-76) titled "Jesus and the Tax Revolt," Rev. Rushdoony categorically argues that the "tax revolt" is a "futile thing, a dead end, and a departure from Biblical requirements." In other words, he is saying that the "tax revolt" is not only an exercise in futility, but that it is also positively sinful.

Rev. Rushdoony advances two substantial arguments in favor of his conclusion. The *first* is that it is wrong to assume that one doesn't have to pay taxes to the government in power because the government in power is not the lawfully constituted government. He uses the distinction between a "de facto" government and "de jure" government. A "de jure" government is one which rules by right of law. In America, a "de jure" government would be one that rules strictly according to the Constitution. On the other hand, a "de facto" government is the one which actually exists and is in power. Rev. Rushdoony argues that just because the government of the United States is allegedly unconstitutional, this is no reason not to pay your taxes. He points out that when Jesus instructed the hypocritical Pharisees to "render therefore unto Caesar the things which are Caesar's; and unto God the things which are God's" (Matthew 22:19-21), He was speaking in the situation of a "de facto" tyrannical Roman government. The Pharisees, and all Jews for that matter, were to pay their taxes regardless of what they thought of the Roman government, because the Roman government was the "de facto" government. His conclusion then is that the "tax revolt" is unlawful because an individual in the "tax revolt" argues the same way the Pharisees did. The "tax rebel" refuses to pay his taxes because the government is unconstitutional; that is, our present Federal Government is not the lawfully constituted government.

64. I realize that both critics wrote their arguments with the libertarian/anarchist versions of the tax rebellion in mind. The position I am surveying is not anarchic, but Constitutional in its presuppositions.

In answer to this first argument, let me first of all point out that in the main body of this article the reasoning I have advanced for participation in the paralegal litigation movement does not include an argument along the lines attacked by Rev. Rushdoony. Nevertheless, Rev. Rushdoony's argument is not acceptable, even if we accepted his reasoning against "tax rebels."

In Christ's day, what "law" were the Pharisees referring to when they said, "Is it *lawful* to give tribute to Caesar, or not?" Were they referring to Roman law, the "de facto" law of the day? Not likely. It is pretty clear they were referring to *the corpus of Jewish law*, which was what the Pharisees considered the "de jure" law within the meaning of Rev. Rushdoony's article. Jesus, of course, answered correctly. Render to Caesar what Caesar's law requires, *but only so long as Caesar's law does not require you to do something that is sinful.* At the same time, give to God what God requires. As Rev. Rushdoony points out, Jesus answered in terms of the existing "de facto" government, to be sure, but the thrust of the passage is tied up in our Lord's qualifying phrase, "Render . . . to God the things which are God's." Jesus not only answered in terms of the "de facto" law, but more importantly, He answered in terms of God and His law, the ultimate "de jure" law which will one day be the universal "de facto" law. The paying of the tax in Christ's day was not unlawful on either account; therefore, the people of Palestine were to pay it.

When we move up to twentieth-century America, let us ask the same question that the Pharisees did: "Is it *lawful* to pay income taxes or not?" Jesus said to "Render unto Caesar the things which are Caesar's. . . ." In the Roman world, Caesar was the supreme law of the land. Who is "Caesar" in twentieth-century America? It would actually be better to ask "What is Caesar?" because *"Caesar" is not an individual in our society.* The supreme "de facto" and "de jure" law of the land in America today is *the United States Constitution.*[65]

65. It is true that legislators, chief executives, jurists, Constitutional law experts, and especially bureaucrats have compromised the "de facto" status of the Constitution's position as "Caesar," but the court system still exists, trial by jury still exists, and we can still appeal to that Constitution.

To answer the question posed above, we need only refer back to the main body of this article. It has been dedicated to proving that unincorporated, "unprivileged" Americans are not required *by law* to pay the "income tax." We have looked at Constitutional issues, excerpts from the Internal Revenue Code, and court decisions. On every account we have found that not only is it not *unlawful* for Americans *not* to pay "income tax," but that *not* to pay "income tax" is perfectly *law-abiding*. The situation in twentieth-century America is not the same as the situation in Palestine of the first century. It is, therefore, improper to apply *wholesale and without qualification* the law of Jesus in Matthew 22. The paralegal litigation movement is not seeking to overthrow our existing law structure, or even to ignore the existing law structure as the Pharisees wanted to do. Rather, its members are intent on *enforcing* the existing law structure. If an official of the civil government tries to require a citizen to do something that the citizen *knows* he is not required to do by law, does the citizen not have the option to point out to the government official that he is not required to comply, and then refuse to do so? I categorically assert that the citizen has that right; that it is not sinful to exercise that right; and that in so doing the citizen is "rendering unto Caesar" in the highest possible way.

The *second* argument of Rev. Rushdoony is that the "Tax Revolt" is revolutionary in nature. He points out that Karl Marx advocated a "tax revolt." He even quotes a statement of Marx's, "Our ground is not the ground of legality; it is the ground of revolution."

From what we previously have said, it is clear that the "ground" of the paralegal litigation movement, including the tax specialists within the overall movement, is *not revolution*. These men do not believe in "the regenerating power of chaos, anarchy, and revolution." *The paralegal litigation movement is not a revolt; it is a movement to enforce the law through political reform.* Nothing that has been asserted in this article is illegal. In fact great pains have been taken to assure the legality of every statement.

### *Jordan*

The second source of criticism comes from the pen of

James B. Jordan. In an article published in *Biblical Economics Today* (Vol. IV, No. 2, April/May 1981) titled "The Christian and Tax Strikes: Pros and Cons," Mr. Jordan offers some "principles which will help the reader as he or she comes to grips with the tax rebellion of the 1980s." He goes on to point out that the basic thrust of the essay is that "the Bible clearly teaches that Christians are to submit to the powers that be and pay whatever taxes are required of them; but citizens of the United States of America may properly raise the question of just precisely what is required of them, and in raising this question may work for reform."

The *first* main argument is that the "Tax Strike" is illegitimate because it seeks spiritual reform through political means. Mr. Jordan argues that "Tax strikes as a Kingdom method are contrary to the teaching of Jesus . . . and Paul." He points out that true liberation has to do *fundamentally* with right worship. When Israel was liberated from Egypt, it was not a political liberation. God insisted that Israel be released in order that they might worship Him. When a culture recognizes who the true God is, and worships Him rightly, then there follows as a result righteous government, lower taxes, and a regular Sabbath rest. Mr. Jordan argues that these *results* are not the *means* to such liberation. He then asserts that "the tax strike and 'liberation theology' obscure this fact."

First of all, I wholeheartedly agree that the worship of the true God is the fundamental element in any cultural reform. It is my personal belief that the "Theonomic" or "Christian Reconstruction" movement has not been more successful precisely because it has neglected the areas of ecclesiology and liturgy. Be that as it may, this criticism is not entirely accurate.

Linking "the tax strike" and "liberation theology" may be valid in some cases, but we believe that it does not apply to the paralegal tax litigation movement. The theology of liberation believes in the regeneration of a culture through political reforms. The paralegal litigation movement is simply endeavoring to see laws observed that are already on the books. Its advocates do not believe in political regeneration of any sort. The paralegal litigation movement is, to be sure, a movement organized for political action. But then so is the Right to Life Committee and other pro-life groups. We do not condemn their activities simply because they are politically oriented, nor should we condemn the paralegal litigation movement simply because it is politically oriented. To be sure, real change will only come when our nation is changed *spiritually*. In the meantime, however, such movements for political reform are important stop-gaps enabling the Church to grow stronger.

The *second* argument of Mr. Jordan's we need to address is really more of a presupposition than an explicit argument. In several of his enumerated headings, the presupposition behind them seems to be that the United States government is a tyranny along the lines of the regimes of "Caesar, Stalin, Hitler, Idi Amin, and Bokassa." He refers to Christians needing to be invisible and superficially cooperative in order to keep oppression to a minimum. There is a sense in which this consideration is valid, but it is not absolute. It is true that the IRS in many respects is approaching a "Secret Police" type agency, but *much of the rest of Federal Government is not at that point yet*. It is for that reason that the tax litigation movement has a very real chance of effecting political reform. The rest of civil government doesn't like the abuses of the IRS, either. Furthermore, part of "counting the cost" of battle is to measure the strength of the opposing forces. *If an individual wishes to join this movement for Constitutional enforcement, then he must first size up the battle ahead of him*. One must not be naive; the IRS is a formidable opponent. "Tank Treads" are not entirely out of the question.

*Third*, Mr. Jordan assumes that it is the *normative will* of Christ to pay the income tax. There is, therefore, *no option* open to the Christian *not* to pay income tax. He writes concerning the tax striker, "Christ has told him to pay, not to strike." Where has Christ said that? He points to Matthew 22:15-22 (the "Render unto Caesar" passage) which we have already looked at. One *can* interpret that as an absolute command to pay any and all taxes to the state, but one does not *necessarily* have to adopt that interpretation. We must note in passing once again that properly to "render to Caesar" is to obey Caesar's law without acquiescing to sin. To become part of the "tax strike" can be eminently legal if the litigant argues so that he *does not violate any laws of the United States Government*.

The paralegal tax litigant *is* "rendering unto Caesar."

Another passage Mr. Jordan refers to Matthew 17:24-27. In this passage Mr. Jordan points out that Jesus miraculously provides tax money for the disciples, even when they are not actually liable for the tax. The message of Christ, according to Mr. Jordan, is that since we are not in bondage to money, we needn't worry about having the money to pay our taxes *and* provide for our daily necessities. God will always provide for us. Once again, the assumption that the motivation to be involved in the paralegal litigation movement is entirely monetary is not entirely correct. To be sure, there are some paralegal litigants who believe they are saving money by not paying taxes. They are mistaken, however, because it is going to cost the paralegal litigant more to fight, than to submit to the unjust demands of the IRS. The main body of this paper has been dedicated to showing one way that "We, the People" can roll back some of the abuses of big government. The motivation is political reform, *not "pure personal covetousness."*

The third passage that Mr. Jordan refers to is Romans 13:1-7. He points out that Christians are "*not* told that each Christian ought to obey God's civil law, willy-nilly, trying to force the hand of the magistrate. Rather, we are told to submit to the existing order, pay our taxes, pray for the conversion of the magistrate, and proclaim the gospel to him and to all men." Further, Mr. Jordan remarks that "Paul does not say in verse 6, 'Pay taxes *whenever* rulers are servants of God,' but rather he says to 'pay taxes *because* rulers are servants of God,' whether they know it or not." In response, I want to emphasize that the tax litigation movement is not setting aside *any law* for *any reason*. Its advocates contend simply that they are not required to pay the income tax. The paralegal litigant is not setting aside a law because the present administrators are not enforcing God's law and Biblical political theory, nor is he setting aside a law because they are simply not observing the Constitution. He contends forcefully that he is obeying the law, and insisting that the administrators of the law do the same.

## *APPENDIX B: How to Use the Jury for Political Reform*

Western Civilization's recognition of a right to a trial by jury goes all the way back to the English Magna Carta in 1215

A.D. Since that time, one of the major purposes of a jury has been *not to convict* under laws they feel are unjust. At the time of the Civil War, northern juries refused to convict under the fugitive slave laws. During Prohibition, government officers found it difficult to get a conviction under the laws against the sale or possession of alcohol. The juries in both of these examples simply refused to convict according to the law because in their judgment, the law was unjust or unfair.

In the main body of this article, we discussed the importance of distinguishing "matters of fact" and "arguments of law." We saw that the courts have jurisdiction in both "matters of fact" and "arguments of law." At the time of the Dred Scott/fugitive slave law decision, the authorities recognized that if juries were allowed to decide on both the facts of a case and the laws applicable to that case, then the "experts"—the judges and lawyers—would lose a great measure of control over the legal system. *They wanted to avoid that at all costs.*

Immediately following the Dred Scott decision, and for some 30 years thereafter, the issue of "jury nullification" was debated back and forth. Some jurists argued that since they were no longer subjects of the King, but were in fact citizens just like everyone else, they could be trusted to have the citizen's best interests at heart. Others argued that if juries were charged with judging the justness of particular laws as well as the facts of the case, it would put too great a mental strain on the jurors.

In 1895 the issue came to a head in a Supreme Court decision. That noble body of jurists ruled that although juries have the right to ignore a judge's instructions regarding the law, *the jury shouldn't be made aware of it.*[66] What hypocrisy! Citizens have a *right* that they shouldn't be made aware of! Judges most assuredly may be trusted with "the citizen's best interests!" Amazing!

Since that 1895 decision, court rulings mention the existence of "jury nullification" only grudgingly. It is not taught in law schools. Judges refuse to tell juries or allow defense lawyers to tell them. It is as if the right of nullification by juries simply dropped off the face of the earth, *but there are faint signs of resurrection!*

The "jury nullification" right is not an oddball, long since

---

66. *Sparf v. U.S.*, 156 U.S. 51 (1895).

obsolete practice. As alluded to, it is beginning to be used today, albeit unselfconsciously. In some areas, the civil government is finding it difficult to get convictions for marijuana violations and other so-called "morals" laws. In Georgia, Indiana, and Maryland, jury nullification is still a constitutional part of state judicial process.

Jurists and courts throughout the history of our nation have affirmed and acknowledged its existence. Listed below are a few selected comments by respected judges and lawyers.

> The jury has the right to judge both the law as well as the fact in controversy. (Chief Justice John Jay, *U.S. Supreme Court Georgia v. Brailsford*, (1794).
>
> The jury has the right to determine both the laws and the facts. (Samuel Chase, Supreme Court Justice, 1804. Signer of the Declaration of Independence).
>
> There are five separate tribunals to veto laws: representative, senate, executive, judicial, and jury. It's the right and duty of juries to hold all laws invalid that are unjust or oppressive, in their opinion. *If a jury does not have this right, the government is absolute and the people are slaves* (emphasis mine). Is it absurd that twelve ignorant men should have the power to judge the law, while justices learned in the law should sit by and see the law decided erroneously? The justices are untrustworthy and are fond of power and authority. To allow them to dictate the law would surrender all property, liberty, and rights of the people into the hands of arbitrary power." (Lysander Spooner, excerpt from "An Essay on the Trial by Jury," 1852).
>
> Jury lawlessness is the great corrective of law in its actual administration. (Dean Roscoe Pound, 44 Am L Rev 12 at 18; 1910).
>
> The jury has the power to bring in a verdict in the teeth of both law and facts. (Oliver Wendell Holmes, *Horning v. DC*, 254 U.S. 135, 138; 1920).
>
> If the jury feels the law is unjust, we recognize the undisputed power of the jury to acquit, even if its verdict is contrary to the law as given by the judge and contrary to the evidence. This power of the jury is not always contrary to the interests of justice. (*US v. Moylan*, 417 F.2d 1002 at 1006; 1969).
>
> The pages of history shine on instances of the jury's exercise of its prerogative to disregard instructions of the judge; for example, acquittals under fugitive slave law. (*US v. Dougherty*, 473 F.2d 1113 at 1130; 1972).

None of the four post-1895 references, when taken in their full context, encourages jury nullification. They simply *recognize* it as part of our history which refuses to die. One modern judge, however, has categorically written in favor of the right. In a dissenting opinion, Washington D.C. Chief Federal Judge Bazelton challenges the hypocritical judicial position regarding jury nullification:

> Deliberate lack of candor . . . sleight-of-hand . . . a haphazard process. Is it true that nullification which arises out of ignorance is in some sense more worthy than nullification which arises out of knowledge? Nullification can and should serve an important function in the criminal process. Trust in the jury is, after all, one of the cornerstones of our entire criminal jurisprudence, and if that trust is without foundation, we must re-examine a great deal more than just the nullification doctrine. The noble uses of the power provide an important input of our evaluation of the substantive standards of criminal law. The reluctance of juries to convict under the prohibition and fugitive slave laws told us much about the morality of those laws. A doctrine that can provide us with such critical insights should not be driven underground. We should grant the defendant's request for a nullification instruction, or at least permit the defendants to argue the question before the jury. *If revulsion against the government has reached a point where a jury is unwilling to convict, we would be far better advised to ponder the implications of that result than to spend our time devising stratagems which let us pretend that the power of nullification does not exist.* (*US v. Dougherty*, 473 F.2d 1113 at 1130; 1972).

It should be obvious to any discerning reader that the right of juries to nullify a law for the particular case they are sitting in judgment on is very important. The most vivid way of describing this important practice is to look at jury duty as a "vote."[67] In this country, the right of choice and a free vote is very important and closely guarded. If a voter walked into a voting booth, and there found a local sheriff's deputy sitting next to the voting machine, he would think that very unusual. If, however, the deputy began to dictate to him how he should vote, the irate voter would probably throw the deputy out on his ear!

Yet, every time a jury is seated in this country, *the judge does just what that hypothetical deputy tried to do!* And no one tries to stop him! The judge tells the jury, "You must uphold the law to the 'nth' degree. You are only authorized to determine whether the facts of the case meet the requirements of the law for conviction." *The judge is telling the jury how to vote!* Although I am not a "conspiracy buff," the effort on the part of the court system to squelch the right of jury nullification is the closest

---

67. This "vote" includes both trial jury and grand jury duty.

thing to a real conspiracy that I have come across.

How can thc right of jury nullification, or jury veto, be used to initiate political reform? Let us suppose that a state government passes a law making it illegal to operate a Christian school without a license. Then officials begin to prosecute parents that send their children to Christian schools, ministers that have a Christian school in their church, and the employees of Christian schools. The District Attorney gets an indictment on the Rev. John Smith on a charge of operating a Christian school without a license. A jury is seated, and the evidence and arguments of the case are presented. The judge then instructs the jury that *if* Rev. Smith is operating a Christian school *then* he is guilty of breaking the law requiring school licensure. He tells the jury that they are *bound* to uphold the law to the "nth" degree. If the facts of the case as alleged by the prosecution are true, then they must convict Rev. Smith.

The jury retires to deliberate. It just so happens that seated on this jury is John "Concerned Citizen." He providentially knows about the right of jury nullification. John tells his fellow jurors that *they have the right to judge both the law AND the facts*. If they believe that the law is unjust, then they don't have to convict, regardless of what the judge said. The jury decides that even though they can't deny Rev. Smith is operating a Christian school, he is *not guilty* of operating a Christian school without a license. They decide to *veto* a bad, unjust law.

Let us expand the situation a bit. Suppose the government is prosecuting churches all across the country. But because juries have been alerted to the fact that they can nullify an unjust law, *the government fails to get a single conviction of any kind!* Just think of the message that "We, the People" would send to Capitol Hill and the Justice Department! Back off the Churches and Christian schools . . . or else!

If we look at the "vote" of a *grand jury*, the significance of jury nullification becomes even more awesome. A grand jury is a jury of *inquiry*. It is called a "grand jury" because it consists of more jury members than a trial jury, usually not less than 12 and not more than 23 members. The grand jury is called to investigate an alleged crime. It is their duty to determine whether "probable cause" exists; that is, whether or not there is enough evidence to indict an individual of a crime. The grand jury has tremendously broad investigatory powers. It can issue summons, and it is not limited to considering only the case or cases that is set before it.

For instance, let us once again assume that the Federal Government is pursuing indictments against individuals in the Christian school movement. The U.S. Attorney brings an allegation against Pastor Sullivan for operating a Christian school. Pastor Sullivan has also refused to turn over all of his records to the Internal Revenue Service, so the U.S. Attorney is also asking the grand jury for an indictment against Pastor Sullivan for "willful failure to file." The U.S. Attorney walks before the grand jury, pats a large stack of official papers representing the allegations against Pastor Sullivan, and says, "This is an open and shut case. Sullivan operates a Christian school and refuses to cooperate with government officials. He is just a trouble-maker. I don't want to take any more of your time than necessary, so if the foreman will simply sign the indictment I have already prepared, you can be on your way."

The foreman of the grand jury, however, is a concerned citizen. He tells the U.S. Attorney that it seems a little premature to indict someone of such a serious crime without even hearing his side of the story. The foreman feels, if none of his fellow jury members has any objections, that it would be best to first talk with Pastor Sullivan before signing anything. The rest of the jury agrees, and Sullivan is brought in.

After about 45 minutes of hearing the horror stories perpetrated against Pastor Sullivan and his Christian school, the grand jury realizes that it must conduct a full investigation. They subpeona government official after government official. They could, if they found enough evidence, *indict every government official* who broke the law when oppressing Pastor Sullivan. The immediate benefit would be, however, that they would "no bill" Pastor Sullivan; that is, they would refuse to indict him on any charge. If enough grand juries exercised their very broad powers, once again "We, the People" would get civil government's attention in a hurry.

In order to take advantage of the jury nullification right, there are several things you must do. First, to be selected for a jury, you must be a registered voter. Second, when selected for jury duty, don't give any indication that you have the least bit of intelligence. *Lawyers prefer to see "no brains" sworn in. An idiot can be controlled and influenced more easily.* Never let them know you have any firm political views or understand the first thing about your constitutional rights. In fact, it would be a good idea to stand in front of a mirror and practice assuming a "blank look" before going to jury duty. Third, when the judge asks if anyone on the jury panel has a problem with the particular laws applicable to the case the panel is up for, just don't respond. You are not bound by oath to answer the judge's every whim. If only those individuals who agree with a particular law are chosen, then what good is the right of jury nullification?

*The bottom line is, do whatever you can within the bounds of the law to be seated on the jury.* Once the jury is seated, and they find out that you are a committed Christian and a concerned citizen, there is nothing they can do.

At that point, do what you are supposed to do. Sit in judgment of fact and law. If the man is guilty of breaking a just law, convict him. If not, then turn him loose. Make the following creed your creed when you are called to jury duty.

*"The Juror's Creed"*[68]

I will not allow myself to be a juror unless I am certain that I can protect the rights of the innocent as well as proclaim the guilt of the criminal.

I will remember that when I take my oath I become a judge and the judge becomes a referee.

I will honor my obligation to be a judge and to judge both the law and the facts as is my right and my duty.

I will not allow the referee, the prosecutor, or the other jurors to talk me out of doing what I know to be right.

I will always be mindful that the accused is innocent until I vote otherwise.

I will claim my right to interrogate the witnesses to eliminate doubt because I will not vote against the accused if I have any doubt.

If I become aware that the Constitutional or other rights of the accused are not being honored, I will automatically vote in favor of the accused, unless I am completely satisfied that harm has truly been done to others by the accused.

I will vote in favor of any defendant who is prevented from presenting to me all of the evidence and testimony he relies on.

I will vote in favor of any defendant who is prevented from telling me why he believes I should find him not guilty.

May I never be an instrument of harm to anyone who does no harm, or who has broken no law.

---

68. I don't know where this "creed" originated. It was sent to the Institute of Christian Economics after being copied.

Finally, *photocopy this section of this article and circulate it in your churches*. The government and the courts are gearing up for a battle with the Church, let's give them one!

## *APPENDIX C: How to Use the Freedom of Information Act and The Privacy Act*

Abraham Lincoln remarked once, "Let the people know the facts and the country will be saved." Walter Lippmann put the issue of public knowledge of government activities in perhaps a little bit better perspective, "Enduring governments must be accountable to someone besides themselves."

We are all aware of the activities of "Big Brother," but up until 1974, we did not have any way to find out just exactly what "Big Brother" was doing. Government agencies could invade our personal privacy, generate personal dossiers, and use the information in any way they wished without "We, the People" finding out about the invasion until it was too late. With the passage of the Freedom of Information Act and the Privacy Act, however, the people have had the means to keep track of "Big Brother."

The original Freedom of Information Act was signed by President Lyndon B. Johnson on July 4, 1966, and went into effect July 4, 1967. The original act, however, had its problems. There were too many obvious loopholes, and the bureaucrats exploited the loopholes to the maximum. It wasn't until 1974 that Congress finally plugged most of the loopholes, and the amended act was passed into law over then President Ford's veto.[69]

It is not possible to discuss fully the meaning, implications, and uses of the FOIA or the Privacy Act. A full text of the FOIA and Privacy Act is published in Title 5, U.S. Code, Section 552. They are also usually reprinted in most of the books dealing with one or both of the acts. Our concern in this appendix is how to invoke and use the FOIA and Privacy Act.

Specifically, the Freedom of Information Act gives the public the guarantee that if they want a certain document or a certain bit of information from a government agency, it will be given to them, subject to specified restrictions. The Privacy

69. For more information on the history of the FOIA, please see L. G. Sherick, *How to Use the Freedom of Information Act*, (New York: Arco Publishing Co.), chapter one.

Act, on the other hand, is designed to give citizens more control over *what information is collected about them* by the Federal Government, and how that information is being used against them.

Uses of the FOIA and Privacy Act that directly apply to the issues dealt with in this essay include: Forcing the IRS to comply with the stipulations of the Privacy Act, using the FOIA or the Privacy Act as a means of discovering what information the government has accumulated on an individual, correcting any misinformation in a government file, challenging any unauthorized information collected, or using the FOIA as a means of "discovery" in a court battle. Other common uses are: exposing possible government wrongdoing, obtaining agency records for a newspaper article, research in academic and historical studies, obtaining factual evidence to challenge a law, for commercial advantage, and to invalidate an activity of a government agency. As one can see, the possible uses of the FOIA and Privacy Act are many, complex, and varied. I have included this list simply to illustrate the breadth of the law. In order to keep the application of these acts straight, I will explain how to invoke and use the Freedom of Information Act first, and then deal with the Privacy Act.

### *Using the FOIA*

There are several preliminary considerations that must be touched upon before we actually write a sample letter. First of all, the law says that one must be able to "reasonably describe" any and all documents or records that are sought under the FOIA. Note, that does *not* mean that an *exact description* is necessary, but enough *identifying* information must be given to enable the FOIA clerks of an agency to find the records or documents.[70]

Second, before using the FOIA, it is important to *review the regulations*, not only the official text of the FOIA, but also *any particular regulations an agency may have pertaining to the FOIA*.

70. An "informal" call to a bureaucrat is sometimes helpful at this point. If you are wise and crafty enough, you can often get the bureaucrat to slip with a name or at least enough information to help you avoid further delays when you finally make a formal FOIA request.

I might also mention at this point that it is most important to keep records or notes of any and all conversations, meetings, etc. with a government official. If possible, tape personal phone conversations and meetings. At the very least make notes immediately after the meeting. Additionally, keep copies of all correspondence.

Getting information from the government is like pulling teeth. If the rules are not followed *exactly*, the government will slip between the cracks. If corners are cut, or the approach is sloppy, the request will fall into the proverbial bureaucratic abyss.

Third, when making the actual request, *give as much identifying information as you have*. Give all the details available. The request should be addressed to the agency having the records to the attention of the general counsel or the agency official designated to handle FOIA requests. Also, write on the outside of the envelope in big, red letters: "FREEDOM OF INFORMATION ACT REQUEST/DO NOT DELAY." The law requires an agency to respond to the request within 10 to 20 days from the receipt of the letter. If, however, you send the letter to the wrong agency, then the time limit does not officially begin until it is received at the proper agency.

Fourth, the law allows the agency to assess "reasonable standard charges for document search and duplication." The law goes on to say that these fees may be waived if the agency decides that release of the information primarily benefits the public-at-large. There are two ways to handle these fees. First, it is always a good idea to place *a maximum authorized dollar amount for the fees* in the request. Additionally, you should always, whenever possible, *claim that the request is for the benefit of the People*, and will be used in support of the public interest.

Fifth, we have already mentioned the 10 to 20 working day response time limit, but if the request is denied within the time limit the agency must also inform you of your right to appeal. The name of the official, usually the director of the agency, to whom the appeal is to be directed, must also be provided. Once again, write on the envelope containing the appeal in big, red letters: "FREEDOM OF INFORMATION ACT APPEAL/DO NOT DELAY." A decision on the appeal must also be made within 20 working days of filing.

Sixth, if you lose the appeal, or simply receive no response within the 20 working day limit, your only alternative is to *file suit in Federal court* where you live, where the agency records are kept, or in the District of Columbia. The court will hear the case "de novo," that is "anew" or "afresh." In other words, the case will not be handled as an ordinary appeal. Furthermore, *the burden of proof is on the agency.* The court even has the prerogative to inspect the withheld information in question to make an independent assessment. FOIA appeals are to be given every priority in the court's docket, so the appeal will be expedited in every way. *The law provides for the recovery of court costs and lawyer's fees and any other litigation fees in cases against the government, provided the government loses*. Finally, when facing a suit in Federal court, the government is required to file an answer within 30 days, unless it wins an extension by proving "exceptional circumstances."

Before we reproduce a sample FOIA request letter, it is important that you are aware of the nine exemptions allowed in the Act. These exemptions should not be looked at as deterrents, but merely as circumstances under which an agency may choose to withhold information. All claims of exemption are subject to appeal.

EXEMPTION ONE: "(a) matters that are specifically authorized under criteria established by an Executive order to be kept secret in the interest of national defense or foreign policy and (b) are in fact properly classified pursuant to such Executive order." Two comments are necessary concerning this exemption. Under the Act, after receiving any request for documents that are classified "SECRET," the agency must re-review the documents to determine whether or not the documents still warrant the "SECRET" classification. Furthermore, always remember that a court may examine any document to verify the claim of "national security." In some past cases, the danger wasn't national security, but political embarrassment.

EXEMPTION TWO: "Matters that are related solely to the internal personnel rules and practices of an agency." This exemption has been very strictly interpreted. It only exempts material that is solely related to internal management or organization. In other words, staff manuals instructing employees on how to perform their jobs, or even job descriptions are *not* exempted.

EXEMPTION THREE: "Matters that are specifically exempted from disclosure by statute." This includes personal income tax returns (when the request is made by a third party), applications for patents, and completed census forms.

EXEMPTION FOUR: "Matters that are trade secrets and commercial or financial information obtained from a person and privileged and confidential." Note the use of the conjunction "and." The material exempted here must be trade secrets *and* commercial or financial information *and* obtained from a person (that is *not* from a government agency) *and* privileged *and* confidential. The "loophole" here is the interpretation of "privileged" and "confidential."

EXEMPTION FIVE: "Matters that are inter-agency or intra-agency memorandums or letters which would not be available by law to a party other than an agency in litigation with the agency." This is probably the stickiest of the exemptions. I suggest you review some of the court cases involving this exemption in order to get a better understanding of it. The problem is, of course, that agencies are very quick to classify a document as "inter-agency" or "intra-agency."

EXEMPTION SIX: "Matters that deal with personnel and medical files and similar files the disclosure of which would constitute a clearly unwarranted invasion of personal privacy." Once again, this looks like a very tight exemption, but look closely at the wording. It doesn't say that just because the request is an invasion of personal privacy, but an *unwarranted* invasion of personal privacy.

EXEMPTION SEVEN: "Matters that are investigatory records compiled for law enforcement purposes, but only to the extent that the production of such records would (a) interfere with enforcement proceedings, (b) deprive a person of a right to a fair trial or an impartial adjudication, (c) constitute an unwarranted invasion of personal privacy, (d) disclose the identity of a confidential source and, in the case of a record compiled by a criminal law enforcement authority in the course of a criminal investigation; or by an agency conducting a lawful national security intelligence investigation, confidential information furnished only by the confidential source, (e) disclose investigative techniques and procedures, or (f) endanger the life or physical safety of law enforcement personnel." Briefly, note that the agency must factually prove that the records requested are investigatory documents *and* that release would involve one of the six types of injuries.

EXEMPTION EIGHT: "Matters contained in or related to examination, operating, or condition reports prepared by, on behalf of, or for the use of an agency responsible for the regulation or supervision of financial institutions." For example, a report the Securities and Exchange Commission may make from time to time on the New York Stock Exchange.

EXEMPTION NINE: "Matters involving geological and geophysical information and date, including maps, concerning wells." For example, information involving oil and natural gas exploration by private firms.

Finally, let me point out that just because an agency deems certain portions of a record to be exempt, they cannot "ipso facto" deem the whole record to be exempt. They do have the prerogative of *deleting certain portions*, but they must honor the request and send any reasonable segregable portions to you.

**Sample FOIA Request Letter**

Name ________________________
Title ________________________
Agency ________________________
Address ________________________ Date ________________
City, State, Zip ________________

RE: A Freedom of Information Act Request

Dear ________________________

1. This is a request made pursuant to the Freedom of Information Act, 5 U.S.C. 552. I agree to pay reasonable costs and fees for locating, copying, or printing the documents.

2. I will pay up to a limit of $20.00. If the amount you want to charge exceeds $20.00, please first make the requested records available for me to inspect and review at the office of yours that is closest to the address given below.

3. I request, however, that fees and costs be waived on the basis that the information sought is for the benefit of the People, generally, and will be used in support of the public interest. If this statement is not sufficient to obtain waiver of fees and costs, please provide me with the forms and information necessary to perfect this request.

4. If you claim that some of the material requested is exempt from disclosure, please send me those portions "reasonably segregable," and provide me with an indexing, itemization, and detailed justification concerning the documents you are not releasing.

5. Please send me a copy of the following:

Cordially yours,

Signature ________________________
Name ________________________
Address ________________________
City, State, Zip ________________

### *The Privacy Act*

As was noted earlier, the Privacy Act is designed to give citizens more control over what information is collected by the Federal Government about them and how that information is used. The Act accomplishes these two related purposes in five basic ways:

1. The act requires all government agencies publicly to report the existence of records maintained on individuals.
2. Information contained in these record systems must be accurate, complete, relevant, and up-to-date.
3. Procedures are outlined whereby individuals are given the opportunity to inspect and correct inaccuracies in almost all Federal files about themselves.
4. Information about an individual gathered for one purpose must not be used for another purpose without the individual's consent.
5. Agencies must keep accurate accounting of the disclosure of records and these disclosures must be made available to the subject of the records (although there are certain exceptions to this rule).

In this day and time, anyone who has had any dealing with the Federal Government has a file kept on him somewhere in the records of some agency. If you believe that an agency has kept records on you, then simply write to that particular agency and ask them. *They are required to inform you whether they have files on you*. Once the specific files are discovered then the procedures are basically the same as with the FOIA. Write a letter along the same lines as the FOIA sample letter above. Insert "Privacy Act of 1974, 5 U.S.C. 522a" in place of the FOIA information. Most of the same ground rules apply to Privacy Act requests as with FOIA requests.

Once you receive the records kept on you, then use the Privacy Act provisions for ensuring the information is accurate, complete, relevant, and up-to-date. *You should always challenge the inclusion of any information in your file describing your religious or political beliefs, activities, and associations;* that is unless you voluntarily gave that information at some point in the past. The reason for this specific challenge is that *the Privacy Act prohibits the maintenance of information regarding the way an individual exercises his First Amendment freedoms.*

**Sample Privacy Act Request to Amend Records**

Date

Name and Address of Government Agency
Washington, D.C. Zip Code

RE: Privacy Act Request to Amend Records

Dear (agency head or Privacy Act officer):

By letter dated ________________, I requested access to (use the same description as in the original letter).

In reviewing the information sent to me, I found that it was (inaccurate) (incomplete) (outdated) (not relevant to the purpose of your agency).

Therefore, pursuant to the Privacy Act of 1974, 5 U.S.C. 552a, I hereby request that you amend my record in the following manner: (Describe errors, irrelevance, etc.).

In accordance with the Act, I look forward to an acknowledgement of this request within 10 working days of its receipt. If you wish to discuss this matter, my telephone number is (890) 123-4567.

Thanking you in advance for your time and consideration, I am,

Sincerely,

Signature
Name
Address
City, State, Zip

If you have trouble determining the location of any personal records, go to a law library and consult the *Federal Register's* compilation of Privacy Act notices. It contains (a) descriptions of all Federal record systems, (b) descriptions of the kinds of data covered by the systems, (c) categories of individuals to whom the information pertains, (d) procedures to follow at the different agencies, and (e) specification of the agency official to whom you should write.

As important as knowing what information the government presently has about you, is the prevention of being forced to give the government any *more* information. The Privacy Act, you will remember, *places restrictions upon how the govern-*

*ment may use information collected*, as well as requiring the government to answer specific questions (when asked) regarding the authority of the agency to gather the information, purposes for the information, uses of the information, and effects of the collected information on the individual. *All of the above restrictions can be invoked prior to the giving of any information.* As you may guess, *it is almost impossible for a government agency to comply with these requirements.*

Let us assume that you have assumed a paralegal tax litigant position and have not "filed a return" for the preceeding ten years. The IRS writes you a letter asking for your "tax returns for the years 1973-1982." The proper response to that letter would be a request for Privacy Act Information (see sample letter on next page).

Another scenario in which the Privacy Act request would be helpful is during the preliminary stages of an investigation of a Christian school. The government might innocently ask for information from the headmaster[71] in the form of a "survey" or some other innocuous information gathering technique. The school's initial response should be the request for Privacy Act information.[72]

The Freedom of Information Act and Privacy Act are very powerful tools when used correctly and appropriately. This appendix is necessarily brief in exploring the possible uses of the FOIA or Privacy Act. For sources of more information, see Appendix D.

## *APPENDIX D: Source Material*

### *The "Tax Movement"*

The best and most useful material on the tax movement is published by the *The American Patriots Association,* 122 Spanish Village #637, Dallas, TX 75248, (214) 644-0420. This is the organization headed by Dr. George Arlen. Dr. Arlen is an expert paralegal specializing in tax matters. *Dr. Arlen and the APA are the best source for practical information regarding resisting the IRS.* Without the work of Dr. Arlen, this article would not have

---

71. The request would have to made to an individual because the Privacy Act only applies to individuals.

72. This assumes that a Federal agency is involved. The Privacy Act is a Federal law, applying to Federal agencies.

## Sample Request for Privacy Act Information

Date

Name and Address of Government Official
Washington, D.C. Zip Code

RE: Your letter dated ____________

Dear ________________________

I have received your letter referenced above, in which you have made a request for information from me. It is my desire to cooperate with you in handling your request, and I want to provide whatever information I am required. I am concerned, however, about your authority and purpose, about your uses of the requested information, and about the effects on me that might result from my responding to your request. In addition there are certain other circumstances that are of concern to me, such as whether your request is an improper or unwarranted intrusion into my personal and private beliefs and affairs.

Therefore, I hereby call upon your cooperation to inform me with true, correct, and complete statements in response to the following statutory requirements of the Privacy Act of 1974, 5 U.S.C., Section 552a, which states in part:

"(e) Each agency that maintains a system of records shall—

(3) inform each individual whom it asks to supply information, on the form which it uses to collect the information or on a separate form that can be retained by the individual—

(A) the authority (whether granted by statute, or by executive order of the President) which authorizes the solicitation of the information and whether disclosure of such information is mandatory or voluntary;

(B) the principal purpose or purposes for which the information is intended to be used;

(C) the routine uses which may be made of the information, as published pursuant to paragraph (4)(D) of this subsection;

(D) the effects on him, if any, of not providing all or any part of the requested information;"

I want to respond to your inquiry in a proper manner, but I do not want to waive or give up any of my rights just as a matter of expediency.

Sincerely,

Signature
Name, address, etc.

been possible.[73] His skilled contribution to the paralegal tax litigation movement is without an equal.

The APA is designed to be a mail-order club. It is quite possible that the IRS monitors his mail. For that reason, when you write for information, *don't put your name or your return address on the outside of the letter*, and specify delivery to a P.O. Box in the letter. You need not give up your Constitutional immunities against unwarranted investigations into your legal, private activities.

The second organization I can recommend is the "Your Heritage Protection Association" in Southern California. Although it is a local group, it publishes a monthly newspaper that is well worth the $25 subscription price. Address: Y.H.P.A., 8769 Garden Grove Blvd., Garden Grove, CA 92644. Same rules: no identifying information on the outside of the envelope you mail to them.

There are other Tax Patriot groups, but no other group offers the quality and consistency of the two mentioned above.

There are also a couple of books on the tax litigation movement that are worth reading:

*The Continuing Tax Rebellion* by Martin Larson. Available from Devin-Adair, 143 Sound Beach Ave., Old Greenwich, CT 06870; $6.95. This book summarizes the history of the Patriot Movement giving brief biographies of important personalities and outlining past strategies.

*How the IRS Seizes Your Dollars and How to Fight Back* by Congressman George Hansen with Larry Anderson. Available from Emissary Publications, P.O. Box 642, South Pasadena, CA 91030. An extremely informative book outlining the many abuses of the IRS along with extensive documentation.

### *FOIA and Privacy Act Information Sources*

There are two books on this subject that will be most helpful. The first is *How to Use the Freedom of Information Act* by L. G. Sherick. Available from Arco Publishing Company, 219 Park Avenue South, New York, NY 10003; $3.50. It is a brief, but useful introduction to the uses of the FOIA and Privacy Act.

---

73. If I had footnoted every point that I learned from Dr. Arlen, readers would have been deluged by citations.

The second book is actually an annual handbook published by the Center for National Security Studies in cooperation with the Freedom of Information Clearinghouse. The title is: *The 1981 Edition of Litigation Under the Federal Freedom of Information Act and Privacy Act*. The handbook is a compilation of the work of various lawyers who specialize in FOIA and related cases. It provides detailed application of the FOIA and Privacy Act. Although designed for lawyers, a knowledgeable laymen can use it without much problem. The handbook also gives a long bibliography and secondary source list for further FOIA studies.

## *Legal Research*

One of the most desperate needs of Christian churches today is well-trained paralegals. A paralegal is someone who has an expertise in law, especially in legal research, but has not graduated from law school, and does not practice law as an attorney. *Every church should appoint one or two interested persons to train as paralegals*. The church should even purchase the basic tools for them. Here is a list of introductory sources that will get anyone interested started as a paralegal.

1) *Black's Law Dictionary* published by West Publishing Company, P.O. Box 3526, St. Paul, MN 55165. $19.95. This indispensable research tool is available at most of the larger bookstore chains (B. Dalton, Walden's). The beauty of this dictionary is its simplicity. The editors have surveyed court opinion after court opinion and then give a very brief synopsis of the legal definition of a word or concept. As a beginning paralegal, one is confronted with hundreds of new terms. *Black's* is a welcome aid when sorting through this new territory.

2) *Gilbert Law Summaries: Legal Research* by Peter Jan Honigsberg. Published by Harcourt Brace Jovanovich Legal and Professional Publications, Inc. Available from Law Distributors, 14415 So. Main Street, Gardena, CA 90248, (213) 321-3275. The *Gilbert Law Summaries* is a series of outlined synopses covering every aspect of the study of law. This particular volume is designed to introduce the student to the world of legal research and law library.

Law is a fascinating study. Our civilization is mature.

There are not many issues or situations that have not been litigated at one time or another. The ability to find your way around a law library will greatly broaden your perspective of what it takes to build a civilization. But more to the point, it will give you the tools to do much of the research yourself. This particular volume of *Gilbert* will guide you step by step through the myriad pathways of a law library. You will be introduced to basic definitions of law, a cursory outline of our legal system, how to find cases and opinions, how to read and understand cases, where to locate a particular statute, how to research the federal codes, the use of secondary source books, what administrative agency material is available, how to use a form book, shortcuts to solving problems and keeping up to date. Although the first book you purchase should be *Black's Law Dictionary*, this handbook on legal research should be the second.

West Publishing Company, the publishers of *Black's Law Dictionary*, also publishes a series of handbooks similar to *Gilbert's* titled the "Nutshell Series." The series also covers every aspect of law, but the format does not make the information as readily available. Each volume of *Gilbert's* is an 8½" x 11", spiral-bound workbook/handbook. The outline of material is very detailed and a good index is included. The print is readable with wide margins for personal study notes. On the other hand, the "Nutshell Series" volumes are small, mass-market size paperbacks. The print is much smaller and the outline and index are not as comprehensive. Overall, if you have the choice between a volume in the *Gilbert's* series and one in the "Nutshell Series," choose the *Gilbert's*.

Although there are more detailed (and more expensive) books available, the beginning paralegal should begin with several volumes from one of these "summary" series. After he becomes thoroughly familiar with the subject matter, it is then time to move on.

## III. OFFENSIVE STRATEGIES OF CHRISTIAN RESISTANCE

# A CHRISTIAN ACTION PLAN FOR THE 1980s

Pat Robertson

*OCTOBER, 1979 marks the 50th anniversary of the Great Depression of 1929—an event which did more to shape the existing framework of U. S. government policy than any other single event in recent history.* Out of the depression came a powerful central government; an imperial presidency; the enormous political power of newspapers, radio, and later television; an anti-business bias in the country; powerful unions; a complexity of federal regulations and agencies designed to control and, in many instances, protect powerful vested interests; and, more importantly, the belief in the economic policy of British scholar John Maynard Keynes, to the end that government spending and government "fine tuning" would guarantee perpetual prosperity.

New Deal Keynesian policies did reverse the economic tragedy of the Depression (with the help of World War II). *But many now feel that the "cure" of the '30s is the cause of the sickness of the '70s.* In fact, many knowledgeable observers are contending that *forces unleashed in the post-Depression days have so weakened Western civilization, and the United States in particular, that a radical change is on the way.* Some feel that *1979 may be the watershed year* for the Western nations as we now know them.

### *Five Critical Problems America Must Face Now*

As we enter the next decade, here are some of the inherited problems which must be dealt with:

(1) *Inflation*

Deficit spending by the federal government, which seemed so appropriate in the Depression and later during

A paper originally published by Pat Robertson in 1979. Reprinted by permission.

World War II, has seized up like a massive narcotic addiction. Presidents Johnson, Nixon, Ford, and Carter could not resist the temptation of the "quick fix." *For 10 years the economy has been on the same cycle: spending, election, monetary contraction, recession, spending, election, etc.* During this time the government has printed vast sums of money, thus ensuring both economic turmoil and the consequent rise in prices. As a result, *the savings of the thrifty have been cut in half, many of the elderly have been beggared, and the Social Security system is approaching bankruptcy.* Reckless borrowers gain and the cautious lose. *Public and private debt has risen into the trillions.* Government has grown so that the load of non-productive governmental interference in the life of every citizen has become insupportable.

(2) *Currency devaluation*

As a Depression measure, President Roosevelt took us off the gold standard and made private ownership of gold illegal. President Nixon completed the action when he removed all monetary backing to the dollar and let if float against all other currencies of the world. When Nixon made his move in 1972, the price of gold was $42 per ounce. In September, 1979, the world price of gold topped $380 per ounce and undoubtedly it will go higher. It could also be said that gold as a commodity has gone up in price in seven years. *It could also be said that the world now regards the U.S. dollar as worth* 1/9 of its 1972 value!

Indeed, in 1979 the dollar is regarded as only about half as valuable against the German mark, the Swiss franc, and the Japanese yen as it was in 1972.

During the last century, the British pound sterling was the reserve currency of the world. It was backed by gold, which was in turn backed by a stable, prosperous empire. In the 1920s Britain removed the backing from its currency. Consequently, one cause of the U.S. Depression was wild speculation brought on by artificially low interest rates in this country, which our Federal Reserve Board permitted in order to protect the then-weak British pound. When the pound fell as a reserve currency, it was every nation for itself. A wave of protective tariffs set in, turning a financial crash into a worldwide disaster.

After World War II, the U.S. dollar became the reserve currency of the world. The dollar was "as good as gold," and became for other nations a store of value. *The policies of the*

*Johnson, Nixon, and Carter administrations have deliberately destroyed the value of the dollar.* Now, instead of currency convertibility and free trade, it becomes again every nation for itself. How do nations protect their dollar reserves, dump unwanted dollars, protect their own currencies? Once again there is talk of trade wars, tariffs, and other protectionist devices.

Further complicating international finance is the OPEC oil cartel. *Oil is priced in terms of dollars. U.S. inflation causes the dollar to drop in value. Whenever this happens, OPEC raises the price of oil to compensate. This causes further inflation and further dollar decline—then another round of a vicious cycle* from which we seem unable or unwilling to extricate ourselves.

(3) *Productivity*

The Depression caused market demand to plummet. Prices crashed along with the stock market. Farm surpluses caused untold misery in America's breadbasket. The New Deal answer was to limit production and competition, kill the little pigs, take acreage out of cultivation, then stimulate demand by massive government spending. In the '30s, it worked.

Now in the '70s, a bewildering array of *New Deal legislation*, coupled with the *Great Society programs* of Lyndon Johnson, coupled with *rigid environmental regulations*, has helped shrink U.S. productivity to record lows.

*More serious is the liquidation of our major industries enforced by inflation.* Here is how it works. A business desires to show profits to its lenders and stockholders. In order to do this, it allows its capital plan to be depreciated at what it cost 10 or 15 years ago, rather than what it would cost now or in the future. *If replacement value depreciation were used, many "profitable" businesses would show substantial losses. Their book "profits" are illusory, nevertheless the businesses pay taxes and dividends on them.*

*Unfortunately, when replacement time comes, the available funds are vastly inadequate to buy modern equipment and factories. So the business*, as in the case of the United States Steel Corp., *closes the old plants and shrinks its output.*

*Unless something is done very soon by government, big business, and the financial community* to recognize the realities of inflation and to make provision for the enormous sums required to modernize our heavy industry, in the 1980s *we will discover that our steel, machinery, and automotive industries have shrunk to the point where they can no longer compete at home or overseas.*

As industries close, the government is forced into additional inflationary spending to care for displaced workers. As productivity drops and government spending accelerates, the pace of inflation speeds up—which in turn further aggravates the plight of industry, which causes a further increase in our trade deficit, causing the dollar to decline again. Dollar decline means we pay more for imported goods and thereby have more domestic inflation.

The cause-and-effect cycle of inflation and industry decline is relatively easy to follow. *It is also easy to understand why the "new breed" of economic conservatives is stressing anti-Keynesian policies of stimulating production and supply while balancing the federal budget* to cool the ruinously inflationary demand side of the economic equation.

(4) *Government*

Until the Depression, the federal government operated largely in keeping with the philosophy attributed to Thomas Jefferson: "That government is best which governs least."

The anguish of the Depression changed all that. *Emergency legislation proposed by President Roosevelt was railroaded through Congress with scarcely a murmur of objection.* The Supreme Court objected on the grounds that the constitution never gave the federal government such power over individual citizens, nor could Congress delegate so much of its authority to the chief executive.

How, for example, could the federal government under our Constitution force a farmer in Iowa to limit his planting of corn and make him kill his little pigs? The Supreme Court struck down item after item of New Deal legislation as unconstitutional. But in effect, Roosevelt said, either approve my laws and regulations, or I will get Congress to expand the number of justices on the Court and then I will "pack" it with people who will do what I want.

This was a dictatorial threat. Roosevelt didn't have the votes in Congress, but a scared Court subsequently backed down. They suddenly discovered that the little pigs in Iowa were a factor in "interstate commerce." Since the federal government had constitutional authority to regulate "commerce," it could limit output of little pigs in Iowa if it wanted to. And it could, in decades to come, control how many channels were on TV sets, who could eat in a restaurant, the working conditions of every business, how many acres a farmer could plant, what wages would be paid to whom. Once the dam was broken, it became hard to conceive of many human endeavors outside of the reach of the federal government.

In fact, under activist presidents, Courts and Congresses, the Commerce Clause and the 14th Amendment have become the vehicles whereby government and its regulations have become the dominant factor in our society today. Federal spending amounts to $2,445 this year for every man, woman, and child in the land, and government debt amounts to $3,998 for each. The load on the family of four will be $9,780 in federal spending this fiscal year, and $15,992 in long-term debt, not including Social Security, Civil Service, and other retirement obligations plus collateral guarantees of federal agencies.

(5) *Rise of Communism*

The Depression idled nearly one of every four workers in America. Businesses failed, banks collapsed, farmers and home owners were evicted from their property, and the life savings of millions vanished. Financial losses triggered the more serious loss of human dignity and purpose.

With the misery came revelations of abuses and scandals, stock manipulations by leading banks, blatant greed and corruption on the part of some of the most respected financial leaders of the day, and massive deception by Wall Street and government leaders.

Sensitive young intellectuals—men like Alger Hiss—became convinced that our system was wrong. Longing for a utopian society to replace it, they became easy targets for the Communist party and Communist fronts throughout the country.

Many of these men and women played a key policy role in education, journalism, religion, labor, foundations, business, and government. They forced a pro-Soviet tilt to U.S. government policy during World War II and in the postwar years.

*It is fair to say that the United States created a world favorable to the growth of the Soviet Union and world communism.* We gave them money, technology, and trade agreements. We allowed them to subjugate Poland, Czechoslovakia, Hungary, Rumania, Estonia, Latvia, Lithuania, Albania, and Manchuria. We permitted a divided Germany and a split Berlin. We established a United Nations charter drafted by Alger Hiss, a reputed Communist party member, which guaranteed the Soviets a veto in the United Nations Security Council.

Our postwar international monetary policy was largely the creation of Harry Dexter White, another reputed Communist party member. And pro-Communist spies in both the United States and Great Britain gave the Soviets access to virtually all of our highly classified nuclear and defense secrets.

Before the Depression, the Bolsheviks were a slightly ludicrous group of fanatics who held dictatorial power in a poverty-stricken land that was still a part of the Middle Ages. Fifty years later, *with our help, they have subjugated one quarter of all the people on earth, and have amassed a war machine that is not equal to but vastly superior to the military capability of the United States and its NATO allies combined.*

*By 1981, the Soviet Union will have such undisputed dominance over the United States that it will be able to move at will against any territory on earth.*

*This would never have been possible had it not been for the Depression-inspired flirtation with Marxism on the part of the U.S. intelectual community—which, unfortunately, in some quarters still continues to this day.*

### *Six Steps to Moral, Political, and Economic Recovery*

As 1979 draws to a close, we are left with a 50-year legacy which should cause alarm. Our domestic strength has been weakened by government excesses and mismanagement; our capacity for national sacrifice and resolute action may have been reduced to a level of ineffectiveness; vital raw materials necessary to our economic and military survival are in the hands of others; and we are confronted by a powerful adversary with both the capability and the desire to destroy us.

*We urgently need two things. First, that God will hold our external enemies at bay while confusing their counsels against us. Second, we need a bold, dynamic plan based on practical reality* which will permit our nation to turn around and begin the slow road to moral, political, and economic recovery.

*A national strategy for the '80s must be formulated.* Each individual needs a similar plan. Here are some suggestions intended to stimulate thought.

(1) *There must be a profound moral revival in the land.*

Not only increased evangelism; not a glib confession of faith, but *a profound commitment to Jesus Christ for biblical Christianity.* There must be true repentence, fasting, prayer, and calling upon God. The "people who are called by His name" need to beseech God with all humility on behalf of our nation and our world. A miracle is needed and we must ask for one.

(2) *Those who love God must get involved in the election of strong leaders.*

Men and women of good will across the land must join together to ensure the election of strong leaders who are beholden to no special interest group; who are pledged to reduce the size of government, eliminate federal deficits, free our productive capacity, ensure sound currency; who are pledged to strong national defense, and do not confuse peace with surrender; who recognize the anti-Christ nature of Marxism and will refuse to permit innocent people to fall victim to Marxist tyranny; who support programs which encourage godliness while resisting programs which result in the triumph of humanism and atheism in our land.

*More than anything we need leaders who are not afraid to demand necessary sacrifices of our people in order to free us from bondage*— whether it comes from the OPEC cartel, from crushing debt, from nuclear blackmail, or from the poverty and helplessness of a portion of our people.

To accomplish this takes work. *Christians must register to vote, work within parties, attend caucuses, mass meetings, and conventions. They need to be informed on issues and know what each candidate stands for. They must be willing to hold public office and, where appropriate, should prepare for government service. They must be willing to write letters, make telephone calls, lobby for legislation, and pray for their leaders.* In short, they must be good citizens. In the Book of Proverbs we read, "The diligent will bear rule, but the slothful will be put to forced labor." If Christians want to rule, they must be diligent. There is no magic shortcut.

(3) *In a moral sense, we must recognize our right to preserve our precious religious heritage.*

Supreme Court decisions are not holy writ. The damage to our spiritual and moral heritage that has been brought on by the Supreme Court school prayer decisions is beyond calculation. President Roosevelt did not hesitate to use power to force the Supreme Court to acquiesce to New Deal legislation. *Christians should not hesitate to use the lawful power at their disposal to secure reversal of onerous Supreme Court decisions.*

(4) *Christians must take action in education.*

The courts and ill-advised federal regulations have often made a mockery of education. Eliminating prayer removed moral restraints; busing tends to remove neighborhood restraints. Many schools have become undisciplined jungles.

Textbooks used in public schools often tend to destroy long-established moral values. *Parents have every right to insist on quality moral education for their children. They should fight for it in public schools, and if good public education is denied them, they must do everything possible to establish an alternative private system of education where Christian values can be taught.*

(5) *Christians must become aware of the awesome power of the media to mold our moral and political consensus.*

*Christians need to do everything in their power to get involved in media* (radio, television, newspapers, magazines). Where possible, *Christians should seek to establish or purchase newspapers, magazines, radio stations, and television stations.*

*Christians should learn motion picture techniques, produce drama, write music, publish books—anything to produce a climate of righteousness and godliness.* They must dispel the sense of nihilism and lack of meaning that is so evident in much that passes for art these days.

(6) *Christians should seek positions of leadership in major corporations and benevolent foundations.*

It has been said that money is the "mother's milk" of politics. It also is the essential nourishment of education, entrance into the media, the arts, and wide-scale evangelism. *Christians should learn the ways of finance: stocks, bonds, banking, commodities, real estate, taxes. More than anything, they should learn and apply the principles of God's kingdom dealing with the acquisition and use of wealth.* When they have accumulated material resources, they should recognize the enormous good they can accomplish with that wealth in unity with other members of the body of Christ throughout the world.

### *The Keys to Success: Faith and Diligence*

The Communists, who espouse a false religion, after only 60 years dominate the world. The reason is simple—they were dedicated to their cause and they worked at it. Except for our Lord's return we cannot expect our nation or our world to be freed from tyranny in one year or even 10 years. But if we are faithful and diligent, with His blessing, it will be done.

"The kingdoms of this world are become the kingdoms of our Lord, and of His Christ; and He shall reign for ever and ever" (Rev. 11:15).

# THE CHURCH AS A SHADOW GOVERNMENT

Ray R. Sutton

HOW many governments are there in the world? One might answer by naming various countries since each nation represents a different government. Another, however, might define government by political ideologies—democracy, socialism, etc.—seeing political structures as the function whereas ideologies are the true forms. Government is ideological, not functional. Thus, the number of governments is equal to the quantity of ideologies.

Third, religion might inform one's determination of the number of governments in the world. Strictly speaking, we are referring to an *archaic* view of religion where politics is an extension of the *priesthood*.[1] In an age such as ours it is presumed that modern democratic societies are not organized around a religious elite.[2] Political theorists try to separate priesthoods and politics by using traditional categories—Christianity, Hinduism, etc.—to sever *religion* from politics. Not only are scholars learning that the latter separation is an illusion,[3] they are realizing that these traditional religious distinctions do not keep priesthoods out of politics. For example, James Billington's *Fire in the Minds of Men* explains the specific tie be-

1. E. C. Wines, *The Hebrew Republic* (Uxbridge, MA: The American Presbyterian Press, 1980), p. 3.

2. True Biblical Christianity—the kind which is developed in Wines's book—avoids the inevitability of the coalescence of priesthood and politics. It says that the civil realm grows out of the *Kingship* of Christ. The church, on the other hand, is an extension of His priesthood. This is the best paradigm known to man for unifying, yet distinguishing, these two spheres.

3. Jungian scholars have been saying this for several years. Mircea Eliade prefers the archaic world view because it more closely approximates reality. Christian thinkers will reject Eliade's presuppositions. Nevertheless, religion and politics are inseparable. Two recent works advocating this position are *The Separation Illusion* by John Whitehead, and *A Christian Manifesto* by Francis Schaeffer.

tween the occult and revolution.[4] He develops in chapter four of the book how the entire organization of revolution rests on occultic priesthoods and ideology.

Thomas Szasz's brilliant work, *The Manufacture of Madness*, describes another kind of priesthood.[5] Comparing the Spanish Inquistions and the mental health movement, he exposes the tyranny of "sanity," and the new psychiatric priesthood. James Thurber's "A Unicorn in the Garden" in the *Thurber Carnival* illustrates. "One morning, a man announces to his wife that there is a unicorn in the garden. She replies: 'You are a booby, and I am going to have you put in the booby-hatch.' The husband, who never liked the words 'booby' and 'booby-psychiatrist' says, 'we'll see about that.' The wife sends for the police and the psychiatrist. They arrive. She tells them her story. 'Did you tell your wife you saw a unicorn?' they asked the husband. 'Of course not,' said the husband. 'The unicorn is a mythical beast.' 'That's all I wanted to know,' said the psychiatrist. . . . So they took her away, cursing and screaming, and shut her up in an institution. The husband lived happily ever after."[6]

Thus, the concept of priesthood is more pervasive than the status quo idea of "minister" or "rabbi." "New" priesthoods are gaining political control under the false notion of separation of religion and state. The latter cannot be separated. The former, church and state, however, can be kept different through a Christian approach to civilization. Here is the dilemma of the modern world. It tries to drive a wedge between that which cannot and should not be separated. In the process, it unites spheres that should be distinct. Archaic priesthoods and their political extensions are still with modern man, therefore, and can be a means of computing the number of governments in the world.

Fourth, one might take a metaphysical approach. Although close to the previous method, it understands governments in terms of good and evil. Thus, the number of governments is two. The Anabaptists of the 16th century contended for a two-government interpretation of the world. In one of their early

---

4. James Billington, *Fire in the Minds of Men: Origins of the Revolutionary Faith* (New York: Basic Books Inc., 1980), pp. 86ff.

5. Thomas S. Szasz, *The Manufacture of Madness* (New York: Harper and Row, 1970).

6. *Ibid.*, p. 44.

creeds, *The Schleitheim Confession*, such a position appears in "The Sixth Article."[7] "We hold that the sword is an ordinance of God, outside the perfection of Christ. Hence the princes and authorities of the world are ordained to punish the wicked and to put them to death. But in the perfection of Christ, the ban is the heaviest penalty, without corporeal death."[8] According to this view, one government is outside of Christ, while the other is "in the perfection of Christ," meaning there are two governments.

### *Calvin's Rejection of Dualism*

This dualistic approach to government was vehemently opposed by John Calvin. In his *Treatises Against the Anabaptists and Against the Libertines* he specifically attacks the statements just quoted from the *Schleitheim Confession*. He says in the chapter on the magistrate: (1) The calling of the civil magistrate is a vocation created by God. (2) The Bible provides set guidelines for magistrates in the Law of Moses. (3) Magistrates are to protect the church. Therefore, although the state is separate from the church, it can exist in the "perfection of Christ." And this avoids a dualistic view of the world which places the civil realm outside of Christ. Calvin expresses these points in the following manner.

"Therefore, let us hold this position: that with regard to true spiritual justice, that is to say, with regard to a faithful man walking in good conscience and being whole before God in both his vocation and in all his works, there exists a plain and complete guideline for it in the law of Moses, to which we need simply cling if we want to follow the right path. Thus whoever adds to or takes anything from it exceeds the limits. Therefore our position is sure and infallible.

"We worship the same God that the fathers of old did. We have the same law and rule that they had, showing us how to

7. *Bruderlich Vereinigung etlicher Kinder Gottes, sieben Artikel betreffend, in Flugschriften aus den ersten Jahren der Reformation*, ed. Otto Clemen (Leipzig: Halle, 1907-1911), vol. 2, pt. 3, as well as in other sources. See John Calvin's *Treatises Against the Anabaptists and Against the Libertines*, tr. by Benjamin Wirt Farley (Grand Rapids, MA: Baker, 1982), pp. 76ff. See John H. Yoder's English translation in *The Legacy of Michael Sattler* (Scottdale, PA: Herald, 1973), pp. 34-43. See also J. C. Wenger, "The Schleitheim Confession of Faith," *Mennonite Quarterly Review* 19 (1945):243-253.

8. Calvin, pp. 76ff.

govern ourselves in order to walk rightly before God. It thus follows that a vocation that was considered holy and lawful then cannot be forbidden Christians today, for a vocation is the principal part of human life and the part that means the most to God. From which it follows that we should not deny ourselves the vocation of civil justice, nor drive it outside the Christian church. For our Lord has ordained it and approved it as good for the people of Israel. And He has appointed His most excellent servants to it and even His prophets.

"They [the Anabaptists] will reply, possibly, that the civil government of the people of Israel was a figure of the spiritual kingdom of Jesus Christ and lasted only until His coming. I will admit to them that, in part, it was a figure, but I deny that it was nothing more than this, and not without reason. For in itself it was a political government, which is a requirement among all people.

"That such is the case, it is written of the Levitical priesthood that it had to come to an end and be abolished at the coming of our Lord Jesus (Heb. 7:12ff.). Where is it written that the same is true of the external order? It is true that the scepter and government were to come from the tribe of Judah and the house of David, but that the government was to cease is manifestly contrary to Scripture.

"But lest we have any doubts about it, we have a still more evident and direct proof. For when the prophets speak of the kingdom of Jesus Christ, it is written that kings will come to worship and pay homage to Him. It is not said that they will abdicate their positions in order to become Christians, but rather, being appointed with royal dignity, they will be subject to Jesus Christ as to their sovereign Lord. Following this, David, exhorting them to do their duty, does not command them to throw down their diadems or their scepters, but solely to kiss the Son, that is to say, to pay homage to Him in order to be subject to Him in His domination over others (Ps. 2:12).

"Without a doubt he is speaking of the kingdom of our Lord Jesus. He admonishes all kings and authorities to be wise and to take heed to themselves. What is this wisdom? What is the lesson he gives them? To abdicate it all? Hardly! But to fear God and give honor to His Son.

"Furthermore, Isaiah prophesies that the kings will become the foster fathers of the Christian church and that queens will nurse it with their breasts (Isa. 49:23). I beg of you, how do you reconcile the fact that kings will be protectors of the Christian church if their vocation is inconsistent with Christianity? If our Lord only bestowed on them that place among His people that He also gave His former prophets, that would suffice to prove our point. But now that He assigns them a place so honorable in the midst of His people as to grant them the honor, I say, of ordaining them 'protectors of His church,' what impudence is it to exclude them from it altogether? Thus we conclude that princes who serve God can be Christians as well, inasmuch as our Lord has given them such a place of preeminence in Christianity."[9]

At other places in Calvin's writings, he used "two-kingdom" language. One was spiritual and the other carnal (carnale). In the latter he placed the secular state, because he believed that Christ *primarily* exercised His offices in the spiritual realm (the church). From the previous quotation, however, this does not mean that he believed in two dialectical governments. Christoph Jungen has correctly pointed out that "spiritual" meant Holy Spirit. Furthermore, "when he [Calvin] talks about 'spiritual,' he is *not talking about Platonic dualism*, but about the work of the Holy Spirit, that is, as particular and 'restricted' as the word of Christ."[10] Thus, his two kingdoms do not equal two governments.

Using Calvin as a guide, the correct view of the number of governments is summarized in the following manner. One, God controls the world from His throne in heaven (Prov. 16:1ff.). This includes "princes" as Calvin has said. Building on him, all the princes of the world serve God's purposes even though they taunt the church. In the early church, Rome's persecution of the church brought its own condemnation. One could say that the church rose to influence through its suffering.

Two, God is a Triune God—three in one and one in three. Calvin expressed this in his spherical view of government. The three spheres are family, church, and state. God governs the world through all three. Thus, we are not advocating a monism that absolutizes one or the other. Luther, for exam-

9. *Ibid.*, pp. 78-79.

10. Christoph Jungen, "Calvin and the Origin of Political Resistance Theory in the Calvinist Tradition" (Th.M. thesis, Westminster Theological Seminary, 1980), p. 56.

ple, absolutized the sphere of the *state*.[11] He believed the princes were the voice of God. This has traditionally led to a top-heavy world view elevating the state to a position of dominance over the church.

Our position, rather, is that the family, church, and state are parallel governments. They are equal in authority. In their respective spheres they discipline and rule. Neither may cross into the other's sphere. The state must not take the children. The church must not take the sword. The family must not become a state as its clan grows in power. They are parallel, and God orchestrates His rule on earth through all three. Even when one sphere revolts against God, the other spheres are used to rule.

Three, this raises a third observation. God works out His purposes progressively. His world is not in a perfected state. No government—civil, ecclesiastical, or familial—is infallible. Nor have they reached their eschatological position. They err to greater or lesser degrees. Even though one sphere disobeys God, however, we are not to conclude there are two governments. Dualism only serves to create a monistic, perfectionistic (infallible) world view.

### *The Effects of Dualism*

Dualism results in abdication of the state to Satan. If there are two governments—presumably God's and Satan's—vying for power, which one represents God? Normally, dualistic thinkers assign the church to God's side. This leaves the state to Satan. Since the church does not concern herself with political matters, the state takes more and more power, as in the case of countries where Lutheranism has had sway. Districts in Northern Europe were the first to fall to socialistic and fascistic ideas. One by one, they were dominated by either Marx or Hitler. In America, the first area to succumb to socialistic ideas was Wisconsin and the north central region. Again we see that the Lutheran Church has historically dominated this area. Thus, viewing the state as belonging to the world breaks a check and balance on power. In the end, the state steals what belongs to the church.

11. Gary North, "The Economic Thought of Calvin and Luther" in *The Journal of Christian Reconstruction*, vol. II., no. 1., pp. 76-108.

Abdication creates another situation. What if a church with dualistic theology happens to influence a whole civilization? In this case, contrary to the previous effect of dualistic theology where the state dominates the church, the church ends up in power. If civilization listens to the teaching of this theological system, it will believe that civil matters are unspiritual. Logically, the Christians will leave vocations concerning the state. Under quasi revival, however, who is left to handle civil affairs? Probably church officials, since they have all the power. Of course, this situation creates a tension for them because their theological position forbids such involvement. So, they will attempt to create a nonpolitical state. Armies and defense systems are dissolved, and crime is not punished. Today, this kind of world is advocated by men such as Art Gish, John Yoder, and other dualism devotees. But the *unspiritual* outcome of this position has already been demonstrated in history.

The early North African Church of the fifth century (Period of Augustine) had become a bastion of the faith. Seminaries flourished—the greatest teachers and apologists coming from there. The whole society had become generally Christian, but had adopted dualistic theology in its last century. The problem was that Manichaean (dualistic) philosophy had infected the church. This form of mysticism taught that the world is evil. Anything physical only hampers the Christian life. Thus, spirituality is determined by what one does *not* have. Furthermore, premillennialism, familiar bedfellow with mysticism, had convinced the Christian world that Christ would remove them from carnal incumbrances. He did, but not the way their theology anticipated.

A false prophet, Mohammed, came down from the mountain with a monistic world view and totally eradicated Christianity in that area. The pacifistic, pietistic church was no match. Did God bless this view of spirituality? No. The church has never regained that area of the world. Today, it is *still* the toughest mission field. Perhaps that is because missions generally have the same theology as the early North African Church.

Therefore, dualism's abdication creates a monistic world. We cannot interpret the presence of evil governments to mean that God and Satan are fighting for control. God has already won the battle at the Cross. There is one government with three spheres. In this world of sin and rebellion, God is establishing His Kingdom as He did Israel in the Promise Land. After they entered, the land belonged to them. Mopping up exercises, however, were needed. That is the status of the development of the Kingdom today. When the civil realm of a country turns from God, He may bring a Christian potentate like William of Orange to bring it back to its Creator and Redeemer. In other cases, God may check disobedient behavior in the civil government by the activity of the other spheres.

This essay focuses on the role of the church, since she consistently finds herself operating in a situation where the state is in rebellion to its God-ordained purposes. Thus, given these initial premises, how does the church function in an age of civil abdication? Moreover, how does it bring the state to Christ?

### *The Church as a Shadow Government*

When one sphere like the state collapses, the church is left to fill the gap. She cannot, however, take the place of the state and pick up the sword. Like a Christian wife married to a rebellious husband, the church must bring the civil sphere to obedience by proper activity in its own category. The best description of this role is shadow government. A shadow government is understood as representing the true government, acting and waiting in the shadows for the present system to fall. When it does, the shadow government becomes the ruling government, or appoints another to take proper rule.

The concept of shadow government is not foreign to our times. Marxism has made unprecedented progress through the implementation of parallel/shadow governments. In Marx's and Engels's "Address Of The Central Committee To The Communist League (1850)," they directed the League to view themselves as the true government. This address was given shortly after the failure of the European revolutions of 1848. The Communist League (formerly the League of the Just) had hired Marx and Engels in 1847 to write the document that we know as the *Communist Manifesto* to help promote this revolution. (As usual, Marx was late; the pamphlet did not appear until after the revolution had already begun in France.) Marx's 1850 address was a blueprint for a period of defensive operations, after the failure of a major offensive campaign against bourgeois society.

Marx said in this address, "While the democratic petty bourgeois wish to bring the revolution to a conclusion as quickly as possible, and with the achievement, at most, of the above demands, it is our interest and our task to make the revolution permanent until all more or less possessing classes have been forced out of their position of dominance, until the proletariat has conquered state power, and the association of proletarians, not only in one country but in all the dominant countries of the world, has advanced so far that competition among the proletarians of these countries has ceased and that at least the decisive productive forces are concentrated in the hands of the proletarians. For us the issue cannot be the alteration of private property but only its annihilation, not the smoothing over of class antagonisms but the abolition of classes, not the improvement of existing society but the foundation of a new one. . . . Therefore, alongside the new official governments [A revolution had just placed a democratic party instead of the communists in power. Marx refers to them here as the 'new official government.'] they [the communists] must establish simultaneously their own revolutionary worker's governments, whether in the form of municipal committees and municipal councils or in the form of workers' clubs or workers' committees."[12]

Marx therefore saw the importance of parallel government. Moreover, he knew these shadow governments would only be effective if implemented at the local decentralized level. Ironic, isn't it? A philosophy of centralization grew in influence by an ideologically contradictory method—decentralized local governments. (Marx personally never organized anything. He specialized only in destruction. But the idea was sound.)

The Soviet Communists followed this approach in their attempts to bring the proletarian revolution to the West. In a Manifesto of July 15, 1920, the International Council of Trade Unions announced: "It is their duty to create everywhere a parallel illegal organization machine which at the decisive

---

12. Marx and Engels, *Selected Works* (Moscow: Foreign Languages Publishing House, 1962), vol. I, pp. 110-112.

moment will be helpful to the party in fulfilling its duty to the revolution. In all countries where the Communists, because of a state of siege and because of exceptional laws directed against them, are unable to carry on their whole work legally, it is absolutely necessary to combine illegal with legal activities."[13]

Marxism, probably unconsciously, stole this from the church. The church has the organizational structure by divine design to be a parallel government to the state. When, however, the state fails to represent adequately the Kingdom of Christ, the church is left as sole reprentative of the government of heaven. She must use her local organizations to model for and train up a Christian state.

In this situation the church is a shadow government. God has given authority into her hands—authority to rule the world *by ruling in her sphere*. What she does affects the world. It must be remembered that God uses church government, normally a parallel government to a Christian state, to function as a shadow government. By implementing the rightful binding and loosing capacities (Matt. 16:16ff.) which God has given her, the church effects political and social change. This means the church plays a strategic role in resistance against tyranny.

It is critical, therefore, that the church understand how to function as a government. The state will collapse. That eventuality is inevitable. If she refuses to raise up an alternative government, God will persecute and chastise. He may raise up an ecclesiastical beachhead in some other part of His world, such as China. Whatever God does, however, He will control the world with His government.

The Church should not forget what happened when the Roman Empire fell. The scenario just described came to pass. The civil government of Rome collapsed. The people of that civilization turned to the church because it represented true government. The Kingdom of God took over a kingdom of the world by default of the latter. In the long run, this was the most effective resistance against tyranny.

History, however, did not stop there. The church was

---

13. Clayton R. Lusk Committee, Senate of New York State: *Revolutionary Radicalism, Its History, Purpose and Tactics*, Part I, vol. I (1920), p. 262; cited in R. J. Rushdoony, *Politics of Guilt and Pity* (Fairfax, VA: Thoburn Press, [1970] 1978), p. 354.

given so much immediate authority and power that it was unprepared to train civil magistrates to step into their rightful positions. Although men sat on the throne, the church, as an institution, was still in control of western civilization. A political tyranny was replaced by an ecclesiastical one. By the time of the Reformation, the princes of Europe supported the rise of the reformers, not so much because they were committed to reformation theology, but because they saw this as their opportunity to escape the hold of the Roman Catholic Church on the state. Now the flow of history indicates that political tyrannies threaten western civilization.

For better or for worse, therefore, the church can create or abolish tyranny. In an age when western civilization stands on the edge of destruction, the question is "how can the church participate in the abolition of tyranny?"

Our position is the church can be the main instrument of change. The weapons God has given her, make the church the most potent army on earth. She is a parallel government—at present she is a shadow government. The state no longer rules for Christ. The church as a shadow government can make the difference.

### *The Theology of the Kingdom*

Ideas are at the base of everything. They have consequences. For the church to function as a shadow government, she must grasp the theology of the kingdom of God to understand her role as a parallel government.

First, God's Kingdom refers to both rule *and* realm. Scholars have used the original language of the Bible to argue that kingdom is either domain or dominion, but not both.[14] An exegetical key found in the word *glory*, however, settles the problem. Paul says to the church at Thessalonica, "That ye would walk worthy of God, who hath called you unto his kingdom and glory" (I Thess. 2:12).[15] It appears that the Apostle is reiterating the coextensiveness of these two terms

---

14. S. Aslen, " 'Reign' and 'House' in the Kingdom of God in the Gospels," *New Testament Studies* 98 (1962): 215-240. Compare another article which differs by G. E. Ladd, "The Kingdom of God—Reign or Realm," *Journal of Biblical Literature* 81 (1962): 230-238.

15. Paul S. Minear, *Images of the Church in the New Testament* (Philadelphia: Westminster Press, 1977), pp. 119-135.

when a familiar Old Testament passage is remembered, "Thine, O Lord, is the greatness, and the power, and the glory, and the victory, and the majesty: for all that is in the heaven and in the earth is thine; thine is the kingdom, O Lord, and thou art exalted as head above all" (I Chronicles 29:11). Also, we are further reminded of the textual variant of the Lord's Prayer which is commonly learned, "for thine is the kingdom, and the power, and the glory, for ever" (Matt. 6:13). In each reference, "glory" is parallel to "kingdom." Thus, we can examine this concept to approximate the meaning of kingdom.

Glory is the image of God which is reproduced as a pattern in several places.[16] In Ezekiel 1 the glory-cloud appears to the prophet with characteristics similar to the heaven into which John was taken (Rev. 1). Looking into the cloud, Ezekiel and John see a throne at the center, fire and lightning, and the people of God with the angels worshipping at God's feet. This liturgical/governmental scene *is the glory of God.*

The glory pattern is also present in the tabernacle/temple, which is a microcosmic picture of the world.[17] It has at its center the ark-throne where God is, and around the walls of the structure are pictures of trees representing people (Psalm 1). The same colors to be noted in Ezekiel 1 and Revelation 1 are also there. These holiness colors often indicate God's presence. Therefore, the tabernacle/temple is both a glory pattern and cameo of what the world ought to be—ordered space around the throne of God. Where God is present, His glory appears. The glory encompasses God as well as what surrounds Him.

Applied to the immediate concern, this information indicates that the Kingdom of God follows the same pattern. This order exists around God's presence. Scripture speaks of the nations of God coming to His holy mountain (Isa. 2). The seventh angel of Revelation depicts the same scene when he says, "And there were great voices in heaven, saying, The kingdoms of this world are become the kingdoms of our Lord, and of his Christ; and he shall reign for ever and ever" (Rev. 11:15). Therefore, the kingdoms, as they come under the Kingdom, become the glory of God. Now it is clear why the words "Kingdom" and "glory" are found parallel to one

16. Meredith G. Kline, *Images of the Spirit* (Grand Rapids: Baker, 1980).

17. *Idem.*

another. Furthermore, we can easily understand how they both include the ideas of ruling and realm. Whatever God dominates, it becomes His *domain*. Sovereignty is not abstracted from an actual *area* of control.

Second, God's rule and realm extend to the world. Some try to equate Kingdom and church. Scripture, however, applies Kingdom to three spheres—the kingdoms of the world (Rev. 11:15), the individual (Lk. 17:21), and the church (Rev. 1:9). Since the fall of Satan at the Cross, God's dominion and domain cover the earth. The Book of Acts tells of the expansion. At the beginning, the Kingdom is as big as Jerusalem. At the end, the remotest part of the earth is included (Acts 1:8). Clearly, the evangelists and Apostles in Acts, therefore, saw themselves as representing God's government before the pagan governments of the world. Indeed, they were going to claim what belonged to God.

This theology provides the rationale for perceiving the *world* as God's *Kingdom*. Thus, the operations of the world are to be viewed according to the inner workings of Christ's Kingdom. Governments that have not come to Christ are not to be seen as outside of God's domain. Rather, they are to be *claimed* for Christ. When civil abdication occurs in a previously Christian society, the state is not to be given up to the Devil. Instead, it must be *recaptured* as that which belongs to God. The church's role, in this regard, is to function as a shadow government. Having introduced a one-government Trinitarian position, the shadow government concept, and the theology undergirding both of these, we now come to specifics. How does the church, therefore, operate in this capacity?

### *Evangelism and Discipline*

The church as a government, essentially, carries on two major functions. First, it sends out ambassador/evangelists to carry the peace treaty of Jesus Christ to the world (II Cor. 5). They go into foreign countries, appear before the leadership, and call them to submit to the King of Kings. The twentieth century seems to have forgotten how Christianity spread across Europe in this manner. An age of nominalism—a time when everything is defined in terms of the individual and particular—makes it difficult to convert whole cultures.

There was a time, however, when a British King converted to Christianity. We know this happened because he wrote to the bishop of Rome, Eleutherius, and asked him how to rule his kingdom as a Christian. The bishop responded by saying, "By divine clemency you have received the Law and faith of Christ, you have the Old and New Testaments, out of them in God's name by counsel of your states take laws, and govern your kingdom."[18]

Notice the pattern. The ambassador goes and sues for peace, claiming the kingdom which is at war with God. The King submits his kingdom to God's government.[19] Evangelism is followed by discipline.

Later in history, we see the same pattern in Calvin's ministry at Geneva. Calvin believed that missionaries should be sent from Geneva into France where the Huguenots, Calvinistic protestants who were predominantly middle class merchants, were being persecuted. Like a government sending out ambassadors, eighty-eight missionaries were sent—so many that the Huguenots were starting to affect the nation as a whole.[20] The following chart is a list of the missionaries and the charge they were given. It is reprinted from the *Registres de la Compagnie des Pasteurs Geneve*.[21]

*Missionaries Sent to France from Geneva*
1555-1562

Normandy: 8 men, 4 churches (3 to Dieppe)
Champagne: 1 man, 1 church

18. Alexander Shiels, *A Hind Let Loose* (Glasgow: Robert and Thomas Duncan, 1770), p. 243.

19. This author recently spoke to a missionary from Africa who related the following story. He told of an entire tribe that converted to the gospel. The evangelical missionaries, however, who first took the gospel encountered some difficulties. It seems that the chief wanted them to only deal with him. They wanted to confront each *individual* to secure an individual decision. The tribe, itself, rejected this procedure. They trusted the judgment of their chief more than their own. When the chief told them to believe, they complied. In an age of individualism, this sounds strange. As far as these missionaries were concerned, it gave them a greater appreciation for a more covenantal approach to evangelism. This same situation occured time and again in the early expansion of Christianity.

20. Janet Glenn Gray, *The French Huguenots* (Grand Rapids: Baker, 1981), p. 65.

21. Robert M. Kingdon, *Geneva and the Coming Wars of Religion, 1555-1563* (Geneva: Librairie E. Droz, 1956), pp. 54-55.

Brittany: 5 men, 4 churches
Touraine: 3 men, 1 church (Tours)
Poitou: 8 men, 3 churches (6 to Poitiers)
Aunis and Saintonge: 5 men, 5 churches
Ile-de-France: 7 men, 2 churches (5 to Paris)
Orleanais: 8 men, 5 churches (3 to Orleans)
Berry: 6 men, 3 churches (3 to Issoudun)
Auvergne: 3 men, 3 churches
Burgundy (really Dombes): 1 man, 1 church
Guyenne, Gascony, Navarre and Bearn: 16 men, 12 churches (3 to Bergerac)
Languedoc: 9 men, 9 churches
Lyonnais: 5 men, 1 church
Dauphine : 7 men, 6 churches
Provence: 6 men, 4 or 5 churches

When the King of France, who was certainly not sympathetic to the protestant cause, learned of the missionary efforts coming out of Geneva, he drafted a letter to the Council at Geneva. Gray summarizes the King's displeasure, "that the seditions and dissensions which had been disturbing his reign for quite some time had their source in the preachers sent by either the governors or the principal ministers of Geneva into his kingdom. He suggested that to maintain peace and avoid further trouble the pastors be recalled and no more sent in the future; he asked for a reply. The council, in a highly secret early-morning session, asked Calvin, Colladon, Beza, Bourgoin, and Michel Cop to explain. They replied to the Council that they were falsely accused, although they admitted that requests for pastors had been answered 'as the Lord commands.' They strongly repudiated responsibility for rebellions in France since the Word of God did not allow such activity.[22]

Calvin was also known for setting up a rigorous discipline at Geneva. Point of fact: He is credited with bringing discipline back to the church.[23] Shortly after he arrived at Geneva, a document was drawn up by him, and presented in the name of the ministers to the Council. It opens with the words, " 'It is certain that a church cannot be said to be well ordered and governed unless the Holy Supper of our Lord is frequently celebrated and attended in it, and that with such good regula-

22. Gray, p. 71.
23. Benjamin B. Warfield, *Calvin and Augustine* (Philadelphia: Presbyterian and Reformed Publishing Company, 1956), p. 16.

tion that no one would dare to present himself at it except with piety and deep reverence. And it is therefore necessary for the church to maintain in its integrity the discipline of excommunication, by which those should be corrected who are unwilling to yield themselves amiably and in all obedience to the holy Word of God.'

"By this programme Calvin became nothing less than the creator of the Protestant Church. The particular points to be emphasized in it are two. It is purely *church* discipline which is contemplated, with none other but spiritual penalties. And the church is for this purpose especially discriminated from the body of the people — the State — and a *wedge is thus driven between church and state* which is bound to separate the one from the other."[24]

Warfield's last comment about Calvin is particularly brilliant. When the church exercises discipline it actually *distinguishes* itself from the state. The nature of this effort draws the line in that the discipline of the church is *restorative* in intent, instead of punitive, as it is with the state. Furthermore, *excommunication* is the means of discipline in the church, while *execution* is to be used by the state. Therefore, the best means of resisting the state is for the church to carry out discipline.

Today, neither church nor state govern as God would have them, and it is not surprising that the two draw closer together. After all, they are alike in that *they both default when it comes to discipline*. Consider, however, what would happen if a few state officials and representatives were excommunicated for their support of the murder of unborn children. The result would be an important polarity.

Polarity is needed. God will put it there when the church quits acting in terms of the same liberal theology as the state. Moreover, God gives the power of binding and loosing to the officers of the church. He expects them to carry out their responsibilities. When they are faithful, He will carry out His judgment on those who apostatize from the faith. Then the world sees that God is actively working in history, and that the covenant is real. Failure to discipline denies a visible demonstration of the reality of Christ and His church.

Thus, from Calvin's activities at Geneva, we see a definite pattern. Together, *evangelism* and *discipline* form the dual thrust

24. *Ibid.*, pp. 17-18.

of an ecclesiastical government. Evangelism expands. Discipline preserves continuity. As we have noted, if the state weakens, one entire sphere necessary to the expansion and preservation of God's Kingdom disappears. When the civil means of governing the world fails, the others must stand in the gap. This situation leaves the church with special opportunity. Using the means God has given her, she unlocks the gates of hell, captures the Satanic city, and eventually re-establishes a Christian government.

### *Gates and Keys*

Christ said to Peter, "And I say unto thee, that thou art Peter, and upon this rock I will build my church; and the *gates* of hell shall not prevail against it. And I will give unto thee the *keys* of the kingdom of heaven: and whatsoever thou shalt bind on earth shall be bound in heaven: and whatsoever thou shalt loose on earth shall be loosed in heaven" (Matt. 16:18-19).

Here is the conflict. The church comes against the gates of hell. One commentator has said this means, "And the gates of hell will never *destroy* it."[25] The Scripture, however, makes the church the aggressor. The conflict occurs at the *gates*. What are they?

It could be argued that gates represent culture, since commerce took place at the gates of a city. Or, since the elders sat at the gate and conducted rule of the city from this location, perhaps the gates represent government. That certainly fits with the premise of this paper. The word, however, is more comprehensive in its symbolism.

Scripture often uses the word gate to refer to the *city* (I Kgs. 3:37; II Chron. 6:28). Specifically, the word gate represents (by metonomy) the people (Ruth 3:11). Thus, the gate stands for a *civilization*—culture, people, and government included.

Christ gives Peter the Keys of the Kingdom, and thereby inaugurates a shift in history. After the fall of man, the Keys were taken from Adam and given to the Cherubim (Gen. 3:24). From this point on in the Old Covenant, angels held predominant sway over the Keys. The New Covenant changes the keeper of the Keys, however, and angels play less of a

25. Dena Korfker, *My Picture Story Bible* (Grand Rapids: Zondervan, 1980), pp. 393-394.

role in this capacity. As to the specific function of Keys, they lock and unlock gates. Thus, in context these Keys of the Kingdom simultaneously lock and unlock the Kingdom as well as the *gates of hell.* A double-entendre is intended. As God's city is opened and locked, an antagonistic city falls.

In these words to Peter, Christ outlines the function of the church as a shadow government. The church must reorient herself around them. Thus, we first examine the city to learn what the church is attacking. In so doing, our conclusions will add insight into the unlocking of the city, which is the process of opening its doors to the kingdom of heaven.

## *The City*

One does not have to read the Bible very far before he realizes the centrality of the city. It is a place of power.[26] Con-

26. Jacques Ellul, *The Meaning of the City* (Grand Rapids: Eerdmans Publishing Company, 1970), pp. 9-10. Ellul refers to the city as a place of power, and notes the following information about the most commonly used Hebrew word-family for the word city.

(1) " *'ar*, the masculine substantive meaning 'city.' This is the term used to designate a (or the) Moabite city granted to the descendants of Lot. But this same word also means 'enemy,' in a spiritual sense: God became Saul's enemy (I Sam. 28:16); and the Psalms speak of the enemies of God (Ps. 139:20). The relation between the two words is explicitly shown in word plays between 'city' and 'enemy' (e.g. Ps. 9:7).

(2) " *'yr*, the verb 'to burn,' in a moral sense—i.e. 'to become angry,' 'to tremble.'

(3) " *'ur*, the verb 'to stay awake,' 'to be watchful.'

(4) " *'yr*, the feminine substantive meaning:

(a) " 'city,' in a very general sense and used very frequently;

(b) " 'guard' or 'sentinel,' usually with respect to the security of a city;

(c) " 'passion,' whether or fear or of anger, although the idea of fear is the more frequent.

(5) " *'yr*, the masculine substantive meaning 'guard' or 'angel.' This meaning, which is found in more recent texts, is obviously derived from the second meaning of the preceding word. Just as guards give security to a city, so do angels. Thus it is a question of guardian angels, vigilant angels. The later development of this sense is easily understood, since it became a part of Hebrew angelology. But the angels of Hebrew angelology are usually condemning angels (Dan. 4:10 [v. 13 in the RSV] and Dan. 4:14 [v. 17 in the RSV]) or evil angels in revolt (Enoch 1:6). They are never guardian angels in the traditional sense and although they are spiritual powers, they always play a baleful role."

trol the city, and one controls the world. The city, therefore, becomes the synthesis of the state when in human hands, and a synthesis of heaven when dominated by the Word of God. At the beginning of Scripture, the world is dominated from the garden. After the fall, man is left wandering.

It is pagan man who builds the first city. He replicates the garden. From that point on, the city is a *place of conflict.* The first city builders, having left the security of God, created a pseudo heaven without God. The city was *a place to contact God*, and thus took on being. It became a *place of salvation* in a total sense. With high walls, and highly developed weaponry, man could be protected from and manipulate the world. The city was a place from which to strike terror and fear into the hearts of the people. The people of God grew to hate the city and its accompanying tyranny. Only under His guiding hand did they ever successfully assault the city.

At the end of the Bible, however, the city/temple comes down on earth (Rev. 21 & 22). It goes beyond paradise. Its dimensions surpass what was in the beginning. God's recreative processes are superior to creation. The holy city displaces the Satanic city, and casts it into the eternal lake of fire. So, writers like Jacques Ellul are wrong to believe the city and technology are inherently wrong.[27] Rather, pagan influence makes them wicked, and the city takes on characteristics of its founder, Cain.

I. *Initiation*

The pagan city was a place of initiation. The name of the first city bears this out. When Cain was driven from the paradise of God, he immediately did two things to relieve his agony. He begat children, and particularly a son. Second, he built a city and named it after the son (Gen. 4:16ff.). Here we see that the city is an extension of one's offspring. *Culture grows out of the son.* Furthermore, the culture will take on the characteristics of the families that comprise it. Thus, we can look at the name Cain gave to his son, and then to the first city in order to discover the kind of cities they would build.

The name of Cain's son and city was Enoch. In Hebrew this was used to mean initiation, inauguration, or dedication. Cain saw his son as *his creation*. Thus, he was dedicating a new

27. *Ibid.*, see Introduction.

world. He was *initiating* his creation. Cain, however, could not create in the true sense of the word. God created the world ex nihilo: "out of nothing" (Gen. 1:1), and Cain attempted to copy so as to become an original creator. His efforts only became imitational and initiatory. The contrast is startling.

One, the Enoch city was one of *pain*. Cain killed. His city was built on human blood and sacrifice. He and his descendants would kill many times over to propagate their race (Gen. 4:23-24).

Two, it was a city of *war*. The Cainites developed the first weaponry. That which God had designed as a tool to cultivate the earth, Cain changed into a device to conquer fellow man. He wanted his name to be remembered. If it took war, he would kill en masse.

Three, the new city was based on *rejuvenation*. He could not maintain the image of God morally and ethically. Rejuvenation was the way to perpetuate man. Thus, pagan man has been obsessed with perpetuating life apart from righteousness. It was the Dorian Grey syndrome.[28] The city was looked upon as a place where man could flee to rejuvenate his life.

Four, the city was built on *generation*, rather than regeneration. Man established the new created order on his seed. He created dynasties. In contrast, the people of God recognized that their children were coming from the Lord. Abel died leaving no children thereby proving that righteousness was not transmitted naturally.[29] Only imputational processes made continued expansion of the race possible. It was by the grace of God that the womb was fruitful. Consistently, the wombs of the wives of the patriarchs and other major women in the Bible were barren. Each time, the text notes that God directly intervened to open the womb. Thus, the Biblical man was not building a dynasty, but the Kingdom of God.

Five, the pagan city became a place where biblical truth was *myth and legend*. The older ones would tell stories of how the world was created, or the entrance of sin. The Word of

28. In Oscar Wilde's *Portrait of Dorian Grey* one sees modern man's quest for longevity of life. Dorian, a nineteenth century figure, wished that his portrait would age instead of him. His wish came true, and the story is about the politics of never aging.

29. *Ibid.*, p. 7.

God, however, was missing. Thus, truth became legend and fiction.

Six, in the city of Cain, *initiation* was the means of entrance. Biblical religion is not a process of initiation. The only rite of passage, perfect obedience to the Law of God, is obtained by Christ's obedience. The religions of man are attainments through some act of heroism or obedience. In a sense, man's labyrinthine rites of passage are new-disobedience designed to earn salvation. Out of this perverted obedience grows all the previous distinctives of initiation. Man is saved, however, by grace through faith (Eph. 2:8-9). Faith is presuppositional. Man cannot seize the Kingdom by any form of initiation. Rather, entrance is like the blowing of the wind (John 3). It comes from the Spirit of God.

II. *Manipulation*

Man's piracy of creation resulted in a city of manipulation. His power avoided some of the effects of the curse. Strong walls stood to keep away the judgment of God. Technology of every kind averted the curse of Genesis 3. Cain spawned the land of Shinar, the cradle of the world.

Shinar is used to mean the "shaker," or "he who throws down." It usually has reference to some kind of evil manipulation through idols, magic, and sin. The word recurs often. Ellul writes: "It was around the King of Shinar that the coalition spoken of in Genesis 14 was formed, the coalition which triumphed over all its enemies, captured Lot, and thereby ran afoul of Abraham. Abraham vanquished the King of Shinar, and Melchizedek, the King of Salem, came out to bless Abraham: the King of righteousness, the prince of peace, the complete opposite of the King of Shinar. Throughout the adventure of the people of Israel, the presence of Shinar is clearly the presence of a spiritual power, of a temptation to evil. It is an object from Shinar that caused Achan's terrible sin (Josh. 7), the transgression of the Covenant. And it is not by accident that such is the case, for this country is typically the country of idols and sin. That is where Nebuchadnezzar took the vessels of God's house to incorporate them into the service of his own god (Dan. 1:2). Daniel purposely calls the country Shinar instead of Babylonia, for he wanted to emphasize that this was a land of thievery and plunder. . . . In the fifth chapter of Zechariah the prophet saw an ephah rising up from the land of Israel, an angel throws a woman—the sin of Israel—into the ephah, and then he covers its mouth with a leaden weight. Then the ephah full of sin is to be carried into the land of Shinar where a house will be built for it."[30]

In every case, Shinar plays a manipulative role. Moreover, other cities grow out of this geographical context. They prove to be as formidable for the covenant people to dominate. These cities are referred to when Scripture says, "And the beginning of his kingdom was Babel, and Erech, and Accad, and Calneh, in the land of Shinar. Out of that land went forth Asshur, and builded Nineveh, and the city Rehoboth, and Calah, and Resen between Nineveh and Calah: the same is a great city" (Gen. 10:10-12).

Like the land around them, these cities convey the idea of manipulation. Symbolically, the names Erech, Accad, and Rehoboth mean respectively, city of long time, city of wilderness, and city of storm. These cities cover the basic dimensions of life: *time*, *space*, and *energy*. They are boundaries that control life. Man knows that the one who controls time, space, and energy manipulates the world. Space and energy are obvious. Time fascinates man. Ancient civilizations tried to manipulate it through their festivals. They ordered this dimension around their gods—perceived to be in control. Modern man is no different. Transversing time still obsesses him.

The name Resen, the great city, means "bridle," or "bit." The bridle and bit may not seem to be important. To the ancient man, they were the key to wealth and power. The bridle was the single item that harnessed the horse. The horse enabled man to conquer his fellow man militaristically, and the ground technologically. With the horse man bridled nature. Thus, the horse is the symbol of "technique, invention, and domination."

The last city, Calah, definitively affected Israel's history. It is the city of deportation. The King of Assyria, Tiglath Pilesar, took Israel captive to Assyria, and the place of captivity was Calah (II Kgs. 17:6). Not coincidentally, the manipulative iron hand of a tyrant brought about God's purposes. We see this in the city of Calah.

30. *Ibid.*, pp. 13-14.

III. *Oppression*

A third characteristic of the city: The people of God found *no rest* in the city. It terrorized them. One bitter moment explaining this fear is actually the *first* experience they had at building—in Egypt. The name of Egypt in Hebrew is Mizraim—suffering or sorrow. Mizraim was the son of Ham, and the theological son of Cain, both men of sorrow. God brought His people to this land. Initially they dominated, but failed to carry out the cultural mandate. Thus, even though their land became a garden—the name Goshen means garden—Egyptian opposition reduced them to slavery on their first building project.

The names of the cities they built were Ramses and Pithom. Pithom means "house of Thom," the sun god. More importantly, they were graineries. Grain reminds of the occupation of Cain. He was a tiller of the ground. When he turned murderer, growth became an obsession. Out of the Cainitic cultures originated the fertility cults. In Egypt, God demonstrated in the exaltation of Joseph to power that he brought growth as well as famine. When Israel retreated from growing and extending the cultural mandate over Egypt, they ended up serving pseudo growers, building graineries for a foreign god.

The name Mizraim implies slavery. Israel did not learn building in freedom, so God made them learn by building pagan edifices. Eventually, a deliverer, Moses, emerged from the training of pagans. Not their skills, however, delivered Israel. Moses was taken to another training ground, the desert, where he learned the Word of God. The church must not forget this experience. God has done it before, and He will do it again.

IV. *Seduction*

The final characteristic of the pagan city is seduction. The first two cities that come to our mind are Sodom and Gomorrah. The clearest example, however, is the urban influence over Solomon and his sons. Scripture says of Solomon, "And this is the reason of the levy which King Solomon raised: for to build the house of the Lord, and his own house, and Millo, and the wall of Jerusalem, and Hazor, and Megiddo, and Gezer . . . and all the cities of store that Solomon had, and cities for his chariots, and cities for his horsemen, and that which Solomon desired to build in Jerusalem . . . (I Kgs. 9:15ff.).

Biblical history keeps the title of builder for Solomon.[31] No other king achieved success in building like the son of David. One detects some problems, however, in the statement in I Kings 9 of his architectural accomplishments. Solomon clearly violated the law of God when he kept in his possession chariots and horses (Deut. 17:16). Why? Horses, remember, were the force of military might. The King of Israel was not to build a military power. *His strength was to be in the Law*. One sees the far reaching effects of that kind of strength when kings and queens from all over the ancient world come to seek Solomon's wisdom (I Kgs. 10:1ff.). Like Samson, *Solomon gave up his true power.* He became like the pagan nations built on power statism. They beguiled him. Two events point out the effect.

One, prophecy was given to the rebellious. Jeroboam learned from Solomon. He failed, however, to gain knowledge of God's wisdom. As Solomon's successor in the Northern Kingdom of Israel, he learned only power. Statism divided the nation. While building one of Solomon's cities, Millo, and learning to build empire instead of Kingdom, the prophet told him of the division to come (I Kgs. 11:26ff.).

Two, his son Rehoboam was also a builder—the greatest besides Solomon. Schism characterized his reign. "Three chapters of the Chronicles are devoted to him. The first tells of the division of the sacred people into two groups because of Rehoboam's blundering. The second tells of his construction of cities and of his idolatry. The third, of his war with the King of Egypt, and of his defeat and death (II Chr. 11:5-12:1)."[32] He built *power cities*, not judicial ones. God brought a pagan power king into the land, Shishak, and struck right at the place where Rehoboam's pride was concentrated.

His power orientation was conspicuous. He was king of the south. With only two out of ten tribes, he offsets the ten tribes with twenty cities. He fills the cities with swords and spears. *He substitutes power for grace*. These were the chosen people with God's promise. Their power was in the Word of

31. *Ibid.*, p. 30.
32. *Ibid.*, p. 33.

God. Rehoboam trusted in his cities, and found that the pagan could match power with power on that level. In the end, he deserted the Law of God.

### *Keys of the Kingdom*

Perhaps one can now comprehend why Christ spoke of Hell as the city. Since the fall of man, the city was a place of initiation, manipulation, oppression, and seduction. With the coming of Christ, however, that changed. He gave the Keys of the Kingdom with which the church would pull down the gates of hell.

Before we proceed to the Keys of the Kingdom, some general observations should be made about the city. They will help to direct our attention to specific tactics for implementing the Keys.

I. *The City: A Weakness, Need, and Strategy*

First, as to an all encompassing weakness, the city is parasitic. It is basically dependent on outside resources to survive. The city absolutely cannot live by itself. "And this, moreover, characterizes all of those works of man by which he seeks autonomy. Everything takes its life from somewhere else, sucks it up. Like a vampire, it preys on the true living creation, alive in its connection with the creator. The city is dead, made of dead things for dead people. She can herself neither produce nor maintain anything whatever. Anything living must come from the outside. In the case of food, this is clear. But in the case of man also, we cannot repeat too often that the city is an enormous maneater. She does not renew herself from within, but by a constant supply of fresh blood from outside."[33] Thus, we can say that the city needs the theology, law, and economics of the church to survive.

Second, as to a basic need of the city, during the middle ages the church gave something to the city that could not be found elsewhere—a program for law and order. Cities were not only created by the spread of Christianity as the Law of God established reliable centers of commerce, but it transformed them from military institutions. The characteristic element was not the wall. "It was its charter. The commercial

---

33. *Ibid.*, p. 150.

and juridical elements were preponderant."[34] Men fled to the city for a fair trial, and to make money.

Third, as to the early church's strategy in the city, Pauline Christianity was entirely urban. "It stood on the growing edge of the Christian movement, for it was in the cities of the Roman Empire that Christianity, though born in the village culture of Palestine, had its greatest successes until well after the time of Constantine."[35]

Paul was a city person. His skills and terminology point to the conclusion that he grew up in a city (Acts 21:39), and he targeted his ministry toward the city. His converts to Christianity continued to live in the city, and to interact with its institutions.[36] Their method was quite effective. What was it? For Marxist revisionists,[37] it was the establishment of the antitheses — class struggles of ancient society. The early Christians, in contrast to Marxism's explanation, saw themselves as the thesis. They built true community, culture, and government. When the Roman Empire fell, the world turned to Christianity out of desperation.

The heart of the thesis they created brings us to the second major feature of Christ's words to Peter. We have examined the gates of hell as they manifest themselves in the cities of Cain, and overviewed their weaknesses. The focus of Christ, however, is the "Keys of the Kingdom."

II. *The Court*

Keys open and shut. As John the Apostle says, "And to the angel of the church in Philadelphia write; These things saith he that is holy, he that is true, he that hath the key of David, he that openeth, and no man shutteth; and shutteth, and no man openeth" (Rev. 3:7).

Keys are an emblem of power (Isa. 22:15-22).[38] They bind and loose (Matt. 16:19). This authority includes "Whose soever sins ye forgive, they are forgiven unto them; whose soever sins ye retain, they are retained" (John 20:23).

---

34. *Idem.*

35. Wayne A. Meeks, *The First Urban Christians* (New Haven: Yale University Press, 1983), p.8.

36. *Ibid.*, p.157.

37. *Ibid.*, p.3.

38. L. Berkof, *Systematic Theology* (Grand Rapids: Eerdmans, 1969), p. 593.

*The Keys are transferred from the apostles to the church.* "That Christ has given power to the Church as a whole, is quite evident from several passages of the New Testament (Acts 15:23-29; 16:4; I Cor. 5:7,13; 6:2-4; 12:28; Eph. 4:11-16)."[39] Thus, the church is vested with a *judicial* authority. The power is real and effective when used properly. The church is not infallible, but when the Keys are applied according to the Word of God, *God stands behind the judicial action of the church.*

In the Book of Revelation, the seven angels of the churches (Rev. 2-3) correspond to the seven angels who pour out judgment (Rev. 8-11). The angels of Revelation 3 are the ones *receiving* the letter. For this reason, they cannot be the angelic beings of Scripture. Thus, these angels are *representatives* —elders—in the church.[40] It is significant that angels symbolize the officers of the church. Earlier we noted a transition from angel to officer as the Keys were transferred from the cherubim to the church. Man once again guards the world. John's language confirms this.

More importantly, they who *receive letters* of commendation or renunciation are the ones who *pour out God's judgment on the earth.* This is done by the blowing of the trumpets. These trumpets are the rams' horns used in the Old Testament (Josh. 6:5; Ex. 19:13: Lev. 25).[41] Their most notable use was

39. *Idem.*

40. Moses Stuart, *Commentary on the Apocalypse* (Andover: Allen, Morrill, Wardwell, 1845), vol. II, pp. 55-56. See also, William Hendriksen, *More Than Conquerors* (Grand Rapids: Baker, 1977), p. 73. In footnote 16 he says the following. "These 'angels' cannot indicate the messengers of the churches sent to visit John, as the Scofield Bible holds. Then the expression: 'To the angel of the church at . . . write' [Rev. 2:1 for example] would have no meaning. Again, real angels, heavenly beings, cannot be meant. It would have been rather difficult to deliver the book or its epistles to them! Neither do we believe that the expression 'angels' can mean the churches as personified or as in the expression 'the *Spirit* of Ephesus.' We seriously doubt whether the expression, thus interpreted, would have been understood by those who first read or heard the book. For an excellent defense of the view that these angels refer to the bishops or pastors or ministers of the churches, see R. C. Trench, *Commentary on the Epistle to the Seven Churches in Asia*, pp. 53-58."

41. The Greek word used in the Revelation passages (Rev. 1:10, 4:1, 8:2,6,13, 9:14) is the same word utilized in the Septuagint to translate the Hebrew word(s) for the ram's horn in the Old Testament. For further study, see the use of *salpigx* in the following work: Edwin Hatch and Henry A. Redpath, *A Concordance to The Septuagint* (Austria: Akademische Druck - U. Verlagsanstalt Graz, 1954), vol. 2, p. 1258.

the announcing of the Year of Jubilee. Christ applies the Year of Jubilee eschatologically to the entire New Covenant Age (Lk. 4:16ff.). The trumpeter of the Old Testament becomes the herald of the New. This connection between blowing the trumpet and proclaiming the gospel, which the Bible makes, clarifies how the judgments of Revelation come. *The heralding of the Gospel draws the Lord near the earth*. When He comes, those who do not know Him are consumed. This phenomenon happens time and again in history.

After Elijah defeated the prophets of Baal, God drove him into a cave (I Kgs. 19:9ff). God passed by, but he was not harmed. Elijah was hidden in the cleft of the Rock. The significance of this unusual event in the midst of victory unfolds as we understand the relationship of the coming of the Gospel and judgment. Elijah had just been victorious. Conceivably, a revival had taken place. The false gods were defeated. But this scene shows Elijah that the consuming fire in the glory/cloud around God would have burned him also, if it were not for the place of salvation which the true God provided. Moreover, we see that the coming of the Lord brings salvation to those in the cleft, but the destruction to all others.

In extra-Biblical history this is confirmed. *Each resurgence of Christianity is accompanied by cataclysmic judgment*. One example will suffice. The infamous 14th century marked a period of wars, famine, and disease (the Black Death).[42] Yet the world was also entering a Renaissance because the Lord was drawing near in the heralding of the Gospel. It was the beginning of the pre-Reformation with the ministries of Wycliffe and Hus. Therefore, the Gospel must not be separated from judgment.

The Gospel tells of the judgment which came on Christ. But the sound of this trumpet speaks of judgment which *will* come on the one who does not trust in Christ's death for salvation. Our study of the trumpet/ram's horn explains.

The ram's horn was also blown whenever the people were drawn near to the Lord for judgment. In Exodus the sound of the trumpet brought the nation to the mountain to receive

---

42. Barbara W. Tuchman, *A Distant Mirror* (New York: Alfred Knopf, 1978), pp.532ff. Tuchman, a master historian, captures the significance of the calamitous 14th century. Interestingly, she compares it to the 20th century—believing this century holds the same potential for catastrophe and conquest.

Yahweh's judgment (Ex. 19:13). At Jericho, however, the same ram's horn that was used to sound the announcement of Jubilee, also brought down the pagan city. In this situation, the nation marched in a liturgical dance/worship around the city. As they engaged in this kind of activity, the trumpet sounded the presence of Yahweh, visible in the Cherubim over the ark of the covenant (Josh. 6:4), and that meant the eminent doom of pagan civilization in God's land. God had raised up His nation of people, had come near with them, and now judgment was coming.

Germane to our study, these trumpets, heralding the Gospel and the judgment to come on those who reject it, are handed to the officers and congregations of the New Covenant Church. Together they are instrumental in simultaneously bringing both the Good News of salvation in Christ alone, and the destruction of Cainitic culture. How is this done?

The Book of Psalms contains *imprecatory* Psalms. Psalms are prayers of the church to be sung liturgically in corporate assembly. Sung at the walls of Jericho, and in New Covenant meetings (Eph. 5:19), they are a primary aspect of bringing down the judgment of God on His enemies. When Paul refers to the singing of Psalms and their relevancy to the New Covenant church (Col. 3:16), he makes no mention of the imprecatory Psalms being deleted. Therefore, consider the words of Psalm 83.

> 1 Keep not thou silence, O God: hold not thy peace, and be not still, O God.
>
> 2 For, lo, thine enemies make a tumult: and they that hate thee have lifted up the head.
>
> 3 They have taken crafty counsel against thy people, and consulted against thy hidden ones.
>
> 4 They have said, Come, and let us cut them off from being a nation; that the name of Israel may be no more in remembrance.
>
> 5 For they have consulted together with one consent: they are confederate against thee:
>
> 6 The tabernacles of Edom and the Ishmaelites; of Moab, and the Hagarenes;
>
> 7 Gebal, and Ammon, and Amalek; the Philistines with the inhabitants of Tyre;
>
> 8 Assur also is joined with them: they have holpen the children of Lot. Selah.
>
> 9 Do unto them as unto the Midianites; as to Sisera, as to Jabin, at the brook of Kison:

10 Which perished at Endor: they became as dung for the earth.
11 Make their nobles like Oreb, and like Zeeb: yea, all their princes as Zebah, and as Zalmunna.
12 Who said, Let us take to ourselves the houses of God in possession.
13 O my God, make them like a wheel; as the stubble before the wind.
14 As the fire burneth a wood, and as the flame setteth the mountains on fire;
15 So persecute them with thy tempest, and make them afraid with thy storm.
16 Fill their faces with shame; that they may seek thy name, O Lord.
17 Let them be confounded and troubled for ever; yea, let them be put to shame, and perish:
18 That men may know that thou, whose name alone is JEHOVAH, art the most high over all the earth.

The magistrate holds the power of the sword. The church is trustee of the Keys of the Kingdom. All things compared, the church has greater power than the magistrate. She can bring down the wrath of God through rulings in her court, and through prayers in worship. Consider what might happen if the Christian elders, pastors, and evangelists of our nation declared an imprecatory day for prayer and fasting. They might choose an infamous day in January when abortion laws were passed, and call down the wrath of God on all those involved in perpetuation of mass murder.

These are the weapons of the church. They are not carnal. Nevertheless, their effectiveness is yet to be seen because the church sleeps. She abdicates the authority God has given her before a state which has given up its responsibilities. By acting judicially and prayerfully, God will bind and loose on earth what has been bound in heaven.

This understanding of the Keys of the Kingdom means the church is a *court*. The Keys are not just for anyone. Nor are they to be applied individualistically. Their place is corporate. The officers of the church assemble the congregation. They lead by pronouncing the anathema of God in the name of the Trinity. The people participate by the imprecatory Psalms, and saying Amen[43] in covenant affirmation.

---

43. Amen means "I affirm this statement, and let the curse of God fall on me and my family if I violate what I am affirming . . . May the birds of the

Historically, the church viewed itself as a court. Paul says to the church at Corinth, "Dare any of you, having a matter against another, go to law before the unjust, and not before the saints? Do ye not know that the saints shall judge the world? And if the world shall be judged by you, are ye unworthy to judge the smallest of matters? Know ye not that we shall judge angels? How much more things that pertain to this life? If then ye have judgments of things pertaining to this life, set them to judge who are least esteemed in the church. I speak to your shame. Is it so, that there is not a wise man among you? No, not one that shall be able to judge between his brethren" (I Cor. 6:1-5).

The early church took Paul's injunctions so seriously that their church buildings were laid out as a court.[44] The area just outside the door was a courtyard with a garden because they saw the church as guarding the *new* garden of God.[45] Just inside the door, the vestibule, was for the hearers, catechumens, and third class of penitents.[46] At the center of the main meeting area was the table where the Lord's Supper was served, and it was called the *Tribunal*, or *Bema*.[47] Since the sacrament was viewed as the locus of discipline, as was the rod in the home, and as was the sword in the hand of the magistrate, the court was held here. Every Lord's Day, when the church met for worship, court was in session. Judgment was rendered through preaching of the Word of God and the administration of the sacraments. People were admitted to the Table and communion of Christ. Sometimes they were dismissed. Furthermore, each Saturday was a time when the Elders met, and people could appear before them to settle their disputes before the Lord's Supper was observed the next day.

From Scripture and its application in history we begin to see the complexity of this court. Although it was judicial in

---

air come down and rip me and my family to pieces if I am found to be unfaithful." Perhaps the word would not be used so capriciously if its true meaning were recognized!

44. Henry R. Percival, *The Seven Ecumenical Councils*, vol. XIV of *The Nicene and Post-Nicene Fathers*, ed. by Philip Schaff and Henry Wace (Grand Rapids: Eerdmans, 1974), pp. 25ff.

45. *Idem.*

46. *Idem.*

47. *Idem.*

nature, disputes were pastorally settled before the elders. Entrance and exit from the church are focused around the sacraments. Worship took a different direction for it was not a form of entertainment, but a time of putting off sin and putting on the new man. Through all of these activities, we now understand how the church unlocks the gates of *Hell.* These are the kinds of efforts that raise up God's government on earth. Thus, we must be more specific as to the use of the Keys of the Kingdom.

A. *Admission*

Since Keys unlock, they are the means of admitting into the church. Baptism admits one into the Church. He enters, however, specific accountability to a local congregation, making church membership important. At baptism, theoretically, he is placed on the church roll. Why is this important? It creates *accountability with consequences.* Properly understood and implemented, church rolls represent God's roll in heaven. One's status on that roll speaks of His relationship with God. Although it is not an infallible guide, nevertheless, the Bible is filled with lists of rolls of God's people. Keeping lists of the faithful and those who belong to the covenant, therefore, helps to maintain the consequences of unrepentant covenant breaking.

Without properly maintained church rolls, people can walk out of the church, and the officers have no way of discipling them out of something they do not belong to. Moreover, if there is no church roll, discipline becomes abstracted —nothing concrete and visible happens to show that the church is being faithful to the Word of God. As a result of this, the person under discipline loses objective perspective on his commitment. There are simply no real consequences.

Churches today neglect these rolls as though they make no difference. God takes them seriously. They are a form of binding. When a person traveled in the early church, he took a letter from the elders of his church stipulating that he was a member in good standing. It obviously indicated that he was accountable with consequences at a local congregation. Thus, if he sinned while away from home, his behavior could be checked by the concerted efforts of the local courts. The letter served as a discipline that makes activities official.

"Officialness" helped the officers to administer God's justice fairly.[48]

B. *Discipline*

Locking, done by Keys, involves discipline. Most church members have never seen discipline. We live in a society that has seldom seen the execution of the criminal, or the excommunication of the apostate. It is a society without discipline!

Discipline is a process of *life through judgment.* At the Cross, God resurrected Jesus only after a lengthy ordeal of suffering, death, and judgment. Life came through these means. Therefore, in the life of the church, life continues to come through judgment. In the first epistle to the Corinthians, Paul emphasized a lengthy ordeal of death on the other side of salvation. He called it mortification in his letter to the church at Rome (Rom. 6:1ff). Resurrection, life, is central, yet tied to dying.

The Corinthians rejected this idea. For them, grace and law—discipline, suffering, obedience, and death—were antithetical to one another. The shortest distance to life was around the Law. They wanted life without death. This problem surfaced in a number of ways. First, they were *negligent in church discipline*, and reluctant to work out problems inside the local congregation. The process of reconciliation was too painful.

Second, the Corinthians wanted *sophisticated, eloquent, and polished preachers* (I Cor. 4:13). Paul was not good enough for them. He was weak, sickly, and not facile of speech. His preaching had the right content (I Cor. 1:18), but external and superficial rhetoric impressed them more than the simple truth and power of the Gospel (I Cor. 3:3-5).

Third, *internal problems* among members of the church bothered them. They wanted a church without problems. They thought a true church should not need arbitration. Resolution was not appealing. Besides, they wanted nothing to do with someone else's problems.

Fourth, *excommunication was unreasonable.* Life with a member in incest was the path of least resistance (I Cor. 5:9ff.). They thought it was too embarrassing to face the cutting off of a brother, and that the community would think Christianity did not work.

---

48. When Paul wanted to commend Onesimus the slave to Philemon, he sent a letter. This serves as a model for the letter of transfer concept.

These are symptoms of people who want *resurrection without mortification*. This is the way of the natural man (I Cor. 2:11ff.) Children never want to be spanked. Why? They want life apart from discipline. Since the fall of man, this is impossible. If God had to sacrifice His only begotten son to secure eternal life, one should expect to find life always attached to death. Even though salvation comes on the basis of *His* death, the life of sanctification is not without sacrifice.

*Life is connected with death* in two spheres of church life. In his *personal life*, a Christian mortifies and puts to death the deeds of the flesh. In the *corporate life* of the church, the elders discipline to restore. Unrepentance leads to excommunication. The guilty party is declared covenantally dead. Even then, Paul says the flesh is turned over to Satan that the spirit might be saved (I Cor. 5:9ff.). God's people are judged unto life, whereas covenant breakers are judged unto death. Therefore, Christians welcome judgment. It gives opportunity to die in order that life might result. Grace and law are not antithetical. Grace comes through obedience to the law. At salvation, it comes through Christ's obedience to the law. In sanctification, it eventuates as the Holy Spirit enables to obey the law. But the process of law, discipline, and judgment is definitely part of the life of the church. With this understanding, several aspects of discipline stand out.

One, *the system of ecclesiastical government is not adversarial.* This adversarial system has its roots in Greek civilization. Although the Bible refers to Jesus as our advocate (I John 2:2), his advocacy contrasts the role of a lawyer. Jesus became *accountable* for our sin. *Lawyers do not have accountability.* They do not die in our place if the case is lost. It would prove to be an interesting twist if lawyers were responsible for their work. Nevertheless, Jesus was a true advocate.

The judicial system of Scripture is *judge* oriented. Jethro directed Moses to establish an appellate system of judges (Ex. 18). The judges of Israel sat between the gates and heard cases. In the New Testament, the procedure laid out in I Corinthians 6 is judge centered. Thus, the impression one receives from reading the Bible is that people simply came to the judges and presented their case. This explains why the Reformers were by and large opposed to the adversarial system. In the church, it tends to fan the flames instead of putting the fire out.

Two, recent writings have sparked interest in Old Testament Law. Most of the response has concerned *civil* law. If one operates on a hermeneutic, however, that perpetuates the civil law, he must be consistent in the ecclesiastical sphere. It too must be extended.

Reformed creeds extend civil law through general equity. For example, the general equity of fences on roofs in the Old Testament is that we prevent the unnecessary loss of life. If we build apartments God expects us to put railings around the flat roof. If we build a swimming pool, some states require fences to be put around the pool to keep little children out. The extension of this precept is by general equity. Why not apply the same idea to the ecclesiastical realm?

Paul does this in I Corinthians 9. In verses 13 & 14 he says, "Do ye not know that they which minister about holy things live of the things of the temple? and they which wait at the altar are partakers with the altar? Even so hath the Lord ordained that they which preach the gospel should live of the gospel." In some sense, the Levitical priesthood equitizes into the ministers of the New Covenant.

At other places in the New Testament (Heb. 9ff.), the Levitical priesthood changes under the New Covenant. Is it completely done away with? No, Paul speaks of the minister of the gospel as being under the remunerative terms of the Old Covenant. On the other hand, the priesthood is definitely changed in that they do not offer up the blood of bulls and goats. They, nevertheless, present living sacrifices to God (Rom. 12:1ff.). These passages equitize the church and priesthood of the Old Testament into the New Testament. The only way to determine the equitization is by organically interpreting the Bible as a whole. One looks at the New in light of the Old, and vice versa. Eventually he begins to see the general equity.

Three, Scripture *requires attendance on the Lord's Day*. According to the writer to the Hebrews, participation in worship is the highest privilege (Heb. 10:26ff.). Unexcused absense is sin. The officers should pursue discipline. In the early church, unexcused absense met with automatic excommunication.[49]

Four, *discipline is processional*. Since the Holy Spirit proceeds from the Father and the Son, as well as the Father

49. Percival, pp. 400, 426, 427.

through the Son, the church has immediate and mediate discipline. When the Lord's Supper is unlawfully taken, God the Son brings immediate spiritual judgment. The process of Matthew 18:15, on the other hand, is mediated *through* the officers of the church—these officially representing the Son. Thus, church discipline is static and dynamic. The double procession of the Holy Spirit keeps discipline from being reduced to either one or the other.

Five, contumacy should be acted on immediately. In the Old Testament, if a man was summoned to stand before the elders or priest, and he failed to come without excuse, he was put to death (Deut. 17:12). Why? A court is only as effective as the penal system attached to it. If someone could avoid coming to trial, he would. Contempt undermines the whole system. Although there is "contempt of court" in both the civil and ecclesiastical realms, an important distinction should be made between the two court systems. The analogy which is otherwise consistent between judicial systems of the two spheres breaks down at the point of contumacy. Discipline in the church is completely *restorative*, and not punitive. There is no gradated system of punishments for someone who refuses to cooperate with the church court. There is simply excommunication, irrespective of the offense which the accused person is being charged with. The offense of contumacy supersedes all other offenses, and the punishment—the announcement of God's death sentence against the sinner—is the maximum ecclesiastical punishment allowed for any offense. For this reason, all sin, if not repented of—and restitution made—becomes contumacy. It means that a relatively small matter can become a major issue of rebellion to the elders in the church. Unchecked, the initial—possibly minor—sin can escalate into contumacy, a great sin.

In the civil realm, however, contempt of court is one among many offenses. A person being tried for murder, if he refuses to cooperate with the court in determining his guilt or innocence, can be held in contempt of court and punished. But the trial can and should go on without his presence, and if he is convicted, he is required by Biblical law to be put to death by the civil government. There are two punishments because there are two separate offenses. In the church, however, the guilty person always has the option of repentance. Hypothetically, the murderer could repent and come back into the church—thus entering the Kingdom, as the thief on the cross did: legitimately condemned for his civil crime, but cleared by God for the ethical rebellion involved in all his transgressions.

Therefore, in the sphere of the church, the sin of one who has not been restored through the "Matthew 18 process" is contumacy. "Excommunication never takes place for committing the sin that occasioned the process in the beginning. Excommunication always occurs when one rejects the authority of the church of Christ; he is excommunicated for contumacy. One is excommunicated, then, not for adultery, but for failure to repent and be reconciled. The sin that occasioned discipline may have been relatively 'small' in its effects, but to *that* sin is added the *enormously* significant sin of the rejection of Christ Himself as He demands repentance through his representatives. Excommunication occurs when men act like Nabal: 'He is such a worthless man that no one can speak to him' (I Sam. 25:17). As Christ puts it: 'He will not hear (listen to) the church.' The people of God were destroyed and God declared that there is 'no remedy,' not because of their sin, but because of their refusal to repent of it; their stiffnecked attitude toward God (cf. II Chron. 36:11-21)."[50]

Six, the advent of American Protestantism has virtually destroyed the concept of *jurisdictional boundaries*. The Old Testament notes the boundaries of the Republic of Israel. In the New Testament the same boundary idea is carried over. Paul acted under strict submission to the other Apostles. He was not free to go anywhere or say anything he wanted.

In the American church, we have the *tyranny of wandering ministers and evangelists*. When someone has a problem, he goes to a neighboring minister and finds acceptance. What does this do to the church? It destroys accountability, escalates problems, and tears the church and churches involved.

The early church observed strict jurisdictional boundaries. If a bishop went into another bishopric without permission, he was automatically defrocked.[51] He never consulted

---

50. Jay Adams, *The Christian Counselor's Manual* (Grand Rapids: Baker, 1973), p. 54.

51. Percival, p. 638. In this section a bishop is forbidden to travel to another city autonomously. He may not usurp another parish. A bishop is excommunicated for communicating with one excommunicated. He suffers deposition for interference of any kind. A presbyter, in other words, had to abide within his bounds.

with members under another bishop's charge without communication to all elders concerned. This keeps one bishop from becoming too dominant. Otherwise, the wandering minister might end up representing whole areas and becoming a miniature pope. In fact, this is precisely what happened at Rome. It was not so much due to the bishop's travel into other areas. Constant appeal by others in the empire to the bishop of Rome gave him more and more influence.

One sees the same concept in practice in the early republic of the Roman Empire. When Caesar crossed the Rubicon, the other Senators wanted to kill him.[52] According to early Roman law, a Senator of one area was not allowed to cross the borders of adjacent territories with his armies. Reason: the empire feared what Julius Caesar eventually accomplished —one man, a tyrant, controlling the empire.

As any church attempts to carry out discipline, it will encounter this problem. People simply leave and go to a neighboring church, perhaps of the same denominational affiliation. Walking out into another ecclesiastical jurisdiction may seem to solve the immediate problem, but it rends the church and creates a worse problem. It leaves differences unreconciled.

Discipline is necessary to the being and well-being of the church. In an essay of this size, only preliminary and introductory considerations appear. Discipline, however, is not the extent of the church court. The court can also function pastorally. It should be a place of reconciliation.

C. *Reconciliation*

Recently, the U.S. Supreme Court has reminded the lower courts that reconciliation outside court should be encouraged. The overload is too much for the system. Traditionally, arbitration on just about anything except a felony, or direct involvement with the government, is acceptable.

Arbitration is sorely needed in the church. Of all places, man ought to find reconciliation before God's throne. Often one does not see this expressed in churches. Most churches do not have a systematic procedure. Unlike the early church whose elders met at the church on Saturdays to hear disputes, people in the church do not know what to do, or where to go.

52. Michael Grant, *The Twelve Caesars* (New York: Scribners, 1975), p. 36.

Another problem is the independent nature of the American church. The majority of successful churches are independent. They have no judicial connections beyond their own deacons or elders.[53] What happens when there is a dispute, and the members cannot work out the problem? If the problem is of major proportion, the church usually splits, and splits, and splits.

Then there is the problem of *divorce and remarriage*. One divorce can start a chain reaction of events that devastates a church. Recently in a church of three hundred people, one of the Sunday school teachers divorced her husband. Within two months, five other divorces had occured *among the Sunday school teachers*. Consider how many families this situation affected. By the time everyone spread into other churches, the fission effect compounded the problems even more. They will probably never resolve the conflicts.

Symptomatic of the need for arbitration, and indicative of the effectiveness of reconciliation is the success of a new organization: *Christian Conciliation Service of New Mexico*. "It is a peacemaking ministry providing Biblically faithful alternatives (options) of resolving legal disputes within the framework of the Christian Church. CCS is staffed in New Mexico by over 200 volunteer lawyers, pastors and laypersons from diverse professional and denominational backgrounds. CCS provides a structure whereby principles and procedures of conflict resolve disputes between Christians."[54]

They see a need for their organization, first, because Scripture commands reconciliation before worship is continued (Matt. 5:23-24). Second, "despite this high priority given to reconciliation, there are thousands of lawsuits in New Mexico each year which pit Christian against Christian. These legal disputes inhibit spiritual growth, create bitterness and divert energies from the building of God's Kingdom. They cost the Christian community millions of dollars in legal fees each year. The Bible clearly states that Christians having disputes with one another should take them to the church rather than the secular law courts (I Cor. 6, Matt. 18:17). CCS

---

53. See James B. Jordan, ed., *The Failure of the American Baptist Culture*, Christianity and Civilization No. 1 (Tyler, TX: Geneva Divinity School Press, 1982).

54. Christian Conciliation Service, 314 Arno N.E., Albuquerque, NM 87102, Telephone: 505/243-6887.

is designed to return the 'ownership' of these conflicts between Christians to the church."[55]

They believe the secular courts should not be used for several reasons. "First, our adversary judicial process is similar to a fight. Far from achieving reconciliation, the system usually heightens animosities and increases hatred between the parties. It is counterproductive to the healing of important Christian relationships which are often permanently fractured in the course of a lawsuit.

"Second, our secular legal process only provides temporary symptomatic relief to the parties in conflict. Underlying the technical legal issues are ignored spiritual needs and problems of unforgiveness, vindictiveness, anger, bitterness, greed, pride, and unbelief. Jesus Christ was concerned with ministering to these deeper causes of conflict.

"Third, the regular court system—with its emphasis on 'rights' and 'technicalities' ignores corresponding responsibilities and neglects what Jesus referred to as the 'weightier matters of the law'—justice, repentance, love, and forgiveness."[56]

The only criticism that could be leveled against CCS is that it is not under the direct oversight of church elders. This mitigates the process laid down in Scripture. Paul, however, says that a "wise man" will suffice (I Cor. 6:1ff.), so, this criticism is not completely valid. All things considered, reconciliation by arbitration should be welcomed in an age of conflict within church, state, and family.

### D. *Healing*

Rationalism has driven healing out of the church. When someone is sick, he generally never considers turning to the elders. How ironic! Healing comes from God, even if He uses the hands of a surgeon.

Healing is one of the functions of the court of Christ. Not exclusively so, but the elders can be appealed to. James says, "Is any sick among you? Let him call for the elders of the church; and let them pray over him, anointing him with oil in the name of the Lord: and the prayer of faith shall save the sick, and the Lord shall raise him up; and if he have commit-

---

55. *Idem.*
56. *Idem.*

ted sins, they shall be forgiven him" (James 5:14).

First, one sees in this passage that the elders are to receive the sick, and pray over them. The elders represent the court of God. Thus, this activity is judicial.

Second, the elders are the ones praying. When James says the prayer of faith heals, he is speaking of the prayer given by the elders of a local church.

Third, the oil was not medicinal, but symbolical (cf. Mark 6:13ff.). Oil in Scripture represents the Holy Spirit as seen in the anointing of priests and kings in the Old Testament. Because oil represents the Holy Spirit, the point of this ritual of going to the elders is that healing comes from God.

Twentieth-century man wants physical healing. Unfortunately, only a few churches have healing services. Historically, the Anglican church has had a *healing liturgy.* This is an important part of ministry. *It is a means of unlocking the city/hell.* A church where there is healing will be appealing to the watching world. As men in Jesus' day came to the pool of Bethesda, they will come to the church for healing.

*Summary*

We have analyzed the Keys of the Kingdom, and noted judicial implications. Specifically, the Keys are in the hands of the officers of the church. Generally, all of God's people hold them. With proper application, the Keys will bring wrath, discipline, reconciliation, or healing. This remarkable authority and power has been given to God's people.

## *Conclusion*

The state of resistance in which the church finds herself, means that difficult days are ahead. She must know how to act. These times can become a period of greatest opportunity which the church has ever known. Or, the church in the Western hemisphere could experience the chastisement levelled on the church of North Africa in the 7th century.

We have considered several points in this essay. First, there is only one government in the world, and it belongs to God. His Kingdom comprehends all nations as well as the church and family. His ways are not always our ways, but He is in control of all things. This means that He desires to govern the earth through three parallel spheres—family, church, and state. When the state abandons its role as an avenger of the wrath of God, however, this leaves the church in a shadowing posture. Outside the family, she is the only institution that models Christian government to the world.

Second, Christ gives Keys to the church which simultaneously open and shut the Kingdom of heaven and the gates of hell. Since the fall of man, the gates of hell refer to the cities of the world. For the church to send ambassadors into these areas and successfully evangelize, she must know the city. It is a place of initiation, manipulation, oppression, and seduction. As formidable as the city has been, it has several weaknesses. By taking advantage of them, the church can conquer.

To be more precise, the Keys given to the church are of such a nature that they are the most effective weapon for conquest. Through their application, the church will win by default. The state will eventually collapse, as it did in the Roman Empire, but the church will be standing with its government intact. Out of last resort, society will again turn to the church. The question is, "will the church be ready?"

In Calvin's day, the burghers asked him to come to their city because they wanted to maintain order.[57] They believed his system of government and theology could restore their city. Unfortunately, the new political right is not courting the religious right for the same reason. All they want are votes. The political right may think it can lead,[58] but it had better understand the role of the church. At the same time, the religious right is not ready to lead either. Its leadership has not begun to see the church as a true government, and temporarily as the civil magistrate's shadow government. Until they do, the gates of hell will prevail.

---

57. Rushdoony, *Politics of Guilt and Pity*, pp. 272ff.

58. Richard A. Viguerie, *The New Right: We're Ready to Lead* (Falls Church, VA: The Vigurie Company, 1981).

# TITHING: FINANCING CHRISTIAN RECONSTRUCTION

James B. Jordan

THE Bible sets forth tithing as the principal means of financing the kingdom of God. Apart from a return to systematic, Biblical tithing, there will be no Christian reconstruction in America. Simply resisting tyranny will accomplish nothing unless a Christian order is built up simultaneously, in order to pick up the pieces.

There is a great deal of confusion in the area of tithing in the church at large today, and in the "Christian Reconstruction" movement as well. Confusion in the latter is largely due to the circulation of a book called *Tithing and Dominion*, by Rousas J. Rushdoony and Edward A. Powell.[1] While there is much of value in this study, it suffers from a failure to grasp properly the nature of the tithe system set up in the Bible. To be specific, Powell and Rushdoony assume that there were three separate tithes, when in fact there was only one with several aspects. They also permit the tithe to be given at random to various kinds of Christian activities, when Scripture requires that it be given to the ecclesiastical order. To a great extent, the essay which follows is designed to correct the faults in Powell and Rushdoony's study. With these things in mind, however, I can recommend the examination of their study, since it does contain much of value.

The problem in the church at large is due to the evil influence of "grace giving." The notion of grace giving places men in bondage, for they never know when they have given enough. It also dishonors God in that it encourages men to give as *they* please instead of as *He* has ordered. Also, in point of fact, men seldom give anywhere near ten percent of their net business income to God, so that grace giving usually means robbing God (Malachi 3:8-12). Tithing liberates men because it tells them exactly how much God requires, and

1. (P.O. Box 67, Vallecito, CA: Ross House Books, 1979).

leaves them free to use the remainder in dominion tasks.

I have set this discussion out in a series of numbered propositions. This is because it makes the various points easier for the reader to isolate, and because it condenses the essay by eliminating transitional sentences and paragraphs.[2] We shall first of all consider the nature and rules concerning Biblical tithing, and then make some practical observations on how these might be implemented in our day.

## *The Melchizedekal Tithe*

1. The Old Covenant was a *provisional* administration of grace and law, while in the New Covenant the kingdom of God and the law of God are established *definitively* (Rom. 3:31). The Cultural Mandate was restricted under the Old Covenant (Gal. 4:1ff.), but fully republished in the New. The restrictive nature of the Old Covenant was due to the fact that the Spirit was not yet given, because Jesus was not yet glorified, and thus power for dominion was limited (John 7:38, 39).

2. Part of these restrictions was a system of laws which kept the people closely tied to an *agricultural economy*. The Old Covenant laws of tithing are couched in this framework, and they cannot directly be applied to all New Covenant situations.

3. Moreover, the Levitical tithe system was intimately tied to the *sacrificial system* and the *centralized sanctuary* of the Old Covenant. The Levitical tithe system is, however, both preceded and succeeded by the Melchizedekal tithe system (Heb. 7).

4. *The Melchizedekal tithe system is permanently obligatory.* Abraham paid tithes (10%) to Melchizedek, and all the true sons of Abraham (Rom. 4, Heb. 7) will also pay the tithe to the greater Melchizedek, Jesus Christ. In return for the tithe, Melchizedek gave Abraham bread and wine. Anyone who refuses to pay a tenth to Christ should also be refused the bread and wine of the Lord's Supper (Gen. 14:18-20).

5. The Melchizedekal priestly order was connected to *sonship* (Heb. 7:3), especially the privileges of the *firstborn*.[3] God

2. An earlier and less complete version of this essay was published by the Institute for Christian Economics, in newsletter form, in 1981.

3. As a type of Christ, Melchizedek is seen as unique. Psalm 110:4 and Hebrews 5:6 speak of the "order of Melchizedek." This is our concern at present.

very meticulously superseded the Melchizedekal order with the Levitical order in Numbers 3. Thus, the Melchizedekal order always underlay the Levitical order throughout the Mosaic period. The Levitical tithe, then, is an extension and specification of the Melchizedekal tithe.

6. The Melchizedekal order was typologically reasserted in the *Davidic Covenant* (2 Sam. 7), which spoke of the king as a son. Psalm 110 and the book of Hebrews must be understood in the light of the Davidic Covenant. Again we see the Melchizedekal order as the foundation for the Levitical, especially as the Davidic kings supported and reformed the Levitical system from time to time. Indeed, the plans for the Temple and the building of the Temple were not given to and accomplished by the Levitical priests, but by the Davidic Kings. (See 1 and 2 Chronicles.)

7. The fact that the Levitical tithe is built on the Melchizedekal means that an examination of how the Levitical tithe functioned in the Mosaic period can provide useful pointers as to how the fully established Melchizedekal tithe should be used in the New Covenant period.

### *The Levitical Tithe*

8. Because of the restrictions on the cultural mandate, and because of its typological nature, the Levitical tithe is always spoken of in terms of the *agricultural year.* The tithe is seen as collected annually, and given to a centralized church order. In the New Covenant, the tithe is given to local churches, and the emphasis is on *weekly* rather than annual contributions (1 Cor. 16:2).

9. Of course, agriculturalists and self-employed persons may and probably should continue to tithe on annual increases. Wage earners, however, should tithe on their paychecks as they arrive, weekly if possible.[4]

10. The stress in 1 Cor. 16:2 on laying aside the tithe on the first day of the week gives a New Covenant focus to the first-fruit offerings of the Old Covenant. The time-honored custom of *paying the church before paying anything else* is based on this.

---

4. Wages must be seen as income, since the *power* to earn wages comes from God, just as the yield of a field or vineyard comes from Him. Thus, clearly a tithe is owed on wages.

11. How many tithes were there? Deuteronomy 14:23 and 12:17 speak of a tithe on "grain, new wine, and oil." Leviticus 27:30, 32 speaks of a tithe on seed, fruit, and animals. If we take these as two different tithes, we should notice that they do not overlap. Together they do not constitute 20% of the whole [$.10(a + b) + .10(c + d) = .10(a + b + c + d)$] Thus, the total tithe remains at 10%.

12. More likely, however, these specifications should not be taken to mean different tithes, but *different aspects of one tithe*. We must beware of an overly nominalistic hermeneutic, which assumes that because different terms are used for the same thing, different things are in fact meant. Leviticus 27 is concerned with vows and their redemption, and the tithe is here seen as a form of vow (cf. Gen. 28:20, where Jacob's tithe is seen as a vow). The fact that Numbers 18 speaks of the tithe as going to the Levites does not contradict Deuteronomy 14:22-19, which tells us that the tithe was used to finance participation in the feast before being turned over to the Levites. The expression "grain, new wine, and oil" is used in Deuteronomy 7:13 as significant of all the blessings of the land.

13. The term 'poor tithe' to refer to the command in Deut. 14:28, 29 is a misnomer. The money was given to the *elders of the gate*, which today are the elders of the local churches (1 Cor. 6:1-5). They determined its use. Part of it went for the poor, but part also for the salary of the local Levite.

14. Contrary to popular ideas, Levites were found in the towns of Israel as teachers in proto-synagogues. Worship was conducted every sabbath and new moon (Lev. 23:3; Deut. 18:6; Jud. 17:7; 18:30; 19:1; Neh. 10:37f.). *The third-year tithe was, then, not a poor tithe, but a local as opposed to a national tithe.*

15. In the New Covenant, since there is no longer any central sanctuary, all tithes go to the "elders of the gate." *We are in a perpetual third-year tithe situation*, until God's great seventh year comes at the Last Judgment. A study of the third-day and third-year concept in the Bible will reveal that just as Christ arose on the third day, we are living in the third day until the seventh day arrives (Gen. 22:4; 42:18; Ex. 19; Num. 19; Hos. 6:2; Jonah 1:17).

16. Under the Old Covenant, in the first and second years the people took their tithes to the sanctuary to celebrate the Feast of Booths (cf. Deut. 14:22-27 with 16:13-14). They used the tithe to finance their participation in the feast. What was

left over, the larger portion by far, was given to the *national Levites*.

17. In the third year, the people took part of their tithes to the sanctuary to celebrate the Feast of Booths (cf. Deut. 26:14), and then returned to their locales, depositing the remainder of the tithe with the elders of the gates.

18. During the year, as various crops came in, and as various animals gave birth to their firstborn, the tithe and firstborn offerings would be laid up. These were apparently delivered in the festival of the seventh month, the Feast of Booths. Cf. 2 Chron. 31:7.

19. The tax of the firstborn was also used first to help finance participation in the Feast of Booths, and then the remainder given to the Levites (Deut. 14:23 & 15:19-20).

20. The Lord's Supper and the Love-Feast of the New Covenant correspond to participation in the *Feast of Booths* (1 Cor. 11:33f., Jude 12). Some churches have occasional Love-Feasts (Agapes, or covered dish meals). Others have them monthly (new moons) or weekly. It is appropriate to use the first part of one's tithe to pay for the dinner you bring to these suppers. The poor, of course, are to be sponsored by those better off.

21. Ordinarily, *the tithe went to the Levites*. The New Covenant affirms that all the Lord's people are Levites (Deut. 33:9 & Matt. 10:35-37, etc.). This does not mean that the Old Covenant people, under the provisional administration of law and grace, were not also priests. Indeed, the Levites came into being as substitutes for the firstborn of all Israel (see #5 above), so that foundationally every household in Israel was a priestly community. What this means is that *the Levites were ecclesiastical specialists*, called to special office.

22. The Biblical view of special office is neither democratic nor aristocratic. Every Christian has the general office. The rationale for special office is in terms of gifts and in terms of the need for good order (1 Cor. 12; 14:40), not in terms of priesthood in any pagan (aristocratic) sense. In times of distress, any general officer may teach, baptize, and administer communion (cf. Ex. 4:25).

23. The tithe went to the Levites because they were ecclesiastical specialists. The elders of the gate *governed* the use of the synagogue's money. Churches which distinguish between preacher-teachers and ruling elders have an analogous system

today.

24. The Levites tithed to the high priest and his family (Numbers 18). Analogous to this, since the high priest was the high court of the church (Deut. 17:8-13), there is a place for a tithe of the tithe to be passed from the local church to larger courts for their purposes.

25. The *local tithe* was administered by the elders for two purposes: the salary of the synagogue Levite and care for the poor (including the widow, fatherless, and alien). The *national tithe* was used by the Levites for a number of purposes, principally educational or cultic in character. An examination of these will show us what the tithe should and should not be used for today.

26. A study of the temple taxes of the Bible will show that the sacrificial system was not maintained solely by the tithe, and so the use of the tithe under the Old Covenant cannot differ greatly from its proper use in the New.[5]

27. Part of the tithe did, of course, go to *maintaining the sacrifices*, offered daily, sabbatically, monthly, etc. We might think the church needs less money today since it no longer has this expense. In the New Covenant, however, there is a great expense connected with *missions* which was not present in the Old Covenant. In the Old Covenant, God located His people at the crossroads of the world, and brought the world to the church. In the New Covenant this is reversed, and money is needed for missions.

### *Education*

28. It is frequently remarked that one of the duties of the Levites was education (Lev. 10:11; Deut. 17:18; 31:9-13; 33:10; 2 Chron. 17:7-9; Neh. 8:9). It is clear from these passages that this education was *training in the Word of God*, not in other matters. Unfortunately, this all-important point has been obscured.

29. Reformed philosophy has in the twentieth century picked up on a shibboleth called 'sphere sovereignty.' Supposedly, life is divided into a series of separate spheres, one of which is the sphere of education. This pattern of thought has

5. See James B. Jordan, "State Financing in the Bible," an essay published in newsletter form by the Institute for Christian Economics, Box 8000, Tyler, TX 75711.

led and continues to lead to confused practices across the Reformed world in the area of education.[6] There is, in fact, no such thing as a 'sphere of education'; rather, education is simply the training arm of each aspect of life.[7]

30. Training of small children in the *basics of life in a given culture* is not the duty of the church (Levites), nor of some "school sphere." It is the *duty of parents*, and is to be *financed by parents*. For parents to use the tithe for this purpose is to rob God. The tithe is for education in the law-Word of God, not for teaching small children to color, read, write, and add. Mothers and fathers took care of this task in Israel, and if they deputize the task to teachers, it is to be a free contractual arrangement, not the business of the church.

31. Powell argues[8] that children do not belong to parents, but to God, and so the tithe should be used to educate small children. This is not a sound argument, because it is true of everything. Everything belongs to God, including my own private business; therefore, I may use the tithe to build up my private business. Not so. God has instructed parents to educate children, not only in the basics of life but also in theological and religious matters (Prov. 1:8; 6:20; 31:1; Ex. 10:2; 12:26; 13:8; Deut. 4:9; 6:7, 20f.; 32:7, 4, etc.). Thus, under normal circumstances, not even the religion class in a grade school should be paid for by the tithe. It is the parents' job.[9]

32. A second aspect of education is *education in a calling.*

---

6. In other words, each social sphere is unique and separate from the others in its government. This is true of church, state, family, and economy. These Reformed thinkers apply this also to the school, so that the school is not under the control either of parents or of the church. The school must have its own "educational creeds." And so forth. In some Calvinistic circles this has resulted in schools which use radical teaching techniques and teach radical humanist ideas, but which are immune from criticism from parents and clergy because of "sphere sovereignty."

7. Those readers aware of the thought of Herman Dooyeweerd will realize that I am not (at this point) criticizing his notion of theoretical law-spheres, but certain radical social applications of a, possibly perverted, understanding thereof.

8. *Ibid.*, p. 106f.

9. On the subject of children's education in Israel, see Roland de Vaux, *Ancient Israel* (New York: McGraw Hill, 1965), pp. 48ff. De Vaux is a liberal, and is often untrustworthy. These few pages, however, simply summarize Biblical information.

This is the duty of the family and also of the individual himself (herself). Again, it is robbing God to use the tithe for this purpose. A man's family might help him with college, and there is always room for charity, but it is not the business of the tithe to finance education in carpentry, medicine, or French literature. Christian colleges should not normally be financed by the tithe. (See #36 below.)

33. A third aspect of education is in the sphere of the *state*. Military schools have a place, but not financed by the tithe.

34. The fourth form of education is education in the *law-Word of God*. This was the duty of the Levites and of the church today. This is what is to be financed by the tithe. At the high school and college level, religion classes may be taught by professional "Levites," and their salaries probably should be paid for by the church and the tithe. This would be analogous to the way the state pays the salary of R.O.T.C. instructors. In some countries, various churches sponsor theological colleges on the campuses of secular universities.

35. Remember, however, that *the tithe also goes for the poor*, and paying the tuition for a poor child to go to a Christian school is entirely appropriate. Education in a calling was accomplished by apprenticeship in the ancient world, and the poor were trained by becoming temporary indentured servants (Deut. 15:12-15). Thus, the tithe probably should not be used to help poor college students, though gifts over and above the tithe are entirely proper. Seminary students (future "Levites") should be sponsored by the tithe. Only in this way will older, more responsible family men be enabled to receive professional theological training.

36. Remember also that in times of persecution many functions must "hide" under the church. In the United States today, it may be necessary for some Christian schools to declare themselves part of the ministry of a local church in order to avoid persecution by the secular state. This temporary measure is not, however, normative.

37. One result of throwing grade school education wholly on the purses of parents is that Christians schools will not have as much money. Is this really a problem? Rushdoony has pointed out that education has a Messianic function in our society.[10] As a result of this salvation function, vast and

---

10. *The Messianic Character of American Education*, available from Thoburn Press, P.O. Box 6941, Tyler, TX 75711.

unnecessary amounts of money are poured into education. *Christian schools, having a more limited and proper role in life, should be less expensive and smaller than Messianic schools*. There is much in the Messianic curriculum which need not be in that of the Christian schools.

38. To take one example, experimental science. Science in the Christian school should take the form of naturalism, study of the "ways" of animals, building on the proverbs and observations of Solomon. Experimentation and dissection are specialized and technical studies, and have more to do with education for a calling than education for whole life.

## *Medicine*

39. Because of the involvement of the Levites in the cleansing rituals of the leper (Lev. 13, 14), it has sometimes been maintained that medicine is a proper use of the tithe. In the Bible, however, there is a difference between sickness as such, which is "healed," and leprosy, which is "cleansed." During a woman's period, she was unclean, but not sick. A child with measles is sick, but not unclean. A leper was both sick and unclean. Uncleanness was "ceremonial" in nature, not medicinal.

40. Most "medicine" in Scripture is *preventative*, a side benefit of the "ceremonial" law, and still instructive for us today. Childbirth and general care of the sick was accomplished by midwives and other semi-professionals within the community. There is really no reason to see the Levites as a class (in part) of professional healers. Medical care should be under free enterprise, and its expenses covered by insurance policies, as we have it today.

41. Care for the poor, in the area of medicine and health in general is, of course, a proper use of the tithe.

## *Advisors to the State*

42. The Levites in Israel served as advisors to the state (Deut. 17:9, 18) and they sat in on court cases to help render judgments by giving professional advice concerning the Law of God (1 Chron. 23:4; 26:29-32; 2 Chron. 19:8-11). They were the closest thing to a professional lawyer class that existed in Israel, for they were experts in the law of God.

43. Thus, the tithe should be used to maintain *a corps of*

professional theologians and legal experts, as well as *educators*. The church must ever advise the state regarding its duties before God. Rightly do the confessions of the Reformation state that the civil magistrate has the power to call church synods to advise him. In light of this, it would be proper for a church to use part of its tithe to assist men in law school, so that they will "know the enemy" better.

### *Worship*

44. The Levites were *professional musicians* within the church. Worship in the Bible centers around teaching, the sacraments, and the response in singing and dancing. The Bible shows us that it is God's will for His people to be trained in proper worship, and to be led by skilled professionals (1 Chron. 15:16-24; 25:1-7; Ps. 149:3; 150:4). This use of the tithe is almost completely overlooked by the conservative and platonic Reformed and fundamentalist churches. The result has been the secularization of music and the reduction of dance to an exclusively erotic function, and the fragmentation of life; not to mention the fact that people don't know what to do with themselves on the sabbath. The reintroduction of wholistic worship to our dying churches will take time, but it is part of the work of the tithe to pay for it.

### *The Foundation of Society*

45. The purpose of the tithe, in sum, is to provide the financial underpinning for the foundational work of society. As such, it finances Christian reconstruction. Society is founded and reconstructed only on the basis of the forthsetting and implementation of the Word. The *capitalization of all of life* is made possible when the tithe is properly paid and directed.

46. The tithe finances the reconstruction of society indirectly, through the proclamation of the Word. This is the meaning of Judges 17-21. *All the disorders in society arose because the Levites were not doing their job*. Every man did that which was right in his own eyes because the Levites were not keeping society conscious of the nearness of the presence of the King (the LORD) and of the demands of His law. They were seeking riches wrongly (Jud. 17). They did not love the people as

Christ loves the church, willing to sacrifice themselves for the bride (Jud. 19). As a result, the people were in open violation of the laws pertaining to the love of God (Jud. 17) and of the laws pertaining to the love of the neighbor (Jud. 19, 21).

47. *Thus, the use of the tithe to pay for the work of the church does not compromise its social use; rather, it constitutes its indispensable social character. Training in the Word and the response of worship are together the bottom line of civilization. Without the forthsetting of the Word, nothing can be accomplished.*

48. The confrontation of God with Pharaoh was precisely over the issue of worship (Ex. 3:18; 4:23; 5:1-3; 8:1). So was the confrontation at the time of the Reformation and the Puritan confrontation with the state church a century later. *The tithe finances social renewal by financing special worship in all its fulness*. People who sing and have memorized the psalms, for instance, are equipped to conquer the world.

49. I cannot go into it here, but the reader should be apprised of the fact that *the central religious disposition of any civilization is revealed in its sacramental theory*. The fact that great religious movements and wars were fought out over transubstantiation, the Real Presence, and theories of baptism—this seems very strange to modern secular man. If we were not so blind to the foundations of our own culture, however, we would realize that *the question of how God makes Himself known, and whether He can be controlled, is the central question of civilization*. Eastern Orthodoxy believes that the world is kept in existence by the proper recitation of the liturgy. Roman Catholicism believes that the world is kept in existence by the perpetuation of the substitutionary dying of Christ. Calvinists believe that the world is kept in order (not in existence) by the work of the Spirit, Who cultivates obedience to the Law and Who makes Christ specially present at His sacraments. Baptists have no theory of social order, for they have taken Western nominalism to its extreme of almost total individualism; for them the sacraments are mere symbols.[11]

50. The reconstruction of society means that foundational attention must be paid to the *reconstruction of worship*. Hard thinking must be devoted to architecture, building churches

---

11. See James B. Jordan, ed., *The Failure of the American Baptist Culture*, Christianity and Civilization No. 1 (Tyler, TX: Geneva Divinity School Press, 1982).

that can accommodate true love feasts, orchestras and choirs, sacramental worship in the round, and even places for sacred dancing. Work needs to be done in music, training in psalm singing and chanting, the development of competent choirs and orchestras, writing music truly worthy of the worship of God (as opposed to the cheap junk of the last century or so). The development of *a professional class of theologians and Biblical lawyers*, who can speak to the legal questions of our day and retrain our civilization in the Word of God, is also a task of the tithe. And of course, the general care and retraining of the poor and helpless is a task of the tithe as well.

### *Should the Tithe Always Go To The Church?*

51. Because of the incredible failure of the church in our day, it is very easy to make a case for giving the tithe to parachurch organizations (non-sacramental teaching orders). I believe that the question here must be approached with care. My thesis is that the *elders of the gate* (the local church) should in normal healthy times administer the tithe, and they may use it in part to support various agencies; but that in times of apostasy the tithe must go to the Lord, and this may mean giving it to non-sacramental teaching organizations.

52. It will not do to say that the general office of all believers means that the tithe may be given wherever the individual wants. Nor will it do to say that the special office in the church is to be given the tithe under any and all circumstances. Rule in the church, including the disposition of the tithe, is representative or covenantal. *Ordinarily, the elders of the gate (church) should determine the disposition of the tithe.* Members should not try to designate where their tithe is to be used. They may, of course, give gifts above the tithe for certain purposes.

53. When the special officers in the church apostatize, or become so delinquent that the general officers (members) come to believe that the tithe properly should be redirected, then *the power of the general office* comes into play. Of course, ideally what should happen is that the true Christians should form a true church, and direct their tithes there. This is not always possible, and people rightly choose to give part of their tithe to the local church and part of it to faithful prophetic organizations outside the strict parameters of any particular church.

54. *The tithe goes to the Lord* (Lev. 27:32; Mal. 3:8). When a church ceases to set forth the law of the King, to make present the reality of the Lord, we are obliged to cut off giving it the tithe. To give the tithe to apostates is to rob God. Thus, in some seasons of the history of the church, the tithe will need to go to parachurch institutions, but only because these are really more fully Levitical than the so-called church itself.

55. Sometimes 2 Kings 4:42-44 is pointed to in this regard. The people evidently brought the tithe to the prophets in Northern Israel. This is interpreted as due to an apostasy on the part of the Levites. While I think that this situation is roughly analogous to what has been set forth in #s 53 and 54 above, it is not as parallel a situation as it might seem. Northern Israel was cut off from Jerusalem and the central Levitical work. It was a separate nation. Many if not most of the Levites migrated from Northern Israel to Judah. *The prophets and the schools of the prophets were simply the churches of Northern Israel.* Of course, they were not the national church, for the officially approved cult of Northern Israel was calf worship, Baalism. The prophets formed a *remnant church*, not a parachurch organization.

56. It was the elders of the gate who directed the local tithe to the poor and to the local Levite (Deut. 14:28f.). Similarly, in early America, the churches contributed part of the tithe to support the American Tract Society, the American Bible Society, and various other tithe-agencies, such as those dedicated to missions among immigrants. As the churches became more institutional and less evangelical, local churches were expected to give only to denominational benevolences. With the splitting of the traditional and now apostate churches in the early years of the twentieth century, the fundamentalist groups frequently returned to the practice of supporting "parachurch" tithe agencies. Thus, God's general principles have been applied in varying ways due to circumstances.

## *How to Tithe*

57. Since all life and strength comes from God, we owe a tithe on whatever our hands produce. The tithe is a return to Him for the strength and capital He has given us. The tithe is paid on the increase, what we make with what we have been given. Those who are paid wages and salaries have little prob-

lem calculating 10% of their gross income and paying it to God.

58. The laws of tithing are phrased in terms of a man's business. Thus, if a man has a herd of sheep, he tithes on all the newborn of the year, not just on the sheep he takes out of the field to eat (Leviticus 27:30-33). Thus, a businessman must tithe not simply on what he removes from his business for his own salary, but on what the business itself produces.

59. Tithing is on the increase. The flock as it exists at the beginning of the year has already been tithed on.[12] The tithe is on the newborn. They are not bred before they are tithed, so that money is not to be used before it is tithed on. I have known men who sought to increase their money by investing it, before tithing on it. This is clearly a violation of principle.

60. In Israel, the tithe would have been withdrawn from the crop or herd before the employees would have been paid. At the same time, the employees would not have tithed on their pay, since the crop or herd had already been tithed upon. Thus, a modern employer might choose to subtract salaries from his gross income before tithing, but he should do so only if he knows that his employees will tithe on it. Otherwise, he should calculate and pay his tithe before paying his employees.

61. How about housing and electricity, and other expenses? God provided these things for Israel in guaranteeing each man a plot of land. In terms of agricultural production, God provides the sun and rain. Thus, it may well be argued that the modern businessman may regard housing and power as part of his capital, and subtract these expenses from his gross income before tithing. These are not part of his profit. At the same time, he must tithe on his profit (increase) *before* moving his company into a newer bigger building. Tithing must come before expansion.

62. We can see that applying the tithe principle to modern business leaves us with some grey areas. Thus, we must be careful in judging others, and leave room for God's assessment. If a man has an attitude of seeking to minimize his tithe by including everything under the sun as a capital expense, God will deal with him. On the other hand, God does not desire men to decapitalize themselves in tithing. What can

---

12. In other words, God does not collect a tithe on capital. He grants it by creation. He demands a tithe on the return of capital, on the increase. Application: no property taxes in a Biblical law system.

fairly be counted as foundation capital, and thus expenses necessary to the production of the profit, should be paid before the tithe is calculated.

63. What about *advertising*? Advertising has two purposes: to set forth a business before the eye of the market, and to expand the business to provide an increase in profit. The first function is a necessary capital investment, and should be paid before the tithe is calculated; but the latter is an expansion, and should only be engaged in after the tithe has been paid. What would be a fair way to calculate the difference? I suggest the following. First, Mr. X (a businessman) should subtract his advertising expenses from his gross income for the year. Then he should work out the percentage of his capital expenses over against his profit. Then, that percentage of his gross income which went to necessary capital expenses is the same percentage of his advertising which was necessary to keep him at last year's level, and should be deducted from his net profit before he tithes.

To take a simple example: Christian Enterprises took in $100,000 last year. During the year, CE spent $10,000 in advertising. CE had $45,000 in capital expenses (rent, power, raw materials), and thus $45,000 in profit. Thus, CE can properly assume that of its $10,000 advertising, half was necessary to get the money to pay for capital expenses, and half contributed to profits. Thus, half of the $10,000 was a capital expense, and so $5,000 should be added to overall capital expenses. This leaves profit at $50,000, so that a tithe of $5,000 is owed to God before the business makes any moves to expand.

64. What about *taxes*? Clearly a man owes God His tithe before he owes the state a tax. On the other hand, confiscatory taxation, more than 10% of income, can be viewed as a plague of locusts or as the damage caused by an invading army. (See 1 Samuel 8, where tyranny is expressed as a government which takes 10% or more in taxes, thus making itself god.) Increase for the year can only be calculated in terms of what is left after the locusts have damaged the crop. In terms of this, it might be proper to consider taxes as part of basic capital expenses, rent paid to the invading army, and to pay the tithe on what remains after taxes. I suggest, however, that a man include in his capital expenses only that amount of tax that goes over 10% of his taxable income. In that way, his conscience can be clear, for he is ascribing to tyranny only what tyranny

takes in excess of what the state might properly take.

65. All of this entails a certain amount of juggling. After all, what the state considers taxable income will not be exactly what a Christian might consider titheable income, so that 10% of tax is only a rough way to do service to the principle outlined in #64 above. Also, the state permits deductions from tax based on tithing, up to a certain amount. Thus, precision in tithing is almost certainly impossible. What God honors, however, is more the intention to tithe than the actual amount. After all, God has infinite resources. He can finance Christian reconstruction at any time He chooses. In terms of that, the widow's mite, faithfully given, does more to honor God and bring about Christian reconstruction than does a large tithe calculated by a niggardly businessman seeking to tithe as little as possible.

66. Finally, we should note that tithing is inescapable. God will take his 10%, either voluntarily, or forcibly. Men who do not willingly tithe a generous 10% will find that God does not prosper them. They will find that God gives them over to a spirit of folly, and they make bad business decisions, and lose money. (The book of Haggai deals with this.) When men do not tithe willingly to God's church, God takes the tithe and gives it to His enemies, to raise them up as a scourge to the church. When Christians return to the practice of faithful tithing, God will begin to decapitalize the wicked, and will give dominion back to His people.

# TACTICS OF RESISTANCE USED BY THE PROTESTANT REFORMERS

Otto J. Scott

THE Reformation came into being in opposition to the Renaissance. Its success in this effort is the major reason why modern anti-Christians hate the very memory of the Reformation and its leaders, though had they not appeared, and had their efforts not been successful, it is doubtful if the West would have survived until today.

The Renaissance, therefore, is essential to a proper understanding of the Reformation. It was defined by Burckhardt, in his brilliant but unfinished opus *The Civilization of the Renaissance in Italy*,[1] as the end of the Middle Ages and the beginning of the modern ages. He described it "from the birth of Dante to the death of Michelangelo, a period as long and at least as variegated as, for instance, the time from Watteau to Picasso, or from Milton to James Joyce."[2]

This period of four centuries altered the life of Europe and the attitude of Europeans beyond recall. The rediscovery of pagan literature, with its vicious splendor, the resurrected arguments of the Sophists, especially Plato, regarding the soul, the afterlife, and the possibilities of power excited scholars and poets, and dimmed the glories of Christianity.

Italian towns argued over whether or not they were the birthplaces of famous Romans, and such disputes gradually displaced the shrines of the Middle Ages. Poetry contests were revived, laurel wreaths bestowed, and Latin schools appeared. Dante's *Inferno* resembled Homer's underworld of dead shades, forced to suffer for earthly sins, replete with topical political references.

Fame replaced immortality as the goal of life. To become famous was to achieve the only possible immortality. In cities

1. Phaidon Publishers, 1965.
2. *Ibid.*, Foreword, by L. Goldschieder, p. xi.

like Florence, where men once wore whatever they pleased, fashions appeared, and styles. The Italians began their famous (and still existing) competition with their own past; their imitations of ages long dead, complete to perversions, conspicuous consumption, dazzling displays, ferocious murders, dizzy struggles for power.

Burckhardt described this as the process of creating a state "like a work of art." A new type of ruler appeared: literate, beautifully dressed, a patron of arts and letters, capable of charming the people—and of ruling absolutely. Life without limits became the goal of many.

The names of these tyrants are still held aloft by some writers as worthy of admiration, but their reality was something different. Ludovici (the Moor) Sforza was a multiple murderer and ruler of Milan. Cesare Borgia prowled the streets of Rome at night with his guards, and committed random murders. But these men, and their counterparts, appreciated poetry and music, painting and sculptor. They employed da Vinci, Michelangelo and others, who produced beautiful works of heavenly bliss: advertisements for a Church eroded by vice.

When Luther went to Rome he was appalled. Poisonings were common. Mercenaries strutted: men like Werner von Urslingen, whose haulberk read: "*The enemy of God, of pity and mercy.*" In this environment, virtue appeared helpless. Satanism and witchcraft flourished, and the Inquisition appeared hard on their heels. Torture—unknown since the time of the Romans—made its reappearance as a respected and common tactic of authority.

All this had started out as an effort to expand life beyond narrow and rigid limits. It was promoted and propelled in large measure by the efforts of men gifted in communication; in writing, who were neither clergymen nor scholars in the restricted sense of the Middle Ages. Unwilling to toil in monastic cells, and unable to lead spiritual lives, they led lives precariously balanced between people with money and power, and the masses. This often led (as today), to desperation and to strange expedients, as well as to the creation of poetry, erotica, sermons, fables, and diatribes—often from the same pens. These Humanists, as they were called, resembled the Greek Sophists on a lower level.

But unlike the Sophists, they were able to change. Let us

say, rather, that some were able to change, and were lucky enough to live, toward the end of the Italian Renaissance, when printing appeared. That was Luther's great springboard.

### *The Printing Press*

It was the accidental sight of a copy of one of Gutenburg's Bibles in the library of the convent of Efurt, where Luther was in training for a monk, that fixed his destiny for life. "I was twenty years old," he said later, "before I had even seen the Bible. I had no notion that there existed any other gospels or episodes than those in the service. . . ."[3]

"He opened it and read with inexpressible delight the history of Hannah and her son Samuel. Oh God!" he murmured, "could I but have one of these books, I would ask no other treasure!" "A great revolution forthwith took place in his soul. . . ."[4]

Prior to printing, hand-copied Bibles belonged to the clergy and were seldom seen or read by others. The printers, who were generally not university men but men who had learned, or made themselves learn, different languages in order to make a living, had to copy edit, which in itself created divisions and argument. Bibles began to appear in the vernacular, despite Church prohibitions and regulations that led to arrests, tortures, and even death. A civilization long accustomed to the idea that there is only one truth was riven by multiple expressions. The natural result was enormous intellectual turbulence and a quickening of discontent with the tawdriness of the Renaissance and the corruption of the Church on the part of younger Humanist scholars.

When Luther listed his Ninety-Five Theses, his agenda for a debate, he was acting well within scholarly conventions and customs. He wrote his Theses, after all, in Latin, and not for the masses. Yet they created an enormous international stir, and Luther—six months later, writing to the Pope—expressed amazement.

"It is a mystery to me how my theses, more so than my

3. Samuel Smiles, *The Huguenots* (NY: Harper & Brothers, 1867), pp. 21-22.

4. *Ibid.*

other writings, indeed, those of other professors were spread to so many places. They were meant exclusively for our academic circle here . . . they were written in such language that the common people could hardly understand them. They . . . used academic categories. . . ."[5]

The answer, according to a fascinating monograph, is that the printers translated Luther's writings into German at first "and then into other vernaculars. How did it happen that, soon after being printed in a handful of towns, such as Nuremburg, Leipzig, and Basel, copies were multiplied in such quantities and distributed so widely that the Theses won top billing throughout central Europe—competing for space with news of the Turkish threat in printshop, bookstall, and country fair?"[6]

The "academic circle" to which Luther referred was greatly expanded after the printing appeared. "The scholarly printer who presided over the new centers of erudition was usually a layman and rarely had a college degree. Although it was closer to commercial crossroads than to cloistered precincts, the printer's workshop attracted the most learned and disputatious scholars of the day."[7]

Eisenstein cites a letter "from Beautus Rhenanus to Zwingli in 1519. . . . He will sell more of Luther's tracts if he has no other to offer, Zwingli was told by Beautus in a letter recommending a book peddler."[8]

By these hard-sell methods, 300,000 copies of Luther's thirty publications were sold between 1517 and 1520 . . . at a time when print had the power of a thunderclap. "For the first time in human history a great reading public judged the validity of revolutionary ideas through a mass-medium which used the vernacular languages together with the arts of the journalist and the cartoonist."[9]

---

5. Elizabeth L. Eisenstein, *The Advent of Printing and the Protestant Revolt: A New Approach to the Disruption of Western Christendom*, p. 238; cf. Robert Kingdon, ed., *Transition and Revolution: Problems and Issues of European Renaissance and Reformation History* (Minneapolis: Burgess Publishing Company, 1974).

6. *Idem.*

7. *Ibid.*, p. 239.

8. *Ibid.*, p. 240.

9. *Ibid.*, p. 235.

*The Counter-Reformation*

Within a generation these developments had created an entirely new intellectual climate, had spurred the study of Greek, Latin, and Hebrew, and switched the brightest of the Humanists into new avenues of thought.

That these avenues were religious reflected the European tradition and environment, and had the effect of pushing the ancients and their presumed glories back toward the cemetery. Persons appeared who scoffed at Aristotle, though Calvin was not one of these; Calvin himself was one of the new breed.

Despite exceptions like George Buchanan, the great poet of Scotland, the intellectuals separated along generational lines. Calvin became a Reformer, and Melancthon became a protégé of Luther, but most older Humanists remained, for the most part, within the safe folds of the Roman Catholic Church.

That Church fell upon great difficulties. The Emperor Charles V had loosed his soldiers upon Rome in a famous Sack. Few events in history have had a greater impact upon a people than the Sack of Rome upon the Italians. It came at a time when they had dissipated nearly all their virtue in the cesspool of the Renaissance. "After the loss of youth, love, and hope," Burckhardt wrote, "the only noble concept left in the wreck of character was honor." That had been the last refuge of the pagans as well. It went hand in hand with vengeance, and with taking the law into one's own hands.

The Sack occurred in 1527, and broke the nerve of Italy, which has never recovered. The glittering days were over, and Italians lived under the contempt of French and Spanish conquerors. The Vatican remained, however, a great power. The Pope had his army and navy, his soldiers, his riches, and his potent network of ecclesiastical courts and laws, of reigning Cardinal and Bishop-Princes, of prelates in high places in other courts, a diplomatic service, and a centuries-old creed with enormous international properties and prestige.

The ferment of the Reformers created a counter-Reformation, in which the Popes, shrewd in the lures of the world, turned to art. The Reformers, in reaction, recoiled from beauty as a snare, an illusion; a worldly diversion of the devil. Their protests took the form of attacking churches and pulling down crucifixes, burning paintings, invading and stopping the Mass.

It was a violent, cruel, and energetic age. The Renaissance had seeped from Italy through France and into England and Scotland, into the principalities of Germany and the reaches of Hungary, Poland, and Spain. In Calvin's France, the Queen Mother, Catherine d'Medici, born in Florence of parents who died of syphilis before she was a month old, maneouvered along the lines of Machiavelli. Descended from Lorenzo the Magnificent, granddaughter of one Pope and niece of another, Catherine operated with the help of a private troop of aristocratic whores who seduced men into her purposes.

In that atmosphere, where poison was considered merciful, youthful Reformers like Calvin lived amid dreadful perils. The Church, alarmed at the numbers of books appearing in vernacular tongues, spurred the authorities into suppressions and punishments. This reaction was evoked by a flood of printed works "which are estimated to have reached four million by the end of the fifteenth century and between 1500 and 1533, eighteen more million. In 1533 there were eighteen editions of the German Bible printed at Wittemberg, thirteen at Augsburg, thirteen at Strasbourg, twelve at Basel, and so on."[10]

By this time people were being punished for possessing these volumes, and tortured and executed for selling and printing them. In Paris, during the six months ending in June, 1534, twenty men and one woman were burned alive. In the following year the Sorbonne, still under the administration of the Church, obtained a royal ordinance forbidding printing altogether.[11]

By then it was, of course, far too late. The Church had been morally declining for a long time. The effects of the Renaissance had traveled from southern to northern Europe, and France was in a state of advanced rot. Printing had provided the Humanists, the young, the unhappy, the uncertain, and the searching with the means of knowledge and discussion formerly unknown. The new learning traveled with the speed of light, and brought in its wake the real people of the Book—the Protestants, whose ranks came from those who could read: the *nobility* and the *bourgoisie*.

---

10. Smiles, *op. cit.*, p. 28.

11. *Ibid.*

### *Calvin and Geneva*

The process started in Germany and moved across Europe, encompassing Switzerland. In Switzerland was the city of Geneva. Geneva was an Episcopal seat ruled by a Bishop who was usually connected by birth to the House of Savoy. Because the Bishop was usually a noble, he seldom lived in Geneva, which was managed by an episcopal Council, headed by a Vicar. The city's noble families came from Savoyard ruling classes. Below the Council were several hundred ordained priests in seven city parishes. The city had church hospitals and schools, legalized prostitutes, ecclesiastical courts, and a pattern of living typical of the Renaissance. That is to say, prosperous but immoral, physically comfortable but spiritually unhappy.

The Reformation changed that. Geneva swung with the new tide, and rebelled against the Bishop and the House of Savoy. The city Council, achieving independence, negotiated with other cities and finally allied with Berne. Berne was a great military power at a time when the Swiss soldiers were considered the most efficient in Europe. Berne came to Geneva's aid when Savoy threatened it, and even won surrounding territories for the Genevans. After various struggles the Bishop fled, followed by the majority of his priests, and the city turned Reformist. Church property was seized, church hospitals closed, and charity became secular. The city formally announced its new beliefs in 1536, the year that Calvin's *Institutes* were printed in Basel.

Farel, an older and brilliant Protestant, was well aware that Geneva needed a structure to hold its new faith together, and persuaded Calvin to come to the city. That was no easy task: ". . . things were very disorderly," Calvin said, "the Gospel consisted mostly of having broken idols . . . there were many wicked people."[12] An entire district of the city was occupied by prostitutes, under the rule of their own *Reine du bordel*, the Brothel Queen.[13]

Calvin, Farel, and their associates launched a strict series of regulations that, within a few years, led to a harsh reaction.

12. Robert M. Kingdon, "Was the Protestant Reformation a Revolution? The Case of Geneva," in *Transition and Revolution*.

13. Will and Ariel Durant, *The Reformation* (NY: Simon and Shuster, 1957), p. 469.

Both Farel and Calvin were removed by the City Council and given three days to get out of town. The people publicly rejoiced.

Calvin went to Strasbourg, where he married and worked hard. In Geneva the ministers who replaced him and Farel proved incompetent. The people relapsed into drunkenness, street brawls, naked wanderings.[14] As disorders mounted, those who voted against Farel and Calvin in the Council fell into difficulties for various crimes. The city reconsidered, and Calvin was persuaded to return. He never again left; his name and that of Geneva became forever welded.

Calvin and Farel, however, were French, not Swiss. All their lives they looked toward events in France. And although Calvin corresponded with people all over Europe, and received visitors from all over Europe, it was France and the French who had his closest attention, always.

This is worth emphasizing because Geneva became the center of Calvinism, and Calvin was the great organizer, theorist, and inspiration of Protestantism after Luther. There might, in fact, not have been any Protestant organization had not Calvin placed his superb mind to the task.

From the first, as in the instance of Luther, Calvin's avenue was through the written and printed word. Not that he did not preach; not that he could not talk. His lectures were generally attended by a thousand persons.[15] But around Calvin at Geneva arose Europe's most centralized and busiest printing industry. Scores of printers, as they were then called, created what today would be known as publishing firms. Each had its editors, translaters, and salesmen, its routes and lists, customers and authors. Geneva also had paper-manufactories and ink-makers. The Fuggers, declining but still immensely wealthy, capitalized some of these efforts.[16]

And beyond the printed volumes, tracts, woodcuts, special brochures, and broadsides that Geneva shot across Europe were the schools and special trainings that the Calvinists created for their training of pastors.

A considerable percentage of those who came to Geneva to be trained were from noble families and a majority from the

---

14. *Ibid.*, p. 471.

15. Robert M. Kingdon *Geneva and the Coming of the Wars of Religion in France* (Geneva: Droz, 1956), p. 15.

16. *Ibid.*, pp. 93-96.

bourgeoise. The intellectual nature of Protestantism and its reliance upon literacy and reasoning militated against candidates from the lower classes in its earlier stages. The city of Geneva did not, of course, consist entirely of candidates for the Calvinist church. The majority of French refugees who flocked into the city were merchants or artisans or displaced nobles whose livelihoods were not involved with preaching. These individuals retained, like refugees around the world, a keen interest in developments in their native land. Many came and went on silent journeys, and it would be naive to assume that either Calvin or his associates kept aloof from these private citizens.

This was especially not practical because Calvin was never the *ruler* of Geneva. He had immense powers of persuasion and his personality was apparently formidable. But he had no armed men, no special authority over the city except eloquence, reason, and moral force.

He relied upon those intangibles at a time of brute power and widespread cruelty so persuasive, so savage, and so gross in its applications, that an ordinary person of that time would be considered nearly monstrous today in his attitude toward punishments, floggings, executions, pain in general.

### *The Secret Army*

When students graduated from the Academy in Geneva, they were assigned various posts, sometimes in France. These were dangerous trips; so dangerous that when the permanent ministers of Geneva went to France they left their families behind, and the city allowed those families to keep the ministerial house and even receive the minister's salary.[17]

Those sent to France were given an accredited letter. These letters were demanded by the receiving congregations; without them, a young preacher could be turned away, and this was an important factor in Calvin's system of discipline and control. On the other hand, the letters had to be well concealed, for if discovered enroute to a congregation, the bearer could be put to death. In 1533, five Lausanne students enroute had been betrayed, and all five were burned to death, one after another, at the same stake in Lyon.

17. *Ibid.*, p. 35.

Among the precautions for travel were *false papers* and *false names*. These disguises were condoned by the authorities in Geneva because of the holy purpose for which they were adopted. Nevertheless, the number of aliases employed confuse the records of Geneva for historians, so that precise identities are sometimes—even now—unknown.[18]

The risks that were taken were as high as any known today, just as the mercilous nature of the authorities then are matched by the totalitarian powers of modern times. Some of the travelers seem to have resorted to obscure mountain routes up into Dauphine. A Dauphine Protestant in the 1950's told historian Robert M. Kingdon that "old folks can still point out the network of mountain paths by which the ministers came into France." The region is still dotted with stone farmhouses that contain secret hiding places behind chimneys or in cellars, a day's walk apart, that were used by the Underground against the Nazis during World War II, and that were created during the period of the French religious wars and the time of Calvin.

Some pastors used commercial routes, and passed themselves off as merchants. The records of the Bernese bailiff in Lausanne contains a copy of a travel document used by preacher Jehan Richard, who went to the church of Crest in Dauphine, bearing a passport written in Latin, made out in the proper form, identifying him as Richardus, a "merchant." Most such documents were destroyed after serving their purpose; this one was overlooked.

False papers and identities, special reports, hidden credentials, and carefully prepared routes dotted with hiding places, lookouts, and helpers, explain why few preachers were captured enroute to their churches. "The majority," according to Kingdon, "(were seized) after arrival in their new parishes when they were actually exercising their religious mission."

As the years passed, the Calvinists established a network of over 2,000 churches and congregations throughout France. The concentrations of these converts were not, of course, uniform. But it should not be forgotten that in those days the pulpit served as a news agency, into which information of a political and economic, as well as religious nature flowed, and

18. *Ibid.*, pp. 33, 35, 38, 39, 40.

from which news was disseminated. The flow of information from France to Geneva was systematic and organized. In effect, Calvin and his associates monitored France.

Their connections were, of course, more widespread than France alone. In the 1550s John Knox of Scotland arrived in Geneva and was more deeply impressed by Calvin and the order he had created in that city than with anyone he met or heard since the early days of his conversion. Knox had grown up in lawless Scotland, where vice of every description reigned with notoriety; he marveled forever over the reins that Calvin had persuaded the Genevans to accept. In Geneva, Knox became a Calvinist, and the structure that Calvin created served as Knox's model when he returned to Scotland.

In 1556, Knox, having lit a series of fires in Scotland, returned to Dieppe and to Geneva. His letters home were signed "John Sinclair," his mother's name.[19] In Geneva, Knox joined a congregation of English refugees (from Bloody Mary), where he was elected a minister. In his conversations with Calvin and Beza, Knox questioned the traditional doctrine of obedience to lawful rulers, irrespective of their policies. He believed, mainly on the basis of the Old Testament, that Christians had a duty to rise against the rule of unbelieving rulers. Judged in that light, virtually all the monarchs of Europe were usurpers. Calvin and Beza were not willing to go that far—at least in public.

In private, however, Calvin from a distance and Beza personally encouraged the House of Navarre, close to the Protestant cause, to compete for control with Catherine d'Medici and her royal sons. In effect, Geneva silently followed a policy that Knox more boldly proclaimed.

Knox was not the only Calvinist moving in this direction in regions beyond the immediate environs of Geneva. The Calvinists of Holland were inching their way toward a break with Catholic Spain and its constricting rule. There were regions in Germany where Calvinists were breaking with both temporal rulers.

Scotland, however, remained an outstanding example of the effectiveness of Calvinist principles when boldly applied. Knox returned there in 1559, after—by correspondence—having indoctrinated the nobility with the idea that it was

19. Hasper Ridley, *John Knox* (Oxford: Oxford University Press, 1968), p. 241.

their duty to organize a Protestant regime over the objections of the Catholic Queen Regent. As part of his campaign, Knox also issued his famous and disturbing *Blasts of the Trumpet* against what he termed *A Monstrous Regiment of Women*, in which Catherine d'Medici, Bloody Mary, and the Queen Regent of Scotland served as horrid examples of all the frailties and follies of the female sex, which Knox regarded as unworthy of rule over males or kingdoms.[20]

Knox's books, which created a sensation, were printed in Geneva. Some of them embarrassed Calvin, who maintained a close and friendly correspondence with the Duchess of Ferrara, an ardent Calvinist and daughter of King Louis XII, but Calvin was not the autocrat of Geneva that history pictures. He had no real control over the printers, who like their breed to this day, would print whoever and whatever would bring in a profit, irrespective of viewpoint, tone, or truth.

If Knox embarrassed in some minor ways, however, he was a brilliant success in many others. He landed in Scotland, and everywhere he toured he left Calvinist crowds that attacked the old Roman Catholic churches and rose against the old regime. By 1559 Scotland was the first completely Calvinist nation in the world; a tremendous triumph both internally and externally; one that changed the mind of the British Isles forever, and through Britain, the world.

The loss of Scotland was a diplomatic blow to France that was accompanied by the rise of Calvinist influence within France itself. Unlike the situation in Scotland, where Knox had successfully enlisted the majority of the Scots nobility, the Calvinists had enlisted only part of the French nobility. They were opposed most effectively by the powerful Guise dynasty, acting through both the Duc and the Cardinal of Lorraine. The Calvinists of France, therefore, had to walk softly.

### *The Calvinist Underground in France*

Each member of a congregation usually had to swear an *oath of secrecy* regarding the identities of his fellow-worshipers. In several instances, and even at one Synod (also secret), some conversation was devoted to the difficulties such an oath

20. This work appeared in 1558, and created more of a stir than any single book since Luther's Theses.

could bring in its wake if a member was arrested, for it was then the custom to force a prisoner to swear to tell the truth. In such an instance, which oath took precedence? The Synod decided that the first oath was paramount, and that the second oath, being under duress, could be broken without sin. Persons in such straits were advised to tell their jailors that they would "reveal nothing which would return to the dishonor of God, or which would damage a neighbor."

Services themselves were also held in secret in private homes, at night, behind heavily curtained windows. Members were checked at the door. Sometimes barns and fields were used. Special care was taken to conceal the identity of the pastor, the main quarry of the authorities. On numerous occasions other men were led away and allowed themselves to be taken, and to suffer, in the pastor's stead. There were instances of daring rescues of pastors who had been captured. Geneva envoy Paumier escaped from the Troyes church "on the night preceding the day on which he was condemned to death, (he was) so subtly and dexterously, without any noise or breaking of doors, taken from the prison, that his enemies circulated a rumor that the devil had saved him."[21]

Each setback seemed to provide the means for an advance of the cause. When Ann du Bourg, a member of the Paris Parlement, was arrested for resisting pressures against "heretics," he smuggled out of prison an attack on the legitimacy of a monarch who attempted to force his subjects to live "contrary to the will of God." This was an important milestone in the development of Protestant thinking regarding the rights of man, and although du Bourg was burned for heresy and sedition at the instigation of the Cardinal of Lorraine, he left a testament that was to help change the world.

Each year, in fact, carried the Calvinists deeper into maneouvers against the old regime. The Conspiracy of Ambois, in which Beza was personally involved, rotated around a reckless plot to kidnap the King and force a change in the royal policy toward Huguenots. It failed, and Calvin denied any complicity. Rumors to the contrary persisted, and eventually Calvin and Beza brought slander charges in Geneva against one persistent gossiper. No evidence of their complicity

---

21. *Geneva and the Coming of the Wars of Religion in France, op. cit.*, p. 51.

was revealed, but on the other hand one would not have expected a Genevan court to convict two such outstanding men for activities that might have changed Geneva's enemies. At the very least the transcripts indicate that Calvin was against the plot on practical grounds and that Beza was more enthusiastic. And at one point, Calvin very significantly told the court that he would have approved of the venture had it been led "by the man who ought to be chief of the Council of the King according to the laws of France."[22] In other words, Antoine de Bourbon, King of Navarre, first Prince of the Blood. This stab at the Duc d'Guise, the actual chief of the Council and leader of anti-Huguenot forces, indicates that Calvin was, by the time of the Ambois Conspiracy, intellectually involved in the political situation in France, and Beza—his number-two man—more personally involved, as the man in the field. It should be kept in mind, however, that Calvin did not act as a modern chief executive, a President or a Premier, or even a Pope. He had no direct authority over Beza or the other ministers; he was not an office-holder in the modern sense, with fixed powers. If some of the ministers of Geneva, including Beza, chose to help political circles in France, this was not Calvin's responsibility. The distinction is important, and important to remember. Calvinism did not freeze its structure during the time of Calvin.

The Conspiracy of Ambois did, however, have a long-lasting consequence. The arguments over the wisdom—both theologically as well as politically—reminded the Calvinists that Beza wrote a book titled *On the Authority of Magistrates in the Punishment of Heretics*. The immediate cause of this book was the storm of criticism that rose in the wake of the burning of Servetus, in Geneva. In his response, Beza argued that heresy could be suppressed by force, if that force was applied by proper and legal authorities. In fact, he went further, and declared that *local authorities could defy even higher national authorities on religious grounds*. It took no great powers of analysis to see in this defense an argument in favor of rebellion, but rebellion led by the Godly, and not by mobs.

"Calvinism began to reach flood tide in France in 1561 and climbed to its crest in 1562, just as the first religious war began."[23] The contemporary estimates were that Calvinists

22. *Ibid.*, p. 69.
23. *Ibid.*, p. 79.

had 2,150 churches and a total estimated membership of 3 million out of a population estimated at 20 million.

This strength was sufficient for the Prince of Conde to rally the Protestants in war against the Crown in 1562. The Calvinists sent so many pastors from Switzerland to help this effort that for a time not one remained in Lausanne. Agents scurried back and forth, and by the time the war ended, two years later, religious toleration, and the rights of the Calvinists, had been expanded.

In the midst of this effort, printing and writing continued as before. In 1561 Calvin produced thirteen titles, in 1562, another thirteen, seven by Beza in 1561, one in 1562, and so on. Nevertheless, there was some slackening of polemics in 1561 and 1562, because the best of the polemicists had gone to the war. Therefore a preponderance of devotional works appeared. But the flood of books, brochures, and tracts continued, and "their cumulative effect must have been profoundly corrosive of Catholic power in France."[24]

Geneva also raised money for the Calvinist cause during the war, and Kingdon terms Geneva "the arsenal of Calvinism" during this period. It was to maintain this role for the duration of the religious wars; a period that was to last some forty years. Such a protracted struggle is too dense with events for detailed description. Let it suffice to say that after Calvin died, on May 24, 1564, Calvinism underwent an alteration.

Theodore Beza, Calvin's successor, was more scholastically learned than his great predecessor, but less theologically original. On the other hand, he had more worldly gifts, was experienced in diplomatic matters, and, being a member of the lesser nobility, had more aristocratic manners and attitudes, and better personal access to higher circles.

Beza, being French, followed but did not direct events in Scotland, Holland, Germany, Hungary, and other regions where Calvinism advanced. His primary interest was in France and French politics—next, of course, to the principles of Calvinism and their expansion. Consequently, a good deal of Beza's attention and that of the Geneva Company of Pastors was focused upon the internal structure of the Calvinist churches, their administration and operations.

---

24. *Ibid.*, p. 101.

These disputes engaged the attention of a number of Synods, while brief localized wars broke out twice more in France. The methods of the Calvinists did not basically alter during these years; they maintained their secret meetings and even though some toleration was gained, deception was essential to survival.

Nevertheless, they seemed to make steady progress culminating in the agreement to have the Prince of Navarre, Henry Bourbon, marry the Princess Margaret, daughter of Catherine d'Medici, in August, 1572.

### *St. Bartholomew's Day: Total War*

Because the previous two years had been the most pleasant and least-disturbed of all those in the years since the French religious wars started, the Calvinists considered themselves secure. The marriage, with its blend of a Protestant Prince with a Catholic Princess, seemed to most the epitome of cooperation and the strongest possible indication of better days and ways to come.

At this moment, when the flower of Protestant nobility had gathered in Paris in honor of their standard-bearer, the Queen Mother Catherine and her son, King Charles IX, summoned the youthful Duc d'Guise, and ordered him to assassinate the Protestant leader, Admiral Coligny. Coligny, already badly wounded by a sniper during a parade, was in bed at the time the order was given, on the dawn of St. Bartholomew's Day. Coligny's house was ringed with royal troops, ostensibly to protect the Admiral from further attacks; they obeyed the orders of the Duc d'Guise, who was accompanied by the Duc de Angouleme. Most of Coligny's attendants, after barring the door, escaped over the rooftops, but the Admiral was too feeble to follow. The soldiers broke the door down and chopped him to death with swords and axes. His body was thrown out the window to the two dukes, one of whom wiped the blood away to verify Coligny's identity.

The mob was summoned by the ringing in the bell tower of St. Germain l'Auxerrois, and gathered around Coligny's cadaver. It was mutilated and separated into parts; the mob surged into the streets and three hundred of the royal guard, wearing white sashes on their left arms and white crosses on their hats for identification, swarmed through the city, leading the attacks upon the Calvinists. Men, women, and children were murdered; the King himself stood in the window of the palace with an arquebus and fired upon people from the Louvre. The massacre lasted three days and thousands of bodies were flung into the Seine.

As news of this proceeding reached other towns and cities of France, similar massacres were conducted. Lyon, Rouen, Dieppe, Havre, and other places were drenched in blood. Estimates vary from 50,000 upward; huge numbers in that time. Arguments persist, as always, over the precision of the statistics, but none is possible over the significance of the event.

That made the Calvinists a minority in France for generations to come, and set the stage for Louis XIV. The Renaissance had won a victory, though it was the victory of a stage, a period.

The Calvinists fled France in great numbers: some to England, some to Switzerland, some to Germany, some to other parts. In England, Elizabeth and the Cecils shook with anger; St. Bartholomew's ended Catholic chances in England. Yet the Vatican rejoiced, and the Machiavellian school approved of a final stroke that ended, it seemed, disorders among the French.

The Calvinists of the Low Countries, however, took the lesson to heart. The realization that there would be no mercy and no reconciliation led to eighty years of struggle against Spain, and the loss to that empire of Holland. The Calvinists, in other words, did not lose heart. The movement proceeded.

### *Renaissance or Reformation?*

One of the reasons for a resurgence of interest in this period and these events has been the steady espansion of despotic anti-Christian power on the part of governments in our own century and in these times. Scholars have begun to look, once again, into the rise of Calvinism and the manner in which it spread across Northern Europe to alter our civilization.

In the view of contemporary historian Robert M. Kingdon, Calvin and Protestantism achieved a genuine revolution by *overthrowing a ruling class*: the Roman Catholic clergy. That class represented a widespread international system using a special elite language, with its own courts and canon law, its own military strength and financial power, its own political connections and official authority.[25]

It would not, of course, have given way under pressure alone had it not been seriously weakened from within by the corruption of centuries. The Renaissance, which represented a turn toward the world and away from religion, was held by Burckhardt to be the declining stage of Christianity. If Protestantism had not arisen, it is conceivable that Christianity would have completely collapsed, à la the religion of the Greeks and the Romans, with similar results, some centuries ago.

As it was, the theories and pattern of the Renaissance remained a part of European thought, to resume a fashionable appeal during the Enlightenment. And although the Enlightenment, which Peter Gay described as "the new Paganism," led directly to the massacres of the French Revolution, the 19th century, once again, with the sanction of Darwinism, resumed the underlying themes of the Renaissance. We today, sated with scenes of vice and the promotion of decadence, are well aware of what it must have been like to have seen Italy through Luther's eyes; something not too different from modern Paris, with its sex shows for tourists, or New York, with its endemic viciousness. The anti-Christian nature of the Renaissance and the Enlightenment, and of Darwinism, Freudianism, and other mind-sets of today pose the same problems and challenges to us that the early Calvinists confronted in their day.

They used, as is clear, the "wisdom of the serpent" in some of their responses. It would be amusing, if it were not tragic, that those who advise some similar ruses today are held to be violating assumed regulations of unnatural purity, drawn up by persons who hold themselves to be holier than God Almighty. One diligent worker for the Gospel for instance, known as Brother Andrew, managed to smuggle a large number of Bibles into Communist China past the noses of the commissars, by printing them in small red-covered books, which resembled the notorious sayings of Mao-Tse-Tung. Brother Andrew was actually criticized by some individuals for this, on the grounds that his tactic was dishonest.

The world will not long respect nor harbor such unworldly

25. *Was the Protestant Reformation a Revolution? passim*. pp. 53-77.

attitudes. The war that engaged all the talents, the strength, the courage, and the wiles of the Calvinists has resumed in our time, and will demand from us as much, or more, than it demanded then from Calvin, Beza, and the Geneva Company of Pastors and their congregations.

## THE USE OF MONEY

A Sermon by John Wesley

*Editor's Introduction*

WESLEY'S sermon on the use of money was one of the most influential he ever preached. The principles he outlined were taken to heart by his followers, and if the truth were known, probably did more to reform their lives than any short-lived emotional revivals could have. In a short span of time, the lower classes in England and America, who had been most responsive to Methodism, began to acquire power and influence, which they put to good use in the economic and social reforms of the next century. In the United States, hard-working and tithing Methodists erected colleges everywhere, many of which are still among the best academically in the nation (e.g., Vanderbilt, Emory, Southern Methodist University, to name but a few).

I have included the sermon here, because what Wesley outlines is one of the most effective of all tactics of Christian Resistance. True resistance is reconstruction, and if Christians return to these principles, we shall overcome secular humanism in a very short time.

(To save space, and to highlight the most important parts of the sermon, I have abbreviated some sections.)

* * * * * *

> *"I say unto you, Make to yourselves friends of the mammon of unrighteousness; that, when ye fail, they may receive you into everlasting habitations" (Luke 16:9).*

Our Lord, having finished the beautiful parable of the prodigal son, which he had particularly addressed to those who murmured at his receiving publicans and sinners, adds another relation of a different kind, addressed rather to the children of God. "He said unto his disciples," not so much to the scribes and Pharisees, to whom he had been speaking before, — "There was a certain rich man, who had a steward, and he was accused to him of wasting his goods. And calling him, he said, Give an account of thy stewardship, for thou canst be no longer steward," verses 1,2. After reciting the method which the bad steward used, to provide against the day of necessity, our Saviour adds, "His Lord commended the unjust steward"; namely, in this respect, that he used timely precaution; and subjoins this weighty reflection, "The children of this world are wiser in their generation, than the children of light," verse 8: those who seek no other portion than this world, "are wiser" (not absolutely; for they are, one and all, the veriest fools, the most egregious madmen under heaven; but, "in their generation," in their own way; they are more consistent with themselves; they are truer to their acknowledged principles; they more steadily pursue their end) "than the children of light"; — than they who see "the light of the glory of God, in the face of Jesus Christ." Then follow the words above recited: "And I," — the only begotten Son of God, the Creator, Lord, and Possessor, of heaven and earth and all that is therein; the Judge of all, to whom ye are to "give an account of your stewardship," when ye "can be no longer stewards"; "I say unto you," — learn in this respect, even of the unjust steward, — "make yourselves friends," by wise, timely precaution, "of the mammon of unrighteousness." "Mammon" means riches, or money. It is termed "the mammon of unrighteousness," because of the unrighteous manner wherein it is frequently procured, and wherein even that which was honestly procured is generally employed. "Make yourselves friends" of this, by doing all possible good, particularly to the children of God; "that when ye fail," — when ye return to dust, when ye have no more place under the sun, — those of them who are gone before, "may welcome you, into everlasting habitations."

An excellent branch of Christian wisdom is here inculcated by our Lord on all his followers, namely, The right use of money; — a subject largely spoken of, after their manner, by men of the world; but not sufficiently considered by those whom God hath chosen out of the world. These, generally, do not consider, as the importance of the subject requires, the use of this excellent talent. Neither do they understand how to employ it to the greatest advantage; the introduction of which into the world, is one admirable instance of the wise and gracious providence of God. It has, indeed, been the manner of poets, orators, and philosophers, in almost all ages and nations, to rail at this, as the grand corrupter of the world, the bane of virtue, the pest of human society. Hence, nothing so commonly heard, as

> *Ferrum, ferroque nocentius aurum:*
> Gold, more mischievous than keenest steel.

Hence the lamentable complaint,

> *Effodiuntur opes, irritamenta malorum:*
> Wealth is dug up, incentive to all ill.

Nay, one celebrated writer gravely exhorts his countrymen, in order to banish all vice at once, to "throw all their money into the sea:"

> *In mare proximum,*
> *Summi materiem mali!*

But is not all this mere empty rant? Is there any solid reason therein? By no means. For, let the world be as corrupt as it will, is gold or silver to blame? "The love of money," we know, "is the root of all evil"; but not the thing itself. The fault does not lie in the money, but in them that use it. It may be used ill: and what may not? But it may likewise be used well: it is full as applicable to the best, as to the worst uses. It is of unspeakable service to all civilized nations, in all the common affairs of life: it is a most compendious instrument of transacting all manner of business, and (if we use it according to Christian wisdom) of doing all manner of good. It is true, were man in a state of innocence, or were all men "filled with the Holy Ghost," so that, like the infant church at Jerusalem, "no man counted any thing he had his own," but "distribution was made to every one as he had need," the use of it would be superseded; as we cannot conceive there is any thing of the kind among the inhabitants of heaven. But, in the present state of mankind, it is an excellent gift of God, answering the noblest ends. In the hands of his children, it is food for the hungry, drink for the thirsty, raiment for the naked: it gives to the traveller and stranger where to lay his head. By it we may supply the place of a husband to the widow, and of a father to the fatherless. We may be a defense for the oppressed, a means of health to the sick, of ease to them that are in pain; it may be as eyes to the blind, as feet to the lame; yea, a lifter up from the gates of death!

It is, therefore, of the highest concern, that all who fear God, know how to employ this valuable talent; that they be instructed how it may answer these glorious ends, and in the highest degree. And, perhaps, all the instructions which are necessary for this, may be reduced to three plain rules, by the exact observance whereof we may approve ourselves faithful stewards of "the mammon of unrighteousness."

### *I. Gain All You Can*

The first of these is, (he that heareth, let him understand!) "Gain all you can." Here we may speak like the children of the world: we meet them on their own ground. And it is our bounden duty to do this: we ought to gain all we can gain, without buying gold too dear, without paying more for it than it is worth. But this it is certain we ought not to do; we ought not to gain money at the expense of life, nor (which is in effect the same thing) at the expense of our health. Therefore, no gain whatsoever should induce us to enter into, or to continue in, any employ, which is of such a kind, or is attended with so hard or so long labour as to impair our constitution. Neither should we begin or continue in any business, which necessarily deprives us of proper seasons for food and sleep, in such a proportion as our nature requires. Indeed there is a great difference here. Some employments are absolutely and totally unhealthy; as those which imply the dealing much with arsenic, or other equally hurtful minerals, or the breathing an air tainted with steams of melting lead, which must at length destroy the firmest constitution. Others may not be absolutely unhealthy, but only to persons of a weak constitution. Such are those which require many hours to be spent in writing; especially if a person write sitting, and lean upon his stomach, or remain long in an uneasy posture. But whatever it is which reason or experience shows to be destructive of health or strength, that we may not submit to; seeing "the life is more [valuable] than meat, and the body than raiment": and, if we are already engaged in such an employ, we should exchange it, as soon as possible, for some, which, if it lessen our gain, will, however, not lessen our health.

We are, secondly, to gain all we can without hurting our

mind, any more than our body. For neither may we hurt this: we must preserve, at all events, the spirit of a healthful mind. Therefore, we may not engage or continue in any sinful trade; any that is contrary to the law of God, or of our country. Such are all that necessarily imply our robbing or defrauding the king of his lawful customs. For it is, at least, as sinful to defraud the king of his right, as to rob our fellow subjects: and the king has full as much right to his customs, as we have to our houses and apparel. Other businesses there are, which, however innocent in themselves, cannot be followed with innocence now; at least, not in England; such, for instance, as will not afford a competent maintenance, without cheating or lying, or conformity to some custom which is not consistent with a good conscience: these, likewise, are sacredly to be avoided, whatever gain they may be attended with provided we follow the custom of the trade; for, to gain money, we must not lose our souls. There are yet others which many pursue with perfect innocence, without hurting either their body or mind; and yet perhaps, you cannot: either they may entangle you in that company, which would destroy your soul; and by repeated experiments it may appear, that you cannot separate the one from the other; or there may be an idiosyncrasy, —a peculiarity in your constitution of soul, (as there is in the bodily constitution of many,) by reason whereof that employment is deadly to you, which another may safely follow. So I am convinced, from many experiments, I could not study, to any degree of perfection, either mathematics, arithmetic, or algebra, without being a deist, if not an atheist: and yet others may study them all their lives, without sustaining any inconvenience. None, therefore, can here determine for another; but every man must judge for himself, and abstain from whatever he, in particular, finds to be hurtful to his soul.

We are, thirdly, to gain all we can, without hurting our neighbour. But this we may not, cannot do, if we love our neighbour as ourselves. We cannot, if we love every one as ourselves, hurt any one *in his substance.* We cannot devour the increase of his lands, and perhaps the lands and houses themselves, by gaming, by overgrown bills (whether on account of physic, of law, or any thing else). . . . Neither may we gain by hurting our neighbour *in his body.* . . . [such] is dear bought gain. And so is whatever is procured by hurting our neighbour *in his soul:* by ministering, suppose, either directly or indirectly, to his unchastity or intemperance; which certainly none can do, who has any fear of God, or any real desire of pleasing him. . . . These cautions and restrictions being observed, it is the bounden duty of all, who are engaged in worldly business, to observe that first and great rule of Christian wisdom, with respect to money, "Gain all you can." Gain all you can by honest industry. Use all possible diligence in your calling. Lose no time. If you understand yourself, and your relation to God and man, you know you have none to spare. If you understand your particular calling, as you ought, you will have no time that hangs upon your hands. Every business will afford some employment sufficient for every day and every hour. That wherein you are placed, if you follow it in earnest, will leave you no leisure for silly, unprofitable diversions. You have always something better to do, something that will profit you, more or less. And "whatsoever thy hand findeth to do, do it with thy might." Do it as soon as possible: no delay! no putting off from day to day, or from hour to hour! Never leave anything till tomorrow, which you can do today. And do it as well as possible. Do not sleep or yawn over it: put your whole strength to the work. Spare no pains. Let nothing be done by halves, or in a slight and careless manner. Let nothing in your business be left undone, if it can be done by labour or patience.

Gain all you can, by common sense, by using in your business all the understanding which God has given you. It is amazing to observe, how few do this; how men run on in the same dull track with their forefathers. But whatever they do, who know not God, this is no rule for you. It is a shame for a Christian not to improve upon *them*, in whatever he takes in hand. You should be continually learning, from the experience of others, or from your own experience, reading, and reflection, to do every thing you have to do better today, than you did yesterday. And see that you practise whatever you learn, that you may make the best of all that is in your hands.

### *II. Save All You Can*

Having gained all you can, by honest wisdom, and unwearied diligence, the second rule of Christian prudence is, "save all you can." Do not throw the precious talent into the sea: leave that folly to heathen philosophers. Do not throw it away in idle expenses, which is just the same as throwing it into the sea. Expend no part of it merely to gratify the desire of the flesh, the desire of the eye, or the pride of life. . . . Who would expend anything in gratifying these desires, if considered, that to gratify them is to increase them? Nothing can be more certain than this: daily experience shows, the more they are indulged, they increase the more. Whenever, therefore, you expend any thing to please your taste or other senses, you pay so much for sensuality. When you lay out money to please your eye, you give so much for an increase in curiosity, — for a stronger attachment to these pleasures which perish in the using. While you are purchasing anything which men use to applaud, you are purchasing more vanity. Had you not then enough of vanity, sensuality, curiosity, before? Was there need of any addition? And would you pay for it too? What manner of wisdom is this? Would not the literally throwing your money into the sea be a less mischievous folly?

And why should you throw away money upon your children, any more than upon yourself, in delicate food, in gay or costly apparel, in superfluities of any kind? Why should you purchase for them more pride or lust, more vanity, or foolish and hurtful desires? They do not want any more; they have enough already; nature has made ample provision for them; why should you be at farther expense to increase their temptations and snares, and to pierce them through with many sorrows?

Do not leave it to them to throw away. If you have good reason to believe they would waste what is now in your possession, in gratifying, and thereby increasing, the desire of the flesh, the desire of the eye, or the pride of life; at the peril of theirs and your own soul, do not set these traps in their way. Do not offer your sons or your daughters unto Belial, any more than unto Moloch. Have pity upon them, and remove out of their way what you may easily foresee would increase their sins, and consequently plunge them deeper into everlasting perdition! How amazing then is the infatuation of those parents, who think they can never leave their children enough! What! cannot you leave them enough arrows, firebrands, and death? Not enough of foolish and hurtful desires? Not enough of pride, lust, ambition, vanity? Not enough of everlasting burnings? Poor wretch! Thou fearest where no fear is. Surely both thou and they, when ye are lifting up your eyes in hell, will have enough both of "the worm that never dieth," and of "the fire that never shall be quenched!"

"What then would you do if you were in my case? If you had a considerable fortune to leave?" Whether I *would* do it or no, I know what I *ought* to do: this will admit of no reasonable question. If I had one child, elder or younger, who knew the value of money, one who, I believed, would put it to the true use, I should think it my absolute, indispensable duty, to leave that child the bulk of my fortune, and to the rest just so much as would enable them to live in the manner they had been accustomed to do. "But what if all your children were equally ignorant of the true use of money?" I ought then, (hard saying! who can hear it?) to give each what would keep him above want; and to bestow all the rest in such a manner as I judged would be most for the glory of God.

### *III. Give All You Can*

But let not any man imagine that he has done anything, barely by going thus far, by "gaining and saving all he can," if he were to stop here. All this is nothing, if a man go not forward, if he does not point all this at a farther end. Nor, indeed, can a man properly by said to save anything, if he only lays it up. You may as well throw your money into the sea, as bury it in the earth. And you may as well bury it in the earth, as in your chest, or in the bank of England. Not to use, is effectually to throw it away. If, therefore, you would indeed "make yourselves friends of the mammon of unrighteousness," add the third rule to the two preceding. Having first gained all you can, and secondly saved all you can, then "give all you can."

In order to see the ground and reason of this, consider, when the Possessor of heaven and earth brought you into being, and placed you in this world, he placed you here not as a proprietor, but a steward: as such he entrusted you for a season with goods of various kinds: but the sole property of these still rests in him, nor can ever be alienated from him. As you yourself are not your own, but his, such is, likewise, all that you enjoy. Such is your soul and your body, not your own, but God's. And so is your substance in particular. And he has told you in the most clear and express terms, how you are to employ it for him, in such a manner, that it may be all a holy sacrifice, acceptable through Christ Jesus. And this light, easy service, he hath promised to reward with an eternal weight in glory.

The directions which God has given us, touching the use of our worldly substance, may be comprised in the following particulars. If you desire to be a faithful and wise steward, out of that portion of your Lord's goods, which he has for the present lodged in your hands, but with the right of resuming whenever it pleases him, first, provide things needful for yourself; food to eat, raiment to put on, whatever nature moderately requires for preserving the body in health and strength. Secondly, provide these for your wife, your children, your servants, or any others who pertain to your household. If, when this is done, there be an overplus still, "as you have opportunity, do good unto all men." In so doing, you give all you can; nay, in a sound sense, all you have: for all that is laid out in this manner, is really given to God. You "render unto God the things that are God's," not only by what you give to the poor, but also by that which you expend in providing things needful for yourself and your household.

If then a doubt should at any time arise in your mind concerning what you are going to expend, either on yourself or any part of your family, you have an easy way to remove it. Calmly and seriously inquire, 1. In expending this, am I acting according to my character? Am I acting herein, not as a proprietor, but as a steward of my Lord's goods? 2. Am I doing this in obedience to his word? In what scripture does he require me so to do? 3. Can I offer up this action, this expense, as a sacrifice to God through Jesus Christ? 4. Have I reason to believe, that for this very work I shall have a reward at the resurrection of the just? You will seldom need anything more to remove any doubt which arises on this head; but, by this four fold consideration, you will receive clear light as to the way wherein you should go.

If any doubt still remain, you may farther examine yourself by prayer, according to those heads of inquiry. Try whether you can say to the Searcher of hearts, your conscience not condemning you, "Lord, thou seest I am going to expend this sum, on that food, apparel, furniture. And thou knowest, I act therein with a single eye, as a steward of thy goods, expending this portion of them thus, in pursuance of the design thou hadst in entrusting me with them. Thou knowest I do this in obedience to thy word, as thou commandest, and because thou commandest it. Let this, I beseech thee, be a holy sacrifice, acceptable through Jesus Christ! And give me a witness in myself, that for this labour of love, I shall have a recompense, when thou rewardest every man according to his works." Now if your conscience bear you witness in the Holy Ghost, that this prayer is well pleasing to God, then have you no reason to doubt, but that expense is right and good, and such as will never make you ashamed.

### *Conclusion*

You see then, what it is to "make yourselves friends of the mammon of unrighteousness," and by what means you may procure, "that when ye fail, they may receive you into everlasting habitations." You see the nature and extent of truly Christian prudence, so far as it relates to the use of that great talent, money. Gain all you can without hurting either yourself or your neighbour, in soul or body, by applying hereto with unintermitted diligence, and with all the understanding which God has given you; – save all you can, by cutting off every expense which serves only to indulge foolish desire; to gratify either the desire of the flesh, the desire of the eye, or the pride of life; waste nothing, living or dying, on sin or folly, whether for yourself or your children; – and then, give all you can, or, in other words, give all you have to God. Do not stint yourself, like a Jew rather than a Christian, to this or that proportion. Render unto God . . . in such a manner that you may give a good account of your stewardship, when ye can be no longer stewards; in such a manner as the oracles of God direct, both by general and particular precepts; in such a manner, that whatever ye do may be "a sacrifice of a sweet smelling savour to God," and that every act may be rewarded in that day, when the Lord cometh with all his saints.

Brethren, can we be either wise or faithful stewards unless we thus manage our Lord's goods? We cannot, as not only the oracles of God, but our own conscience beareth witness. Then why should we delay? Why should we confer any longer with flesh and blood, or men of the world? Our kingdom, our wisdom, is not of this world: heathen custom is nothing to us. We follow no men any farther than they are followers of Christ. Hear ye him: yea, today, while it is called today, hear and obey his voice! At this hour, and from this hour, do his will: fulfil his word, in this and in all things! I entreat you in the name of the Lord Jesus, act up to the dignity of your calling! No more sloth! Whatsoever your hand findeth to do, do it with your might! No more waste! Cut off every expense which fashion, caprice, or flesh and blood demand. No more covetousness! But employ whatever God has entrusted you with in doing good, all possible good, in every possible kind and degree, to the household of faith, to all men! This is no small part of "the wisdom of the just." Give all ye have, as well as all ye are, a spiritual sacrifice to him, who withheld not from you his Son, his only Son: so "laying up in store for yourselves a good foundation against the time to come, that ye may attain eternal life."

# LEVERS, FULCRUMS, AND HORNETS

Gary North

*Introduction*

IN terms of its potential for Christian social change, I believe that the suggestions I present in the following essay are the most important I have ever written. I have discussed the details of this project with numerous Christian and conservative leaders, and they all agree: this could be a turning point.

In the fall of 1982, I was invited to meet in Virginia Beach, Virginia, with Pat Robertson, who heads "The 700 Club" and the Christian Broadcasting Network. He wanted suggestions about what needed to be done to reverse the drift into humanism by the United States. Also invited were Francis Schaeffer, his son Franky, and John Whitehead, the lawyer who specializes in defending Christian causes. The meeting was held on November 11, 1982. Ted Pantaleo, the head of the Freedom Council, also attended, as did several of Mr. Robertson's staff members.

John Whitehead and the Schaeffers made a plea for support of Mr. Whiteheads's newly formed legal organization, the Rutherford Institute. I also recommended such support, but my presentation was much broader. I believe that the Rutherford Institute's efforts could be far more effective if tied to a comprehensive program of satellite communications. I handed Mr. Robertson a preliminary draft of the following article, along with copies of the support materials mentioned in the footnotes.

It is my view, as I told him, that he is in a temporarily unique position. He has mastered the satellite television medium and has a powerful tool at his disposal. No other Christian leader presently in possession of such a tool has a broad enough vision of the kingdom of God to use it in the way I have outlined in this article. This communications tool could be used to transform American Christian higher education within a decade, and it could lay the foundation for a true Christian society by the end of the century. As I said to him, "You have the choice of becoming a chapter in some future history of Christianity rather than a footnote."

Mr. Robertson asked me to meet with two of the men in charge of CBN University the next day. We met for an hour, and one of them wrote a report. I do not know what happened to it.

I believe that the preliminary phases of the following proposal could be implemented within a year, and that the whole program could become a reality within five years. I believe that it is technically and financially possible for Mr. Robertson's various organizations to implement it. It might not receive the public support I envision, but it should nevertheless be attempted.

I am not absolutely certain that Christians are ready to make effective use of the information that CBN University could deliver to them via the CBN Satellite. I *do* know that if CBN University were to hire the best people in the nation to produce the programs—the sort of people who wrote the essays in this issue of **Christianity and Civilization**—American American Christians would have no excuses left for their political impotence. They could not stand before God on judgment day and say, "but we didn't know." If the CBN Satellite were put to the uses I describe in the following presentation, it would make available to American Christians the tools of Christian reconstruction.

Unquestionably, it will take time, money, and effort even to begin to test my project. There is a real possibility that it is premature. I have decided to publish it because I want people to consider its potential. Christians may find themselves institutionally defeated temporarily before this century is over. If this happens, I do not want future historians to claim that the Christian church in the final years of the twentieth century was defenseless. Rather, Christians *chose* not to defend their faith adequately.

### *Comprehensive Salvation*

American Christians for a century have sought to influence the way that others think about God, salvation, and the church. They have not been equally concerned about influencing people's thoughts about society—not since the

Prohibition movement, anyway. They have not bothered to examine the Bible in a search for the first principles of society that lead to progress and wealth. They have allowed humanists to capture the seats of influence and power in every institution. As Campus Crusade for Christ's brochure for its International School of Theology puts it: "According to a 1980 Gallup Poll, 50 million Americans identify themselves as born-again Christians. Yet where is our effect on our nation?"[1] Some 50 million self-professed "born again" Christians have become, in effect, a political minority, while an elite group of humanists has taken over the key institutions of society.

Today, slowly but surely, Christians are beginning to realize that there is no neutrality before God.[2] This means that there is no neutrality possible in law, politics, and education. Thus, it is either the principles of the Bible that will rule supreme on earth, or other principles opposed to the Bible. But some principles must be supreme.[3] *There are no moral vacuums, intellectual vacuums, or power vacuums*. To cite an example: Law makers and courts have only two choices concerning abortion: a baby in its mother's womb is going to be allowed to live or someone is going to be allowed to abort it. There is no "neutral" place for the baby to hide, or for us to hide from this question. Christians finally have been forced by the present lawlessness of our legal system to come to grips with a moral, legal, and political issue which cannot be decided neutrally.

Another example is education. It is now becoming clear to a growing minority of Christians that education is not neutral.[4] A few of them now see that the public schools are the tax-supported established church of secular humanism, where humanism's priesthood indoctrinates our children. A new, unfamiliar set of problems now faces American Christians. How

1. *New Distinctives in Theological Education* (1982).

2. For a popular discussion of this point, see Franky Schaeffer, *A Time for Anger: The Myth of Neutrality* (Westchester, IL: Crossway Books, 1982).

3. R. J. Rushdoony, *By What Standard?* (Tyler, TX: Thoburn Press, [1958] 1983).

4. R. J. Rushdoony's book, *Intellectual Schizophrenia: Culture, Crisis and Education* (Philadelphia: Presbyterian & Reformed, 1961), was one of the early books to defend this thesis. See also Alan Grover, *Ohio's Trojan Horse* (Greenville, SC: Bob Jones University Press, 1977).

can they create an alternate set of private educational institutions? How can they reduce the tax burden associated with the financing of the public schools? Can Christian schools take tax money and simultaneously escape public control over their schools? Can they take tax credits and still avoid control? Most important, should they seek to take over the control of the public schools, either to close them down or to make them decent again. Which?

Christians are beginning to face the reality that the myth of neutrality helped to hide from them for centuries: *religion involves morality, morality involves civil law, civil law means politics, and politics means power*. There is no way that Christians can escape the implications of this syllogism and still remain faithful to the *comprehensive gospel* and its *comprehensive salvation*.

The word "salvation" comes from the same root as "salve." A salve is a *healing ointment*. Salvation is also a means of healing. Christians have always recognized that salvation provides healing for the *soul*. Some Christians have recognized that salvation can also involve the healing of the *body*. But what only a handful have recognized is that salvation also involves the healing of the *body politic*. Because Christians have generally failed to recognize this last form of healing, they have allowed the humanists to capture the political process *by default*. The same process of default has led to the humanists' capture of our educational institutions. *This process of "defeat by default" must be reversed.*

We want to influence events. How can we do it? It will take a multi-tiered program of Christian reconstruction. This program will involve several aspects. While they may not be able to be achieved simultaneously, given our limited resources, the goal should be to develop a full-scale program which eventually will include all six:

Spiritual awakening
Education
Motivation
Communication
Legal confrontation
Political mobilization

How can we achieve these goals? We must recognize and acknowledge without any qualification whatsoever *the sovereignty of God*. We must submit ourselves to His will. We must seek out his will through prayer and a study of His word.

But haven't Christians always done this? We have not. If we had, then we would not be so far behind the humanists. There is a reason why so many Christians have been remiss for so long in failing to acknowledge and defend the sovereignty of God: they have failed to recognize the ordering principle of the universe—a principle which reflects the very being of God. We have not taken seriously the central intellectual and organizational problem of man: *the problem of the One and the Many.*[5]

### *The One and the Many*

Men who are in rebellion against God have a desire to achieve autonomy from God. There are two ways that men have attempted to do this: *anarchism* and *statism.* Rebellious men seek either total independence from God and God's ordained institutions—an imitation of the aseity (self-contained independence) of God—or they seek power through empire—an imitation of the kingdom of God. They seek anarchy or statism. In our day, obviously, statism is the most powerful influence. Godless men are seeking to construct a new humanist empire, a one-world State. There are Communism's rival empires, and they face (and are also subsidized by) the West's rival empires: NATO, the European Economic Community, the New World Order (northern, industrial), the New International World Order (third world), etc. *When men cannot find meaning in life, they seek power.* The only alternative to the quest for power in a meaningless universe is *escape from power.* Alert humanists know this. In Aldous Huxley's *Brave New World*, we see both: a total State, with total planning, and a passive population which is hooked on, and controlled by means of, orgies and drugs.[6]

---

5. R. J. Rushdoony, *The One and the Many: Studies in the Philosophy of Order and Ultimacy* (Fairfax, VA: Thoburn Press, [1971] 1978). See also *Preface 2* for my analysis of this book. Published by the Institute for Christian Economics, P.O. Box 8000, Tyler, TX 75711.

6. It is one of those oddities of history that three men died on November 22, 1963: Aldous Huxley, C. S. Lewis, and John F. Kennedy. The first was the most eloquent and intellectually incisive heir of the world's most consistently atheistic and evolutionistic family; the second was the most eloquent Christian of his generation; and the third was the humanists' incarnation of magical Camelot, the last major representative of the "end of ideology" or "can-do" humanist technicians. Three months later, the Beatles arrived, and launched the counter culture in America.

What is the Christian approach to the problem of the One and the Many? *We must begin with the doctrine of the Trinity.* God is three and He is one. He is both unity and diversity. Neither unity nor diversity is paramount in the created realm. Neither unity nor diversity is to be divinized. Every institution is to reveal both unity and diversity. The guide to the proper balance or mixture of unity and diversity is found in biblical law.

As we seek to reconstruct the humanist culture of our day, bringing it back to Jesus Christ, we must honor the principle of unity and diversity in the construction of *alternative Christian institutions*. These reconstructed institutions are eventually to replace the humanist institutions of our era. Rather than an appeal to armed revolution, American Christians initially need to use the existing legal order—which was originally Christian in origin—to *recapture* these institutions or else (e.g., tax-supported education) *abolish* them.

This was Horace Mann's strategy when he created the first state school system in Massachusetts in the early 1830s. He wanted to replace sectarian Christianity with a universal institution, the public school, which was to be organized in terms of the supposedly universal principles of natural law.[7] "Neutral" natural law was to replace biblical morality as the standard of civil justice.

Humanists in the United States since the early 1800s have sought to capture those offices that bear authority in the West: the *judges*, the *pastors*, and the *teachers*. The mark of authority of these offices is the right of the office-holder to wear a black robe.[8] The humanists have been remarkably successful in their strategy. They have completely fooled Christians into believing that the authority of the "robes" has nothing to do with the biblical principles that originally undergirded these God-ordained offices. The humanists have clothed their own anti-God principles with the robes that they stole from the Christians, and the Christians have been so hypnotized by the sight of the robes that they have not fought to return the robes to the rightful owners, namely, those who profess faith in, and conform their authoritative judgments to, the law of God.

7. R. J. Rushdoony, *The Messianic Character of American Education* (Nutley, NJ: Craig Press, 1963), ch. 3.

8. Gary North, "Capturing the Robes," *Christian Reconstruction,* VI (Sept./Oct., 1982). Published by the Institute for Christian Economics.

Humanists wear most of the robes today, not Christians.

The *myth of neutrality* has been the primary tool of deception used by the humanists in this strategy. "Robes" are supposedly nothing more than neutral symbols of authority; whoever wears them has the right to impose any law-order—especially an anti-Christian law-order—on all those under his rule. Thus, America's institutions—indeed, the West's institutions since the French Revolution—have been totally restructured by humanists to conform to anti-God presuppositions.

What should Bible-based institutions look like? They must be simultaneously unified and diverse. How? The biblical answer is found in I Corinthians 12, where Paul sketches the outline of church government. Christ is the head; we are the body. Eyes should not complain that they are not feet, and feet should not complain that they are not eyes. All receive their purpose and meaning from the head. They are part of an integrated whole. But that whole is neither "essentially" centralized nor "essentially" fragmented. The whole is based on a *covenant*: an agreement among men, under God, to work together in *specified and limited ways*, to achieve *specified and limited goals*, in order to subdue the earth to the glory of God. No single institution has absolute power, for no institution is divine. Institutions are supposed to be *ministerial*, not soteriological. God saves men; institutions minister to men, under God.

Local organization is important; general (central) goals and strategies should grow out of co-operation. Acts 15 records the results of the Jerusalem council, where a few general guidelines were imposed on all church members, but not many. Any voluntary institution which is organized in terms of the *empire principle*—a top-down chain of command—will become paralyzed. But any organization that ignores the need for some degree of centralized decision-making will become scattered. Yet centralization must be limited. As Lamennais, the early 19th-century French social philosopher, once commented, "Centralization induces apoplexy at the center and anemia at the extremities."[9]

9. Cited by Robert A. Nisbet, *The Sociological Tradition* (New York: Basic Books, 1966), p. 115.

### *The Lever*

*Leverage*: investors use it, politicians use it, anyone seeking to influence the outcome of an event uses it. It is the factor which gives the one who possesses it more impact on events than he could have without it. In business, it means OPM (other people's money). In politics, it can mean money, or votes, or trading something the other man wants for what you want. It may mean "calling in past debts." In religion, it means prayer and conformity to God's will.

"Leverage" comes from the word "lever." "Give me a long enough lever and a firm spot to stand on," Archimedes supposedly said, "and I can move the world." But Archimedes would have needed more than a lever and a firm spot to stand on; he would have needed a *fulcrum*. A lever with no fulcrum is like a child's see-saw with no fulcrum: a useless device that sits on the ground. To begin the process of recapturing the institutions of authority, we need some means of centralized communication. In the American Revolution, Sam Adams's Committees of Correspondence served this function. In our day, the direct-mail *newsletter industry* is the equivalent of Adams's Committees. In the future, the microcomputer telecommunications industry will become crucial. But by far the most powerful untapped communications resource today is the *CBN Satellite*.

Isolated individuals need to know that they are not alone. The isolation of churches and Christian day schools today is very great. There are a few co-ordinating organizations, but they are very weak. A good way to go bankrupt is to mail unsolicited materials to churches or Christian schools. Headmasters have not been willing to fight until their own schools are being attacked. By then, it is too late. The *Sileven case* is the first one in which this pattern of isolation has been broken.

We have to examine the cause of Sileven's notoriety. One word describes the difference: *television*. Several of the "electronic churchmen" devoted time on their shows to Sileven's plight. This media coverage did for Sileven what it did for Martin Luther King. It brought to light what the bureaucrats were doing. I was amused at the ABC TV report. They interviewed one woman, a supporter of the local public school, who said, "I think Nebraska's affairs should be run by Nebraskans, not all these outsiders." This was the same argument Southern whites used in 1962, the "outside agitators" argument. Television coverage made the difference for King. It could make the difference for Christians who want to recapture the nation.

The existence of satellites and cable channels has at last broken the hold of the major TV networks. The level of information provided by a 30-minute interview is far greater than that provided by a 2-minute news snippet. News snippets are designed to hold an impersonal audience's attention long enough to sell a percentage of them some soap. There is no dedicated group of viewers who are emotionally committed to an anchorman. On the other hand, there are millions of viewers who are personally committed to one or another of the electronic churchmen. Thus, they will sit in front of the screen and listen to a lengthy interview, and even try to understand it. *This puts a major educational tool into the hands of Christian leaders*—a tool which the humanists cannot match on television because of the "least common denominator" principle which governs the Nielson rating wars.

The lever of television gives the local Christian soldier hope. He knows there is a potential army of supporters behind him, if he gets in a difficult situation. His supporters can be mobilized rapidly and inexpensively if a particular electronic churchman gets his case before the viewers. The problem of anonymity which the local Christian pastor faces in any confrontation with the bureaucrats can now be overcome overnight. This is what Martin Luther King discovered, and it led to the creation of a successful resistance movement in 1956. *Bureaucrats run from adverse publicity the way cockroaches run from light.* This weakness must be exploited by Christian activists.

The very existence of the CBN satellite in itself is a mobilization tool of great importance. It is safe to say that few men are willing today to take the risks necessary to stand up to the various state and Federal bureaucracies. *The very presence of the satellite gives CBN an important edge in getting its people involved in Christian activism.* Without a means of publicizing a crisis, few pastors will take a stand. The CBN-mobilized leaders could easily take positions of leadership locally that other pastors would not dare to take, since they would not have the potential back up of the CBN Satellite. The satellite is like a howitzer on a battlefield in which Christians have been fighting with pistols and slingshots.

Men need motivation. The existence of the satellite network offers men motivation. They can join together in a coordinated effort to roll back humanism at every level. This is the approach I call *brush-fire wars*.[10] It can work well for legal resistance, but it can also work for political action, education, and almost everything else. It is a fundamental tool of resistance. But it takes a combination of *centralized strategy* and *local mobilization and execution*. It takes, in short, the application of the One and the Many principle.

### *The Fulcrum*

Those who have been most successful in developing the lever of satellite communications and cable TV distribution have been skilled practitioners of media communications. Understandably, there has been a tendency to emphasize the impact of the media. But a medium needs a message; it is not (contrary to McLuhan) itself the message. The message has, until recently, been limited: personal salvation, personal healing, family solidarity, and musical entertainment.

Those who have been in the "fulcrum production business" have been inept at developing levers. They have not written widely read books, nor have they pioneered the use of TV communications or motion pictures. The few exceptions: the Schaeffers, the various Christian counsellors—Dobson, Gothard, and Adams—and the six-day creationist movement (including the old Moody science films). But with respect to positive programs of Christian reconstruction, there has been no successful program so far—graphically or politically.

What is now needed is a bringing together of the lever and the fulcrum. Those who have built up large audiences must begin to join hands with those who have developed specific programs of reconstruction: education, legal defense, political training, etc. The "electronic churchmen" have got to begin to target specific segments of their audiences who are ready for specific programs: first by education, second by organizational mobilization. In short, *we need feet, hands, and eyes*, and each subgroup within various large television audiences needs

10. See my essay elsewhere in this journal, "The Escalating Confrontation with Bureaucracy."

specific guidance and training in order to become proficient.

There is no doubt that CBN would be better able to begin this program of specialized training than any of its competitors. It has the broadest audience. Scattered within any given prime-time audience, there are more people who might be interested in getting involved in a particular action program. CBN is on the air 24 hours a day. It can therefore devote specific time slots to identifying and developing segments of the overall viewing audience, but without alienating the viewers as a whole. Also, Pat Robertson, not being a pastor, is less of a threat to the egos and programs of the nation's pastors.

CBN University offers an institutional base for launching an educational program. The Freedom Council offers an institutional base for the creation of political education and training. If each of these two organizations can recruit the services of outside specialists in the particular areas, then the expertise of the "fulcrum developers" can be put to use. I have in mind such non-profit organizations as the Free Congress Foundation, the Rutherford Institute, the American Vision, the Foundation for American Christian Education, the Foundation for Christian Self-Government, the Institute for Christian Economics, the various creation research organizations, Western Goals Foundation, Chalcedon Foundation, and other educational groups. A body of explicitly Christian literature in several areas has been produced over the last two decades. These educational resources should be integrated into an overall program of education and mobilization.

In the past, there has been a problem of communication between "lever builders" and "fulcrum builders." The "lever builders" have been fearful of getting too intellectual, too controversial, and too action-oriented to maintain their large, essentially passive Christian audiences. The risk of controversy has been too great. The "fulcrum builders" have resented pressure from the "levers" to "water down" their message in order to meet the needs and intellectual abilities of mass audiences. They have chosen instead to gather still more footnotes, develop still more complex theories, and publish ever fatter books in the quest for the near-perfect intellectual equivalent of Augustine's *City of God* or Calvin's *Institutes*.

In the providence of God, both sides have been correct, up until now. The levers are longer, and the fulcrums are stronger, than they would otherwise have been had the developers in each camp been too concerned with imitating the other. But now the levers are in place, and the fulcrums are as ready as they need to be at this moment in history. Christian viewers are not nearly so passive any more. They see clearly the threat of humanism for the first time. Therefore, it is time to meet the newly felt needs of these viewers. There is always a need for larger audiences and more footnotes, but there is a far greater need today to get the existing footnotes in bite-sized portions to the existing hungry multitudes. Christ fed the multitudes with two fish and five loaves of bread; we can feed them with our existing body of materials. While they are digesting what we can deliver today, the fulcrum experts can crank out more footnotes.

### *The "End Run"*

The humanists captured the mainline denominations, the universities, the major news media, the entertainment media, and the public schools. In short, *humanists captured the giant institutions*. But look at what is happening. The generalized institutions are losing their share of the market. What is clearly taking place is a shift: *from the generalized to the specialized*, from the large to the small. *Life* and *Look* along with the original weekly *Saturday Evening Post*, did not survive. The proliferation of special-interest magazines and newsletters has enabled advertisers to target specific audiences and increase their revenues per advertising dollar spent. Now the same phenomenon is taking place in the television industry. Like the Model T Ford, which could not compete once General Motors offered five or six cars with numerous models, so is the modern TV network. The networks look strong today, just as the Model T looked in 1914. Looks are often deceiving.

The humanists captured the national political parties, but today we find that single-interest voting patterns are tearing the national parties apart. Direct-mail campaigns allow these groups to target their audiences, producing more votes per invested dollar, and more ulcers per elected politician. What Alvin Toffler has predicted in *The Third Wave*, and what John Naisbett has predicted in *Megatrends: Ten New Directions Transforming Our Lives*, is the coming decentralization. In short, in the face of excessive centralization and statism, we are seeing a countertrend, or better put, multiple countertrends. We are being given an opportunity to attain a better balance between the One and the Many.

Christians are in an excellent position to take advantage of this reversal. Christianity is decentralized—indeed, "fragmented" better describes our condition. If the Christians can assemble themselves into loosely organized but well trained special-interest blocs, while today's centralized humanist culture is disintegrating, the result could be *the creation of a new cultural synthesis*, one based on biblical law rather than some version of humanistic natural law, meaning a version of the myth of neutrality.

What we need, therefore, is *a technological "end run" around today's entrenched, centralized, humanist institutions*. We have begun to do this in television. The development of an alternative information network through newsletters has also made an impact. The development of direct-mail lists has increased our ability to get a specific message to a specific audience. We have a real edge in communications. The Christian day school movement has made a substantial dent in the humanist monopoly of information. Where we have not yet been successful is in the areas of higher education, political training, and legal defense.

### *Higher Education*

Technology is why CBN University is in a position of strength. This strength is presently only potential. The long-run potential could be nothing short of revolutionary.

Where will the graduates of the Christian day schools go? Few Christian colleges are straightforwardly Christian.[11] They are expensive. State universities offer socialism at socialism's State-subsidized prices; Christian colleges too often offer socialism at free market prices.

How can Christians provide a low-budget Christian alternative to humanistic higher education? Simple: by creating a low-tuition, institutionally decentralized educational system which requires minimal capital expenditures, but which has access to an integrated, biblically based curriculum taught by the best teachers in each field.

---

11. Gary North, "The Impossible Dream," *Christian Reconstruction*, VI (May/June, 1982).

Impossible? Not at all. As they say on those late-night Ronco Products TV ads, "Here's how it works!" CBN University decides on a series of 35-hour, one-semester academic courses. It hires the best people in each discipline to teach them. Each instructor is then brought in for two weeks to put his course onto videotape. He is paid, say, $2,000 plus expenses for two weeks of lecturing. If CBN can locate stock footage (e.g., recent U.S. history, political science, economics), fine. If not, the talking head approach is all that a classroom normally has anyway.

Each instructor is required to produce, in advance, a workbook which will be the basis of the course's outline. The workbooks will be sold by CBN University as part of the educational package. The profits can be split between CBN University and the author on a 50-50 basis. This is the author's chief financial incentive.

CBN University can hire good men during the summers. Summer employment means extra money to the instructors. It also means that there are no continuing salary expenses for CBN University. This drastically lowers the cost of operation. Also, no large library is mandatory initially. No dorms are necessary. No large administrative staff, groundskeeping staff, or secretarial staff is necessary. CBN has thereby reduced all the major expenses of running a college.

How to get this material to the students? Simple: you take advantage of the *CBN satellite lever*. From midnight until five A.M., or from one A.M. to six A.M., CBN University broadcasts each course. In one week, 35 hours of lectures can be put onto seven videotapes in the extended play mode. (You use 5-hour segments for the convenience of Betamax users; VHS units allow 6 hours). This is the equivalent of a 3-unit (3-semester hour) college course. One course per week could be beamed down to viewers.

The users will set their videotape units' automatic timers and go to bed. Next morning, they will wake up possessing five more hours of the course. In a week, they will own a 3-semester-hour course. Total cost per course to the user of "hiring" a permanent professor: $10 per cassette times seven. Try to match this salary scale in any other university! Who will be the people who record the courses? They could be students, but this is unlikely. The owners will probably be Christian day schools, local churches, existing colleges, Christian businesses, and missionaries. These tapes will become permanent additions to a training library in these local institutions. Tape owners will then be able to go out and attract students. Students can be instructed by local pastors or teachers, or they will be able to take the courses for credit through correspondence from CBN University.

What if the tapes are "pirated"? That is the whole idea. The courses are tied to the workbooks. Anyone who wants full use of the course needs to order a workbook. When he does, CBN University then gets his name and address. This goes on the mailing list, and can be rented by other CBN-related organizations. Students are now identified. Their progress can be traced over the years. Whenever a Christian organization wants a specialist in a given field, he calls CBN, pays a fee, and is given a print-out of the names of students (auditing or correspondents), their particular specialties, and their attainments. CBN University could become the foremost clearing house of Christian talent in the world. It could get paid for its trouble, too. But this would take place only after several years of operations.

Initially, the University gets money for the workbook (say, $25). What about selling textbooks by mail? Courses will require textbooks in addition to workbooks. This could prove very profitable. It could even develop that CBN University will begin to publish textbooks, which could be even more profitable than printing workbooks.

So far, we have only been talking about people who "audit" ("vidit"?) the courses. What about a person who wants to take a course for *full academic credit?* He will send in, say, $100 per course for his tuition in order to receive credit for the course. Paying $100 for a 3-hour, one semester course is a bargain in today's college world. CBN University takes, say, 50%, and the instructor takes 50%. The student writes two term papers and takes two locally monitored exams. These are sent to CBN University's correspondence division and forwarded to the instructor. Total time needed to grade these? Possibly an hour. What teacher wouldn't be happy to make $40 or $50 an hour in his spare time? This could become the best retirement program in the history of education. He gets residuals on his workbook plus a big chunk of any future tuition payments. Think he won't do his best to create an interesting, popular course? At last: a faculty payment schedule based on actual performance!

Pastors or other entrepreneurs will be encouraged to set up *totally autonomous local colleges* that use the CBN University tapes and workbooks. The more, the merrier. More to the point: the more schools there are, the tougher it will be for the bureaucrats to bottle up these materials. If a headmaster of a Christian day school wants to start a junior college program using CBN University materials, that is to CBN University's advantage. CBN University accepts no responsibility for the final educational product, makes money selling the workbooks and textbooks, and sees the creation of dozens of new colleges.

But what about *accreditation?* Well, what about it? First of all, who needs it?[12] Employers are buying competence, honesty, and people who are willing to work hard. If a student can show that he read the material (in his library) and he has the grades, what does the recruiter care about accreditation? Furthermore, graduate schools are willing to accept a college graduate's test scores on the various Graduate Record Exams in lieu of grades. Second, those who want accreditation can take the courses from CBN University directly. Third, CBN University can set up its undergraduate division, if necessary, in whichever state in the U.S. has the easiest accreditation requirements. Nothing says the undergraduate program has to be located in Virginia. Offer an accredited home study degree. But never forget: *it is better never to have received accreditation than to have received it, and subsequently have it revoked.*

The humanists who control the accreditation committees understand this. Once they accredit a school, they possess a powerful lever. Why give them a lever to use against us? Why should humanists and compromised Christian academics certify our competence? Will we not judge the angels (I Cor. 6:3)?

What about *transferring credits?* Again, this is not a very big problem. These days, independent Christian colleges are in deep financial trouble. What if CBN University offers a junior college program? The director of the CBN University correspondence division can send out a letter offering the following deal: "Accept the graduates provisionally, Mr. College Presi-

12. Gary North, "Who Should Certify Competence?" *Biblical Economics Today*, IV (Feb./March, 1981). Published by the Institute for Christian Economics.

dent, and don't grant any credit for previous work unless the graduate gets at least a B– average in his upper division major during his first semester or quarter, and at least a C average in his non-major course work. If you will grant this, sir, we will put you on our recommended college list." What will the rational president's response be? He is being offered access to bright students. (The less bright will pay their tuition for at least a semester and then leave.) The regional accreditation committee cannot complain, since all these students are accepted only provisionally—a reasonably common practice. And the college taps into the largest single base of Christian college students in the nation. Almost any Christian college president will agree to the deal. Anyway, several dozen will. All you need is a dozen, perhaps fewer.

Where will graduates want to go to *graduate school?* How about CBN University? By creating videotaped undergraduate college courses, CBN University positions itself in the future market for graduate studies. Students who have been trained in an explicitly Christian world and life view will be valuable commodities in the future. CBN University will be able to attract a far better prepared student body because it has provided the undergraduate training materials in the first place. Furthermore, the population base of students who have received an integrated Christian curriculum will be far larger than it is today, which also serves as a means of upgrading CBN University's graduate program. There will be more students to attract.

*CBN University could create a decentralized educational revolution within ten years.* The whole program could be packaged at the junior college level within two years. If demand is high, CBN can add the upper division courses later on, but at least offer the first two years of academic course work. Before any Christian student walks into the lions' den of a humanistic college classroom, he can already possess the philosophical and biblical training necessary to "gird his loins" for an intellectual battle. Why send them in unarmed at age 17 or 18?

Who wins in this program? 1) Students who cannot afford college. They can work for two years, take cheap tuition courses, and save money for upper division. 2) Younger students who are not yet emotionally or intellectually prepared to face the intellectual and moral battlefield of university life; 3) Married students who cannot afford the move. They need their local employment. They study part time, at their own pace. 4) Families who prefer not to send 17-year-old children off to college just yet. 5) Headmasters who want to expand into a junior college. 6) Pastors who do not want to see young people turned into humanists.

Who loses? State universities, state accrediting agencies, and the compromised Christian colleges that demand high tuition for third-rate courses in baptized humanism.

Who cares about these losers?

### *Political Education*

The first step is to create awareness of the Christian background of *American Constitutional liberties*. Viewers should be aware of this history, as well as the specific provisions of the Constitution. A one-week, all-night TV, citizens training course on the Constitution could be produced by CBN University which could also serve as a college course on the Constitution. It could be taught by John Whitehead, Dr. James McLellan, Prof. M. E. Bradford, and possibly others. Once in the possession of each local Freedom Council unit, these videotapes could be used over and over to educate members in the nature of Constitutional law, and the humanist distortions thereof. They could also be shown to churches as part of the Freedom Council's ongoing educational ministry in the local Christian community.

Once the basic educational tapes have been shown to local members, the Freedom Council's national office would then bring in the Free Congress Foundation and other skilled political technicians and have them record *detailed programs on how to mobilize*. These would *not* be shown on CBN TV. They could be used in travelling seminars and shown only to those members who have been screened through regional weekend training programs or other means. The information possessed by these experts could wind up in the videotape files of local branches of the Freedom Council. This could become a major incentive for highly action-oriented Christians to join the local Freedom Council.

*Mailing lists* that are developed locally could go to Freedom Council's national offices twice a year. On the other hand, names generated by means of 700 Club appearances by Freedom Council representatives could be directed to the appropriate regional data banks. This honors the principle of the

One and the Many. The POLSYS computerized program for local political action, which uses the inexpensive Radio Shack TRS-80 Model III or 4 computers, is ideal for such a training program. The developers of POLSYS, Frank Slinkman and Larry Pratt, could be brought to the CBN studios to videotape a training program in the use of POLSYS. This cassette tape would go to all regional units of the Freedom Council.[13]

What is needed is a generation of *trained, dedicated political activists* who can learn leadership skills at the local level. They can serve in local governments in order to build political buffers to the illegitimate extension of Federal power. We need men who will, if necessary, serve initially as dogcatchers, so that they can later serve as county commissioners, state legislators, and Congressmen. Not everyone needs to start at the top. Most people shouldn't. Elders need to serve first as deacons; this principle is a good one for political action.

First approach: a local church uses the POLSYS program for development of its own *door-to-door evangelism-survey program*[14] It thereby builds up a local data base. This data base could be rented later on to political candidates who want to use a direct-mail campaign. By renting the list, the church avoids suspicion about "mixing church and State." But the church is under no obligation to tell every local candidate that it rents its list or even has a list to rent. Presumably, the elders will want to screen the candidates very carefully.

Second approach: if local churches are unwilling or unable to adopt this sort of evangelism strategy, then *local units of the Freedom Council* can do it. These surveys become sources of names for the creation of local data bases, as well as a national data base. Again, we are honoring the One and the Many principle: a national strategy that offers incentives, benefits, and responsibility to local branches.

Third approach: a local Christian businessman uses the POLSYS program, or other data base program (Datafax, etc.) for business-related mailings. He can deduct the cost of the computer and the program as business expenses. At some point, he rents the list to political action committees or candidates. This transfers power to him, as the man who controls

13. Gary North, "A Politic Move," *Desktop Computing* (June, 1982).

14. Gary North, "Bread-and-Butter Neighborhood Evangelism," *The Journal of Christian Reconstruction*, VIII (Winter, 1981).

a very valuable asset, a mailing list which is specifically designed for political campaigns. He screens the candidates by controlling access to his data base.

*By developing local data bases, Christians can become enormously influential.* Over the next decade, direct-mail campaigns will become even more important than they are today. Christians need to learn the techniques of building, maintaining, and using local public opinion data bases. Few local groups are today assembling such data bases. Those groups that do will exercise political leverage way out of proportion to their numbers over the next decade.

### *Legal Defense*

The Rutherford Institute could be used to produce *motivational and training videotapes* for pastors and headmasters. A series of four or five half-hour programs could be broadcast by the 700 Club during prime time. These films would encourage viewers to send in $50 to buy a *legal defense manual* that would enable them to gain extra time when any bureaucratic agency begins to interfere with their Constitutional liberties. The manual could generate income for both CBN and the Rutherford Institute, and the films would begin to mobilize the viewers for the battles in the courts that are already here.

The Rutherford Institute could use its share of the funds from sales of the defense manual to finance its program of *training local Christian lawyers in the techniques of a Constitutional defense of religious rights.* There is a great need to train up lawyers in each region who know the proper legal defense approach. *We need a L'Abri for lawyers.* If they know what to do in advance, and if they are continually receiving updated materials on court decisions, these lawyers will not have to charge their Christian clients $100 an hour to learn the field. They will also win more cases.

*The present approach to defending the schools and churches is all wrong.* It is *centralized,* even more than the humanists' program of attack is. The Federal bureaucrats use local officials to serve as their agents. In contrast, Christians have a handful of overworked lawyers who run all over the country trying to defend everyone. They cannot prepare their cases properly, and they are losing. This establishes legal precedents that later go against other Christians. What is wrong here? Clearly, it is the *empire-building impulse of a handful of Christian lawyers*. They are unwilling to decentralize the defense program, and then use their research skills to prepare an integrated, continually updated, effectively packaged, national Christian legal defense program which local lawyers can implement, case by case, state by state. In short, the present legal defense program violates the principle of the One and the Many. It is too centralized. It is doomed to failure.

The present legal defense programs do not train up local church members to be *paralegals*. This is desperately needed. The bureaucrats have limited resources. The first contact with the church or school is probably initiated by very low-level officials. A skilled paralegal could probably deal with these officials for several months. Then an expensive lawyer can be called in. There are paralegal research programs today that train average but motivated people to be quite effective at the local level. These training programs can be videotaped and used by the Freedom Council or CBN University. It might even pay to broadcast these training tapes over the air, midnight to five. This would drive the humanists crazy.

If pastors were told in advance on the 700 Club that a series of very important tapes would be shown beginning at midnight on such and such a date, they could tune in and get them recorded before any government agency could complain to CBN. Once out, they could circulate widely. There would not need to be any advance statement on the 700 Club about the nature of the message—just a warning that all pastors and headmasters should tune in and record the broadcast. This is a kind of *electronic "hit and run" guerrilla attack*. The CBN satellite could become a high-order weapon in the battle against bureaucracy.

The local Freedom Council units must become comprehensive clearing houses for information on how the churches, schools, and businesses can fight back. The Freedom Council does not need to become a law office. What it needs to do is to assemble materials, including videotapes, and make available information to members on *how to begin*. Those first steps—deciding how to respond, writing the initial responding to the bureaucrats, selecting a lawyer—can "set in concrete" the organization's legal strategy. If Christians knew where to look for assistance, they could save themselves a lot of money and a lot of grief. The Freedom Council can and should become the first line of defense for Christians in the war against the humanist State.

I can see a market for training tapes and manuals among small businessmen whose enterprises are threatened by bureaucratic intimidation. They simply don't know where to start when they are hit by an official demand for compliance —a demand which may well be unconstitutional. What if every local church had videotaped training programs to assist small businessmen, if only to delay a crisis until the right lawyer could be located?

*It is time to fight back, at every level, with every tool available.* A Christian legal defense program could increase the cost to the State of infringing on our Constitutional liberties. It could also lower our costs of defense, especially initial costs. If Christians think they cannot afford to fight, many of them will quit.

### *Hornets and Revival*

Christians pray for revival. It is doubtful that they are ready for revival. Consider the implications of a revival today. The myth of neutrality has faded, not only in Christian circles but also on the campus. The work of Thomas Kuhn in the physical sciences and the work of Karl Marx and others in the social sciences have destroyed men's faith in neutral human reason. The educated man's faith in natural law has been destroyed by the Darwinian revolution.[15]

We now face a crucial problem. If there were a great outpouring of Christian faith tomorrow, what would be the answer of the Christian world to the inevitable question of the newly converted: "How should we then live?" To say, as most Christians do, that "the Bible has the answer to every question," implies that Christians have studied the Bible and have asked a lot of questions which the Bible has answered. Is this the case? Have Christians actually gone to their Bibles in search of answers to life's questions? "How should we then live?" is a broader question than "How should I treat my wife?" or "Should I stop being a prostitute?" or even "Is the required mode of baptism by immersion only?" Do we have a

15. Gary North, *The Dominion Covenant: Genesis* (Tyler, TX: Institute for Christian Economics, 1982), pp. 24f., 300, 409ff.

developed body of practical answers to the questions that a newly converted world will raise?

If our answer is "No, we do not have such answers," then we are in the unenviable position of a newly elected President who has no program. *We will have to stall for time.* We will have to announce, "We can get the answers, but we will need a little time." After 2,000 years, and still no answers, how much more time can we reasonably ask for? How can we ask a newly converted world to wait patiently, as the humanist culture is collapsing, while we figure out *specific, concrete answers to specific, concrete problems?* If we ask for more time, won't we make fools of ourselves? Does Christ want us to make fools of ourselves? If not, what does He expect us to do in order to prepare for a truly biblical revival?

If we cannot come before the world, as the prophets came, in the name of God and His law, then how can we legitimately expect to get a revival? What kind of revival will it be? A biblical revival? Did the prophets ask for an emotional revival apart from a turning away from sin by the king, rulers, and common people? Did the prophets not call for *comprehensive repentance?* Were not the people of Israel in *comprehensive rebellion?* Did the prophets offer not offer a message of *comprehensive redemption?*[16] Did they not come before Israel with *comprehensive answers?* Isn't this the kind of preaching that produces biblical revival? Can any other kind of preaching produce biblical revival?

If we are unprepared to answer the burning issues of the day, then we are unprepared for revival. *To call for revival prematurely is to call for the public humiliation of the church.* Christians will be revealed as incompetents before the world. Christians talk as though they expect revival to be some sort of zero-responsibility event—a kind of cosmic bail-out for the 20th-century church. Was the Hebrews' return to the land in Nehemiah's day a bail-out for Nehemiah? Wasn't it an era of major decisions? If Christians refuse to think about revival in these terms, then they do not understand the comprehensive implications of revival. *Those who preach revival must begin to take steps to prepare for the social and institutional effects of revival.*

The Israelites in Moses' day were told that they would not

---

16. Gary North, "Comprehensive Redemption: A Theology for Social Action," *The Journal of Christian Reconstruction*, VIII (Summer, 1981).

replace the Canaanites overnight, however evil the Canaanites were. "And I will send hornets before thee, which shall drive out the Hivite, the Canaanite, and the Hittite, from before thee. I will not drive them out from before thee in one year; lest the land become desolate, and the beast of the field multiply against thee. By little and little I will drive them out from before thee, until thou be increased, and inherit the land" (Ex. 23:28-30). *Deliverance demands dominion.*

We are no different in our struggle to take the land. We are unprepared to occupy the land overnight. The world must roll along during the period of transition. If revival comes overnight, how will we reconstruct the institutions of our era? Will we tell men to continue as they did before conversion? Then we are not preaching comprehensive repentance from comprehensive sin. If we tell them that they are new creatures, but that they need not change the daily routines of their lives, including their work's goals and routines, then we are *not* really saying, "Behold, *all things* have become new." If we stand mute and tell them nothing, then we are not preaching at all. *Preaching the gospel means preaching total reconstruction.* Nothing lies outside the judgment of God.

Nevertheless, we must expect to reconstruct "Canaan" overnight. We must begin to prepare Christians to begin to take the reigns of power, at every level, in every institution, across the face of the earth, *before* we call on God to bring an overnight revival. What we need is *revival with hornets*. We need a steady spread of the gospel, meaning an expansion of the rule of Christ's people. We need *on-the-job training*. Let the hornets of our age—herpes, drought, war, depression, inflation, doubt, fear, and consternation—confound the Canaanites and drive them out of the seats of power. *Let us recapture the robes*. But it will not happen in a year.

We should not expect revival overnight. If some wave of emotional outpourings should come before Christians are ready to lead, then either it is a false revival, or else we will be hard-pressed to give direction to the new converts. *Let us not pray for overnight revival unless we are ready to offer comprehensive counsel overnight*. Let us strive to raise up Christians who will be ready to offer counsel overnight, in every area of life, at every level of leadership. *If we are not involved in a program of raising up such comprehensive counsellors, then God will not take seriously our call for overnight revival.*

### *Household Evangelism*

The importance of the household in evangelism is not generally understood. We invite people to worship in God's house, but we fail to see that we are also to invite people into our homes as a way to introduce outsiders to the household of faith. They see the *whole Christian man* within the framework of *a crucial area of responsibility and dominion*. They see the outworking of the household's faith, from the discipline of the children to the orderliness of the house. This testifies to the existence of *God's order*. This calls to the attention of unregenerate people the possibilities of peace and tranquility in a key biblical institution, the family.[17] They see the outworking of God's social order in a familiar and universal institution.[18]

The success of *neighborhood Bible studies* in bringing millions of people to Christ testifies to the importance of the household. But few Christians seem to understand why home evangelism works so well. They do not understand the *theology of the household*, that the household is an aspect of the kingdom of God. The Hebrews were forced to come to grips with this aspect of the kingdom because of Passover. The father became a priest in the household who directed family worship and trained the children through the ritual of the Passover (Ex. 12:26-28). *The father as household priest* is not taught in churches today.

The problem we face today is the lack of skilled Bible teachers for these neighborhood study programs. Few men have the biblical knowledge and self-confidence necessary for them to initiate a weekly Bible study in their homes. They expect church officers to lead such worship services. There are not enough church officers to accomplish this.

The existence of the CBN satellite offers a solution to the problem on a scale never before possible. Here is how it could be used.

#### *Videotaped Bible Studies*

CBN creates a series of half-hour Bible study packages. These would be specific and practical in nature. They could

17. James B. Jordan, "God's Hospitality and Holistic Evangelism," *The Journal of Christian Reconstruction*, VII (Winter, 1981).

18. R. J. Rushdoony, *Foundations of Social Order* (Fairfax, VA: Thoburn Press, [1968] 1978). See my analysis of this book in *Preface 1*.

include very simple introductions to the plan of salvation, but that would not be the overall approach. These would be *packaged, topical courses*. Many Christians feel embarrassed to bring up an intimate topic like salvation. They feel as though they are invading another person's privacy, thereby invading his "sacred space." In a very real sense, this is exactly what the presentation of the gospel does do. But millions of Christians hesitate at this point. The Bible study programs I am recommending overcome this psychological barrier by making the presentations intensely practical and not visibly denominational. They would offer *specific, Bible-based solutions to universally perceived needs*. Courses on the following subjects could be produced:

Family finances
The drug problem
Alcoholism
Child discipline
Neighborhood crime
Marital dissention
Occupations
Teaching children
Dealing with teenagers

Each course would be four weeks long. Up to 13 courses could be presented in a year in any given household, but 10 or fewer would be more likely. Each segment would be no longer than a half hour. (Studies on learning have indicated that the learning curve drops off rapidly after 25 minutes. People retain very little after 25 minutes, unless the teaching has been truly inspirational.) Families in the neighborhood would agree to come for a full course. This gets people into the *discipline of a covenant*. They are committed to perform a minimal set of tasks. It makes the course appear to be important, which it is.

Each Bible study would last exactly one hour, with refreshments served afterward. The cost of refreshments could be borne through the local church (tax-deductible), since they are an aspect of an evangelism program. By fixing the time involved, people would know that they could schedule their evening rationally. A predictable schedule also testifies to godly order.

CBN could hire the best men in each field to teach the course. Then each course can be recorded and beamed down to local churches all over North America. Each church will purchase a $3,500 receiving dish and several videotape recorders. The recorders would record each course, and then they could be borrowed by Bible study leaders each week to play in their homes. A four-part course will fit on a two-hour cassette in the high speed mode which is necessary for the highest quality reproduction.

These courses would be broadcasted three or four at a time. Each church would then have several to select from. Different families could select the course most suited to their immediate skills. Then each family could rotate the courses, so that a new course could be offered each month. These courses would constitute a comprehensive introduction to *applied, practical Christianity.* People in the neighborhood could gain access to material available nowhere else in such bite-sized portions. They would receive this information in godly homes.

Each family would receive a *study leader's guide* produced by the course's instructor and sold to local churches. The master copy could be photocopied locally. The study leader's guide would contain relevant Bible verses, explanations of how they apply, suggested questions for discussion, and hints on how to keep the discussion alive. This would further reduce fear on the part of home Bible study leaders.

To raise money for both the church and CBN, these courses could be made available on audio cassettes, but only to those who take the course and participate in the discussions. This is not simply a way to transfer intellectual information; this approach involves the *whole man strategy.* It needs the household as its institutional focus.

The Bible teacher improves his knowledge of the Bible. He learns to lead a discussion. He learns to spot people's responses, so that he can better communicate with them privately later on. He takes notes on the responses each person makes in the discussion. This arouses no suspicion; people like to have others pay attention to what they say. Over several weeks, the discussion leader can get a pretty good feel for what interests and bothers the participants. Such information is impossible to obtain in the normal, anonymous, middle-class suburban neighborhood.

The Bible leader also identifies himself as a potential counsellor and leader in the neighborhood. He has access to answers. He understands the Bible. Over time, the courses will impress upon the participants the fact of just how comprehensively the Bible speaks to all areas of life. And *this* man understands this amazing book! The home in which the Bible study is conducted should, over time, become *the single focal point of order in the neighborhood.* He is its one source of true *community.*

When this man presents the gospel, or invites a neighbor to church, he is not some unknown person standing in the doorway. He is someone commanding respect and even authority in the neighborhood. God has already begun to deal with the whole neighborhood through this man's household. He is no longer a stranger to other residents. The unregenerate person who senses his need may respond openly to his perception of the other person's authority—an authority which extends from an orderly household which manifests the *presence of God.*

### *Teleconferences*

Having gained the confidence of neighborhoods all over town, the participating churches that had set up reception dishes could get out the word: CBN or some other organization with access to the CBN satellite is going to present a special conference dealing with an important topic of interest to viewers. How would CBN know what topics interest viewers? Local churches could take a survey, either through the household evangelism programs (preferable) or by means of the survey technique.[19]

These conferences would be equally practical. They might be like Bill Gothard's *Basic Youth Conflicts.* In any case, the authority developed by the neighborhood Bible studies could be transferred in part to the churches, and then indirectly to the teleconference's sponsoring organization.

*Incentives:* Churches would have a new incentive to purchase a receiving dish. Not only will they be able to develop programs of higher education, legal resistance programs, and political motivation programs, but the CBN satellite will also provide a revolutionary program of neighborhood evangelism. Any church that refuses to participate will be at a

19. North, "Bread-and-Butter Neighborhood Evangelism," *op. cit.*

competitive disadvantage. The first churches to get their members involved will identify themselves early as candidates for future influence in their communities.

*Speed is of the essence.* Communities are beginning to pass ordinances banning satellite receiving dishes, or place them under severe restrictions. While this may be overcome in several ways, it is best to act now.

In the future, direct broadcast satellite (DBS) technology may make programs like this universal, but today, CBN and the other Christian television networks have the advantage. The question is: Will the directors of these mighty tools of evangelism see their full potential now, or will we have to wait a decade or more?

### *Latin American Evangelism*

Consider the possibilities of the CBN satellite. It is located 23,000 miles above the earth close to the equator. Its broadcasts reach Mexico, Central America, and much of South America. What if missionaries were given satellite receiving dishes, videotape machines, and power generators? They could set up Spanish-speaking or Portuguese-speaking broadcasts by Latins brought to CBN specifically for this program.

First, the broadcasts could cover agriculture. What kinds of agriculture are appropriate to various regions, given the capital base? The best scientific minds could be hired to produce the scripts for such broadcasts.

Next, a series on basic health care. What about nutrition and hygiene? What about childbirth? What about infant diseases? What are steps that villagers can take to decrease the rate of infant mortality? The videotaped broadcasts could provide answers.

What about "appropriate" technology—low-cost technology that is suitable for rural villages? What about Christianity's struggles with Marxism and "liberation theology"? What about the Bible's laws concerning restitution, forgiveness, and so forth?

The missionary who has access to the tools of the satellite is in a position to become the dominant influence in a region. He could become a local high school. He could possess a near-monopoly of advanced education in many regions.

Pat Robertson is in a position to reshape Latin America within a generation. The satellite is a powerful tool.

### *Conclusion*

By using the lever of the CBN satellite communications network, and by using the existing skills of a group of outside Christian experts in several academic and practical fields, CBN is in a position to change the direction in which the United States is headed. By using Spanish-speaking and perhaps even Portuguese-speaking translators, it is conceivable that the whole Western hemisphere could be transformed. The Marxists cannot match this. The cults cannot yet match this. Why not press our advantage while we possess it? The satellite is temporarily an exclusively Christian educational tool. The only other group that seems to be making effective use of satellites to change society is the pornography industry. Pornography works against the humanists' culture more than it works against dedicated Christians, who are less likely to become addicted.

There are still communities in which cable has not been installed, or cable systems that do not carry CBN. By advertising the educational program, CBN might persuade individual churches and schools in these areas to install a reception dish. They will not merely be missing talk shows; they will be missing an opportunity to reshape the American Constitutional republic. If CBN could make available at "cost plus shipping" satellite reception dishes, as well as cheap videocassette recorders, to local churches and Christian day schools, CBN could broaden its market for all the other programming.

In short, *CBN has within its reach the position of number-one international Christian educator*. The whole decentralized Christian education system could be intellectually restructured by midnight-to-five broadcasts of supplemental classroom programs for the Christian day school movement, not just in the United States but all over the world. It could begin with kindergarten and carry through graduate school. We could see the creation of independent Christian schools in regions where they do not exist today. Any threat to the schools could be met almost overnight by full-scale mobilization.

The lever is already in place. The fulcrum is waiting on the sidelines. The game is in progress. The score is humanists

80, Christians 12. We may not know what quarter we're in, but we know this much: the game isn't over yet. CBN has the technological capacity to change the score for the better.

What will CBN have to give up? Mainly, the advertising revenues generated from reruns of the thirty-year-old situation comedies that are broadcast after midnight. On the other hand, the sales of workbooks, textbooks, and even tuitions could compensate CBN for the loss of these advertising revenues. In any case, the 20th century is not going to be reshaped in terms of the standards of the gospel through reruns of "My Little Margie" or "The Life of Riley," however harmless these shows were in 1952. *Now is not the time for harmlessness; now is the time for hornets*. CBN's satellite is a perfect lever for stirring up God's hornets, all over the world.

### *Postscript*

I have passed along copies of this proposal to Jerry Falwell, of the Moral Majority, and Bill Bright, of Campus Crusade. If Pat Robertson is unwilling to take full advantage of his own satellite, then perhaps other ministries with a broad outreach could buy the time on the midnight-to-five A.M. time slot. They could prepare the necessary training materials and hire the teachers. If they could reimburse CBN for the revenues forfeited by the network by removing "The Life of Riley" and other ancient sitcoms from the air, perhaps CBN's management would allow others to use this tool more effectively.

# TOOLS OF BIBLICAL RESISTANCE

Lawrence D. Pratt

SHOULD Christians be involved in politics? And, should they be willing to break the law? When, if ever, should they be willing to take up arms against tyranny?

The Biblical answer is clear: "We ought to obey God rather than man" (Acts 5:29b). God, who knows man's heart, warns against taking the law into our own hands: "Vengence is mine; I will repay, saith the Lord" (Romans 12:19b). Government is ordained of God, and we are enjoined to be subject to it: "Let every soul be subject unto the higher powers. For there is no power but of God: the powers that be ordained of God" (Romans 13:1).

While each person is to be subject to higher powers, government is also constrained by God: "For rulers are not a terror to good works, but to the evil. Wilt thou then not be afraid of the power? Do that which is good, and thou shalt have praise of the same" (Romans 13:3).

Biblical Christianity goes beyond our own personal relationship with Christ and our church activities. For Christianity to be limited to a private matter concerning ourselves and our local congregation is to surrender a great deal of God's creation to His enemies. Passive, uninvolved Christianity will inevitably lead to prohibitions on teaching the gospel and the jailing of faithful Christians, just as the Jews of the Old Testament were oppressed when they departed from the will of the Lord.

Martyrdom and incarceration should be something a Christian works tirelessly to avoid. Avoidance of oppression goes well beyond our personal comfort. A peaceful land glorifies God. We are told in I Timothy 2:1-4 to pray for peace that all men might be saved. The Kingdom of God will not grow in jail as well as it can in a free and peaceful land.

It was to establish a free and peaceful land that our forefathers established settlements in America. They made every effort to have their laws in the New World conform as closely as possible to the Law in the Bible. Most people are not aware of this because the educational system has expunged everything that does not fit the prevailing orthodoxy—the religion of secular humanism.

### *Tool No. 1: Education*

The issue of Christian resistance to tyranny has already been faced by Christian educators. Christians have been jailed and threatened with jail for not teaching the state religion in their schools.

Christian parents used to control the education of their children in this country. Today, unless a parent carefully selects a private Christian school, the education of his children is calculated to turn them into pagan socialists whose only concept of freedom is self-gratification which leads to self-enslavement. This leaves the state, and the bureaucrats who run it, free to work their will unimpeded by a citizenry single-mindedly pursuing "their own thing."

The history of Israel in the Old Testament spells out what happens when parents neglect the education of their children in the Lord. The first generation following the conquest of the Promised Land was a faithful one: "And the people served the Lord all the days of Joshua, and all the days of the elders that outlived Joshua, who had seen the great works of the Lord, that he did for Israel" (Judges 2:7).

While this generation served the Lord, the same chapter indicates that they overlooked the education of their children, and the terrible consequences that followed: "And there arose another generation after them which knew not the Lord, nor yet the works which he had done for Israel. And the children of Israel did evil in the sight of the Lord and served Baalim. . . . And the anger of the Lord was hot against Israel and he delivered them into the hands of spoilers that spoiled them, and he sold them into the hands of their enemies round about, so that they could not any longer stand before their enemies . . . as the Lord had sworn unto them" (Judges 2:10-11 and 14:-15).

The Christian origins of our country have been completely excluded from most curricula, unfortunately in private as well as public schools. No longer is the historical experience of our founding fathers woven around the theme of II Corinthians 3:17b: "Where the Spirit of the Lord is, there is liberty."

Christians have too often bought the lie put forth by Norman Lear's audacious theft of the meaning of the "American Way." Now, in our anti-Christian culture, pluralism means about what it did in first-century Rome—we are free to believe anything we want to as long as all of our action is predicated on the official faith of the state. This is what pluralism means in the Soviet Union, too. Gone is the Christian meaning of pluralism practiced in Colonial America which legally tolerated the existence of non-conformist local communities as long as they did not try to overthrow the Christian foundation of their own liberty.

Christians have yielded control of the education of their young to the secular humanist priests of the National Education Association teachers union and to the curricula which they dictate must be taught in the nation's classrooms. Pluralism now means that Christians are free to be Christians as long as they bow to the God of the humanists. The humanist priests make known their God's teaching in classrooms they control to the exclusion of parents, taxpayers, and elected officials.

The NEA platform is an amazing document supporting abortion, privileges for homosexuals, and busing, as well as opposing voluntary prayer in schools. Crossing a picket line is deemed unprofessional behavior.

The NEA, with its multi-billion dollar annual budget, has increased its leverage on the taxpayer by control of public education from the top down (the Federal Department of Education along with its equivalent in each of the 50 states). Operation of this supposedly public structure more closely resembles a private instrumentality of the NEA rather than a servant of the people.

Instead of an education based in Christian liberty, American education, with its secular humanist foundation, is using the techniques of Values Clarification to expunge the last vestiges of Christian morality. In place of traditional morality students are being taught the situation ethics of secular humanism.

Values Clarification makes it appear to the child as if he, through questions, experimentation, and role playing is arriving at his own answers to the fundamental questions of right and wrong. Students thus learn that Christian concepts regarding the value of human life and the integrity of the traditional family are "not necessarily valid for all people in all circumstances." Instead, the governing ethic of secular humanism is implanted: "If it feels good, do it."

The secular humanist understands the impossibility of a valueless fact better than does the contemporary Christian. This has resulted in a rather ineffectual opposition to such failures as the New Math. At best we hear complaints that it doesn't work. From the point of view of the secular humanist, the failure of this generation to be able to make change at the cash register is not relevant. Secular humanism has succeeded when they have the child believing (or assuming, if he is not interested enough to be aware of his beliefs) that *HE* decides whether or not 2 + 2 = 4.

As with morality, so with the nature of the universe, humanism places man at the center as the arbiter of all reality. Humanists are offended at the notion that children should simply be told that 2 + 2 = 4 because God set it up that way.

In other words, the God of our public school religious instruction is the Man of secular humanist mythology. That was the same sin of Adam and Eve when they decided that they would determine whether or not they would die if they ate of the forbidden fruit. That sin led to lawlessness, suffering, and death when Adam and Eve tried it, and our culture is headed the same way courtesy of humanist doctrine and the abdication of the Christian in the face of the Old Time Sin.

The secular humanists have controlled the educational system so long that Christians generally agree strongly with the "need" for their abdication from government. Christians have allowed their faith to be spiritualized into a religion unattached to the material world of God's creation. Christians have been convinced that there is not one reality, created entirely by God, but rather, autonomous areas of knowledge and existence, each with rules that man sees fit to apply in each independent area.

For too many Christians, Darwin's theory of evolution has replaced the account of creation set forth in Genesis. Even though evolution has never been proven on a single point, its utility for the humanist stems from the fact that while few Americans say they believe it, they act in terms of its premises. The assumption that evolution accounts for the creation of the world and the presence of man on the face of the earth frees the humanist to "discover" for himself the underlying principles of reality, and of right and wrong.

Evolution has gradually been applied to the fundamental premises of not just education, but law and politics as well. The result has been removal by secular humanists of Christ from the center and foundation of our law and politics following the removal of Christ from education. They then have the effrontery to turn about and intimidate any Christian attempt to repair the damage and restore Christ to law and politics. The humanist warns against violation of the "well-known" constitutional doctrine of separation of church and state, which of course, is to be found nowhere in the Constitution. (Look for yourself—the Constitution doesn't read at all as rendered in the media.)

The Declaration of Independence refers to inalienable rights. To be inalienable, a right must be created by God, and thus unchangeable, and then bestowed by Him on individuals. Humanist law recognizes no inalienable rights. For example, the very right to life itself has been subordinated to an invented right of privacy. In the name of "quality of life," America has stained the land with the aborted blood of over 1.5 million unborn children a year.

Who have the humanists established to determine the quality of life? Clearly, the Bible is no longer available as the bedrock of law and society as it was for our founding fathers. In place of the Bible, the ultimate law in the America of the secular humanists has become the Supreme Court. In the name of a "living constitution," nine men and women have taken the authority to find rights that never existed and take away rights bestowed by God and set forth in the Constitution drawn up 200 years ago.

The politicians have found this arrogation of power by the Supreme Court to be quite acceptable. Do you think abortion should be illegal? Elected officials quickly point out that they had nothing to do with that. What can they do? The Supreme Court says that it is legal.

For the "Me" generation, educated by the humanists to believe and act according to the ethic of "If it feels good, do it," abortion is an important part of the social safety net that government must provide for those devoted to self-gratification. (Of course, abortion is more discreet than the apostasy of Baal worship which called for throwing excess children into the flames burning inside idols.)

Local government is weakened when local politicians willingly surrender authority and responsibility to the central, Federal government. The reason for this is simple. Taxes must be raised incessantly in order to provide for the socialized welfare programs humanist government has yanked from churches and private charity.

Charity delivered through churches tends to prevent abuse because it is administered by people who know each other. The administrators are accountable to a congregation that, if it is Biblical, places a limit on welfare: "that if any would not work, neither should he eat" (II Thessalonians 3:10b).

The goal of Christian welfare is *restoration*—to return an individual to *self-reliance under God*. The goal of the statist welfare of the humanist is dependence. Dependence is facilitated by training up a generation in the nurture of self-gratification and the admonition to ignore the future. After all, even though we have lost our right to life before we are born, at least we have a right to live thereafter in whatever style we can vote for.

To try and pay for all this bloated government at the local level would be impossible. The American political scam has shifted the taxing responsibility increasingly to the central government. To raise these taxes at the local level not only involves risk of political defeat for local politicians, it also runs the risk that neighboring localities will not behave as irrationally as their neighbors, thus producing negative results for the high tax locality.

In brief, here is what has happened over the last few decades in America. We have taken Christ out of education, and replaced Him with a man-centered doctrine called secular humanism. This new religion has encouraged people to act as if there were no tomorrow, with only the moment to concern them. This has fostered a Christless politics which removes responsibility and accountability from local government because voters generally are not interested in exercising control over local politicians who increasingly are little more than local administrators of Federal policy who dole out Federally raised revenues.

This is extremely convenient for all politicians. When an

occasional concerned citizen voices objection to some tax or regulation, the local politician can point to Washington, or perhaps to the state capital. It is from there, the uppity citizen will be told, that "we were told we had to do it to you." The higher level of government "mandated" the program.

The concerned citizen will find it almost impossible to discover who in the state capital, let alone in Washington, is lording it over him and eating out his sustenance. And the congressman can throw up his hands and sigh that the program is "mandated." It is considered bad taste and politically irresponsible to suggest that Congress "un-mandate" its whoppers.

Ultimately, there is no middle ground in this battle. As Christ said in the Sermon on the Mount, "No man can serve two masters; for either he will hate the one, and love the other; or else he will hold to the one, and despise the other" (Matthew 7:24). Yet, Christians are trying to serve two masters indeed when they try to instill biblical precepts in their children while most of the week the priests of secular humanism are teaching their ethic and destroying the child's belief in God and His law. What is not taken care of at school is handled by the TV.

We are on the threshold of overt prohibitions against teaching Christianity. Already in the name of the non-Constitutional doctrine of "separation of church and state" and "academic freedom," Christianity cannot be taught in public institutions. Depending on which judicial circuit one lives in, it may even be illegal to use a public school room for a Christian meeting.

It is so true that the power to tax is the power to destroy. Even Christians often buy the pagan notion that the church's tax exemption is a "benefit" bestowed by government. This view has already lead to substantial restrictions on Christian schools via IRS regulations. Forgotten is the Christian notion of our founding fathers that the church's tax exemption is not a benefit, but a recognition that the state has no authority over the church. (That is the first amendment statement of church-state relations.)

At the moment, the battle centers around the effort by the benevolent humanists in Washington to prevent any church school from "benefitting" from tax exemption if it practices racial discrimination. Since there is a large consensus in the U.S. which disapproves of racial discrimination, the real issue conveniently has been obscured—namely, should the state have any say whatsoever over the terms of the church's exemption from taxation?

Here is what South Carolina Senator Ernest Hollings recently wrote to a constituent: "But when religious belief is contrary to the law of the land, then it is the law, not religion, that must be sustained."

Right now, Christians are only being asked to pay an unfair (higher) price monetarily for being Christians. We must pay taxes so that unborn children can be aborted through government sponsored "services," and we must pay taxes for religious indoctrination in public schools even if we place our own children in private, Christian schools.

The groundwork has been laid for more than just hitting up Christians for a surcharge for the practice of their beliefs. The foundation has been laid for an assault on Christian practice, and then we will have to choose to serve God or mammon. The choice at that time will cost us more than money. As Francis Schaeffer put it in *A Christian Manifesto*: "If there is no final place for civil disobedience, then the government has been made autonomous, and as such, it will have been put in the place of the Living God."

The secularization of our education, politics, and law puts Christians on a collision course with the state. Discussion of civil disobedience has to be taken seriously if we are to take our Christianity seriously. If God is the center of our lives, then He must be the center of our national life as well. Liberty comes from the Lord. "Where the Spirit of the Lord is, there is liberty."

For the moment there are ways short of civil disobedience and revolution to turn this bad situation around. As God told Israel in II Chronicles 7:14, "If my people, which are called by my name, shall humble themselves, and pray, and seek my face, and turn from their wicked ways; then will I hear from heaven and will forgive their sin, and will heal their land."

When the Lord used Gideon to remove the oppression of the Midianites from Israel, he had Gideon first seek the face of the Lord. Israel was in subjection to the Midianites because it had turned its face from God to Baal. Gideon was ordered to destroy his father's temple to Baal. In Schaeffer's words, there was "no final place for disobedience" under the Midianites—choosing God and destroying one's own idol demanded the death penalty. When Gideon's father Joash refused to turn Gideon over to the mob, the war was started.

To make sure that Israel would not think they had saved themselves, God reduced the troops available to Gideon from 32,000 to 300. Then, with 300 men, God used Gideon to annihilate the Midianites.

*Tool No. 2: A Well-Armed Local Militia*

The American Revolution was born when the Colonists, in Schaeffer's words again, felt that "there was no final place for civil disobedience," and that "the government had been made autonomous, and as such, it had been put in the place of the Living God."

The English Parliament had stated in the Declaratory Acts that the Parliament had the power to regulate every aspect of every Englishman's existence wherever he lived. Right there, they had declared that they were severing English law from what theretofore had been its basis in Christ.

When the Colonists declared that their American government was independent from a British Parliament which claimed to be autonomous from the Living God, there was a price to pay. In an effort to collapse the wherewithal of colonial independence, British authorities—in Massachusetts and in Virginia—endeavored to disarm the Americans by confiscating their arms and powder. That provoked the war and triggered the shot heard around the world.

The right of free persons to keep and bear arms traces back to Anglo-Saxon jurisprudence long before the discovery of America. Under the laws of Alfred the Great, who reigned in the ninth century, all English citizens (nobles and peasants alike) were obliged to purchase weapons and to be available for military duty. These laws were in force approximately 1,100 years before enactment of the Kennesaw, Georgia, ordinance requiring able-bodied heads of households to own firearms and ammunition.

According to our best information today, the term "militia" was first used during the Spanish Armada crisis of 1588 to refer to the entirety of the armed citizenry.

Virginia, in 1623, forbade people to travel unless they were well armed, and in 1631, the Colony required colonists to have target practice on Sunday. Virginia's Kennesaw precedent was enacted in 1658 when the Colony required every householder to have an operable firearm in his house. In 1673, Virginia law provided for government purchase of a firearm for the indigent, although repayment was required as the person was able.

The Massachusetts legislature required freemen and indentured servants alike to own firearms, and in 1644 went so far as to impose a six shilling fine upon a disarmed citizen.

After successfully throwing off the chains of a standing army, the former colonists made sure that the Constitution of the new Republic protected the people from such an affliction.

In Elliot's *Debates in the Several State Conventions* published in 1826, we have a precise record of what the framers meant by "militia" and the language of the second amendment. George Mason, author of the Virginia Bill of Rights, pointed out that the British had tried "to disarm the people—that was the best and most effective way to enslave them . . . by totally disusing and neglecting the militia."

Who are the militia, Mason asked? "They consist now of the whole people, except a few public officers."

Patrick Henry put it this way: "The great object is that every man be armed and everyone who is able may have a gun."

In a pamphlet aimed at swaying Pennsylvania toward ratification of the Constitution, Noah Webster argued: "Before a standing army can rule, the people must be disarmed as they are in almost every kingdom in Europe. The supreme power in American cannot enforce unjust laws by the sword, because the whole body of the people are armed, and constitute a force superior to any band of regular troops that can be, on any pretense, raised in the United States."

(If anyone doubt the continuing efficacy of Webster's statement, consider the Afghan resistance to Soviet invasion. For nearly two years a poor people armed with mostly World War I rifles have been able to stalemate the most sophisticated army of aggression the world has ever seen.)

The author of the second amendment, James Madison, mentioned in Federalist Paper 46 that: "The advantage of being armed, which the Americans possess over the people of all other countries [and that] notwithstanding the military establishments in the several kingdoms of Europe, which are carried as far as the public resources will bear, the governments are afraid to trust the people with arms."

The second amendment was passed by the House of Representatives with its present language: "A well regulated militia being necessary to the security of a free state, the right of the people to keep and bear arms shall not be infringed." In the Senate, an amendment was rejected which would have limited the keeping and bearing of arms to just "the common defense."

To subordinate this second amendment right of the *people* to the police power of the state, as a Federal judge did in upholding the Morton Grove handgun ban, is to side with the British against the Colonists—for oppression and against freedom.

Today, as in the past, that government which endeavors to disarm its people is trying to enslave the citizenry. Any supposed security from violence that would allegedly benefit us from disarmament can only be purchased in exchange for our freedom. Once we have lost our freedom, we lose the promised gain of security as well.

The right to keep and bear arms is just as important today as when the Bill of Rights was drafted. The right to keep and bear arms will be important until Christ comes again, because until then, people will be sinful. Crooks will steal, and murderers will kill, and government officials will tyrannize. The common thread is man presuming to make himself into a God. "Professing themselves to be wise, they became fools" (Romans 1:22).

Christ told us to "Occupy till I come" (Luke 19:13). It's hard for Christians to occupy while crooks, murderers, and tyrants are running around loose. Anti-Christian governments such as we have in the United States cannot be counted on to keep the peace. At the same time that we have two-bit despots on the Morton Grove Village Board making it illegal to possess a handgun, a Federal court in Washington, D. C. is ruling that the police do not have a responsibility to protect individuals—only to protect society as a whole!

If anybody thinks that that kind of government will keep them safe, then perhaps they are so far "off" mentally that they should not have a firearm. But the rest of us should.

*Tool No. 3: Electronic "Committees of Correspondence"*

While the nature of force has changed very little from the time of the American Revolution, communications have changed dramatically.

Paul Revere had to ride around all night in the cold to alert his neighbors about the British arrival. Today he would have picked up the phone, or gotten word out over his own radio telecommunications system. And now that the Federal Communications Commission has ruled that individuals can put up their own roof-top satellite receiver dishes, the prospect for variety and independence in transmission is virtually limitless.

At least until the advent of the personal satellite receiver in the mid-80s, the communications media, including radio, television, newspapers have been dominated by the liberal, humanist establishment.

One medium, however, has remained competitive. Conservatives have proven to be the most effective users of the mails. This skill has enabled conservatives to add a brand new aspect to the governmental decision making process, namely, grassroots lobbying.

Starting with Richard Viguerie, conservative direct mail professionals have enabled conservative groups and candidates to transmit their messages directly to their audiences without the constant distortion resulting from communicating through the liberal-dominated media. Those who support the causes and organizations who communicate through the direct mail then become the identified voice of a particular constituency that can be mobilized to speak out almost instantly on a particular issue.

The ability to elicit the input into a governmental body of thousands of postcards, calls, and letters has often changed the outcome of a rule awaiting promulgation or of a bill about to be enacted. Even the lowly, "mass-produced" postcard has real impact because it is a real message from a real voter.

The aspect of grassroots lobbying that most enrages those entrenched in power is the knowledge that the shift of power away from the local level has not completely obscured all of the antics of our public "servants." They react about as sweetly as a child caught with his arm in the cookie jar when the cards and letters start rolling in. They all but articulate the opinion that the peasants should not be so uppity.

Government has gotten so big at all levels that a real need for grassroots lobbying exists even in large counties, not to mention every state of the nation.

National issues can support, because of the tens of thousands of donors, full time staff to coordinate grassroots lobbying at that level. With few exceptions, this is not possible at the state and local level.

That is where the computer system originally developed for my state legislative campaigns comes in. Frank Slinkman, then my campaign supporter and now my partner in our company, Political Data Systems, has written such amazing programs that we are able to use a $2,000 Radio Shack computer to drive an $8,000 printer which produces 17,000 labels an hour or 3,000 to 4,000 letters per day, and with unparalleled selectivity. Apparently the programs will continue to improve as they have so often in the last three years. For instance, just recently, Slinkman discovered how to push a single mailing list size from 25,000 records to 50,000—all using five-inch minifloppy disks. Each record carries complete contributor information, volunteer history, and issue interests—in all, nearly 50 variables.

The first major use of our system outside the campaign arena occurred in 1980, when I was in the Virginia legislature. The State Board of Health was committed to putting in a regulation that would have used public funds to finance abortions. We figured that the vote would be 7 to 2, or 8 to 1 in favor.

We think the Board tipped off the pro-abortion forces in May, 1980, that there would be public hearings in September. The opposition had almost five months to organize. Even though I was in the state House, I didn't hear anything about the hearings until mid-August. But I did have my computer program, POLSYS™, and they didn't.

I went to my basement and pulled together a total of 7,500 anti-abortion names. The printer cranked out the labels, and almost as fast, I had a letter in the mail asking anti-abortion advocates to write to the Board of Health, both as a group and as individual members. I gave people the date of the hearing and the address of each of the Board of Health members.

The result? Within two weeks, the Board received 9,000 letters, petitions, and telegrams. In five months the pro-abortion forces, using traditional methods, had mustered only 2,000. In addition, more than 500 anti-abortionists showed up at the hearing and swamped the chamber.

It was incredible. My letter didn't mention the Governor, but he was getting copies of all the public input directed to the Board of Health—plus all the mail that was sent spontaneously to him directly.

He told me later that in his term of office this issue had produced one of the three top responses. The Board voted in favor of the pro-abortion regulation, 5 to 4. The Governor vetoed it, as well as two related bills that passed the 1981 session of the legislature.

With what was then less than $6,000 in equipment, we killed the abortion bills and raised $3,000 for the Virginia Society for Human Life. (We had asked for money for the group in the same letter in which we asked people to write to the Board of Health.)

I started out with about 3,500 pro-life names (plus another like number from pro-life groups in the state) in the 1980 project. We have carried out the project another time, and now my computer is able to disgorge over 20,000 labels and/or letters of pro-life people (some with volunteer contributor information, but most simply having come on board by signing a petition). This size list would be equivalent to nearly 1,000,000 names and addresses nationally.

We found that a list consisting of petition signers, that would be *worthless* for fundraising for a *national* organization, could accomplish fast turnaround legislative projects, pay for the mailing, and produce some net money on top. We think that this experience would be true for others, assuming the issue is state or local, the group making the mailing is state or local, and the project is a hot one, which clearly abortion funding is.

But POLSYS™ works on other issues, too, and at the county level as well. One evening an activist in the Fairfax County Taxpayer Alliance called. She was concerned that the petition drive to force a recent property tax increase into court was not going well.

The petition process is almost totally unknown in Virginia, but state law provides for automatic appeal into the county court of a new property tax levy within thirty days—if one percent of the voters of the county sign a petition for that purpose. For someone living in California, one percent does not sound like much, but in Virginia, we are not very experienced in collecting petition signatures. Furthermore, at the time I was called, over half the 30-day limit had expired.

We decided that we could afford the time and money to get a mailing of 1,000 out right away. After doing several "selects" on the computer, I found 957 names in Fairfax County who qualified on these criteria: either anti-tax or anti-ERA, who also had done any kind of volunteer work. Within ten days' time, the recipients generated most of the two percent of the voters who signed the petition. Frankly, the county officials were stunned (and privately outraged) that the Taxpayers Alliance had succeeded.

I asked for money in the letter, too, and $450 came in to the Fairfax County Taxpayers Alliance.

POLSYS™ was also used in the conservative takeover of the Fairfax County Republican Party. In Virginia, party elections are done by caucuses which we call mass meetings (at the sub-county level) and county conventions.

As the recruitment time drew to an end with the approach of the filing deadline, recruiters were beginning to exhaust their lists of conservatives who had previously attended conventions, friends at church, etc. We went into the computer file and developed two different "profiles" which turned out to be the winning margin needed in the party contest to put conservatives in charge of the Republican Party in a county of nearly 610,000 people. All this with only a few thousand dollars invested in computer equipment.

## *Conclusion*

Christians have the means to resist the approach of tyranny in the United States. We have technologies such as POLSYS™ and a political process that together permit Christians to organize, to lead, and to rule—but only if we are determined to be politically active in the Lord.

Tyranny, as in the case of Old Testament Israel, comes when education is forfeited to God's enemies. Such a generation couldn't care less about the threat of tyranny—"eat, drink, and be merry, for tomorrow we die." When a generation acts as if there is no tomorrow, there is always a tyrant around willing to steal their tomorrow.

Christ told us, "Occupy till I come." Either we occupy, or we will be occupied by His enemies.

Continued uninvolvement of the Christian community could well put us in the position that some of our brothers have already faced in the U.S. — run a pro-atheist "Christian" school or go to jail. It would be a pity to have to fight the American Revolution a second time. It would probably be harder, because rather than a King with a funny accent living several thousand miles away, the present situation is, as Pogo put it, "I have seen the enemy, and he is us."

It is an indictment of German Christians that they surrendered their government to an occultist like Hitler. With none of the higher powers ruled by Godly men, and with Hitler's Gestapo in complete control of the guns, Germans could only practice civil disobedience and suffer the consequences if caught. Harbor a Jew in one's house and ride with him to the concentration camp. When Israel rose up against a Parliament that oppressed through law severed from Christ, it was through higher powers (governments). Israel did not rebel under the leadership of self-appointed "freedom fighters," nor did the Americans. The American Revolution, as well as the restorations of Israel, were precisely that — restorations. Restorations of government under the law, not of men.

American Christians should welcome, and encourage, such movements as the Sagebrush Rebellion. The "Sagebrush Rebellion" is an effort by Western state legislatures to re-establish state authority over public lands now controlled by the Federal government. Since the movement has been lead by duly constituted authorities — the state governments — the Rebellion is proper. Movements such as the Sagebrush Rebellion are blessed opportunities to encourage state and local politicians to relearn their proper responsibilities and regain authority they have surrendered to the Federal government.

By the same token, Christians should be in the forefront of efforts to amend the Constitution in order to limit the excesses of Congress, the Supreme Court, and the Federal bureaucracy. Our efforts should also include support of legislation designed to withdraw jurisdiction from the Supreme Court under the powers of Article III Section I.

Biblical resistance to tyranny is not something that can be put off by American Christians. First we must pray. Pray for the peace of the land. Pray that we all would humble ourselves and turn from our wicked ways and seek the Lord. We are still free to put on the armor of God—his Word.

We are not yet at the point of our forefathers, or of Gideon, where seeking the face of the Lord and turning from evil is a capital offense. But we have no one to blame but ourselves if we do not, prepared by prayer and protected by the armor of God, go out to restore liberty to our land with a generation brought up in the nuture of the Lord.

"Where the Spirit of the Lord is, there is liberty."

# POLITICAL RESISTANCE TACTICS

Paul M. Weyrich

## *When To Fight*

WHEN we get into the question of legislative battles, the first question that has to be asked is, "When do you fight? When do you want to make the all out effort to win?" And the answer to that question is relatively simple: Whenever there is a basic principle at stake. Whenever there is a basic principle at stake you need to make a fight, regardless of how the situation looks, because failure to fight when there is a basic principle involved can mean a loss later on. It can mean that an opportunity is wasted—even though you don't have the numerical superiority.

In Washington, the prevailing attitude among current House and Senate legislative leadership of the republican party is the opposite. They will look at the matter and will take some preliminary soundings. Of course, nobody ever wants to commit initially unless the issue is very clear cut, so most of the legislators don't want to commit, and so the leadership will conclude that the issue can't be won. And so when it comes to a question of whether to fight or not, they will generally recommend: Don't fight. They will say: "You can't win that one and there is no point to fighting it—it would be an exercise in futility." Well, I totally disagree with that philosophy.

Let me give you a couple of stories that illustrate why I disagree. First of all is the story of Walter Hickel. I was in Washington when Walter Hickel was nominated by President Nixon to be Secretary of the Interior. The Senator for whom I worked at the time, Gordon Allott of Colorado, told the President in my presence that if he nominated an Easterner to be Interior Secretary, he, Allott, would see to it that the name never came out of the Senate Interior Committee. Allott and a group of other Westerners were pushing former Senator and

Governor Ed Meechem of New Mexico, but he was not acceptable to Nixon. So, they came up with Walter Hickel, Governor of Alaska. He was a Westerner and pro-development, and therefore, came close to satisfying the pro-development Western Senators on the Interior Committee. So, Hickel was nominated. Then his hearings came up, and every left-wing environmental protection group raised a cry of outrage against him. Now it's very interesting that they did that. They understood him better than we did. Senator Allott and Senator Clif Hansen of Wyoming and Senator Fannin of Arizona and some other Senators from the West went all out to defend Hickel. But throughout those days and days of testimony, which got a lot of headlines, Hickel was sitting through all this testimony listening, and something interesting was happening. He was confirmed, the vote was overwhelmingly in his favor. There were only 16 votes against his confirmation. If you look at that vote, you would say that was an overwhelming defeat for the people who waged the battle against Wally Hickel, because they only got 16 votes. The fact of the matter is, they won the war. Because while they cranked up all this campaign, the whole situation affected him to the point that when he got in, he spent the rest of his term accommodating those people who had criticized him. He became somewhat anti-development in the policies he introduced. The very people who had defended him were disappointed. By the time that he left office, the people who had defended him in his confirmation hearings were not sorry to see him leave. Those who attacked him in his confirmation hearings were praising him by the time he left. Who is to say that the liberals' fight, although getting only 16 votes, was the wrong fight from their point of view? After all, they ultimately got what they wanted out of the Secretary of Interior.

I'll give you another example: When the news came that Sandra Day O'Connor had been nominated to the Supreme Court, I had a meeting in my office of 50 different pro-family and conservative organizations. Since I have done some head-counting in the Senate on numerous legislative battles, I was asked in this meeting my assessment of the situation. If we went all out in the conservative movement, and we did everything we could, what would the results be in the Sandra O'Connor nomination fight? I said that, barring some secret revelation that would prejudice her case, in my opinion, if we did everything right, we would have at most five votes against her, and that we could well have even fewer votes simply because I knew the attitude of the Senators toward a woman appointee. If we have to have a woman, it doesn't matter what her philosophy is; as long as she looks like a woman, and talks like one, they'll vote for her. Based on that assessment, then, why then did the conservative movement, and the pro-family movement go all out on the Sandra O'Connor fight? You would think that with those numbers that would be suicidal. If under the best of circumstances, you get five votes, that's embarrassing, and if you get zero, that's more than embarrassing. As a matter of fact, there were a lot of arguments after she was confirmed by a 100-to-zero vote that the conservative movement has no clout in Washington. We reasoned, however, that if we didn't make the fight against her confirmation, particularly on right-to-life issues, then we would never have an opportunity to let her know the sentiment of the country. We made her sit through days and days of hearings. She made comments to various Senators involved, to the effect that she really hadn't understood a lot of the right-to-life issues before. In a head-to-head private session with one leading conservative Senator, she assured him, that come a vote on the abortion issue, she would not be on the wrong side of the issue. Now that she's on the Supreme Court, she could decide she doesn't want to keep that pledge, but assuming she is an honorable person, the fight was worth waging. First, she gave that commitment, and second, she learned things she otherwise would not have. She listened to the Freeman Institute tapes on the Constitution,[1] for instance, something she certainly wouldn't have done if that kind of fight hadn't been waged against her.

So, when you look at the situation, if you look only at the numbers, you can say, well, never wage a fight where it looks like you are going to get beat, that's political suicide. On the other hand, I think if you look at the confirmation of Sandra O'Connor, it's clear that some gain was made with her personally by our fighting that nomination with all our energy. I think that it made an impression on her. One last point: in the course of the battle, Administration people had special

1. "The Miracle of America" by Dr. W. Cleon Skousen. This excellent series of 12 cassette tapes and a study guide are available for $60 from The Freeman Institute, P.O. Box 31776, Salt Lake City, UT 84131.

meetings with us to say: Granted, we can't do anything about this appointment, and we know that you don't like it, but let's talk about the next one. Let's talk about future appointments. And as a matter of fact, two pro-abortionist women have since been eliminated from consideration as nominees for the District Court level because of that fight. We made it clear, if they wanted to go all out and fight for those, then they'd have a fight. The White House is very pragmatic (*very* pragmatic), and they don't like a lot of battles from any side. And so, if they are going to have to put up with a lot of grief, they would rather accommodate you in the meantime.

### *The Mentality of Legislators*

Let me explain the mentality of the average legislator. I have done training conferences all over the country, from Alaska to Florida, and made this explanation. Every time we have either a legislator or a former legislator in the audience, whether it's a Member of Congress or State legislator, every one of them has said, yes, that's really the way it works.

The diagram that I'm going to use is of the United States Senate in the 97th Congress (1981-82), because I'm not very good at arithmetic, and there are 100 people in the Senate, which makes for nice easy numbers. In this United States Senate, if you were to divide the Senate philosophically, you would have a group of conservatives on one side. These are people who vote for limited government, free enterprise, strong defense, and traditional values without being heavily lobbied. That's how I define a reliable conservative: Someone who votes that way in the absence of a national outcry to do so. In other words, if somebody sponsors an amendment, and there is no great deal of press coverage on it, but it is a clear

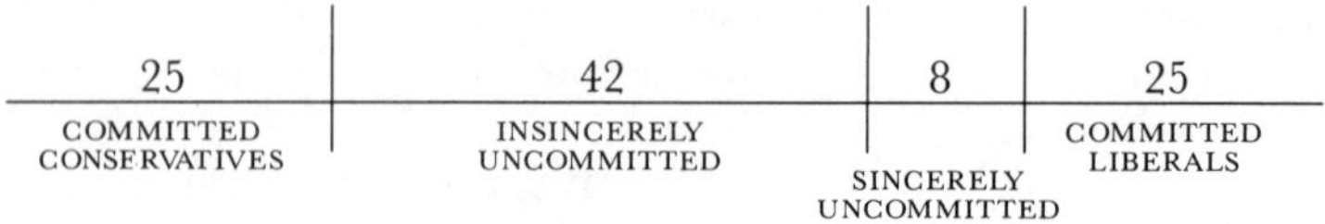

cut philosophical amendment, without a major campaign, you will get 25 votes in the Senate. That's up from only 12 or 14 a couple of years earlier.

Opposite them are the liberals, the people who are committed to bigger government, unilateral disarmament, more government regulations, and are opposed to traditional values. Today, if, say, Howard Metzenbaum sponsors an amendment, and there's no national campaign to that amendment, he will get, as it turns out, about 25 votes. Now, sometimes you will get 29 here or 29 there, but this is an average.

What all this means is that one half of the United States Senate is available—up for grabs by whoever can exert the strongest pressure. The Senators have *preferences rather than principles*. A lot of these folks here in the mushy middle would love it if they could get elected and for six years would never have to cast a roll call vote. That way they could say one thing to a group on one side, "I am really with you," and then they could come over to the other side and say to those who are on the opposite side of the first group, "I'm really with you," and nobody would ever know because you could never pin them down. Even as it is, with roll call votes, it is very difficult to pin them down. We almost have to be there to outsmart them and out-talk them because they'll be able to rationalize whatever they've done and tell us, "You really don't know what you are talking about." But nevertheless, one half of the United States Senate is uncommitted in the philosophical sense, and as I say, they tend to go one way or the other. But in the true philosophical sense, in terms of whether they have a world view, these Senators are uncommitted. And they are the people that you want to focus your attention on in a legislative battle.

For practical purposes, I divide these legislators into categories of Saints, Saveables, and the Sinners. I'm going to recommend something that is bad theology but good politics. In a theological context, you ought to spend a lot of time with the sinner to try to convert him, because there is more rejoicing in heaven over one sinner who returns than there is over all the just, but in political terms, it is a mistake. Because, in a political context, if you spend a lot of time with the committed leftwingers, you're going to expend enormous amounts of energy, time, and effort, and you're going to get virtually no result. Let me give some specifics. Ted Kennedy and Alan Cranston fall into this "Sinners" category. Jeremiah Denton and Jesse Helms fall into this "Saints" category. You don't have to worry about how Jesse Helms is going to vote; in all the years that he's been in the Senate, he has voted wrong so few times, nobody can remember. You don't have to have a national campaign to get him to vote right. Likewise, the liberals don't have to have a national campaign to get Kennedy or Cranston to vote for them.

The point is: in the legislative context, your efforts should be with the Saveables, because these are the people who exemplify the point made by the late Everett Dirksen: "When I feel the heat, I see the light." Now the "Saveables" group is divided into two parts, as follows: the *sincerely uncommitted*, of whom there are about 8, and the *insincerely uncommitted*, of whom there are about 42.

The *sincerely uncommitted* are people who are, as best I can describe it, of small vision. They have trouble making up their minds. You know, first of all, they can't decide which restaurant to go to, and when they finally make up their minds on that, they can't decide what to eat or what to have for dessert. Those are the people who can't decide what tie to wear in the mornings. In any case, these are the people who always see the small picture and yet have enormous, complicated questions. When you examine a bill, and say to yourself, "The whole world is at stake in this bill," you will find this group talking about some little clause being out of place in the text of the legislation. These people don't have an overall perspective. The "Saints" and the "Sinners" on either side, tend to see the large picture. The "Saints" tend to see the large picture that we would probably agree with, and the "Sinners" tend to see the picture that we wouldn't agree with; but nevertheless, in philosophical terms, both groups have a world view. They are doing things because they have a vision of how they think the country ought to be run.

The *sincerely uncommitted* simply have no vision. The group of 8 over here simply don't have a vision, and you've got to meet their little objections. There was a Senator, when I came to Washington, by the name of Jack Miller, from Iowa. Jack Miller was one of those people who had a small vision of things. He had an old typewriter in the cloakroom and he would come in, and for every major bill that came out, he would bang out 30 unprinted amendments. Other Senators would jump to get on Jack Miller's unprinted amendments because whoever would show him enough accommodation would wind up getting his vote in the end. These amendments did things sometimes like rearranging the commas. You would sit in wonder at some of these amendments because he seldom looked at the big picture, but usually dealt with something small. In sum, it pays to try to accommodate that individual because if you can reach his small objection, he will probably come your way.

To give an example: I was in a meeting with one newly elected Senator who won in 1980, and the Hyde Amendment was coming up on the Senate floor. Connie Marshner and I had gone over there to visit him on a different matter, that didn't have anything to do with the Hyde Amendment. We were talking to him and all of a sudden he said, "By the way, where do you people stand on the Hyde Amendment?" (The Hyde Amendment prevents Federal funding of abortions.) To me, that is as clearcut an issue as you will find in the country. From my philosophical perspective, it is unbelievable that somebody wouldn't have a clear cut view of that, one way or the other. But anyway, he said, "Where do you people stand?" Both of us said we favored the Hyde Amendment. He said, "I would like to be with the Hyde Amendment too, but. . . ." He got up and started pacing back and forth and said, "but you know, I don't see that right to lifers who are concerned about that, are doing anything for the poor people who are brought into this world. This bothers me, and I don't see how I can vote for that when I don't see anything being done to help them once they're born." Now, to me that is, first of all, confusing issues, and second, a perception that doesn't coincide with reality. But it was his concern. It so happened, we had some very recent information of a program that Senators Jepsen, Armstrong, and others were involved in, which is now called the STEP Foundation. It is a foundation to help the poor, using the resources of the conservative churches. So we told this Senator about this foundation for the poor, and it was like taking a great load off of his shoulders. While we were talking to him the bell rang and he had to leave, and when I looked at the roll call the next day in the *Congressional Record*, he had voted right. I am absolutely convinced, that if we hadn't been there at that particular time, and able to meet his objection, we wouldn't have gotten his vote. I may be wrong, but in many cases with the people who have a small vision of a large problem, it pays to listen, because they are sincere. There is no question in my mind that this Senator was sincere.

There is also a sort of subcategory to the *sincerely uncommitted*, and not all legislatures have it. But they may if they have old members. The U.S. Senate has a number of examples. Senator Len Jordon of Idaho was one, as was Senator Milton Young of North Dakota in his final years. These are people who are very inflexible. They become so touchy that any kind of lobbying at all will tend to send them in the opposite direction. Perhaps they want to feel that they are not going to be bought by anybody and nobody is going to control them, and so on. If you have somebody genuinely like this, it is best to stay away from him. As a matter of fact, what I used to do in the case of Len Jordon, I would put out the word to the opposition that we just couldn't pin down Len Jordon, and were worried about his vote. They would go all out and try to get him. And as soon as they did that then he would come running right into our hands. If you have somebody unusual like that, make sure the opposition pressures him, and you'll get his vote. If you pressure them, they go the other way, regardless of their history or their philosophy, their previous votes and everything else.

To know who's in what category you must get information from inside the legislature. People ask me, "How do you come up with a chart like this?" My answer is, you have got to work with somebody on the inside and force him to put legislators into these categories. A lot of times people don't want to do that. But if they have a reasonable good power of observation, you will be able to get them to break down your state legislature or your City Council or whatever it is into these categories. Then you'll know who to work with. But be sure you pick the right person to talk to. Some people don't have good powers of observation.

The hardest work in the legislative battle is with the *insincerely uncommitted*. The insincerely uncommitted have only one issue that's important to them: their *re-election*. The people who manage to get their votes are the people who make the linkage between their issue and the legislator's future. In the past, these people tended to virtually and completely go to the liberal side, because Washington was wired in such a way that the only people making a fuss, and the only people making a fuss at the grassroots level, were all liberal. For example, a lot of people voted for the ERA Time Extension who were not really for it, but they were convinced they had to do that because not to do it would mean the feminists would harass them in the future.

Now we have a somewhat different situation. It's very interesting. You may have heard, for example, that the Religious Right is causing a great constitutional crisis in the country and everybody's religious liberty is at stake because religious people are out working in the political process. Understand that what is being said hasn't anything to do with religious liberty—nobody's future is at stake—and the Constitution is safe. What's happening is that these *insincerely uncommitted*, who formerly had it very easy, now have hard choices to make. It used to be that, whenever it came time to choose, they got pain from only one side, the left. So following the pain-pleasure principle, in order to relieve the pain they went to the left. The reason they complain that we have a great constitutional crisis now is that pain is being inflicted from both sides, and that means they have got to choose. Now they have to figure out, "Let me see: if I go one way, I'm going to get beat up over here, and if I go the other way, I'm going to get beat up over there." They hate that more than anything else. That means they could be in error. In the past, they would just go toward the liberal side and would get praise from the media, and all the liberal grassroots groups would praise them, and while the conservatives would grumble, they were never well organized to do anything about it. A Southern Democrat from South Carolina was once very candid with me when I talked to him about a particular bill and he said, "You know, I recognize the majority of people of my district are opposed to this legislation, but, the ones who get out and work, the liberal activists who opposed me in my election, they're for it. I'm going to be in favor of it because the other people don't count, they don't organize, they don't vote, they don't work." Of course, he was absolutely right, until more recent times.

The question is how to deal with these insincere people. What you have to do—if not in reality, at least in perception—is to persuade them it is more costly to cross you than it is to cross the opposition. If you are able to make that case, you will have a chance at getting their vote.

* * * * * *

A footnote to Mr. Weyrich's essay: In *Christianity Today* for 15 July 1983, page 30, it was reported that the U.S. Supreme Court has extended the 1973 *Roe v. Wade* decision, "by nullifying state laws that require women to be hospitalized for late abortions, to be informed about fetal development, and to be given a 24-hour waiting period before going through with the operation."

Leading the dissent, however, was Justice Sandra Day O'Connor. The article goes on to say that leaders of the right-to-life movement praised O'Connor's stance, but that she has taken "biting criticism from women's rights groups" for it.

# HOW TO LOBBY

Connie Marshner

THIS is a preliminary introduction to lobbying. The first thing to do is to make sure that you feel comfortable with thinking of yourself as a lobbyist. The word itself has a sort of negative connotation. The image of smoke-filled rooms, behind closed doors where mysterious and unethical things take place is one that lobbyists have had for some time. But you should come away from such negative connotations or you will not be an effective lobbyist. The *Federalist Papers*, Federalist 10 in fact, describes what basically amounts to the process of lobbying. The very first lobbyist recorded in our country's history was a Methodist minister named Isaiah Cutler who went to the First Continental Congress and said, "Listen, I would like you folks to give me some land, and in turn, I promise to build a school on a portion of it." Eventually, that idea became the Land-Grant College concept.

Lobbying is not a matter of forcing people to do things that are wrong. It is not a matter of forcing your will on people. Lobbying is a matter of communication between who is being represented and who is doing the representing. It's communication between human beings. A baby who wakes up at 2 o'clock in the morning and cries for a meal, is a lobbyist. He is letting you know what he wants. Now, he may not be very effective at it, because the secret of effective lobbying is that it is pleasant for both parties, and 2 o'clock in the morning has limited pleasant aspects. But that baby is a lobbyist, so be comfortable with the concept of yourself as lobbyist. Lobbying simply means that you're communicating with an elected representative and telling what you want him to do and what you need. And as a voting member of the public or a member of an organized group, you are entitled to do that; in fact, you ought to do it.

### *How a Congressional or Legislative Office Functions*

You can tell a great deal about what your Congressman's intentions are by looking at how he organizes his office. Congressmen and Senators in Washington have a certain staff allowance and a certain office allowance. They have a lump sum of money they can spend however they feel best to help them carry out their duties. They may have as many offices as they want. And you can tell by looking at the configuration what your Congressman is interested in doing. If he has six different regional offices, and a minimum crew in the Washington office, then you can know that he is more interested in mending fences back home than he is in his legislative function. On the other hand, many Congressional offices are very top heavy in Washington; for instance, they may have umpteen lawyers on the staff and numerous research assistants. That office is interested in being a legislator. Once you know what type you have, you have a better idea how to proceed to lobby him. If he's very interested in what the folks back home are thinking, that's where you ought to put your pressure. If he's very Washington oriented, and has most of his researchers in Washington, then that gives you the clue that if you're going to get to him, you must get to the people in the Washington office.

Let's now look at various sources of pressure that can be brought to bear on legislators.

### *Media*

Obviously, the media are a major source of pressure. Some staffer in every Congressional office reads the hometown newspaper every day. The folks who read it in the district office call the Washington office every day and give an account of what the editorials said, and the letters-to-the-editor, and the news topics. Indeed, they will keep very close to what the hometown press says. That's why it is worth your time to get letters to the editor in your hometown paper. Learn how to write succinct, thoughtful, interesting letters to the editor, and then send them in. Practice writing them until you learn how.

Most Congressional offices also read the *New York Times* and the *Washington Post*, faithfully, every day. The Congressmen and their staff also watch *Good Morning America* and the *Today Show* and the weekend news interview shows. Legislators are very conscious of the media—you can say that with a certain validity. Some Congressmen at times are terrorized and refuse to take action because they are afraid of what the media will think of them. For many of them, principle takes a back seat to perception. In politics, perception is 99% of reality. And until the *New York Times* or the *Washington Post* has given respectability to something—the right-to-life movement, for example—the right-to-life movement doesn't exist in the eyes of these weak members. And that's true of any issue. Suppose you're trying to get parents' rights in sex education to be an issue of concern to your State representatives. If you can get factual coverage in the newspapers locally, then you have established some credibility that your issue is real. Until a politician reads it in the newspaper, he doesn't believe it is real. So media is very important pressure on a legislator.

### *Peer Pressure*

The second major source of pressure has the potential of being more destructive than any of the others. This is peer pressure. Peer pressure and, of course, party pressure. If a legislator is of the party in power, then he's subject to Administration pressure from the President in Washington or, in his state, from the Governor. How does this peer pressure operate? Look at it from the point of view of the establishment vs. the non-establishment. The establishment, in the party context, is essentially dedicated to just moving along in a nice comfortable way.

Let me give you an example of that. Say a hard-charging freshman Congressman gets elected and comes to Washington to fight for social issues. He gets taken aside by the party leader, who says, "Listen, Joe, we really like you, but if you hang around with people like the New Right, then you're not going to get along." Most Congressmen want to get along, they want to get invited to the right cocktail parties, and they want to get invited to the right dinner parties, and in order to achieve that, they don't offend the people who send the invitations. So the average fellow, when he gets taken aside like this, will respond like a puppy to the sight of food. They want to follow the establishment, that's human nature. Sometimes, after two or three years, they realize the leadership has sold them a bill of goods, and they begin to become leaders in their own right. It takes a couple of years. I've seen that happen, but in the meantime, they're little more than a vote.

It's only human to want to do what your peers want, you know. When someone you respect says, "I wish you would stop talking about that," it really makes you feel uncomfortable. Unless you are really committed in principle, you are likely to say, "Well, gee, I didn't mean to offend you." This very strong social pressure is the reason why so many politicians work within the party structure, thinking that when they get to the top of the party establishment things might be different. In the meanwhile, this sort of peer pressure tends to push Congressmen away from being hard-chargers.

### *Staff and Interns*

If you are a Congressman or a Senator, and/or to a certain extent, a State legislator, you have, like the rest of the world, a 24-hour day. But in Congress you have about 64 hours worth of work to put into those 24 hours. You have thousands of letters a day, most of which you'll never see. You have hundreds of phone calls a day, most of which you'll never be able to return. Hundreds of people are demanding, begging, pleading, and cajoling to see you, most of whom you'll never be able to see. So what do you do? You delegate your authority. You've got to delegate; you've got to rely on other people to do these things, and to provide you with information because you haven't got time to do it yourself. Whom do you rely on? You rely on your staff. If you ever go to Washington when Congress is in session, station yourself on the corner of Independence Avenue by the Capitol. There you can watch the Congressmen walking over to the Capitol to vote. Almost always they have a staff member trotting alongside of them, and the conversation goes something like this:

> Congressman: "Hey, John, what are we voting on here?"
> Staff person: "This is the Health Care Financing Bill."
> Congressman: "Well, how should I vote on it?"

Votes are cast that way many times. Occasionally there are some major issues where the Congressman actually forms his own opinion. These tend to be either big national issues or big local issues which a Congressman can't avoid knowing about. Then you do have people who take an issue to heart and make it their personal cause. Then they know what they think about it. But in general, for the run of the mill issues, most votes are cast that way, by relying on staff analysis and recommendation.

Staff work is certainly how they answer their letters. A Senator sees very few letters. The staff writes them. Therefore the staff is in the powerful position of putting words into their mouth. Staff also writes statements for newsletters, speeches for debates, comments for newsletters. Staff keeps the Congressman's calendar. Congressmen only rarely write those committee reports or the amendments to bills; the staff does all of that. The staff is more powerful than the legislator in some instances.

Don't get the impression I'm belittling staff. Not at all. A reliable, honest, hardworking staff person is as valuable a friend as a legislator can have. Former staffers occasionally run for Congress themselves, and do as well—or better—a job than anyone else. The reality is that an efficient staff person becomes very powerful. Power, like handguns, is morally neutral. Whether it's good or bad depends on how it is exercised. Being a staffer to a legislator is an opportunity to serve the Lord. Discharging properly your duties there has intrinsic benefit to the nation, as well as the intrinsic value to your soul of doing any job well and faithfully. And right now, there is not enough conservative staff to go around. If you have any sons or daughters who are conservative, college-educated, and looking for a career, talk to them. Urge them to come to Washington. It takes three or four years for somebody to get a foundation of Hill experience, and to learn how to be effective, but once those skills are mastered, if the individual is committed, there's no limit to how far he or she can go.

The last couple of years, the conservative movement had the problems of being asked by good newly elected conservatives to help find them a staff. The bottom of the barrel was scraped in 1981 on Capitol Hill by legislators who were looking for conservative staff. There are plenty of liberals. For example, Strom Thurmond, a strong conservative Republican, of South Carolina, is the Chairman of the Judiciary Committee in the Senate. His chief staffer is a former Kennedy staffer, because there wasn't anybody else to take the job. There you are talking about a position for which experience is the critical qualification. That staffer had worked for the other side and he knew what the bills were, and what the amendments were, and what section 5205 of this means, and what the Smith Amendment to that means, and so on. He could make a case for himself, saying: "I am not biased by any one fact or world view, I just know the facts." That's the problem: if you're a Senator, say on the Interior Committee, and you are dealing with oil reserves, or deep sea mining, you need a staffer who is a conservative and who also knows deep sea mining or whatever, *and* has the Capitol Hill experience so he knows how to write a bill and how to draft a committee report and amendments and all of this kind of thing. You're talking about a person with extensive qualifications. The point is: There is a shortage of qualified conservative staff.

Liberals have a system for developing competent staff. This is the *intern system*. It goes back to the 60s, when liberals would take the best and the brightest, the most ambitious college students from all over the country and bring them into Washington to work in the summers or during a semester, sometimes receiving college credit for it, in a Congressional office. The zealous, enthusiastic, energetic kids don't think anything of working 12 hours a day and welcome the opportunity. It gives them a boost in their career. The intern system has not been effectively supported and utilized by conservatives. There has been one program in Washington in which Christian colleges try to cooperate, but it is not a very large program, and it does not outreach to conservative students. Conservative legislators, when they get interns, like them to be conservative, and they also like them to be intelligent. Internships are a way of learning to become a Capitol Hill staffer, so bear that in mind. At one point, Jacob Javits, a former liberal Senator from New York, had on his staff, all told, something like 50 lawyers—that doesn't count legislative aides or professional staff researchers or anything of that sort, just lawyers. And they were there cranking up bright ideas. You can understand how important the pressure of the staff is.

### *Bureaucracy*

Next is a source of pressure you cannot overlook. That's the bureaucracy. In politics, as in most walks of life, *knowledge is power.* Information is power. And who controls information, has power. If you were a state legislator, and you were trying to formulate a conservative education policy for your state, and you were sitting there thinking, "I'm going to write a bill to turn the education system in this state right side up," you realize very quickly, that you need to know how the Education Department is organized, where it gets its money, and what the money is used for. And where do you go to get that information? Most likely, you'll go to the Education Department and you'd bring out the friendly bureaucrat and you'd say, "I'm Senator X and I need to know where you get your money and what you're doing with it." And then what happens? They tell you what they want you to know. The political appointees in a bureaucracy may be fine, solid fellows, but even they have to rely on information from their bureaucrat staff. They only know what the staff tells them.

As a grass roots activist, if you can provide information from other sources, you have yourself some leverage. For instance, if there's a legislator trying to improve the education system, the State Education Department representative tells him: "We need more money for the sex education program because we were only able to reach 15,000 students last year and we have a problem with teenage pregnancy. If we could only reach more sooner then we can do something about that problem." Your average politician will say, "Okay, fine, good point." If you as a parent or activist have information that is documented and can stand up to scrutiny, you can go to the legislator and say, "Listen, let me give you some information about what this sex education program is really doing." Show him the material, underline it, prove to him that the State Department of Education funded it, and so forth. Show where the bureaucrats are wasting money, or where the money is being misspent or where the program is a little behind. If you can do that, then what you are doing is counter-balancing that pressure, because you're providing information; you're countering a monopoly of information.

Often grassroots people have access to lots of information, but don't always know what to make of it. There's danger, of course, of blowing something out of proportion. The danger is that you lost your credibility. And that, of course, is a fatal mistake. Don't ever use any information that you cannot prove. As an activist and a leader, *your credibility is the most precious thing you have.* If you go to a politician or to the press and say something, you have got to be able to prove it. Not just by hearsay or "I heard somebody on the radio say it." You've got to get proof in writing. Only then you can counter that monopoly of information.

The courts are also a source of pressure on legislators. Courts make decisions on which way the wind is blowing politically, even the U.S. Supreme Court. There was an article in the *Washington Post* a couple of years ago about, "Why has the Supreme Court not taken a case about homosexual rights?" And the point of the article was basically that the public was not ready for a decision on the issue. There have been many times when a conservative amendment has not been added to a bill, or a conservative bill has not been introduced or brought to the floor, because a politician has said, "Well, while I like the idea, I'm afraid the courts will find it unconstitutional." So, instead of saying, "Let's pass it and let the courts challenge it," the legislators back off. The courts are very much a part of the political pressure system.

### *Special-Interest Groups*

Then there are the special-interest groups. This has become a dirty word in the last couple of years, because suddenly conservatives have been organizing their own special-interest groups. Until recently, there were the old-line special-interest groups: The League of Women Voters; the American Civil Liberties Union; Ralph Nader's many consumer front groups; the professional welfare workers societies—which go by deceptive names like Child Welfare League of America; the environmentalist extremes like National Wildlife Federation and the Sierra Club; the teachers unions' National Education Association and American Federation of Teachers; the professional pacifists. More recently there are such stars in the constellation as the National Abortion Rights Action League, the National Gay Task Force, the National Organization for Women, and such fringe groups as animal rights groups. Recently also are conservative right to lifers, and a conservative pro-family movement which are not quite balancing the pressure simply because they are new at it. Our people don't have the channels of communication and organizational structure necessary for maximum effectiveness. But we're learning.

The great pressure generated by special-interest groups

results from their making a connection between the Congressman's future and their issue. You know how the ERAers did it? Senators who didn't believe in ERA, voted for ERA. Why? Because they were scared that if they went home, having not voted for the ERA, they would be picketed, and there would be nasty letters to the editor, and the Women's movement in their state would de-elect them. Senators who didn't believe in the thing, voted for it because the pressure was so strong!

### *Local Government*

State and local government can be another source of pressure on a Congressman. You'd better believe when a State legislature passes a memorial asking Congress to do something, it is noticed by Washington. Early in 1981, I was in a room with a group from the distiller's lobby, and they were in a state of distress because the state of Utah had just passed a memorial to Congress, asking Congress to enact a law putting warning labels on alcoholic beverages: "Caution, this can be dangerous to your health." These lobbyists were as nervous as house cats because Orrin Hatch, who is Chariman of the Senate Human Resources Committee, is from Utah, and they figured Hatch would be starting a campaign in Washington to do the same thing.

Another example of how local activity can have impact on Washington comes from Maryland. Recently a group of parents who were bound and determined to do something about drugs got organized. They got their state legislature to pass laws outlawing the sale of drug paraphernalia. That issue has since turned into a nationwide campaign. In Maryland, one of the most interesting things to happen was that these mothers went to their U.S. Senator Charles Mathias, a liberal Republican, and all of a sudden he became a real believer. He never paid attention before, but all of a sudden he began to get the message. The activity in the State wasn't trying to influence him because it was focusing on the State legislature. He had his finger in the wind and decided to be friendly to the winners. So when you have the opportunity to make waves at your state level, be aware that this may indirectly affect your federal legislators in Washington. So that in itself can be a very important factor.

### *Think Tanks*

What is a think tank? A think tank is basically a hothouse of ideas. It is a research institute, generally of 501(c)(3) tax status, a non-profit, non-political organization. Its purpose is to provide a nesting place for people with bright ideas, provide them with a place to do their own research, provide them credibility and prestige. They sit there and think up new ideas, and then document the needs of their new ideas.

The left wing has had think tanks for ages and ages. You may be familiar with the Brookings Institute, the Aspen Institute, the Institute for Policy Studies, the Childrens Defense Fund, and a lot more. Conservatives have recently begun competing in this arena with groups like the Heritage Foundation or the Free Congress Foundation. The latter deals with social issues, while Heritage researches mostly business and foreign policy issues.

### *Grass Roots Activity*

The last source of pressure on the chart is the grass roots. Grass roots are distinguished from special interest, in that grassroots activists do not make money from their concern. Also, grassroots folks are more spontaneous and often not as well organized.

Let me give you a case study of how all these things interact. Back in 1970, there was a White House Conference on Children and Youth. It was a Republican Administration, but the thing was run by the HEW bureaucracy. The White House Conference on Children cranked up an idea for federal child care. They said millions of children are not meeting their full potential, so we need child development programs. They took that idea to Congress, where the staff of senator Walter Mondale of Minnesota wrote up the bill and got him to introduce it. There was working at the Brookings Institute think tank a woman by the name of Alice Rivlin. She began cranking out scholarly monographs and research papers on the need for federal day care. She found other people, and they helped fund other studies to show how there were X number of children of X number of working mothers in need of day care, and so forth. The legislation began moving through in Congress. When it got close to the point of being voted on, Alice left her job at Brookings and went over to the *Washington Post*, where she cranked up editorials and news articles to support further the general thrust of calling attention to this terrible national problem. The bill passed the House, and it passed the Senate, and it went to the President. Meanwhile, conservatives got the word out, and the President vetoed it. At the time there was an unprecedented flood of mail to the White House demanding a veto. They were very surprised by this spontaneous overflow of powerful feeling. It proved to be the beginning of the pro-family movement historically. Now you may have heard of Alice Rivlin recently, because like a bad penny she doesn't disappear. The first sour note in Reagan's honeymoon was sounded by the Congressional Budget Office, which proclaimed that Reagan's figures were inflationary. Who was it who was directing the congressional budget office? Alice Rivlin, that's right. She had at this point moved on to the staff level. You can see how all these different institutional forces work together.

## CONTRIBUTORS

**Harry Caul** writes for *Popular Communications* magazine.

**David Chilton** works for the American Bureau of Economic Research, Tyler, Texas, and is the author of *Productive Christians in an Age of Guilt-Manipulators*.

**Louis DeBoer** is a minister in the American Presbyterian Church.

**Michael R. Gilstrap** is the Administrator of Geneva Divinity School Press.

**A. Richard Immel** is a contributing editor of *Popular Computing* magazine.

**Wayne C. Johnson** is a specialist in political direct-mail campaigning, and resides in Sacramento, California.

**James B. Jordan**, Th.M., is an instructor in theology at Geneva Divinity School, Tyler, Texas.

**Douglas Kelly**, Ph.D., is a Research Associate of the Chalcedon Foundation, and currently teaches at Reformed Theological Seminary, Jackson, Mississippi.

**Francis Nigel Lee**, Ph.D., Th.D., is a Professor of Theology at Emmanuel College, Queensland University, Australia.

**Connie Marshner** is a researcher at the Free Congress Foundation, Washington, D.C., and has been active in the Pro-Family movement.

**Gary North**, Ph.D., is the editor of *Remnant Review*, an economic newsletter. His most recent book is *The Last Train Out*.

**Lawrence D. Pratt** is the national lobbyist for Gun Owners of America, and co-owner of Political Data Systems, Inc.

**Pat Robertson** is the creator of the CBN television network, and host of the "700 Club."

**Rousas John Rushdoony**, M.A., B.D., is the president of the Chalcedon Foundation. His most recent book is *Law and Society.*

**Herbert Schlossberg**, Ph.D., is a professional economic advisor, and author of *Idols for Destruction*.

**Otto J. Scott** is a noted Christian author. His most recent book is *The Secret Six*.

**Wayne C. Sedlak** is a pastor of Reformed Bible Church, Brookfield, Wisconsin.

**Ray R. Sutton**, Th.M., is a pastor of Westminster Presbyterian Church, Tyler, Texas.

**John Wesley** was the founder of the Methodist movement in England and America.

**Paul M. Weyrich** is director of the Free Congress Foundation, and also of the Committee for the Survival of a Free Congress. He is a specialist in the field of political mobilization.

# ABOUT CHRISTIANITY AND CIVILIZATION

*Christianity and Civilization* is published occasionally, at least twice annually. Subscribers are sent each issue as it is published, postage free, and receive a 10% discount. Address: 708 Hamvasy Ln., Tyler, TX 75701.

Essays in *Christianity and Civilization* are intended to be scholarly, but non-technical, and are aimed at the literate layman. It is intended as a forum for serious discussion within Christian circles. The perspective of *Christianity and Civilization* seeks to be thoroughly Biblical, comprehensively catholic, and distinctively Reformed.

*Geneva Divinity School,* which sponsors the journal, is located in Tyler, Texas. The school is a ministry of Westminster Presbyterian Church, a member of the Association of Reformation Churches. In addition to *C&C,* Geneva issues four monthly newsletters (available upon request): *Calvin Speaks, The Geneva Papers, The Geneva Review,* and *The Phineas Report.* Geneva Divinity School Press publishes both reprints and new works, designed to assist the work of Christian reconstruction in our day. There is a six-week Summer Training Program for college and seminary students, which provides lectures and assignments in the Christian view of theology, politics, economics, the arts, and more. Finally, Geneva Divinity School offers parts curriculum in the form of correspondence courses. Tapes of lectures are also available. For information on any of these ministries, write to 708 Hamvasy Ln., Tyler, TX 75701.

## *Geneva Divinity School*

Founded in 1980, Geneva Divinity School was set up to fill a gap in existing theological education. Virtually all existing theological seminaries have adopted either a position of studied indifference to the problems of contemporary civilization, or a position embracing to one degree or another the solutions to those problems advocated by modern humanism and revolutionary Marxism. Sadly, this is the case not only in liberal seminaries, but also in evangelical and

Reformed theological schools as well. The purpose of Geneva Divinity School is to provide ministerial and academic training to Christian leaders, training which reflects historic Biblical Christianity, a Protestant perspective on the Bible, and the desirability of building a Christian civilization (Gen. 1:26-28; Matt. 28:18-20).

Though there are many obstacles to Christian civilization arising from the world, the flesh, and the devil, there are also obstacles within today's church. Five of these obstacles which are of particular importance are "pietism," intellectualism, revolutionism, ignorance of Scripture, and ignorance of the Biblical doctrine of justification.

The attitude which we call "pietism" is characterized by the belief that the Christian community *should not* try to reform society. Rather, all our efforts should be directed toward producing Christian character in individuals, and generating a healthy family and church life. Society will be changed indirectly by the influence of Christian individuals, but the church should not prophesy to society, and no program of reform should be constructed. We at Geneva Divinity School agree with "pietism" that the foundations of Christian culture are the Christian home and the local church, and that the first work of the churches must be to build Christian character into individuals and families. We believe, however, that Scripture requires us to think hard about the nature of Christian civilization, to try to develop the Biblical alternative to humanistic civilization, and to prophesy Biblically to the cultural problems of our age.

A second problem is intellectualism. There is much fine scholarship being generated in Christian circles today, but for the most part it is characterized by a studied indifference to the problems of civilization. We at Geneva Divinity School intend to make the most of true Bible-believing scholarship and intellectual endeavor, but to join this with a strong concern to reconstruct our culture on a Biblical foundation.

A third obstacle to Christian civilization, manifest within the churches and seminaries, is revolutionism. Increasing every year is a revival of anabaptistic perspectives, theologies of liberation, and egalitarianism within the evangelical and Reformed theological seminaries. We at Geneva Divinity School stand opposed to this kind of political theology, with its emphasis on rights instead of duties, its evident commitment to socialistic violation of the Eighth Commandment, and its rejection of the Biblical, covenantal form of society in favor of the modern humanistic theory of total equality. We agree that the Christian community must address itself to modern social problems, such as poverty, crime, abortion, and war;

but we insist that the Bible's solution to these problems is not simply a watered down humanism.

A fourth difficulty is ignorance of Scripture. For a variety of reasons, a great many believers in the churches today are ignorant of vast portions of Scripture. Partly this is due to the influence of liberalism, which disparages the Old Testament and most of the New. Partly this is due to the influence of some extreme dispensational theories which also throw out the Old Testament. We at Geneva Divinity School are whole-Bible Christians as well as New Testament Christians. We believe that the whole Bible should be studied and taught, and that God's basic principles for life have not changed from Bible times. Now that Jesus Christ has been enthroned on high, we must call the world to bow the knee, and adopt His entire Word as our rule for life. The New Testament does not abolish the Old Testament, but completes and fulfills it. Thus, the curriculum of Geneva Divinity School entails a study of every book of the Bible.

A fifth difficulty is ignorance of the Biblical doctrine of justification. Scripture declares that the perfect righteousness of Christ and His death for our sin, imputed to His people, is the sole ground of their justification. Those who receive this imputed righteousness by saying "amen" to God—covenant faith—are cleared of sin and guilt before the law-court of heaven. While this doctrine is given lip-service on all sides, it is effectively denied by much modern evangelical teaching and preaching. We are told that we should feel guilty about the poor, feel guilty about the heathen, and so forth. Biblical Christianity does not, however, try to motivate believers by guilt. Believers are to be motivated by love and obedience, not by guilt. Those who are justified are freed from guilt.

People who are not freed from guilt will seek release in other ways. It is no accident that the theology of liberation, which seeks freedom apart from the Protestant doctrine of justification, is immensely popular in Roman Catholic and neo-anabaptistic circles. Those who reject the Biblical doctrine of justification are today seeking to work off their sense of guilt through revolutionary activity.

Furthermore, those who cling to their guilt and seek to make other Christians feel guilty, necessarily also reject the blessings of God's covenant. The guilty man is embarrassed by riches and blessing, because he feels he does not deserve them. True, none of us deserves God's blessing, but the justified man, confident in Christ, can rejoice in prosperity. The neo-anabaptistic movement assumes that all prosperity is sinful, and teaches that it is a sin to be wealthy and enjoy life. We may contrast this attitude with that of Job, who was the richest man in the East (Job 1:3), who used his wealth wisely and did not give it up foolishly (Job 31:13-23), and who was rewarded by God with even more riches (Job 42:10-17). The same may be said of Abraham, the father of true believers (Gen. 13:2).

We at Geneva Divinity School assert the Biblical doctrine of justification by faith, and confidence before God. What the modern church needs is not more guilt but release from guilt, and confident service before the face of God.

### *Statement of Belief*

Geneva Divinity School is committed to the absolute authority and inerrancy of the Holy Scripture of the Old and New Testaments. We affirm that these contain all that is necessary for faith and life, so that all aspects of society must be governed by the Word of God, and all men are held accountable to Scripture by God.

We affirm the historic Christian faith, as summarized in the Apostles' Creed, the Nicene Creed, and the Athanasian Creed. Further, we affirm the theology of the Reformation, as summarized in the Belgic Confession, the Heidelberg Catechism, the Canons of Dordt, the Westminster Confession of Faith, and the Westminster Larger and Shorter Catechisms.

Finally, we affirm that human reason is subject to the Scriptures at all points, and we look forward to the advance of the gospel, amidst tribulation in the world until all nations have received the blessings of the Kingdom of Christ.

# PUBLICATION SCHEDULE

Listed below are the symposium topics for the next two issues of **Christianity and Civilization.** Manuscripts dealing with the topics are now being reviewed for publication. Anyone wishing to submit a manuscript for consideration would be wise to clear the topic in advance with the editor. Manuscripts should be between 20 and 40 pages in length, typewritten, double-spaced. A *Style Sheet* for **C&C** is available from Geneva Divinity School. It is imperative that each writer consult this style sheet before submitting a final draft of any manuscript. If accepted, **C&C** will pay the author $100 upon publication. Shorter manuscripts (under 20 pages) receive $50. Book reviews (5-10 pages) receive $25; books dealing with the symposium's topic are preferred. Suggestions concerning the reprinting of important documents or published articles, if accepted, are worth $35, if accompanied by a clear photocopy of the recommended piece.

Although the author is paid, copyright remains with the individual author.

**Topics and Deadlines:**

No. 4: **THE RECONSTRUCTION OF THE CHRISTIAN CHURCH**
(James B. Jordan, editor) 15 December 1983

No. 5: **CHRISTIANITY, WAR, AND TERRORISM**
(Gary North, editor) 15 February 1984

**Christianity and Civilization**
708 Hamvasy Lane
Tyler, TX 75701